Houghton Mifflin Company Editorial Adviser in Education

HEROLD C. HUNT

Charles William Eliot Professor of Education
Harvard University

SECONDARY

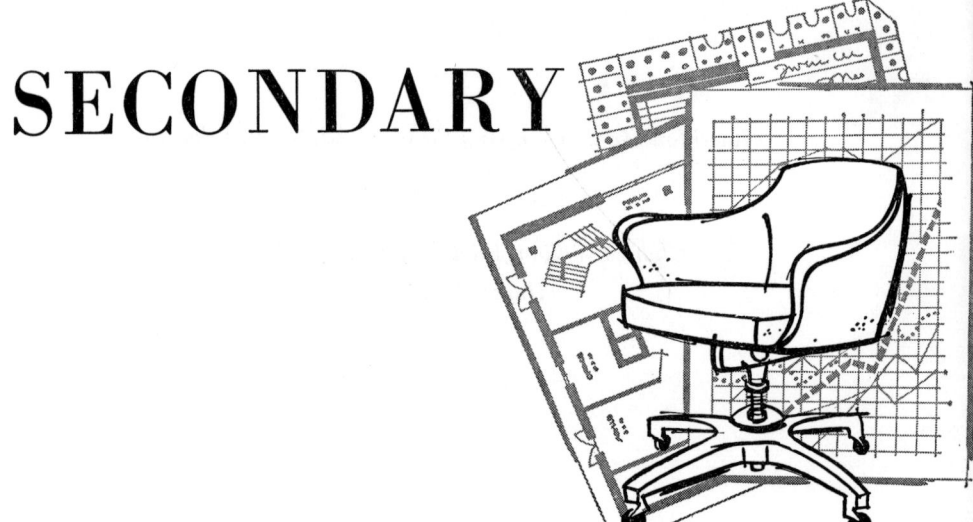

SCHOOL ADMINISTRATION

LESTER W. ANDERSON
University of Michigan

LAUREN A. VAN DYKE
State University of Iowa

HOUGHTON MIFFLIN COMPANY • BOSTON

Andrew S. Thomas Memorial Library
MORRIS HARVEY COLLEGE, CHARLESTON, W. VA.

53438

Copyright © 1963 by Lester W. Anderson and Lauren A. Van Dyke.
All rights reserved, including the right to reproduce this book
or parts thereof in any form.

HOUGHTON MIFFLIN COMPANY • BOSTON
PRINTED IN THE U.S.A.

PREFACE

Secondary school administrators occupy a sensitive position in the field of education because they can influence many of the conditions affecting instruction within a school. Although administrators need to be skillful in assisting teachers with instructional problems, efficient in securing the things that teachers need to do a good job of teaching, and competent in managing the details of the educational enterprise, they also need to be knowledgeable about educational theory and trends. We have therefore sought to combine theory and principles of leadership in administration with numerous suggestions for the day-to-day management of the school.

This book is designed to serve as a textbook for the basic course in secondary school administration usually required in the preparation of high school principals. Although it is addressed primarily to the beginning student of secondary school administration, experienced principals should find it a convenient guide to research and new developments in the field.

The book is developed around six major areas or parts. Part I, "The Secondary School Administrator," consists of an orientation to positions and careers in secondary school administration. Part II, "The Changing Role of Secondary Education in America," presents background information needed to develop a perspective on contemporary practices, conflicts, and theories in secondary education. Part III, "Organization and Direction of the Educational Program," deals with the design of the curriculum and the task of organizing it for instructional purposes. Guidance services, extraclass activities, and the library are discussed in their relationship to the administration of the instructional program. Part IV, "Staff Organization and Relationships," suggests a number of principles and practices relating to staff selection, organization, and utilization, staff morale, and in-service procedures. Part V, "Student Relationships," outlines the role of the principal in discipline and in the administration of pupil personnel records and reports. Part VI, "Management and Community Relations," deals with the business management of the school, public relations, and the role of the principal in school plant planning.

A viewpoint that prevails throughout the book is that effective administrative leadership is based on democratic principles and the participation of the staff in policy formulation. This does not mean that the secondary school administrator should be primarily a master of process; he must also be a man of vision and insight with respect to the entire field of education. And he must, of course, assume responsibility for making decisions which are properly his. This book attempts to portray the ideal secondary school administrator as a man of action, a man who possesses strong leadership qualities, a man who is knowledgeable in the broad field of secondary education, a man who is sensitive to the problems of human relations, and a man who is master of the techniques of administration. It is our hope that this book will make a contribution to the development of such men in secondary school administration.

LESTER W. ANDERSON
LAUREN A. VAN DYKE

CONTENTS

PREFACE ... v
LIST OF FIGURES ... xi
LIST OF TABLES ... xiii

Part I THE SECONDARY SCHOOL ADMINISTRATOR

1. *Careers in Secondary School Administration* ... 5
   Evolution of the High School Principalship • Preparation and Personal Qualities of the Successful Principal

2. *The Principal as an Educational Leader* ... 25
   The Nature of Leadership • Professional Growth of the Principal

Part II THE CHANGING ROLE OF SECONDARY EDUCATION IN AMERICA

3. *The Secondary School in Transition — Perspective* ... 45
   Great Expansion • Development of Secondary Schools • The First Secondary Schools (1635–1780) • The American Academies (1751–1860) • Early Public High Schools (1821–90) • Development of the Modern High School (Since 1890) • Changes in Public Perceptions of Secondary Education • Changes in Objectives • Changes in the Educational Program

4. *Structure, Size, and Relationships of Secondary Schools* ... 77
   Structure of Secondary Schools • Size of Secondary Schools • Relationships with Other Schools and Agencies • Relationships with Governmental and Extralegal Agencies

CONTENTS

Part III ORGANIZATION AND DIRECTION OF THE
EDUCATIONAL PROGRAM

5. *Curriculum Planning and Design* — 109

Curriculum Planning • Organizational Design of the Curriculum • General Education to Serve Common Needs • Programs for Specialized Education

6. *Organization of the School Schedule and Calendar* — 151

The Daily and Weekly Schedule • Types of Schedules • Characteristics of Conventional Schedules • Types and Characteristics of Variable Schedules • Building a Schedule • The School Year

7. *Administration of the Guidance Program* — 189

Definition and Point of View • Need for Guidance Services • The Effectiveness of Guidance • Organizing the Guidance Program • Guidance Services • Physical Facilities for Guidance

8. *Extraclass Activities and Their Management* — 221

Factors in the Growth of the Activity Program • Functions and Purposes of the Extraclass Program • Administrative and Organizational Policies for the Extraclass Program

9. *Administration of Major Types of Extraclass Activities* — 247

Student Participation in Government • Homerooms • Assemblies • School Publications • Music Activities • Speech and Dramatics • Social Life and Activities • Physical Activities — Athletics • School Clubs • Extraclass Finances

10. *The Library as an Instructional Center* — 280

Definition and Role of the School Library • The Present State of School Libraries • The Role of the Administrator • Characteristics of Good School Libraries • Library Quarters and Physical Facilities

CONTENTS

Part IV Staff Organization and Relationships

11. *Staff Organization and Utilization* — 301
Line and Staff Organization · Organization of the High School · Staff Utilization

12. *Staff Morale* — 330
Definition · Factors Affecting Morale

13. *Developing a Democratic In-Service Program* — 350
Faculty Meetings · Educational Workshops · Preschool Conferences · Faculty Committees · Administrative Advisory Councils · Individual Conferences

14. *Selection of the Staff* — 376
Who Selects Teachers? · How Can Teaching Success Be Predicted? · What Procedures Should Be Followed in the Selection Process?

Part V Student Relationships

15. *The Principal's Role in Discipline* — 407
Definition of Discipline · Establishing Policies and Procedures · Administrative Guides in Discipline

16. *Pupil Personnel Records and Reports* — 428
Guiding Principles · Types of Records

Part VI Management and Community Relations

17. *The Secondary School and Community Relations* — 467
Growing Importance of School Public Relations · Nature of the Problem · Responsibility and Coordination · Principles and Policies · Procedures and Media

18. *Business Functions and Responsibilities of the Principal* — 495
General Operations · Business Management of Extraclass Activities

CONTENTS

19. *Office Management and Program Accounting*   530

    Office Services • Personnel and Facilities • Educational Program Accounting

20. *The Role of the Principal in School Plant Planning*   550

    Nature and Purpose of Educational Specifications • Contents of Educational Specifications • Process of Developing Educational Specifications • Innovations in School Buildings

INDEX   575

FIGURES

1.	A Comparison of Median Salaries Between Classroom Teachers with Five Years of College, Secondary School Principals, and Superintendents of Schools, 1958–59, Urban Districts from 10,000 to 30,000 in Population	19
2.	Types of Organization of Public Secondary Schools	84
3.	Program of Studies for a Four-Year Junior High School	132
4.	Section of a Block-Time Schedule	162
5.	One-Week Schedule for a Ninth-Grade Student — Floating Period Schedule	163
6.	Program for an Eleventh-Grade Student — Varied-Period Schedule	164
7.	How a Student Might Spend His Time in the Secondary School of the Future	165
8.	Conflict Chart of Single-Section Courses	174
9.	Pupil Schedule Card	177
10.	Marginal Punch Card	178
11.	Keysorter and Pupil Schedule Cards	180
12.	Guidance Organization for a Small School System	202
13.	Guidance Organization in a Medium-Sized School System	203
14.	Relative Location of Guidance Quarters	217
15.	Guidance Area	218
16.	Line Type of Organization	303
17.	Line Type of Organization	304
18.	Line and Staff Organization	305
19.	Departmental Plan of Organization	309
20.	Coordinate Line and Staff Organization with Cabinet and Advisory Councils	310
21.	Proposed Organization of Instruction	324
22.	Cumulative Personnel Record	436
23.	Permanent Record Form	440
24.	Transcript of Credits	444
25.	Additional Fact Sheet Used by Ann Arbor High School, Ann Arbor, Michigan	446

FIGURES

26. Report Card Used by Tappan Junior High School, Ann Arbor, Michigan — 455
27. Typical Attendance Record Card — 457
28. Form for Reporting Absence — 460
29. Typical Inventory Card — 505
30. Organizational Chart for Business Management of Extraclass Activities in a School System with a Unit Type of Organization — 510
31. Official Receipt — 520
32. Activity Purchase Order — 521
33. Fund Balance Record — 522
34. Receipts Distribution Ledger — 523
35. Expenditures Distribution Ledger — 524
36. Monthly Summary Statement for All Funds — 525
37. Floor Plan for Administrative Offices in a High School of 2000 Students — 541
38. Accumulated Number of Needed Classrooms in the Regular Public Schools of 48 States and the District of Columbia: 1959 to 1969 — 551
39. Dearborn Public Schools Organization for Development of Educational Specifications for School Building Projects — 558

TABLES

1. Percentage of Time Estimated to Be Spent by Assistant Principals in Los Angeles and Twenty-Three Cities with Populations over 400,000 — 12
2. Minimum Requirements in Teaching Experience, Degrees, and/or Semester Hours for Secondary Principal's Certificate, 1960–61 — 15
3. Recommended Maximum Salaries for Secondary School Principals and Assistant Principals, Stated in Percentage Ratio Above Teachers' Maximum Salaries — 20
4. Median Salaries of Principals and Other Professional Persons as a Per Cent of Median Salary of Classroom Teachers, by Size of Place, 1958–59 — 21
5. Gains in Enrollments in Grades 9–12 in Public and Private Secondary Schools in Relation to Population 14–17 Years of Age — 55
6. Changes in Number of Independent School Districts in the Continental United States, 1932 to 1961 — 57
7. Physics Test Results for Boys at Three Levels of Quantitative Ability — 82
8. Trigonometry Test Results for Boys at Three Levels of Quantitative Ability — 82
9. High School Per-Pupil Costs in Iowa, 1957–58 — 92
10. Relationship Between School Size and Achievement on ITED (Composite) for Iowa High Schools from 1956 to 1958 — 92
11. Importance of Ten Areas for NCA Action Regarding Closer High School-College Articulation — 99
12. Per Cent of Schools Requiring Units in Each Subject Field and Average Number of Units, if Required, by Courses of Study — 129
13. Number and Per Cent of Junior High Schools Requiring Certain Courses — 131
14. Per Cent of Junior High Schools Permitting Number of Elective Credits — 131
15. Per Cent of Midwestern Senior High Schools Employing Advisory Curricula, Offering Each Special Curriculum in 1954–55 — 133

TABLES

16.	Mean Load per Teacher by Type of Schedule	156
17.	Comparison of Distributions of Intelligence Test Results for Certain Secondary School Populations from 1919 to 1960	192
18.	Trends in Occupational Distribution, 1900 to 1975	195
19.	Summary of a Five-Year Follow-Up Study on Occupational Adjustment	199
20.	Subject Grade Coefficients for Use in the Teaching Load Formula	320
21.	Distribution of Local Educational Expenditures by Function or Object, 1957–58	377
22.	Rank Order of Traits Mentioned by Pupils of Ages 14 and Higher	385
23.	Number of Teachers in Public Secondary Schools, by Sex, School Years 1947–48 to 1957–58	391
24.	Selected Items Discussed in Less Than 20 Per Cent of 106 Initial Interviews	399
25.	The 25 Most Frequently Discussed Items During Initial Conferences with 35 Hiring Officials	400
26.	Major Business Functions and Responsibilities of High School Principals for General Operations (Exclusive of E.C.A.)	497
27.	Functions and Responsibilities of High School Principals in Planning the General Budget	499
28.	Responsibilities and Functions of Principals for Activity Fund Management	508
29.	Media Used by High School Principals in Communicating	533

SECONDARY SCHOOL ADMINISTRATION

I

The Secondary School Administrator

Many teachers seek careers in educational administration in order to improve their professional status, to exercise leadership within their professional ranks, to secure greater financial rewards for their services, or to satisfy other ambitions. There are teachers, however, who are ambivalent as to whether or not administration provides the opportunities appropriate to their interests and abilities. Regardless of their initial commitment to enter secondary school administration, a number of questions need to be investigated by prospective administrators. For example, how many positions are available in secondary school administration? How much and what kind of formal and informal preparation is required in order to enter the field? What are the advantages and disadvantages in the position of high school principal? These and similar questions are discussed in Chapter 1.

Chapter 2 analyzes one of the most important responsibilities of the principal: his work as an instructional leader. In addition, the nature of leadership, with special attention to "democratic administration," is discussed.

The person who has finished his formal graduate study and become a high school administrator is faced immediately with the never ending task of keeping himself informed and up to date in the field of secondary education. He is also expected to improve his own skill as an instructional leader. Some of the typical ways in which school administrators continue their in-service growth are discussed in Chapter 2.

In general, Chapters 1 and 2 of this book are intended to present an overview of the positions in secondary school administration and to assist those interested in the field to plan their preparation.

CHAPTER 1

Careers in Secondary School Administration

For a young person to take a hard look at a profession in order to determine what it has to offer and what he has to offer it is an indication of mature judgment. A position in secondary school administration may, and often does, appeal to young teachers as an opportunity to advance within the field of professional education. Probably some teachers are attracted by the relatively good status enjoyed by principals within and outside the profession; others are interested in the opportunities for service or the higher earning potential of the position. The prospect of managing and coordinating a large enterprise may appeal to still others. Whatever their specific reasons, many young teachers do enroll in graduate courses in secondary administration to explore the possibilities of a career in the field or to begin actual preparation for it.

A field which draws so many prospects must have some reasonably attractive features about it. It would be naïve to assume, however, that it has no unattractive features. Students who are contemplating entering secondary school administration certainly will want to give some thought to the nature of the position, its advantages and disadvantages, the type of person most likely to succeed, and the training and experience required.

Perhaps some insight into the high school principalship may be gained from an examination of its evolution as a part of the teaching profession in America.

Evolution of the High School Principalship

The colonial secondary school had little need for a principal. These schools were small, often with one teacher in charge of the entire educational program. Whatever little supervision or administration was needed was provided by a board of laymen, serving as examiners. This arrangement was satisfactory as long as only small numbers of teachers and pupils were involved. The situation changed, however, as the population began to expand in the eighteenth century, and more young people sought the opportunity to attend secondary school.

During the second half of the eighteenth century, mounting enrollments forced towns to organize multiple-room secondary schools which required the services of several teachers within one building. As these schools evolved, it became necessary to devise some type of organization for coordinating the instructional services of the entire school. No one on the staff had any real authority except in his own classes. Such elementary things as determining the time of opening and closing school, scheduling classes, securing supplies and equipment, taking care of and managing the building, and communicating with parents and patrons began to pile up and demand so much time that the trustees had to appoint a "head teacher" to perform these duties. From this position of "head teacher" the secondary school principalship gradually emerged.

The first principals were appointed from the ranks of classroom teachers and, in most cases, did not give full time to administering the school. Since the early administrator generally served as a teacher as well as a principal, a close relationship was maintained between the administrative and instructional programs of the school. This close identification of the principal with teachers, pupils, and instructional activities is characteristic of most schools today. Initially, the teacher assigned to administrative duties was called the "principal teacher," but later the title was shortened to "principal."

In addition to being responsible for the instructional program of the school, the principal dealt with problems of grade placement of pupils, discipline, care of the building, and assignment of teachers. A statement by Cubberley, however, calls attention to the continued importance of the supervision of instruction as a professional responsibility of the principalship.

> . . . Yet the supervision of instruction that the education of children may proceed under better conditions and be more effective in results, is the prime reason for freeing the principal from teaching and is the end goal toward which the organization and administration should tend.[1]

---

[1] Ellwood P. Cubberley, *The Principal and His School* (Boston: Houghton Mifflin Company, 1923), p. 43.

Originally, the principal also served as the liaison person between the board of education and the teachers. As such, he was the prototype of the superintendent of schools. It is noteworthy that the principalship was the first administrative position in American education. A single administrator was adequate until communities grew so large that a number of schools were required to serve their educational needs. At this stage an additional problem of coordinating the activities of the various schools developed, and the task of general administration became too time consuming and complex for a board of laymen. The position of superintendent of schools was created in Buffalo, New York, in 1837, and a similar position was established in Louisville, Kentucky, the same year.

Following the establishment of the superintendency, a change occurred in the principal's role, since he no longer worked directly with the board of education. The principal became responsible to the superintendent of schools and served as the liaison person between the central office and the teachers in his school.

Another early characteristic of the high school principalship was the relatively high status that the principal enjoyed within the community. Often he was referred to as "The Professor," being looked upon as a person who was scholarly, highly cultured, and an intellectual leader in the community. Some duties associated with the position, however, seem rather strange and amusing today. In addition to teaching and administering the school, the principal often served as town clerk, church chorister, official visitor of the sick, bell ringer of the church, gravedigger, court messenger, and occasionally in other capacities.[2] These duties were probably important functions in the community at that time.

Favorable status continues to be one of the attractive features of the position of high school principal in most communities. The principal is still expected to take an active part in local cultural and civic affairs. It is not uncommon to find school administrators busily involved in service clubs, PTA, community fund drives, music and art societies, drama clubs, and other special civic projects. Not only is membership in such groups usually open to the principal, but very often his services are sought, and if he does not overdo it, he may derive considerable satisfaction from the leadership and service he can offer.

Similarly, his social life is limited largely by his own interest and available time. As a matter of fact, it is frequently necessary for him to budget his leisure time carefully in order to participate in the many affairs in which he is interested and obligated. The community status enjoyed by most secondary school administrators, therefore, might be considered one of the attractive features of the position. Not only is it highly satisfying to be in a position of responsibility in one of the most important

---

[2] Paul B. Jacobson, William C. Reavis, and James D. Logsdon, *Duties of School Principals* (New York: Prentice-Hall, Inc., 1950), p. 727.

enterprises in the world, the education of children, but it is also gratifying to be recognized as a leader within one's own community.

By the late 1800's, the high school principal had become established as the actual administrative head in many secondary schools. This does not mean that all principals were given full responsibility for administrative leadership in their schools. Wide differences still exist from school to school in the opportunity principals are given to serve as the administrative head of the high school. An examination of duties and time available for administrative functions in various sized schools discloses these variations and the types of administrative positions found in today's secondary schools.

Administrative Aide

High schools with a small enrollment, approximately 100 or less, generally employ an administrative assistant who is also a full-time teacher. His administrative duties are usually confined to clerical tasks associated with pupil attendance, report cards, and disciplining pupils. They have little to do with the selection and assignment of teachers or the supervision of instruction. The latter responsibilities belong to the superintendent of schools, who is the actual administrative head of the high school. A good description of the status of such an administrative aide is reported by Austin:

> ... And then there is the case of a principal in a school with an enrollment of 126 who writes "In my school I am so busy with the five classes daily and coaching two sports plus study hall, etc., that many of the things I think are important I cannot do. Also, I do some things that I think are unimportant because I have them shoved off on me. I have little authority in running the school, just disciplining the children."[3]

It is probably inaccurate to classify this type of position as a principalship. A more realistic view would regard the person employed in such a position as a head teacher who assists the superintendent of schools with some clerical duties and serves as a disciplinarian.

Although the nonteaching duties of an administrative aide are only nominal, there are teachers who find satisfaction in serving in this capacity. Usually the salary is slightly higher than that paid to regular classroom teachers, but the amount is hardly enough to make the position attractive from a financial point of view. A teacher who is interested in going into secondary school administration probably would not want to consider this type of position as a permanent career. Nevertheless, it does afford some excellent experience which may be extremely valuable in qualifying for a position with greater administrative responsibility.

[3] David B. Austin, "Characteristics of a Successful Principal," *The Bulletin* of the NASSP, April, 1956, 40:445.

Part-Time Principal

Schools with a pupil enrollment of approximately 100 to 250 usually employ a *bona fide* principal who may also be a part-time teacher. The amount of teaching time varies from school to school, but it is quite common to find principals assigned to one-third time in teaching and two-thirds time in administration.

Many of the administrative duties assumed by the part-time principal are similar to those of the administrative aide, such as keeping pupil records, checking attendance, counseling, and disciplining students. There are two major differences: the part-time principal is usually responsible for administering the extraclassroom activity program and for arranging the schedule of classes. The latter duty involves him in the selection and assignment of teachers; at least, the superintendent usually consults with him prior to the final selection of new teachers. The part-time principal may also be in charge of supervising the building, securing instructional supplies, and managing auxiliary services such as the cafeteria, the health service, and transportation. He is not likely to have major responsibilities in the areas of public relations, supervision of instruction, or finance. These duties are retained, for the most part, by the superintendent.

A secretary or clerical assistant may be provided, but many part-time principals have only high school pupils as assistants in their offices. Additional assistants — a counselor, a cafeteria manager, and an athletic director — are sometimes provided in schools of this size. Coordination problems begin to appear in these schools and offer an opportunity to develop organizational and leadership competencies. A report of a follow-up study of thirty beginning principals illustrates the variety of experiences and problems they have had. The following are typical of the comments of these principals about their jobs:

> I have some difficulty helping a beginning teacher, appearing before the public, planning the activity period, managing pupils during the noon hour.

> I have difficulty getting teachers to take full advantage of the library facilities; in knowing how a library should operate to obtain maximum efficiency.

> The cafeteria manager is not trained to do her job.

> There is a lack of secretarial assistance.

> Parents are not interested in school functions and are not willing to encourage their children to do good school work.

> Good bus drivers are hard to find and keep because of low pay.

The superintendent's wife is a member of my faculty and, although she is a fine person, the other teachers do not feel at ease in her presence.[4]

A part-time principal who has the good fortune to work with an experienced and skillful superintendent will find this position excellent preparation for assuming full responsibility for the administration of a secondary school. The beginning principal is likely to secure his first administration position in a small school and may use it as a stepping stone. There is also the possibility that he may move into a superintendency after a few years of experience. Because administrative turnover is relatively high in small school systems, they provide numerous opportunities for a young principal to get started. However, they also offer him an opportunity to enter a permanent career if he chooses to remain in a small community.

Full-Time Principal

The greatest satisfaction in the principalship is usually realized when the principal can devote full time to professional duties. High schools with 250 or more pupils need a full-time principal who is capable of serving as a real administrative head. He is looked upon as the educational leader of his school and generally is responsible for the following:

1. Leadership in curriculum planning.
2. Study and discussion of educational theory and current developments in secondary education with the professional staff and school patrons.
3. Organization of a program of studies appropriate to the needs of the pupils, community, and nation.
4. Development of guidance and counseling services.
5. Management of auxiliary services such as health, transportation, and cafeteria.
6. Procurement and organization of library and instructional facilities and services.
7. Participation in the selection of teachers and organization of the faculty to provide high-quality instruction.
8. Development of conditions within the school conducive to high morale and development of good citizenship on the part of students.
9. Development and maintenance of good faculty morale.
10. Development and maintenance of an effective program of in-service education for the faculty.
11. Development and maintenance of a sound program of extraclassroom activities for all pupils.
12. Organization of the school day and year so that the instructional program functions effectively.
13. Organization and management of records and office routine needed for the effective educational and business management of the school.

[4] Ben H. Horton, Jr., "School Principals Look at Their Problems," *The Bulletin* of the NASSP, September, 1959, 43:115.

14. Provision of leadership for participation of citizens in school affairs.
15. Interpretation of the program of the school to the community, the superintendent of schools, and the board of education.
16. Participation in coordinating educational services for youth in the community.
17. Management and supervision of the maintenance of the high school plant and other physical facilities.
18. Participation in the development of plans for future buildings.
19. Maintenance of cooperative and effective relations with legal agencies, accrediting agencies, and other educational institutions.
20. Contributions to the advancement of the teaching profession.

The truly professional principal must be competent to perform the above duties effectively. Although it is likely that only full-time principals will be expected to assume all the duties listed, part-time principals must be prepared for these responsibilities if they wish to advance to a full-time position in secondary school administration.

It is apparent that the principal who does well all of the things he is expected to do is a very busy person. The job does not lend itself to a time-clock routine. Anyone seeking a forty-hour week with evenings and week ends free for leisure would do well to avoid the field of high school administration. A study of the high school principalship in Pennsylvania,[5] in which approximately 500 principals replied to a questionnaire concerning the amount of time they spent on their jobs over and above the regular school day, showed that they devoted about 520 hours per year of extra time to their work. This amounts to thirteen forty-hour weeks, or about three months of extra time per year.

Principals of large schools find it necessary to delegate many managerial and administrative tasks so that they can concentrate on instructional and leadership responsibilities. The increasing complexity of school populations, organizations, and curricula has resulted in the necessity for a degree of specialization in administration. Some very large schools may have an assistant principal who specializes in college entrance and scholarship counseling while other assistants are concerned primarily with student activities or other special services.

Assistant Principal

There is no general agreement as to the title that should be given to persons holding administrative positions subordinate to the principal. The term "assistant principal" is used most frequently and "vice-principal" is the next most popular choice. "Assistant principal" seems to be as appropriate as any to designate administrative assistants who do not have highly specialized functions.

[5] "A Study of the High School Principalship in Pennsylvania," *The Bulletin* of the NASSP, December, 1953, 37:119.

The number of administrative assistants in a school will vary according to the wealth of the district, the nature of the program of studies, the physical makeup of the building, the size of the student body, the other youth agencies in the community, and other factors which make administration of the school complex. The need for assistants to the principal in large schools is recognized by the North Central Association of Colleges and Secondary Schools, which now requires member schools with 500 pupils and above to have at least one part-time administrative assistant. The trend appears to be in the direction of having a ratio of one administrator for every 500 pupils or major fraction thereof.

Selection of an assistant should be made by the principal with whom he will work, since it is most important that the two be compatible and qualified to complement each other in their professional functions.

Although the duties of assistant principals vary from school to school, a review of some of their typical responsibilities will indicate the general nature of the job. Jarrett's study in 1957 compared duties of assistant principals in Los Angeles and in twenty-three other cities in the United States whose population exceeded 400,000.[6] A striking similarity was shown in the percentage of time estimated to be spent by assistant principals in the six major responsibility classifications used in the study. Table 1 presents a summary of this report.

TABLE 1

Percentage of Time Estimated to Be Spent by Assistant Principals in Los Angeles and Twenty-Three Cities with Populations over 400,000

Responsibility Classification	Los Angeles Vice-Principals	Twenty-Three Largest Cities
Administration of the education program	19	25
Pupil personnel services	45	45
Administration of the cocurricular activities	13	12
School management	12	8
Community relations	6	4
Professional and in-service training	5	6

It may be seen that the assistant principal's time is distributed over a variety of duties but that he assumes a major role in pupil personnel services and in closely related duties, such as discipline and attendance. Most principals in large schools seem to be disposed to delegate discipline problems to an assistant. The second most frequently occurring area of

[6] Richard W. Jarrett, "The Activities of the Assistant Principal in Secondary Schools," *The Bulletin* of the NASSP, September, 1958, 42:28–32.

responsibility for assistants is the management of the educational program. Building the class schedule, enrolling pupils, and administering the record system are often included in this category.

Seventy per cent of the time of assistant principals in the twenty-three largest cities was spent working in the combined areas of administration of the educational program and pupil personnel services. A similar pattern was found by Weiss in his report on a study of the duties of sixty-six vice-principals in the Middle Atlantic states.[7] A rank order of duties placed management and pupil problems at the top of Weiss's list and the supervision of teachers and community activities at the bottom.

A majority of assistant principals recognize and accept the assignment of responsibilities dealing primarily with pupil welfare and administrative details of the school, but they also aspire to the position of a full-time principal and look upon their present position as a training period for promotion to the principalship.[8] This is especially true in large cities where it is the accepted practice to promote personnel from within the system to the principalship except in the case of women assistants. At the present time most women assistant principals are likely to find that their position is as high as they can go in school administration. They may not approve the obvious discrimination against women in administrative positions, but they appear to be realistic in their expectations. Morale among women assistants is usually relatively high in spite of the terminal nature of the position.[9] Exceptions have been made to the general practice of nonpromotion of women to the principalship, but they are rare. During the 1958–59 school year, there were only thirty-nine women principals — 1.3 per cent — in the 3,091 public high schools accredited by the North Central Association.

Preparation and Personal Qualities of the Successful Principal

It is important for a student thinking about a career in secondary school administration to take into account preparation requirements, both legal and extralegal, and personal qualities usually considered important in achieving success as an administrator.

Certification Requirements

Certification for school administrators is a legal requirement in most states. The prospective principal must plan his preparation specifically

---

[7] G. A. W. Weiss, "The Duties of the Secondary School Vice-Principal," *The Bulletin* of the NASSP, December, 1953, 37:109–17.

[8] H. F. Bolden, "Attitudes of High School Assistant Principals Toward Their Duties and Responsibilities," *The Bulletin* of the NASSP, November, 1956, 40:24.

[9] Evelyn B. Martin, "A Profile of Women as Secondary School Vice-Principals," *The Bulletin* of the NASSP, March, 1958, 42:77–83.

to meet this requirement in order to be licensed by the state to administer a school. Qualifying for a principal's certificate is complicated by the fact that there are no nation-wide standards; each state determines its own standards. Graduate students preparing for secondary school administration should investigate the requirements of each state in which they hope to secure a position.

Although there are differences in the standards in the various states, there are also many similarities. For example, an analysis (see Table 2) of the minimum requirements in teaching experience, degree, and specific graduate courses in administration and supervision needed for a secondary principal's certificate reveals that (1) all except five states and territories require some teaching experience, with thirty-three requiring three years; (2) thirty-two states call for a master's degree or a minimum of thirty semester hours of graduate work; (3) forty-four states require specific preparation in courses dealing with administration and supervision, ranging from three to thirty semester hours, the median being twelve semester hours; (4) Michigan and the District of Columbia do not issue a special certificate for school administration.

These data indicate that the student working toward a certificate in secondary school administration should plan to take at least twelve semester hours of graduate study in administration and supervision, earn a master's degree, and secure at least three years of teaching experience. This preparation would meet the certification requirements in a large majority of the states. On the other hand, some states have special requirements which must be considered. Arizona, for example, requires all school administrators to complete a course in the school laws of Arizona.

It should be noted also that the preceding standards are minimum for a beginning certificate. In states which have more than one secondary principal's certificate, additional graduate work is usually necessary to obtain the most advanced certification. Certification requirements are being revised in some states and lists soon get out of date. It would be desirable, therefore, to check with the proper officials for the latest requirements in a state in which the student is interested.

In addition to state certification requirements, it is necessary to meet the criteria of regional accrediting associations if the employing school is a member of such an association.

Accreditation and Professional Organization Requirements

School standards in most states are influenced by the criteria of one of the five regional accrediting associations. Accreditation requirements differ from state certificate requirements in being extralegal in nature. In other words, since membership in regional accrediting associations is voluntary, schools do not have to meet their standards in order to operate.

TABLE 2

Minimum Requirements in Teaching Experience, Degrees, and/or Semester Hours in Administration and Supervision for Secondary Principal's Certificate, 1960–61

States and Territories	Graduate Hours or Degree[a]	Hours in Administration and Supervision	Years of Teaching Experience	State	Graduate Hours or Degree[a]	Hours in Administration and Supervision	Years of Teaching Experience
Alabama	B.A. + 9	9	3	Montana	M.A.	10	3
Alaska	B.A. + 16	16	3	Nebraska	B.A. + 15	15	3
Arizona	M.A.	9–12	3	Nevada	B.A. + 16	16	3
Arkansas	M.A.	15	3	New Hampshire	B.A. + 18	6	3
California	48	[b]	2	New Jersey	B.A. + 24	24	3
Colorado	M.A.	10	3	New Mexico	M.A.	16	3
Connecticut	M.A. + 6	9	3	New York	B.A. + 6	6	2
Delaware	M.A.	9	5	North Carolina	M.A.	12	3
District of Columbia	No certificate granted			North Dakota	B.A. + 8	8	3
Florida	M.A.	30	3	Ohio	B.A. + 12	12	3
Georgia	M.A.	30	3	Oklahoma	M.A.	8	2
Hawaii	B.A. + 6	10	5	Oregon	M.A.	8	3
Idaho	M.A.	12	3	Pennsylvania	M.A. or 30	[b]	5
Illinois	M.A.	20	4	Puerto Rico	B.A. + 15	15	3
Indiana	M.A.	18	3	Rhode Island	M.A. or 30	15	3
Iowa	M.A.	20	4	South Carolina	M.A.	18	3
Kansas	M.A.	8	2	South Dakota	B.A. + 21	9	2
Kentucky	B.A. + 15	15	3	Tennessee	30	10	3
Louisiana	M.A.	12	3	Texas	M.A.	30	3
Maine	B.A. + 18	6	3	Utah	M.A.	12	3
Maryland	30	[b]	4	Vermont	30	18	2
Massachusetts	B.A.	3	0	Virginia	M.A.	[b]	3
Michigan	No certificate granted			Washington	B.A. + 16	16	3
Minnesota	B.A. + 6	6	1	West Virginia	M.A.		3
Mississippi	B.A. + 12	12	2	Wisconsin	M.A.	[b]	0
Missouri	M.A.	20	0	Wyoming	M.A.	24	3

[a] M.A. degree is used as a general term to refer to any master's degree.
[b] Preparation is required but no specific number of hours is stated.

The principal must meet regional association standards, however, if his school is a member of such an agency. Failure to do so places the accreditation of the school in jeopardy. There are many advantages to graduates of accredited high schools, such as acceptance by colleges of credits earned in high school without a written examination and eligibility for a number of college scholarships. Usually there is much public interest in a high school's membership in a regional association, and certainly the principal should not be responsible for jeopardizing the status of his school.

Following are the preparation requirements for high school principals in the five associations:

1. Southern Association of Colleges and Secondary Schools. The administrative head of the system (superintendent) and of the school (principal, headmaster, etc.) shall have received a graduate degree from an institution approved by the Association, and the major portion of one year of such advanced study shall be designed as preparation for administrative and supervisory functions.[10]
2. The Northwest Association of Secondary and Higher Schools. High school principals new in their positions shall qualify for one of the following:
   a. Have a master's degree which includes 24 quarter (16 semester) hours of graduate work in education, or
   b. Have 57 quarter (38 semester) hours in graduate work, 30 quarter (20 semester) hours of which must be in education.[11]
3. Middle States Association of Colleges and Secondary Schools. Matters of this type are left in the hands of the State Department of Education in each state (see Table 2).
4. North Central Association of Colleges and Secondary Schools. The principal of a member school shall hold a master's degree with at least twenty semester hours of graduate work in education with major emphasis on administration and supervision. This preparation should include such graduate courses as educational philosophy, secondary administration and supervision, curriculum, guidance, educational psychology, and related courses. He shall have had a minimum of two years of successful teaching experience.[12]
5. New England Association of Colleges and Secondary Schools. No specific training requirements are demanded for high school administrators by this Association.

Professional organizations have played an important part in the upgrading of preparation requirements for school administration. In Febru-

---

[10] Southern Association of Colleges and Secondary Schools, *Principles and Standards*, The Commission on Secondary Schools, 1959, pp. 7–8.

[11] The Northwest Association of Secondary and Higher Schools, *Manual of Accrediting Secondary Schools*, Commission on Secondary Schools, 1959 revision, p. 10.

[12] North Central Association of Colleges and Secondary Schools, *Policies and Criteria for the Approval of Secondary Schools*, 1960 revision, p. 13.

ary, 1959, the American Association of School Administrators voted favorably on the following amendment to its constitution:

> Beginning on January 1, 1964, all new members of the American Association of School Administrators shall submit evidence of successful completion of two years' graduate study in university programs designed to prepare school administrators and approved by an accreditation body endorsed by the Executive Committee of the AASA.

Requirements of the AASA, like those of the regional associations, are extralegal. The membership requirement just cited should stimulate administrators to continue their formal education at least one year beyond the master's degree, which is higher than most of the present state or regional association standards. It is certainly a step forward in achieving genuine professional status for school administrators. The action of the AASA may bring similar action by members of the National Association of Secondary School Principals. At least it seems probable that preparation requirements for the principalship will continue to be raised. It is also probable that principalships in larger cities will require considerable preparation beyond the master's degree.

Many universities also have been devoting considerable attention to keeping up with the general expectation of increased preparation for administrators. A six-year program has been developed which usually leads to the Specialist in Education degree (Ed.S.), a diploma, certificate, or some other appropriately designated award. This program provides advanced preparation in professional areas where the master's degree is not sufficient and where the doctor's degree is not necessary. The trend toward increased professional preparation seems well established, and beginning principals should consider this factor in planning their careers.

Personal Qualities of Successful Principals

Personal qualities necessary for success in secondary school administration are difficult to identify. There is a large body of material, however, based on the opinions of practicing principals which provides some valuable leads for prospective principals.

The high school principal spends a big part of his working day in face-to-face relationships with a great variety of people, including students, teachers, parents, custodians, city officials, and salesmen. Much of his time is occupied with problems of other people. Certainly a person who is so engaged, day after day, must have a genuine interest in, and respect for, all kinds of people. On the other hand, a person who is self-centered and insists that his problems be the center of attention will find little satisfaction in school administration. The high school principal who does not have a strong desire to be of service has little to contribute to education.

In addition to a general interest in people, the really fine principal will feel a very special concern for the professional growth of his faculty. If he is able to assist a teacher who is in difficulty, or if a teacher makes an outstanding contribution, the principal should experience genuine satisfaction. One of his major functions is to help teachers develop professionally so that the educational program of the school may benefit.

Edwin Willard has this to say about his feelings upon returning to a high school principalship after a successful career as a diplomat:

> I have come back, after almost seven years away from the field of education, to being a High School Principal once again. And I like it. I have given up a successful career in the government; I have taken a thirty-six hundred dollar cut in salary; I have moved my family away from the excitement of life in Washington to the reality and down-to-earth living of a small town near the eastern seaboard; and I have found contentment and the self-satisfaction that was lacking in my other way of life. . . .
>
> While searching for personal satisfaction and gratitude from work in the embassy, I would suddenly be confronted by a student tourist who would look me up and thank me, as he successfully approached his last year in college, for having directed him toward his college or for having helped him in search for a career. Other former students, when I would meet them, might reminisce on some slight influence I had brought to bear, an influence I had forgotten I had ever exerted, if I had known at all. Some of my former teachers also would come abroad. I remember one especially. Thrilled with her first sight of Europe, she reminded me that it was I who had originally stimulated her to travel. I found more and more that I longed for that satisfaction of helping an individual find his way. . . .[13]

Anyone who deals with a great variety of problems finds it difficult not to base decisions on emotions rather than on philosophy or principles. But decisions which reflect maturity of judgment and wisdom are usually based upon a rational personal philosophy. A school principal is expected to be a person with good judgment and one who is consistent in his point of view. Students and teachers should be able to anticipate where he will stand on important issues.

Consistency derived from rational philosophy should not be confused with rigidity and inflexibility. Education in our democratic society is attended by constant change, and the principal must demonstrate a capacity for making logical changes. If a school is fortunate enough to have a faculty which is creative and interested in the continued development of the school, there will be a never ending flow of ideas across the principal's desk. Successful principals seem to be able to surround themselves with people who have ideas; and an attitude of sincere interest on the part of the principal does much to encourage the expression of ideas by the faculty.

[13] Edwin A. Willard, "A High School Principal Comes Back," *The Bulletin* of the NASSP, November, 1956, 40:17.

A mature sense of humor is an important asset in the principal's day-to-day relationships with people. The ability to see the lighter side of things makes one more relaxed and approachable. The principal is expected to be a person of integrity and sincerity, but it does not follow that he cannot have a little fun on the job. Teen-age students are especially responsive to a principal who can see the humor in a situation.

The school administrator needs poise, and a "thick skin" may help upon occasion. No matter how hard-working or sincere he may be, there are usually some people who become disgruntled and critical of him and of the school. Such reactions are likely to develop in any community and the principal can meet them most effectively by not allowing himself to become easily disturbed.

Economic Aspects of the Principalship

It is to be expected that the prospective principal will be more than mildly interested in the economic aspects of the job. At least, this is one of the most frequent considerations mentioned by classroom teachers in response to the question "Why do you want to become a school administrator?" Men who are interested in continuing in the field of profes-

FIGURE 1

A Comparison of Median Salaries Between Classroom Teachers with Five Years of College, Secondary School Principals, and Superintendents of Schools, 1958–59, Urban Districts from 10,000 to 30,000 in Population

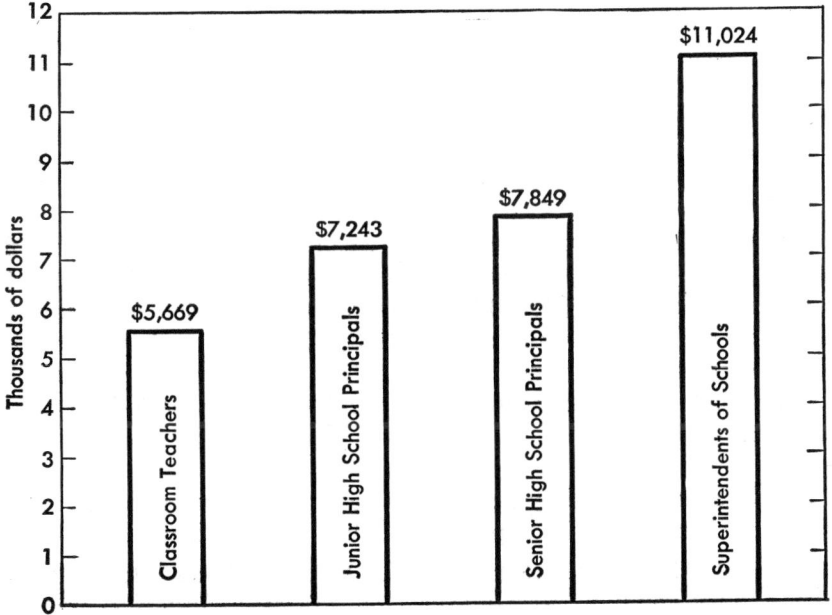

sional education usually want to know whether they can expect to earn a salary adequate to maintain a decent standard of living for their families.

A comparison of salaries of high school principals and teachers shows that salaries are substantially better in administration than in classroom teaching. A research report of the National Education Association on school salaries in urban districts from 10,000 to 30,000 in population showed that the median for all teachers with five years of college preparation was $5,669.[14] The median salary reported for junior high school principals in the same school districts was $7,243. Senior high school principals received a median salary of $7,849, and the median for superintendents of schools in the same districts was $11,024.

TABLE 3

Recommended Maximum Salaries for Secondary School Principals and Assistant Principals, Stated in Percentage Ratio Above Teachers' Maximum Salaries

(Teachers' maximum salary with master's degree = 1.00)

Suggested Size of Enrollment[a]	Principal	Assistant Principal[d]
A. Secondary schools under 500	1.60[b] 1.40[c]	
B. Secondary schools 500–1,000	1.80[b] 1.60[c]	1.50[b] 1.30[c]
C. Secondary schools 1,000–2,500	1.95[b] 1.75[c]	1.65[b] 1.45[c]

[a] No special recommendation for secondary schools over 2,500 enrollment.
[b] 12-month employment, with 3–5 weeks vacation allowance during the summer period.
[c] 10-month employment, with 8–10 weeks vacation allowance during the summer period.
[d] If an assistant principal has a regular teaching assignment, the differential may be less in a proportional amount.

The difference in median salaries between classroom teachers with five years of college preparation and senior high school principals as reported in this study amounted to $2,180 a year. Over a period of twenty-five years, this differential would amount to $54,500. Comparing the median salary for classroom teachers with that for superintendents of schools, we find that the difference over a twenty-five-year period would be $133,875.

The differential in salary also is reflected in the proposal of the Executive Committee of the National Association of Secondary School Princi-

[14] National Education Association, Research Division, "School Salaries, 1958–59, Urban Districts 10,000 to 30,000 in Population," *Reseach Bulletin*, May, 1959.

pals. This proposal bases the principal's maximum salary on a percentage ratio above the maximum teachers' salaries in the same school. According to the recommendations presented in Table 3, the salary for high school administrators should be from 30 to 95 per cent above the maximum for classroom teachers.

Current practice is consistent with these suggested percentage differentials, as is shown, for example, in a survey by the National Education Association comparing median salaries of principals and classroom teachers (see Table 4).[15]

TABLE 4

Median Salaries of Principals and Other Professional Persons as a Per Cent of Median Salary of Classroom Teachers, by Size of Place, 1958–59

(Median salary of classroom teachers = 100)

Size of Place		Junior High School Principal	Junior High School Asst. Principal	Senior High School Principal	Senior High School Asst. Principal
Group I	500,000 and over	174.2	144.3	188.0	162.4
Group II	100,000–499,999	164.8	141.1	177.8	153.8
Group III	30,000– 99,999	157.7	138.7	171.9	150.9
Group IV	10,000– 29,999	147.7	134.3	159.8	144.4
Group V	5,000– 9,999	136.0	132.7	149.6	146.9
Group VI	2,500– 4,999	134.1	—	138.3	129.5

Read as follows: In cities of 500,000 and over, the median salary of the junior high school principals is 74.2% greater than the median salary of the classroom teachers in cities of that size.

In reviewing salary levels, it is important to keep in mind that the amount of salary paid to secondary school administrators is positively related to the size of the school. Larger schools pay higher salaries than do smaller schools. A typical distribution of salaries according to the size of schools may be seen from the results of a study of Michigan salaries for the year 1959–60.[16] Average salaries for the principals were as follows: $10,876 for Class A schools (800 or more pupils); $7,572 for Class B schools (325–799 pupils); $6,700 for Class C schools (150–324 pupils); $5,973 for Class D-E schools (less than 150 pupils). The top salary paid to a Michigan secondary school principal in 1959–60 was $13,000.

[15] National Association of Secondary School Principals, *Spotlight*, November–December, 1959, No. 40.
[16] Michigan Association of Secondary School Principals, *Bulletin*, 1960, Vol. 1, No. 4.

Most principals start their careers in small schools in the lower salary brackets, but many advance to positions in schools which pay higher salaries. On the other hand, it is well to remember that there are more small high schools than large high schools. To be realistic, a person preparing to become a principal should regard the median figures as the best estimates of financial potential. However, a top man can reach the $15,000 to $20,000 bracket in secondary school administration in some regions.

Salary is also an important factor in the decision of many high school principals to accept a superintendency. Just as the principalship draws many classroom teachers to administration because of the higher economic return, so the superintendency appeals to experienced principals.

Job Opportunities

Opportunities in secondary school administration are related to the number of high schools operating in the United States and to job turnover. It is impossible to state accurately how many high schools are in existence at any one time; the number is changing constantly owing to school district reorganization and the organization of new schools. The National Association of Secondary School Principals estimated that there were approximately 28,000 principals and assistant principals in public high schools throughout the United States in 1959–60.

We mentioned earlier that opportunities for women in secondary administration are limited. About 1 to 2 per cent of the principalships in public schools are available to them. Many women, however, serve as assistant principals, deans of girls, or in some other supplementary administrative position, and their contributions to the administration of secondary schools is substantial in such roles.

A person seeking a position as a beginning principal must consider whether he wants to enter administration in a relatively large school or a small school. The usual route to the principalship in a large school is through a succession of promotions — from classroom teacher to department head or counselor to assistant principal and finally to principal. Competition is usually keen. A teacher's chance of becoming a principal under these conditions is much less than if he is willing to leave his teaching position in a large school and seek a principalship in a small community.

Opportunities to become a principal at a younger age are much more prevalent in small schools than in large schools, since the former commonly seek a principal from outside the school system. A younger man is often preferred in the small school. But even here the trend appears to be toward giving careful consideration to successful teachers on the present staff before seeking applicants from outside. If a person is especially anxious to secure a principalship in a particular community, he probably would enhance his chances by first serving as a classroom teacher there. This is a slower route to administration, but it does allow the candidate to demonstrate to the local community that he has the potential to become a successful principal.

Some teachers become principals with the object of using the position as a stepping stone to a superintendency or to a supervisory position. There is considerable logic in this point of view, since boards of education often do regard experience as a high school principal as excellent training for the superintendency. On the other hand, the high school principalship has come to have sufficiently high status and leadership opportunities so that it is attractive to many as a lifetime career.

Questions and Group Projects

1. Invite a panel of high school principals to meet with the class to discuss the pros and cons of becoming a high school principal.
2. Compile a list of reasons for wanting to become a high school principal as presented by the various members of the class.
3. Have a member of the class interview a director of a placement bureau to secure tips on how to secure a position as a high school principal.
4. Interview a principal to determine the extent of his participation in community affairs.
5. Determine the number of new principals placed during the past year by the university's placement bureau. Compare this figure with the number of graduates in administration and supervision in the same institution for the past year. Discuss the implications of these figures for a person interested in becoming a principal.
6. Identify and discuss the specific certification requirements for the position of high school principal in your state. Do the same for the requirements of the regional accrediting agency that serves the schools in your state. What are the differences between the state requirements and those of the regional accrediting agency?

Selected References

Austin, David B. "Characteristics of a Successful Principal," *The Bulletin* of the NASSP, April, 1956, 40:441–46.

Beach, Fred F. "Professionalization of Educational Administration," *School Life*, October, 1959.

Boardman, G. W., J. M. Gran, and A. E. Holt. "The Duties and Responsibilities of the Assistant Principal in the Secondary School," *The Bulletin* of the NASSP, March, 1946, 30:3–11.

Bolden, H. F. "Attitudes of High School Assistant Principals Toward Their Duties and Responsibilities," *The Bulletin* of the NASSP, November, 1956, Vol. 40.

Brandes, Louis Grant. "The Position of the Subordinate Administrator in the Secondary School," *The Bulletin* of the NASSP, May, 1956, 40:46–52.

Cubberley, Ellwood P. *The Principal and His School*. Boston: Houghton Mifflin Company, 1923.

Eikenberry, Dan Harrison. "Training and Experience Standards for Principals of Secondary Schools," *The Bulletin* of the NASSP, November, 1951, 35:16.

Ensign, Forest C. "Evolution of the High School Principalship," *School Review*, March, 1923, 31:181–82.

Farmer, F. M. "The Public High School Principalship," *The Bulletin* of the NASSP, April, 1948, 32:82–91.

French, Will, J. Dan Hull, and B. L. Dodds. *American High School Administration*. New York: Rinehart and Company, rev. ed., 1957.

Horton, Ben H., Jr. "School Principals Look at Their Problems," *The Bulletin* of the NASSP, September, 1959, 43:115.

Hunt, Herold C., and Paul R. Pierce. *The Practice of School Administration*. Boston: Houghton Mifflin Company, 1958.

Jacobson, Paul B., William C. Reavis, and James D. Logsdon. *Duties of School Principals*. New York: Prentice-Hall, Inc., 1950.

Jarrett, Richard W. "The Activities of the Assistant Principal in Secondary Schools," *The Bulletin* of the NASSP, September, 1958, 42:28–32.

Martin, Evelyn B. "A Profile of Women as Secondary School Vice-Principals," *The Bulletin* of the NASSP, March, 1958, 42:77–83.

National Association of Secondary School Principals. "A Study of the High School Principalship in Pennsylvania," *The Bulletin* of the NASSP, December, 1953, 37:118–20.

National Education Association, Research Division. "School Salaries, 1958–59, Urban Districts 10,000 to 30,000 in Population," *Research Bulletin*. Washington: The Association, May, 1959.

Weiss, G. A. W. "The Duties of the Secondary School Vice-Principal," *The Bulletin* of the NASSP, December, 1953, 37:109–17.

Willard, Edwin A. "A High School Principal Comes Back," *The Bulletin* of the NASSP, November, 1956, 40:17–19.

CHAPTER 2

The Principal as an Educational Leader

The chief function of a school is the education of boys and girls. To achieve this it is necessary to have good facilities, excellent teachers, adequate supplies and equipment, and community interest and support. But crucial to all instructional activities is the skill with which the principal plays his role as an educational leader. Leadership is a matter of enlisting and coordinating the efforts of members of a group to accomplish the purposes of the group. The managerial activities of the principal are of little consequence if they do not further the educational aims of the school. The operation may run smoothly, but it contributes little unless it has purpose.

Under our state system of education most of the control of public schools is delegated to local boards of education, who are accountable to the electorate of their districts. The major responsibility for professional leadership is centered in local officials. State and federal educational agencies assist local schools by providing information, technical consultation, special instructional materials, special supervisors, and other related administrative services. But the effectiveness of these services is dependent upon the cooperation and competence of local administrators and local boards of education.

A progressively more important aspect of educational leadership is that of working effectively with citizen committees. Since 1950, there has been a marked increase in the participation of local citizens in school affairs. In 1950 citizens' advisory committees were practically nonexistent, whereas in 1960 there were approximately 20,000 such groups throughout the United States. This growth is due in no small degree to the influence of the National Citizens Council for Better Schools, which has demonstrated that people are interested and capable of participating in school affairs when proper leadership is provided.

The National Citizens Council for Better Schools discontinued its promotional activities December 31, 1959. It had given outstanding leadership in arousing local public interest in providing better schools. The Parent-Teacher Association continues to offer an avenue for effective cooperation between lay and professional personnel. The point is that lay groups are interested in their schools and willing to work constructively to further excellence in schools. It is the responsibility of local school administrators to capitalize on this interest and to assume leadership in utilizing it for the continued improvement of education. Without sound leadership, citizen interest can become destructive rather than constructive.

An effective job was done in Michigan, for instance, by a committee of high school principals working with the League of Women Voters. The League, interested in promoting study of the forthcoming constitutional convention in Michigan, asked the Contests and Activities Committee of the Michigan Association of Secondary School Principals for permission to sponsor a state essay contest on the convention. In this situation the motives of both groups were good, but there was a direct conflict in the means for achieving the desired study, because the principals had taken a firm stand that essay contests should not be encouraged in the schools. As a result of working together cooperatively, however, it was agreed that the League of Women Voters would supply materials and consultants to assist schools in conducting mock constitutional conventions. This approach was very successful; the initial interest and drive had come from a lay group and the suggestion for the specific learning experiences from the secondary school principals.

Although the principal should be closely associated with school patrons, his most immediate responsibility for leadership is with the school faculty and student body. It is with them that he works daily, and it is with them that he must develop a favorable climate for the operation of the school. Teachers usually want professional leadership from the principal. This concern is expressed emphatically by Wernick:

> ... My concern of late is that I am in a group that may soon be given up to disaster.
> It seems to me that our leaders should be doing more than they are doing. Exactly what? I don't know. ... However, I do know that I am not intensely proud of the records of my national and state leaders; I am not fiercely loyal to these spokesmen for my basic concerns; and I

do not care to be in this awkward position, professionally exposed to every pot-shot some public figure throws in the direction of education. My leaders owe it to me morally to make use of their values in difficult times. They must make clearer, more vigorous policies to stand up to the increasing number of challenges made to the education profession. . . .

If others feel as I do, resurgence of the moral constituents of educational leadership might energize not only the teaching profession, but also the entire human community. The moral demands of leadership press heavily upon our profession, if we are a profession. How many more times must we hear the clarion ring out the call for responsible direction from authoritative moral sources. . . .[1]

There is considerable support for Wernick's plea at the local level as well as at the state and national level. Many administrators have not given adequate time and attention to this responsibility. High school principals commonly spend much of their time taking care of routine details which have only an incidental relationship to educational leadership. There are numerous cases of discipline waiting to consume the principal's time and energy; an irate parent refuses to talk to anyone but the principal; transportation must be arranged for the football team; the dishwashing machine breaks down; or some visitors want a conducted tour of the building. Administrative detail is indeed a part of the principal's duties, but it should not take priority over professional leadership with the faculty, students, and community.

Concern over conditions in secondary education has been widely voiced by friends and critics alike. For example, the following statement is by a strident critic of American secondary education who has found fault especially with the provisions made for educating the gifted child and has advocated the adoption of European standards in our schools.

> The American public school today does not, by and large, offer this kind of equality and opportunity. Even among professional defenders of the educational status quo, few are so hardy as to allege that the superior student is being regularly called upon to work at the top of his capacity in the typical high school, or that he is being challenged by standards as exacting as those imposed without question upon candidates for advancement up the educational ladders of most European countries. . . .[2]

A concern for the need of generally higher standards in our high schools was expressed by the editors of *Changing Times* and quoted by Scott and Hill:

[1] Walter Wernick, "The Moral Emasculation of Educational Leadership," *Phi Delta Kappan*, February, 1960, 41:202–3.
[2] C. Winfield Scott, Clyde M. Hill, and Hobert W. Burns, *The Great Debate, Our Schools in Crisis* (Englewood Cliffs, N.J.: Prentice-Hall, Inc., 1959), p. 78.

> . . . The trouble with education in this country is that we made things too easy for our kids. What they need is the kind of intensive drilling that children in European countries are given. Over there standards are high and youngsters really have to toe the mark. When those kids go to college, they're really prepared.[3]

No attempt will be made at this point to undertake an extensive review of criticisms of secondary education, but many schools face problems which need thoughtful study on the part of local school faculties. It is doubtful that high school administrators have ever faced a greater challenge to become "educational statesmen" than they do today.

What are some of the factors in leadership which have important implications for secondary school administration? What do theory and research say about the process of leadership in education? The present chapter considers these key questions.

The Nature of Leadership

Leaders in any major enterprise need a basic philosophy if they are to be effective. In education in a democratic society consistency in viewpoint is essential if the administrator is to secure the maximum cooperation of those with whom he must work. The authors hold that acceptance of a "democratic" concept of leadership by the high school administrator is basic in schools committed to preparing future citizens for responsible participation in our free society.

Democratic Administration

A half-century ago school administration was characterized by autocratic practices. Superintendents and principals regarded themselves as "experts" in education who knew the best answers to the educational problems within a school. Few people questioned the propriety of their authoritarianism, since this was the accepted pattern of administration in other institutions.

During the first quarter of this century a growing interest in pragmatism with its great emphasis on democratic values had considerable influence in bringing about a revolt against autocratic school administration. Some of the pragmatists' more common criticisms included the following: (1) The American school system was being administered upon a pattern diametrically opposed to democracy; (2) in the autocratic school organization there is a dichotomy in planning and performance; (3) there is a clamor for loyalty up the line, but no loyalty down the line; (4) the supervision is dictatorial; (5) the teacher occupies a subordinate position in American education; (6) the teacher's personality is violated; (7) the pupil's personality is violated; (8) autocratic supervision violates

[3] *Ibid.*, p. 141.

the spirit of science — it does not ask what is right, but who is right, and the highest official is always right; (9) autocratic supervision breeds the cult of blind obedience; (10) classroom procedures are correspondingly dictatorial; (11) efficiency is the god of administration; (12) our schools have ignored the social challenge, i.e., the local community must not be touched; and (13) supervision has been centered in subject matter.[4]

John Dewey wrote of the need for democratic action in school administration as early as 1903.

> ... But until the public school system is organized in such a way that every teacher has some regular and representative way in which he or she can register judgement upon matters of educational importance, with the assurance that this judgement will somehow affect the school system, the assertion that the present system is not, from the internal standpoint, democratic seems to be justified. Either we come here upon some fixed and inherent limitation of the democratic principle, or else we find in this fact an obvious discrepancy between the conduct of the school and the conduct of social life, a discrepancy so great as to demand immediate and persistent effort at reform.[5]

As these views have gained stature in educational circles, efforts have been made to develop correspondingly democratic administrative procedures which would help establish more effective working relationships in the operation of schools.

In recent years democratic administration has been characterized by a point of view which holds that in the management of local school affairs policy making should be shared by the board and the professional staff and that the responsibility for implementation of policies should be assumed by all members of the staff. It is an approach to administration which depends upon the cooperative effort of every individual in the school organization to achieve the aims and purposes of the school.

The concept of democracy in the operation of schools is basic to consideration of the nature of effective leadership in education. But merely describing certain processes which distinguish democratic administration is not adequate. Also to be considered with respect to the role of the high school principal are (1) the personal-qualities theory, (2) status leadership, and (3) functional leadership.

Personal-Qualities Theory

For many years it has been popular to analyze the personal qualities or traits of people who are recognized leaders and to assume that anyone who possesses such traits has the potential to become a leader. This point

---

[4] John T. Wahlquist, *The Philosophy of American Education* (New York: The Ronald Press Company, 1942), pp. 210–11.
[5] John Dewey, "Democracy in Action," *The Elementary School Teacher,* December, 1903, 3:194–95.

of view holds that leaders are born, not made; either they have the qualities which make them leaders or they do not.

The influence of personal qualities of leaders may be especially effective in times of crisis. Franklin D. Roosevelt's famous first inaugural address, in which he stated, "We have nothing to fear but fear itself," came at a time when there was a need to bolster the confidence of people struggling with a paralyzing depression. No doubt the note of courage in President Roosevelt's speech was an important factor in his role as leader in that critical period.

Winston Churchill through his inspiring oratory and personal courage led the people of England to heroic efforts in the early months of World War II. The common people responded almost miraculously to his personality.

One of the problems in this approach to leadership is to determine which traits are characteristic of effective leaders. Research studies have not been able to discover universal qualities of leadership. Although studies are contradictory, Trow did conclude that "some leader superiority is usually found in various groups in intelligence, scholarship, dependability, and responsibility, activity and social participation, and socioeconomic status. . . ."[6]

Even though research studies have failed to identify universal qualities of leadership in education, there is considerable evidence that certain of the qualities described in Chapter 1, such as sincere interest in people, concern for the professional growth of the faculty, a consistent philosophy, open-mindedness to change, a mature sense of humor, and good emotional control, are present to a greater degree in acknowledged administrative leaders than in the average professional worker. Many educators, however, are unwilling to accept the personal-qualities theory as an adequate explanation of leadership. They have turned their attention to an analysis of leadership behavior as it relates to status and to leadership within a particular situation.

The Principal as a Status Leader

Status leadership is associated with an official position held by an individual. Assumption of the position results automatically in acceptance of authority and certain responsibilities. A person is expected to serve as a "status leader" because he holds a specific position, as in the case of the high school principal. For example, most principals are in charge of curriculum development in their schools. Such responsibility requires a number of faculty decisions relating to instruction; there are minor problems, such as whether credit should be allowed for participation in band,

---

[6] William Clark Trow, "Leadership," *Encyclopedia of Educational Research* (New York: The Macmillan Company, 3rd ed., 1960), p. 607.

and significant problems, such as those of joint teacher-citizen planning and whether algebra should be taught in Grade 8 or 9. Faculty decisions require leadership, and the principal as a status leader is likely to be the person who is expected to provide it.

Or it may be necessary for teachers to secure permission from the principal before initiating a certain change which deviates considerably from previous practice, since the proposed change might raise some serious public support problems. For example, suppose the teachers of social studies and English in a particular school want to attempt a core curriculum type of teaching in their classes. Up to now the teaching of these subjects has followed a conventional method, and a core program would be a rather drastic departure. In such a situation, the principal might reserve the right to decide on the wisdom of making the change at the time, in view of all factors affecting the school. In so doing, he would exercise the authority of his position and act as a status leader.

Some principals think leadership is based exclusively on status and become autocratic in their relationships with people. Apparently they feel that if a responsibility has been assigned to them it is their job to make all of the decisions pertaining to it. An administrator who looks upon leadership in this manner seems to consider it a sign of weakness to enlist others in the decision-making process. Unfortunately, he has a very narrow understanding of the role of administration, and his reluctance to share policy decisions prevents him from providing effective leadership.

It is possible, however, to make a farce out of enlisting the faculty in decision making. Some responsibilities associated with the position of high school principal have to do primarily with administrative routine and do not involve the exercise of leadership. Clerical work, management of supplies, and handling common discipline cases fall in this category. The skillful status leader is able to judge which problems should be referred to the faculty for consideration. Usually he refers only those which involve policy determination or major program changes. Once policy has been determined, the principal should see to it that it is carried out effectively. Teachers are often impatient if they are asked to perform strictly administrative tasks, such as recording marks on cards. On the other hand, they are usually glad to take part in policy formulation with respect to the school's system of reporting marks. They also feel strongly about participating in plans for important program changes.

Whenever the faculty or some other responsible group appears to be concerned with a school problem, the principal should be alert to the possibility of including them in a study of the problem even though he may have the authority to make the decision on his own. The fact that a person is a status official does not imply that he should carry out his duties without advice and suggestions from the faculty. Assume, for example, a situation in which the superintendent of schools informs the principal that the board of education is considering initiating a plan of merit pay for teachers. The superintendent suggests that the opinion of the principal would be helpful in the deliberations of the board. In this case the principal could give his opinion without discussing it with his faculty. On the other hand, he should be aware that the proposal will be of great interest to the faculty. In considering this type of problem, it is highly important that the principal consult the faculty before submitting his ideas to the superintendent. In so doing, he recognizes that the members of the faculty are vitally concerned and should participate in a solution so that the program of the school may benefit from their thinking. It is likely that the principal who works with his faculty in this manner will become a stronger and more effective leader and the faculty will become a stronger and more effective faculty.

The Principal as a Functional Leader

Functional leadership (sometimes referred to as situational leadership) differs from status leadership in that any individual in a group may become a functional leader whereas only a person holding an official position which carries some authority may serve as a status leader. It is inherent in functional leadership that a member be recognized by the group as a leader. This type of leadership must be earned through demonstrated competence in a situation of concern to the group.

The situational theory of leadership suggests that personal qualities of leaders are related to conditions and personnel within a particular situation. The assumption is that when a group of people are confronted with a problem someone in the group may suggest a possible solution or course of action, supply appropriate information, or do something which makes it possible for the group to proceed toward a solution.[7] The person who provides leadership to the group in one situation may not be the one to whom the group turns in a different situation. It depends upon a cluster of forces operating at a particular time and place.

Ability to provide leadership is dependent on the competences of a leader under a particular set of circumstances. It is necessary also that people trying to solve a problem be willing to recognize and accept leadership from an individual or group. A member of the group may have the necessary information to solve a problem but lack the ability to make himself understood. He cannot be effective as a leader of the group in this situation. Another person may have the necessary information and skill of communication, but the group may have rejected him previously and be unwilling to accept his leadership in any situation.

[7] C. A. and Mary E. Weber, *Fundamentals of Educational Leadership* (New York: McGraw-Hill Book Company, 1955), p. 49.

To illustrate how situational leadership may operate, suppose that the faculty of a suburban high school has been disturbed over the recent dismissal of a teacher who has attained tenure status. After considerable discussion of the problem, the faculty decides that it wants to do something about it but is not certain what course of action will be helpful. At this point, Lee Perkins recalls that the matter of teacher tenure was discussed in a graduate course in which she was enrolled last summer at the University. She also recalls that any teacher dismissed under the provision of the tenure law in her state must be given reasons for the dismissal and an opportunity for a hearing before the board of education. These provisions were not met in this case.

She presents this information to the faculty with the recommendation that the members take formal action requesting the board of education to follow the dismissal procedures established under the state tenure law. The faculty votes unanimously to follow her suggestion. In this situation Miss Perkins emerged as the leader because of the information she possessed and because the group was willing to accept her suggestion for an appropriate course of action.

The same faculty might be involved in trying to decide on the merits of grouping talented students for instruction in English. But in this situation Miss Perkins has neither reliable information nor strong convictions on the question. As a matter of fact, she is quite neutral on the subject and is willing to let someone else provide the leadership needed in reaching an acceptable solution. Leadership must be consonant with the nature of the problem, the abilities of the members of the group, and their willingness to accept an individual as a leader.

The personal-qualities theory and the functional theory of leadership are not mutually exclusive but complement each other. Effectiveness in leadership depends upon the possession of desirable personal qualities and the ability to exercise these appropriately in relation to a particular problem and to the people involved.

Although the principal is assured of being the status leader of his faculty, it is not at all certain that he will become its functional leader. In order to become a functional leader he must demonstrate his willingness to work as a member of the group and not remain outside because of his official position. In many respects the principal has a harder time becoming a functional leader than do other members of the faculty, since he must be able to discount his authority and be willing to have his ideas and suggestions stand on their merits. It is also rather difficult for a faculty member not to give undue weight to his suggestions, since the teacher knows that the principal is in a position of authority over him. It is unrealistic, of course, to expect that these conditions will not prevail to some extent in all school situations, but they can be minimized to a degree which permits the principal to be effective as a functional leader.

As long as there is a threat to an individual's security, he is likely to be somewhat fearful and reluctant to try out new ideas. It is difficult for some teachers to differ with their principal, because they feel a certain amount of threat to their security if they antagonize him. A principal who wishes to become a functional leader, as well as a status leader, must recognize this factor and guard carefully against the use of any type of threat to teachers because of differences in views. The extent to which he is successful in becoming a functional leader depends largely on how effectively he can practice democratic principles in his relations with the staff.

A few years ago an intensive study on the nature of leadership provided by secondary school principals was conducted in the Denver high schools. One of the important areas considered was the way a high school principal provides instructional leadership. Mackenzie reported that there were four basic methods that principals could adopt, namely, force, bargaining, paternalism, and determining goals and means in a mutually acceptable manner.[8] The conclusion was that a principal who aspires to be a functional leader must work cooperatively with the faculty in the determination of goals and means which are mutually acceptable to the group. It is interesting to note the reasons reported as to why the other methods of operating are not acceptable. The following is a brief summary of the four methods as reported by Mackenzie:

1. Force. The principal has the authority to force his point of view upon the group. He may not be aware that he is using force, but the faculty is very sensitive to any coercion and will usually react negatively to this type of behavior. Whenever decisions are rushed, when a principal is required to take certain actions without consulting his staff, and when he assumes he already knows the best method of working or the best action to be taken, it is likely that teachers will interpret the principal's proposal for action as an order. The implication of this reasoning seems clear: any time the principal finds himself taking action on policy matters without consulting his faculty, he is decreasing his chances of serving as a functional leader of the group.[9]

2. Bargaining. This method of dealing with teachers implies that the principal offers the teacher some favor, assignment, or benefit if the teacher will do something desired by the principal. The principal might suggest that teachers who agree to take tickets at the basketball games will receive special consideration on room assignments for next year. Or he might merely imply that if the teachers will support his plan of

---

[8] Gordon N. Mackenzie, Stephen M. Corey, and associates, *Instructional Leadership* (New York: Horace Mann-Lincoln Institute of School Experimentation, Teachers College, Columbia University, 1954), pp. 24–41.

[9] *Ibid.*, pp. 24–27.

school assemblies he will do his best to lighten teacher loads next year. Mackenzie suggests that this way of exercising leadership, if mutual confidence exists, is often better than the method of force. The leader's power is reduced, and the teacher's freedom of choice is increased. Mackenzie emphasizes, however, that bargaining places serious restrictions on the effectiveness of both teachers and status leaders. Mutual confidence is usually lacking, and a great deal of energy and time are expended by each side in enforcing the bargaining arrangements. Accusations of bad faith are common. The implications seem to be that the welfare of teachers or status leaders, not that of children, is paramount.[10]

3. Paternalism. Paternalism is a special kind of bargaining in which the principal creates the image of himself as doing his utmost to promote the welfare of the faculty or is always going out of his way to do nice things for them. Decision making still lies completely with the principal, but he expects the faculty to support his actions because they are intended to be in the best interests of the group. Mackenzie suggests that paternalism has an advantage over force in that it stresses reward rather than punishment, but it also implies, as does force, that teachers and status leaders have different objectives. The official leader helps teachers get what they want and then expects them to help him get what he wants. Paternalism also violates an important psychological principle with respect to the sequence of reward and activity. Instead of feeling rewarded for their professional activity, teachers get certain rewards first and then are expected to do what the status leader wants in order to earn what they have already received. This may result in increasing expectation on the part of teachers without any feeling that effort on their part is a prerequisite of such benefits.[11]

4. Determination of mutually acceptable goals and means. This method of leadership is dependent upon the principal's working cooperatively with the faculty in determining goals and courses of action which are in the best interests of all concerned. The faculty has an active part in forming policy, and the principal assumes a nonauthoritative role within the group. Goals of the principal are more likely to become compatible with goals of the faculty, and the group is then more likely to look upon him as a co-worker in achieving the objectives of the school. Mackenzie points out, however, that achievement of mutually acceptable goals by the teachers and the principal is sometimes difficult. The process appears to necessitate a climate in which the status leaders and teachers work together with mutual trust and in a spirit of free inquiry. When this spirit exists, the conditions are primarily democratic

[10] *Ibid.*, pp. 27–28.
[11] *Ibid.*, pp. 28–29.

and allow the principal to become a functional leader as well as a status leader.[12]

Whether or not a principal can become an effective leader within his faculty will depend upon his ability to achieve a thorough understanding of the strengths and weaknesses of group processes and to apply them wisely and discriminatingly. It is not feasible to present a complete discussion of the techniques and principles of group planning in a book concerned with secondary school administration in general. Some consideration is given to this problem in Chapters 12 and 13, which deal with the application of democratic principles to administrative tasks and to the development of good faculty morale. The authors also have attempted to describe administrative techniques and principles throughout the book which are realistic and in harmony with a democratic concept of administration and which stress both the status and the functional leadership roles of the principal.

Each principal must develop his own approach to meeting the challenge for effective leadership. It is doubtful that any principal can be entirely consistent in his philosophy or procedures as an educational leader. At times he will have to exercise his authority as a status leader, but at other times he can and should seek to achieve a high degree of functional leadership with his faculty and community. Some situations will require that he enlist the skills, abilities, and experience of others in order to solve certain types of educational problems.

Excellence in leadership demands versatility in employing appropriate techniques as a situation develops. We believe, however, that leadership based on democratic principles will be most effective. The major concern of educational leadership should be sound instruction implemented through democratic relationships between principal and teachers and between teachers and students.

It should be anticipated that the principal will experience some setbacks in his efforts to develop in leadership. A person who is charged with coordinating and integrating so many values and points of view in a dynamic field full of controversies, such as education, is bound to have some disappointments. Skill in democratic problem solving comes slowly and sometimes painfully. In this highly complex enterprise the old slogan "If at first you don't succeed, try, try again" makes some sense.

An educational leader should recognize that he must seek to continue to grow in his professional competence as a leader. There are many things which can be learned through experience and study in preparation for a career in secondary school administration, but the role of an educational leader is a dynamic one and demands continued growth. At best, a pre-service training program can help prepare a person only as a "beginning" administrator.

[12] *Ibid.*, pp. 29–30.

Professional Growth of the Principal

Secondary education is a changing field which requires continuous effort upon the part of professional workers to keep pace. There is little chance for the administrator to rest on his oars unless he chooses to go downstream. More than casual planning is necessary to enable him to profit from opportunities for in-service growth. To be sure, there are some areas of professional activity which contribute to the principal's growth in the normal business of administering a school, but other areas may escape him if he fails to make a systematic effort to include them. One of the most likely avenues for growth is through participation in professional organizations on both the state and the national levels.

Professional Organizations

High school principals should belong to at least two types of professional organizations: those designed to keep them informed on curriculum developments and methods of instruction, and those which foster growth in administrative and leadership skills. Membership in several organizations will insure adequate coverage of professional developments; certainly a principal should be a member of the National Education Association, his state education association, the National Association of Secondary School Principals (NASSP), and his state association of secondary school principals. There are a number of other associations in which he should elect to participate according to his interest and needs.

The National Association of Secondary School Principals is the one organization which has as its major purpose improvement in the quality of administration of secondary schools. Its monthly publication, *The Bulletin,* is outstanding in providing current ideas about secondary school administration. The annual national convention of the Association brings together members working in the field of secondary education from all sections of the United States so that they may share ideas and information related to their profession. In addition to serving as a clearinghouse of information, the NASSP supports and encourages research and the promotion of activities designed to improve secondary education. For example, one of its outstanding projects has been the establishment and continued sponsorship of the National Honor Society for recognition of high achievement by high school students.

Membership in the NASSP brings valuable information to the high school principal through the Association's publication and reports, but the principal who wants to get the most out of belonging to it should try to contribute to its success by active participation in its affairs and programs. Invitations received for committee membership or participation in a special project should be welcomed by the practicing principal as a means of professional improvement.

Although it is not possible for every principal in the United States to participate directly in the working committees of the NASSP, all states have affiliated associations which usually carry out projects, hold conventions, and conduct research at the state level just as the national organization does throughout the country. Some of the larger states also have organized county or regional groups within their boundaries.

Professional Reading

Teachers and laymen frequently turn to the principal for assistance in dealing with educational and instructional problems and they expect him to be well informed on such matters. If he is to meet this expectation, it is imperative that he have a knowledge of developments in secondary education. The most reliable method for developing this competence is through extensive reading of professional literature.

The volume of literature available on secondary education is so extensive, however, that it is virtually impossible for any one person to read everything in the field. A careful selection has to be made, since the principal has only a limited amount of time for reading and he cannot afford to waste it on second-rate material. Book reviews and articles in the journals of professional organizations are likely to provide his best leads.

It is important for the principal to be well read not only in his own field but also in contemporary affairs and cultural subjects; he will need to include diversified material in his reading to improve his own general knowledge as well as his professional power. The high school principal who desires to keep pace with his profession can look forward to a lifetime of study. It is doubtful whether anyone who does not enjoy scholarly pursuits should aspire to a career in secondary administration. On the other hand, the person who continues his intellectual development, both professionally and generally, is likely to find great satisfaction in his role as high school principal.

Cultural Activities

One of the more attractive features of a career in secondary school administration is that there are many opportunities for identification with a variety of cultural activities in the community. In small towns the school is often the cultural center. Certainly, few other professions offer as many occasions to gain cultural experiences as does the education profession.

The principal should take the initiative in encouraging the highest possible level of cultural programs in his school. Concerts, art exhibits, dramatic productions, book clubs, and similar endeavors should be the best that the school and community can provide. Participation in one way or another will not only contribute to the principal's pleasure but also make him a more interesting and enlightened person, thereby enhancing his leadership potential in the community.

Professional Writing

Sharing experiences, research, and ideas with colleagues through writing adds a dimension to the principal's professional life which is difficult to secure in any other way. Considerable satisfaction as well as increased professional effectiveness may be derived from organizing and presenting ideas in writing, especially if an article has sufficient merit to be accepted by a professional journal. Recognition by the profession through the publication of articles may give a needed boost to a principal's morale.

Few effective writers are born. Most of them have to work hard at the business of producing cogent and interesting prose. There is no substitute for practice in writing, and the sooner a principal tries his hand at it, the sooner he will achieve the degree of competence required for having his work appear in professional journals.

Practice in writing will also help to improve the administrator's ability to communicate with teachers and patrons through bulletins, brochures, newspaper articles, and other types of publications. This is a skill which the principal should cultivate early in his career in the interest of his own professional development as well as for its functional values in strengthening support for the program of his school.

Public Speaking

A principal who is not an effective speaker is handicapped in carrying out his leadership and public relations responsibilities. There are few experiences quite so dull or disappointing to teachers as to be forced to sit through a meeting of the faculty, P.T.A., or some other group while a school administrator, or anyone else for that matter, rambles on in a disjointed or uninspiring manner. On the other hand, the prestige of the administration may be considerably enhanced if he has the ability to speak effectively to a group. The importance of facility in public speaking is compounded by the fact that frequent demands are made upon him to speak at a variety of affairs such as school assemblies, service club meetings, public forums, and student and parent conferences. These occasions call for considerable versatility in oral presentation.

Speaking is much like writing in that it takes practice and careful preliminary work. When the principal receives speaking invitations, he should accept those for which he has time to make adequate preparation and should look upon each as an opportunity for improving his skill as a speaker. The 1960 Yearbook of the American Association of School Administrators stresses the advisability of accepting only those talks for which the administrator has time to do the necessary research:

> Knowing he is vulnerable to the call for declamation from many quarters, and knowing his time for this phase of work is limited, the superintendent should accept only those invitations for public speaking for which he can conscientiously prepare. Only such addresses will earn the respectful ear of discriminating listeners. Only such addresses will add to his own in-service growth.[13]

This advice is just as appropriate for the principal as it is for the superintendent of schools.

Improvement in public speaking is very likely to come with practice if one is willing to look at his performance objectively and to accept constructive criticism. It is good strategy to utilize the services of speech teachers or other critics in seeking assistance. Many speakers like to plant a "listener" in the audience to catch its reaction to his speech. Undoubtedly there are thousands of brave wives of school administrators throughout the United States who have served in this capacity many times. One need not become a golden-voiced orator, but to be able to express ideas clearly and interestingly is essential. The spoken word is likely to be one of the principal's most effective means of enlisting public support for his school.

Advanced Study

Some consideration was given in Chapter 1 to the pre-service preparation of the principal. It was pointed out that at least a master's degree is generally needed to enter the field of school administration. The following materials are concerned with formal study after the master's degree has been won and the principal has had some administrative experience.

Additional study at a first-rate college or university has much to commend it. It is especially important for those who wish to become principals of larger high schools, which often require preparation beyond the master's degree. Programs of study leading to the Ed.S., Ph.D., or Ed.D. degree are being pursued by an increasing number of school administrators who find the necessary time and money to undertake them. Many universities, however, recognizing that not all principals can complete the work for an advanced degree, offer a number of non-degree programs or short-term courses which even the busiest administrators should be able to attend. Two-week workshops held in the summer or even full summer sessions afford a welcome change of pace and

---

[13] American Association of School Administrators, *Professional Administrators for America's Schools*, Thirty-Eighth Yearbook (Washington: National Education Association, 1960), p. 93.

can be of considerable help in providing programs and facilities for some concentrated study.

Formal study, of course, is not the only way for the administrator to continue his professional growth, but there is no substitute for a periodic return to the campus, with its library facilities, professors, and atmosphere of scholarship. Many principals have been gratified by their own motivation for formal study when they returned to the campus. It is stimulating also to gain new insights into old problems, catch up on recent developments, and have one's thinking challenged by other competent administrators and professors.

Selection of an institution and a specific program to be pursued should be made with an individual's own needs in mind. Sometimes it is desirable to choose a particular professor with whom to study. In any event, the choice of a place to study should be based upon the greatest return to the individual in terms of his professional growth rather than upon proximity to a particular institution.

Research

It is a real challenge to the administrator's creative ability in education to conduct good research, since he is forced to become thoroughly acquainted with related literature and to plan a course of action leading to the solution of his problem. His direction of the educational program is likely to proceed with greater confidence when based on insight gained through careful investigation. In many respects research is the backbone of modern education; without it there is little hope of achieving real professional improvement. Every teacher and administrator has an obligation to assist in this endeavor.

The testing laboratories for new theories in education are the schools themselves. Thus educators and scientists are faced with quite different situations: The scientist can conduct most of his experiments in industrial or university laboratories; the high school principal actually directs the major research laboratory for secondary education. Cooperation between the public schools and research specialists is important, therefore. It would be desirable for all principals to have the time and the competence to carry on local research, but if this is not possible, they can at least work closely with others and encourage research in their schools. Simply demonstrating a positive attitude toward research and a willingness to cooperate in it will do much to stimulate research activities within their schools. Utilization of experimental data tested in a local school as a basis for changing the instructional program or administrative practices is likely to be the soundest approach to improvement of the educational program. Participation in research also contributes to the professional growth of the secondary school administrator.

Questions and Group Projects

1. Make a list of all of the opportunities for professional activity available to a principal in your state. Rate this list in terms of priority, assuming you are the person to take advantage of them.
2. Try to recall a situation in which a principal you know achieved functional leadership. Why do you feel he was successful in this situation?
3. Some people claim it is impossible for a principal to achieve functional leadership within a faculty because of the authority inherent in his office. Do you agree with this viewpoint? Explain your reasons for agreeing or disagreeing.
4. One principal in a secondary school made the following statement: "None of this democratic administration for me. I was hired to run this school, and that is what I am going to do." Try to anticipate some of the problems likely to evolve during the career of this person.

Selected References

American Association of School Administrators. *The Superintendent as Instructional Leader.* Thirty-Fifth Yearbook. Washington: National Education Association, 1957.

Brownell, John A. "What Infirmities of Administrators," *Phi Delta Kappan,* November, 1959, 41:53–56.

Bush, William T. "What Administrators Do to Improve Instruction," *Phi Delta Kappan,* November, 1959, 41:64.

Chandler, B. J., and E. T. McSwain. "Professional Programs for School Administrators," *Phi Delta Kappan,* November, 1959, 41:61–63.

Christophe, LeRoy M. "The Principal and the Improvement of Relationships," *The Bulletin* of the NASSP, October, 1957, 41:55.

Dewey, John. "Democracy in Action," *The Elementary School Teacher,* December, 1903, 3:194–95.

Durgan, Guy Adrian. "A Study of the Principal's Role in a Curriculum Improvement Project," Ed.D. dissertation, Wayne University, 1953.

Mackenzie, Gordon N., Stephen M. Corey, and associates. *Instructional Leadership.* New York: Horace Mann-Lincoln Institute of School Experimentation, Teachers College, Columbia University, 1954.

Trow, William Clark. "Leadership," *Encyclopedia of Educational Research.* New York: The Macmillan Company, 3rd ed., 1960, p. 607.

Wahlquist, John T. *The Philosophy of American Education.* New York: The Ronald Press Company, 1942.

Weber, C. A., and Mary E. Weber. *Fundamentals of Educational Leadership.* New York: McGraw-Hill Book Company, 1955.

Wernick, Walter. "The Moral Emasculation of Educational Leadership," *Phi Delta Kappan,* February, 1960, 41:201–3.

II

The Changing Role of Secondary Education in America

The secondary school administrator who is competent to provide strong educational leadership must have educational perspective and statesmanship. He must be able to stimulate, to coordinate, and to direct the educative process. There is no shortage in the supply of educational technicians. We have an ample number of people with principal's certificates in the United States who can perform the technical tasks of operating a school. They are competent office managers, organizers, keepers of records, and schedule makers. But there is a pressing need for high school administrators who have the capacity to see the broad design of secondary education — how it has developed, where it is going, the theoretical framework, and the philosophical issues.

A textbook on school administration can present little more than a rough sketch of the broad design of education. However, the authors believe that such a sketch will serve as a backdrop against which the specialized tasks and responsibilities of the administrator may be seen.

In Chapter 3 we review the historical development, emerging theories, and various views of the functions and objectives of secondary education. The matter of the structure and size of secondary education is discussed in Chapter 4. Available evidence and arguments concerning minimum and maximum size and the troublesome question of the secondary school's relationships with elementary schools and colleges are reviewed. We have directed attention also to the position of local schools vis-à-vis the federal and state governments and various extralegal agencies.

CHAPTER 3

The Secondary School in Transition — Perspective

The first requisite in planning a sound educational program is perspective with respect to where education has been, where it is, and where it should go. Without perspective, schools are apt to go from one popular whim to another, getting nowhere and confusing a lot of students in the process. One of the strange paradoxes in American secondary education today is that, despite the great volume of materials written on the theory and aims of education, a majority of schools have no well-defined philosophy.

It is also paradoxical that, in the contemporary tumult over American high schools, so many critics have overlooked so much educational history. If a major issue — as suggested by much of the recent debate over education[1] — is whether a selective high school with a prescribed academic program or a comprehensive school with broad functional offerings is better, then it would seem important that teachers and administrators examine the reasons why we have moved so far from the first toward the second over a period of three hundred years. What changes have taken place in the functions and aims of the secondary school as this nation has developed from a collection of small theocratic, agricultural, and trading colonies to a great democratic and industrial republic? Have these changes resulted from the theories of educators and psychologists or from the demands of the public that the schools change to meet changing conditions outside the school?

[1] H. G. Rickover, "European vs. American Secondary Schools," *Phi Delta Kappan,* November, 1955, 30:60–64.

The administrative head of a secondary school is responsible for providing the leadership required to give direction to its educational program. If the program is to have perspective, *he* must have perspective, plus the ability to stimulate and to coordinate the efforts of various groups who have a responsible voice in the direction of education. It is with this responsibility of the secondary school administrator in mind that we review some of the trends and current issues in American secondary education.

Great Expansion

One of the most significant trends in American secondary education in this century has been the great expansion in educational opportunities and the remarkable increase in the number and proportion of youth taking advantage of those opportunities. However, the United States has not yet achieved the goal of getting all of its educable youth to complete high school voluntarily. We are plagued by the problem of racial discrimination in certain sections, many young people do not have access to schools that are large enough to provide the offerings commensurate with their needs, and the dropout rate is high among culturally deprived students and students of below average academic ability. By 1961, however, almost 90 per cent of all youth between the ages of fourteen and seventeen were enrolled in school despite the fact that in most states school attendance is voluntary after age sixteen or completion of the eighth grade.

Substantial gains also have been made in the proportion of youth graduating from high school. In 1957–58, 64.9 per cent of the total seventeen-year-old population graduated, as compared to 6.4 per cent in 1899–1900. A study by Thorndike published in 1907 shows that only 18.3 per cent of the children who started to school from 1900 to 1904 completed the ninth grade.[2] Bonner, in a study made in 1917–18, reported that, for every 1,000 pupils in the fifth grade, 32.4 per cent entered high school and 13.9 per cent graduated.[3] In 1954, out of every 1,000 pupils who entered the fifth grade in 1946–47, 55.3 per cent graduated from high school. Of those pupils who actually entered the ninth grade in 1954, 65.9 per cent graduated in 1958.[4] Spot studies in various states indicate that this figure had increased to around 70 per cent by 1960–61.[5]

[2] E. L. Thorndike, *Elimination of Pupils from School,* U.S. Bureau of Education, Bulletin No. 4 (Washington: Government Printing Office, 1907), pp. 11–12.
[3] H. R. Bonner, "Statistics of State School Systems" (1917–18), *Biennial Survey of Education, 1916–18* (Washington: Government Printing Office, 1920), p. 82.
[4] U.S. Office of Education, *Progress of Public Education in the United States of America, 1959–60* (Washington: Government Printing Office, 1960), p. 12.
[5] "Hopeful Second Chance," *Life,* May, 1960, 48:102–9.

Development of Secondary Schools

As the proportion of youth attending and graduating from American secondary schools has increased, the functions and programs of the schools have undergone significant changes. The story of secondary education suggests a cause-and-effect relationship between these factors, but it also suggests the importance of other factors in shaping the schools. The interaction of the many social, philosophical, economic, and political changes affecting the growth and development of secondary education is too complex to consider here. But knowledge of the major changes and some of the forces that brought them about is essential for the school administrator charged with leadership in educational planning. Without this sort of perspective, he and the school which employs him may be unduly influenced by interest groups who are opposed to, or fail to understand, the significance of a comprehensive program of secondary education in our society.

The first 250 years of secondary education in this country was occupied largely with establishing schools and developing the types of institutions and programs that were suited to the needs of Americans. Viewed from the vantage point of the 1960's, this period constituted an extended and sporadic struggle, closely paralleling the fortunes and misfortunes of the young republic.

The slow growth in numbers of schools and enrollments was geared to the pace of our national economy and to the changing status of the family and of children. During the colonial years much of the time and energies of entire families was required to make a living. The school is an institution dependent upon a society which has economic resources in excess of its needs for survival and which is in a position to release its children from the business of providing the necessities of life. Even though some of the colonial governments recognized the essential relationship between popular education and popular government, for more than a hundred years they could not afford to do much about it. Neither could many parents afford to spare the services of their children from family labors or to pay the cash cost of schooling. Under these circumstances, the first schools were highly selective, serving mostly the children of the elite.

The First Secondary Schools (1635–1780)

The first schools in America were Latin grammar schools. At the peak of their popularity, in the mid-1700's, several different types were in operation. Their principal functions appear to have been (1) to prepare boys for college and eventually for the ministry, (2) to develop sufficient skills in language, especially Latin, to enable students to read and to understand the scriptures, and (3) to provide religious and moral training for young men who were to become leaders in the church and government of the colonies. Since records for the Latin grammar schools are sketchy and their aims and programs have had to be pieced together from personal letters, speeches, and newspaper advertisements, any statement of their functions represents some conjecture on the part of historians. An authentic and direct statement, however, is contained in the first paragraph of the famous "Old Deluder Satan Act" passed in 1647, by the colonial legislature of Massachusetts:

> It being one chiefe project of ye ould deluder, Satan, to keepe men from the knowledge of ye Scriptures, as in former times, by keeping ym in an inknowne tongue, so in these lattr times by peswading from ye use of tongues, yt so at least ye true sence and meaning of ye originall might be clouded by false glosses of saint seeming deceivers, yt learning may not be buried in ye grave of or fathrs in ye church and commonwealth, the Lord assisting or endeavors. . . .[6]

Most historians of education agree that the Boston Latin School, established in 1635, was the first American secondary school. It was a transplant of the most popular type of secondary school in England during that period. Although some European schools, such as Vittorino da Feltre's school at Mantua, Italy, the Ritterakademien in Germany, and Mulcaster's Merchant Taylors School in England, had broken with the narrow scholasticism that had dominated secondary education in Europe from the Middle Ages, the first American schools reflected little of this reform movement. Since the first American teachers were educated in Latin schools, the available textbooks were written for them, and they embodied the educational traditions of the homeland, it would have been strange indeed if the first schools in America had not been Latin schools.

The immediate purpose of the early colonial Latin schools was to prepare boys for admission to college, and Harvard was the principal college. The entrance requirements for Harvard, as stated in 1734, indicate the content of the curriculum of the secondary schools:

> Whoever upon examination by the President, and two at least of the tutors, shall be found able extempore to read, construe and parse Tully, Virgil, or such like common classical Latin authors, and to write true Latin in prose, and to be skilled in making Latin verse, or at least the rules of Prosodice, and to read, construe and parse ordinary Greek, as in

---

[6] As quoted by E. E. Brown in *The Making of Our Middle Schools* (New York: Longmans, Green and Company, 1921), pp. 64–65. (From the Records of the Governor and Company of the Massachusetts Bay in New England.)

the New Testament, Isocrates, or such like, and decline the paradigms of Greek nouns and verbs, having withal good testimony of his past blameless behavior, shall be looked upon as qualified for admission into Harvard College.[7]

Like any institution which is borrowed from one nation and superimposed upon another without regard for differences in the cultures and social conditions of the two peoples, the Latin grammar school was ill suited to changing conditions in the New World. It did, however, make important contributions to American education. Especially did it serve to institute formal education in the colonies and to provide a foundation for a system of publicly supported common schools.

Evidence of dissatisfaction with the curriculum and purposes of the Latin schools may be found in modifications made during the second half of the eighteenth century. Sentiment developed for instruction that was more functional for life in the colonies than the study of Latin and the scriptures. Private-venture grammar schools advertised in the newspapers that they offered instruction in the English branches including writing, arithmetic, natural philosophy, rhetoric, and geometry. They also listed courses in the practical arts, such as navigation, surveying, dialing, and gauging.[8] That the demand for change came from the public is supported by the fact that the private-venture schools were well patronized and steadily increased in number.

The American Academies (1751–1860)

Dissatisfaction with the Latin schools continued to grow during the first half of the eighteenth century. As new groups such as the Separatists, French Huguenots, German peasants, English bond servants and Scotch-Irish individualists migrated to the colonies, the Puritan doctrines of social class and theocracy met strong resistance. A prospering merchant class along with a growing number of freeholders, craftsmen, and free laborers became an influential social block challenging the power of the clergy and the customs and traditions imported from England.

As the principle of separation of church and state gained popular support, a demand grew for schools that were more directly under civil control and that stressed preparation for citizenship more than classical and religious instruction. The merchants, freeholders, and tradesmen wanted an education for their children which was both cultural and

---

[7] Benjamin Pierce, *History of Harvard University* (from 1636 to 1769) (Cambridge, Mass.: 1833), Appendix, p. 125.

[8] Robert Francis Seybolt, *Source Studies in American Colonial Education: The Private School*, Bulletin No. 28, Bureau of Educational Research, University of Illinois, 1925, p. 99.

practical. The idea of broader offerings to serve differences in aptitudes and future plans of students took root and resulted not only in popular criticism of the rigid Latin curriculum but also in the establishment of more private-venture schools.

Benjamin Franklin and some of his friends in Philadelphia became the most articulate group of critics of the Latin schools. They contended that knowledge was for use and could best be gained through the study of science and man's environment, that the language of instruction should be the vernacular, and that the common schools should devote most of their efforts to instruction in the English branches. They held also that the secondary school should assume dual functions, preparing some youth for college and some for business and the trades.

In 1749 Franklin, in his famous essay entitled "Proposals Relating to the Education of Youth in Pennsylvania," wrote,

> As to their Studies, it would be well if they could be taught *everything* that is useful, and *everything* that is ornamental; but Art is long, and their Time is short. It is therefore propos'd that they learn those things that are likely to be *most useful* and *most ornamental*. Regard being had to the several Professions for which they were intended.[9]

Franklin's proposals reflect the beginning of a general sentiment for the extension of educational opportunities to more youth. They also reflect a growing conviction among many of his contemporaries that the success of a democratic form of government requires more than bare literacy on the part of the electorate. Franklin's views on curriculum indicate that the doctrine of mental discipline was losing some of its popular support and that many of his followers had come to believe that an appropriate program of secondary schooling should make provisions for youth of diverse abilities.

The curriculum outlined by Franklin placed priority on basic courses in English composition and literature, speech, history, mathematics, and science. Franklin also proposed "that to keep them in Health and render active their Bodies, they be frequently exercised in Running, Leaping, Wrestling and Swimming."[10] He declared that all should *not* be *compelled* to learn Latin, Greek or the modern foreign languages, but that all who desired to study languages should be given an opportunity to do so. In addition, he recommended instruction in such practical subjects as agriculture, mechanical theory, drawing, and commerce.

Franklin was successful in raising funds for the establishment of the type of secondary school that he had proposed, and in 1751 the Phila-

---

[9] Edgar W. Knight and Clifton L. Hall, *Readings in American Educational History* (New York: Appleton-Century-Crofts, Inc., 1951), pp. 76–77.

[10] T. H. Montgomery, *A History of the University of Pennsylvania* (1749–1770) (George W. Jacobs and Co., 1900), pp. 497–500.

delphia Public Academy opened its doors. But Franklin's curriculum was too advanced for the educators, and the courses actually taught in the early academies were little different from those of many private-venture grammar schools.

The growth of the academy was interrupted by the occupation of the colonists with the revolution and the turbulent conditions which immediately preceded and followed it. But after the critical business of winning independence, adopting a constitution, and establishing a federal system of government was largely accomplished, people turned again to the task of earning a living, building homes, and founding communities. No mention of education was made in the federal Constitution. Of the numerous explanations advanced for the failure of its framers to include any provisions for education, the following appears to be most credible:

> Perhaps the most significant as well as the simplest explanation is the undoubted fact that schooling in those days was not considered a government function in any sense of the word; it was all under the aegis of church and home. Thus, and almost by default, public education in America fell into a state and local framework where it has remained ever since.[11]

Throughout the history of public education in the United States, local communities have enjoyed a large measure of actual control over schools, but this authority has been delegated to them by the states. The "residual powers" interpretation of the Tenth Amendment of the Constitution has resulted in the several states' assuming both responsibility for and control over the public schools within their borders. The academies, like the Latin grammar schools, were local institutions — controlled and supported by churches, community associations, or private corporations. Consequently, the principle of local control became more firmly entrenched than ever during the period of the American academy.

Until the early part of the nineteenth century, the academy seems to have been well accepted by most Americans as the type of educational institution which could best serve their purposes. It grew rapidly and by 1850 there were about 6,085 academies enrolling approximately 260,000 students.[12]

The academy movement, however, did not live up to its early promise. Teachers and headmasters were not trained for the kind of functional curriculum that Franklin had proposed, many parents wanted to make certain that their children were eligible for admission to college if it

[11] Emery Stoops and M. L. Rafferty, Jr., *Practices and Trends in School Administration* (Boston: Ginn and Company, 1961), pp. 17–18.
[12] "Educational Statistics of the United States in 1850," *American Journal of Education*, March, 1856.

developed that they could afford to send them, and trustees tended to be conservative and were faced with the difficult job of providing finances. The college preparatory function therefore became the dominant aim of a majority of the academies, and classical languages, mathematics, geography, ancient history, and English grammar constituted most of the curriculum. Because the academy was too expensive for children from low-income families, because its curriculum gradually became more academic, and because its philosophy lagged behind progress in other aspects of American life, agitation again developed for a different type of secondary school.

Nevertheless, substantial educational advances were made during the life of the academy. (1) Opportunities for secondary education were extended to a larger portion of youth than was true during the period of the Latin schools. Girls were admitted to secondary schools for the first time and coeducation had its beginnings. (2) The curriculum was expanded to include several subjects dealing with the contemporary scene plus a number of additional vocational offerings. (3) Preparation for citizenship became an important aim of secondary education, and less attention was given to sectarian religious training. Character training, however, remained a major aim in most of the academies. (4) Although the theory of mental discipline continued to enjoy general credibility, a growing belief in the concept of education for social utility was reflected in such offerings as composition, speech, bookkeeping, carpentry, commerce, state and national history, stenography, and surveying.[13]

Early Public High Schools (1821–90)

The egalitarianism which gained momentum in the early part of the nineteenth century made a strong impact on education along with other social and political institutions. During this period the resistance of propertied classes to taxation for the education of other people's children was overcome in large measure. "For a nation of farmers and mechanics, bent on self-government and possessed of the ballot, there was only one kind of educational program in keeping with self respect, namely, a free and open school system supported by taxation and nonsectarian in its control."[14]

The extent to which the struggle for free public education had pro-

---

[13] George F. Miller, *The Academy System of the State of New York*, Fifteenth Annual Report of the New York State Education Department (Albany: University of the State of New York, 1922), Vol. 2.

[14] Charles A. Beard and Mary R. Beard, *The Rise of American Civilization* (New York: The Macmillan Company, 1930), p. 810.

gressed by the early 1800's is evidenced by the establishment of a free public high school in Boston in 1821. Known as the English Classical School, it was a response to the petitions of small merchants, mechanics, and other middle-income groups for a school for their children that offered a practical education, was free, and provided equality of opportunity for all youth with the requisite ability. The first public high schools were new chiefly in the sense that they were under public control, were tax supported, and charged no tuition. Despite much agitation for a more functional type of education, the curriculum was changed very little. Their great contribution was that they initiated a program of free public education at the secondary school level which has become one of our nation's great strengths.

That the high school was regarded by the people as a logical upward extension of the common schools and, therefore, entitled to financial support from tax funds, is reflected in a series of state court decisions dating from the 1850's. The most famous of these was the Kalamazoo decision handed down in 1874 by the Supreme Court of Michigan. In substance, it held that a Michigan law passed in 1850 clearly authorized a system of free schools in every district of the state as well as a state university, and that the law expressed the desire of the people for a complete system of free public education. The court ruled, therefore, that tax funds could be employed by primary school districts for the support of high schools and that the high schools could use such funds to provide instruction in languages and other academic subjects.

These decisions furnished the legal precedent for tax support for public high schools in other states and cleared the way for their rapid growth at the expense of the academies. The number of public high schools increased from 321 in 1860 to 2,526 in 1890.[15]

Public high schools were organized so fast, especially in New England and the frontier states, that by the late 1880's curricula in the various schools had become extremely diverse, not only in course offerings but in time allotments, grade placement, and standards for promotion. The colleges were more than mildly disturbed over the incongruities in preparation presented by candidates for admission and urged public school officials to put their house in order.

The National Education Association appointed its famous Committee of Ten in 1892, to make a nation-wide study of the high school curriculum and submit recommendations for improvement. President Charles Eliot of Harvard was appointed chairman and the membership included five other college faculty members, one public school principal, two headmasters of private schools, and the United States Commissioner of

[15] U.S. Bureau of Education, *Report of the Commissioner of Education for the Year Ending June 30, 1904* (Washington: Government Printing Office, 1904), Vol. 1, p. xvii.

Education. Their report, published in 1893, did much to standardize the length, content, and sequence of academic courses. Four parallel curriculum sequences were recommended: (1) the classical, (2) the Latin-scientific, (3) the modern language, and (4) the English.[16]

The major differences in these curricula were in the amounts of time allotted to classical languages, modern languages, science, and mathematics. The offerings in each sequence were limited to academic subjects. The English curriculum presumably was intended for terminal students, since it included no Latin, but the other three were strictly college preparatory sequences. Even in the English curriculum no provisions were made for any practical subjects although two business subjects were mentioned as possible substitutions.

Despite the efforts of Benjamin Franklin and many groups of merchants, mechanics, and farmers, extending over a period of more than one hundred years, to free the secondary school from college domination, the report of the Committee of Ten attempted to continue that control. The modest gains that had been made by secondary schools toward providing practical training for terminal students, general social and civic education, and instruction in the fine arts were completely ignored by the Committee. At the same time, the Committee's report did bring some much needed organization and unification to the curriculum.

But the report of the Committee of Ten was addressed largely to the past rather than to the future of American secondary education. Rapidly changing social and economic conditions during the first half of the twentieth century soon made its proposals unrealistic. Within ten years high school enrollments had doubled and, with the exception of the World War II years, they have increased in great amount every decade since 1890.

Development of the Modern High School (Since 1890)

The years since 1890 in secondary education have been marked not only by spectacular gains in enrollments and schools but also by extensive changes in the purposes and nature of the high school program. The twentieth century has been a period of high controversy in education. At times relations between groups with conflicting views and interests have become so strained that the survival of the high school as an institution has been threatened. But the high school has proved hardy and has continued to grow and to gain public support despite many attacks and crises.

The number of public high schools increased from 2,526 in 1890 to

[16] *Report of the Committee of Ten on Secondary School Studies*, U.S. Bureau of Education, Bulletin No. 2–5 (Washington: Government Printing Office, 1893).

24,549 in 1950. Between 1950 and 1960, there was a slight decline due to extensive school district reorganization in some sections of the nation.[17] Except for the decade of World War II, high school enrollments have gained by more than one million students every ten years since 1910. From 1950 to 1958 they increased by two and one-half million students, reflecting the enormous rise in births during the 1940's.

TABLE 5

Gains in Enrollments in Grades 9–12 in Public and Private Secondary Schools in Relation to Population 14–17 Years of Age

School Year	Enrollment, Grades 9–12 and P.G.		Population, 14–17 Years of Age		Number Enrolled per 100 Persons 14–17 Years of Age
	Number	Per Cent Increase	Number	Per Cent Increase	
1889–90	359,949		5,354,653		6.7
1899–1900	699,403	94.3	6,152,231	14.9	11.4
1909–10	1,115,398	209.9	7,220,298	34.8	15.4
1919–20	2,500,176	594.6	7,735,841	44.5	32.3
1929–30	4,804,255	1,234.7	9,341,221	74.5	51.4
1939–40	7,123,009	1,878.9	9,720,419	81.5	73.3
1949–50	6,453,009	1,692.8	8,404,768	57.0	76.8
1957–58	8,930,000[a]	2,490.0[a]	10,164,000[a]	89.8[a]	87.9

[a] Preliminary data.

Source: U.S. Office of Education, "Progress of Public Education in the United States of America," *Biennial Survey of Education in the United States, 1954–56* (Washington: Government Printing Office, 1959), p. 11.

Tentative figures show that enrollments in public and nonpublic high schools for 1961–62 were almost ten million, and statistical projections indicate that they will increase to about thirteen million by 1970. While the general youth population increased 90 per cent from 1890 to 1958, secondary school enrollments increased almost 2500 per cent. Further, the percentage of youth of secondary school age enrolled increased from 6.7 per cent to 88 per cent during these years.

Consequently, the differences in abilities, plans, interests, and backgrounds among high school students have become progressively greater. For example, according to early records the entering freshman class in colleges in 1890 was about 70 per cent of the number of high school

[17] U.S. Office of Education, "Statistical Summary of Education, 1955–56," *Biennial Survey of Education in the United States, 1954–56* (Washington: Government Printing Office, 1959), p. 28.

graduates for that year, whereas in 1958 only 35 per cent of the graduates entered colleges.[18] Even though preliminary counts indicate that this figure had increased to about 40 per cent for the fall of 1961, it is evident that the future educational plans of high school graduates today are much less homogeneous than for the graduates of 1890.

No intelligence test results are available for high school students for 1890, but with only 6.7 per cent of the youth population enrolled, the spread in academic aptitude must have been relatively small. In contrast, the intelligence quotients for 13,000 high school students as reported in a nation-wide study published in 1960 ranged from 50 to 159.[19]

In addition, the 88 per cent of our youth enrolled in secondary schools in 1957–58 came from extremely diverse home backgrounds. Some were from the highest-income families and some from the lowest; some of their fathers were professional men, corporation executives, and statesmen, and some were unemployed and unskilled laborers. Approximately 8 per cent of the parents of these students had some college education, but almost 40 per cent had only an eighth-grade education or less.[20]

A key question facing high school administrators and teachers in planning future educational programs is whether these trends will continue. Will enrollments keep going up and will student bodies become even more heterogeneous? The answer seems to be yes, with some qualifications concerning the second part of the question.

As noted previously, projections indicate that enrollments in Grades 9 through 12 will increase at least 25 per cent by 1970, largely due to the rise in youth population. Some of these children are already in the primary grades. However, the rate of increase will not be as high as it has been during the past twenty to thirty years. The rate of increase from 1950 to 1960 was about 39 per cent, as compared to an anticipated increase of 25 per cent between 1960 and 1970.

At the same time, it is probable that the high school retention rate will continue to rise, largely because job opportunities for youth without a high school diploma will decline. There is little reason to expect that such long-time economic trends as automation, increased production per man-hour, greater number of married women in the labor market, shorter work week, and restrictions on the employment of young workers by organized labor will not continue.

---

[18] U.S. Office of Education, "Progress of Public Education in the United States of America," *Biennial Survey of Education in the United States* (Washington: Government Printing Office, 1959), p. 13.

[19] J. G. Umstattd and Robert D. Thornton, "Secondary Education — Student Population," *Encyclopedia of Educational Research* (New York: The Macmillan Company, 1960), p. 1280. (Based on a study by Blyth C. Mitchel and Roger T. Lennon of the World Book Company.)

[20] Paul E. Opstad, "Non-Scholastic Factors Associated with Drop-Outs in Iowa High Schools," unpublished Ph.D. dissertation, State University of Iowa, 1958.

Another factor working to keep youth in school is the declining need for their services around the home. Social changes such as the rural-urban movement, the increasing dependence of the family on other sources for goods and services, and the growth in multi-unit dwellings have resulted in fewer work responsibilities for urban youth at home and more idle time on their hands.

Since the well-being of the individual and the strength of our society require more and better education for all youth, the retention rate of secondary schools seems certain to continue to rise. It will probably climb from the present figure of 70 per cent to 80 per cent by 1970 and then to 90 per cent by 1980. On the other hand, the differences among students in intelligence, family background, special talents, temperament, and educational and vocational interests have almost reached the extreme ends of the spectrum. Some of the current generation of high school students have IQ's below 60. It is doubtful that these young people belong in a comprehensive secondary school; certainly those with less ability should be in special institutions where they can be properly cared for and trained.

However, the heterogeneity in individual schools may increase as the characteristics of communities change and as small schools are consolidated into larger units. The school district reorganization movement has made substantial progress in several states since 1950 and should gain momentum during the 1960–70 decade. The decline in number of school districts from 1951–52 through 1956–57, as shown in Table 6, reflects the extent of reorganization which took place during this period. Most of the decrease in the number of independent school districts may be attributed to the consolidation of small districts into larger ones, and this trend will very probably continue.

TABLE 6

Changes in Number of Independent School Districts in the Continental United States, 1932 to 1961

Year	Number of School Districts	Per Cent of Decrease
1932	127,649	
1948	105,971	16.98
1953	67,075	36.70
1961	36,402	45.73

Source: American Association of School Administrators, *School District Organization — Journey That Must Not End* (Washington: National Education Association, 1962), p. 4.

In summary, it seems likely that during the next decade or two (1) high school enrollments will continue to rise because of the increase in general population, continued reduction in the dropout rate, and the needs of our society for a better-educated citizenry; (2) the national student population will become only slightly more heterogeneous since the diversity in characteristics is now almost as great as it can become; and (3) some individual school populations will become more diverse as school districts are reorganized and communities change. These changes will require further changes in the purposes and characteristics of the high school's educational program.

But modifications in the educational program are influenced as much by public beliefs about the functions of an educational institution and the nature of the educative process as they are by the size and composition of the school population. Perspective in educational planning also requires knowledge of the expectations of the supporting public.

Changes in Public Perceptions of Secondary Education

Some observers of American education attempt to link most of the changes in school programs to those in institutions outside the school. On the other hand, many critics attribute most of the innovations in school programs to educational theory. We suggest that changes in educational functions and practices cannot be explained unilaterally either on the basis of modifications in institutions outside the school or on the basis of new philosophies and theories. Both have had an important impact on the program of the American secondary school in the past and both undoubtedly will continue to influence it in the years ahead.

What the relative influences of theory and changes in the economic and social setting of the school have been is largely a matter of conjecture. Some shifts in educational theory undoubtedly are the products of educators' efforts to rationalize adjustments in the school which have been made to meet changing external conditions. But other developments in theory have evolved from research in the psychology of learning and child growth and from the works of philosophers. Whatever the reasons, important changes have occurred during this century in the basic beliefs of the American people as to whom the public high school should educate, what the ends of secondary schooling should be, and what means of accomplishing those ends should be used.

Equal Educational Opportunities for All Youth

The most fundamental tenet in American secondary education is that all youth should have an opportunity to secure a secondary schooling. The idea took root in the early 1800's and provided the theoretical support for the organization of the first public high school. Currently, few but the racial segregationists openly dispute the principle, and the segregationists protest that they seek equal, but separate, educational facilities for the races.

However, the principle of equal educational opportunity is not an absolute. To a majority of the American people equal opportunity means that tuition-free, tax-supported secondary schools should be made available to all youth regardless of personal characteristics such as race, creed, and economic status. In most states free transportation also is provided, and free textbooks are furnished in some. But the popular view does not hold that all costs of a secondary schooling should be borne by tax funds. Subsistence and incidental costs must be paid by students or their parents.

In addition, the doctrine does not imply that secondary education should be the same for all youth. The program may vary depending upon the talents and needs of students and their future educational and occupational plans.

In practice, educational opportunities for youth have a rather wide range from state to state and from community to community. Some states with a large ratio of children to adults, such as Mississippi and Arkansas, are the least able to support a good educational program. The personal income per school child in Maine and Florida was in excess of $12,000 in 1954–56, while in Mississippi and Arkansas it was less than $4,000.[21] Within each state, the valuation per school child among individual school districts varies in great amount. For example, Harris County, Texas, had an economic index of 13.996 in 1959–60, whereas another Texas county had an index of only 0.021.[22]

Real differences in educational opportunities also exist between small and large high schools. A school of around fifty or sixty pupils usually employs only four or five teachers and offers as few as seventeen to twenty courses, while high schools of around a thousand students employ fifty to sixty teachers and offer as many as seventy to eighty courses. These differences are discussed in greater detail in the next chapter.

Nevertheless, substantial progress is being made toward reducing differences in educational opportunities. Some federal funds are now available to all states on a per-pupil or teacher-unit basis for instruction in special fields, and federal allocations are made to local districts which have abnormally heavy enrollments because of the location of federal installations within their areas. More than forty states now have a foundation program of some type to attempt to provide reasonably equitable educational opportunities for all boys and girls regardless of

---

[21] U.S. Office of Education, "Progress of Public Education in the United States of America," p. 38.

[22] *Economic Index Exhibit,* Texas State Board of Education, March 2, 1959.

where they may live. In addition, the reorganization of many small high schools into larger units has helped to equalize the curriculum offerings and the special services available.

Mounting public support for equal educational opportunities is further evidenced in the favorable reaction in most sections of the nation to the United States Supreme Court decision in the Brown case in 1954. This decision held that segregated public schools for children of different racial origin are in violation of the Fourteenth Amendment to the federal Constitution.[23] As the tenet of equal opportunity gains increasing popular acceptance, our laws and methods of financing the public schools are being strengthened. The ideal is becoming a reality for a steadily growing portion of our youth population.

Voluntary Completion of High School by All Educable Youth

It is one thing to give all youth a chance to complete a secondary schooling and another to persuade all of them to take advantage of it. Although tuition-free schooling from the first grade through high school is now available to almost everyone in the United States, it is a hard fact that in 1960 only 70 per cent of those who entered the ninth grade in 1956 actually graduated from high school.

Steady gains have been made in the percentage of youth completing high school, however, and, as noted before, this trend seems certain to continue. One reason for optimism is that in recent years community groups and leaders all over the nation have been trying to convince youth of the importance of completing high school. Further evidence of the attitude of the public is reflected in the increased taxes that have been approved in local districts for guidance services, expanded curricula, new buildings, and student activities.

Although economic factors are operating to reduce job opportunities for youth and to persuade them to remain in school, the American people have sought to influence even more youth to continue through high school because the strength of our society, as well as their personal well-being, is enhanced by the completion of a secondary school program. It is both wise and feasible for this country to provide an educational program which makes it possible for each person to develop his potential and to contribute as much as possible to the nation.

Recent events in domestic and world politics, along with developments in science, technology, and social institutions, have imposed increasingly complex problems on each adult citizen in our democracy in his role as voter, taxpayer, and participant in civic affairs. Making informed and responsible decisions in meeting these problems requires more than mere literacy; it requires at least as much knowledge, social understanding,

---

[23] Brown vs. Board of Education, 347 U.S. 483, 74 S. Ct. 686 (1954).

intellectual curiosity, and personal responsibility as can be developed in a full-length elementary and secondary school program.

At the same time, the American people have hesitated to make secondary education compulsory. By 1954, five states had extended their compulsory age limit to age eighteen, but thirty-nine states required school attendance only to age sixteen. Since 1954, eight southern states have repealed or suspended their compulsory attendance laws because of the United States Supreme Court's ruling against segregation in the Brown case. Consequently, in all but five states students complete high school because they elect to do so, and in those five states any students over eighteen who graduate do so voluntarily.

One argument often made in opposition to compulsory secondary education is that most students have developed deep-rooted attitudes toward education by the time they reach sixteen. If their attitudes are negative, they probably will not gain much from being forced to attend school, and they may have an undesirable influence on other students. Often a boy or girl who is forced to attend school after reaching mid-adolescence tends to resist the help of teachers.

In addition, a small percentage of youth are uneducable because of mental or physical handicaps. Blind and deaf students may complete a secondary schooling if given appropriate instruction, but this requires specialized personnel and facilities. Again, a small percentage of youth are so retarded mentally that they are barely trainable and therefore must be provided for in special institutions. The popular phrase "universal secondary education" expresses an important American attitude, but in the literal sense it is unattainable, since there will always be some persons who are uneducable. Nevertheless, we are moving closer each year to the goal of secondary schooling for all educable youth. And in many communities the secondary school is being extended upward to include the junior college to meet our fast-growing needs for more education for more people.

Provisions for Individual Differences

Until Benjamin Franklin and his supporters began to puncture some of the long-entrenched educational views of their times, few Americans questioned the appropriateness of a classical education for everyone who aspired to be educated. Furthermore, it was not until well into the twentieth century that a substantial body of knowledge concerning the nature and extent of individual differences had been compiled and that schools were attempting to do something about it.

Although the lag between theory and practice has been great, it appears now that practice is catching up. Since 1950 the percentage of schools employing ability grouping, remedial classes, multi-track curricula, unit assignments, course enrichment, and guidance services has increased by very considerable amounts. In 1953 only 37 per cent of the large schools in the Midwest were using some type of ability grouping.[24] Five years later almost 70 per cent of these schools had adopted it.[25]

Currently, most of the proponents of mental discipline would disregard the great diversity among our students as well as most of the research in the psychology of learning and have our schools return to the single curriculum of European secondary schools. But a large majority of the American people have demonstrated through local actions their belief that the school should do as much as possible to adapt instruction to the different needs and abilities of students. It is as logical to argue that all children should be taught in the same way in school as to argue that all children should be reared and disciplined in the same way in the home. It is as logical to force a boy with an IQ of 70 to compete in the classroom with the intellectually talented as to force a boy with little physical stamina to scrimmage each day with the varsity football squad.

Growing public support for provisions for individual differences in secondary schools is indicated in the greatly expanded number of electives in the curriculum, especially in such high-cost fields as vocational education, music, advanced science, remedial reading, and foreign languages (with laboratories).

General and Specialized Programs

In a great majority of secondary schools in Europe the dominant purpose has long been to prepare students for the universities. This was also the primary purpose of American secondary schools for more than two hundred years. But it became evident during the nineteenth century that this traditional function was ill suited to the educational needs and conditions of American democracy.

Experience has demonstrated that under our form of government and in our type of society all people require certain common skills, information, and values which will equip them for freedom and for their responsibilities as participants in government and in civic affairs. In combination, these outcomes define the scope of general or basic education in the United States. These are the things that we have come to regard as essential in the education of all students — college preparatory and terminal.

Supporters of the European system hold that whatever program is suitable for preparing students for college is the best program of general education for all youth. But the typical college preparatory program

---

[24] Dean A. Crawford, "The Administrative Organization of the Curriculum in Midwestern High Schools," unpublished Ph.D. dissertation, State University of Iowa, 1955.

[25] L. A. Van Dyke and Jack N. Sparks, *Four-State Survey of Secondary School Marking Practices*, Research Digest No. 2 (Iowa City: Iowa Center for Research in School Administration, 1960).

places emphasis on the academic aspects of our cultural heritage and is only incidentally concerned with the contemporary social-civic scene and with such outcomes as health, personal adjustment, and social relationships. Most Americans now reject this restricted view of basic education.

General education, as it has evolved in American secondary schools during the twentieth century, is directed toward promoting competence in the basic skills, health, knowledge of the American heritage, moral and ethical values, social understanding, civic responsibility, preparation for family living, and appreciation of the arts. Over the past half-century the American people have given approval to a program of secondary education which makes these the basic educational goals for all students. And most youth now are required to devote about one-half of their time in high school to studying courses designed to implement these common aims.

But American parents and educators believe that the secondary school also should offer some specialized education. By the time adolescents reach the tenth or eleventh grade, most of them have demonstrated some special abilities and have developed interests in further education or in some type of occupation. With increased enrollments and a concomitant increase in the heterogeneity of the secondary school population, it has become necessary for high schools to provide both college and vocational preparatory courses in order to serve the needs of all their students. Without some exploratory and specialized courses in the vocational field, many students who do not have the talent and/or finances for college tend to lose interest in high school and drop out. Since we are committed to a program of voluntary secondary education for all educable youth, it follows that our secondary schools need to provide specialized as well as general studies in order to implement that program.

The critical question is how to achieve these dual purposes. Out of the great volume of knowledge, what knowledge is most appropriate for the general and specialized education of adolescents? And within the time available, should the curriculum of the high school be designed to provide a survey of all the major organized fields of knowledge or should it be developed around persistent social problems and youth needs? Public opinion seems to be moving toward support of a program that places greater emphasis on social needs and values and the needs of students.

Emphasis on the Needs and Values of Our Society

Until well into the twentieth century, the American secondary school curriculum was composed primarily of those organized bodies of knowledge that scholars considered most appropriate for transmitting the cultural heritage and for training the powers of the intellect. The assumption was that these subjects provided the best educational foundation to prepare the individual for future responsibilities in adult life. We recall that it was Benjamin Franklin who first voiced dissent: "It is therefore proposed that they learn those things that are likely to be *most useful* and *most ornamental.*"[26] Franklin contended that rhetoric, American literature, writing, United States history, government, and certain of the practical arts should be included in the curriculum to perpetuate the values and to serve the needs of American society.

Instruction dealing with the distinctive values and important needs of our society was also proposed by Thomas Jefferson and other prominent statesmen during the eighteenth and nineteenth centuries. But changes in the educational program came slowly. Not until after the beginning of the great expansion of knowledge in the twentieth century did educators face up to the necessity of defining criteria for the selection of curriculum content. From that time on, statements of educational aims included such social-civic objectives as "civic responsibility," "economic efficiency," "family living," and "human relationships."

Since the 1920's, course offerings in history and the social studies have been greatly expanded, and the content of these courses, as well as those in other fields, have placed greater emphasis on social relationships, civil liberties, economic competence, civic responsibilities, the nature of a free society, and representative government. They also have dealt with such important and persistent problems as international relations, family instability, unemployment, social security, public health, and intergroup conflicts. But these changes have been directed largely to the future needs of youth in an adult world. And youth have asked for help with their own problems.

Provisions for Youth Needs in the Curriculum

Research concerned with the developmental problems of youth has focused attention on the nature and importance of physiological and social adjustments of adolescents in our society. From the early 1930's to the middle 1950's a great volume of materials on youth needs was addressed to parents and to secondary school faculties. Yearbooks, research reports, textbooks, and literally hundreds of articles were devoted to the special characteristics and problems of adolescents. Some were sound, identified problems significant to the educational growth of youth; some were trivial and amounted to little more than gossip.

Out of the profusion of pronouncements an important principle emerged and gained wide acceptance: Adolescents have in common many problems of adjustment to physiological changes, to social relations within peer groups, and to adult standards of behavior; and it is a proper func-

---

[26] Knight and Hall, *op. cit.*, pp. 76–77.

tion of the secondary school to assist students in meeting these problems.

A statement of the developmental tasks of adolescent boys and girls which has gained wide currency is the following, formulated by Havighurst and his associates:

1. Achieving new and more mature relations with age-mates of both sexes.
2. Accepting a masculine and feminine social role.
3. Accepting one's physique and using the body effectively.
4. Achieving emotional independence of parents and other adults.
5. Achieving assurance of economic independence.
6. Selecting and preparing for an occupation.
7. Preparing for marriage and family life.
8. Developing intellectual skills and concepts necessary for civic competence.
9. Desiring and achieving socially responsible behavior.
10. Acquiring a set of values and an ethical system as a guide to behavior.[27]

Few educators or laymen hold that these tasks should serve as the framework for the curriculum, but most would agree that they are legitimate concerns of secondary education. If guidance is accepted as an important service of the secondary school, then the needs of youth constitute educational goals of some consequence, since the problems of students are the chief concerns of guidance. That guidance has been widely accepted as having a major place in secondary education is reflected in the number of organized guidance programs developed in schools since 1950. It is also reflected in the volume of articles on the subject appearing in popular magazines and newspapers and by the action of Congress in appropriating several million dollars under the National Defense Education Act for the training of school counselors.

Academic Freedom Vital to a Free Society

Freedom of speech and freedom of the press were written into the Bill of Rights of the federal Constitution because the American colonists had learned through a long and painful experience that a free society cannot exist without these guarantees. Academic freedom *per se* was not provided for in the Constitution, but over the years the American people have extended more freedom to teachers to deal with controversial matters in educating youth. It would be wishful thinking to assume that high school teachers enjoy a full measure of academic freedom even in this century of scientific progress. Nevertheless, they now possess a much greater degree of freedom in teaching scientific facts and in dealing with

[27] Robert J. Havighurst, *Human Development and Education* (New York: Longmans, Green and Company, 1953), Chaps. 9–11.

controversial issues in the classroom than did their predecessors of only thirty or forty years ago.

Since the famous Scopes trial in Tennessee in 1925, in which a state law prohibiting the teaching of the theory of evolution in the public schools was tested, the public has grown progressively more liberal in permitting teachers to present scientific facts. But in the realm of social thought, the American people have been much more jealous of their prerogative to approve what is to be taught in the schools. Probably parents will continue to hold some reservations with respect to the degree of freedom extended to teachers in determining what shall be taught to immature children. Nevertheless, teachers have gained greater freedom as they have demonstrated sound judgment and a mature sense of responsibility. In addition, the American people have come to recognize that the vitality of a free society depends in great degree upon the free exchange of ideas, whether in the press or in the classroom.

These views, based on experience, deliberations, and research during the twentieth century, provide a framework of public opinion within which the program of the high school has been built. That they are also the views of a majority of the public has been demonstrated through legislative acts, support of tax levies, approval of local curriculum plans, and direct expressions of opinion. Other beliefs, equally or more influential, have persisted over a longer period of time. Since the background of these concepts was reported in the historical sketches of early types of secondary schools, we simply call attention to them here:

1. The critical and sustaining role of popular education in a democracy.
2. Local control of public schools — the delegation of major control to executive boards representing the people in local districts.
3. The supplementary role of the school — the school in a supporting role to the home and other institutions in the education of the young.
4. Separation of church and state — in the control of schools and in the teaching of religion.

Along with growing enrollments and extensive changes in the composition of the high school population, these widely held beliefs have shaped the special objectives of the high school. Some idea of the shift in emphasis in objectives may be gained by comparing statements formulated by national committees over a forty-year period.

Changes in Objectives

Probably the best-known statement of objectives for the high school, the "Cardinal Principles of Secondary Education," was authored by the Commission on the Reorganization of Secondary Education in 1918. The objectives are (1) health, (2) command of fundamental processes, (3) worthy home membership, (4) vocation, (5) civic education, (6) worthy use of leisure, and (7) ethical character.[28]

Although this statement often has been employed by both elementary and secondary school faculties, it has also been sharply criticized. It is a statement by adults specifying qualities that they regarded as desirable for adult citizens. It overlooks the developmental problems of adolescents, and it fails to include such educational outcomes as social responsibility, economic competence, intellectual growth, international understanding, and scientific knowledge, which many educators now consider as important as the ones listed by the Commission. At best, it is an incomplete list of broad areas of instruction for the secondary program.

Twenty years later the Educational Policies Commission undertook to draft a statement which would fill in some of the gaps in the "Seven Cardinal Principles" and give more specific direction to curriculum planners. This statement was published by the National Education Association in 1938 under the title, *The Purposes of Education in American Democracy.*[29]

The Commission classified the objectives of education under four broad headings. In the words of the Commission,

> These aspects center around the person himself, his relationships to others in home and community, the creation and use of material wealth, and socio-civic activities. The first area calls for a description of the educated *person;* the second, for a description of the educated *member of the family and community group;* the third, of the educated *producer or consumer;* the fourth, of the educated *citizen.*[30]

The statement of the broad purposes and specific objectives proposed by the Commission follows:

I. THE OBJECTIVES OF SELF-REALIZATION

The Inquiring Mind. The educated person has an appetite for learning.
Speech. The educated person can speak the mother tongue clearly.
Reading. The educated person reads the mother tongue efficiently.
Writing. The educated person writes the mother tongue effectively.
Number. The educated person solves his problems of counting and calculating.

[28] Commission on the Reorganization of Secondary Education, *Cardinal Principles of Secondary Education,* U.S. Office of Education, Bulletin 1918, No. 35 (Washington: Government Printing Office, 1918), p. 9.
[29] Educational Policies Commission, *The Purposes of Education in American Democracy* (Washington: National Education Association, 1938).
[30] *Ibid.,* p. 47.

Sight and Hearing. The educated person is skilled in listening and observing.

Health Knowledge. The educated person understands the basic facts concerning health and disease.

Health Habits. The educated person protects his own health and that of his dependents.

Public Health. The educated person works to improve the health of the community.

Recreation. The educated person is participant and spectator in many sports and other pastimes.

Intellectual Interests. The educated person has mental resources for the use of leisure.

Esthetic Interests. The educated person appreciates beauty.

Character. The educated person gives responsible direction to his own life.

II. The Objectives of Human Relationship

Respect for Humanity. The educated person puts human relationships first.

Friendships. The educated person enjoys a rich, sincere, and varied social life.

Cooperation. The educated person can work and play with others.

Courtesy. The educated person observes the amenities of social behavior.

Appreciation of the Home. The educated person appreciates the family as a social institution.

Conservation of the Home. The educated person conserves family ideals.

Homemaking. The educated person is skilled in homemaking.

Democracy in the Home. The educated person maintains democratic family relationships.

III. The Objectives of Economic Efficiency

Work. The educated producer knows the satisfaction of good workmanship.

Occupational Information. The educated producer understands the requirements and opportunities for various jobs.

Occupational Choice. The educated producer has selected his occupation.

Occupational Efficiency. The educated producer succeeds in his chosen vocation.

Occupational Adjustment. The educated producer maintains and improves his efficiency.

Occupational Appreciation. The educated producer appreciates the social value of his work.

Personal Economics. The educated consumer plans the economics of his own life.

Consumer Judgment. The educated consumer develops standards for guiding his expenditures.

Efficiency in Buying. The educated consumer is an informed and skillful buyer.
Consumer Protection. The educated consumer takes appropriate measures to safeguard his interests.

IV. THE OBJECTIVES OF CIVIC RESPONSIBILITY

Social Justice. The educated citizen is sensitive to the disparities of human circumstance.
Social Activity. The educated citizen acts to correct unsatisfactory conditions.
Social Understanding. The educated citizen seeks to understand social structures and social processes.
Critical Judgment. The educated citizen has defenses against propaganda.
Tolerance. The educated citizen respects honest differences of opinion.
Conservation. The educated citizen has a regard for the nation's resources.
Social Applications of Science. The educated citizen measures scientific advance by its contribution to the general welfare.
World Citizenship. The educated citizen is a cooperating member of the world community.
Law Observance. The educated citizen respects the law.
Economic Literacy. The educated citizen is economically literate.
Political Citizenship. The educated citizen accepts his civic duties.
Devotion to Democracy. The educated citizen acts upon an unswerving loyalty to democratic ideals.

This statement has provoked mixed reactions among reviewers. Those who regard themselves as humanists question the emphasis on social adjustment and vocational preparation. They also are critical of the casual nod given to intellectual development. The functionalists, on the other hand, have been critical of the failure to recognize the growing-up problems of adolescents. Both groups point out the fact that some of the outcomes are far from comparable in importance. Although some of the specific objectives have become badly dated, the complete statement provides a useful guide for local schools.

In 1944 a committee of the National Association of Secondary School Principals drafted a list of "The Imperative Needs of Youth": (1) salable skills; (2) health and physical fitness; (3) citizenship; (4) family life; (5) purchase and use of goods and services; (6) scientific knowledge and methods; (7) appreciation of beauty; (8) wise use of leisure time; (9) respect for others, ethical values, and cooperation; and (10) ability to think, express thoughts, read, and listen.[31] This statement has been used extensively by faculties of local schools and focuses attention on im-

[31] National Association of Secondary School Principals, *Planning for American Youth* (Washington: National Education Association, 1944).

portant outcomes. However, it is essentially an expansion of the "Seven Cardinal Principles" and is successful chiefly in identifying desirable qualities of a well-rounded citizen. The imperativeness of the needs identified by the committee is based on the judgment of a group of adults rather than young people. Several of the developmental tasks of adolescents described by Havighurst and his associates apparently were not regarded as imperative by the committee.[32]

A more recent statement of purposes was drafted by the 1955 White House Conference on Education. It borrows liberally from each of the earlier statements but appears to reflect current public opinion, since laymen were in the majority in the conference.[33]

What Should Our Schools Accomplish?

1. A general education as good or better than that offered in the past with increased emphasis on the physical and social sciences.
2. Programs designed to develop patriotism and good citizenship.
3. Programs designed to foster moral, ethical, and spiritual values.
4. Vocational education tailored to the abilities of each pupil and to the needs of the community and nation.
5. Courses designed to teach domestic skills.
6. Training in leisure time activities such as music, dancing, avocational reading, and hobbies.
7. A variety of health services for all children including both physical and dental inspections and instruction aimed at bettering health knowledge and habits.
8. Special treatment for children with speech or reading difficulties and other handicaps.
9. Physical education, ranging from systematic exercises, physical therapy, and intramural sports, to interscholastic athletic competition.
10. Instruction to meet the needs of abler students.
11. Programs designed to acquaint students with countries other than their own in an effort to help them understand the problem America faces in international relations.
12. Programs designed to foster mental health.
13. Programs designed to foster wholesome family living.
14. Organized recreational and social activities.
15. Courses designed to promote safety. These include instruction in driving, swimming, civil defense, etc.

This list is a mixture of goals and services, but it provides a helpful set of guides for educational planning. Moreover, a fine distinction between

---

[32] Havighurst, *op. cit.*, Chaps. 9–11.
[33] The Committee for the White House Conference on Education, *A Report to the President* (Washington: Government Printing Office, 1956), pp. 8–9.

goals and services is probably of little practical importance in the functioning of a school. The Conference statement emphasizes a sound basic education but calls for the inclusion of instruction in social values, social needs, health, recreation, practical arts, and moral values. In addition, it points to the need for special educational provisions for gifted and handicapped students.

Changes in the Educational Program

The typical high school today resembles the typical high school of 1890 about as closely as a modern aircraft plant resembles the Wright brothers' shop at Kitty Hawk. The lag between theory and practice may be greater in education than in business and industry, but the gap is no wider than in other enterprises dependent on public control and public support. Since 1950, changes in the educational program have kept pace with changes outside the school more closely in the high school than in other branches of education.

Lee A. DuBridge, President of California Institute of Technology, declared recently that the average college freshman in 1961 ranked far higher on major aptitude tests than did his counterpart in 1951. And 148 of 182 freshmen at Cal Tech in 1961 came from public high schools. DuBridge says the 1951–56 improvement in student levels is so marked that many colleges are having to advance the quality and content of their courses to keep up with the students. "But recent reports from some of the toughest and most demanding colleges in the country — Harvard, Yale, Princeton, Chicago, Stanford, California Institute of Technology, and Massachusetts Institute of Technology — indicate that many of our high schools are turning out a far better product than they did a dozen years ago."[34]

Fast-shifting economic, political, and social conditions along with changing educational theories and school enrollments have forced secondary schools to make extensive changes in their curricula and special services. Seventy years ago such subjects and services as vocational education, music, art, economics, social problems, speech, journalism, guidance, bus transportation, and food services were rarely, if ever, found in a high school program. Today they are commonplace.

Expanded accounts of developments in these fields will be included in later chapters. The following summary is presented as an overview of the scope and direction of changes during the growth of the modern high school.

[34] Bruce Biossat, Newspaper Enterprise Association, reprinted in Iowa City *Press Citizen*, May 2, 1962, editorial page.

Curriculum

1. Marked increase in total course offerings (over 1,000 per cent).
2. Extensive gains in vocational offerings stimulated by federal appropriations — the Smith-Hughes (1917), George-Deen (1936), and George-Barden (1945) acts.
3. Development of fused survey courses (general biology, modern problems, world history, etc.).
4. Decline and rise of enrollments in academic courses (e.g., geometry down from 21 per cent to 11 per cent and back up to 15 per cent).
5. Increased provisions for individual differences (such as ability grouping, honors programs, remedial courses, advanced placement, and work-study programs).
6. More emphasis on contemporary affairs and works.
7. Growth of core programs — especially block-time programs in junior high schools.
8. Greater emphasis on socio-civic outcomes.
9. Inclusion of guidance materials within regular courses; attention to problems of adolescents.
10. Incorporation of some student activities into organized courses (e.g., music, speech, and journalism).
11. Increase in experimental programs (such as modern mathematics, advanced placement courses, etc.).
12. Substantial gains in science and mathematics offerings and enrollments since 1950 (materially aided by funds authorized by the National Defense Education Act of 1958).
13. Large increase in fine arts offerings — especially in music, art, and dramatics.
14. Marked gains in number of schools engaging in local cooperative curriculum planning.
15. Development of curriculum materials by national committees composed of high school and college teachers (such as the physical sciences and biological sciences curriculum study committees).
16. Increased participation by laymen in local curriculum planning.
17. Establishment of physical education and health as a required field in the secondary school curriculum.
18. Abandonment of the single curriculum and adoption of constants-with-variables and multi-curriculum types of organization.
19. Gradual shift from rigid time allotments to flexible schedules.

Instructional Methods and Materials

1. Increasing provisions for individual differences (e.g., directed study, differentiated assignment, projects, multiple readings, unit method, and independent study).
2. Greater use of supplementary materials (multiple texts, library references, flat file materials, paperback books, etc.).
3. Improvement of assignments — use of pretests, student planning, motivational procedures, and similar methods.

4. Marked increase in extent of participation by students in classroom activities — reports, discussions, dramatizations, panels, committee work, etc.
5. More frequent use of technological aids such as filmstrips, models, television, sound films, tape recorders, overhead projectors, language laboratories, and the like.
6. Inception of team teaching and teacher aides, with large-group instruction, small discussion groups, independent study, readers for English teachers, etc.
7. Use of diagnostic and remedial procedures.
8. Much more extensive use of active learning procedures, such as demonstrations, field trips, and laboratory procedures.
9. Extensive use of objective tests, both teacher made and standardized.
10. Development of new evaluation procedures such as pupil conferences, observations, rating scales, problem-solving situations, case studies, and the like.
11. Development of new grading and reporting procedures.
12. Development and growing use of programmed teaching materials — in both textbooks and teaching machines.
13. Growing emphasis on quality; insistence that students do well those things they undertake to do.

Guidance Services

1. Marked increase in number of schools employing trained counselors, especially since World War II.
2. Expansion in types of guidance services from early emphasis on vocational advisement to inclusion of personal and educational counseling, information services, etc.
3. Development of closer working relationships between counselors and classroom teachers in guidance.
4. Inclusion of guidance materials in regular school subjects.
5. Buildup of collections of guidance materials in school libraries.
6. Marked increase in availability and use of standardized instruments for measuring academic abilities, attitudes, special aptitudes, social adjustment, etc.
7. Improved and more comprehensive student records.
8. Provision of suitably designed guidance facilities and equipment.

Extraclass Student Activities

1. Shift from faculty opposition to recognition and then to active sponsorship of activities as a part of the educational program.
2. Extensive growth in the number and types of student activities sponsored by high schools.
3. Growth of programs for student participation in government (such as student councils, homerooms, and *ad hoc* committees).
4. Increased efforts to provide equal opportunities for all students to participate in activities.
5. Improved faculty sponsorship of activities.

6. Organization of state associations for correcting overemphasis and abuses (e.g., state athletic, music, and speech associations).
7. Improvement of business and financial management of student activities.
8. Substantial progress in scheduling activities so that all may participate and conflicts with regular classwork are minimized.
9. Improvement of systems of rewards and recognition.
10. Progress in relating extraclass and classroom activities.
11. Progress in screening and developing a sound emphasis in competitive activities.
12. Progress in protecting students from exploitation and injury during participation in activities.

Auxiliary Services

1. Marked growth in number of pupils being transported to schools at public expense.
2. Enormous growth in number of schools providing food services and numbers of pupils being served, due largely to federal aid in the form of surplus commodities and financial grants.
3. Improved health services including services of school nurses, physicians, and dentists, plus health examinations and comprehensive health records.
4. Expansion and improvement of library services.

Our intent in outlining these changes has been to show in condensed form the direction in which the secondary school has been moving. The foregoing list of changes is not complete but includes most of the highlights. Even a condensed version indicates the dramatic shifts that have occurred in secondary education during the modern period. Although much of the time and resources of high school faculties have had to be devoted to quantitative matters during these years of rapid growth, increasing attention has been directed to quality. We anticipate that the search for better services and better results will occupy the major energies of secondary school faculties during the remainder of this century.

Questions and Group Projects

1. Compare the curriculum offerings of an early American academy with those of a modern-day German *Gymnasium* and an English public grammar school. What philosophical concepts seem to be common to these programs?
2. Trace some of the major social, economic, and political changes which appear to have been influential in the establishment of the first public high school and in the decline of the academy.
3. Compare some of the dropout studies made in the 1930's with several made in the 1950's. What are some of the important similarities and

differences in students' reasons for withdrawing from school during these two periods?

4. Compare the objectives of secondary education embodied in the "Seven Cardinal Principles of Secondary Education" with those listed in more recent statements. Which changes appear to have resulted primarily from changes in educational theory and which from changes in conditions outside the school?

5. What social and economic factors have contributed most to the rapid growth in high school enrollments since 1900? What is likely to happen to enrollments and to the composition of the high school population during the next ten years?

6. Outline an affirmative or negative brief on the proposition: Universal secondary education is both possible and desirable in the United States.

7. Define general education. What courses are most frequently offered in junior and senior high schools in your state to implement their programs of general education?

8. What additions would you make to the list of significant changes in the program of the public high school since 1890, as outlined by the authors in this chapter?

Selected References

Briggs, Thomas H., J. Paul Leonard, and Joseph Justman. *Secondary Education*. New York: The Macmillan Company, 1950.

Brown, Elmer E. *The Making of Our Middle Schools*. New York: Longmans, Green and Company, 1902.

Butts, R. Freeman. *A Cultural History of Education*. New York: McGraw-Hill Book Company, 1947.

Clark, Burton R. *Educating the Expert Society*. San Francisco: Chandler Publishing Company, 1962.

Commission on the Reorganization of Secondary Education. *Cardinal Principles of Secondary Education*, U.S. Office of Education, Bulletin 1918, No. 35. Washington: Government Printing Office, 1918.

Conant, James B. *The American High School Today*. New York: McGraw-Hill Book Company, 1959.

Cubberley, Ellwood P. *Public Education in the United States*. Boston: Houghton Mifflin Company, 1934.

Educational Policies Commission. *The Purposes of Education in American Democracy*. Washington: National Education Association, 1938.

French, William M. *American Secondary Education.* New York: The Odyssey Press, 1957.

Kandel, I. L. *History of Secondary Education.* Cambridge, Mass.: Harvard University Press, 1957.

Meyer, Adolphe E. *An Educational History of the American People.* New York: McGraw-Hill Book Company, 1957.

National Association of Secondary School Principals. *Planning for American Youth.* Washington: National Education Association, 1944.

Report of the Committee of Ten on Secondary Schools. U.S. Bureau of Education, Bulletin No. 2-5. Washington: Government Printing Office, 1893.

Trump, J. Lloyd. *Images of the Future.* Urbana, Ill.: Commission on the Experimental Study of the Utilization of the Staff in the Secondary School, NASSP, 1959.

Trump, J. Lloyd, and Dorsey Baynham. *Guide to Better Schools — Focus on Change.* Chicago: Rand McNally and Company, 1961.

Uhl, Willis L. *Secondary School Curricula.* New York: The Macmillan Company, 1927.

U.S. Office of Education. "Statistical Summary of Education, 1955–56," *Biennial Survey of Education in the United States, 1954–56.* Washington: Government Printing Office, 1959.

CHAPTER 4

Structure, Size, and Relationships of Secondary Schools

The secondary school, like politics, is a subject upon which most people have strong opinions, but few have been able to agree on a definition. If an attempt is made to define the secondary school in terms of years or grades, there are so many variations that it requires a major prophet to reconcile them. There are six-year, five-year, four-year, three-year, and two-year secondary schools. A few include Grades 7 through 14, 40 per cent embrace Grades 7 through 12, and about one-third extend from Grade 9 through Grade 12. In addition, there are a number of special local variations based on expediency.

The matter of definition becomes no simpler in terms of the age levels of students served. Some youth enter the seventh grade at the age of ten, many at twelve, and some at thirteen or fourteen. Most students graduate at seventeen or eighteen, but almost half a million adults are enrolled in secondary courses of one sort or another — in evening schools, correspondence study, adult education classes, and similar special programs.

Nor can the secondary school be defined accurately in terms of special functions, control, or support. It is a "middle school" and many of its operations overlap with those of the elementary school and the college.

However, according to prevailing practice, secondary education in the United States includes Grades 7 through 12, and any school composed of some or all of these grades has come to be regarded as a secondary school. It is a school for youth in their early and middle adolescent years. Its primary functions are to continue the program of general education begun in the elementary school and to initiate exploratory and special preparatory education.

Although some writers and professional groups hold that Grades 13 and 14 in a community college are a part of secondary education, a large majority of these institutions concentrate on two-year liberal arts and advanced technical programs and serve older youth and adults. They are usually accredited as colleges and seem to be more closely associated with higher education than with secondary schools.

Structure of Secondary Schools

Horizontal Organization — Comprehensive or Specialized

A comprehensive high school is one which provides educational opportunities for all types of youth — bright, average, not-so-bright, rich, poor, college preparatory, and terminal. It offers basic general courses and a wide range of courses in special fields — academic, vocational, and avocational. Also, it provides a broad program of extraclass activities, guidance, and community-related experiences.

A majority of high schools in the United States are not really comprehensive, since they are too small to give a broad educational program. United States Office of Education figures for 1959 showed that there were 11,000,000 students enrolled in 24,000 public secondary schools of all types — junior, senior, four-year, and junior-senior.[1] The average enrollment was 458. The average enrollment in four-year high schools (grades 9–12) was 330. Actually, 68.4 per cent of the public secondary schools enrolled fewer than 300 students in 1952.[2] These small schools cannot be truly comprehensive; they have neither the students nor the program.

However, a *comprehensive* high school has come to mean any non-specialized high school. It is a school that is available to all youth in a community, provides a program of general education, and offers a variety of elective courses. A *specialized* high school, on the other hand, provides a program that is designed for a selected and relatively homogeneous body of students with a dominant educational objective such as college preparatory, vocational, scientific, or fine arts.

One of the earliest and most influential recommendations in support

---

[1] Edmond A. Ford, "Organization Pattern of the Nation's Public Secondary Schools," reprint from *School Life* (May, 1960) (Washington: U.S. Office of Education, OE–23010, 1960).

[2] U.S. Office of Education, "Statistics of Public Secondary Day Schools, 1951–52," *Biennial Survey of Education in the United States* (Washington: Government Printing Office, 1954), Chap. 5, Table D.

of the comprehensive high school as the most suitable type for the United States was made in 1918 by the Commission on the Reorganization of Secondary Education.³ And in 1959 Conant stated,

> I should not want to argue for the elimination of selective academic high schools in the cities in which these schools are now successful, but I would raise many questions about the establishment of such a school in another city. . . . The improvement of the comprehensive high school would seem to offer far more promise for the improvement of American education than the introduction of selective academic high schools into communities where, hitherto, they have not existed.⁴

Here, as in most matters of education, some argument is inevitable. Rickover asks rhetorically, "Why do most of our public schools fail in the objectives I have mentioned?" He then ventures the opinion that "One reason is that we are wedded to the concept of the comprehensive high school."⁵ Conant, however, based his views in support of the comprehensive school on observations of many schools, a review of many facts, and discussions with many people.

Regardless of the argument, most public and many nonpublic high schools in the United States are more comprehensive than specialized, and the American people seem to be persuaded that this is the most appropriate type for our democratic way of life. There are no accurate data available on the number of specialized high schools in the United States, but they are limited largely to public schools in large cities and to schools provided by certain private and church organizations. Probably not more than 2 per cent of the 27,000 public and nonpublic secondary schools in this country are specialized schools, unless the segregated schools in the South are counted. Fortunately, much progress has been made toward desegregation. As of 1960, 27 per cent of 2,840 school districts with a Negro population in seventeen southern states had desegregated.⁶ Moreover, 29 per cent of the Negro youth in these districts were in integrated schools.

An American Contribution. The comprehensive high school originated in the United States and represents a significant innovation in secondary education among the nations of the world. However, the first secondary schools in this country were specialized academic schools modeled after

---

[3] Commission on the Reorganization of Secondary Education, *Cardinal Principles of Secondary Education,* U.S. Office of Education, Bulletin 1918, No. 35 (Washington: Government Printing Office, 1918), pp. 8–9.

[4] James B. Conant, *The American High School Today* (New York: McGraw-Hill Book Company, 1959), pp. 90–91.

[5] H. G. Rickover, *Education for Freedom* (New York: E. P. Dutton and Company, 1959), p. 135.

[6] *Southern School News,* October, 1960, 7:1.

those of England and continental Europe. Although this type of school continues to predominate in most European countries, several of these countries also maintain special vocational schools.

Soviet secondary schools, on the other hand, offer both academic and practical subjects and enroll a higher proportion of youth than do schools in western Europe. But the Soviet schools are much more selective than ours and the curriculum is entirely prescribed.

Our broad base of secondary education with its dominantly comprehensive school, where youth of all types and backgrounds learn to get on with each other and where many provisions are made for differences in abilities, talents, and interests, has attracted world-wide interest.

> Each month [writes Lawrence Derthick, former United States Commissioner of Education] visitors from all over the world come to study our comprehensive schools. They see two distinct advantages in them: (1) the building of social unity by lowering class barriers and (2) the preparation of more young people for life in societies which, like our own, are demanding increased numbers of graduates.[7]

Reforms underway in secondary education in several European and Latin American countries are in the direction of increasing the number of comprehensive schools. Many educators and laymen in the free countries recognize that the implementation of democracy in this century of rapid scientific and technological progress requires an educational system that is much broader and more capable of raising the educational level of all of the people than is their traditional system. They recognize also that through a broad system of comprehensive schools designed to educate children of all classes and talents, more potential leaders are likely to emerge and make substantial contributions to their countries.

Since the passage of the Fisher Act in 1944, England has been steadily extending its base of secondary education. There are now approximately fifty genuinely comprehensive schools and over 3,700 *secondary school moderns* in England. Although the latter enroll only non-college preparatory students, they provide a broad curriculum of general and practical courses. A beginning toward the comprehensive secondary school has been made in West Germany with the establishment of a few *Einheitschulen* in such city-states as Bremen and Hamburg.

Values. There are many questions in education that cannot be answered objectively and categorically, and one of them is whether or not comprehensive schools are superior to specialized schools. Nor can it be demonstrated conclusively that a multi-purpose university is superior to specialized institutions for medicine, law, engineering, and other professions. But higher education in the United States is moving in the

---

[7] "Schools in Our Democracy," report to the Congress by Lawrence G. Derthick, 1960.

direction of large multi-purpose universities; many former specialized institutions are being converted to this type. The case for comprehensive high schools appears to be even stronger than the case for multi-purpose universities, since the first function of the high school is to provide general education for all youth.

It seems highly logical that students will be aided in developing democratic attitudes toward individuals and groups who are "different" if they associate with them in the classroom and in school activities. It seems logical also that the development of a sense of social, civic, and moral responsibility will be enhanced in a school environment which enables youth to take part in many group enterprises with peers from all family backgrounds, races, and creeds.

On the other hand, the social stratification in specialized high schools in large metropolitan centers is probably not as pronounced as it is in small cities and rural areas. Specialized schools in big cities are usually large and include students from all social classes.

We are inclined to agree with Conant that the comprehensive high school can supply as good a quality of education for students with special abilities and interests as can specialized schools and that youth are more likely to develop desirable social attitudes and associations in comprehensive schools. In smaller cities and in rural county systems, it is likely that the segregation of youth into specialized schools would promote social divisions as well as a certain amount of social conflict.

The principal argument advanced by proponents of the selective and specialized high school is that it provides more intensive and better academic or vocational education. But, as Conant has reported, the academic education now offered by many of our large comprehensive high schools is of high quality. Multi-track programs, ability grouping, and advanced placement programs are being offered with increasing frequency in comprehensive schools large enough to support such programs.

When graduates of comprehensive public high schools are compared with graduates of private preparatory schools on academic tests and achievement in college, the public school graduates come off with as many or more honors. In 1957 Herbert L. Brown, Jr., Managing Editor of *Changing Times,* reported the latest results of the College Entrance Examination Board tests. In eight of the ten subject areas on the achievement tests the comprehensive public school students made higher average scores than the private preparatory school students.[8]

Conant compared test results for students from thirteen comprehensive public high schools with those for students from four specialized academic public schools. The tests used were the School and College Ability

[8] Herbert L. Brown, Jr., "Are the Public Schools Doing Their Job?" *The Saturday Evening Post,* September 21, 1957, 230:39.

Test, published by the Educational Testing Service, the Cooperative Trigonometry Test, and the College Entrance Examination Board Physics Test. The results are shown in Tables 7 and 8.

TABLE 7

Physics Test Results for Boys at Three Levels of Quantitative Ability

Ability Level	Type of School	SCAT-Q Range of School Means	Physics Score Range of School Means
High	Control	331–333	564–609
	Comprehensive	329–334	502–692
Medium	Control	319–320	506–598
	Comprehensive	318–320	459–568
Low	Control	303–309	474–535
	Comprehensive	294–307	416–513

TABLE 8

Trigonometry Test Results for Boys at Three Levels of Quantitative Ability

Ability Level	Type of School	SCAT-Q Range of School Scores	Trigonometry Score Range of School Means
High	Control	329–334	55.2–66.9
	Comprehensive	326–334	54.1–66.7
Medium	Control	319–321	52.7–60.0
	Comprehensive	319–321	47.5–61.2
Low	Control	304–309	46.8–57.9
	Comprehensive	299–313	44.9–58.7

Conant concludes, "There was no important difference, as revealed by these tests, in the degree of mastery of trigonometry and physics by the students tested in the comprehensive high schools and those in the four control high schools."[9] Comprehensive schools not only offer as good academic training as special academic schools but provide a breadth of social relations not found in most of the latter.

Vertical Organization — Traditional and Reorganized Schools

The debate over education extends to the question of the most appropriate way to group grades into administrative units for educational

[9] Conant, *op. cit.*, pp. 33–35.

purposes. Is the 8–4, 6–3–3, 6–6, 6–4–4, or some other type of vertical organization most suitable to accomplish the objectives of American education? Discussion centers largely around the relative merits of the traditional (8–4) type and the reorganized (6–3–3, 6–6, 6–4–4, etc.) types.

The traditional vertical organization provides an eight-year elementary school, frequently with a kindergarten added, and a four-year high school including Grades 9 through 12. The reorganized type usually provides a six-year elementary school, plus a kindergarten, with a six-year secondary program. The six-year secondary often is divided into a junior high school for Grades 7 through 9 and a senior high school for Grades 10 through 12. However, the junior-senior high school may be undivided. In addition, about 5 per cent of the secondary schools in the United States are organized with a two-year junior and a four-year senior high school, and some educators believe that the secondary school should be extended upward to include Grades 13 and 14 of the public junior or community college.

Trends in Vertical Organization. The traditional 8–4 organization was modeled after the Prussian school system and introduced in this country around 1850. By the early 1900's it had become the standard type of organization and it continued to predominate until about 1950. However, in the early 1950's the reorganized type of vertical structure was being used by more school systems than the traditional, and more students were enrolled in reorganized schools.

The reorganization movement in secondary education actually got under way in the first years of the twentieth century. Even as early as 1893 the Committee of Ten, under the chairmanship of President Eliot of Harvard, had recommended that "it is feasible and desirable that all of the principal subjects (except Greek) which are offered in the secondary schools should be begun in grades before the high school." The Committee of Ten and other educators of that period were chiefly concerned with economy of time. They believed that in Grades 7 and 8 pupils spent too much time repeating materials learned in the lower grades. They proposed that much of the curriculum content of the first two years of high school be moved down into the elementary school and that some freshman college courses be shifted to the high school.

One of the most influential study groups in the history of American secondary education, the Commission on the Reorganization of Secondary Education, recommended in its 1918 report that the traditional 8–4 organization be changed to a six-year elementary and a six-year secondary.[10]

The rapid growth of the reorganization movement since 1920 is

---

[10] Commission on the Reorganization of Secondary Education, *op. cit.*, 32 p.

shown in Figure 2, based on a 1959 report from the U.S. Office of Education. In 1920, 94 per cent of all public schools were traditional (8–4) and only 6 per cent were reorganized; in 1959, only 24 per cent were traditional and 76 per cent were reorganized. Of the public secondary schools, 42 per cent were undivided junior-senior high schools, 21 per cent were separate three-year junior high schools and 7 per cent were separate three-year senior high schools.

In 1920, traditional high schools enrolled 84 per cent of all secondary students, while in 1959 they enrolled only 18 per cent. Since that time

FIGURE 2

Types of Organization of Public Secondary Schools

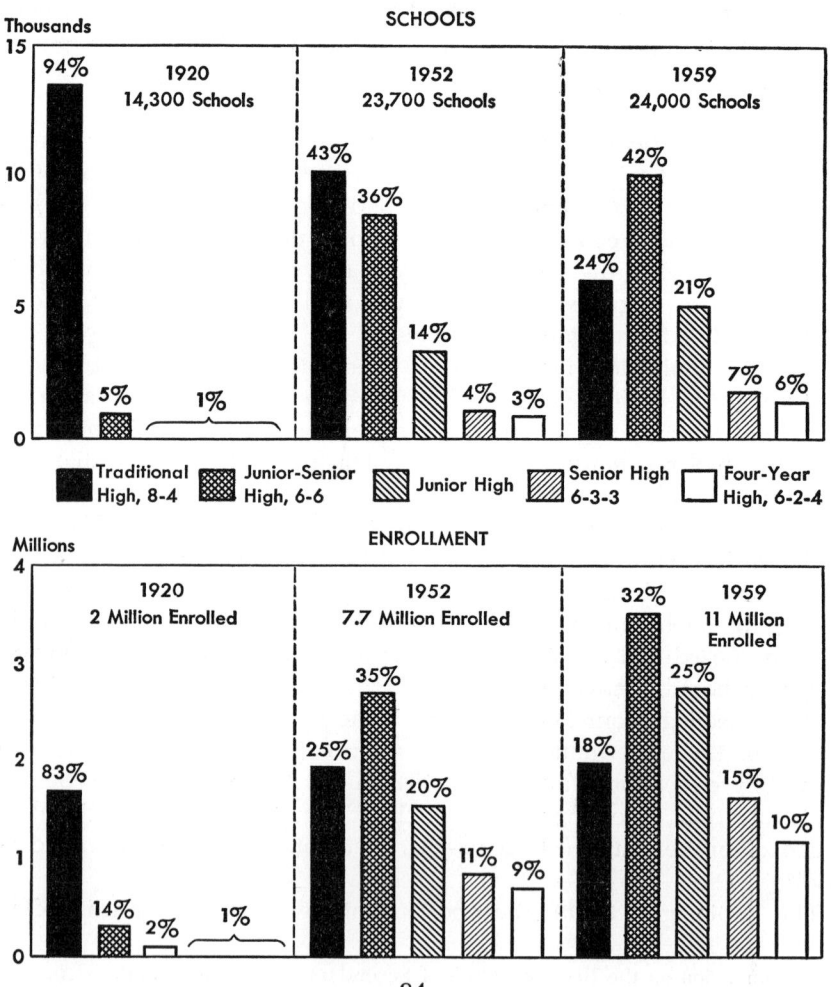

the percentage of enrollments in reorganized schools has increased from 17 to 82 per cent.[11]

Although there may be room for some argument over the relative merits of traditional and reorganized schools, public opinion seems to favor the reorganized type. At any rate more and more of the latter are being established. A professional publication in 1960 had this to say about trends in organization: "Pattern of school organization will vary according to conditions in the community or district. A program of high quality, well supported financially, can function in almost any type of school organization. Even so, reorganized systems (6–3–3 and 6–6) will continue their established pattern of growth."[12]

The lack of agreement in figures on public junior colleges reflects the uncertainty over the classification of these institutions. Should they be regarded as the upper division of secondary education or the lower division of higher education? The several regional accrediting associations classify them as colleges and the U.S. Office of Education puts them under "Higher Education" in its statistical reports. The 1956–58 *Biennial Survey* of the Office of Education reports 283 public junior colleges in the United States, enrolling 297,680 students.[13] During the ten years from 1945 to 1955 there was no substantial increase in the number of public junior colleges, but enrollments increased over 50 per cent.

Advantages Claimed for Traditional and Reorganized Schools. Educators have had little more success in proving that a reorganized school is superior to a traditional school, or vice versa, than they have in securing evidence of the superiority of comprehensive over specialized schools. About all we have to go on is observation, opinion, and a few quantitative measures such as a comparison of facilities and services.

Conant sums up the situation as follows:

> Because of wide diversity in school organization, professional disagreement, and my own observations, I conclude that the place of grades 7, 8, and 9 in the organization of a school system is of less importance than the program provided for adolescent youth. When enrollments are large enough, I am convinced that it is possible to provide for pupils in grades 7, 8, and 9 the kinds of experiences they need regardless of the structure of the school system.[14]

[11] Ford, *op. cit.*
[12] National Association of Secondary School Principals, *Spotlight*, November–December, 1960, No. 45, p. 1.
[13] U.S. Office of Education, "Statistical Summary of Education, 1957–58," *Biennial Survey of Education in the United States, 1956–58* (Washington: Government Printing Office, 1962), p. 37.
[14] James B. Conant, *Education in the Junior High School Years* (Princeton, N.J.: Educational Testing Service, 1960), p. 12.

Such professional organizations as the National Association of Secondary School Principals, quoted earlier, tend to agree with Conant. But they maintain that, while it is *possible* to provide just as good education under one type of organization as another, the facts are that we have not provided as good facilities, as well-prepared teachers, and as broad a program of educational services in the traditional as in the reorganized school.

Case for Reorganized Schools — The Separate Junior High School. The arguments most frequently advanced for the separate junior high school are these:

1. It provides a school environment most suitable for young adolescents who are at a similar stage of physiological and social development. Youth between the ages of twelve and fifteen are in their early adolescence. It is true that some enter puberty earlier than others and it is also true that wide individual differences exist among students of this age group with respect to social maturity. But the great majority of girls enter puberty between ten and twelve and boys between eleven and thirteen. Since these youngsters face many common developmental problems, there are important advantages in having them in a school where young children are not associated with them and where they are not associated with older and more mature youth.

2. Seventh- and eighth-grade students are provided a broader curriculum, programs better geared to accommodating individual differences, and more and better special services in separate junior high schools than in traditional elementary schools. Most junior high schools require courses in industrial arts, home economics, physical education, group guidance (orientation, library, etc.), art, and music.[15] On the other hand, a majority of elementary schools do not offer more than a few minutes per week of instruction in these subjects in the seventh and eighth grades, and many do not offer them at all. Since 1957, many junior high schools have added modern foreign languages — still uncommon in the upper two years of the eight-year elementary school.

Since the seventh and eighth grades in the traditional elementary school usually are parts of small schools, very often the buildings are not equipped with a central library, science laboratory, industrial arts shop, home economics laboratory, and music room. In contrast, a large percentage of separate junior high schools have these facilities. For example, Grim found that of thirty-eight separate junior high schools in

---

[15] Walter H. Gaumnitz and others, *Junior High School Facts — A Graphic Analysis*, publication of the U.S. Office of Education (Washington: Government Printing Office, 1954), p. 51. (From the Ed.D. thesis of Edward G. Fennell, Cornell University, 1953.)

Iowa in 1956 the percentages having special physical facilities were: gymnasium, 95 per cent; science laboratory, 90 per cent; library, 92 per cent; music room, 87 per cent; home economics room, 76 per cent; and shop, 78 per cent. The figures for unreorganized elementary schools were very different: gymnasium, 20 per cent; laboratory, 30 per cent; library, 64 per cent; home economics room, 12 per cent; and shop, 10 per cent.[16]

It is evident from this comparison that the opportunities for exploratory study and activities in specialized areas, as reflected in the physical facilities available, are usually greater in separate junior high schools than in the seventh and eighth grades of traditional elementary schools.

3. Young adolescents have better opportunities to participate and to develop leadership in extraclass activities in separate junior high schools than they have in six-year or four-year secondary schools. In the six-year school, the senior high school students tend to dominate activities and to receive preferential treatment in the use of facilities. Frequently they also get more attention from teachers and coaches. In the four-year high school, ninth-grade youngsters find themselves in much the same disadvantageous position as do junior high students in a six-year school.

4. Junior high school students have an opportunity to study with teachers who are better prepared in special subject fields than are most elementary school teachers. Although the seventh and eighth grades may be partly departmentalized in the eight-year elementary school, the major portion of the students' day is spent with one broadly trained teacher without depth of preparation in such areas as science, mathematics, music, art, shop, physical education, and home economics. In junior high schools, teachers usually are assigned to fields in which they have an undergraduate major or minor. Fennell's study shows that in 224 outstanding junior high schools in several different states the following percentages employed teachers in certain special fields: boys' physical education, 93 per cent; girls' physical education, 91 per cent; home economics, 86 per cent; art, 86 per cent; and industrial arts, 85 per cent.[17]

5. Junior high schools generally have better guidance facilities and personnel than do elementary schools. Few of the latter have guidance libraries, counseling facilities, or trained counselors. Junior high schools, on the other hand, are developing guidance services rapidly. The report by Gaumnitz, cited previously, shows that 47 per cent of the junior high schools in Fennell's study employed guidance counselors.[18] Undoubtedly

---

[16] Mary Grim, "The Program of Studies for Junior High Schools in Iowa," unpublished master's thesis, State University of Iowa, 1956.
[17] Gaumnitz, op. cit., p. 51.
[18] Ibid.

the number has increased substantially since 1953 when his study was made.

6. The transition from the self-contained classroom of the elementary school to the departmentalized secondary school is made by pupils with less difficulty if an intermediate junior high school unit is provided.

Case for the Undivided Junior-Senior High School. All but two of the principal arguments in support of the separate junior high school may be made with equal logic in support of the junior-senior (six-year) secondary school. The exceptions are (1) the assertion that a more suitable environment is provided for young adolescents and (2) the argument that better opportunities are made available for younger students to participate in the extraclass activity program. The claims of broader curriculum offerings, better prepared teachers in special subject fields, better special facilities, better guidance services, and a smoother transition from elementary to secondary are as valid for combined as for separate junior and senior high schools.

In addition, the undivided school may be more economical with respect to construction costs, the utilization of professional personnel, and the provision of special physical facilities. Expensive items such as the auditorium, gymnasium, central library, shops, home economics suite, and music rooms need not be duplicated for the junior and senior divisions in a six-year secondary organization as long as enrollments in each division do not exceed 500 to 750 students. When a 6-6 organization is employed, building costs are distributed over more students and special facilities do not stand idle as much of the time.

Case for Traditional 8-4 Organization. Most of the advantages claimed for the traditional organization have to do with costs. But if the people of local communities bought as much in the way of educational services and physical facilities under a traditional as under a reorganized system, there would be little difference in costs. They do not, however, and per-pupil costs are therefore not as high for seventh and eighth grades in 8-4 systems. There is very little difference in per-pupil costs in the upper secondary grades under either system.

Elementary per-pupil costs in 1952–53 were about $180 in 52 cities of 100,000 or more and $150 in 82 cities of 2,500 to 9,999. Junior high school average costs were about $260 per pupil in the large cities and $190 in the small cities. Costs in regular four-year high schools were about $290 per pupil in large cities and $230 in small cities, while the senior high school figures were around $300 in large cities and $270 in small cities.[19] Although these costs have gone up considerably since 1952–53, the ratios undoubtedly hold true at the present time. At any

[19] *Ibid.,* p. 41.

rate, elementary school per-pupil costs averaged from 26 to 30 per cent less than junior high costs, and costs in traditional four-year high schools (Grades 9–12) averaged from 3 to 17 per cent less per pupil than senior high school costs (Grades 10–12).

Supporters of the 8–4 system also argue that there is less danger that seventh- and eighth-grade pupils will develop too rapidly in social tastes and activities if they remain in the elementary school and that the pressure for overemphasis on interscholastic athletics and competition in music, speech, and other types of activities is less.

An additional argument for the 8–4 system is that the curriculum does not become as fragmented in a school where students spend a major part of the day in self-contained classrooms under one teacher.

Most of the reasons advanced for reorganized schools are criticisms of traditional schools and vice versa. As noted earlier, the advantages and disadvantages are not inherent in the type of organization but are frequently found in each type as it now functions. For example, the advantages claimed for traditional schools with self-contained classrooms may be offset in junior high schools with block-time scheduling and homerooms. Actually, in 1957 almost 50 per cent of the junior high schools over the nation employed block-time classes. To some extent the form of organization has to be adapted to existing buildings, financial resources, and related factors in a local school system. But the arguments and trends favor the reorganized school. Where costs for buildings and other facilities are within the financial means of a community, we believe that the three-year junior and three-year senior high school organization has important advantages over other types.

Size of Secondary Schools

In view of soaring school enrollments, costs, and district reorganizations, administrators frequently are called upon to wrestle with the problem of minimum and maximum size for secondary schools. At the same time, the controversy over large and small schools has become extremely bitter in several states. What are the most appropriate minimum and maximum limits? Are there points when a high school becomes too small or too large? Research and the professional literature provide some evidence and guides on the matter of minimum size, but little more than logical argument is available on the question of maximum size.

Minimum Size

Most specialists in school administration, officials in state departments, and professional organizations in school administration agree that average per-pupil costs in small high schools are too high and that their programs are inferior in quality to those of large high schools. However, they are not always in accord on a definition of a small school. Conant says,

> The enrollment of many public high schools is too small to allow a diversified curriculum except at exorbitant expense. The prevalence of such high schools — those with a *graduating class of less than one hundred students* — constitutes one of the serious obstacles to good secondary education throughout the United States.[20]

Conant's minimum of 100 students in the graduating class would mean a total enrollment in Grades 9 through 12 of from 450 to 500 students.

Other writers and professional organizations and agencies have recommended a minimum size of from 200 to 300. The figure suggested in a U.S. Office of Education report is 300.[21] On the other hand, a committee of the American Association of School Administrators defines a *small* school as one with fewer than 200 students and does not make an unqualified recommendation as to minimum size.[22]

Since one of the major arguments is that a small high school is unable to offer a comprehensive curriculum, there is considerable logic in defining minimum size in terms of minimum course offerings and educational services. An absolute minimum enrollment figure cannot be established which is equally appropriate for all states, or even for regions within a single state, because of transportation problems, distribution of population, and related factors. The North Central Association, therefore, has defined the minimum size for member schools as a program including at least twenty-six units of course work with adequate guidance, library, and extraclass services.[23] The twenty-six units may appear to be a very modest figure, but diverse conditions in the nineteen states of the Association must be taken into account. Distances and winter travel conditions in Wyoming, North Dakota, and Kansas are quite different from those in Ohio, Indiana, and West Virginia. Smaller school units closer to the students' homes are more logical in the former states than in the latter.

Another argument against small high schools is that they are too expensive — at least, the per-pupil costs are much higher than for large high schools. The National Commission on School District Reorganization states,

---

[20] Conant, *op. cit.*, p. 77.
[21] Walter H. Gaumnitz and Ellsworth Tompkins, *How Large Are Our Public High Schools?* U.S. Office of Education Circular No. 364 (Washington: Government Printing Office, 1959), p. 15.
[22] American Association of School Administrators, *The High School in a Changing World,* Thirty-Sixth Yearbook (Washington: The Association, 1958), p. 280.
[23] North Central Association, of Colleges and Secondary Schools, "Policies and Criteria for the Approval of Secondary Schools" (Chicago: Commission on Secondary Schools, 1960), p. 6–10.

Size of school and cost of education are directly related. In general, the smaller the school the higher the cost per pupil, and the smaller the administrative unit the smaller the schools maintained. Thus the organization of administrative units is closely related to the per-pupil cost of education.[24]

Woodham used teachers' salaries as a cost measure and breadth of program as a quality measure in a study in Florida in 1951. He found that the relationship between secondary school size and cost per pupil is inverse and that costs per pupil are greatest as the size falls below 350 pupils. When he related cost per pupil and breadth of program in a single cost measure as a cost per pupil per unit of educational opportunity, he found a significant negative relationship between this measure and size of school. In other words, in schools enrolling fewer than 350 students, the smaller the school the higher the costs of units of educational service.[25]

In a review of more than thirty studies Mort states,

> Every empirical study of the relationship between expenditure level and quality of education adds its bit to the presumption that the relationship is strong. Studies of the relationship in acceptably organized districts suggest that schools that spend more contribute more to . . . the social and economic strength of Americans as a people.[26]

A direct relationship between per-pupil cost and size of school is shown in Table 9, for a single state for the 1957–58 school year.

The Iowa figures show that the most expensive schools in terms of per-pupil costs were those enrolling 300 or fewer students. Schools with fewer than 100 pupils were by far the most expensive. The lowest per-pupil costs were for schools between 300 and 499, but costs started to increase again in schools of 500 and more students. These size categories and cost figures may not hold true for large industrial states but probably are representative for midwestern states with many small school districts in rural areas.

Another Iowa study shows a similar correlation between school size and pupil achievement. Gray studied the relationship between school size and mean gains in achievement of students who took the Iowa Tests of Educational Development in the tenth grade in 1956 and again in

---

[24] National Commission on School District Reorganization, *A Key to Better Education* (Washington: National Education Association 1947), p. 89.

[25] William Jesse Woodham, Jr., "The Relationship Between the Size of Secondary Schools, the Per Pupil Cost, and the Breadth of Educational Opportunity," unpublished Ed.D. dissertation, University of Florida, 1951.

[26] Paul R. Mort, "Cost-Quality Relationship in Education," *Problems and Issues in Public School Finance* (New York: Bureau of Publications, Teachers College, Columbia University, 1952), p. 9.

TABLE 9
High School Per-Pupil Costs in Iowa, 1957–58

Size of School	Number of Schools	Average per Pupil
0–24	3	$599.41
25–49	115	635.83[a]
50–74	108	576.32
75–99	105	530.09
100–149	138	520.65
150–199	70	498.93
200–299	72	488.04
300–399	27	456.02
400–499	19	398.05[b]
500–599	11	452.39
600–Above	26	447.45
Totals	694	$535.25

[a] Highest.
[b] Lowest.
Source: Iowa Department of Public Instruction, "High School Tuition Costs in the 694 Districts Maintaining Approved Public Four-Year High Schools" (Des Moines: State of Iowa, December, 1958).

TABLE 10
Relationship Between School Size and Achievement on ITED (Composite) for Iowa High Schools from 1956 to 1958

Size of Schools	Number of Schools	Mean 10th-Grade Score ITED, 1956	Mean 12th-Grade Score ITED, 1958	Mean Gain from 10th to 12th Grade
D 149 and under	10	14.40[a]	17.73	3.33
C 150–399	10	15.62	19.38	3.76
B 400–999	10	15.85	19.81	3.96
A 1,000 and over	10	14.92	18.97	4.05

[a] Standard score units.
Source: Stuart Gray, "Relationships Between Size, Costs, and Quality of Program in Iowa Secondary Schools," unpublished Ph.D. dissertation, State University of Iowa, 1961.

the twelfth grade in 1958.[27] The schools were classified by the four size groups shown in Table 10. Only ten Class A schools administered the tests both years, so all of these schools were included. An equal number of schools were selected at random in each of the other size categories. Students in the small schools, of 149 and under, scored lowest each year

[27] Stuart Gray, "Relationships Between Size, Costs, and Quality of Program in Iowa Secondary Schools," unpublished Ph.D. dissertation, State University of Iowa, 1961.

and made the least gain. Students in the two middle groups made the highest average composite scores, but students in Class A schools, of 1,000 and over, made the largest mean gain from the tenth grade to the twelfth.

However, the advantage is on the side of the small school with respect to close personal relationships between teachers and pupils. In an effort to combine the advantages of large and small schools, a few small high schools in certain regions have pooled their resources to provide more comprehensive curriculum programs, more adequate special services, and improved instructional facilities. The Upper Catskill Area Project in New York State has demonstrated that small neighboring high schools can increase the quantity and quality of their educational programs by sharing facilities, equipment, and personnel.[28] The theory underlying the project is that the small high school offers some important advantages to students. Six techniques are being employed: (1) multiple classes, (2) shared services, (3) technological communication, (4) school aides, (5) flexible scheduling, and (6) supervised correspondence study. Shared services, for example, include the cooperative use of personnel such as counselors and language teachers and special facilities such as shops and art rooms. Several of the schools are cooperating in providing a special seminar for gifted students. A similar project involving seven small schools, known as the Rocky Mountain Project, is being conducted in Colorado.

In most areas, however, it is more economical and provides better opportunities for students when two or more small high schools join in forming a single reorganized district. Perpetuation of very small high schools because of community pride and for the benefit of local sports fans is a luxury that we can ill afford in American education.

Maximum Size

The evidence is not as convincing on maximum size as it is on minimum size. Some writers and professional organizations suggest a maximum of 1,000 to 2,000 students, but the supporting research is rather thin. Michael pinpoints one of the major concerns of large schools: "Many of our large high schools show a real concern for the individual student and his identification with the school and its program. But some of the accepted values of smallness are lost unless they are so organized as to insure proper regard for the individual pupil."[29]

Among the more common criticisms directed toward the very large high school are the following: (1) Teachers tend to know students chiefly as

---

[28] Mildred Whitcomb, "A Living Laboratory for Improving the Small School," *Nation's Schools*, March, 1959, 63:53–58.

[29] J. Lloyd Michael, "Innovations in Organization," in Francis S. Chase and Harold A. Anderson, eds., *The High School in a New Era* (Chicago: University of Chicago Press, 1958), p. 234.

names on a list; the only ones they know well are the very good, the very bad, and the athletes. (2) Most students do not have an opportunity to participate in all-school activities such as varsity athletics, dramatics, band, chorus, school paper, and student council. (3) In order to administer a large school, many rules and regulations are necessary, and very often students are caught unjustly in them. (4) Teachers in different departments do not become well acquainted and frequently compete for students; the result is likely to be an exaggerated compartmentalization of the curriculum. (5) The dropout rate is higher in large schools in large cities, in some degree because of the feeling of anonymity upon the part of students.

Per-pupil costs are higher in large urban centers of 100,000 and over than in small urban centers of 2,500 to 9,999. The average per-pupil cost for senior high schools in large cities in 1952–53 was $300; in small cities, $270.[30] Cost figures are not reported for extremely small high schools in rural districts in the Office of Education survey, but the Iowa data, shown in Table 9, indicate that these are the highest among all size groups.

Schunert, in a study of mathematical achievement, found that students in high schools enrolling 100 to 500 scored higher on a mathematics achievement test than students in smaller or larger schools.[31] In a study of relationships of high school size to staff relations conducted by Shapiro in California, high schools of 800 to 1,199 ranked higher on staff communication, group cooperation, and teacher effectiveness than did high schools of 1,200 and over. No difference was found in teacher load and routines, but the schools enrolling 1,200 to 1,600 were ranked superior to smaller and larger schools on supervisory relations. The very large schools of 1,600 and over did not rank at the top on any staff relations factors.[32]

The case for a limit on the maximum size of a secondary school is not convincing on the basis of available studies comparing costs, student achievement, staff relations, and other factors. Nevertheless, they do show some disadvantages for large schools as enrollments exceed the 1,500 to 2,000 range.

More impressive is the fact that a number of experienced staffs in large schools are convinced that they are losing something important in the way of close personal relations among students and between students and faculty. They also feel that in a large school a majority of students are at a disadvantage with regard to opportunities for valuable experiences and recognition through the activity program. As one principal put it, "Too many of our students lose their identity and are merely customers in an educational super-market."

[30] Gaumnitz, *op. cit.*, p. 41.
[31] Jim Schunert, "The Association of Mathematical Achievement with Certain Factors Resident in the Teacher, in the Teaching, in the Pupil, and in the School," unpublished Ph.D. dissertation, University of Minnesota, 1950.
[32] Daniel F. Shapiro, "Relationship of High School Size to Staff Relations," unpublished Ed.D. dissertation, Stanford University, 1958.

The important thing, of course, is whether students obtain a good education. Many laymen and educators believe that small schools, more often than large schools, afford individualized attention and promote the development of desirable social attitudes. In a small school teachers know each student and take a personal interest in him. And all students gain valuable group experiences through extraclass activities. But the curriculum offerings are narrow, teacher turnover is high, and facilities and special services, such as guidance, usually are limited.

The large high school, on the other hand, presents a broader curriculum, makes better provisions for individual differences in academic ability, has a better-trained and more stable faculty, has better library and laboratory facilities, and provides more adequate special services.

Some large-school faculties believe it is possible to combine the best features of large and small high schools within a single framework. In the so-called "schools-within-a-school" and "house" plans a large school is organized into two or more small schools of from approximately 250 to 600 students, on the same campus. Each small school has it own faculty and building area but shares some special facilities and personnel with other "little schools." Additional information concerning this type of organization is included in Chapter 11.

Relationships with Other Schools and Agencies

The contemporary American high school, unlike its early counterparts, is part of a large, complicated, and somewhat sprawling educational organization.

First, it is a part of a joint elementary-secondary system. And since it draws most of its students from affiliated elementary schools, it has a large stake in the articulation of its program with the work being done in the elementary schools.

Second, the typical high school sends approximately 40 per cent of its graduates to college or to some kind of advanced institute. Although the high school is not directly affiliated with these institutions, it must fit into the hierarchical structure.

Third, public secondary schools are a part of a state system of education. They are accredited by the state, receive some funds from the state, and must operate within state laws and regulations. Nonpublic high schools also are subject to certain state controls, such as teacher certification and basic curriculum offerings.

And fourth, most high schools belong to some extralegal accrediting and/or regulatory agencies and must meet the standards of these bodies to retain membership. Included are such organizations as state activities associations and regional accrediting organizations.

The matter of articulating the program of the secondary school with various institutions and agencies is an important aspect of administration. Educational articulation has to do with the coordination of programs from one level to another and from one department or service to another. Its purpose is to provide an administrative and curriculum organization which facilitates the educational progress of students from one level to the next and helps relate subjects and services so that the student's educational experiences do not become fragmented. The first relationship, coordination between levels, is termed *vertical* articulation and the second, correlation among subjects and services, is termed *horizontal* articulation.

Vertical Articulation

One of the common weaknesses in school organization is that too many duplications, gaps, and conflicts develop between levels. These are especially commonplace and damaging between the elementary and the high school and between the high school and college. Various studies show that between 20 and 25 per cent of the high school graduates who enter college drop out during their freshman year. One of the several factors contributing to this high rate of attrition is the lack of continuity between the instructional programs of the two types of institutions. Part of this may be attributed to weaknesses in the college program, but some of it is due to inertia, inadequate counseling, and inappropriate instruction at the high school level.

Breaks and wasteful duplications also occur between the elementary and high school programs. For example, a majority of systems teach the entire span of American history in the fourth or fifth grade, again in the seventh or eighth grade, and for a third time in the tenth or eleventh grade. Although methods and emphases differ, the basic content of the course at these three levels is the same.

Similarly, gaps and conflicts occur in special services and administrative policies. Not infrequently students are caught in the middle of differences in policies between elementary and secondary school with regard to such matters as marking, promotion, and homework. Perhaps most students should be able to make adjustments from one level to another without undue direction from teachers, but they cannot do much to overcome built-in conflicts and breaks.

Good vertical articulation does not require much added financial support, but it does call for some time, effort, faculty cooperation, and organization. Among the measures that have been employed by various school systems with good success are the following:

1. A central council on curriculum and policies. A central council should include teachers from both elementary and secondary schools together with administrative and supervisory officials. It should function primarily as an advisory and communicating agency. Members should provide two-way communication between the faculty and administration

and should advise on matters of policy, curriculum, and staff relationships. With all levels and divisions represented in its membership, the composition of the council is such that it should facilitate articulation.

2. Longitudinal supervisory assignments. In large systems vertical articulation may be strengthened by assigning some subject field supervisors to Grades 1 through 12. For example, a head supervisor in language arts might effect good articulation by developing continuity between grade levels and eliminating needless duplication. Although teachers need the assistance of some specialists for the grade levels in which they are working, they also need someone who has an over-all view of the program to help them develop coordination between levels. Usually special supervisors are not within the financial means of small schools, but in some rural sections they have been made available to neighboring small schools through intermediate county units.

3. Intervisitation. Articulation may be strengthened through visitation of elementary classes by high school teachers and of high school classes by elementary teachers. It would be inadvisable, however, for administrators to initiate such a program without careful preparation, since it could result in irresponsible criticism and some personal antagonisms. Nevertheless, when accompanied by proper preparation, scheduling, and methods of interpretation, intervisitation has helped to effect better articulation.

4. Joint elementary-secondary curriculum committees. With the exception of vocational education, the central curriculum committee in each subject area should include both elementary and secondary members. It is through such committees that matters of scope, sequence, instructional materials, and evaluation for each major curriculum area may be coordinated most successfully.

Other methods which have been used to further good articulation include staff newsletters, supervisory bulletins, joint elementary-secondary faculty meetings, and curriculum bulletins.

However, the preceding measures are useful primarily within a single school system and do not lend themselves to the more complicated and difficult problems of articulation between secondary schools and colleges. Since World War II, college and high school relationships have deteriorated noticeably. This state of affairs has produced much "viewing with alarm" but little action. To some extent the strains in high school-college relations have been due to the critical attitude of college faculties toward high schools, but inadequacies in high school programs and facilities also have been contributing factors. In addition, the facts that colleges and high schools operate under independent boards of control and that the machinery for articulation is badly designed have made effective coordination difficult.

The most common trouble spots have been identified in a recent study conducted by the North Central Association of Colleges and Secondary Schools.[33] These are reported in Table 11.

One important move toward bettering high school-college articulation has been the preparation of outlines and textbooks for certain advanced high school courses by joint national committees. Since 1957 several committees such as the Physical Science Study Committee, the Curriculum Study Group of the American Institute of Biological Studies, and the Division of Chemical Education of the American Chemical Society, composed of both high school and college teachers, have developed some excellent materials for high school science. In addition, these cooperative projects have brought about better understanding between high school and college teachers. Joint committees of teachers and professors also have produced courses and examinations for use in advanced placement programs in several academic areas. More than 12,000 students in over 650 high schools participated in these programs in 1959.[34]

The regional accrediting associations have made sporadic efforts to promote good high school-college relations and, after a lapse of several years, seem to be directing renewed attention to this problem. For example, the North Central Association now has a committee of secondary school and college representatives seeking answers to the problems raised by the multiplicity of external testing programs being imposed on high schools by colleges and commercial testing agencies. The cumulative amount of time and expense that these programs require of high school students has become a matter of great concern among high school faculties — especially since most of the tests serve about the same purpose and one is little better than another. The Joint Committee on Testing reports that "Even today there are more than twenty national testing programs being administered. . . . In some cases the cost of testing alone adds an appreciable financial burden to families of low or modest means."[35] Its report was based on a study sponsored jointly by the National Council of Chief State School Officers, the National Association of Secondary School Principals, and the American Association of School Administrators.

Some individual states such as Michigan and Illinois have made substantial progress toward improving high school-college articulation through joint committees of secondary school administrators and college officials. Important advances have been made in these states toward developing realistic college admissions policies, more uniform college

---

[33] North Central Association, "Importance of Ten Areas for N.C.A. Action Regarding Closer High School-College Articulation," *North Central Association Quarterly*, January, 1960, 34:207.

[34] Lawrence G. Derthick, "Review of the American Educational System," *Hearings*, U.S. House of Representatives, Committee on Appropriations, (Washington: Government Printing Office, 1960), p. 20.

[35] Joint Committee on Testing, *Testing, Testing, Testing* (Washington: AASA, CCSSO, and NASSP, 1962), pp. 12 and 15.

TABLE 11

Importance of Ten Areas for NCA Action Regarding Closer High School–College Articulation

Problem Area	Level	Very Much			Somewhat			Total		
		Number	Per Cent	Rank	Number	Per Cent	Rank	Number	Per Cent	Rank
1. Curriculum articulation	High school College	35 31	73 75	1 1	12 10	23 25	9 9	50 41	96 100	1 1
2. Proficiency assessment	High school College	13 13	25 32	7 8	22 19	42 46	5 2	35 32	67 78	9 6
3. College admissions process	High school College	34 15	65 37	3.5 7	15 16	29 39	7.5 4.5	49 31	94 75	3 8
4. Test programs for college scholarships and admissions	High school College	34 17	65 42	3.5 5	15 12	29 29	7.5 8	49 29	94 71	3 9
5. Transition from school to college	High school College	21 19	40 47	6 4	24 16	46 39	2.5 4.5	45 35	86 86	6 4
6. Communication between schools and colleges	High school College	24 27	47 66	5 2	22 10	43 24	4 10	46 37	90 90	5 2
7. Motivation of students for college	High school College	19 18	36 45	6 5	24 17	46 42	2.5 3	43 35	82 87	7 3
8. High school multiple tracks and differentiated diplomas	High school College	9 12	16 30	9.5 9	28 19	53 47	1 1	37 31	69 77	8 7
9. Articulation between elementary and secondary education	High school College	9 6	16 15	9.5 10	20 14	38 35	6 6.5	29 20	54 49	10 10
10. "Advanced placement and credit" in college	High school College	37 20	71 50	2 3	11 14	20 35	10 6.5	48 34	94 85	3 5

Source: "Importance of Ten Areas for N.C.A. Action Regarding Closer High School–College Articulation," *North Central Association Quarterly*, January, 1960, 34:207.

admissions forms, standardized high school transcripts, improved reporting procedures from colleges to high schools, advanced placement programs, and similar instruments and procedures.

Horizontal Articulation

The problems of articulation between departments, activities, and special services at a particular level in the school program are of no less consequence than vertical articulation problems. Many of the procedures described in the preceding section should be equally suitable in effecting good horizontal relationships. A central steering committee may serve as a means of bringing together personnel from different departments and service divisions to plan cooperative programs. Special supervisors, intervisitations, area curriculum committees, bulletins, and joint faculty meetings may be as effective in dealing with horizontal as with vertical articulation.

But the matter of horizontal articulation involves some special types of problems and requires some special tactics. One of the more common problems is the tendency of teachers in different fields to become so preoccupied with their own courses that they lose sight of the over-all program and of relationships between what they are teaching and what is being taught in other subjects. Sometimes this results in conflicts and sometimes only in the failure to coordinate learning experiences when such coordination would be helpful. In either event, students are the losers.

For example, conflicts develop when teachers who are uninformed about another field attempt to discredit the value of that field. This practice not only is unethical but may be damaging to students in that it restricts their educational outlook and deters them from obtaining valuable educational experiences. It is certain to be detrimental to intrastaff relations and, therefore, to the cumulative effectiveness of the school's program.

Equally serious is the failure to connect content and activities in two or more subject fields when logical and useful relationships could be exploited. Not infrequently, high school mathematics courses are taught as if they had little in common with science, and little effort is made to relate history courses to literature or vice versa.

Consequently, the principal needs to devote some time and effort to working with his staff on matters of interdepartmental relationships. In addition to the suggestions made earlier, the following may be helpful in promoting horizontal articulation: (1) team teaching, (2) regular conferences of teachers and counselors at each grade level, (3) coordinated scheduling of homework, (4) joint assignments for student reports and research papers, (5) cooperative unit teaching by members of different departments, and (6) block-time or unified studies programs.

The attitude of teachers is sure to be one of the major factors in articulation and is likely to be influenced to a great extent by the administrator's attitude toward teachers. If he is friendly, shares responsibilities, and words cooperatively with members of the faculty, the prospects are good that they will work cooperatively with one another.

Relationships with Governmental and Extralegal Agencies

Teachers and administrators in local schools tend to become so engulfed in the immediate tasks of teaching school that they lose sight of the fact that all public schools are a part of a state system and all nonpublic schools are subject to certain state laws and constitutional provisions. Furthermore, the programs of all schools — public and nonpublic — are affected substantially by federal laws, court decisions, and/or conditions for participation in aid programs.

Federal Relationships

Even though the federal Constitution is silent on education and the tradition of state and local control is deeply rooted in American thought, the federal government is a very real force in shaping the program of our schools, especially at the secondary level. It exercises influence principally by (1) protecting the rights of citizens under the Constitution and statutes of the nation and (2) providing financial aid for certain types of programs.

Any illusions entertained by the several states that they are omnipotent in matters of education have been rather thoroughly dispelled by some history-making decisions of the United States Supreme Court, especially those dealing with religious instruction and racial segregation in the public schools. In a decision rendered on September 29, 1958, the Supreme Court strongly confirmed the principle that a citizen's constitutional rights take precedence over state powers to control education:

> It is, of course, quite true that the responsibility for public education is primarily a concern of the States, but it is equally true that such responsibilities, like all other state activities, must be exercised consistently with federal constitutional requirements as they apply to state action. The Constitution created a government dedicated to equal justice under the law. (27LW4006)[36]

The federal government also has given financial aid to public education from the time of the passage of the Northwest Ordinance in 1785. Such statutes as the Morrill Act of 1862, the Smith-Hughes Law of 1917, the George-Deen Law in 1936, and the George-Barden Act of 1946 have provided federal funds for education — especially for vocational training.

---

[36] Cited in William M. Alexander and J. Galen Saylor, *Modern Secondary Education*, (New York: Rinehart and Company, 1959), p. 678.

Most recently, the National Defense Education Act of 1958 has allocated millions of dollars of additional federal money for a large variety of educational programs and services. Under the provisions of this act secondary schools benefit directly from funds to upgrade programs in mathematics, science, foreign languages, and guidance. And they benefit indirectly from aid for such programs as summer institutes for teachers, counselors, and gifted students.

Federal funds for education amounted to almost two billion dollars in 1956–57,[37] and were appropriated for many purposes. Some were allotted to the United States Office of Education for research, leadership, information, and consultation; some for direct subsidies to vocational classes; some for the operation of special schools such as those for dependents on military posts overseas; some for research grants; some for hot-lunch programs in the form of surplus commodities; and some as loans and/or grants for equipment and other facilities. Even though we have no national system of schools, federal support plays a significant role in shaping American education.

State Relationships

Despite the many facets of federal influence,

> The State bears legal responsibility for the public education of its citizens. . . . Wherever possible each state delegates responsibility to local agencies. . . . The State agencies generally promote the cause of education through exercising leadership, administering essential state-wide programs, and providing services for the public schools.[38]

Participation in, and control over, public education by the several states varies widely in degree. For example, 40 per cent of all funds for public elementary and secondary schools came from state sources in 1957–58.[39] But in Delaware, Louisiana, and Georgia the proportion was over 70 per cent, while in Nebraska, New Hampshire, and South Dakota it amounted to less than 10 per cent. Forty-seven states require a certain number of specific courses to be taken by all students for graduation from high school, but the amount specified ranges from one-half unit in Michigan to eleven units in Missouri. A bulletin published prior to the admission of Alaska and Hawaii as states reported that the state department of education accredited high schools in forty states and exercised varying amounts of responsibility in six states. The state university accredited them in two states.[40]

---

[37] U.S. Office of Education, *Progress in Public Education in the United States — 1958–59* (Washington: Government Printing Office, 1959), p. 7.
[38] *Ibid.*, p. 2.
[39] *Ibid.*, p. 20.
[40] U.S. Office of Education, *State Accreditation of High Schools* (Washington: Government Printing Office, 1955), p. 72.

The states directly influence public secondary schools through (1) constitutional provisions, (2) statutory regulations, (3) appropriations of state funds, (4) court decisions, and (5) powers and duties delegated to a state board and/or chief state school officer, including approval.

The constitution and/or statutes in all states have created a system of public schools. In addition, they have provided for the creation of local school districts, empowered them to levy taxes for the construction of buildings and the operation of schools, and delegated certain powers and duties to local boards and professional personnel. The state laws and regulations affecting the operation of local schools are many and diverse. They range from the certification, duties, and powers of teachers to the health, welfare, and safety of students and to regulations for financing buildings and raising taxes. In some states the laws even specify that certain subjects shall be offered and the minimum amount of time that these subjects shall be taught.

Perhaps the most direct and powerful influence of the state in public education comes through its financial support and control. State support means state accounting — and therefore some degree of state control. State monies usually are allotted for specific purposes, e.g., general operation, transportation, textbooks, tuition, supplemental building aid, vocational education, and the like. Through its power of audit, the state exercises substantial control over local programs. School administrators and board members are held legally responsible to the state in accounting for, and in the proper expenditure of, all school monies, state and local.

In all but a few states the chief state school officer, as executive officer of the state board of education, is assigned extensive authority over the public schools — usually much more than he chooses to use. Although education is legally a state function, there are no state systems of schools in the sense that they are centrally administered, and in most states the chief state school officer and his staff limit their activities to regulatory, leadership, and operational functions.[41]

Relationships with Extralegal Agencies

Certain types of extralegal associations also influence the nature and quality of secondary school programs. These are associations, established by representatives of local schools, in which membership is voluntary. Their purpose is to provide both leadership and controls in order to promote sound policies and practices in the operation of local programs. They also serve to protect schools against irrational and damaging pressures from special-interest groups, such as local sports fans who demand an excessively large number of games.

The most influential type of extralegal association, in terms of the

[41] National Council of Chief State School Officers, *The State Department of Education* (Washington: The Council, 1952), pp. 17–30.

number of schools involved, is the state association for the control of extraclass activities and competitions. Most secondary schools, both public and private, belong to the state activities association or associations in order to be eligible to compete in athletics, speech, music, and so on. Such organizations are voluntary, but members are not permitted to compete against nonmembers. Consequently, all schools desiring to compete must be members.

Some states have a single state activities association, which provides leadership and controls for all interscholastic competitions; others have several associations, each functioning in a single activities field, such as athletics or music. The trend is toward a single state organization for the control of all interscholastic activities. Regulations usually cover student eligibility, number of contests per season, amount of practice time, professional status of coaches and sponsors, safety of participants, limits on values of awards to students, qualifications of officials, types of events, and official rules governing specific types of contests.

Many secondary schools also belong to one of five regional accrediting associations which include both colleges and secondary schools in their membership: the Middle States, New England, North Central, Southern, and Northwest.

Membership in these associations is voluntary and is attractive to secondary schools that can qualify because it enables them to join with schools in other states to work for better programs, conduct needed research and experimentation, and exchange information about new and successful practices. Regional associations also bring colleges and secondary schools closer together and assist individual schools in acquainting local patrons with desirable standards for maintaining a good educational program. In addition, membership serves to protect a school from actions by local pressure groups which might have an adverse effect on the school.

Some of the associations require applicants to undergo a comprehensive evaluation using the instruments and procedures of the *Evaluative Criteria*.[42] And all but one of the associations have their own policies, regulations, and criteria which schools must meet in order to be admitted and must continue to meet in order to retain their accreditation. The standards employed in accreditation are developed by representatives of the member schools and are approved by majority action.

Questions and Group Projects

1. Define secondary education and write a brief statement in support of your definition.

[42] *Evaluative Criteria* (Washington: National Study of Secondary School Evaluation, 1960).

2. Distinguish between a comprehensive and a specialized high school. Present the principal arguments and research evidence in support of each type.

3. Review a recent descriptive account of Soviet secondary schools. In what respects do they resemble and differ from our comprehensive public high schools?

4. Prepare in outline form a review of the highlights of the reorganization movement in American secondary education.

5. Assume that you are chairman of an advisory committee to the board of education in a city of 40,000 which is considering the question of shifting from an 8–4 organization to a 6–3–3 or 6–6 organization. Disregarding the initial costs for plant construction, prepare a brief to be presented to the board on the type of organization that you would recommend. Support your recommendations with evidence from research studies.

6. Defend or criticize the proposition: The public community college should be regarded as an upward extension of the senior high school.

7. Is there a point at which a senior high school may become too large? Present arguments, research evidence, and authoritative opinions to support your position.

8. Should the minimum size for a high school be established on the basis of number of students or scope of its program? Present arguments in support of your position.

9. Summarize what is being done in your state to effect better articulation between high schools and colleges.

10. Examine the accreditation standards for one of the regional accrediting associations. How do they compare with those of the state department of education in your state?

Selected References

Alexander, William M., and J. Galen Saylor. *Modern Secondary Education.* New York: Rinehart and Company, 1959.

American Association of School Administrators. *The High School in a Changing World.* Thirty-Sixth Yearbook. Washington: The Association, 1958.

Commission on the Reorganization of Secondary Education. *Cardinal Principles of Secondary Education,* U.S. Office of Education, Bulletin 1918, No. 35. Washington: Government Printing Office, 1918.

Conant, James B. *The American High School Today.* New York: McGraw-Hill Book Company, 1959.

———. *Education in the Junior High School Years.* Princeton, N.J.: Educational Testing Service, 1960.

Douglass, Harl R. *Secondary Education.* New York: The Ronald Press Company, 1952.

Evaluative Criteria. Washington: National Study of Secondary School Evaluation, 1960.

Faunce, Roland C., and Morrel J. Clute. *Teaching and Learning in the Junior High School.* New York: Wadsworth Publishing Company, 1961.

Ford, Edmond A. "Organization Pattern of the Nation's Public Secondary Schools," *School Life,* May, 1960.

French, William Marshall. *American Secondary Education.* New York: The Odyssey Press, 1957.

Gaumnitz, Walter H., and others. *Junior High School Facts — A Graphic Analysis.* Publication of the U.S. Office of Education. Washington: Government Printing Office, 1954.

Kefauver, Grayson U., Victor H. Noll, and C. Elwood Drake. *The Horizontal Organization of Secondary Education,* National Survey of Secondary Education, Bulletin, 1932, No. 17. Washington: Government Printing Office, 1934.

Koos, Leonard V. *Junior High School Trends.* New York: Harper & Brothers, 1955.

Michael, J. Lloyd. "Innovations in Organization," in Francis S. Chase and Harold A. Anderson, editors, *The High School in a New Era.* Chicago: University of Chicago Press, 1958.

Mort, Paul R. "Cost-Quality Relationship in Education," *Problems and Issues in Public School Finance.* New York: Bureau of Publications, Teachers College, Columbia University, 1952.

National Commission on School District Reorganization. *A Key to Better Education.* Washington: National Education Association, 1947.

National Council of Chief State School Officers. *The State Department of Education.* Washington: The Council, 1952.

Noar, Gertrude. *The Junior High School.* New York: Prentice-Hall, Inc., 1953.

North Central Association of Colleges and Secondary Schools. "Policies and Criteria for the Approval of Secondary Schools." Chicago: Commission on Secondary Schools, 1960.

U.S. Office of Education. *Progress of Public Education in the United States, 1958–59.* Washington: Government Printing Office, 1959.

———. "Statistical Summary of Education, 1957–58," *Biennial Survey of Education in the United States, 1956–58.* Washington: Government Printing Office, 1962.

Van Til, William, Gordon F. Vars, and John H. Lounsbury. *Modern Education for the Junior High School Years.* Indianapolis: The Bobbs-Merrill Company, 1961.

III

Organization and Direction of the Educational Program

The reason schools were organized by various peoples in the first place was to provide an educational program for children that would be superior to that which most parents could provide. Since this is the principal reason for the existence of schools, other professional activities in which teachers and administrators engage are justified only to the extent that they contribute to the effectiveness of the educational program.

In addition to students and teachers, the main ingredients of the high school program are classroom instruction, extraclass activities, guidance services, and instructional materials. Collectively, the learning experiences available through these components of a school make up the curriculum — although the curriculum is also thought of in the more restricted sense of course offerings and their content.

Leadership in planning and implementing the curriculum is the most important single responsibility of a high school principal and therefore is considered first in this section on the educational program (Chapter 5).

Chapter 6 deals with the scheduling of classes and activities during the school week and school year. Although scheduling is a technical aspect of school administration, it can do much to facilitate the successful operation of the educational program.

Chapter 7 directs attention to the nature and organization of guidance services in the high school. Guidance now enjoys widespread popular support, and much of the responsibility for selecting good personnel and making it possible for them to do a successful job rests with the secondary school administrator.

Since extraclass activities have become solidly established in high school programs, and many serious problems develop from these activities, the authors have devoted Chapters 8 and 9 to this aspect of school administration. The extraclass program requires prudent and courageous direction if it is to be a real asset to education, and the high school principal is the person whom the public expects to provide such direction.

Chapter 10 is devoted to an important and often neglected division of the high school — the school library. Here again, the key person in building and maintaining adequate services is the principal.

CHAPTER 5

Curriculum Planning and Design

Curriculum Planning

The curriculum is the main business of the school. It is the substance of what pupils learn and the methods by which they learn. Other enterprises involved in the operation of a school, such as supervisory services and business management, have value chiefly as they contribute to the strength and implementation of the curriculum. In our locally controlled system of education, curriculum planning involves the participation of many people and the reconciliation of many ideas. Because of its educational import and the complexities of the planning process, the curriculum demands more skillful leadership than any other aspect of the school program.

Definition of Curriculum

Most laymen view the curriculum as the content of a collection of courses taught in a school. This may be a serviceable popular definition, but the value of the curriculum is dependent not only on the nature of its content but also on the quality of the learning activities in which students engage. Moreover, students learn many valuable things in school outside of the content of organized courses.

Educators, therefore, have come to view the curriculum as including all of the constructive learning experiences in which students engage under the direction of the school. The emphasis is on the *constructive* nature of these experiences, whether gained through classroom instruction, guidance services, or extraclass activities. Although few educators would argue that everything engaged in by students in school is educative, most would contend that the curriculum extends beyond the classroom and that all constructive experiences which contribute to the objectives of the school are educative. Collectively, these experiences constitute the curriculum.

Need for Curriculum Planning

The observation that the curriculum of the school is shaped by the values and characteristics of the society in which it functions may be slightly worn, but it states a fundamental consideration in educational planning. As social conditions change, the curriculum changes — perhaps slowly, but it changes. If social change is accelerated through new developments in political affairs, economic conditions, or scientific and technological know-how, gaps develop between the curriculum and life outside the school. Such shifts occur in any type of society, democratic or totalitarian.

In the 1950's, gaps appeared between the curriculum and the needs of American society in science, technology, national purposes, and moral values. But they also developed between the needs of European societies and their school curricula. For example, Premier Khrushchev of the USSR declared in a speech in 1958, "The system now produces too many pampered intellectuals, boys and girls who have lost their respect for manual labor."[1] Soon after this speech, most students in the Soviet Union were required to engage in work as a part of their secondary schooling.

In a democracy, and especially under the American system of local control of education, major curriculum changes seldom are made with such dispatch. Occasionally the hiatus between social change and the curriculum reaches a critical state while we argue.

It appears that the American secondary curriculum is in such a state at the present time. Prominent scientists and statesmen warn that scientific discoveries and developments in atomic energy, space exploration, electronics, and chemistry are pushing us into a period of precipitate change in technology and industrial production. These developments, in combination with modern automation, are now revolutionizing our ways of making a living and our manner of living.[2] It has been estimated that within two decades almost one-half of our labor force will be employed in the manufacture of products that are not now known.

While such monumental changes have been in the making, the secondary school has been sputtering along with an old-model curriculum, not because teachers and administrators have been unmindful of the need for a new model but because other things have seemed to require our

[1] Roy Essoyan, "Russian School System Has Critics," an Associated Press news story appearing in *The Press-Citizen*, Iowa City, Iowa, September 28, 1959, p. 9.
[2] Rockefeller Report, *The Pursuit of Excellence—Education and the Future of America*, Special Studies Project Report V (Garden City, N.Y.: Doubleday and Company, 1958), pp. 1–48.

immediate resources. First the urgent demands of World War II, and then the enormous growth in enrollments, the acute shortage of qualified teachers, and the financial demands for new buildings and equipment have made it exceedingly difficult to find time and resources for substantial curriculum revision.

The net result is that the secondary school has been teaching too much that is outmoded in the fields of mathematics, science, vocational education, and the social sciences. Attempts to make provision for adolescent needs often have been based on studies conducted in the depression years and are as dated as dance marathons and NYA projects. A striking example of current lag is the fact that in a world dependent for survival on mutual understanding among nations, less than 10 per cent of our high schools offer courses in world geography.[3]

More fundamental, however, is the inadequacy of provisions for the academically talented and culturally deprived and for differences in abilities and special interests all along the line. These deficiencies are not due to the failure of professional educators to recognize the problems or their lack of desire to do something about them. The Educational Policies Commission published a comprehensive study on the education of the gifted child eight years before Conant made his first report, and many professional articles had appeared on the subject prior to 1950.[4] Furthermore, some of our better-financed and larger school districts have provided excellent programs for gifted students for many years. But the great majority of secondary schools are too small and lack sufficient financial resources to provide first-rate programs. Conant states, "I should like to record at this point my conviction that in many states the number one problem is the elimination of the small high school by district reorganization."[5] At another point he observes,

> To provide adequate teachers for specialized subjects is extremely expensive. Furthermore, to maintain an interest in academic subjects among a small number is not always easy. . . . The situation in regard to nonacademic elective programs in a small high school is even worse.[6]

A sound answer to the problem of providing for individual differences requires not only broad offerings and special administrative devices such as grouping and remedial classes but also effective classroom procedures in working with students as individuals. Even though district reorganization and more adequate finances may be needed in a particular com-

---

[3] U.S. Office of Education, "Offerings and Enrollments in High School Subjects," *Biennial Survey of Education in the United States, 1948–50* (Washington: Government Printing Office, 1951), Chap. 5, pp. 107–8.

[4] Educational Policies Commission, *Education of the Gifted* (Washington: National Education Association, 1950).

[5] James B. Conant, *The American High School Today* (New York: McGraw-Hill Book Company, 1958), p. 38.

[6] *Ibid.*, p. 37.

munity, this is not a valid reason for deferring all aspects of curriculum improvement. Certain types of improvements can be made even with limited resources. For example, one of the most persistent blocks to curriculum improvement is the lack of careful instructional planning by classroom teachers. At the present time a majority of high school teachers depend on a basic textbook for course organization as well as content. They conduct recitations out of the book, they make all assignments out of the book, and they make up examinations out of the book. The basic textbook serves an important function in classroom instruction, but by itself it is a highly restricted educational diet.

Responsibility for Leadership

The extent and quality of curriculum planning in a school system will depend largely on the competence and efforts of administrative leaders. It is sometimes true that the curriculum is weak in a school with good administrative leadership, but it is rarely true that the curriculum is good in a school with weak leadership. In the first situation, there may be certain factors such as lack of funds, inadequate size, athletic pressure groups, and/or a superannuated faculty which are inherited by an administrator and cannot be corrected immediately. In the second situation, there is little hope for the curriculum without a change in administration. Even though teachers and parents may be interested in curriculum improvement, they cannot secure the necessary time, money, and materials to do a competent job without the support of the administration.

The key people in local curriculum planning, therefore, are the superintendent of schools and the principals of individual school units. Without enterprising, informed, and imaginative leadership in these positions the curriculum is likely to become a disjointed collection of courses. With such leadership, it may become the constructive force that it should be in the education of children.

The high school principal is responsible for leadership in curriculum improvement in his school. If nothing of consequence is happening to improve instruction, he may well look at himself. Most people tend to give priority to those things in which they are interested. If the high school principal is interested in entertainment and public relations, he will probably devote much of his time, beyond the routine tasks of his job, to the promotion of entertainment and publicity. If he is interested in the educational program, he will find ways to improve it. In most systems in cities of 20,000 and over, curriculum consultants are available on the central office staff to assist the principal in curriculum planning. But consultants are not in a position to make contributions if the principal does not utilize their services. In a small high school, if the principal is a principal in fact, progress in curriculum improvement will depend to a considerable extent upon his ability to stimulate and coordinate the efforts of his teachers. He will need the support of the superintendent, but much of the real business of planning and improvement will stem from his own interest, drive, and knowledge.

Leadership in curriculum work, however, is not the exclusive responsibility of administrators and supervisors. Their initiative is a requisite, but as the program develops, leadership should shift within the faculty according to the nature of a problem and the special competences of members of the staff. If the focal point should become the articulation and planning of the science sequence from the primary grades through the senior high school, qualified science and elementary teachers should assume much of the leadership. Effective curriculum planning is a cooperative process, and the competent administrator will make use of, and seek to develop, the potential of his staff.

Much of the effectiveness of the principal in his role as a curriculum coordinator will depend upon his ability to understand and to work with people. Within most faculties, individuals vary considerably in temperament, abilities, and experience. At times, certain teachers may be enthusiastic over the prospects of curriculum planning and need only encouragement, time, and facilities in order to get under way. But other teachers may be indifferent or obdurate regardless of the efforts of the principal and other staff members to get them to move. The first responsibility of the principal is to his students and to the educational program of his school. If some staff members consistently malinger or obstruct, he must reach a clear understanding with them about their professional functions. Democracy is not all "togetherness" and "consensus"; it fixes responsibilities and each person should be expected to assume his share of them.

Guides in Curriculum Planning

Curriculum planning cannot be reduced to a series of steps or a set of rules. Situations, problems, and personalities vary widely among different communities and schools, and planning procedures must be adapted to local conditions in order to effect constructive results. Nevertheless, the authors believe that the following procedures have been sufficiently well tested under a variety of circumstances to justify their being stated as guides for local faculties. They may not be appropriate in all situations, but they have proved to be sound in a large number of schools and communities.

1. *Reach agreement on key issues and objectives early in the program.* Many administrators have discovered, in their haste to get started on specific curriculum problems, that much time and effort have been wasted because of failure to agree on basic issues and aims early in the program. It does not follow that curriculum planning should get under way with a systematic study of educational philosophy or the drafting of a formal

statement of objectives. Such an approach not only is likely to be dull but usually contributes very little to instructional practice. However, the discussion of educational issues which have meaning to teachers and which are basic to the design of the curriculum need not be dull and should facilitate agreement on policies and on the outcomes of instruction. For instance, should all youth in the community be encouraged to complete high school? Is ability grouping likely to promote undesirable social attitudes? Should promotion be based on certain fixed minimum standards of achievement? Is it a proper function of a secondary school to provide technical vocational instruction? Should all academically talented students be required to take advanced courses in mathematics and science?

It is far better to reach a consensus on such questions in the early stages of a local program than to arrive at a stalemate halfway through and be compelled to discard much of the work completed by a hardworking committee. Experiences of this nature soon dampen faculty enthusiasm for curriculum work.

The chief purpose of such agreement, of course, is to give direction to the program. With a definitive statement of goals and agreement on key issues it is possible to develop a design that has direction and a rational emphasis. Without them, the curriculum is likely to embody contradictions and much needless duplication.

2. *Proceed on an evolutionary basis.* The real test of curriculum planning is whether it results in better education for students. Teachers must understand and support contemplated changes, since they are charged with implementing them. Sudden and sweeping changes tend to cause confusion and disagreement among teachers. Often such confusion is transmitted to patrons, and the program becomes a target for attacks primarily because it is not understood.

In some schools, however, the situation may have deteriorated so badly that a new administration finds it necessary to move rapidly and to make drastic changes in the best interests of students. Needless to say, in such cases the program is likely to be extremely controversial, and the administration will need the full support of the board of education and community leaders. Whether much is gained over a long period by a "shock" treatment is questionable. If such therapy is contemplated, the administrator should be certain of his diagnosis and convinced of the urgency of changes.

Solid curriculum gains depend upon improved instructional practices; these, in turn, depend upon the attitudes and understanding of classroom teachers. If a procedure is employed which seriously undermines teacher morale, little real gain is likely to accrue even if the new program looks good on the drawing board. Adequate time and preparation at an early stage usually bring more solid long-term improvements.

3. *Begin with a limited number of projects and see them through to tangible results.* Some writers refer to the concentration on a few cur-

riculum projects at a time as a "demonstration" approach as opposed to a "unified front" approach. As observed earlier, there are few generalizations on curriculum procedure that apply to all situations. It has been the experience of many school faculties who have attempted a broad frontal attack on the curriculum that some working groups get bogged down and never succeed in producing anything really worthwhile. Frequently, teachers who have had this type of experience become disillusioned and develop negative attitudes toward curriculum work in general.

On the other hand, concentration on a manageable number of projects until substantial improvements are observable is likely to be rewarding to the participants and result in favorable attitudes on the part of other members of the staff. The chances for success are enhanced under this approach, since the time and energies of the staff and other available resources are not spread so thin that the quality of the work suffers.

Local circumstances may be such, however, as to warrant a comprehensive program. If sufficient funds, teachers, time, and supervisory assistance are at hand, it may succeed.

4. Develop and maintain good faculty morale. Morale as defined in Chapter 12 is the feeling of well-being that a person has toward himself and his group, plus desire and effort to accomplish the common goals of the group. It is a significant force in the success of any group enterprise. With it a school faculty can accomplish solid results in curriculum improvement. Without it curriculum work has little chance of getting beyond the conversational stage.

A discerning school administrator should be able to recognize the symptoms of good or poor morale in his faculty. If the signs point to good morale, he may anticipate that the faculty will be ready and willing to make the kind of effort required for curriculum improvement. If the symptoms are negative, he may expect little faculty support.

The factors which research has shown to be most closely related to teacher morale are discussed in Chapter 12. In general, studies show that teacher-administrator relationships and rapport among members of the staff are two of the most influential factors and that administrators who are professionally competent, friendly, and sympathetic contribute positively to morale. Opportunities to participate in policy making, community support, favorable salaries, adequate instructional supplies, and reasonable teaching loads are additional factors. Back slapping and pep talks are synthetics and contribute little to the morale of a group of intelligent people.

5. Provide opportunities for all faculty members to participate. A faculty must draw upon many areas of knowledge and many types of learning experiences in developing a suitable curriculum. Consequently, it is important to the strength of the curriculum that all teachers be familiar with the purposes and design of the total program and appreciate their respective responsibilities for its success.

A comprehensive approach to curriculum planning, involving all teachers at the same time, carries the risk that the program may become mired from its own weight. But there are certain aspects, such as agreement on aims, scope and sequence, formulation of policies, provision for individual differences, and coordination of classroom teaching and counseling, which depend for their success upon the cooperation and participation of the entire faculty.

Perhaps the most important benefit to the curriculum resulting from participation by all staff members is that the potential of the entire group may be brought to bear on educational problems. Without group participation, some teachers with excellent ideas may feel that their opinions are not solicited and therefore may be reluctant to express themselves. Under such circumstances the curriculum is the chief loser.

Techniques for securing effective teacher participation should be consistent with the size and composition of the group. Any procedure which promotes a favorable atmosphere for the exchange of views and which stimulates creative and constructive thinking is desirable. Approaches such as brainstorming and group dynamics have a place but involve the risk that means may be confused with ends. Cohesiveness and harmony are admirable group qualities, but some problems require a certain amount of old-fashioned conflict and argument if the staff is to make progress in curriculum improvement.

Most faculty members also will profit from participation in the planning of specific departmental, guidance, or student activity projects. Such experience contributes to their professional growth and, in turn, to the strength of the curriculum.

6. *Reach agreement on areas of responsibility and relationships.* Much curriculum planning involves group work of some type by teachers, patrons, and pupils. If a group is to come out somewhere, participants should know the ground rules, including lines of responsibility and working relationships. It is an imposition on conscientious workers to permit them to devote a large amount of time and effort to some project only to discover that they are in direct conflict with, or have been duplicating the work of, another group. This is also an excellent way to bring curriculum planning to a sudden impasse or to precipitate a beautiful Donnybrook.

In a relatively small school with few curriculum workers the entire faculty may serve as a steering committee to define responsibilities and relationships before individual and committee planning gets under way. In a larger system, a central planning committee may serve effectively to interpret policies, specify responsibilities, and clarify relationships. Regardless of the size of the school, it is the function of school administrators to make certain that organizational and procedural matters are clearly described and that members of curriculum groups recognize that final authority rests with the board of education.

7. *Provide adequate time, materials, and personnel.* In too many

schools curriculum work is literally a "moonlighting" type of job. Committee meetings and general faculty meetings are held after school or on Saturdays, and individual teachers are expected to work on materials during their spare time. Many faculties do not accomplish much in the way of curriculum planning largely because boards and superintendents have made inadequate provision for it in the school budget. It has been the observation of the authors, however, that the failure of boards to provide funds for curriculum improvement is as often due to the failure of administrators to inform them of the need as to their reluctance to allocate money for such purposes. Once board members understand what is required for curriculum planning, they usually are willing to appropriate the necessary funds.

Good curriculum planning makes heavy demands on the time of the people involved. It also requires adequate library materials and some expert consultant services. If a school expects to do any really solid curriculum work, teachers serving on key committees need to be released from part of their regular teaching duties or to be employed during the summer for this specific purpose.

In addition, a curriculum library and materials center is almost a necessity. Professional reference books, yearbooks, and journals are needed along with a good collection of course guides, resource units, textbooks, and other instructional materials. Funds should be made available, too, for the employment of special consultants to supplement the regular supervisory staff.

8. Enlist the cooperation and participation of representative citizens. Under our system of local control, states delegate much of the responsibility for the operation of public schools to citizens in local districts. Their educational interests and views are ordinarily reflected in the actions taken by an elective board of education. In small systems the composition of the board may be such as to provide adequate communication with the public on curriculum matters. In large systems, however, the relatively small number of members on the board usually does not permit effective two-way communication with school patrons. Policies, objectives, and the general design of the curriculum are joint responsibilities of teachers and lay citizens, with authority for final approval residing with the local board and the state government.

It is difficult in a large community for citizens to become articulate or to keep informed about the curriculum. One means of achieving these ends is through an organized body of laymen such as the Parent-Teacher Association or a citizens advisory council. Such groups serve in an advisory capacity to the board of education. They are not legislative bodies nor are they professional curriculum workers responsible for detailed planning of courses and other materials. Nevertheless, they may make valuable contributions to the curriculum by reviewing proposals, making recommendations, and communicating with other patrons.

At times some members of a lay advisory group may lose sight of their functions within the legal framework for the operation of schools. But the positive aid of citizen planning groups generally far outweighs their occasional excursions into areas which are beyond their advisory role. A growing number of laymen are beginning to take a discerning interest in education and to bring a fresh point of view to the curriculum. Their interest and cooperation should be welcomed and encouraged by teachers and school administrators.

9. Encourage student participation in some aspects of curriculum planning. The student is the forgotten person in much of the recent popular debate on education. It seems that almost every adult has plans for doing things for, and to, students. A school board member writing in a weekly magazine declares with some pride, "We are going to stuff solid courses in history — ancient, medieval, modern, and United States — down the gullets of the high school youngsters."[7] Presumably she should add, "or else." Probably many youngsters will elect the "or else" option if this becomes the prevailing attitude of board members and teachers. Undoubtedly some, but not all, high school students can profit from a renewed emphasis on so-called "hard-core" subjects. But in the final analysis the desire of students for education is the most potent force in determining how well they learn. Stuffing courses down their gullets is one of the best ways known to encourage them to become disillusioned with the whole business of formal education.

Most high school students are immature and lack the knowledge and experience needed to make significant contributions to the over-all design and objectives of the secondary school curriculum. But they know whether or not they are getting anything of consequence out of their courses. In addition, they may want to know how certain courses and methods contribute to their educational purposes. If they are bright, they will be especially anxious to know. Sound curriculum planning provides opportunities for students to raise questions and to make suggestions. It also seeks to give them rational answers.

Tasks in Curriculum Planning

Groping, exploration, and trial and error are inevitable in an enterprise as complex and controversial as planning for the education of the young. Consequently, curriculum planning cannot be organized as a series of orderly operations. It may, however, be described in terms of major tasks or phases. The following procedures are not presented as distinct and sequential steps, but somewhere along the line they fit into the total process and each serves important purposes. Although it is logical that some of them should precede others in a long-range plan of curriculum

---

[7] Bianca Bradbury, "We're Always on the Spot," *The Saturday Evening Post*, November 14, 1959, p. 69.

improvement, most of them will function concurrently. Evaluation and community relations, for example, are continuous procedures and are essential in all aspects of curriculum improvement. We submit these suggestions, then, as descriptive phases of the over-all process of local curriculum planning.

Appraisal of the Current Program. In education, as in business, government, or any other institution, the first step toward improvement is to find out where you stand. How well is the program accomplishing the things it is supposed to accomplish?

In business the evidence is fairly objective: it is largely a matter of determining profit or loss. But in education a balance cannot be struck quite so neatly. In the first place, the end products cannot be as clearly defined; and in the second place, the results are much more difficult to measure. Nevertheless, education cannot progress without appraisal. If educators cannot manage it, the public will.

The first requirement in determining how well a school is doing is to reach agreement on what it is expected to do. In a public school this involves the joint efforts of laymen and educators in defining the goals of the program. From there, the process becomes one of trying to measure or judge how well the school is accomplishing the purposes agreed upon.

Among the procedures that have been used successfully for such judgment are the following:

1. Analysis of underachievement on the basis of standardized aptitude and achievement test results.
2. Follow-up studies of graduates.
3. Studies of dropouts — causes and adjustments.
4. Surveys of teacher and parent opinion.
5. Student interviews.
6. Self-evaluation by faculty, using such instruments as the *Evaluative Criteria* (published by the National Study of Secondary School Evaluation, Washington, D.C., 1960 edition).
7. Observation of classroom instruction by supervisors and consultants.
8. Review of curriculum content by consultants.
9. Survey of community resources and needs and analysis of the educational program in relation to the findings.
10. Pupil inventories and case studies.
11. Diagnostic tests to determine student learning problems.
12. Survey of adequacy of the student activity program and extent of student participation.

Basic to all of these is a sound and comprehensive system of student records. A description of such records and their uses is presented in Chapter 16.

Study and Planning. After a local faculty and board have gathered information about the results of the program, someone needs to decide whether they are good, bad, or indifferent and what should be done about them. Under our system of local control, this is the legal responsibility of the board of education. But the board will need expert advice on some problems and community support on others.

Local boards may, and sometimes do, make important decisions affecting the curriculum without consulting teachers and patrons. This may speed up the decision-making process but it often results in poor implementation and/or strong opposition. Cooperative study and planning by teachers and lay groups not only bring the talents of these people to bear on curriculum problems, but generally serve to clarify points of dispute and to enlist their assistance in gaining public support for needed improvements.

It does not follow, however, that all or even most decisions affecting the curriculum should be made jointly by teachers and citizen groups. Course organization, course sequences, grade placement, and the like should be determined by professionally trained teachers. But such matters as defining general goals, reviewing over-all policies, recommending the relative emphasis to be placed on major fields, and securing resources have a much better chance of being implemented if they have been jointly settled on by teachers and lay groups. Furthermore, those decisions affecting the curriculum which are the primary responsibilities of teachers are likely to be carried out most successfully if they are based on cooperative study and planning by the faculty as a group.

The chief functions of school administrators in this aspect of curriculum planning are to arrange the setting, expedite the conduct of meetings, provide for records and follow-up, and secure the information needed for intelligent deliberations. Although administrators ought to become involved as active participants, they should not seek to impose their views on study groups.

The immediate goal of this phase of curriculum planning is to enlist the thinking of teachers and laymen by effecting a good two-way flow of ideas. The most effective media are likely to be PTA meetings, joint teacher-citizen committees, local curriculum workshops, and individual and small-group teacher-parent conferences.

Preparation of Curriculum Materials. Although substantial progress may be made toward upgrading local curriculum programs without undertaking the preparation of resource units, course guides, and instructional handbooks, work on such materials often brings sizable dividends in the form of higher teacher competence as well as better unity and direction in classroom procedures. Frequently, however, production work is attempted too early in local curriculum planning. The result is waste motion and confusion because the staff is not certain where it is trying to go. Under such circumstances teachers grow weary, nerves become frayed, and the quality of the product suffers.

Among the guides for curriculum planning described earlier, the following are prerequisites for good planning at the local level: (1) early agreement on issues and aims, (2) good staff morale, (3) agreement on responsibilities and relationships, and (4) adequate personnel, time, and resources. Adequate time is an essential condition for teachers, administrators, and laymen to reach agreement on the over-all design and central purposes of the curriculum. And agreement on design and central purposes is an essential condition for successful planning of course content and learning activities.

But with these cautions, the preparation of curriculum guides and publications may make solid contributions to the quality of the instructional program. First, good planning is an essential ingredient in good classroom instruction, and work on course guides and resource units provides the teacher with a reservoir of materials and procedures to draw upon for day-to-day instructional plans. Second, teachers working on production committees share their views and do considerable research in locating fresh ideas and materials. As a result, references are updated and teachers are encouraged to try new and imaginative techniques and media. And third, the publication of bulletins on special instructional procedures such as programmed learning, group planning, directed study, and the use of student data permits all members of the faculty to have access to recent research and the experience of other school systems with these media and materials.

Experimentation. Instructional procedures and materials which may be successful in one system under a particular set of circumstances may not be successful in another system under different conditions. Consequently, if a school staff is to come up with some better ways of doing things, it has to undertake a manageable number of experimental programs and evaluate them in terms of their effectiveness under local conditions.

Local experimental programs are sometimes referred to as "action research," since they do not ordinarily employ the sophisticated controls and analyses that are commonly used by research specialists and organizations. However, it does not follow that local experimentation cannot be designed so as to discover important ways of improving instruction. If the design, collection and treatment of data, and interpretation of results are done as carefully as possible under working conditions, noteworthy curriculum advances may come out of this type of research.

The lack of ideal experimental conditions and facilities should not deter a staff from attempting and evaluating new types of programs. Some of the most significant breakthroughs in curriculum improvement have come out of experimentation under typical school conditions and from evaluations based, in part, on the subjective judgment of teachers.

For example, because certain variables such as teacher bias and the composition of classes cannot be controlled, it may not be possible for a local faculty to determine whether the placement of biology in the ninth grade results in statistically significant gains or losses in pupil achievement. However, if one or two sections of biology are tried in the ninth grade and the teachers are convinced that freshmen understand the material about as well and show as much interest as sophomores, such evidence merits careful consideration in making a decision about the grade placement of biology. It may not be adequate in itself, but it is as important to a working program as standardized test results and other more sophisticated methods of evaluation.

Maintenance of Two-Way Communication with the Public. The support of patrons in the community, necessary to successful innovations in the school curriculum, is dependent on reliable information. If, for example, the faculty and board of education should decide that there is a need for a directed work experience program in business education, and the public gains the impression that students are going to replace full-time workers, the program will encounter strong opposition and have little chance for success.

However, if citizens are given the supporting facts and have an opportunity to meet with members of the staff to discuss the implications, the chances are good that they will back the proposal. If a major move is made without acceptance by the people, they may properly exercise their right to change the administration of the schools. With public understanding and support, however, teachers and administrators need have little fear of attacks from pressure groups and should feel encouraged to seek new and better answers to educational problems. More important, they are likely to get some first-rate suggestions from laymen.

Continued Evaluation and Follow-Up. Any discussion of evaluation *per se* duplicates some of the discussion of other phases of curriculum planning, since it is an integral part of each of the other phases. The appraisal of strengths and weaknesses in the curriculum, for example, is a process of evaluation. However, evaluation must extend into other phases of curriculum improvement in order to determine their effectiveness. Evaluation of the curriculum should never end, because curriculum change should never end. Consequently, the school administrator who is concerned with the level of educational performance in his school has a continuing job to do in evaluation.

In summary, the principal tasks involved in evaluation include (1) *formulating objectives* in terms of desired changes in pupil behavior; (2) *securing information* indicating whether or not these changes are occurring, by means of procedures such as those listed under Task 1, "Appraisal of the Current Program"; and (3) *analyzing and interpreting* the information secured.

It is hardly necessary to point out that evaluation becomes merely an academic exercise without follow-up procedures. Its chief purpose is to secure information needed to make further improvement in the educational program. If the information reposes in the files in the principal's office it is about as useful as a stack of old newspapers.

Curriculum planning is a complex, demanding, and frequently contentious task. But the curriculum is the chief vehicle for education in a school; its design and implementation, therefore, are the major professional functions of teachers and administrators. Even though the process of improvement is often erratic, appraisal, joint study, production, experimentation, two-way communication, and evaluation are essential ingredients and must somewhere be involved if a school is to move ahead.

Organizational Design of the Curriculum

The design of the curriculum embodies its scope and sequence. *Scope* refers to the composition and breadth of the curriculum, the nature of the learning experiences that the school seeks to provide for pupils. *Sequence* deals with the order and relationships of learning experiences, their grade placement and continuity in the program of the school. Effective articulation, both vertical and horizontal, is a major concern in planning sequence.

If the curriculum is regarded as all of the constructive learning experiences in which pupils engage under the direction of the school, the scope of the curriculum includes not only organized knowledge and classroom instruction but also extraclass activities, guidance, and certain community-related experiences. Each of these fields is of sufficient breadth and importance, however, to be the subject of entire volumes. Separate chapters are devoted to the administration and organization of the extraclass and guidance programs in this text. The present section, therefore, will be limited to a consideration of the nature and organization of course offerings, generally referred to as the program of studies, and of certain related administrative procedures.

The Program of Studies

Schools were devised by parents to secure greater depth, efficiency, and economy of time in the education of their children than most of them were able to provide at home. The ancient Romans employed tutors, who presumably possessed more knowledge and were more skilled in methods of instruction than the citizens who employed them. Parents have been arguing with teachers about these matters ever since.

After some two thousand years of trial, error, and research, it appears that some type of logical and sequential arrangement of courses and activities in relation to the maturity of students and to the logical sequence of subject matter enhances learning in schools. In modern educational planning, the term "program of studies" is used to designate the courses offered by a school and their arrangement into sequences and patterns so as to best serve the needs and interests of students. For secondary schools this involves (1) the selection of organized bodies of knowledge and learning experiences to achieve the objectives of the school, (2) the arrangement of materials and experiences in sequences appropriate to the maturity of students and to providing continuity in learning, (3) the selection of materials and experiences which best serve the *common* needs of students and the needs of society, (4) provisions for organized experiences to serve the *special interests, needs,* and *abilities* of students, and (5) provisions for articulation between grade levels and areas of instruction.

Criteria for Organizing the Program of Studies

No administrative plan can insure a high degree of learning, but administrative arrangements may serve to facilitate effective learning and instruction. Over a period of years certain empirical criteria for planning the program of studies have been developed by professional workers in the field of secondary education. One of the guides widely employed by regional accrediting associations in evaluating member schools is that of the Cooperative Study of Secondary School Standards.[8] This set of criteria, based on more than twenty years of research and experience follows.

General Principles

The program of studies:

1. Is based on an analysis of the educational needs of youth.
2. Provides a wide variety of experiences to meet both the common and individual educational needs of youth.
3. Is planned to help meet both present and probable future needs of pupils.
4. Provides opportunities for pupils as well as staff members to participate in the planning and development of curriculum activities.
5. Provides for relating subject-matter fields to life problems of pupils.
6. Emphasizes critical and thoughtful approaches to present-day problems.
7. Provides opportunities for experiences especially adapted to the superior or advanced pupils.
8. Provides opportunities for experiences especially adapted to slow-learning pupils.

[8] Cooperative Study of Secondary School Standards, *Evaluative Criteria* (Washington: The Study, 1950), pp. 49–52.

9. Provides organized sequences of courses carrying on through several grades.
10. Provides for coordination of educational experiences within each grade.
11. Places emphasis on broad concepts taught for transfer value.
12. Is flexible in time allotments to meet individual pupil requirements (e.g., variation in number of periods for elective subjects, periods allotted to special-help and remedial work, or time devoted to pupil-initiated course work).
13. Provides for the evaluation of pupil achievement in the program in terms of each individual's aptitudes and abilities.
14. Recognizes the contributions made by the pupil activity program.
15. Encourages enlargement and enrichment of the pupil's scope of interests.

Types of Programs of Studies

During the 300-year history of secondary education in America four basic types of organization for the program of studies have been employed:

Single Curriculum. This is the traditional European pattern employed in the German *gymnasium* and the French *lycée*. The same courses are prescribed for all students. No electives are provided, and students with different interests select different schools. Few secondary schools in the United States have employed a single curriculum since the Civil War.

Multiple Curricula. Under this type of organization a school provides two or more parallel curricula to serve the special interests of different groups of students, such as college preparatory, business, and trades. In its pure form, all courses within a curriculum are prescribed. Students electing one curriculum are not permitted to elect courses from another. The Committee of Ten recommended this type of pattern for the organization of the program of studies, and it was widely used from the 1890's until around 1910. This pattern is at present limited largely to intensive vocational programs in a few large high schools.

Constants-with-Variables Type. Certain courses (constants) are prescribed as requirements for graduation for all students, and other courses (variables) are designated as free electives. The chief restriction on student elections is the grade level of a particular course, although students usually are counseled in their selection of courses in terms of their abilities and future plans. The constants-with-variables organization gained steadily in popularity from 1910 to 1960. A National Education Association survey shows that almost 80 per cent of the 866 schools responding used a constants-with-variables pattern.[9]

---
[9] National Education Association, Research Division, "High School Graduation Requirements," *Research Bulletin*, December, 1959, 37:121.

Advisory or Combination Pattern. This is a mixture of the multiple and constants-with-variables types. Certain specific, or constant, courses are prescribed for all students as in the constants-with-variables plan, and advisory curricula for special-interest groups are outlined for guidance purposes. Students electing a college preparatory or business curriculum, however, are not restricted to that program and may elect courses in other sequences.

General Education to Serve Common Needs

Most definitions of liberal and general education tend to be rather extensive but non-controversial, until someone attempts to reduce them to prescriptions. At this point people tend to become emotional and it becomes apparent that the fine rhetoric about liberal and liberating education and educating the young for rational and responsible citizenship means many things to many people. But in the ordinary business of organizing a school it becomes necessary to translate the rhetoric into some sort of systematic program. In modern democratic administration school officials tend to "share" this privilege with committees.

Whether or not the responsibility is shared, the secondary school administrator needs a definition of a program of general education for his school in terms of courses or some other scheme for organizing subject matter and activities. Some of it may be defined by state law. The school statutes and/or state department regulations in several states require certain subjects such as United States history, American government, driver education, and physical education to be completed for high school graduation. The local school administrator must first provide for such state requirements in the design of the program of general education for his school.

Ideally, the program should be defined in terms of criteria and objectives. What are the most important skills, concepts, and attitudes that all students should be expected to have by the time they complete the secondary school? And what proportion of the student's time in high school should be occupied with the study of these things? The neohumanists would answer these questions in terms of a prescribed list of academic courses such as those found in the *gymnasia* of Germany and the *lycées* of France. The functionalists or experimentalists would answer them in terms of the contemporary values and needs of American society and the common needs of youth.

Under our system of local control of education, the school administrator has no real right to make final decisions on curriculum offerings for a community. Most of the authority is delegated by the state to local boards of education and therefore to the electorates of local districts. Consequently, the "sharing" of responsibility for planning the program of general education with committees of teachers and laymen is a matter not of shifting responsibility but essentially of recognizing legally constituted authority. In most school districts, however, the people properly turn to the professional staff of the school for leadership and recommendations.

It is the point of view of the authors that the most defensible criteria for defining a set of guiding objectives for general education are (1) the distinguishing values of American culture, (2) the important and persistent problems of our society, and (3) the significant and common developmental problems or needs of adolescents. Several national and state organizations have drafted statements of objectives based on these criteria which should serve as valuable guides for local schools in undertaking a statement of their own. The authors suggest that the complete statement drafted by the Educational Policies Commission under the title *The Purposes of Education in American Democracy*, as outlined in Chapter 3, may guide local committees.[10] However, it should be adapted to the contemporary needs of students and of the community.

The aim of any program of general education in our society is to bring about such changes in the behavior of youth as the American people believe are desirable. Consequently, a definition of these changes in terms of behavioral goals is a logical step in planning the scope and sequence of a program of general education. One of the better-known attempts at such definition is the report of a large group of educators under the direction of the Educational Testing Service, the National Association of Secondary School Principals, and the Russell Sage Foundation. Space does not permit a reprint of this complete set of goals but the school administrator should find the report by French very helpful.[11]

Organization of Programs for General Education

In most secondary schools planning groups have translated the objectives of general education into a pattern of conventional courses. In a small percentage of schools, a different type of pattern has been adopted which is characterized by a reorganization of content and activities into a "core" program cutting across conventional subject boundaries. The common experiences of general education are organized around social themes and youth problems. Core programs usually are referred to as "unified studies," "common learnings," or "block-of-time" curricula. Most core programs are found in junior high schools, generally in Grades 7

[10] Educational Policies Commission, *The Purposes of Education in American Democracy* (Washington: National Education Association, 1938), pp. 39–50.
[11] Will French, *et al., Behavioral Goals of General Education in High School* (New York: Russell Sage Foundation, 1957), p. 235.

and 8. A nation-wide survey conducted in 1956–57 reports that approximately 19.3 per cent of the public junior and senior high schools in the United States offered some type of block-time classes.[12] However, a study made by a committee of the National Association of Secondary School Principals in 1955–56 shows that 57.3 per cent of 1,200 junior high schools employed some block-time classes. And of the large schools of 1,000 or over, 72.5 per cent scheduled these classes.[13]

It appears that over 80 per cent of the four-year and three-year senior schools in the United States employ a conventional subject organization for the design of the curriculum and that the program of general education prescribes specific courses to be completed by all students. Moreover, a large majority of schools with block-time courses (about 70 per cent) employ conventional subjects within the block of time.

Provisions in Four-Year and Three-Year Senior High Schools

The following are Conant's recommendations for graduation requirements in grades 9 through 12:

> *General Education.* The requirements for graduation for all students should be as follows: four years of English, three or four years of social studies — including two years of history (one of which should be American history) and a senior course in American problems or American government — one year of mathematics in the ninth grade (algebra or general mathematics), and at least one year of science in the ninth or tenth grade which might well be biology or general science.[14]

The principal differences between current practice and Conant's recommendations are that a majority of schools now specify one unit in physical education (Conant did not specify any), three units of English rather than four, and two units of social studies rather than three.

A survey of graduation requirements was conducted by the National Education Association for the 1958–59 school year. Table 12 reports the findings of that study, which included replies from 866 high school principals in all sections of the country. The NEA study reports that almost 80 per cent of the high schools employed a constants-with-variables organization, called "Single" in the table. The average number of total units required for graduation was 16.5 in Grades 9 through 12, of which 9.7 were constants or specified and 6.8 were variables or electives. Over half of the high schools (53 per cent) had increased their graduation requirements in the last five years. Almost 12 per cent had increased requirements in mathematics, 10 per cent in science, and about

---

[12] Grace S. Wright, *Block-time Classes and the Core Program in Junior High Schools*, U.S. Office of Education, Bulletin 1958, No. 6 (Washington: Government Printing Office, 1958), pp. 5–6.

[13] Ellsworth Tompkins, "The Daily Schedule in the Junior High School," *The Bulletin* of the NASSP, May, 1956, 40:177.

[14] Conant, *op. cit.*, p. 47.

TABLE 12
Per Cent of Schools Requiring Units in Each Subject Field and Average Number of Units, if Required, by Courses of Study

	Schools with Single Course of Study[d] (79.8 per cent)[a]		Schools with Multiple Courses of Study						
			General Courses (19.3 per cent)[a]		Academic Courses (20.1 per cent)[a]		Commercial Courses (13.7 per cent)[a]		Vocational Courses (11.4 per cent)[a]	
Requirement	Per cent	Average number of units required[b]	Per cent	Average number of units required[b]	Per cent	Average number of units required[b]	Per cent	Average number of units required[b]	Per cent	Average number of units required[b]
English	100.0%	3.6	100.0%	3.7	100.0%	3.8	100.0%	3.7	100.0%	3.4
Social studies	99.0	2.3	100.0	2.5	99.0	2.6	100.0	2.4	100.0	2.2
Mathematics	94.5	1.4	95.5	1.4	100.0	2.4	98.7	1.4	97.4	1.4
Science	94.1	1.5	93.7	1.5	97.1	2.2	89.9	1.4	89.5	1.4
Foreign languages	0.8	2.0	1.8	*	61.5	2.1	3.8	*	—	—
Health and physical education	62.5	1.1	68.5	1.1	62.5	1.1	62.0	1.1	68.4	1.0
Home economics	11.8	1.2	10.8	1.2	8.7	0.9	5.1	*	23.7	3.3
Business education	4.6	1.2	5.4	1.2	5.8	1.3	100.0	4.5	10.5	*
Industrial arts	6.3	1.0	9.0	1.5	4.8	0.9	1.3	*	18.4	2.4
Vocational education	6.3	1.4	2.7	*	3.8	*	3.8	*	86.8	4.3
Music	3.0	0.6	4.5	0.5	1.9	*	1.3	*	—	—
Art	2.1	0.6	3.6	*	1.0	*	1.3	*	2.6	*
Driver education	1.9	0.5	6.3	0.5	3.8	*	5.1	*	10.5	*
Elective units	100.0	6.8	100.0	6.4	100.0	3.4	100.0	2.4	100.0	2.8
Units in specified fields	100.0	9.7	100.0	10.1	100.0	13.2	100.0	14.2	100.0	13.6
Total units[c]	—	16.5	—	16.5	—	16.6	—	16.6	—	16.4

* No average computed on fewer than five cases.
[a] Schools offering these courses as a per cent of the total number of schools.
[b] Average for the schools which require courses in these fields.
[c] Average for all schools offering the course of study indicated.
[d] Most commonly called "constants-with-variables." (Authors' note.)
Source: National Education Association, Research Division, *Research Bulletin*, December, 1959, 37:125.

9.5 per cent in both English and social studies. Small percentages of schools had added physical education, driver education, and foreign languages as requirements.

Recent surveys and reports indicate the following trends in provisions and characteristics of the program of general education in four-year and senior high schools:

1. An increase in the total number of units required for graduation, from 16 to 17 or 18.
2. An increase in the number of specific courses required, from 8 to 9 plus. The most common subject requirements are English, 3.5 units; social studies, 2.5 units; mathematics, 1 unit; science 1.5 units; and physical education, 1 unit.
3. Provisions for optional courses within required subject fields. For example, four years (units) of English may be required, but students may be assigned to courses designed for different ability levels in the first two years, such as English I (M) for students with average ability, English I (R) for students needing remedial instruction, and English I (H) for honor students. In the junior and senior years students may be required to take English but may choose, with the advice of counselors, general English (composition and reading), journalism, college grammar, English or American literature, dramatics, or writing workshop. Two years of science may be required, but students may elect either general science or biology in the first two years and physics, chemistry, or physical science survey in the last two years.
4. Major and minor sequences. Frequently students must complete a major of three or four units in English and one other major of three units plus two minor sequences of two units each.
5. Character and citizenship standards. Students must be rated by teachers as being of good character and have a good citizenship record in order to qualify for a diploma.

Junior High School Programs of General Education

In practice, most of the program of the junior high school is regarded as general education; few electives, therefore, are provided in grades 7 through 9. Table 13 reports course requirements as determined in a study by Fennell of 224 junior high schools in 1953.

Another study (reported in Table 14) shows the percentage of junior high schools permitting a certain number of electives in each grade, thus indicating the relative emphasis placed on general and special education.

Although the program of studies illustrated in Figure 3 is for a four-year school, the offerings in Grades 7 to 9 are representative of those found in many three-year junior high schools. It provides a block-of-time program under one teacher in Grades 7 and 8 with one elective subject in both of these grades, and two electives in Grades 9 and 10.

TABLE 13
Number and Per Cent of Junior High Schools Requiring Certain Courses

Course	Number of Schools	Per Cent of Schools	Course	Number of Schools	Per Cent of Schools
English	221	98.7	Social studies	171	76.3
General science	219	97.8	Health	166	74.1
Physical education	218	97.3	Library	157	70.1
General mathematics	212	94.6	U.S. history	112	50.0
Music	203	90.6	Civics	112	50.0
Home economics	192	85.7	State history	109	48.7
Industrial arts	188	83.9	Ancient history	32	14.3
Art	183	81.7	Agriculture	19	8.5

Source: Edward G. Fennell, "An Analysis of Programs of Outstanding Junior High Schools in the United States," unpublished Ed.D. thesis, Cornell University, 1953, as reported in *Junior High School Facts*, U.S. Office of Education Bulletin, Misc. No. 21 (Washington: Government Printing Office, 1955), p. 51.

TABLE 14
Per Cent of Junior High Schools Permitting Number of Elective Credits

Grade	None	½	1	1½	2	3	No Reply
7th grade	61%	7%	22%	1%	3%	0	6%
8th grade	37%	8%	29%	4%	10%	0	12%
9th grade	8%	2%	22%	5%	46%	8%	9%

Source: John H. Lounsbury, "The Rate and Status of the Junior High School," unpublished doctoral thesis, George Peabody College for Teachers, advanced tabulations as reported in *Junior High School Facts*, U.S. Office of Education Bulletin, Misc. No. 21 (Washington: Government Printing Office, 1955), p. 50.

Programs for Specialized Education

In terms of common practice, the four broad institutional functions served by secondary schools are: (1) general education for citizenship, plus the specialized functions of (2) preparation for college, (3) preparation for employment, and (4) development of avocational interests. Although each of these may be implemented to some extent through extra-classroom activities and through guidance services, in most schools elective courses and special organizational provisions within the structure of the program of studies are the principal means of implementation.

FIGURE 3

Program of Studies for a Four-Year Junior High School

CURRICULUM

Redwood has over sixty different course offerings. All children must take certain subjects to fulfill either state or district requirements. Other courses may be selected by the student — "electives."

PROGRAMS REQUIRED BY THE STATE AND LOCAL BOARD TO ASSURE SOUND BASIC EDUCATION

SEVENTH	EIGHTH	NINTH	TENTH
Orientation English Social Studies Arithmetic Physical Education	English Social Studies Arithmetic Science Physical Education	English Social Studies Mathematics Physical Education	English Biology Physical Education
same teacher	same teacher	different teacher each period	different teacher each period

Elective courses are available for exploration: to develop hobbies, prepare for courses, or just to gain an appreciation of something — art or music.

... for a profession	... career in a trade	... office worker	... the arts
French	Wood Shop	Typing	Instrumental Music
Spanish	Electric Shop	Business Training	Vocal Music
Latin	Metal Shop	Office Practice	Arts & Crafts
Algebra	Mechanical Drawing		Ceramics
Geometry		**... farmer**	Newswriting
Science	Math	Science	Speech & Drama
World History		Agricultural Mechanics	**... develop a hobby**
		Agricultural Science	Fine Arts
			Shops
			Physical Education

... or just to gain an appreciation of what the other fellow does .. shops — fine arts — cadets — conversational Spanish ...

Source: Redwood Junior High School, "This is Redwood," dedication brochure, Napa Public Schools, Napa, California, 1957, p. 2.

Two types of curriculum organization designed to serve the specialized interests and abilities of students are employed in about 99 per cent of the senior high schools in the United States: (1) the constants-with-variables plan, in which all electives are free electives, and (2) the advisory curricula (combination) plan, in which parallel curricula are outlined for special interest groups. The latter plan may also provide multiple-track programs for students of different ability levels. Usually the parallel curricula are planned for college preparatory, business, trades and industries, and agriculture students. According to the NEA study previously referred to, about 20 per cent of all the schools surveyed used this type of organization. On the other hand, 37 per cent of the large schools with enrollments of 1,000 and over employed it.[15] Table 15 shows the percentage of schools in a study by Crawford that offered each type of special curriculum.

TABLE 15

Per Cent of Midwestern Senior High Schools Employing Advisory Curricula, Offering Each Special Curriculum in 1954–55

Curriculum	Per Cent of Schools Offering
College preparatory	100.0
General	92.6
Commercial	91.2
Industrial arts	63.2
Homemaking	61.8
Agricultural	38.2
Miscellaneous	20.6

Source: Dean A. Crawford, "The Administrative Organization of the Curriculum in Midwestern High Schools," unpublished Ph.D. dissertation, State University of Iowa, 1955, pp. 41–42.

Conant maintains that students should not be classified on the basis of special interests and suggests a multi-track type of organization based on ability. He argues that the special-interest curricula promote undesirable social divisions but apparently does not believe that separating students into high-ability and low-ability groups would have this effect. A few large high schools now provide recommended sequences for groups of students at the extreme ends of the spectrum of academic talent, such as the mentally retarded and the academically gifted. Most multi-track programs, however, are based on ability grouping within subjects and do not attempt to set up entire curriculum sequences for special groups of students.

Conant states, "It should be the policy of the school that every student

[15] National Education Association, *op. cit.*, p. 121.

has an individualized program; there would be no classification of students according to clearly defined and labeled programs or tracks such as the 'college preparatory,' 'vocational,' 'commercial.' "[16] It seems to the authors that Conant is raising an issue where none exists. The old rigid multiple-track system to which he appears to be referring is no longer found in more than a handful of high schools.

The advisory curricula plan, on the other hand, is characterized by its flexibility and readily permits the individualization of a student's program. As it is usually administered, students electing a college preparatory sequence may take courses in the business sequence and vice versa without any serious difficulty. The purpose in outlining the special sequences in the advisory plan is to assist students in the selection of courses. It has proved to be very helpful to students and to parents at registration time in many schools. Furthermore, it permits ability grouping as readily as does any other plan. Because of its value in providing recommended sequences for the guidance of students and to inform parents, and because of the flexibility usually employed in its administration, the authors believe it is superior to other types for all but junior high schools and very small four-year high schools. The latter provide so few electives that there is little need to outline advisory curricula.

Examples of Programs of Studies

The following programs of studies are examples of various types being employed in senior high schools of different sizes and in different sections of the country.

Advisory Curricula — Large Midwestern High School.[17]

COLLEGE PREPARATORY COURSE
RECOMMENDED

Sophomore Year		Junior Year		Senior Year	
English II	1	English III	1	English IV	1
Plane Geom.	1	Amer. Hist.	1	Prob. of Dem.	1
Latin I or II	1	Latin II, III	1	Chemistry	1
French I	1	French II	1	Adv. Biology	1
Spanish II	1	Physics	1		
Biology	1	Adv. Biology	1		
World Hist.	1	Phys. Ed.	½		
Phys. Ed.	½				

One unit of laboratory science is usually required. Biology, Physics, Adv. Biology or Chemistry is recommended.

[16] Conant, *op. cit.*, p. 46.
[17] "General School Policies and Registration Procedure," West Senior High School, Aurora, Ill., 1959–60.

CURRICULUM PLANNING AND DESIGN

ELECTIVE

Sophomore Year		Junior Year		Senior Year	
Algebra I	1	Adv. Biology	1	Algebra III	½
Art I	1	Algebra III	½	Algebra IV	½
Biology	1	Arch. Draw.	1	Adv. Biology	1
Bookkeeping	1	Mach. Draw.	1	Mech. Draw.	1
Typing I	1	Com'l. Art	1	Mach. Draw.	1
Wood Shop I	1	Advanced Art	1	Adv. Mach. Draw.	1
Printing I	1	Bookkeeping	1	Arch. Draw.	1
Metal Shop I	1	Math. Funds.	½	Physics	1
Mech. Drawing	1	Homemaking I	1	Com'l. Art	1
World Hist.	1	Homemaking II	1	Advanced Art	1
Math. Funds.	½	Homemaking III	1	Bookkeeping	1
World Geog.	½	Home Mgt.	½	Dress Design	½
Driver Training		Dress Design	½	Print. I or II	1
and P.E.	½	Journalism	½	Adv. Arch. Draw.	1
Activities		Pers. Typing	½	Homemaking III	1
		Latin I	1	Home Mgt.	½
		Latin II	1	Journalism	½
		Latin III	1	Chemistry	1
		French I, II	1	Pers. Typing	½
		Spanish II	1	Solid Geom.	½
		Spanish III	1	Latin II	1
		Physics	1	Latin III	1
		Solid Geom.	½	French II	1
		Plane Geometry	1	Spanish III	1
		Speech	½	Speech	½
		Art I	1	Trigonometry	½
		Activities		World Geog.	½
				Analytic Geom.	½
				Math. Funds.	½
				Phys. Ed.	½
				Activities	

There is a continued demand for well-trained young people to take positions as accountants, bookkeepers, billers, collectors, business machine operators, general office workers, sales clerks, secretaries, stenographers, typists, etc. The business education course is designed to prepare students for these positions. Each year many graduates find employment in local firms.

BUSINESS EDUCATION COURSE
RECOMMENDED

Sophomore Year		Junior Year		Senior Year	
English II	1	English III	1	Com'l. Eng.	1
Bookkeeping	1	Amer. Hist.	1	Prob. of Dem.	1
Typing I	1	Shorthand I	1	Office Practice	1

ORGANIZATION AND DIRECTION OF THE PROGRAM

Sophomore Year		Junior Year		Senior Year	
Phys. Ed.	½	Typing II	1	Shorthand II	1
		Phys. Ed.	½		

ELECTIVE

Art I	1	Adv. Biology	1	Adv. Biology	1
Biology	1	Com'l. Art	1	Com'l. Art	1
Math. Funds.	½	Advanced Art	1	Advanced Art	1
Homemaking I	1	Algebra III	½	Dress Design	½
Mech. Draw.	1	French I	1	Homemaking I	1
Printing I	1	French II	1	Homemaking II	1
World Hist.	1	Spanish II	1	Home Mgt.	½
World Geog.	½	Latin I, II, III	1	Journalism	½
French I	1	Speech	½	Mech. Draw.	1
Spanish II	1	Journalism	½	Shorthand I	1
Latin I	1	Dress Design	½	Shorthand II	1
Driver Training		Homemaking I	1	French II	1
and P.E.	½	Homemaking II	1	Spanish III	1
Activities		Home Mgt.	½	Speech	½
		Mech. Draw.	1	World Geog.	½
		World Geog.	½	Latin II, III	1
		Activities		Art I	1
				Math. Funds.	½
				Phys. Ed.	½
				Activities	

This school also offers vocational printing and industrial arts curricula, but the two curricula shown illustrate the type of organization employed.

Constants-with-variables with Multi-Tracks in Academic Subjects — Large New England High School.[18] Noteworthy provisions in the following program of studies are the multi-track programs for groups of different abilities in English, foreign languages, American history, and science. These are designated as basal, standard, and honors sections with a remedial section in ninth-grade English. There are also advanced placement sections in English, foreign languages, science, social studies, and mathematics. An unusual feature is the list of noncredit courses under the heading of "personal service courses."

NINTH GRADE

Subject	Periods	Subject	Periods
Required Subjects		Mathematics	
*English I		Algebra I	5
Basal	4	General Mathematics I	5

[18] "Educational Opportunities in Brookline High School," Public Schools of Brookline, Mass., 1957–58.

Subject	Periods	Subject	Periods
Honor	4	Music	
Standard	4	Band	1–5
Remedial	5	Choral Music & Voice	
Physical Education	2	Training	1–5
		Orchestra	1–5
Elective Credit Subjects		Music Theory	4
Art		Science	
Art I	5	General Science	5
Business		Social Studies	
Junior Bus. Trng.	5	Human Relations	5
Foreign Languages		World Civilizations	5
French I (honor, basal,		Speech	
standard)	5	**Elements of Speech A	5
German I	5	**Extemporaneous Spkg. B	5
Latin (honor, basal,		Drama	5
standard)	5		
Spanish I (honor, basal,		Personal Service Courses (noncredit)	
standard)	5	Application of Design	1–2
Homemaking		Art Appreciation	3
Clothing I	5	Avocational Shop (boys and	
Foods I	5	girls)	1–4
Industrial Arts		Chef's Club (boys)	1
**Automobile Shop A	5	Corrective Speech	1
**Electrical Shop A	5	Handwriting	1
**Machine Shop A	5	Party Foods (girls)	1
**Printing Shop A	5	Public Speaking	1
**Woodturning Shop A	5	Wardrobe Planning (girls)	1
**Mechanical Drawing A, B	5		

* Placement by testing and recommendation from elementary school.
** Semester courses are indicated by letters of the alphabet.

TENTH GRADE

Subject	Periods	Subject	Periods
Required Subjects		Music	
*English II		A Cappella Choir	
Basal	4	(for the better voices)	5
Honor	4	Band	1–5
Standard	4	Chorus	3
Remedial	5	Music Appreciation	5
Physical Education	2	Music Theory	5
		Orchestra	1–5
Elective Credit Subjects		Science	
Art		Biology (honor or standard)	5
Art I, II	5	Social Studies	
Business		††Far East A	4
Bookkeeping I	5	††Latin America A	4

ORGANIZATION AND DIRECTION OF THE PROGRAM

Subject	Periods	Subject	Periods
Junior Bus. Trng.	5	Human Relations	5
Typewriting	5	††New England A	4
Foreign Languages		††Social Geography A	4
**French I or II (honor, basal, standard)	5	World Civilizations	5
		Speech	
**German I or II	5	††Elements of Speech A	5
**Latin I or II (honor, basal, standard)	5	††Extemporaneous Speaking B	5
**Spanish I or II (honor, basal, standard)	5	Drama	5
Homemaking		Personal Service Courses (noncredit)	
Clothing I or II	5	Application of Design	1–2
Foods I or II	5	Art Appreciation	3
Homemaking	5	Avocational Shop	
Industrial Arts		(boys and girls)	1–5
Automobile Shop A or I	9–10	Chef's Club (boys)	1
Cabinet Shop A or I	9–10	Corrective speech	1
Electrical Shop A or I	9–10	Handwriting	1
Machine Shop A or I	9–10	Party Foods (girls)	1
Mechanical Drawing A, B, C, D	5	Personal Use Typewriting	2–3
		Public Speaking	1
Printing Shop A or I	9–10	Wardrobe Planning (girls)	1
Mathematics			
Algebra I	5		
**General Mathematics I or II	5		
†Mathematics (advanced pl.)	5		
Plane Geometry	5		

* Placement by testing and achievement.
** To be elected for the first time or continued from the first year.
† Requires department head's approval.
†† Semester courses are indicated by letters of the alphabet.

ELEVENTH GRADE

Subject	Periods	Subject	Periods
Required Subjects		Mathematics	
American History (honor or standard)	5	**Algebra I or II	5
		**General Math. I or II	5
American History †(advanced placement)	5	†Mathematics III (advanced placement)	5
*English III		Plane Geometry	5
†Advanced Placement	4	Music	
Basal	4	A Cappella Choir	5
Business	4	Band	1–5
†Creative Writing	4	Chorus	1–5
Honor	4	Ensemble	2–5

CURRICULUM PLANNING AND DESIGN

Subject	Periods	Subject	Periods
Standard	4	Music Appreciation	5
Physical Education	2	Music Theory	5
		Orchestra	1–5
Elective Credit Subjects		Science	
Art		Biology (honor, standard)	5
Art I, II, or III	5	Chemistry (honor, standard)	5
Business		†Chemistry (advanced pl.)	5
Office Practice I	5	Physics (honor, standard)	5
Stenography I	5	Social Studies	
Bookkeeping II	5	††Far East A	4
Typewriting II	5	††Latin America A	4
Foreign Language		††New England A	4
**French I, II, or III		††Social Geography A	4
(honor, standard)	5	Speech	
**German I, II, or III	5	††Elements of Speech A	5
**Latin I, II, or III		††Extemporaneous Spkg. B	5
(honor, standard)	5	Drama	5
**Spanish I, II, or III			
(honor, standard)	5	Personal Service Courses (noncredit)	
Homemaking		Application of Design	1–2
Clothing I, II, or III	5	Art Appreciation	3
Foods I or II	5	Avocational Shop	
Foreign Foods	5	(boys or girls)	1–5
Nutrition	4	Chef's Club (boys)	1
Social Customs	4	Corrective Speech	1
Home Management	4	Family Living	1
Industrial Arts		Home Nursing	1
Automobile Mechanics		Home Planning	1
A or I	9–10	Party Foods (girls)	1
Electricity A or I	9–10	Personal Use Shorthand	3
Printing A or I	9–10	Personal Use Typewriting	2–3
Woodworking A	9–10	Public Speaking	1
Machine Shop A	9–10	Wardrobe Planning (girls)	1
**Mechanical Drawing			
A, B, C, D	5		

† Requires department head's approval.
* Placement by testing and achievement.
** Elect the year applicable to your program.
†† Semester courses are indicated by letters of the alphabet.

TWELFTH GRADE

Subject	Periods	Subject	Periods
Required Subjects		Mathematics	
#American History		Algebra I or II	5
(honor or standard)	5	General Math. I or II	5
*English IV		†Math. (adv. pl.)	5
†Advanced Placement	4	Plane Geometry	5

ORGANIZATION AND DIRECTION OF THE PROGRAM

Subject	Periods	Subject	Periods
Basal	4	Solid Geometry & Trig.	5
Business	4	Music	
†Creative Writing	4	A Cappella Choir	5
Honor	4	Band	1–5
Standard	4	Chorus	3–4
Physical Education	2	Ensemble	2–5
		Music Appreciation	5
Elective Credit Subjects		Music Theory	5
Art		Orchestra	1–5
Art I, II, III, or IV	5	Science	
Business		Biology (honor or standard)	5
Bookkeeping	5	Applied Biology	5
Office Practice	5	Chemistry	
Stenography	5	(honor or standard)	5
Typewriting II	5	†Chemistry (adv. pl.)	5
Business Law	5	Physics (honor or standard)	5
Senior Business Trng.	5	†Physics (adv. pl.)	5
Foreign Languages		Social Studies	
French II, III, or IV		†American History (adv. pl.)	5
(honor or standard)	5	†European History (adv. pl.)	5
†French (adv. pl.)	5	Modern European History	5
German II or III	5	Problems of Democracy	5
Latin II, III, or IV		World Civilization	5
(honor or standard)	5	Speech	
†Latin (adv. pl.)	5	††Elements of Speech A	5
Spanish II, III, or IV		††Extemporaneous Spkg. B	5
(honor or standard)	5	Drama	5
Homemaking			
Clothing I, II, or III	5	Personal Service Courses (noncredit)	
Foods I or II	5	Application of Design	1–2
Home Management	4	Art Appreciation	3
Nutrition	5	Avocational Shop	
Social Customs	4	(boys or girls)	1–5
Industrial Arts		Chef's Club (boys)	1
Auto. Mechanics A,		Corrective Speech	1
I, or II	8–10	Family Living	1
Electricity A, I, or II	8–10	Home Nursing	1
Machine Shop A, I, or II	8–10	Home Planning	1
Printing A, I, or II	8–10	Party Foods (girls)	1
Woodworking A, I, or II	8–10	Personal Use Shorthand	3
Mechanical Drawing A,		Personal Use Typewriting	3
B, C, D	5	Public Speaking	1
Shop Mathematics	3	Review Mathematics	2

\# If credit not received last year.
* Placement by testing and achievement.
† Requires department head's approval.
†† Semester courses are indicated by letters of the alphabet.

CURRICULUM PLANNING AND DESIGN

Constants-with-Variables — Small School (250).[19] A feature of this program is the use of semester hours rather than Carnegie units in an effort to secure greater flexibility. The program of studies is organized around six broad divisions.

1961–62 CURRICULUM

DIVISION OF LANGUAGE AND LITERATURE		DIVISION OF SCIENCE AND MATHEMATICS		DIVISION OF SOCIAL SCIENCES	
	s.h.		s.h.		s.h.
English		*Mathematics*		*History*	
English 1	10	Basic Mathematics	10	World History	10
English 2	10	Algebra 1	10	U.S. History	10
English 3	10	Accel. Algebra 1	10		
English 4	10	Plane Geometry	10	*Government*	
English 5	10	Algebra 2	10	U.S. Government	5
		Trigonometry	5		
Speech		Principles of Math	5	*Economics*	
Speech Fundamentals	5			Senior Economics	5
		Science			
Latin		General Science	10	*Geography*	
Latin 1	10	Physical Science	10	Geography	5
Latin 2	10	Biology	10		
		Chemistry	10	*Sociology*	
Spanish		Physics	10	Sociology	5
Spanish 1	10				
Spanish 2	10			*Psychology*	
				Psychology	5
DIVISION OF FINE ARTS		DIVISION OF APPLIED ARTS AND SCIENCES		DIVISION OF HEALTH, SAFETY, AND PHYSICAL EDUCATION	
	s.h.		s.h.		
Music		*Home Economics*			
Applied: Vocal	10*	Home Economics 1	10		s.h.
Applied: Instrum.	10*	Home Economics 2	10	*Physical Education*	
		Home Economics 3	10	Boys' Phys. Educ.	4*
Art				Girls' Phys. Educ.	4*
Art 1	10	*Business Education*			
Art 2	10	Typewriting 1	10	*Safety Education*	
		Typewriting 2	5	Driver Education	0
		Bookkeeping	5		
		Shorthand 1	10		
		Shorthand 2	10		
		Industrial Arts			
		Industrial Arts 1	10		
		Industrial Arts 2	10		
		Maintenance & Repair	10		
		Industrial Arts 3	10		
* non-solid credit		Industrial Arts 4	10	* non-solid credit	

[19] "The Instructional Program," Emmetsburg High School, Emmetsburg, Iowa, 1961–62.

ORGANIZATION AND DIRECTION OF THE PROGRAM

REQUIREMENTS FOR GRADUATION

The Emmetsburg High School requires for graduation 176 semester hours of credit, at least 160 of which must be from subjects other than those listed as "non-solid" above. Ten semester hours are equal to one Carnegie Unit of credit. A student must have completed at least four years of English, two of science, one of mathematics, one year each of world history and U.S. history, one semester of U.S. government, one semester of economics, and four years of physical education to qualify for graduation.

Special Administrative Plans to Provide for Individual Differences

Among the most frequently employed administrative plans for organizing the curriculum to provide for differences in student capacities and interests are (1) elective courses, (2) ability grouping, (3) multi-track plans, (4) acceleration, (5) advanced placement courses, and (6) remedial classes. Enrichment, the unit method, and differentiated assignments are employed by classroom teachers, but these are instructional methods rather than organizational plans.

It is probably true that the most effective provisions for differences in student capacities and interests are made within the classroom through the day-by-day work of teachers with students, but special administrative plans may assist teachers in providing for individual differences. Following is a brief description of some of the more common administrative plans.

Elective Courses. The most common and oldest plan is the use of elective courses. There is little disagreement over the value of elective courses for meeting various student interests and future plans, but there is a marked lack of agreement concerning the value of electives in providing for differences in student abilities. Some educators argue that (1) the elective system is practical and democratic because it permits a student to select the type of course work in which he is interested and in which he has ability; (2) students in elective courses are not grouped upon the basis of arbitrary criteria such as intelligence quotients, and therefore the plan is not as vulnerable as some to the charge that it promotes undemocratic segregation; (3) elective courses effect voluntary ability grouping — the bright students tend to elect advanced academic courses and the low-ability students to choose courses in the general or practical arts fields. However, other educators maintain that electives, at best, serve only as a partial means of providing for individual differences since instruction is usually the same for all students and wide differences exist among pupils within elective classes. Secondary school staffs generally agree that electives are an essential part of the curriculum but leave much to be desired as the principal means of coping with individual differences.

Ability Grouping. The subject of much controversy since it was first employed more than fifty years ago, ability grouping in secondary schools consists of the classification of students for a particular course into two or more levels upon the basis of their ability as determined by performance on standardized aptitude and achievement tests, teacher judgments, and mental age as measured by intelligence tests.

Regardless of the arguments over the plan, it has been gaining ground rapidly during the last five or six years. In 1955 Crawford conducted a study in five midwestern states and found that 37 per cent of the schools studied were using some form of ability grouping.[20] Van Dyke and Sparks made a study in four of the same states in 1959 and found that 68 per cent of the schools at that time were employing some form of grouping.[21]

What have we learned about grouping in fifty years of research and experience? Briefly, the following seem to be the most pertinent findings:

First, we have learned that grouping *per se* has little, if any, effect on student achievement. It is an administrative arrangement whereby the range of individual differences in a particular class may be reduced. Individual differences still exist in grouped classes and the use of grouping does not insure that teachers will do anything about them.

On the other hand, in experiments in which materials and methods have been adapted to ability levels, greater gains in student achievement have been secured in homogeneous classes than in heterogeneous classes. Among the experimental studies showing superior results for grouped classes are those by Billett,[22] Justman,[23] and Barthelmess and Boyer.[24]

In addition, Cornell reports that

> One of the most consistent results has been the possibility of increased speed in covering a given amount of work on the part of bright students. It has been found repeatedly that bright students . . . can do the usual

[20] Dean A. Crawford, "The Administrative Organization of the Curriculum in Midwestern High Schools," unpublished Ph.D. dissertation, State University of Iowa, 1955, p. 151.
[21] L. A. Van Dyke and J. N. Sparks, *Four-State Survey of Secondary School Marking Practices,* Research Digest No. 2 (Iowa City: Iowa Center for Research in School Administration, 1960), p. 1.
[22] Roy O. Billett, "A Controlled Experiment to Determine the Advantages of Ability Grouping," *Educational Research,* Bull. VII, April 4–8, 1928, pp. 133–96.
[23] Joseph Justman, "Academic Achievement of Intellectually Gifted Accelerants and Non-accelerants in Junior High School," *School Review,* March, 1954, 62: 142–50.
[24] Harriet A. Barthelmess and Phillip A. Boyer, "An Evaluation of Ability Grouping," *Journal of Educational Research,* December, 1932, 26:284–94.

work of any grade in about half the usual time, and in general the bright classes can save two or three years in their progress through school and at the same time have an enriched curriculum.[25]

Reviewers of research on grouping tend to agree with Ekstrom that "In experiments that specifically provided for differentiation of teaching methods and materials for groups at each ability level and made an effort to push bright homogeneous classes, results tended to favor the homogeneous groups."[26]

Even though most of the experimental studies have not been well designed, the few that have been show that ability grouping *can* secure improved student achievement. It is possible, of course, that similar results could be obtained through the use of the same methods in heterogeneous classes, but teachers find it extremely difficult to employ differentiated procedures in ungrouped sections and most of them do not attempt it.

Second, the claim that students are more likely to develop undesirable social attitudes in grouped sections than in ungrouped sections is not well founded. Studies by Goldberg,[27] Justman,[28] and Bell[29] show little difference in the social and personal attitudes of students growing out of the two plans for sectioning students. Some of these studies employed standardized attitude scales, some employed opinions of graduates, teachers, and parents, and some made use of both.

Most of the researchers who have investigated this problem in recent years agree with Goldberg's conclusion that "There is no evidence to support the notion that grouping has adverse effects on the social or personal attitudes or behavior of children."

Third, studies of teacher preferences indicate that a large majority of teachers experienced with both grouped and ungrouped classes favor ability grouping. Drews found that teachers like ability grouping because it enables them to work with a narrower range of abilities, devote more time to the needs of individual students, and do a better job of planning materials and methods for their classes.[30] Although teachers generally

[25] Ethel Cornell, "Effects of Ability Grouping Determinable from Published Studies," *Grouping of Pupils*, Thirty-Fifth Yearbook, National Society for the Study of Education, Part I (Chicago: University of Chicago Press, 1936).

[26] Ruth Ekstrom, "Experimental Studies of Ability Grouping," *School Review*, Summer, 1961, 69:216–26.

[27] Miriam L. Goldberg, "Research on the Talented," *Teachers College Record*, December, 1958, 15:157.

[28] Joseph Justman, "Personal and Social Adjustment of Intellectually Gifted Accelerants and Non-accelerants in Junior High Schools," *School Review*, November, 1953, 61:468–78.

[29] Mary Bell, "A Comparative Study of Mentally Gifted Children Heterogenously and Homogeneously Grouped," Ed.D. thesis, Indiana University, 1957.

[30] Elizabeth Drews, "The Effectiveness of Homogeneous and Heterogeneous Ability Grouping in Ninth Grade English Classes with Slow, Average, and Superior Students," Cooperative Research Program, U.S. Office of Education, No. 608, E-2, 1959.

express no great enthusiasm for low-ability sections, they are willing to work with some low-ability groups in order to gain the general advantages of grouping. This in itself seems to be a strong recommendation for ability grouping.

Fourth, research shows that students should be assigned to groups separately in each subject rather than to the same ability level in all subjects. It is true that some students will be in the honors group in all subjects and some will be in the low group, but subject variability is so great for so many students that across-the-board assignments result in many misplacements. Therefore, assignment should be based on ability in a specific subject rather than on measures of general ability.

Studies by Hull,[31] Burr,[32] and Hollingshead[33] show that the range in achievement variability within a single class, when students are grouped on general ability, is reduced only about 20 per cent. Hull's study reveals that trait differences for the average pupil are approximately 80 per cent as great as those among all pupils within a particular class. Lindquist, in a study on overlapping in achievement, found that on the same test about 16 per cent of the sixth-grade pupils typically exceeded the median for eighth-grade pupils and about 30 per cent exceeded the median for seventh-grade pupils; also that about 15 per cent of the eighth-graders fell below the sixth-grade median and 32 per cent fell below the seventh-grade median.[34] With this much variability in achievement between grades in a single subject, it is clear that grouping must be according to subjects if we are to achieve more than a slight reduction in the range of abilities.

Fifth, evidence from research and experience strongly supports the conclusion that students should be identified and selected for grouped sections on the basis of multiple measures of aptitude rather than on the basis of a single measure. Few studies have been conducted on the relations of various predictive measures to the appropriate assignment of pupils to ability sections because of a lack of agreement on criterion measures of appropriateness. However, many studies have investigated the predictive value of certain measures of aptitude to general academic success in high school and college. These studies usually obtained correlations of from about .35 to .70 between general achievement and such single predictive measures as intelligence test scores, achievement test

[31] Clark L. Hull, "Variability in the Amount of Different Traits Possessed by the Individual," *Journal of Educational Psychology*, February, 1927, 18:77–106.

[32] Marvin Y. Burr, *A Study of Homogeneous Grouping*, Contributions to Education, No. 457 (New York: Teachers College, Columbia University, 1931).

[33] A. D. Hollingshead, *An Evaluation of the Use of Certain Educational and Mental Measures for Purposes of Classification*, Contributions to Education, No. 302, (New York: Teachers College, Columbia University, 1928).

[34] E. F. Lindquist, *et al.*, "Manual for Administration and Interpretation of 1938, Iowa Every-Pupil Test of Basic Skills," Bureau of Educational Research and Service, State University of Iowa, 1938, p. 23.

scores, previous school marks, and teachers' estimates. But when two or more of these measures were used in combination and multiple correlations obtained, the correlations increased to between .75 and .80.

Multi-Track Plans. Use of multi-tracks is an adaptation of ability grouping, but it provides for special sequences of courses for students of different levels of ability rather than sectioning courses for groups of students. For example, students may be classified as "honors," "standard," "basal," or "remedial" in mathematics on the basis of results of a mathematics aptitude test, previous scholastic records, and recommendations of former teachers. Special mathematics sequences such as the following may be developed for all four of these groups of students:

Grade	Track I Honors	Track II Standard	Track III Basal	Track IV Remedial
9	Intermediate Algebra	Algebra I	Basic Math	Computational Skills
10	Integrated Geometry	Plane Geometry	Algebra I	Consumer Math
11	Advanced Placement Algebra	Intermediate Algebra	Refresher Math	
12	Advanced Placement Trigonometry and Analytics			

Similar tracks may be worked out in English, science, and social studies. This type of plan is being employed in an increasing number of large high schools, but it is beyond the facilities of most small high schools.

Acceleration. Any plan which permits a student to progress through school at a more rapid pace than normal is termed acceleration. Thirty or forty years ago students were accelerated by letting them "skip" a grade. In recent years, however, high school students have been accelerated primarily by permitting them to complete courses in less than the usual length of time or to take more than the usual number of courses.

The principal reason for acceleration is that it enables a student to progress as rapidly as his ability will permit. It is claimed that the gifted student achieves better under this plan because he is not held to the pace of his less gifted classmates. He can finish his general program in a shorter time and proceed to studies in the field of his special talent and interest.

Opponents hold that this plan causes students to be thrown into groups which are extremely diverse from the standpoint of physical and social maturity. Academically talented youngsters move up into classes with students who are older and larger and so encounter difficulties in social adjustments. It is contended also that accelerated students miss some important background material, which lack may prove to be a serious handicap in later years.

Research indicates that acceleration during the secondary school years may be desirable for some superior students, but not for all of them. Enrichment of the gifted student's program and of his course work has been recommended by certain professional groups, such as the Educational Policies Commission, as a sounder method for providing for bright students.[35]

At the present time, however, some promising experiments are being conducted in early admission of gifted high school students to college. The experiment carried on under the Ford Foundation Fund for the Advancement of Education from 1951 to 1955 included about 1,350 high school students, selected upon the bases of superior academic ability and social maturity. These students were admitted to twelve colleges one or two years before they were scheduled to graduate from high school. Coombs reported in 1954,

> Academically, the first two classes of Early Admission Students have far out-performed their classmates generally. Interestingly enough they have also tended to out-perform their matching students in the comparison groups. . . . The colleges rated both the scholars and their comparison students quite satisfactory on mental and physical health.[36]

Advanced Placement Courses. The School and College Study of Admission with Advanced Placement, which was conducted from 1952 to 1955, met with so much success that it stimulated a great amount of interest in this method of providing for gifted students and has resulted in a steady increase in the number of high schools participating in it. The plan calls for the development of college courses for superior students which they may take while in high school under the direction of high school teachers. Examinations constructed by committees of college and high school teachers are administered upon the completion of the courses. After graduation from high school, students who make a satisfactory score on these examinations may be admitted to a cooperating college with advanced standing in the subject fields in which they were examined.

---

[35] Educational Policies Commission, *Education of the Gifted* (Washington: National Education Association, 1950).

[36] Philip H. Coombs, "Lessons from Recent Experiments in Articulation and Acceleration," *Current Issues in Higher Education, 1954,* Proceedings of the Ninth Annual National Conference on Higher Education (Washington: National Education Association, 1954), p. 274.

Since 1955 the College Entrance Examination Board has administered this program on a national basis, and the number of cooperating colleges and high schools has expanded. Some states have developed cooperative programs, with most of the colleges participating. Derthick reported that more than 12,000 students in 650 high schools took advanced placement courses in 1959.[37] And Douglas made the following comment about the joint planning involved:

> But even more far-reaching in the writer's opinion has been the splendid way in which college professors and capable secondary-school teachers have come to a position of mutual understanding and appreciation for each other's problems. Out of the Advanced Placement conference held annually in June has come a warm respect for the abilities of those at both levels in our educational structure.[38]

Remedial Classes. Students with deficiencies in certain subjects or skills, but with average or better ability, may benefit from remedial or clinical instruction. Remedial classes are usually limited to skill subjects such as reading, writing, speech, and mathematics and are likely to be most effective at the junior high school level of the secondary school.

When a student enters high school with a serious deficiency in a fundamental skill, the faculty should be willing to do everything possible to help him overcome it. Even though the basic problem is one of improving the instructional program in the lower grades, the youngster who is in the secondary school now and has weaknesses needs assistance. Whether remedial instruction should be given in regular classes rather than in special sections depends upon the qualifications of the regular teachers to direct it, the availability of suitable materials, and the gravity of the problem.

Determining whether or not a case is remediable requires someone on the staff who is well trained in diagnosing individual student problems. Regular classroom teachers seldom have the training necessary to do this competently. Students with low intelligence are certain to have deficiencies in reading and arithmetic skills, but these are not remediable cases and should be placed in special classes for the mentally retarded.

Students with average or near-average intelligence may be helped to overcome deficiencies in certain skills. The best results with seriously retarded readers have been secured in special classes which permit individual instruction by a trained teacher and with appropriate materials and equipment.

---

[37] Lawrence G. Derthick, "Review of the American Educational System," *Hearings*, U.S. House of Representatives, Committee on Appropriations (Washington: Government Printing Office, 1960), p. 20.

[38] Edwin C. Douglas, "The Advanced Placement Program of the CEEB," *The Bulletin* of the NASSP, May, 1959, 43:94–95.

Questions and Group Projects

1. Prepare a list of brief summary statements of major social and technological developments in the United States during the last quarter of a century. What changes in the curriculum do these suggest? To what extent have high schools made such changes?

2. Make a case study of a local curriculum program in which it is known that major conflicts developed and which was abandoned for a time. What were the sequential steps taken in this program? In the opinions of staff members, what were the major points of conflict? Do these reflect lack of concern or neglect of the guides proposed in this chapter?

3. Prepare a proposal for a comprehensive appraisal of the curriculum program of a high school with which you are familiar. Describe the instruments and procedures that you would use.

4. Visit a curriculum center or library. What types of materials are being prepared in largest volume by various local curriculum committees? Prepare a summary description of the provisions most commonly included in these publications.

5. Define the term "program of studies." Examine several curriculum bulletins or handbooks for local high schools. What type of organization do these schools employ for their programs of studies?

6. Define the term "general education." What are the most common provisions for general education in high schools in your state? Which ones are prescribed by state law or regulation? Is this desirable?

7. Some critics of American high schools charge that we provide too many electives and permit students to "nibble" on too many courses without gaining any depth of knowledge. What is your reaction to this charge?

8. What is the evidence that ability grouping does or does not result in the development of undemocratic social attitudes?

9. Write a paper comparing the advantages of early admission to college and advanced placement programs.

10. Make a survey of research studies on special remedial programs in secondary schools. Differentiate between a low-ability and a remediable student.

Selected References

Alcorn, Marvin D., and James M. Linley. *Issues in Curriculum Development.* Yonkers-on-Hudson, N.Y.: World Book Company, 1959.

American Association of School Administrators. *American School Curriculum.* Thirty-First Yearbook. Washington: The Association, 1953.

Bereday, George Z. F., and Joseph A. Lawerys, editors. *The Yearbook of Education, 1958, The Secondary School Curriculum*. London: Evans Brothers Ltd., 1958.

Chase, Francis S., and Harold A. Anderson, editors. *The High School in a New Era*. Chicago: University of Chicago Press, 1958.

Conant, James B. *The American High School Today*. New York: McGraw-Hill Book Company, 1958.

Douglass, Harl R., editor. *The High School Curriculum*. New York: The Ronald Press Company, 1956.

Educational Policies Commission. *Education for All American Youth — A Further Look*. Washington: National Education Association, 1952.

———. *Education of the Gifted*. Washington: National Education Association, 1950.

Harvard Committee on General Education. *General Education in a Free Society*. Cambridge, Mass.: Harvard University Press, 1945.

Herrick, Virgil E., and Ralph W. Tyler. *Toward Improved Curriculum Theory*. Chicago: University of Chicago Press, 1950.

Krug, Edward A. *Curriculum Planning*. New York: Harper & Brothers, 1957.

———. *The Secondary School Curriculum*. New York: Harper & Brothers, 1960.

Leonard, J. Paul. *Developing the Secondary School Curriculum*. New York: Rinehart and Company, 1953.

National Society for the Study of Education, *Curriculum Reconstruction*, Forty-Fourth Yearbook. Chicago: University of Chicago Press, 1945.

Romine, Stephen A. *Building the High School Curriculum*. New York: The Ronald Press Company, 1954.

Saylor, J. Galen, and William M. Alexander. *Curriculum Planning*. New York: Rinehart and Company, 1954.

Shertzer, Bruce, editor. *Working with Superior and Talented Students*. Chicago: North Central Association of Colleges and Secondary Schools, Science Research Associates, 1960.

U.S. Office of Education. "Offerings and Enrollments in High School Subjects," *Biennial Survey of Education in the United States, 1948–50*. Washington: Government Printing Office, 1951, Chap. 5.

CHAPTER 6

Organization of the School Schedule and Calendar

The Daily and Weekly Schedule

The daily and weekly schedule of a school often reflects the philosophy of its educational program and the administrative competence of its principal. If the schedule is inflexible, stereotyped, and packaged in old containers, it is generally symptomatic of a static and routine educational program. If it is carelessly drafted and generates confusion, it usually reflects an inept or inexperienced administrator. Conversely, if the schedule shows modern offerings, makes provisions for student differences, provides flexible time blocks, and functions smoothly, the chances are good that it expresses a well-designed educational program and a competent administrator.

But a schedule does not make an educational program; it merely provides a format. An experienced, sympathetic, and intelligent corps of teachers *can* do a first-rate job of teaching in spite of a disreputable looking and outmoded schedule. Sometimes an old nag turns out to be a champion jumper, but usually an old nag turns out to be an old nag.

In a Mark Hopkins log–boy educational setting, schedules are unimportant. But in a school with many students, various Mark Hopkinses, and specialized logs, some sort of systematic arrangement is necessary to get them together at the most suitable times and places. The purpose of the schedule is to facilitate the operation of the educational program, not to straitjacket it. In view of present-day overcrowded school facilities, a shortage of qualified teachers, heavy demands for specialized courses, and widely diverse student abilities, the process of building a good schedule calls for an uncommon amount of know-how and imagination on the part of school administrators.

The *Dictionary of Education* defines the daily program, or schedule, as "A chart or general plan of action by which the different activities of the curriculum involving pupils, teachers, and other school personnel are accorded a sequence and location."[1] This is probably as good as any short definition, but a short definition does not convey more than a general idea of what a schedule is and does. Specifically, a school schedule should show the following:

1. The name of the school, the community in which it is located and the administrative heads of the school.
2. The dates for which the schedule is to be operative.
3. The organization of the school day and week including the times for opening and closing, the number and length of class periods, the time between classes, the lunch hour, and provisions for homeroom and activity periods.
4. The names of all teachers, the courses and sections to which they are assigned, their conference and planning periods, and, if necessary, the study halls to which they are assigned.
5. The course sections and/or activities scheduled each period.
6. The number of the room in which each class section usually will meet.
7. The days of the week that each class section will meet.
8. The number of pupils assigned to each class section.
9. The grade level (or levels) of pupils enrolled in each course section.
10. Such special provisions as seminars, large-group sessions, floating periods, and block-time classes.

Types of Schedules

For descriptive purposes, high school schedules may be classified as (1) conventional or (2) variable. *Conventional* schedules are characterized by periods of fixed length, classes meeting at the same hour each day, assigned study halls, and similar uniform provisions. *Variable* schedules introduce a degree of flexibility by means of functional variations in length of periods, hours and days of class sessions, activity periods, and so on. Although the number of schools employing some form of variable schedule is relatively small, several imaginative versions have been developed in individual schools in all sections of the country. These are too diverse to classify, but they include such departures as "blocktime" for core classes, the "'floating period" or revolving schedule,

---

[1] Carter V. Good, *Dictionary of Education* (New York: McGraw-Hill Book Company, 1945), p. 311.

in which classes meet at different times each day of the week, and the flexible type of program with classes scheduled for a varied number of hours during the week. The latter includes the schedule employed in some of the team-teaching experimental programs under the joint sponsorship of the National Association of Secondary School Principals and the Fund for the Advancement of Education.

Characteristics of Conventional Schedules

Even though conventional schedules are marked by uniform provisions within a particular school and possess many common features from one school to another, several different patterns are employed. The most familiar types are the basic eight-period, seven-period, and six-period schedules. The term "basic" may appear to be superfluous, but it is a serviceable adjective in view of the fact that a school using an eight-period schedule for classes and study halls may also provide a short homeroom period and an activity period; nevertheless, it has a "basic" eight-period schedule for classes.

Various studies indicate that from 90 to 95 per cent of the four-year and senior high schools in the United States employ some type of conventional schedule. Sturges reports that in 1958–59, 92 per cent of 938 North Central Association high schools operated with a conventional schedule, 41 per cent with a six-period schedule, 29.5 per cent with a seven-period schedule, and 21.7 per cent with an eight-period schedule.[2] The percentage of small schools (enrollments of 249 and under) operating with an eight-period schedule was 31.9 per cent, as compared to 18.1 per cent for schools with enrollments over 249. On the other hand, MacKenzie reported that 70.8 per cent of the schools that he studied in the Northwest Association used a six-period schedule.[3]

Length of Periods

Some state departments of education and some regional accrediting associations have adopted minimum standards for the length of periods or minimum weekly time allotments for various courses. The principal should make certain that these standards are met in the schedule. Sturges found that 43 per cent of the schools in his study employed a class period that was from 55 to 59 minutes in length. Periods of mixed length were used in 26.7 per cent of the schools and periods of from 40 to 44

[2] Allen W. Sturges, "Techniques and Practices in Scheduling in Midwestern Secondary Schools," unpublished Ph.D. dissertation, State University of Iowa, 1959, pp. 41–60.

[3] Charles MacKenzie, "Scheduling Practices of Secondary Schools in the Northwest Association of Secondary and Higher Schools," unpublished master's thesis, Linfield College, 1954, p. 7.

minutes in 15.6 per cent. The mean lengths of class periods in schools using the three most popular types of schedules were 57.6 minutes in schools with a six-period schedule, 55.6 minutes in schools with a seven-period schedule, and 45.5 minutes in schools with an eight-period schedule.[4]

Conant recommends a seven- or eight-period day with forty-five minute periods and double laboratory periods.[5] His chief reason is that the short-period schedule permits academically talented students to enroll in more electives. However, Conant reports considerable disagreement among administrators in the schools that he visited over the question of short or long class periods.

The persisting trend has been toward long periods. In 1934 Hotz found that 37.9 per cent of North Central Association high schools employed long periods,[6] while in 1959 Gibson reported that 78.8 per cent scheduled long periods.[7] The principal arguments for long periods are as follows: (1) The long-period schedule provides time for both recitation and directed study under the same teacher; (2) long periods make it unnecessary to schedule double laboratory and shop periods; (3) long periods allow time for projects, audio-visual procedures, demonstrations, panels, and similar activities with fewer interruptions; (4) the long period schedule provides substantially more instructional time during the school year, and, therefore, better student achievement is likely to result; and (5) the use of a schedule with six or seven long periods reduces the number of study halls and the number of students that must be assigned to each study hall.

Research on relative achievement in long and short periods shows no significant differences. Sparks made a study comparing factors in twenty Iowa high schools in which students made the greatest growth in mathematics with twenty schools in which students made the least growth from Grades 9 to 12.[8] Advance in achievement was measured by the test on Quantitative Thinking in the battery of the Iowa Tests of Educational Development. The twenty high- and twenty low-achievement schools were paired for general academic ability by means of the composite scores of the ITED. Sparks found that the median length of class periods in the high-achievement schools was fifty-four minutes as compared to forty-seven minutes in the low schools. But the differences were not statistically significant.

[4] Sturges, *op. cit.*, p. 54.
[5] James B. Conant, *The American High School Today* (New York: McGraw-Hill Book Company, 1959), p. 65.
[6] H. G. Hotz, "Trends in the Development of Secondary Schools," *North Central Association Quarterly*, January, 1936, p. 290.
[7] A. J. Gibson, "Trends in Secondary Schools," *North Central Association Quarterly*, July, 1959, p. 137.
[8] Jack N. Sparks, "A Comparison of Iowa High Schools Ranking High and Low in Mathematical Achievement," unpublished Ph.D. dissertation, State University of Iowa, 1960, p. 142.

Mowrer found no significant differences in achievement in English for students graduated from schools with periods of fifty minutes or more and students from schools using periods of less than fifty minutes.[9] The students in Mowrer's study were matched in ability on the basis of scores on the Ohio State Psychological Examination, Form 23. Achievement was measured by grades made in first-semester English courses at the University of Missouri and scores on the Cooperative English Test A: Mechanics of Expression, Form 1 and the Cooperative English Test B2: Effectiveness of Expression, Form S.

McElhinney studied the relationship between length of class periods and progress in academic achievement of secondary school pupils during 1959–60.[10] He investigated eleven schools which used both long and short periods for the same courses in English, science, mathematics, and social studies, comparing educational growth in sixty-six pairs of classes for the same courses. Each pair included one section scheduled for a short period of forty-five minutes or less and one section scheduled for a long period of fifty-five minutes or more. Both classes in a pair were taught by the same teacher and the same basic instructional materials were used. Achievement gains were measured by the Iowa Tests of Educational Development, administered in September, 1959, and September, 1960. The classes included eighteen pairs in the ninth grade, twenty-three in the tenth, and twenty-five in the eleventh. The students numbered 1,379 in English, 474 in mathematics, 364 in science, and 892 in social studies.

McElhinney concluded that, although the test results favored the long period in a majority of the comparisons, none of the differences was significant at the 5 per cent level of confidence. This held true for all four subject fields; for ninth-, tenth-, and eleventh-grade classes; and for pupils of low, average, and high ability. The statistical design used was treatments by levels by repetitions and analysis of variance to test for significance of differences.

Nevertheless, teachers tend to favor long periods. Sturges found that teachers in schools with long periods (55 to 59 minutes) rated the length of class periods and the length of the school day as more satisfactory than did teachers in schools with short periods (40 to 45 minutes). Forty-five per cent of the teachers in the schools with an eight-period day said the classes were too short.[11] McElhinney also found that teachers preferred long periods to short ones.[12]

---

[9] George E. Mowrer, "A Study of the Effect of the Length of the High School English Class Period on Achievement in English," unpublished Ed.D. dissertation, University of Missouri, 1956.

[10] J. Howard McElhinney, "The Length of the High School Class Period and Pupil Achievement," unpublished Ph.D. dissertation, State University of Iowa, 1961, pp. 136–45.

[11] Sturges, *op. cit.*, p. 158.

[12] McElhinney, *op. cit.*, p. 145.

On the other hand, if getting more courses into the school day and cutting costs per class section are the most important considerations, short-period schedules have advantages over long-period schedules. According to Sturges, schools using an eight-period schedule (40- to 45-minute periods) offered 21.4 per cent more class sections per teacher than did schools with a six-period schedule (55- to 59-minute periods), and schools using a seven-period schedule offered 12.2 per cent more class sections per teacher than did schools with six periods.[13]

The economy of the eight-period schedule over the six- or seven-period schedule, however, is effected at the expense of the classroom teacher. As may be seen in Table 16, teachers in eight-period schools teach more classes per day, supervise more study halls per day, and teach more students per week than do teachers in schools with six periods.

TABLE 16

Mean Load per Teacher by Type of Schedule

Mean	6-period		7-period		8-period	
	N[a]	Average	N[a]	Average	N[a]	Average
Mean number of classes daily	407	4.47	225	5.01	117	5.42
Mean number of study halls daily	410	0.45	227	0.60	118	0.79
Mean number of students weekly	415	540.84	229	520.56	117	554.83
Mean number of classes plus study halls daily		4.93		5.61		6.21

[a] N is the total number of teachers included under each type of schedule and for each item.
Source: Allen W. Sturges, "Techniques and Practices in Scheduling in Midwestern Secondary Schools," unpublished Ph.D. dissertation, State University of Iowa, 1959, p. 135.

It is the view of the authors that the evidence and arguments tend to favor a schedule with six or seven long periods of fifty-five minutes or more over one with eight or nine short periods of forty-five minutes or less. Any advantages for short periods in terms of reduced costs appear to be more than offset by more reasonable teaching loads and teacher satisfaction with long periods. Since the evidence available indicates no significant differences in student achievement, we believe that teacher preferences should prevail.

Conant's objection to the six-period day as being too restrictive could be met by adding a somewhat shorter period for activities and personal

[13] Sturges, *op. cit.*, p. 158.

service courses. This would give academically talented students an opportunity to elect music, art, typing, shop, homemaking, or other courses of a similar nature. Although the addition of a seventh period would lengthen the school day if the other periods retained their full time, this is a reform long overdue. The school day in the United States is shorter than that in most other countries of the world.

Length of Day

The most appropriate length for the school day depends on community and individual school factors, which may vary considerably from one community to another. In the Midwest, the modal length is about seven clock hours including lunch time.[14] The North Central Association requires member schools to provide a school day of at least six hours exclusive of lunch periods,[15] and several states have enacted laws requiring schools to conduct classes for a minimum of five to six clock hours daily. Some large city schools have been forced to operate with overlapping shifts in a single building because of overcrowding, and the school day in a particular building may be as long as ten clock hours, although it usually is only five or six hours for each shift of students and teachers.

A school day of approximately seven clock hours will accommodate six periods of fifty-five minutes each, allow adequate time between classes, and permit a lunch hour of about thirty minutes and an activity period of forty to forty-five minutes. Most school programs will fit satisfactorily into a day of that length. An increasing number of schools are employing a seven-period day with periods of different lengths. Some long periods are scheduled for laboratory and shop classes and short periods for recitation-discussion classes. Reactions to this type of schedule are mixed; it complicates the job of schedule building, but it accommodates more courses and provides greater flexibility than a six-period schedule.

Opening and Closing Times

Transportation problems, such as rush hours on public transit lines in cities, long bus routes in rural districts, and other local characteristics, must be considered in determining the times for opening and closing the school day and the length and time for the lunch hour. The safety and welfare of students must be a primary consideration. The principal should clear with the superintendent and the board of education before making decisions on these matters. Sturges found that the modal time

[14] *Ibid.*, p. 50.
[15] North Central Association of Colleges and Secondary Schools, "Policies and Criteria for the Approval of Secondary Schools" (Chicago: Commission on Secondary Schools, 1960), p. 22.

for opening the school day was between 8:30 and 8:39 A.M. for the 938 secondary schools in his study and that the modal dismissal time was between 3:30 and 3:39 P.M.[16]

Lunch Periods

Sturges reported a wide variety of practices in scheduling lunch periods.[17] Very few schools had a completely "closed" lunch period, in which no students were permitted to leave the campus. Several principals said, however, that their lunch period was too short to permit more than a few students to go home for lunch and that these students were required to have permits. In an increasing number of schools, students are not permitted to drive their automobiles during the noon hour.

The mean length of the lunch period was 46 minutes in the schools studied by Sturges; the range was from 19 to 120 minutes. Sixty-seven per cent used a "single" lunch period; that is, all students ate lunch at the same time. Six per cent used a "split" noon hour, in which students went to lunch during part of the noon hour and attended classes during the remainder. The most common pattern for split periods was to divide the student body into three shifts: While Group A was at lunch, Groups B and C were in class; then Group A returned to class, Group C remained in class, and Group B went to lunch; next Group C went to lunch and Groups A and B were in class. Usually in schools with a split noon hour, the over-all length was ninety minutes with three thirty-minute shifts. Twenty-seven per cent of the schools used a "staggered" lunch hour plan, which provided a lunch period during more than one class period.

A majority of the principals interviewed by Sturges expressed a preference for the split lunch period, and several who were using a single period were planning to shift to the split type. This type of lunch period reduces the problem of supervision of students during the noon hour and virtually eliminates "ramming" around in automobiles, loitering in nearby hamburger joints, and similar practices.

Activity Periods

A 1950 United States Office of Education survey shows that 66 per cent of 10,925 secondary schools reporting scheduled an activity period within the school day.[18] The length was 275 or more minutes per week in 8.2 per cent of the schools, 175 to 274 minutes in 19.3 per cent, 75 to 174 minutes in 18.9 per cent, and less than 75 minutes in 19.5 per cent. Sturges found no clear-cut pattern with respect to the time of day for this period,

---

[16] Sturges, *op. cit.*, pp. 47–49.
[17] *Ibid.*, pp. 70–77.
[18] U.S. Office of Education, *Activity Period in Public High Schools*, Bulletin 1951, No. 19 (Washington: Government Printing Office, 1951), pp. 1–10.

but more schools placed it immediately after the lunch hour than at any other time.[19]

Schools with enrollments of 249 and under, and with a high percentage of students transported on buses, generally scheduled the activity period late in the school day. Seventy-one per cent of these schools included football and basketball practice during the school day, but during a physical education period rather than during the activity period. In contrast, 70 per cent of the schools enrolling 250 or more students scheduled these practices outside of the school day and made special arrangements for transportation of rural participants.

Music had a regular period within the school day in 91.5 per cent of the schools that Sturges studied and before school in the morning in 8.5 per cent. The activities most frequently scheduled during the activity period were student council, newspaper staff, yearbook staff, clubs, and assemblies.

In the authors' view, athletic practices should be scheduled outside of the regular school day, and the activity period should be reserved for assemblies, clubs, council meetings, publications staff meetings, and certain speech and music activities. It is virtually impossible to crowd both music and athletics into the regular school day without seriously limiting the academic program and some of the other activities. If athletic practices are held outside of the regular schedule, most of the conflicts with music can be eliminated. Even the coaches agree that a single activity period is too short for boys to dress and shower and accomplish much in the way of individual and team practice. Many schools with a high percentage of rural students have worked out special transportation for boys in athletics through car pools, service club volunteers, auxiliary school buses, and other cooperative plans. Athletics serve an important need in a secondary school program, but to attempt to build an academic schedule around them indicates loss of perspective on the part of someone in authority.

Homeroom Periods

In most three-year senior and four-year senior high schools the homeroom period is actually a short administrative period. Frequently it is only ten to fifteen minutes in length and is scheduled just prior to the first class period in the morning. It is used primarily for checking attendance, making announcements, and collecting fees, and so is not a homeroom but merely an administrative unit.

In some schools, however, the period is lengthened to thirty or forty minutes once or twice a week and is used for group guidance purposes.

---

[19] Sturges, *op. cit.*, pp. 90–96.

The homeroom may also function as a basic unit in the program of student participation in government. It is discussed in greater length in Chapters 7 and 8, on guidance and extraclass activities.

Laboratory and Shop Periods

The beginning principal will need to become familiar with state department and regional accrediting association regulations concerning the time requirements for laboratory and shop courses. These requirements vary considerably from state to state, especially in the field of vocational education.

In a majority of states biology, chemistry, physics, home economics, typewriting, bookkeeping, office practice, and a few other business education subjects are considered laboratory subjects. If a school operates with a short-period schedule (40- to 45-minute periods), two double laboratory periods per week usually are required for these subjects if a full unit of credit is to be granted. A school employing a long-period schedule (55- to 60-minute periods) need not include extra laboratory periods. The North Central Association specifies 275 minutes per week in these subjects, but the arrangement of laboratory periods is left to the local school.[20]

Requirements in industrial education and agriculture vary with respect to time allocations. As a rule, the standards for shop periods for general industrial arts courses are about the same as for science courses. If a school employs short periods, general courses such as diversified shop, mechanical drawing, woodworking, sheet metal working and auto mechanics usually must be scheduled for at least seven periods per week, and in some states, ten. However, a school can meet most state and regional association time requirements for these subjects with five long periods per week.

For the vocational education courses which are reimbursable in part from federal and state funds the time regulations are varied. The principal will need to secure the latest regulations from the vocational education division of his state department before scheduling vocational subjects. In the field of vocational agriculture, two plans for scheduling are widely employed. Under one plan, high school classes are approved on the basis of 300 minutes per week provided the vocational agriculture instructor also teaches some classes for adult farmers. The other plan applies if the agriculture teacher does not teach these adult classes. In this case the usual time requirement is 420 minutes per week for each high school class in agriculture. Federal and state regulations for reimbursable trades and industries vocational classes such as machine shop,

---

[20] North Central Association, *op. cit.*, p. 2.

electricity, and auto mechanics usually require boys to be scheduled for shop classes for at least one-half of the school day. In certain other vocational courses, however, five periods of fifty-five to sixty minutes each are sufficient to satisfy federal and state regulations.

Criticisms of Conventional Schedules

The conventional schedule has invited many criticisms over the years, most of them directed at its inflexibility. Manley criticizes it on the following counts:

1. The conventional daily schedule lacks flexibility.

2. The conventional schedule does not permit adequate coordination of the efforts of teachers.

3. The conventional schedule greatly hampers attempts to make guidance and instruction integral parts of the total learning activity.

4. The conventional schedule does not reflect the aims or philosophy of the school attempting to develop a program of evaluation that promotes integration.[21]

Some of these criticisms appear to the authors to be pertinent to the schedule, while others are such that they could not be met by any type of administrative pattern. Still others stem from the limited financial and personnel resources of many schools rather than from the schedule. For example, providing time for teachers for conferences and cooperative planning is not a function of the *type* of schedule, but of financial resources and administrative policy. On the other hand, the rigid time allocations for all courses, regardless of their nature, are a function of the schedule and can be corrected by modifications in its structure.

Types and Characteristics of Variable Schedules

There is a limit to the amount of educational theory that can be built into administrative structure, but in the case of the school schedule, some modifications have been developed that appear to be more compatible with contemporary educational theory than the characteristics of conventional schedules. As previously noted, the variable types of schedules represent efforts to introduce flexibility through functional changes in time provisions. The most common variable schedules are (1) the block-time type, (2) the floating or revolving periods type, (3) the varied-period type, and (4) the modular type schedule.

[21] C. B. Manley, "Secondary School Organization and Schedule Making for the Integrating Curriculum," Type B Project, Teachers College, Columbia University, 1941, pp. 141–44.

Block-Time Type

The block-time schedule is an offshoot of the core curriculum movement but has proved to be hardier. Essentially, it allows one group of pupils to have two or three consecutive periods under one teacher or a team of teachers. Most frequently two courses, such as English and social studies, which may be correlated are scheduled in the long time block. The block-time schedule shown in Figure 4 is an example of one for the seventh and eighth grades in a junior-senior high school.

FIGURE 4

Section of a Block-Time Schedule

Teacher	Homeroom 8:45-3:57	Periods						
		I 9:00-9:57	II 10:00-10:57	III 11:00-11:57	Lunch 12:00-12:40	IV 12:40-1:37	V 1:40-2:37	VI 2:40-3:37
Miss A	8th 219	Eighth, English, Social Studies		Conference		Eighth, English, Social Studies		Conference
Mr. B	8th 320	Eighth, English, Social Studies		Eighth Reading		Ungraded 8-9 Eng.	Remedial 8th Eng.	Conference
Mrs. C	7th 217	Remedial 8th Eng.	Ungraded 10-11 Eng.	Ungraded 8-9 Eng.		Seventh Reading	Conference	Reading Testing
Mrs. D	7th 114	Eighth, English, Social Studies		Conference		Seventh Reading	Eighth, English, Social Studies	
Miss E	7th 216	Conference	Seventh, English, Social Studies ⟶				Seventh, English, Social Studies	

Adapted from "Schedule of Classes," Webster Groves, Mo., High School, first semester, 1959–60.

Considerable flexibility to accommodate a variety of learning activities is introduced through the two- and three-period blocks in this schedule. Time is provided for guidance activities by the homeroom teachers who are assigned to block-time sections. Time for conferences is scheduled for each of the block-time teachers. The degree of integration secured between English and social studies will depend upon the course organization and the type of learning activities that take place under the direction of teachers. The block-time schedule should facilitate, but is no guarantee of, integration. Faculties employing it generally agree that it makes for better transition for students from the self-contained classroom of the elementary school to the departmentalized junior high school and that it provides a better organization for guidance purposes than does a conventional schedule.

Floating Period or Revolving Schedule

The label for this modified version stems from the provision for one or more courses to meet at different times on successive days and for an activity period which "floats" in the sense that it occurs at a different time each day or week. Several variations of this type of schedule may be found in secondary schools over the country, but the example shown

FIGURE 5
One-Week Schedule for a Ninth Grade Student — Floating Period Schedule

Period	Monday	Tuesday	Wednesday	Thursday	Friday
A	English	English	English	English	Algebra
B	Civics	Civics	Civics	Algebra	Civics
C	General Science	General Science	Activity Homerooms	General Science	General Science
D	Band	Algebra	Band	Band	Band
E	Algebra	Physical Education	Physical Education	Physical Education	Physical Education

in Figure 5 is fairly representative. Periods A to E are all seventy minutes in length and each class meets four times per week. Anderson cites the following advantages for this type of schedule as employed in some Michigan schools:

> (1) To provide a larger amount of time for supervised study under the direction of the teacher for whom the work is being prepared, (2) To make possible the elimination of large study halls, (3) To provide a longer period for laboratory classes and field trips, and (4) To provide a longer activity period once a week.[22]

Anderson also reports that teachers in these schools liked the schedule because it provided more continuous time for supervised study and for work with individual students. Teachers of laboratory and shop classes were pleased because the long periods permitted them to conduct uninterrupted projects, assemble equipment, take field trips, and engage in other special activities.

Varied-Period Schedule

A few secondary schools have adopted the varied-period schedule employed in colleges in an effort to break with the illogical uniformity of

---

[22] Lester W. Anderson, "What Is the Most Effective Way of Arranging the Length and Use of the Class Period?" *The Bulletin* of the NASSP, April, 1959, 43:162.

ORGANIZATION AND DIRECTION OF THE PROGRAM

conventional high school schedules. Probably a change to the semester hour plan of granting credit would be necessary, but colleges and accrediting associations generally accept credits on this basis, and it is much more flexible than the Carnegie unit system. Some high schools place students on their own time between classes, but usually they are required to remain on the premises. Others assign them to study halls as under a conventional schedule.

The program shown in Figure 6 is typical for an eleventh-grade student in a school using a college-type schedule. Some courses meet only two or three times per week while others meet six or seven periods each week.

FIGURE 6

Program for an Eleventh-Grade Student — Varied-Period Schedule
(Second Semester)

Period	Monday	Tuesday	Wednesday	Thursday	Friday
I 8:15	American Literature Lecture	Quiz–Study Section B	American Literature Lecture	Quiz–Study Section B	American Literature Lecture
II 9:15	French III	Art III	French III	Art III	French III
III 10:15	American History Lecture	American History Lecture	American History Lecture	Quiz–Study Section D	Quiz–Study Section D
IV 11:15	Algebra IV		Algebra IV		Algebra IV
V 1:00	Physical Education		Physical Education		Physical Education
VI 2:00	Chemistry	Chemistry	Chemistry	Chemistry	Chemistry
VII 3:00	Band	Laboratory	Band	Laboratory	Band

The American literature and history lectures are large sections of 100 or more students and the quiz-study sections are limited to about fifteen students. Each of these courses carries five semester hours of credit. The French and algebra courses carry three semester hours of credit, and art carries two semester hours. Chemistry is also a five-semester-hour course, and credit is optional for band and physical education. The chemistry lecture-study and laboratory sections are flexible and may be employed as the instructor chooses.

The principal advantages claimed for the varied-period plan are that it permits students to enroll in more courses during each semester and that time allocations for courses are more realistic than the periods of uniform length and number of hours per week provided under a typical high school schedule.

Modular Type Schedule

In 1956 the Commission on the Experimental Study of the Utilization of the Staff in the Secondary School was appointed by the National Association of Secondary School Principals to conduct a number of experimental programs, make evaluations, and hold workshops on more efficient utilization of staff and instructional aids. The Commission was awarded a grant by the Ford Foundation to finance its project.

One of the major provisions of the project was the employment of teaching teams composed of master teachers, who lectured to large sections, and professional teacher aides, who conducted small-group-discussion and study sections. Nonprofessional helpers and clerks also were employed to assist with routine clerical, managerial, and mechanical tasks. Emphasis was placed on a flexible schedule composed of short time modules of 20 to 30 minutes which could be shifted to accommodate the different activities.

The several experimental programs conducted in local high schools in various sections of the country required extensive revision of the curriculum, teaching procedures, and schedules. Figure 7, showing how a student might spend his time, also presents variations in the schedule suggested for schools participating in this project.

FIGURE 7

How a Student Might Spend His Time in the Secondary School of the Future

Period	Monday	Tuesday	Wednesday	Thursday	Friday	Saturday
8:30 9:00 9:30 10:00 10:30 11:00 11:30	Large Group Instruction Small Group Discussion Large Group Instruction	Individual Study Large Group Instruction	Large Group Small Group Large Group	Large Group Individual	Large Group Small Group Individual Study	Individual
12:00	Lunch and Activities					
1:00 1:30 2:00 2:30 3:00 3:30	Individual Study Small Group	Small Group Large Group Individual Study	Small Group Individual Study 	Small Group Individual Study	Large Group Small Group	Individual

Source: J. Lloyd Trump, *Images of the Future* (Urbana, Ill.: Commission on the Experimental Study of the Utilization of the Staff in the Secondary School, 1959), p. 12.

Evaluations of the effectiveness of the different types of local experiments have been reported in several issues of *The Bulletin* of the NASSP.[23] A more complete description of these experimental programs and their evaluations is included in Chapter 11, "Staff Organization and Utilization," since the project is directed primarily to staff utilization. In general, the evaluations show teacher and parental approval, extensive cooperative activity on the part of participating faculty members, wider and more effective use of audio-visual procedures, considerable saving in teachers' time, and good behavioral and social adjustment on the part of students. Few significant differences in academic achievement for students in the experimental classes and control classes are reported by most of the schools. The participating schools also reported little difference in operating costs between team teaching and conventional classes.

The team teaching plan appears to be more feasible for large high schools than for small schools, at least until such time as coordinated regional television instruction becomes a reality in all states. Nevertheless, some promising innovations in scheduling have been developed in the participating schools. As more refined evaluation techniques and teaching procedures appear, some of the key questions about team teaching may be answered more conclusively.

Building a Schedule

Some operations in the business of constructing a daily schedule are routine, but the influence of a well-designed schedule on the successful operation of a school makes this one of the important professional responsibilities of a high school principal.

To free the principal of some of the time-consuming technical work involved in schedule making, some of the tabulations may be done by machines, and in large schools many of the routine tasks may be delegated by the principal to assistants. In all schools, however, important decisions with respect to such matters as the bases for sectioning students, lengths of periods for various types of classes, assignment of teachers to courses for which they are best qualified, and optimum teacher loads must be made by a principal who knows his business.

Criteria of a Good Schedule

The items to be included in a schedule have been listed at the beginning of the chapter, but the schedule must be judged in terms of how well

[23] National Association of Secondary School Principals, "Progressing Toward Better Schools," Third Report on Staff Utilization Studies, *The Bulletin* of the NASSP, January, 1960, Vol. 44.

it does what it is supposed to do. The authors suggest that a good schedule should:

1. Be sufficiently clear and complete to assist materially in the effective operation of the daily program on opening day.
2. Function with a minimum of confusion and change from the first days of the school year.
3. Contain no conflicts between courses for all but a very small percentage of students. It may be necessary for a few students (1 or 2 per cent) to change one of their electives in order to resolve a conflict. Such changes should be made prior to the opening day.
4. Provide for good balance in the distribution of class sections throughout the school day.
5. Assign teachers to courses for which they are qualified and, insofar as possible, those for which they have a preference.
6. Provide good balance in section size and in the number of students and class sections assigned to teachers.
7. Provide at least one open period for planning and conferences for each teacher.
8. Provide for optimum utilization of all rooms in relation to the capacity of the building and the enrollment.
9. Meet all minimum standards for time allocations as designated by the state department of education and other accrediting agencies.
10. Serve the characteristics and preferences of the community with respect to time limits for the school day.
11. Provide for some degree of flexibility in the length of certain periods, meeting times for certain sections, and programming of various activities within the school day.
12. Make provisions for ability groups, seminars, remedial sections, and other programs to allow for differences in ability.

Information Needed in Building a Schedule

Some of the information and decisions needed before the construction of the schedule may be attempted have been discussed in the section on characteristics of conventional schedules. For example, such things as time for opening and closing of the school day, length of class periods, time for lunch periods, and the number of teachers that may be employed will have to have been decided on. In addition, the principal will need the following information:

Offerings and Organization of the Curriculum. Besides the design of the curriculum, discussed in Chapter 5, course offerings, requirements for graduation, provisions for grouping, specialized sequences, remedial courses, advanced placement and/or acceleration programs, types of activities, and group guidance provisions must be known.

Student Election of Courses — Preregistration. The schedule maker will need to know as nearly as possible the number of students enrolled in each course in order to determine how many sections, teachers, and rooms are necessary. This information may best be secured by means of a preregistration held a few weeks before the end of the school year or semester. Preregistration plans and adjustments for failures and transfers will be discussed more fully in the following section on procedures.

Bases for Sectioning and Assignments to Special-Ability Classes. The selection of students for special-ability sections, such as remedial courses and ability groups, must have been made so that the principal will know how many sections of special groups will be required and where to post other courses so as to avoid conflicts. If ability grouping is employed, pertinent information on all students enrolled in each grouped course should be reviewed by the principal in consultation with teachers and counselors. Students then should be assigned to appropriate sections on the basis of the recommendations made by the conferees. If students are to be grouped differently in each subject — as in English and mathematics — it will be necessary to know their ability level in each subject. The grouped sections should be posted first in the schedule for each grade level in order to hold conflicts to a minimum.

Class Size and the Number of Sections Needed in Each Course. The number of sections may be determined tentatively from the data secured from the two preceding operations and the maximum and minimum size of class sections decided upon. In courses in which grouping is not a factor, only the total number of preregistrations in each course and the desired size of class sections need be known. Often some slight revision is necessary in the limits agreed upon for the size of class sections owing to unexpected shifts in enrollments in certain departments; upon occasion, it may be appropriate to defer a course offering until the following year.

Research and recommended practices with respect to class size will be reported in the section on teacher loads in Chapter 11. The Commission on Teacher Education and Professional Standards recommended that "twenty-five pupils should be the maximum number enrolled in any class or grade taught by one teacher."[24] In laboratory, shop, and remedial classes, however, the special problems of supervision and instruction involved justify the limitation of sections to approximately twenty students. In certain courses such as typewriting, music, and physical education larger sections may be both justified and necessary. And in team teaching programs some large lecture sections are required along with small groups.

There is little support for making a recommendation on minimum class

[24] National Education Association, Research Division, "Teaching Load in 1950," *Research Bulletin*, February, 1951, 29:47.

size other than the argument that it is difficult to defend the expense of tutorial sections for two or three students in a public school. In general, the minimum cutoff point for class size will depend on local policy and the financial ability of the school district. Sometimes the problem of small enrollments in advanced courses, such as French III and IV, can be met by scheduling them together or by offering them in alternate years. Some schools employ accredited supervised correspondence courses, offered by several colleges and universities, to meet the needs of a small number of students interested in a specialized type of course.

The entire question of class size is in a state of flux at the present time because of the many experimental programs with TV instruction and the project of the Commission on the Experimental Study of the Utilization of the Staff in the Secondary School.[25] Certainly the teaching load becomes greater and a close personal relationship between teacher and students is difficult to develop with large classes. To compensate for these losses, the aforementioned commission of the NASSP on utilization of the staff recommends the use of assistants with master teachers and the provision of adequate clerical workers to handle nonprofessional chores and thereby give teachers more time to work with students.

Teachers Needed and Their Qualifications and Preferences. The finished schedule should show the teachers assigned to each class, homeroom, and study hall. The number of teachers needed will depend upon the number of course sections and the number of sections to be assigned to each teacher as determined by administrative policy. Five class sections in a six-period schedule and six class sections in a seven- or eight-period schedule are as many as an individual teacher should be expected to assume in most subject fields. Certainly every teacher should have at least one open period each day for conferences and planning.

The schedule maker must be familiar with the experience and training of each teacher and should know his preferences for certain courses. No teacher, of course, should be assigned to a subject in which he has had little or no preparation. Most states and regional accrediting associations require a minimum number of semester hours of college preparation for teachers in each subject to which they are assigned. The North Central Association requires at least eighteen semester hours in most fields as minimum preparation.[26]

It is highly improbable that the principal will be able to assign every teacher to the courses that he prefers, but teacher preference should be honored whenever possible. The principal's and teacher's first concern,

[25] J. Lloyd Trump, *Images of the Future* (Urbana, Ill.: Commission on the Experimental Study of the Utilization of the Staff in the Secondary School, 1959), pp. 15–27.
[26] North Central Association, *op. cit.*, pp. 15–17.

however, should be the best interests of students and it is not unreasonable to expect a teacher to accept some course assignments that do not represent his first choices.

The Number, Size, and Special Facilities of Classrooms. The principal will need a floor plan of his building facilities showing the types of rooms available and a brief description of their capacity and special equipment to guide him in making room assignments in the schedule. If office space for teachers is not available, an effort should be made to assign each teacher to a room that he may regard as his base of operations and in which he will meet most of his classes. With the exception of certain special-purpose rooms such as the cafeteria, library, and auditorium, the principal should attempt to schedule each room for instructional purposes at least 80 per cent of the school day. A study of room use in secondary schools in Ohio revealed that the average room use was 85 per cent of the day for interchangeable rooms and 71 per cent for special rooms.[27] These figures are in approximate agreement with other studies and with recommendations made by school building specialists.

The Organization of the School Day. The factors to be considered in the organization of the school day have been discussed previously in this chapter. The specific decisions needed before attempting to block in the schedule have to do with (1) time of opening and closing, (2) organization and length of the lunch hour, (3) length and number of class periods, (4) time between class periods, (5) homeroom, activity, and assembly periods, (6) laboratory and shop periods, and (7) provision for overlapping sessions, if necessary.

Scheduling Procedures

The process of building a schedule so that all of the components are well coordinated and the whole fits the educational program requires some expert direction and a little trial-and-error manipulation. Some principals take the job rather lightly and simply warm over the old schedule from year to year. Others, alert to the implications of changes in institutions outside the school and in pupil needs, work hard on curriculum improvement, and that generally requires some imaginative adaptations in the schedule. For example, a program of ability sectioning in which students are grouped on the basis of aptitude in each subject, rather than by some general classification, calls for a substantial amount of work and no little professional knowledge on the part

[27] W. R. Flesher, E. B. Sessions, and T. C. Holy, *A Study of Public School Building Needs* (Columbus: Bureau of Educational Research, Ohio State University, 1947), p. 50.

of schedule builders. But it can be and is being achieved in many secondary schools whose faculties are primarily interested in developing an educational program that meets the needs of students.

There is disagreement among school administrators over the best time of the year for building the schedule; some prefer to do it in the spring and some during the summer. Probably the technical work such as posting courses in a time chart should be done during the summer. But if the process of registering students and helping them plan their high school program is to be made an effective means of group guidance, it is necessary to get under way early in the spring. A second advantage in starting to work on the schedule in the spring is that the principal can confer with teachers and enlist their thinking in planning a sound schedule. Regardless of the timing, the chief tasks involved in schedule building are the following:

Securing Estimates of Course Enrollments — Preregistration. The first step is to get an estimate of the number of students who will be enrolled in each course for the following year or semester. This information may be secured through preregistration for students currently enrolled in the high school or its associated elementary and junior high schools. Estimates for students who transfer into the high school district during the summer will have to be based on previous transfers or on information about new residents obtained from the chamber of commerce or other community agencies. Late transfers, of course, cannot be taken into account in setting up the master time schedule.

Preregistration should be held a few weeks before the end of the school year (during the first semester in schools with numerous mid-year changes) in order to give students time to discuss choices with their advisers and parents and to enable the principal to tabulate the data and make up a preliminary schedule. The program may be conducted through homerooms or other small advisory groups with the assistance of faculty advisers. In some schools a series of parent nights is scheduled, usually for one grade at a time, to permit parents to take an active part in planning a program for their son or daughter with faculty advisers and other school personnel. Certainly parents should assume some of this responsibility and a parents' night is an excellent means of providing them with an opportunity to do so.

A printed or mimeographed curriculum bulletin showing required and elective courses by grades and advisory curricula for special-interest groups should be issued to each student. Many schools also include summaries of graduation requirements, department sequences, and admission requirements for area colleges in their curriculum bulletins. Along with the bulletin, a preregistration blank goes to each student.

It should provide space for the student to record his present program, the courses that are required, and those that he wants to elect. The form also should allow for a tentative choice of activities.

Students probably will need a week or two to study the bulletin with their parents and to confer with their class or homeroom adviser, counselor, and other faculty members in order to make appropriate elections. At the end of this time each student should indicate his choices of elective courses on the preregistration blank — preferably a card for ease in processing. The completed blank should be signed by the student and one of his parents and returned to his adviser. The adviser then sends the cards to the principal's office for tabulation.

Preregistration may be an effective guidance procedure if the faculty is oriented toward that purpose. Counselors, administrators, and teacher-advisers should work together as closely as possible to help students make appropriate course elections. A number of high schools have students outline their entire three- or four-year program when they first register and the program is kept in the files of the student's counselor for guidance purposes. Plans may be changed with the approval of parents and counselors, but most schools with a good counseling program find that only a small percentage of students request changes in their study programs.

A number of interesting and effective plans are employed in conducting preregistration for incoming students from the eighth or ninth grades of associated schools. Some senior high schools send counselors to the junior high schools or elementary schools in the spring to meet with students and their teachers and counselors and to discuss the high school program. They also may administer standardized tests and assist students in selecting a tentative high school sequence of courses. In addition, it is helpful to invite prospective students to spend a day together in the high school in order to become better acquainted with it. Student council members may act as guides and participate in a planned orientation day. At the end of the preregistration period the incoming students should meet with counselors to fill out registration materials. Rural high schools may, and some do, conduct this type of program for eighth-graders from surrounding elementary schools. Needless to say, orientation day programs require cooperative planning by the faculties of the feeder and receiving schools if they are to be successful.

Tabulating Registrations and Conflicts. The second step is the tabulation of course registrations from the preregistration forms. This may be done manually by clerks in the principal's office or by homeroom or class advisers with the assistance of students. In an increasing number of schools, however, marginal or machine punch cards are used in preregistration and tabulations are made with the aid of a tool sorter or a machine. For courses in which there is no ability grouping, the total number of registrations divided by the desired size of sections indicates the number of sections needed. For courses in which grouping is employed, the students assigned to each ability classification must be counted separately and these totals divided by the desired size of grouped sections to determine the number of sections at a particular ability level. For example, if out of a total of 175 students to be grouped in English II, 40 are ranked superior, 43 are ranked low, and 92 are ranked average, and the maximum size of sections is set at 25, it will be necessary to schedule two high sections, two low sections, and four average sections.

It will save time and assist materially in building a sound schedule if possible conflicts are tabulated at this point. Several different procedures may be employed, but most of them involve using either a conflict chart or a marginal punch system with punched and notched individual student program cards. The conflict chart is compiled manually and probably is most practical in schools of around 500 or fewer pupils. It consists of a chart for each grade, such as that shown in Figure 8, on which are listed all course sections in which the registration, as shown by the general tabulation of all student preregistrations, is sufficiently small to justify only one section. Courses with enrollments large enough to require two or more sections need not be tabulated on the conflict chart, since most conflicts involving these courses may be resolved by shifting students from one section to another. The single-section courses are listed across the top and in the same order down the left side of a paper ruled into rectangular spaces, as in Figure 8.

All of the preregistration cards for one grade then are assembled and those for students enrolled in two or more single-section courses are sorted out. These are the students with possible conflicts. Clerks then tabulate the number of possible course conflicts from these registration cards. For example, if Bill Jones has registered for French I and English II, a tally should be entered on the conflict chart in the vertical column labeled French I and the horizontal column labeled English II. Similarly, if Sarah Smith has elected the single-section courses French II, English III, and Home Economics III, tallies should be made for each combination.

At the conclusion of the tabulation, the chart will show how many students have conflicts between each specific pair of one-section courses. The schedule maker should attempt to block in the schedule so as to avoid placing these sections in the same period. From Figure 8 it may be seen that French I and English II, French II and English II, Vocational Agriculture III and English III, and Home Economics III and English

III should not be scheduled during the same period. The other conflicts involve only two students each and it may be necessary to persuade them to adjust their registration. However, the number of students who are required to change their registrations should be very small.

FIGURE 8

Conflict Chart of Single-Section Courses

	English II	English III	French I	French II	Home Ec. III	Voc. Ag. III	Mech. Dr. II
English II			12	6			
English III			2	7	7	2
French I							
French II							
Home Ec. III							
Voc. Ag. III							2
Mech. Dr. II							

Posting Sections on the Master Schedule. After information on the number of sections needed for each course, possible conflicts, and teaching personnel have been assembled, the next step is to post course sections on the master schedule.

Some type of skeleton layout with the numbers of each period across the top and the names of each teacher down the left-hand side or vice versa is in order for this procedure. A plywood panel hung on the wall, with vertical columns for each period and horizontal columns for each teacher painted on it and with screw hooks inserted in each rectangular space, is used by some principals and seems satisfactory. In schools with machine equipment a large card bin is used as a framework for the schedule. Names of teachers may be printed on cards and fastened to the chart with thumbtacks. Names and numbers may be printed on metal-edged cardboard disks for each course section and hung on the chart in a period space opposite the name of the teacher to whom the section is to be assigned. A different-colored disk for each grade makes checking for conflicts easier.

In large senior schools and junior high schools, students may be scheduled by blocks or groups in certain required and popular elective courses if they are not grouped independently in two or three courses on the basis of ability. Many large schools now use this system of ability grouping, however, and it virtually eliminates block or group scheduling.

Filling in the master schedule involves a certain amount of trial and error and is sometimes referred to as the "mosaic" method. Nevertheless, there are important sequential steps and priorities to be kept in mind if the schedule is to have good balance and serve the educational program of the school satisfactorily. Some of the more important sequential steps and priorities are as follows:

1. If short periods — less than fifty-five minutes — are to be used, begin with the predominantly senior courses and post those for which there will be only one section and which require double periods, such as physics, machine shop, and vocational agriculture. Place these on the master chart so that no two courses for which conflicts are shown on the conflict sheet are assigned to the same period.

2. Next post the single-section senior courses that do not require double periods. Insofar as possible, avoid placing any two with conflicting registrations in the same period. Write in nonteaching assignments for teachers, such as counseling or newspaper staff work, on the master chart at this time, since these assignments usually tie up a single period for each of the teachers involved.

3. Then assign the senior courses with two sections. Some of these probably will have to come at the same time as some of the single-section courses. Most students with conflicts can be shifted to a duplicate section of the double-section courses. If a few seniors have difficult conflicts, keep shifting the sections around in an effort to work them out, or consider a third section, since the seniors will not have an opportunity to defer a desired course.

4. Next post the senior courses with more than two sections. These courses should be scheduled so that no two sections conflict with both divisions of a two-section course. It may be necessary to schedule two of the three sections during the same period, but usually this does not result in conflicts.

5. After the courses that are predominantly for seniors are scheduled, proceed in the same manner with courses that are primarily for juniors, primarily for sophomores, and so on down the line.

6. In scheduling courses for underclassmen in which ability grouping is used, it probably will be necessary to post ability sections first except in very large high schools. Ability grouping increases the probability of conflicts, and the most likely way to reduce conflicts is to assign the ability sections first. Other special provisions, such as clearing a certain period for band, should be made along with posting the single-section courses.

Assigning Teachers to Courses for Which They Are Qualified and Balancing Loads. With a few exceptions, the number of classes and study halls and the total number of pupils per week assigned to teachers should be balanced. First-year teachers should be given a lighter load if at all possible because of their inexperience and need to devote time to planning their courses. The number of pupils per week assigned to music, typewriting, and physical education teachers may be somewhat larger than that given to teachers of academic subjects. If readers are not provided for English teachers, their class load should be reduced to permit them time to read papers and to consult with individual pupils. Teachers of certain advanced academic subjects such as foreign languages, mathematics, and science may be expected to have a smaller pupil load than teachers in most other fields. Teachers should be assigned to not more than two subject fields and, if at all possible, only to their major fields.

Some principals in large schools find it worthwhile to duplicate copies of the tentative schedule and distribute it to the faculty for study and suggestions. In small schools with only ten or fifteen teachers the tentative master chart may be brought into a faculty meeting and discussed there. Although the principal must assume primary responsibility for blocking in the schedule, the over-all design should be a cooperative faculty enterprise. Teachers may offer valuable suggestions as well as profit from a study of the problems involved.

Making Room Assignments. After adjustments have been made for conflicts, sections equalized as nearly as possible, and teacher assignments balanced, rooms should be assigned. Working from a floor plan of the building, the principal should enter on the schedule the number of the room in which each class section will meet. An effort should be made to schedule all sections for each teacher in the same room except where the special nature of a class does not permit it, such as certain sections of music, laboratory, and shop. Room facilities for these special courses must be cleared of conflicts.

After room assignments have been completed, a check should be made to determine whether good use is being made of all rooms. However, the principal will be limited in his control of this factor by enrollments and the capacity of buildings.

Printing or Duplicating the Operating Schedule. At this point the operating schedule for final pupil registration should be ready and copied from the large working model. Sufficient copies should be printed or duplicated to supply all teachers and students and to provide an adequate reserve. Some principals prefer to run off the operating copy a week or two before the end of the semester or year, and others prefer to do it during the summer. If the schedule is printed early, it cannot be in final form, since there may be some faculty changes and unexpected shifts in student enrollments before the beginning of the new year or semester.

ORGANIZATION OF THE SCHOOL SCHEDULE AND CALENDAR

FIGURE 9
Pupil Schedule Card

Central High School, River City, Mountain State
Pupil Schedule Card, 19 63

Name: Ray L. Hicks   Parent's Name: George Hicks   Phone: 2-3861
Home Address: 2256 N. Pine, River City   Date: 9-3-63
Class: Freshman   Home Room: 201   Locker: 1108

Course	Sec.	Period	Day	Room	Instructor
Algebra I	H	1	D	201	Sherman
English I	S	2	D	342	Wright
Study		3	TTh	NSH	Mangum
Physical Ed.		3	MWF	B. Gym	Swearingen
W. Geography		4	D	225	Vaughn
Biology	B	5	D	112	Knight
Band		6	D	224	Maupin

Programming Students. Students will need to have a copy of the schedule of their courses showing periods, rooms, and teachers on the opening day of the new semester or year. A considerable saving in time and reduction in confusion can be effected if pupil programs are made up a week or two before the end of the semester or during the summer. The programming will differ considerably in small and large schools using manual methods and still more in schools using a tool-sorter or machine techniques.

In getting ready for the new school year, many principals prefer to have clerical personnel prepare pupil schedules during the summer months in order to reduce errors, equalize the assignment of pupils to sections, make adjustments for failures, and register students transferring into the district during the summer. In most schools the number of changes in the program at midyear is small, and pupils can enter changes in their schedule in homerooms with the assistance of their faculty advisers.

The pupil schedule cards are made up from the students' preregistration forms, which have been approved by parents and advisers. Required courses may be printed on cards for each grade with space for section numbers to be filled in by the secretaries. The cards should be made out in duplicate or triplicate so that one copy may be retained by the student on opening day. In addition to such information as parent's name and address, homeroom, class, and telephone number, the card should show all courses and study halls by periods, the names of the instructors, the days of the week that each course meets, the room number, and the section number. Figure 9 shows a student schedule card.

Machine and Marginal Punch Card Programming and Registration

The number of schools using marginal punch card and electronic machine equipment in registration and scheduling has increased rapidly during the last few years. In large schools the amount of clerical and teacher time saved makes the use of a machine-processing system an economical investment. There are several different systems of machine and marginal punch card programming available, and descriptions and sample forms may be secured by writing to the various companies that produce them. Machines can reduce computational errors and take over many tedious tasks of processing data, but machines cannot think, and the composition of a sound master schedule requires some careful thought.

Marginal Punch Card. This method employs special preregistration cards with holes punched around the edges which are keyed to course titles and notched for courses elected by the student. A sort of elongated ice pick with technological refinements is used as a tool. Figure 10 shows the type of card employed.

The major advantages of the marginal punch card system are that it speeds up the preparation of a conflict sheet and the sorting of cards in assigning students to homerooms and class sections. The procedure in several schools using this method is as follows:

1. The preregistration process is conducted in the sequence described previously for manual scheduling.

2. Special coded registration cards are issued to all students in homerooms, where they fill in personal information and the names of the courses in which they desire to register for the following year. The cards are checked for accuracy by the homeroom teacher, and the pupil makes a copy in his notebook for his own record.

3. The registration cards are sent to the office, where clerks punch or notch each student's card around the margin for each course in which he is registered. The clerks then sort the cards and tabulate registrations for each course.

4. The cards are sorted again to determine possible conflicts between single-section courses. The single-section courses may be readily identified from the tabulations made of all student elections in Step 3. Courses with approximately twenty-five or fewer registrations usually are classified as single-section courses. In order to check conflicts for single-section subjects, all of the cards for a certain grade are placed in a box or bin and a sorting tool is inserted in the holes for a specific single-section

FIGURE 10

Marginal Punch Card

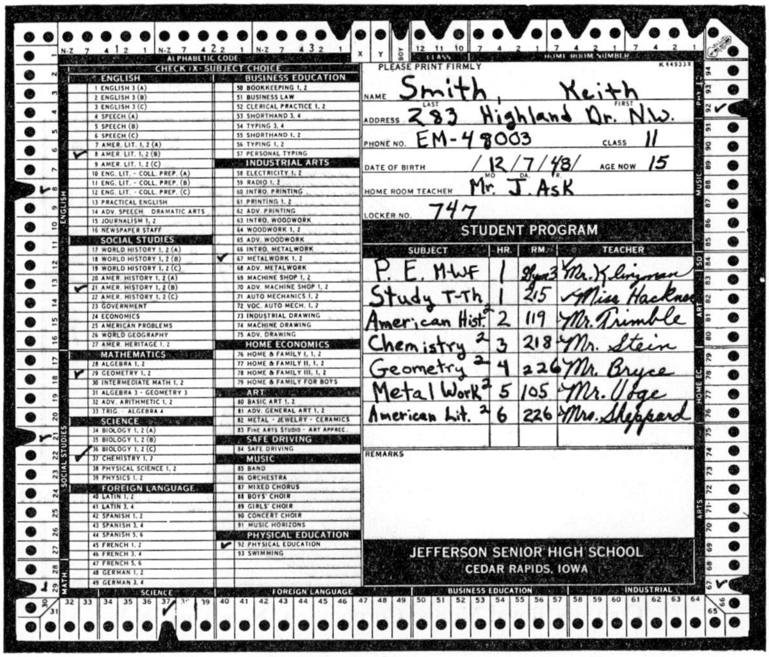
ALPHABETIC CODE

CHECK (X) SUBJECT CHOICE

ENGLISH
1 ENGLISH 3 (A)
2 ENGLISH 3 (B)
3 ENGLISH 3 (C)
4 SPEECH (A)
5 SPEECH (B)
6 SPEECH (C)
7 AMER. LIT. 1, 2 (A)
8 AMER. LIT. 1, 2 (B) ✓
9 AMER. LIT. 1, 2 (C)
10 ENG. LIT. - COLL. PREP. (A)
11 ENG. LIT. - COLL. PREP. (B)
12 ENG. LIT. - COLL. PREP. (C)
13 PRACTICAL ENGLISH
14 ADV. SPEECH DRAMATIC ARTS
15 JOURNALISM 1, 2
16 NEWSPAPER STAFF

SOCIAL STUDIES
17 WORLD HISTORY 1, 2 (A)
18 WORLD HISTORY 1, 2 (B)
19 WORLD HISTORY 1, 2 (C)
20 AMER. HISTORY 1, 2 (A)
21 AMER. HISTORY 1, 2 (B) ✓
22 AMER. HISTORY 1, 2 (C)
23 GOVERNMENT
24 ECONOMICS
25 AMERICAN PROBLEMS
26 WORLD GEOGRAPHY
27 AMER. HERITAGE 1, 2

MATHEMATICS
28 ALGEBRA 1, 2
29 GEOMETRY 1, 2 ✓
30 INTERMEDIATE MATH 1, 2
31 ALGEBRA 3 - GEOMETRY 3
32 ADV. ARITHMETIC 1, 2
33 TRIG. - ALGEBRA 4

SCIENCE
34 BIOLOGY 1, 2 (A)
35 BIOLOGY 1, 2 (B)
36 BIOLOGY 1, 2 (C)
37 CHEMISTRY 1, 2 ✓
38 PHYSICAL SCIENCE 1, 2
39 PHYSICS 1, 2

FOREIGN LANGUAGE
40 LATIN 1, 2
41 LATIN 3, 4
42 SPANISH 1, 2
43 SPANISH 3, 4
44 SPANISH 5, 6
45 FRENCH 1, 2
46 FRENCH 3, 4
47 FRENCH 5, 6
48 GERMAN 1, 2
49 GERMAN 3, 4

BUSINESS EDUCATION
50 BOOKKEEPING 1, 2
51 BUSINESS LAW
52 CLERICAL PRACTICE 1, 2
53 SHORTHAND 3, 4
54 TYPING 3, 4
55 SHORTHAND 1, 2
56 TYPING 1, 2
57 PERSONAL TYPING

INDUSTRIAL ARTS
58 ELECTRICITY 1, 2
59 RADIO 1, 2
60 INTRO. PRINTING
61 PRINTING 1, 2
62 ADV. PRINTING
63 INTRO. WOODWORK
64 WOODWORK 1, 2
65 ADV. WOODWORK
66 INTRO. METALWORK
67 METALWORK 1, 2 ✓
68 ADV. METALWORK
69 MACHINE SHOP 1, 2
70 ADV. MACHINE SHOP 1, 2
71 AUTO MECHANICS 1, 2
72 VOC. AUTO MECH. 1, 2
73 INDUSTRIAL DRAWING
74 MACHINE DRAWING
75 ADV. DRAWING

HOME ECONOMICS
76 HOME & FAMILY I, 1, 2
77 HOME & FAMILY II, 1, 2
78 HOME & FAMILY III, 1, 2
79 HOME & FAMILY FOR BOYS

ART
80 BASIC ART 1, 2
81 ADV. GENERAL ART 1, 2
82 METAL - JEWELRY - CERAMICS
83 FINE ARTS STUDIO - ART APPREC.

SAFE DRIVING
84 SAFE DRIVING

MUSIC
85 BAND
86 ORCHESTRA
87 MIXED CHORUS
88 BOYS' CHOIR
89 GIRLS' CHOIR
90 CONCERT CHOIR
91 MUSIC HORIZONS

PHYSICAL EDUCATION
92 PHYSICAL EDUCATION ✓
93 SWIMMING

PLEASE PRINT FIRMLY

NAME Smith, Keith

ADDRESS 283 Highland Dr. N.W.

PHONE NO. EM-48003 CLASS 11

DATE OF BIRTH 12/7/48 AGE NOW 15

HOME ROOM TEACHER Mr. J. Ask

LOCKER NO. 747

STUDENT PROGRAM

SUBJECT	HR.	RM.	TEACHER
P. E. M-W-F	1	Gym 3	Mr. Klingman
Study T-Th	1	215	Miss Hackner
American Hist. 2	2	119	Mr. Trimble
Chemistry 2	3	218	Mr. Stein
Geometry 2	4	226	Mr. Bryce
Metal Work 2	5	105	Mr. Uge
American Lit. 2	6	226	Mrs. Sheppard

REMARKS

JEFFERSON SENIOR HIGH SCHOOL
CEDAR RAPIDS, IOWA

Courtesy, Cedar Rapids Public Schools,
Cedar Rapids, Iowa

course, such as chemistry. The tool is raised so that the cards notched for chemistry drop down. Then to check for conflicts between chemistry and another single such as French III, the tool is inserted in the hole for French III in the bunched chemistry cards and raised. All of the French III cards then drop. A count of these gives the number of conflicts between chemistry and French III. All possible conflicts between single-section courses may be checked in this manner and recorded on a conflict sheet. See Figure 8.

5. The master schedule is made up at this point using the procedure previously described. Some principals employ a large cabinet with card bins as the framework for the master schedule.

6. Clerks record the period, room number, and teacher for each course on the student's schedule card during the summer.

7. The cards are then sorted by homeroom numbers and distributed to the homeroom teachers during the preschool conference in the fall. At the opening session of school the homeroom teachers give each student his card to copy his schedule. The cards then are collected by the homeroom teacher and returned to the office.

The student also fills out a coupon card for each course in which he is registered. These are sorted in the office by clerks and serve as class rolls for teachers.

FIGURE 11

Keysorter and Pupil Schedule Cards

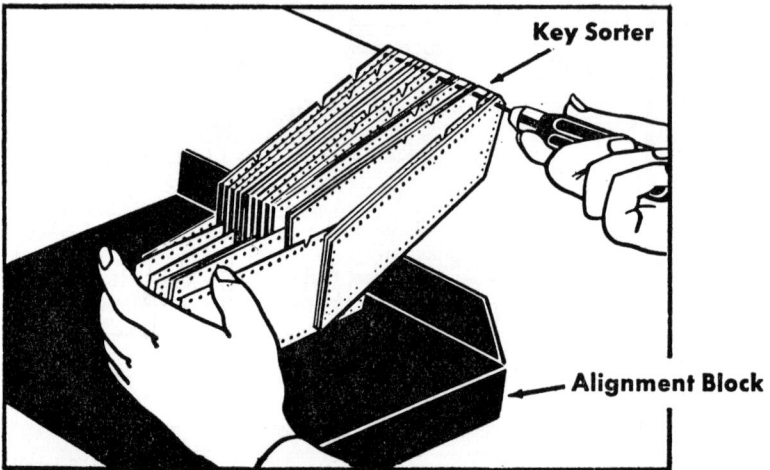

Courtesy Royal McBee Corporation, New York, N.Y.

Matulis, in describing the system of marginal punch cards used in his school of 1,500 students, lists the following advantages:

(1) Total scheduling for the new school year was completed only one week after the end of the old year, (2) On the second day of the new school year, the halls were as quiet as at mid-term, (3) The system helped end platooning at Taylor High by eliminating errors in scheduling, and (4) The subject demand for the coming school year is indicated in pretty definite terms by this system early in the last semester of the current year.[28]

Machine Processing. Schools employing machine data-processing equipment also make use of punch cards. The cards are punched for the student's name, sex, course sections, homeroom, and other desired information. The process of tabulating enrollments in each course is done by a machine rather than manually. Printed lists of students in each section may be prepared for teachers' class rolls with machine equipment.

Although machine procedures appear to be most feasible in large schools at the present time, it is probable that machine service centers

[28] Anthony S. Matulis, "Foolproof Scheduling in Record Time," *School Management,* March, 1960, 4:69–74.

will be established in areas close to smaller schools within a few years and that the costs will become reasonable enough to justify their use. Certainly machine techniques greatly speed up the technical process of registration and schedule building.

The School Year

A little confusion probably is inevitable in the operation of a school and, at times, may relieve the monotony of bells, forms, and close routine. But a little confusion, like a little inflation, can get out of hand. Careful planning of the school year will conserve valuable instructional time and reduce misunderstanding and conflict among members of the staff. The principal is primarily responsible for working out the high school calendar and organizing the opening and closing events of the school year. Needless to say, it is essential that he consult with the superintendent, members of the teaching staff, and leaders of church and civic organizations in planning the high school calendar.

Length of the School Year

The responsibility for fixing the length of the local school year properly belongs to the board of education and its executive officer, the superintendent of schools. The individual high school calendar must be coordinated with the calendars of other schools in the system. Minimum lengths usually are set by each state and by accrediting agencies. The North Central Association requires member high schools to schedule a school year of at least 180 days with classes in session for at least 175 days.[29]

Trends in Length of Traditional School Year. Otto reports that the long-time trend has been toward a longer school year. In 1870 the average length of the school year for all types of schools in the United States was 132 days.[30] In 1944 it was 175 days in urban school systems, and in 1955 it was 180 days in these systems.[31] Although the school year in the United States has been growing longer, it is still much shorter than in many other countries. In England, Germany, and France it generally runs from 220 to 250 days. The year usually is ten or ten and one-half months in length, and classes are conducted five and one-half to six days per week.

[29] North Central Association, *op. cit.*, p. 22.
[30] Henry J. Otto, "Elementary Education, Organization and Administration," *Encyclopedia of Educational Research* (New York: The Macmillan Company, 1950), p. 369.
[31] U.S. Office of Education, "Statistical Summary of Education," *Biennial Survey of Education in the United States, 1954–56* (Washington: Government Printing Office, 1959), p. 44.

Trends Toward an Extended School Year. A small proportion of secondary schools have conducted summer programs for many years, but these have been designed primarily for students who needed to make up credit because of failure. Recently, however, there has been a rapidly growing interest on the part of laymen as well as professional educators in extending the school year to include a summer session for purposes of enriching the educational program and making greater use of the school plant.

The motives of various groups of laymen who have proposed an extension of the school year appear to be mixed. One group seems to be concerned chiefly with economies that might be effected through the use of school buildings the year around, not as a means of enriching the school program, but as a means of reducing school costs by housing more students in limited building facilities. Among other proposals of this group is a trimester plan under which each one-third of the student body would attend school for two 16-week terms. This would reduce the needed building space by approximately one-third. The plan undoubtedly would serve that purpose, but it would reduce the period of instruction for each student by at least two weeks and seriously limit educational opportunities for some students in certain types of activities. Furthermore, it would interfere with summer employment for students enrolled during the summer term and conflict with family vacation and travel opportunities. Because of these problems, the trimester is not likely to become common in American high schools.

Other laymen and educators are interested in promoting summer sessions because of the possibilities of enriching the educational program and better serving the needs of boys and girls. Although up-to-date, nation-wide figures on summer schools are not available, regional and small sample studies indicate a rapid gain since 1955. The Research Division of the National Education Association, in a survey of a sample of 302 urban school systems, found that 256, or 84.7 per cent, conducted summer schools in 1959. The range in length of terms was from four to ten weeks with a median of 7.3 weeks for secondary schools.[32]

Schools with summer sessions in over 3,500 North Central Association high schools in nineteen states increased from 15.1 per cent in 1955–56 to 29.4 per cent in 1959–60.[33] The NEA study reports that the dominant purpose of summer sessions in 1959 was enrichment.

As noted previously, the traditional summer school program has been conducted largely to permit students to make up credit lost through fail-

---

[32] National Education Association, Research Division, "Summer Schools = Opportunity," *Research Bulletin*, February, 1960, 38:23-24.

[33] From the summary statistical reports on file in the office of Gordon Cawelti, Executive Secretary, Commission on Secondary Schools, North Central Association of Colleges and Secondary Schools, Chicago, Illinois.

ure, illness, or some other circumstance that has hampered their regular progress. There is a need for this type of opportunity in most communities, but it should be a minor purpose of the program. The major intent should be to provide educational experiences for students which they need and desire and which supplement those of the regular school year. The types of experiences most frequently provided in secondary school summer programs are the following:

1. *Enrichment of the academic program,* including such offerings as writer's workshop, biological and geological field studies, advanced science and mathematics courses, and foreign languages.
2. *Supplementary personal-use courses,* such as homemaking, typewriting, industrial arts, and mechanical drawing for college preparatory students.
3. *Extended work experience* and vocational courses, including distributive education, diversified occupations, vocational agriculture projects, and building trades.
4. *Driver education,* to meet an important need and to relieve the overcrowded curriculum of the regular school year.
5. *Fine arts,* such as music camp, summer dramatics playhouse, and art workshop.
6. *Remedial and makeup classes* for students with deficiencies in skills or to meet the long-standing problem of students who need to make up courses failed.
7. *Acceleration,* so that a few mature students may earn additional credit during the summer in order to graduate in less than four years. Most schools discourage summer school attendance for this purpose, but in some individual cases it may be desirable. Permission to take summer work for purposes of acceleration should be based upon the recommendation of counselors and the student's parents.
8. *Recreational program,* to provide constructive leisure-time activities for children during the summer. Many schools conduct some type of summer recreational program, frequently in cooperation with the city recreational department. It may include a wide range of activities from playground games and swimming to little theater and camping.

About 64 per cent of the schools in the NEA study previously mentioned charged tuition for summer school, although in some states summer school tuition has been ruled illegal. Certainly there seems to be little justification for it other than expediency. The authors suggest that charging tuition is an unwise expedient in that it sets a precedent that could easily carry over to the regular school year and weaken the foundation of free public secondary education.

Organization of the School Year — The School Calendar

One of the most useful devices for teachers, patrons, and students during the school year is a published calendar of events. It facilitates long-range planning of course work and activities and encourages teachers and students to get together to coordinate various activities and events for the new school year. Although dates for all events cannot be determined before school opens, the dates for opening and closing, vacation periods, holidays, convention days, and traditional community affairs can be set and included on a tentative calendar.

Planning the calendar provides a good opportunity for a cooperative project by a committee of teachers and students working with the principal. Members of the staff who are responsible for areas in which numerous special events are scheduled during the year are likely to be the most valuable members of the committee and, in working together on the calendar, should be able to resolve serious conflicts in dates. In addition to the principal, the guidance director, director of student activities, director of athletics, head of the music department, head of the speech and dramatics department, student council adviser, and faculty chairman of assemblies should be included on the committee. A few members of the student council or other student leaders also should serve on it.

In small high schools the entire faculty might act as a committee to draw up the calendar. The most desirable time to prepare the calendar is late in the spring so that teachers and students may make plans in accordance with the opening of school in the fall. If it is impractical to set up the entire calendar in the spring, a workable compromise might be to compile the calendar for September, publish it in tentative form, and then make up the complete calendar after school opens. In most schools the calendar committee will have to make revisions from time to time.

The following items are generally included on the schedule calendar:

1. Dates of opening and closing the school year.
2. Schedule of events for the first week of school.
3. Schedule of events for the closing days of school, including commencement and senior class events.
4. Recesses for holidays, teacher conventions, and such traditional community affairs as may be considered by the board of education to be of sufficient importance.
5. Local staff meetings such as preschool conferences, workshops, system-wide faculty meetings, and regular faculty meetings.
6. Special student activities including
    a. Major social events.
    b. Athletic contests.
    c. Assemblies.
    d. Dramatic productions.
    e. Speech and forensic events.
    f. Music concerts and productions.
    g. Competitions such as scholarship exams, state meets, etc.
    h. Student council events, including elections.
7. Dates for examinations and testing programs.
8. Administrative procedures such as dates for reporting grades to par-

ents, parent conferences, due dates for teachers' reports to the principal, dates for administering supplies and equipment, student registration, American Education Week, and open-house observances.
9. Group guidance events, such as career days and special conferences.
10. Community-school events such as PTA meetings, adult education classes, community forums, and concerts.

Getting Under Way

A good opening week does not make a successful school year but it helps. If the opening days are well organized, materials are on hand, and classwork is started promptly, a desirable pattern is formed for the year ahead. The authors recognize that most veteran principals have developed appropriate procedures and schedules for their schools and that they are not especially concerned with this problem. The beginning principal, however, may find a brief checklist of opening events helpful. The following list is a composite of opening procedures and events scheduled in a number of different schools.

1. Distribute teacher's handbooks by mail about a week or ten days before the opening faculty meeting. A personalized cover letter should be included with the handbook.

2. Hold registration for new students who have moved into the district about one week before the opening date of the school year. Make announcements through the press and local radio stations.

3. Announce a date for the consideration of changes in student programs two or three days prior to the opening of school. Have adequate counselors available to confer with students on program changes.

4. Hold a preschool conference or faculty meeting immediately preceding the first day of school. One session should be set aside for the orientation of new teachers. Preschool conferences usually are scheduled for two or three days and, in addition to discussion meetings and the distribution of supplies, may include community tours, a social event such as a dinner meeting or picnic, and some time set aside for teachers to work on their own plans and materials. A growing number of schools conduct a preschool workshop for a week or ten days in which some curriculum planning is done along with committee work on special problems.

Although most of the problems of getting the school under way can be anticipated and adequate provisions made, it is not unusual to have a number of unexpected complications arise. Beginning principals may find some comfort in knowing that "first-day jitters" plague experienced administrators as well as the neophyte. Nevertheless, careful attention to the many details discussed in this chapter should assist the beginning principal considerably in facing his first major administrative test, namely, getting the school year launched smoothly and effectively.

ORGANIZATION AND DIRECTION OF THE PROGRAM

Questions and Group Projects

1. Examine ten or twelve schedules for high schools in your area and tabulate the information shown on them. How do they compare with the items listed by the authors?

2. For the schedules examined in the preceding exercise, what is the average length of periods, length of variable periods, time for opening and for closing, length of science laboratory and of vocational periods, and length of lunch periods? How do these compare with general practice?

3. What does research show about relative achievement in long and short periods? Is this adequate information upon which to base a decision regarding the length of periods for a local school?

4. Secure used preregistration cards from a nearby high school and data on the preparation and course preferences of teachers. Prepare a schedule for that school.

5. Review recent reports on team teaching and summarize the modifications made in the schedules of the schools using it. Compare these with recommendations made in J. Lloyd Trump's report, *Images of the Future*.

6. Summarize the advantages claimed for block-time courses and scheduling.

7. Visit a nearby high school in which the principal is using machine processing in building his schedule. Prepare a diagram of the process, step by step.

Selected References

Anderson, Lester W. "What Is the Most Effective Way of Arranging the Length and Use of the Class Period?" *The Bulletin* of the NASSP, April, 1959, 43:161–63.

Austin, David B., Will French, and J. Dan Hull. *American High School Administration*. New York: Holt, Rinehart, and Winston, Inc., rev. ed., 1962.

Catskill Area Project in Small School Design. *Guidebook on Flexible Scheduling*. Oneonta, N.Y.: The Project, 1959.

Conant, James B. *The American High School Today*. New York: McGraw-Hill Book Company, 1959.

Douglass, Harl R. *Modern Administration of Secondary Schools*. Boston: Ginn and Company, 1954.

Edmonson, J. B., Joseph Roemer, and Francis L. Bacon. *The Administration of the Modern Secondary School*. New York: The Macmillan Company, 1953.

Eveslage, D. C. "Scheduling Balanced Classes," *The Bulletin* of the NASSP, October, 1950, 34:47–60.

Faunce, Roland C. *Secondary School Administration.* New York: Harper & Brothers, 1955.

Glenn, Burvil H. "The Length of the School Day," *The Bulletin* of the NASSP, October, 1956, 40:63–66.

High School Registration and Class Organization. New York: International Business Machines Corporation, 1959.

Hooker, C. P., and C. M. Lindvall. "Student's Day Hasn't Changed Much or Enough Either," *Nation's Schools,* June, 1957, 59:48–49.

Ivok, Leo. *How to Prepare a Schedule for a Secondary School.* Harvard Graduate School of Education, Harvard Workshop Series, No. 5, Cambridge, Mass., 1944.

Langfitt, R. Emerson. *The Daily Schedule and High School Organization.* New York: The Macmillan Company, 1938.

McKenna, Bernard H. "Greater Learning in Smaller Classes," *National Education Association Journal,* October, 1957, 46:437–38.

Manley, C. Benton. "Secondary School Organization and Schedule Making for the Integrating Curriculum." Type B Project, Teachers College, Columbia University, 1941.

Matulis, Anthony S. "Foolproof Scheduling in Record Time," *School Management,* March, 1960, 4:69–74.

National Education Association, Research Division. "Summer Schools = Opportunity," *Research Bulletin,* February, 1960, 38:23–24.

North Central Association of Colleges and Secondary Schools. "Policies and Criteria for the Approval of Secondary Schools." Chicago: Commission on Secondary Schools, 1960.

"Progressing Toward Better Schools" (third report on Staff Utilization Studies), *The Bulletin* of the NASSP, January, 1960, Vol. 44.

Rinker, Floyd. "Subject Matter, Students, Teachers, Methods of Teaching and Space Are Redeployed in the Newton, Massachusetts, High School," *The Bulletin* of the NASSP, January, 1958, Vol. 42.

Royal McBee Corporation. *Keysort Notching and Sorting. . . .* Royal McBee Corporation, Data Processing Division, New York, N.Y.

Sturges, Allen W. "Techniques and Practices in Scheduling in Midwestern Secondary Schools," unpublished Ph.D. dissertation, State University of Iowa, 1959.

Templeton, F. L. "The Use of IBM Techniques in Program Making and Class Scheduling," *The Bulletin* of the NASSP, October, 1950, 34:15–22.

Tompkins, Ellsworth. "Desirable and Undesirable Policies for Extra Class Activities," *School Activities,* February, 1955, Vol. 26, No. 6.

Trump, J. Lloyd. *Images of the Future.* Urbana, Ill.: Commission on the Experimental Study of the Utilization of the Staff in the Secondary School, 1959.

U.S. Office of Education, "Statistical Summary of Education," *Biennial Survey of Education in the United States, 1954–56.* Washington: Government Printing Office, 1959.

Wrightstone, J. Wayne. "Class Organization for Instruction," *Research Bulletin* (National Education Association), October, 1957, Vol. 35, No. 3.

CHAPTER 7

Administration of the Guidance Program

John Jay Chapman once protested, "Is the education of the young the whole of life? I hate the young — I'm worn out with them. They absorb you and suck you dry and are vampires and selfish brutes at best. Give me some good old rum-soaked clubmen who *can't* be improved — and let me play checkers with them and look out of the club window and think about what I'll have for dinner."[1]

It is understandable that at times a teacher may grow weary of trying to be tutor, parent, and confidant to a varied assortment of adolescents. It is also understandable that, when guidance people insist that teachers must play a *key* role in guidance, teachers protest that they are already attempting to do so much they cannot do anything very well.

Although the education of the young may not be the whole of life, it is one of the chief means of perpetuating our democracy, and that makes teaching as important as any job in America, and more important than most. Consequently, most career teachers are more than willing to explore and master new procedures which show promise for improving the education of the young.

Teaching at the college level is directed largely to the intellectual development of students. But at the elementary and secondary levels teaching must be concerned with the personal and social development of children as well as with their intellectual growth. Since guidance is primarily oriented to helping pupils become self-sufficient in making choices and

---

[1] As quoted by Mark Van Doren in *Liberal Education* (New York: Henry Holt and Company, 1943), p. 16.

adjustments, classroom teaching and guidance complement each other and are mutually dependent.

In the early years of the guidance movement many teachers were disposed to agree with the old cliché, "Guidance is nothing more than good teaching." They believed it, in part, because the pioneer exponents of guidance were preoccupied with its vocational aspects and rather vague in their attempts to define its personal-social and educational functions. They tended to be evangelistic in their approach and engaged in sermonizing on the importance of knowing children, individualizing instruction, and dealing with causes of maladjustment. Good teachers recognized the importance of these things, were trying to do something about them, and rather resented the implication that they were being remiss. At the same time, guidance people were not convincing in their explanations of how guidance services could be of substantial help to teachers in working with progressively larger and more diverse groups of students.

Since the 1940's, popular views of guidance have changed rapidly — perhaps too rapidly. In less than twenty years the attitude of educators and parents toward guidance has changed from rather superficial skepticism to equally superficial acclaim. In 1958 Congress passed the National Defense Education Act, which included an appropriation of several millions of dollars to stimulate and strengthen guidance services in the schools. And in 1959 Conant recommended that every high school employ one full-time counselor for every 250–300 students.[2] The guidance movement had advanced in the period immediately following World War II, but with these assists, it literally mushroomed. In one year, from September, 1958, to September, 1959, the number of counselors employed in the nation's schools increased 29.6 per cent.[3]

But guidance is not a panacea; it is simply one of several basic educational services. Along with classroom instruction and extraclass activities, it is an integral part of the curriculum. In the day-by-day work of teachers and counselors with students, it is difficult to determine where classroom and extraclass experiences end and guidance begins. Each blends into the other in an effective and balanced educational program.

Definition and Point of View

Although classroom instruction, extraclass activities, and guidance are closely related, each has special functions. Smith defines guidance as follows: "The guidance process consists of a group of services to indi-

---

[2] James B. Conant, *The American High School Today* (New York: McGraw-Hill Book Company, 1959), p. 44.
[3] Kenneth B. Hoyt, "Research Evidence of the Effectiveness of Guidance in Secondary Schools," unpublished paper, State University of Iowa, 1959.

viduals to assist them in securing the knowledge and skills needed in making adequate choices, plans, and interpretations essential to satisfactory adjustment to a variety of areas."[4] Collectively, guidance activities amount to something distinguishable from classroom teaching, although good classroom teaching makes frequent use of guidance services. On the other hand, guidance involves special procedures which classroom teachers find difficult to employ without the know-how and assistance of trained guidance personnel.

The special functions of the guidance program have been described by Hatch and Stefflre as follows:

1. *Inventory service* — the primary appraisal program of the school, with emphasis on the collection of data that accentuate the uniqueness of the individual.
2. *Information service* — which consists of three major areas and has been conceived as a way of eliminating omissions and increasing the pertinency of the data to each individual. The three parts are *occupational, educational, and personal-social.*
3. *Counseling service* — a process in which the pupil is approached on an individual basis by means of interviews and other techniques.
4. *Placement service* — the continuing adjustment service to pupils. . . . It assists them in such post-school activities as selection of an appropriate occupation, educational institution, and part-time employment.
5. *Follow-up service* — through a continuing follow-up of students, the educator learns of their problems, and failures, and . . . obtains their suggestions for improvement.[5]

It is true that some aspects of these services have been provided in schools without an organized guidance program or trained personnel, but usually such efforts have been too incidental to be effective.

Need for Guidance Services

Research shows that youth believe the school should provide more and better guidance. Remmers reported in a study of 2,000 American teen-agers that "In planning their education as in making their choice of a job, 60 per cent said that they would like more help from teachers and school authorities than they are now getting."[6] Romine made a study of youth

---

[4] Glenn E. Smith, *Principles and Practices of the Guidance Program* (New York: The Macmillan Company, 1951), p. 5.
[5] Raymond N. Hatch and Buford Stefflre, *Administration of Guidance: Organization, Supervision, Evaluation* (Englewood Cliffs, N.J.: Prentice-Hall, Inc., 1958), p. 25. By permission.
[6] H. H. Remmers and D. H. Remmler, *The American Teenager* (Indianapolis: The Bobbs-Merrill Company, 1957), p. 121.

TABLE 17

Comparison of Distributions of Intelligence Test Results for Certain Secondary School Populations from 1919 to 1960

Year	1919	1932	Reported in 1960	1958	1958
Study	Terman	National Survey of Secondary Education	World Book Company	Carroll County Iowa	Omaha Nebraska
Number	107	2,906	13,049	165	568
Test	Stanford-Binet	Otis-Pressey	Terman-McNemar	California Mental Maturity	Terman-McNemar
Range	79–136	Not reported	50–59 to 150–159	72–136	53–150
Median	105	101	102	106	113
Q_1	Not reported	92	92.5	94	101.7
Q_3	Not reported	110	114	113	123.9
Grade	Ninth	Tenth	Tenth	Tenth	Tenth

interests as reported by 1,816 pupils in 37 Colorado high schools.[7] The areas of highest interest were how to study and do better in school; how to plan for future education; how to act — manners and etiquette for business; worries, feelings of inferiority and self-consciousness; how to find a job and how to apply for a job; how to discover personal interests and abilities; training for a job, where to get it and the cost; and deciding what occupational field to enter. Each of these is a problem with which guidance is directly concerned.

Youth want more and better guidance services, and changes taking place in our society and our schools support the need for such services.

Range in Student Abilities

A comparison of data from different intelligence tests administered to different populations at different times has severe limitations, but it provides a rough estimate of trends in the level of scholastic aptitude of the populations being studied. Table 17 presents data from five studies in which intelligence tests were administered to five high school populations over a period of forty years. The Omaha Central High School data have been included to show the great range in abilities in a large public secondary school which is predominantly a college preparatory school.[8] Al-

---

[7] Stephen Romine, "Youth Interests and the Educational Program of Secondary Schools," Bureau of High School Counseling and Accreditation, University of Colorado, 1951, p. 3–8.

[8] Omaha Public Schools, "Central High School," mimeographed bulletin from the office of the curriculum director, 1959.

though 72 per cent of the 1958 graduates of this school entered college, the range in IQ scores was from 53 to 150. The National Survey of 1932[9] and the Mitchel and Lennon study compiled in the late 1950's[10] show very little difference in the norms for contemporary high school students and for students enrolled thirty to forty years ago. However, the range in IQ's from 50 to 159, reported in the latter study, is considerably greater than the range of 79 to 136 reported by Terman in 1919.[11] Unfortunately, the range is not reported in the 1932 National Survey of Secondary Education. The Carroll County, Iowa,[12] data were obtained from four small rural high schools in a prosperous agricultural area. Each of these schools enrolled about 200 pupils and about 33 per cent of the graduates entered college over an eight-year period. Even for this rather homogeneous economic and social population there was a spread of sixty-four points in the IQ scores for tenth-grade students.

Although the median intelligence of the student population in secondary schools has not changed substantially between 1919 and 1960, the range has increased and the percentage of extremely low-ability students has increased. When it is considered that students also vary in their interests, special talents, and attitudes, the evidence points strongly to the need for more and better guidance services. Classroom teachers need more information than they have time to secure through their own efforts in order to adapt instruction to the needs of individual pupils, and students who vary widely in abilities and interests need the aid of counselors who know them and who are well informed about educational and vocational opportunities.

Expansion and Specialization in the Curriculum

As schools increase in size, they offer more courses and more specialized curriculum patterns. More specialized curriculum patterns raise the number of options available to students and the number of important decisions that they must make while in school.

As noted in Chapter 3, high school course offerings increased from about 60 in 1900 to over 600 in 1948. The number of elective courses tends to go up in direct proportion to the size of the school, and schools are growing larger in most sections of the nation. The mean enrollment

[9] National Survey of Secondary Education, *The Secondary School Population,* Bulletin 1932, No. 17, Monograph No. 4, U.S. Office of Education (Washington: Government Printing Office, 1933), p. 21.

[10] J. G. Umstattd and Robert D. Thornton, "Secondary Education — Student Population," *Encyclopedia of Educational Research* (New York: The Macmillan Company, 1960), p. 1280. (Based on a study by Blyth C. Mitchel and Roger T. Lennon, World Book Company.)

[11] L. M. Terman, *The Intelligence of School Children* (Boston: Houghton Mifflin Company, 1919), pp. 80–81.

[12] Carroll County, Iowa, "Curriculum Study," mimeographed report by L. A. Van Dyke, State University of Iowa, 1958.

in public secondary schools (Grades 9–12) increased from around 180 in 1930 to almost 350 in 1960.[13]

Consequently, students need counseling in planning a curriculum program that is appropriate for their talents and interests, and faculties need guidance services in assigning students to appropriate sequences, ability groups, and special courses.

Changing Social Environment

In 1930 one-fourth of the population of the United States lived on farms; in 1960 only one-tenth lived on farms. People are moving to the cities and the suburbs. In many families both parents must work to pay off the mortgage and to meet the payments on cars, boats, and household appliances and this leaves children without adequate parental supervision. Youth on the farm want to know whether they should stay on the farm or look for a job in the city. Small-town young people are asking "Is it better to move to a big city or stay in my home town?" "Should you stay where you are known or should you get out and make new friends?" "If a couple moves to a city suburb, will both the husband and wife have to work to make ends meet?"

High school students also wonder about the cold war and whether another war is inevitable. Youth inventory returns often include the statement "I'm worried about the next war." And boys ask, "Should I go to college or get my military service out of the way first?" Girls ask, "Should we get married before my fiancé goes into the service?"

Students are concerned, and more than a little confused, about other equally fundamental changes in our rapidly moving social scene. They ask about integration and mixed marriages, about moral values and the ethics of business and politics, about economic conditions, and about family life and rearing children.

Life was simpler and the future more predictable before automation, jet planes, atomic bombs, missiles, compulsory military service, big business, big government, and international politicking. No one has the answers to the many questions raised by these developments, and certainly it is not a function of guidance to attempt to supply the answers. But it is a duty of guidance to assist youth to identify alternatives, to get information, and to learn more about themselves for purposes of making satisfactory adjustments.

Changing Occupational Scene

A large number of the questions students ask on open-ended questionnaires have to do with preparing for, and getting, a job. It is common knowledge that the number of jobs and the nature of jobs have undergone extensive changes during the last thirty or forty years. Automation in

[13] U.S. Office of Education, *Progress of Public Education in the United States of America, 1959–60* (Washington: Government Printing Office, 1960), pp. 10 and 67.

business and industry, and mechanization in agriculture have become realities. The tasks that people are called on to perform to keep our economy going are becoming more complex and more demanding each year.

The Rockefeller Report on Education sums it up this way: "As a result, we are experiencing a great variety of shortages of human resources in fields requiring a high competence and extended training."[14] The actual shift in the percentage of workers in types of occupations from 1900 to 1950, together with predictions to 1975, are shown in Table 18.

TABLE 18
Trends in Occupational Distribution, 1900 to 1975

Occupation	1900	1950	1965	1975
White-collar workers	17.6%	36.6%	42.5%	46.6%
Professional, technical, and kindred workers	4.3	8.6	11.3	14.0
Managers, officials, proprietors	5.8	8.7	10.3	10.8
Clerical workers	3.0	12.3	14.4	14.4
Sales workers	4.5	7.0	6.5	7.4
Manual and service workers	44.9	51.6	49.9	48.0
Craftsmen, foremen	10.5	14.1	13.5	13.7
Operatives	12.8	20.4	19.6	17.5
Industrial laborers	12.5	6.6	5.0	4.4
Service workers	9.0	10.5	11.8	12.4
Farm workers	37.5	11.8	7.6	5.3
Farmers and managers	19.9	7.4	7.6	5.3
Farm laborers	17.7	4.4	7.6	5.3

Source: David L. Kaplan and M. Claire Casey, *Occupational Trends in the United States, 1900–1950*, Working Paper No. 5, as quoted in National Education Association, Research Division, "Occupational Trends," *Research Bulletin*, February, 1959, 37:24.

Every sign in our economy points to a speeding up rather than a slowing down in the growth of jobs requiring specialized training at a higher level. Someone in the school needs to know what is going on in the world of work; youth need information on changing job opportunities, the type of training needed, where they can get it, and what it costs. They need to know as much as possible about themselves, their interests, talents, and temperaments for different types of occupations. Securing this information and making it readily available to students are additional tasks of guidance.

[14] The Rockefeller Report on Education, *The Pursuit of Excellence — Education and the Future of America* (Garden City, N.Y.: Doubleday and Company, 1958), p. 7.

Growing Percentage of Youth Attending Higher Institutions

The gains in types of occupations demanding more specialized training have resulted in a steady increase in the percentage of high school graduates going to college and to technical institutes. Twenty-three per cent of all high school graduates entered college in 1935, compared to 35 per cent in 1958. When the number entering technical schools is included, about 45 per cent of today's high school graduates are continuing their formal education beyond the secondary level.

Unfortunately, many graduates are going to college who probably should not, many are not going who should, and many are going to the wrong institutions. Wolfle reports that only 43 per cent of the top fifth of all high school graduates go to college and only 59 per cent of the top 1 per cent actually graduate from college. On the other hand, 17 per cent of the lowest one-fifth enroll in college.[15] A score of 110 on the American Council on Education Psychological Examination is recommended by the Commission on Financing Higher Education as a minimum for college matriculation, but Corcoran and Keller report that only 40 per cent of the Minnesota high school graduates going to college scored that high and probably the same would hold true for most other states.[16]

According to a United States Office of Education study in 1956, 43 per cent of the students entering college do not go beyond the second year and 57 per cent do not graduate from the institution they enter.[17] However, some of these transfer and later graduate from another institution. How many graduates select the wrong type of institution for them is not known, but the high attrition rate during the first two years of college is a good clue that the number is large. Certainly, these statistics suggest that a better job of counseling needs to be done with students in high school who are considering college.

The Dropout Problem

Guidance must be concerned not only with potential graduates and those going to college but also with youth who leave high school before graduation. About 42 per cent of the children who enter the fifth grade in the United States drop out of school before high school graduation, and about one-third who enter the ninth grade leave school early.[18] These

[15] Dael Wolfle, *America's Resources of Specialized Talent* (New York: Harper & Brothers, 1954).

[16] Mary Corcoran and R. J. Keller, *College Attendance of Minnesota High School Seniors* (Minneapolis: Bureau of Institutional Research, University of Minnesota, 1957).

[17] Robert E. Iffert, "Drop-Outs: Nature and Causes, Effects on Student, Family, and Society," *Current Issues in Higher Education* (Washington: National Education Association, 1956), pp. 94–102.

[18] U.S. Office of Education, *op. cit.*, p. 13.

are national averages and vary considerably from state to state and from school to school.

Because youth who do not graduate from high school find it difficult to get employment except in unskilled jobs, because the rate of delinquency is much higher among dropouts, and because our democracy needs citizens who possess the tools of learning and a common background of information, the present high rate of dropouts represents a misfortune for the individual and for the nation. It is tragic that around 17 per cent of the students with IQ's of 120 or above withdraw.[19] "The drop-out problem is extremely complex, involving personal characteristics of students as well as characteristics of the school, the home, and the community. A cluster of forces acts to influence an individual student to persist in, or to withdraw from, high school."[20] Personal characteristics such as low ability, poor grades, poor home background, and failure to get along with other students are positively related to withdrawal from school. Since it is possible to identify a high proportion of potential dropouts when they enter high school, a good guidance and counseling program is the first requirement in the efforts of a school to retain a higher percentage of its entering students. At least, the school should do everything possible to encourage students to continue in school as long as they can benefit from its program.

Adolescent Developmental Tasks

Adolescence is a period of normal growth and development. Most adolescents, however, face problems in adjusting to physiological changes and to adult social standards that sometimes prove extremely difficult for them as individuals. Several statements of such problems have been drafted, but the developmental tasks identified by Havighurst and reported in Chapter 3 have gained wide acceptance among counselors and teachers.[21]

Some of these overlap with certain adjustment problems discussed earlier; the needs of students cannot be neatly categorized. Neither can they be regarded as the special responsibilities of any one area or group of professional workers in the school. However, someone in the school needs to be able and willing to assist individual students in identifying and making adequate adjustments to these tasks — especially those youngsters whose parents do not have the time, background, or disposition to help them. Alert and sympathetic classroom teachers may help some of them,

---

[19] L. A. Van Dyke and K. B. Hoyt, *The Drop-Out Problem in Iowa High Schools*, State University of Iowa and Iowa State Department of Public Instruction, 1958, p. 84.

[20] *Ibid.*, p. 81.

[21] Robert J. Havighurst, *Developmental Tasks and Education* (New York: Longmans, Green and Company, 1950), pp. 30–63.

The Effectiveness of Guidance

Some teachers and parents are dubious about the value of guidance and, before endorsing proposals to add new personnel and services, may demand some supporting evidence. Can guidance do what it claims to do? What does research show? The principal will need to be prepared to answer these questions if he hopes to make a case for guidance in his school. Guidance operates under the same limitations as any other aspect of the educative process when it comes to demonstrating cause-and-effect relationships. Most of the outcomes sought in education are exceedingly difficult to measure, as are relationships in other areas of human behavior.

Automobile manufacturers use the most scientific techniques available to predict public acceptance of a new model, but sometimes they miss. Public opinion pollsters usually come within a few percentage points in predicting elections, but a sudden increase in unemployment may make their predictions go far astray. Methods of experimentation and measuring instruments in education have been improved in recent years, and a fairly extensive number of experimental studies are now available which demonstrate what *did* happen under certain conditions even though they may have shortcomings in predicting what *will* happen.

The experimental evidence on the effectiveness of guidance is becoming more impressive each year. The following studies on the relationships of guidance and counseling to scholastic achievement, realistic educational and occupational choices, personal adjustment, and job success and satisfaction are a part of the growing body of information on the values of guidance.

Scholastic Achievement

Serene studied the extent of agreement between scholastic achievement and intelligence as an outgrowth of counseling in the Ambridge (Pennsylvania) Senior High School.[22] The experimental group was the eleventh grade and the control groups were the tenth and twelfth grades. Counselors interviewed the experimental group with respect to their abilities, study techniques, actual achievement, and reasons for higher achievement. The control groups were not counseled on these problems. At the end of the school year, school marks and intelligence test scores were correlated for members of the three groups and significant differences were found in favor of the experimental group.

[22] Michael Serene, "An Experiment in Motivational Counseling," *Personnel and Guidance Journal,* February, 1953, 31:319–24.

TABLE 19
Summary of a Five-Year Follow-Up Study on Occupational Adjustment

Factor	Experimental Group	Control Group	Difference of Means
1. Mean annual earnings	$3,105	$2,614	$491
2. Mean job satisfaction score (Hoppock Blank)	22.4	19.0	3.4
3. Per cent liking job	87%	69%	18%
4. Per cent who thought seriously of changing jobs	26%	62%	−36%
5. Per cent satisfied with job	77%	45%	32%
6. Would choose present job again	55%	17%	38%
7. Would not change job	45%	17%	28%
8. Said they got more pleasure from jobs than from leisure	61%	21%	40%

Stasek conducted a study with high school sophomores and seniors in which he identified underachievers and counseled a random sample of these students in each class.[23] He then compared their improvement in grade-point average with that of a control group of underachievers from the same classes. The results showed improvement in favor of the experimental group in terms of the number of students making gains in grade-point average and in the degree of improvement in grade-point.

Educational and Vocational Choices

Another pertinent question is whether counseling aids students in making realistic educational and vocational choices. Several studies indicate that it can do so. A study conducted by Hedge and Hutson with a group of 422 high school juniors and 79 seniors showed a reduction in the number of students with college aspirations, especially among those with IQ's of less than 100.[24] A program of vocational lessons and voluntary interviews resulted in a higher median IQ for the group planning to go to college at the end of the experimental period and also showed an increase in the average class range for this group.

Cuony and Hoppock conducted a one-year and a five-year follow-up study of thirty-five high school graduates who had completed a vocational guidance course.[25] The control group consisted of thirty-five graduates who had not taken the course. Both groups had been counseled, but the members of the experimental group had requested more counseling

---

[23] Erwin D. Stasek, "The Effects of Specialized Educational Counseling with Selected Groups of Underachievers at the Secondary School Level," unpublished Ph.D. dissertation, Northwestern University, 1955.

[24] J. W. Hedge and P. W. Hutson, "A Technique for Evaluating Guidance Activities," *School Review*, June, 1931, 39:508–19.

[25] E. R. Cuony and R. Hoppock, "Job Course Pays Off," *Personnel and Guidance Journal*, March, 1957, 32:116–17.

than the control group. The results for the five-year follow-up are given in Table 19. This study shows not only higher earnings for the group that had taken the occupations course but also a considerably higher degree of job satisfaction.

Rothney, in an eight-year study of high school graduates after they had been out of school two and one-half years and again after they had been out five years, also found that his experimental subjects were getting along better on the job.[26] The five-year group had clear advantages with respect to the proportion owning their own business, having better jobs, getting promotions faster than usual, and getting promotions on schedule. Fewer of the experimental group remained at the same job level, were demoted, or were dismissed.

Personal and Social Adjustment

Cantoni, in a ten-year follow-up study of counseled and noncounseled high school graduates, found that the experimental group had improved while the control group had regressed on scores made on the Bell Adjustment Inventory.[27]

Caplan held small group sessions with thirty-four junior high school boys who were discipline problems.[28] He used individual and multiple counseling procedures over a ten-week period and made a comparison with a similar group of boys who did not have counseling. There were significant increases in correlations between "self" and "ideal self" ratings and decreases in "poor citizenship" grades for the experimental group. The control group showed no improvement on these measures.

Additional studies support the results reported in the preceding summaries. On the other hand, some studies show no significant differences between counseled and uncounseled groups of students. But the studies cited present evidence that guidance services and personnel *can* accomplish the purposes that they are intended to accomplish.

Organizing the Guidance Program

Davis reported in 1953 that California secondary school principals spent an average of about 14 per cent of their time organizing, administering, and improving the guidance program.[29] And in 1958 McAbee reported

[26] J. W. M. Rothney, *Guidance Practices and Results* (New York: Harper & Brothers, 1958).

[27] L. J. Cantoni, "Reunion Party: An Unorthodox and Enjoyable Follow-Up of the Subjects of a 1939–43 Guidance Experiment," *Clearing House*, April, 1955, 29:466–69.

[28] Stanley Caplan, "The Effect of Group Counseling on Junior High School Boys' Concept of Themselves in School," *Journal of Counseling Psychology*, Summer, 1957, 4:124–26.

[29] H. Curtis Davis, "Where Does the Time Go?" *California Journal of Secondary Education*, October, 1953, 28:349.

that Oregon principals devoted 8.4 per cent of their time to pupil personnel work.[30] Guidance of some type long has been an important part of the principal's job and it continues to rank as one of his top three or four professional duties as measured by the amount of time put into it.

In any school large enough to have a *bona fide* principal, the nature and effectiveness of the guidance program will depend largely on his leadership. In very small schools the superintendent is actually the principal and is primarily responsible for organizing and administering guidance services. In large schools there may be a director of guidance for the school system, but the program in each secondary school building depends to a great extent on the leadership and interest of the principal. In schools of all sizes, the principal not only must be a moving force but usually must spend considerable time in actual counseling.

Regardless of the number of specialized guidance people on his staff, the principal needs to maintain a face-to-face relationship with students in order to keep in touch with their points of view and problems. If he loses his personal associations with students, he loses much of the satisfaction in his job. The principal of a large high school cannot hope to confer with all students, but he certainly should be able to devote some of his time to direct student relations.

To be most successful, the guidance program must be well coordinated with the classroom and extraclass functions of the school. Teachers, counselors, and administrators must work together closely in their efforts to meet the needs of individual students. There is small virtue in having counselors confer with students on selecting courses in relation to their abilities if principals and teachers make little effort to provide for individual differences through the organization of the curriculum and through classroom instruction.

If the guidance program is to receive support and cooperation from the faculty, teacher loads must be adjusted to compensate for the additional time demanded for guidance. Without teacher support, guidance is in trouble, since it depends to a great extent upon the cooperation of teachers in securing information about individual pupils, in dealing with students in the classroom, in counseling, and in conducting case conferences. If guidance functions are imposed on overloaded teachers without relief somewhere, the program is certain to encounter serious faculty opposition. And teacher attitudes usually are reflected in student attitudes.

The principal must assume much of the responsibility for getting the necessary funds for guidance personnel, supplies, and equipment. Ordinarily he prepares the budget requests for his school, and it is up to him to present the case for guidance at budget time. If he hopes to receive adequate support, he must be thoroughly familiar with the nature and

[30] Harold V. McAbee, "Time for the Job," *The Bulletin* of the NASSP, March, 1958, 42:41.

potential of guidance services. As noted earlier, these include (1) individual student inventory, (2) information, (3) counseling, (4) placement, and (5) follow-up services. The following sections deal briefly with each of these areas and with organizational patterns for guidance.

Organization and Personnel

The type of guidance organization most appropriate for a school will depend upon such local factors as size, financial ability, administrative and supervisory personnel, teacher and community relations, and institutional objectives. Figures 12 and 13 show suggested organizations for small and medium-size school systems. The organizational outline for the guidance program at San Bernardino, California, illustrates the type of structure being employed in some large city systems with several secondary schools. Organizations for large school systems usually have evolved as the system has grown and vary considerably depending on local needs and personnel. Consequently, little purpose would be served by charting one of these unique local organizations.

FIGURE 12

Guidance Organization for a Small School System
(200 to 300 pupils in the high school)

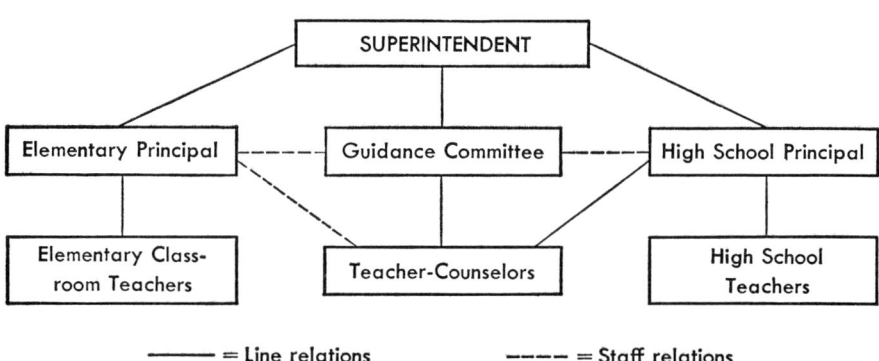

In the organization shown in Figure 12, the superintendent serves as the general coordinator and the high school principal as the direct administrative head of the program in his school. The counselors are part-time teacher-counselors on the high school staff and are responsible directly to the high school principal and through him to the superintendent. The guidance committee may well include the elementary and high school principals, the counselors, and some elementary and high school teachers. Although counselors are not members of the elementary school staff, they should advise with elementary teachers and the principal in securing articulation between the elementary and secondary school programs. They are also responsible for coordinating the guidance program in the elementary school. Counselors should do the major share of counseling in the high school and, with the principal, should plan and coordinate group guidance activities. Their professional status and salary should be the same as that of the classroom teachers. Counselors are co-workers with teachers and not administrative superiors.

FIGURE 13

Guidance Organization in a Medium-Sized School System
(500 to 1,000 students in the senior high school)

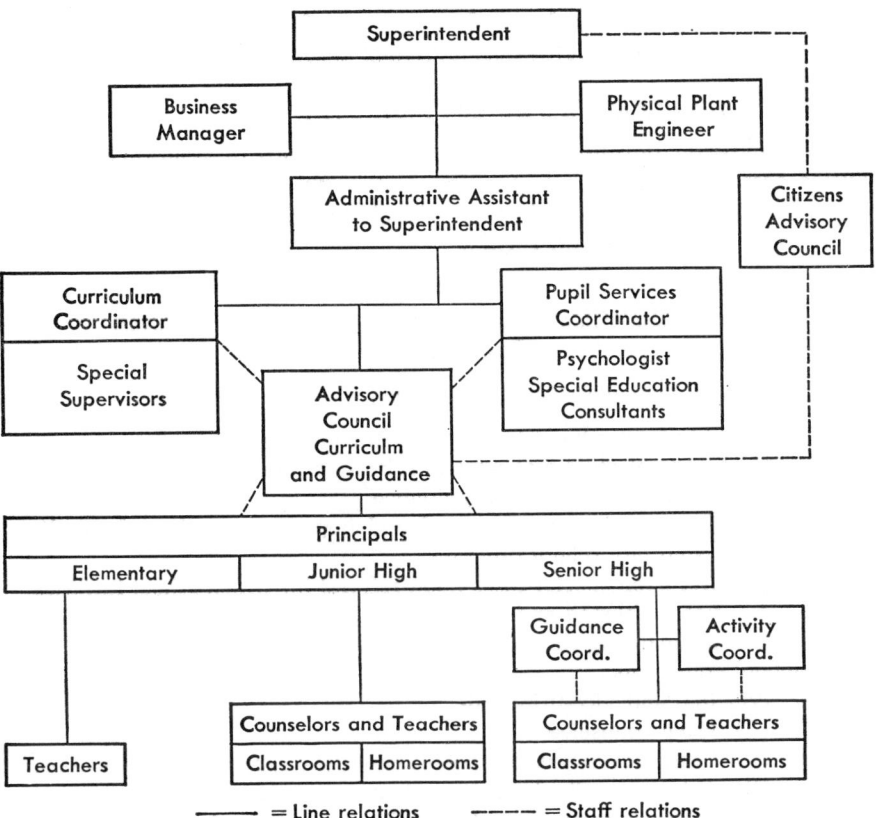

In a medium-size school system a coordinator of pupil services is needed and should be responsible for directing guidance services in all schools as well as for coordinating other pupil personnel services. As in the case of small schools, the counselors in medium-size school systems should have the same professional status as classroom teachers. Their line responsibility should be to their respective principals, but they also should have a line responsibility through the principals to the coordinator of pupil personnel services. The advisory committee should serve principally in a consultative capacity but should also coordinate the instructional and pupil personnel programs and be an agency for two-way communication between teachers and administrators.

Since the senior high school may have several teacher-counselors, a full-time guidance person may be needed to act as coordinator. He should be responsible to the coordinator of pupil personnel services and should work directly with teachers and teacher-counselors in planning and conducting guidance services. The coordinator of pupil personnel services, in addition to coordinating all guidance services in the system, sometimes is expected to direct the program of special education for the school system and supervise psychological services.

Guidance Organization in a Large School System

The following outline describes personnel, lines of relationships, and duties associated with each position in the guidance organization for a city of about 200,000 population.[31] Each teacher-counselor is assigned about 100 counselees in this system.

Duties and Relationships of the Personnel Involved in Guidance Services
San Bernardino, California, Public Schools

1. Consultants from administrative departments
    a. Supervisor of child welfare and school psychologists
    b. Supervisor of research and guidance
        (1) Give services as requested and improve operation of coordinated city school program.
        (2) Act upon special cases upon referral for which school facilities not developed or inadequate and work with school counselors in following through on case work.
2. School counselors
    a. Principal and vice-principals
        (1) Have counselee load.
        (2) Used for referrals on specific cases, such as disciplinary actions.
        (3) Act as consultants to counselors.
        (4) In administrative meetings with counselors set up policies and procedures for current operations.
    b. Head counselor
        (1) Coordinates work of counseling staff.
        (2) Sets up tentative schedules for specific counseling and guidance functions, such as testing.
        (3) Disseminates data compiled from various sources.

[31] San Bernardino Public Schools, *Counselors Handbook*, 1950, pp. 11–12.

c. Counselors
  (1) Counselees for each one based on scholastic and vocational interests.
    (a) Academic
    (b) Vocational
    (c) Business education
    (d) Remedial
    (e) General
    (f) Mental retardation
    (g) Special problems
  (2) Scholarship counselor for gathering and distributing pertinent information to all students who qualify for consideration.
  (3) Attendance counselor for specific problems related to this area.
3. Relationships
  a. By referral, all cases may cut across lines and several counselors may give guidance as coordinated unit.
  b. By weekly conferences, problems and action may be determined for individual and/or group cases.
  c. Volunteers among all referred to herein may assume certain temporary duties to alleviate duplication and to make consistent plans.

Guidance Services

Inventory Services

Inventory or appraisal procedures in guidance involve collecting, recording, and using information which will be helpful to the faculty in understanding students and to students in understanding themselves. McDaniel states that the following types of data should be included in an adequate set of student inventory records: (1) personal (identification), (2) home and community, (3) scholarship, (4) test scores and ratings, (5) school attendance, (6) health, (7) employment, (8) activity records, (9) anecdotal records, (10) interview notes, and (11) follow-up records.[32]

The basic student record is the *cumulative* card or folder. Most secondary school administrators use a printed folder but a few use a single printed card in a visible index file. Examples of these are shown in Chapter 16. Although cumulative forms for administrative purposes include much of the same data employed in counseling, another set of cumulative records for each student is needed for the day-by-day use of counselors and teachers. The second set need not be recorded on a printed form but may be filed in plain Manila folders, as inserts.

Although the administrative and guidance cumulative records dupli-

[32] Henry B. McDaniel, with G. A. Shaftel, *Guidance in the Modern School* (New York: The Dryden Press, 1956), pp. 187–89.

cate each other to a considerable extent, having a set in the guidance office makes these records available *when* they are needed and *where* they will be most used. The categories of information that appear to be most useful are those previously cited from McDaniel's list. The basic criterion for determining what pupil information should be collected and filed is its *usefulness* to the educational program. If certain items are not being used, there is no point in spending time and money to collect and record them.[33]

The business of housing, recording, and transferring pupil inventory records usually calls for some administrative resourcefulness. The main housing requirements are safety, confidentialness, convenience, and space. All records worth collecting in the first place should be protected against loss by fire, theft, or vandalism. The *administrative* records should be located in the principal's office in fireproof filing cabinets or a vault. *Counseling* records should be housed in the counselor's office or a special guidance record room in fireproof cabinets.

There are certain legal aspects related to student records with which the principal and his staff should be familiar. In general, confidential pupil information for use by school faculties has been held by the courts to be conditional privileged communication. As long as the staff has treated it as confidential information, members have not been held liable for defamation of character, even though the information was derogatory. But if teachers engage in malicious or careless gossip, they may be held liable. Law enforcement officials have the power to subpoena school records. Administrators and counselors need to consider carefully the type of derogatory information they record about students, since their confidential relationships with counselees may suffer irreparable damage if such information should be subpoenaed by outside agencies.

Some of the *inserts* for the guidance folders may be recorded on mimeographed or printed forms. A number of schools print insert forms on cards of different colors for ease in identification. Other inserts may be detached from tests, inventories, and rating scales. Inserts recommended by various writers as most useful are (1) student's autobiography (2) interview records, (3) anecdotal records, (4) student data blanks, (5) student's three- or four-year curriculum plans, (6) teacher ratings of students, (7) student's self-rating, (8) sociometric charts, (9) placement and follow-up records, (10) health records, and (11) test and inventory records.

Standardized test records are an essential part of the student's cumulative inventory. The types of tests to be administered in a local school will depend on the disposition of the faculty to make use of them. It

---

[33] Some of the states with well-designed cumulative record forms are Nebraska, Minnesota, Missouri, Oregon, California, and Florida.

is a waste of time and money to administer tests if teachers and counselors do not employ the results in working with students and in planning the instructional program. However, a minimum testing program in a secondary school for effective counseling should include (1) intelligence or mental abilities tests, (2) standardized achievement and reading tests, (3) personality inventory, (4) special subject and vocational aptitude tests, and (5) vocational preference inventory.

Anecdotal records also may be a valuable part of the student inventory even though some teachers object to spending time in preparing them. However, these reports usually prove extremely useful in counseling and in adapting instruction to individual student needs. Their value will depend largely upon the objectivity of teachers in reporting and upon their ability to select significant examples of a student's behavior. Anecdotal reports are of sufficient potential worth to justify holding a series of in-service conferences on their use and preparation.

The blanks employed for anecdotal reports may be quite simple. They should provide spaces for a brief description of an incident, comments by the teacher, and his recommendations for follow-up. Anecdotal reports should be made for all students, not merely for those who are disciplinary and/or maladjusted cases.

Information Service

A second basic guidance service is that of acquainting students with information about occupations, educational opportunities, and materials on personal-social problems. There appears to be some difference of opinion among administrators and guidance people over who should provide such information and how it should be done, but its importance to the guidance program is rarely disputed. Some school personnel hold that guidance information should be provided by teachers as a part of classroom instruction; others maintain that it should be given by counselors through the specialized guidance program. The authors subscribe to the view that the provision of such information is a function of all branches of the educational program and that all faculty personnel have an important part to play. Teachers may do much in regular courses and in activities, and counselors may contribute through group conferences and personal interviews. Also the guidance collection in the library may be of substantial help.

The first task is to build a good collection of informational materials. Since this requires financial support, administrators will need to enlist the aid of counselors and librarians in organizing and presenting a well-documented budget request to the board. Many good free or inexpensive materials are available from educational institutions, government agencies, and industrial concerns. Probably these should be secured first and then supplemented with more expensive reference books, periodicals, and visual aids. Excellent paperback units and booklets are available from commercial publishers.

The organization and housing of the collection should be planned to encourage extensive use. The books and periodicals may be located to advantage in a special section of the central library or in an adjacent room. The bulletins and flat file materials should be placed in convenient cabinets in the library or in the counselor's offices. Some of these materials should be displayed prominently on racks and bulletin boards to promote student reading. A few schools have established a guidance reading room in the counselors' suite, but this arrangement does not seem to be as effective as locating the collection in the central library. The main point is that such materials should be located in a place where they will be most accessible to the greatest number of students.

Opinions and research evidence are divided on the value of organized guidance courses. The study by Cuony and Hoppock[34] cited earlier, reports success with this type of course, while a study by Hutson and Webster[35] reports that no significant differences in realistic occupational and educational choices were obtained for tenth-grade students who had taken a weekly guidance course and a matched group of students who had not had the course. Apparently the differences in results were due to the nature of the course, time allocations, and teachers. However, it has been demonstrated that these courses may be successful in effecting desired changes under favorable conditions.

Some administrators and guidance people prefer to include units on various student problems in established courses rather than to organize guidance classes because of the crowded state of the program of studies. Excellent units on personal and social relations, family living, planning for a vocation, and planning for college may be found in problems courses in social studies and in some English courses. Courses in mathematics, science, business, and other subjects may include units on careers in those fields.

The homeroom is being employed as a guidance medium in an increasing number of schools. Some schools schedule a long (thirty- to forty-minute) homeroom period once or twice a week and attempt to present most of their group guidance information then. As in the case of special classes, much of the success of the homeroom depends upon materials and teachers. The most common weaknesses are that some teachers are not qualified and are not sympathetic with the purposes of the homeroom. Consequently, the program is likely to be very spotty. If

---

[34] Cuony and Hoppock, *op. cit.*, pp. 116–17.

[35] P. W. Hutson and A. D. Webster, "An Experiment in Educational and Vocational Guidance of Tenth Grade Students," *Educational and Psychological Measurement,* Spring, 1943, 3:3–21.

it is contemplated that the homeroom is to be used for group guidance, in-service programs for teachers, teaching guides, and materials for students should be provided.

Counseling Services

The third major service area of the guidance program is counseling. McDaniel quotes a doctoral candidate as writing on his examination, "Counseling appears to be the most defined yet least understood aspect of the total guidance process."[36] There are several schools of thought and approaches to counseling, and each group defines counseling in terms of its own emphasis and techniques. We believe that the following definition by Froelich is an appropriate one for a secondary school program:

> Counseling provides a relationship in which the individual is stimulated: (1) to evaluate himself and his opportunities, (2) to choose a feasible course of action, (3) to accept responsibility for his choice, and (4) to initiate a course of action in line with his choice.[37]

It is beyond the scope of a book on administration to delve into the special techniques of counseling and the relative merits of the directive, nondirective, and eclectic schools of thought.

We believe, however, that counseling, as Froelich has defined it, is an essential part of guidance and that an important part of an administrator's job is to make plans for counseling services in his school. He should be informed about counseling, know what he expects of teachers and counselors, know what it takes to do effective counseling, and be able to do some himself. In order to discharge these responsibilities, the secondary school principal should have some formal training in guidance and should keep informed on developments in the field through professional journals and conferences.

The factors that support the need for a guidance program are the factors that support the need for counseling services. Students are confronted with a confusing number of choices and adjustments in an increasingly complex social environment. Someone on the staff should be trained and have the time to assist them — without making the decisions for them. Counseling is much more than simply knowing a student and his family, important as that may be, and then advising him what to do. The purpose is to assist the student to know himself, to recognize his problems, to know his opportunities, and to become increasingly self-sufficient in making decisions. This requires much more than friendly advice; it requires appropriate techniques employed by trained people.

[36] McDaniel, *op. cit.*, p. 120.
[37] Clifford P. Froelich, *Guidance Services in Schools* (New York: McGraw-Hill Book Company, 1958), p. 16.

Ideally, every high school should have at least one full-time counselor on the staff with a master's degree in guidance. But this is unrealistic at the present time for most high schools of 200 or fewer pupils. The North Central Association recommends at least one half-time counselor with a minimum of fifteen hours of graduate work in guidance for schools enrolling fewer than 200 students and one full-time counselor for every 300 students in larger schools.[38] As reported previously, Conant recommends a full-time counselor for every 250 to 300 students.[39]

Counselors in small schools should be teacher-counselors rather than administrator-counselors because administrators rarely are able to adhere to a systematic counseling schedule. Too many things come up unexpectedly for the administrator to attend to, and his first responsibility is to the over-all program of the school. In addition, his general responsibility for discipline tends to conflict with counseling.

The issue of full-time counselors versus part-time counselors in large schools is a difficult one to resolve. Both types of organization are being employed successfully at the present time. If it works, the pros and cons can be disregarded. The authors favor full-time counselors because they are more likely to carry through with a schedule of systematic interviews and are more readily available to students when they desire a counseling session. There also seems to be some logic in the argument that a full-time counselor is in a position to concentrate more on his cases and do more follow-up work. On the other hand, a counselor should regard himself and be regarded by others as a teacher. Unfortunately, some full-time counselors seem to lose sight of this role, thereby raising barriers between themselves and classroom teachers. This isolation, in turn, limits their effectiveness as counselors.

If counselors are to realize their aims, they must work cooperatively with classroom teachers and enjoy their respect and confidence. School counselors are not junior-grade psychiatrists practicing in the public schools. They are members of the teaching profession charged, along with other teachers, with the educational growth of students. To do their job well, they must get certain kinds of information from teachers and secure the cooperation of teachers in following through with students in the classroom. They cannot do these things properly if they consider themselves a special cult of professionals simply attached to the schools. Counselors should be prepared as teachers and have experience as teachers before specializing, if they are to deal successfully with the types of guidance problems that are most important in schools.

Teachers are also key people in the school's counseling program. If a

---

[38] North Central Association of Colleges and Secondary Schools, "Policies and Criteria for the Approval of Secondary Schools" (Chicago: Commission on Secondary Schools, 1960), p. 17.

[39] Conant, op. cit., p. 44.

counselor is working with sophomore Jerry Jones and Jerry is having a struggle in his course work, getting no encouragement to stay in school from his family, and feeling insecure because of the bigness of high school, all he needs to convince him that school is no place for him is to have some of his teachers treat him critically and coldly. The counselor must have some help from teachers in understanding and working with Jerry. And it should help if the teachers have had some training in guidance.

In addition to counseling students, school counselors must work with teachers and administrators in coordinating guidance services with other aspects of the educational program. Dugan states that the school administrator may expect the counselor to:

1. [Do] individual student counseling — 50 per cent of his time.
2. Provide consultant services to teachers.
3. Develop and maintain cooperative working relationships with parents.
4. Supply technical leadership to the program of testing and cumulative records.
5. Provide a channel of communication with other community agencies.
6. Pay special attention to group procedures in guidance.
7. Conduct service studies and research to help gain a better understanding of students.[40]

Perhaps one of the most important things for the principal and superintendent to keep in mind in planning the guidance program is that counselors need time to counsel. A common weakness is that administrators tend to draft guidance people to do numerous administrative chores at the expense of counseling students. Patrons are beginning to ask some pertinent questions about what they are getting for their money in guidance, and if trained guidance people are forced to spend their time checking attendance, building schedules, and doing routine clerical work, public support for guidance in the schools is likely to deteriorate rapidly.

Some guidance writers recommend that counselors hold two scheduled interviews each year with all senior students and at least one interview with all other students. In addition, counselors need adequate time to hold follow-up interviews with some counselees and to confer with students who are referred to them. If these interviews average about thirty minutes each, and a counselor has a load of 300 counselees, he must spend from 250 to 300 hours per year in individual counseling. Including the time required to prepare for each interview, he should spend at least 50 per cent of his time in counseling, as Dugan has recommended.

[40] Willis E. Dugan, "If I Were a School Administrator, This Is What I Would Look for and Expect from a School Counselor," *Epsilon Bulletin,* Phi Delta Kappa, State University of Iowa, 1960, 35:8–10.

The remainder of his time will be needed for testing, administering inventories, conducting group sessions, conferring with parents, consulting with teachers, doing placement and follow-up work, and maintaining records.

Placement Services

Matching students and jobs, steering students into suitable courses and programs, and getting them into the right type of higher institutions is referred to as "placement" in guidance circles. Whether the choice of terms is fortunate or not, the service is important and constitutes one of the principal functions of guidance. Many parents and teachers tend to regard placement as having to do with locating people in jobs, but educational placement, both within the high school program and in higher institutions, is also a central function of this aspect of guidance.

As high schools grow in size, the design of their programs tends to become more complex in order to serve the needs and abilities of a heterogeneous student population. Consequently, the process of getting the right students into the right courses and programs becomes both complicated and demanding. Much of the process takes place at registration time, especially during preliminary registration. In some schools, counselors are assigned the task of assisting their counselees with preliminary registration; in others, homeroom advisers are given this responsibility. Under either plan, counselors play a major role. In the latter plan, they act as coordinators and assist homeroom teachers in securing the information they need about each pupil.

In schools employing ability grouping, multiple curricula, and special programs such as remedial and advanced placement, the information that counselors secure about each student is indispensable to teachers and administrators in making student assignments. Helping students select an appropriate curriculum in accordance with their future plans and abilities is a substantial part of placement. Not only is counseling of students and parents involved, but preparing materials such as handbooks describing the school's offerings and summarizing information on college entrance requirements is essential in the registration of students.

When ninth- or tenth-graders first enter high school they should make up a tentative long-range study program. This requires the cooperative efforts of counselors, advisers, and students and means that counselors must confer individually with each enrollee about his program. In a number of cases, it also means a conference with the student's parents.

Placement services within the high school are also concerned with getting each student into at least one extraclass activity and, insofar as possible, into one that is suitable for him. The "insofar as possible" qualification seems necessary because many schools do not have balanced extraclass offerings.

Placement in colleges and advanced technological schools is becoming more difficult each year as enrollments climb and facilities for higher education lag. Finding the right school for the right student and helping him to gain admission is a substantial part of a counselor's job. For many students who are interested, and who have the ability to go to college, finances is a major problem. Counselors can be of invaluable service in securing information about scholarships, part-time work opportunities, loan funds, and installment financing. Just keeping track of all the external admissions and scholarship testing programs is a time-consuming job these days in a large high school.

For students interested in continuing their education in a business, technical, or nurses' school, the counselor should assist in locating reputable and good-quality institutions. Unfortunately, there are numerous "diploma mills" operating at this level, and students need all the reliable information they can get about a prospective school.

The job placement function of guidance involves placing students in part-time jobs while they are in school and in full-time jobs after they leave school. The counselor must determine which students want jobs, which teachers are able and interested in assisting with placement, what jobs are available, and what other community agencies provide placement services.

Job placement requires that someone in the school keep well informed on job opportunities in the area. One way to do this is to designate the counselor or guidance coordinator as director of job placement so that he will be recognized by employers as the individual in the school to whom job openings are referred. He should also become the liaison person between the school and the state employment service. A close working relationship with this agency usually is a valuable aid to the school's guidance program.

Follow-Up Services

Without follow-up studies of its present and former students, a school has no basis for judging its program. Information on how students are getting along in the next higher level in school or on the job and their evaluations of their school experiences are requisites in educational planning. This too, is a major function of the guidance program.

Teachers and administrators do not view their program from the perspective of students. Not that the students are always right, but their viewpoint is important in evaluating the appropriateness and success of educational services. One of the authors made a school survey in a city of about 50,000 in 1959–60 in which the administrative and guidance personnel rated their counseling program as excellent, but 53 per cent of over 400 former students stated that they had never had a counseling interview and 82 per cent of those employed stated that they had received no help from the school in locating a job. If a majority of students are convinced that certain courses or services are ineffective, educators would do well to take a hard look at them.

Follow-up services are not limited to studies of former students. They are concerned equally with pupils currently enrolled — their success and adjustment as they go from one level of the school program to the next; how effective counseling has been in assisting them to get into suitable courses, ability groups, and extraclass activities; how many are retarded and why; the effectiveness of remedial programs.

The follow-up program usually includes (1) studies of graduates and dropouts, (2) studies of pupils now attending school, and (3) studies of the relationship between instructional and guidance services. The close relationship which should exist between guidance and the classroom program is pointed up clearly in conducting follow-up studies. It is virtually impossible to attempt to study the effect of one without evaluating the composition and influence of the other. For example, a seventh-grade orientation program in the junior high school cannot be evaluated apart from such factors as the preparation of students in reading and other skills in the elementary school and the provisions for individual differences in junior high school instruction.

The school needs information from two groups of former students: graduates who continue their formal education in college or technical schools, and graduates and dropouts who enter employment immediately after high school. Some information on the success of the general education program may be secured from both groups.

The most serious blocks to good follow-up studies have been the inability of schools to locate their ex-students and the lack of a sufficient response to provide a reliable sample. Schools cannot keep track of all students over a long period, but they can maintain up-to-date addresses and other basic information for four or five years after the students leave school.

The percentage of returns to follow-up questionnaires will be increased if they are kept short and only essential information is called for. College records for graduates may best be secured from official transcripts from the colleges. Information from former students which is likely to be most useful includes (1) personal data — name, class, address, etc.; (2) occupational information — student, worker, military, housewife, earnings, how job was secured, satisfaction with job, occupational plans, etc.; (3) student status — institutions, courses, major, plans, satisfaction; (4) marital status — present status, children, etc.; (5) civic activities — participation in politics, community affairs, etc.; (6) recreational activities — leisure interests, time, etc.; (7) suggestions for the high school program — courses, guidance services, extraclass activities.

Excellent suggestions for conducting follow-up studies are published in various issues of *The Bulletin* of the National Association of Secondary School Principals,[41] and state departments in several states, such as New York, Illinois, Iowa, Maryland, and Oregon, have developed useful forms and guides.

Questionnaires also may be sent to drop-outs, but more valid results will be obtained by means of interviews. A word of caution concerning drop-out studies: Statements by drop-outs as to their reasons for leaving school have not proved to be sufficiently reliable to justify conclusions about the educational program. This type of information needs to be supplemented by an analysis of test results, personality inventory data, scholastic records, extraclass records, and interviews with former teachers and with parents. A small number of carefully conducted case studies probably will be worth much more to the school than a large number of superficial replies to questionnaires.

If the guidance program is effective, it will make a difference in the growth and adjustment of students while they are still in high school. In order to appraise the contributions of guidance to student growth and adjustment, follow-up information will be needed with respect to (1) academic growth in relation to ability as shown by standardized test scores, (2) regularity in attendance, (3) student conduct and citizenship, (4) appropriateness of placement in ability groups, (5) extraclass participation, (6) voluntary requests for counseling interviews, (7) stability of educational and vocational choices, (8) growth in self-concepts.

This information also will be essential in evaluating the success of the instructional program. Follow-up of students in school should include studies of their success in the next higher level of the educational program — as they move, that is, from elementary to junior high and from junior to senior high.

Determining the suitability of guidance procedures involves some carefully designed action research similar to the studies reported earlier in this chapter. It also involves the use of self-evaluation instruments by guidance personnel and periodic evaluations from students, teachers, parents, and administrators. Evaluations should be coordinated carefully, and all members of the staff should participate in some phase of follow-up procedures. Roeber, Smith, and Erickson comment, ". . . the follow-up service need not require provisions beyond the financial resources of any school district. Most follow-up studies require more inspiration and perspiration than anything else."[42]

[41] Three articles on follow-up studies are included in *The Bulletin* of the NASSP, February, 1960, Vol. 44, No. 253.

[42] Edward C. Roeber, Glenn E. Smith, and Clifford E. Erickson, *Organization and Administration of Guidance Services* (New York: McGraw-Hill Book Company, 1955), p. 22.

Physical Facilities for Guidance

Counselors are employed to do guidance work and should be given time to do it. They also need a suitable place to work. It is exceedingly difficult to establish a confidential relationship with a student counselee in one corner of a study hall or in the principal's outer office.

It might be profitable to outline specifications for some model guidance suites if every school were in a position to build a new building and had adequate funds. However, many schools must convert some space in a building that was constructed before guidance had gotten much beyond the textbook stage, and even in communities with new buildings in prospect local guidance requirements make model plans largely academic. The description of physical facilities and sketches presented in this section, therefore, will be general and intended to serve merely as guides for local planners.

The following general provisions and characteristics should be considered in planning the guidance quarters:

1. The guidance quarters should be located near, but not necessarily adjacent to, the principal's office. This location tends to facilitate conferences on problems between the principal and the guidance personnel, permit the joint use of some secretarial and clerical personnel, and provide for joint access to student records. Coordination and conferences among student services personnel will be facilitated if these services are located in the same building area.

2. The guidance quarters should be attractively decorated and furnished so as to encourage students to visit counselors for interviews.

3. The guidance quarters should be near the main flow of student traffic, directly accessible from a corridor, and not far from the main entrance to the building for the benefit of patrons.

4. Each counselor should have a small private office where he can confer with individual students and small groups without distractions. The counselor's office should be reasonably well soundproofed to safeguard the confidentialness of his communications with students.

5. There should be a waiting area, either a combination reception room and secretarial office outside the counselor's office or a large joint reception and reading room serving several adjacent counselors' offices. This area should have comfortable seating for two or three clients for each counselor.

6. There should be sufficient closet and storage space for tests, printed forms, booklets, filmstrips, tapes, office supplies, information files, inventory files, and similar materials.

7. If at all possible, there should be a room available which is suitable for individual testing, for committee meetings, and for occasional use

ADMINISTRATION OF THE GUIDANCE PROGRAM

FIGURE 14

Relative Location of Guidance Quarters

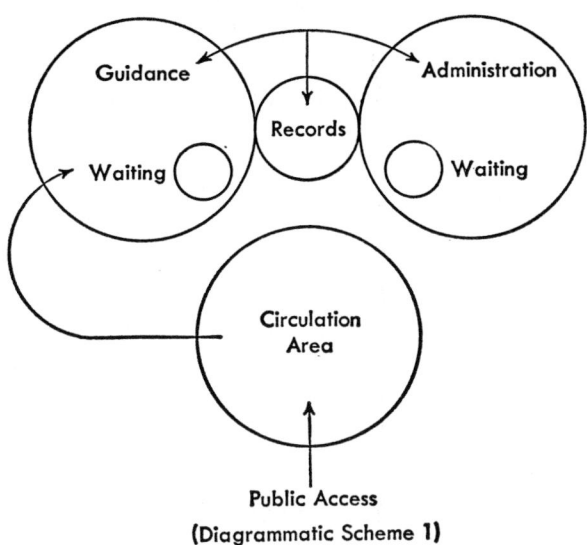

(Diagrammatic Scheme 1)

by such personnel as college admissions counselors, visiting teachers, school psychologists, and others.

8. If counselors teach special classes in group guidance, a multi-purpose room of standard classroom size near the guidance quarters is highly desirable. This room may be used for many other purposes, such as group testing, teacher-counselor conferences, and meetings with parents.

A national committee on physical facilities for school guidance services states that

> Preconceived, detailed plans are likely to stereotype the design of guidance facilities. Plans which have been designed for a given program of guidance services in one school may not be adapted functionally to the program of guidance in another. It is better, therefore, for each school to develop its own plan for guidance facilities.[43]

The committee presents the diagrammatic schemes shown in Figures 14 and 15 as general guides showing the suggested location of the guidance quarters in relation to administrative offices and the special areas within the guidance quarters. The figures are adaptations from the sketches in the U.S. Office of Education brochure. These diagrams

[43] U.S. Office of Education, *Physical Facilities for School Guidance Services* (Washington: Government Printing Office, 1960), p. 5.

indicate only the relative locations and size of the various areas and are intended only as suggestions for local boards, administrators, and architects. Diagrammatic Scheme 1 shows the relative positions of the guidance and administrative quarters with respect to the records and circulation or main foyer areas. Diagrammatic Scheme 2 shows the relative positions and size of the special areas within the guidance quarters.

FIGURE 15
Guidance Area

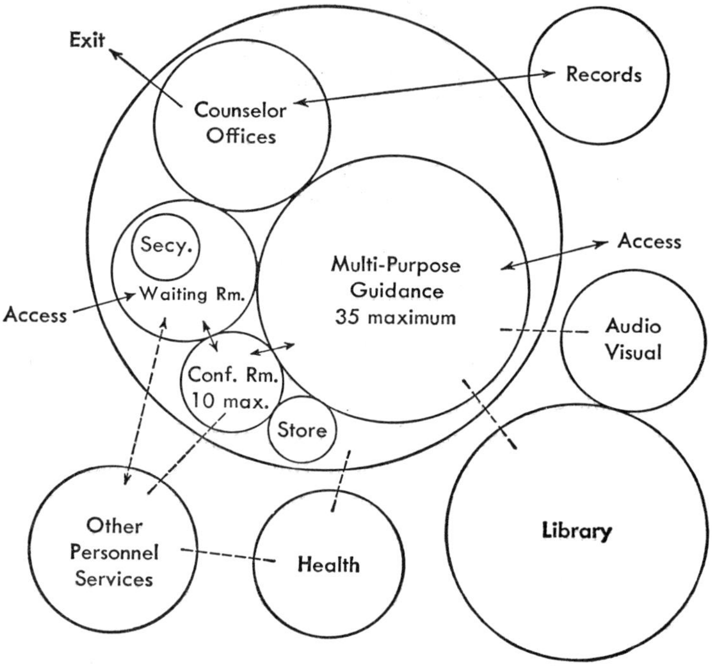

[Diagram showing circles labeled: Exit, Counselor Offices, Records, Secy., Waiting Rm., Access, Multi-Purpose Guidance 35 maximum, Access, Audio Visual, Conf. Rm. 10 max., Store, Other Personnel Services, Health, Library]

(Diagrammatic Scheme 2)

QUESTIONS AND GROUP PROJECTS

1. Examine the definitions of guidance in several different textbooks. What are the main points of agreement and disagreement?

2. How do various writers in the field of guidance reconcile the view that counselors should not solve problems for counselees and the view that counselors should help underachievers to improve their classwork?

3. Examine several reports of follow-up studies of high school students. How do students rate the guidance they had in high school?

4. Review several college drop-out studies. What are the most frequently listed reasons for withdrawal from college? What are the implications for high school guidance?
5. Review several high school drop-out studies. What are the implications for guidance in these?
6. Write a paper summarizing the research showing the influence of counseling on student achievement.
7. Secure summaries of intelligence test scores for entering students in 1930 and in 1960, from two or three different high schools (check the annual reports of principals or superintendents). How do these sets of scores compare? What are the implications for the guidance program?
8. Visit several high schools and ask to see the records used by counselors. Which items on the cumulative record forms are most frequently recorded and which least frequently?
9. Discuss the desirability of having counselors certificated as teachers. Should counselors be required to have had teaching experience before going into counseling?
10. Examine some floor plans for guidance suites in new high school buildings and draw a plan which is a composite of what you consider to be the best features in them.

Selected References

Conant, James B. *The American High School Today.* New York: McGraw-Hill Book Company, 1959.

Erickson, Clifford E., and Glenn E. Smith. *Organization and Administration of Guidance Services.* New York: McGraw-Hill Book Company, 1947.

Froelich, Clifford B. *Guidance Services in Schools.* New York: McGraw-Hill Book Company, 1958.

Germane, Charles E., and Edith G. Germane. *Personnel Work in High School.* New York: Silver Burdett Company, 1941.

Hatch, Raymond N., and Buford Stefflre. *Administration of Guidance Services.* Englewood Cliffs, N.J.: Prentice-Hall, Inc., 1958.

Havighurst, Robert J. *Developmental Tasks and Education.* New York: Longmans, Green and Company, 1950.

McDaniel, Henry B., with G. A. Shaftel. *Guidance in the Modern School.* New York: The Dryden Press, 1956.

National Study of Secondary School Evaluation. *Evaluative Criteria.* Washington: The Study, 1960.

North Central Association of Colleges and Secondary Schools. "Policies and Criteria for the Approval of Secondary Schools." Chicago: Commission on Secondary Schools, 1960.

Ohlsen, Merle M. *Guidance — An Introduction.* New York: Harcourt, Brace and Company, 1955.

Roeber, Edward C., Glenn E. Smith, and Clifford E. Erickson. *Organization and Administration of Guidance Services.* New York: McGraw-Hill Book Company, 1955.

Rothney, J. W. M. *Guidance Practices and Results.* New York: Harper & Brothers, 1958.

Smith, Glenn E. *Principles and Practices of the Guidance Program.* New York: The Macmillan Company, 1951.

Wrenn, C. Gilbert, and Willis E. Dugan. *Guidance Procedures in High Schools.* Minneapolis: University of Minnesota Press, 1950.

CHAPTER 8

Extraclass Activities and Their Management

The meaning of "extra" in extraclass activities is a matter of some dispute. To most high school students and their parents it means practical and recreational school experiences as distinct from the academic proceedings of the classroom. They regard activities as "practical" in the sense that students learn certain nonacademic things that they will need after they get out of school: getting along with people, sharing in community service, speaking before groups, managing finances, and developing recreational interests.

On the other hand, some people hold that the "extra" means dispensable. These partisans maintain that extraclass activities are largely a waste of the students' time and of the taxpayers' money and that the business of schools is to teach children the things that they cannot learn outside of school. They argue that the chief function of the school is to impart knowledge and intellectual discipline and that these result primarily from the systematic study of organized subjects. Regardless of the pros and cons, it is apparent that extraclass activities have become as much a part of the American high school scene as textbooks, report cards, and algebra.

The authors have elected to use the term "extraclass" rather than the more familiar "extracurricular" because the latter term implies that such activities are something apart from the curriculum. We support the point of view that all student activities which are conducted under the direction of the school and which provide desirable learning experiences are integral parts of the curriculum. Although extraclass activities usually take place outside of regular course work and carry no credit, they serve educational purposes that are as valid as those of classroom instruction. They may or may not be as important, but they serve special objectives that have a legitimate place in the educational program.

Other authors have used the terms "co-curricular," "allied activities," "collateral activities," and "out-of-class activities" to make the distinction between classroom and extraclassroom education. We recognize that one label is about as suitable as another but suggest that there is little profit in arguing terminology; the most important consideration is the extent to which a faculty succeeds in making activities a constructive part of education.

The large amount of time and attention devoted to student activities is a characteristic of secondary education that is not peculiar to the United States. So-called "extracurricular" activities have been a part of student life in European schools since the early Greek period. Elected student "Scholarchs" participated in the government of Plato's academy and of Aristotle's *lyzeum*. During the Reformation period in Germany the *Ritterakademien* taught dueling, riding, gunnery, music, and heraldry.[1] In England's great "public" grammar schools — Eton, Harrow, and Rugby — the training of character and gentility through activities, especially sports, has been a major part of the education of boys for more than three centuries.

During the depression of the 1930's one of the most common criticisms of the high school was that there were too many "fads" and "frills." The words had changed by the late 1950's, but not the music. As public opinion became aroused by the press and other mass media following the USSR's success in launching the first satellite, supporters of a strictly academic curriculum raised pointed questions about most things non-academic in the schools. Representative of that viewpoint is the following comment by Professor Commager, well-known historian at Amherst College and Columbia University:

> Instead of being a device whereby the community is persuaded to take an interest in the high school, football and basketball have become, in all too many communities, devices whereby the high school entertains or profits the community. More and more the athletic tail is wagging the academic dog.[2]

[1] R. Freeman Butts, *A Cultural History of Education* (New York: McGraw-Hill Book Company, 1947), p. 272.
[2] Henry Steele Commager, "A Historian Looks at the American High School," *The High School in a New Era*, papers presented at the Conference on the American High School, October, 1957 (Chicago: University of Chicago Press, 1958), p. 11.

Some critics would go farther and generalize Commager's criticism of athletics to all high school activities. But many people, including more than a few college staff members, do not share Commager's views. Colleges have set the pace for the high schools in extraclass activities. Postseason bowl games, huge marching bands, dancing baton twirlers, fraternities and sororities, and elaborate social events are norms of college life. Every year college representatives seek out star high school athletes and offer them more remunerative scholarships than are offered to prospective Phi Beta Kappas.

High school administrators have been caught in the middle of a large-scale hassle over school activities, and the American people have been inconsistent in their views on the subject. Some organized groups insist that activities be de-emphasized; other groups demand bigger and better programs. Although some prominent Americans warn that "the tail is wagging the dog," others sing the praises of activities. The late President Lotus Coffman of the University of Minnesota declared a few years ago that "The fads and frills have become the fundamentals of education."[3]

Factors in the Growth of the Activity Program

If contradictions exist in a local activity program — and in most schools they do — the administrator has the responsibility of assessing the forces that tend to set the pattern in his school, informing community and faculty leaders of the facts, and enlisting their support for changes. In his capacity as an educational leader the high school principal must weigh the interests of different groups and the relative educational values of different types of school activities.

The vigorous growth of the extraclass program since 1900 cannot be explained simply on the basis of adolescent whims. There have been solid educational reasons, and secondary school people need to be cognizant of these reasons if the program is to have competent direction. It is with this need in mind that we call attention to the factors that have been most influential in the development of the activity program.

The Interest and Persistence of Students

The most sustained demand for school activities has come from students. During the early years of the American high school the interest of students and their convictions that activities had important values prompted them to initiate and take part in these affairs in defiance of strong faculty opposition.

[3] As quoted by Louis R. Kilzer, Harold H. Stephenson, and H. Orville Nordberg, *Allied Activities in the Secondary School* (New York: Harper & Brothers, 1956), p. 1.

Perhaps as important as any factor in the motivation of students to promote activities has been their desire for relaxation. Youth and adults alike need a change of pace from the tedium of work. In the case of students the desire was, and still is, to seek relief from the regimented atmosphere of the classroom. Efforts by adults to prevent youth from engaging in things that are interesting to them and that are commonplace in life outside the school are rarely successful. Parents and teachers may succeed in banning student activities from the school, but they have had little success in preventing youth from participating in such affairs outside the school. Youth of high school and college age are going to dance, associate together in organizations, compete in sports, and engage in other activities with or without the blessing of the school. It would seem to be a matter of wisdom, therefore, for faculties to channel student interests into desirable learning experiences.

Contributions to Educational Needs of Students

In his book on educational psychology Stroud writes,

> At the high school level the various extra-class functions are particularly important because of the recognition and prestige they command. The athletic program, dramatics and music, public speaking, and student government are activities in which pupils may develop their resources and win recognition and security.[4]

Adolescents have in common certain developmental problems which are important to them and which they believe are served effectively through extraclass activities. For example, most adolescents feel the need to achieve independence from adults. In the words of one high school boy,

> Everywhere we go, all day long, they organize the heck out of us. We rush from home in the morning to get to school where we're regimented all day. . . . Even at home, there are music lessons, swimming lessons, and gosh knows what other kinds of lessons. It's one great big rat race all the time. But at the Corral, we don't do anything. We loaf. We cork off. We just sit. Nobody organizes us; nobody tells us what to do. We like that and we're willing to work once in a while to keep it that way.[5]

Forty years ago, about all that teachers and administrators had to guide them in their work with high school youth was personal observation plus homespun philosophy. Some of this was sound and some of it was romantic and superficial. Today educators have access to a large

---

[4] James B. Stroud, *Psychology in Education* (New York: Longmans, Green and Company, 1946), p. 276.

[5] From an interview with Joseph N. Bell, quoted in "Teen Trouble in the Suburbs: One Answer," *The American Home*, May, 1960, p. 8.

body of competent research on adolescent psychology and characteristics, and this knowledge suggests that student activities have an important role in meeting youth needs.

In assessing the contributions of extraclass activities to the educational program, educators have more to go on than general impressions. Studies such as Hamilton's, on opinions of students and teachers with respect to the values of activities, show that the people most directly involved rate activities highly.[6] Hamilton secured evaluations of the contributions of the activity program to the educational needs of youth as defined by the Cooperative Study of Secondary School Standards.[7] The ratings were obtained from 180 activity sponsors and 2,061 high school seniors in 24 high schools in Texas.

Hamilton found that the outcomes of activities rated highest by students were in the areas of socialization (3.86), mental health (3.69), guidance (3.65), preparation for further education (3.62), reasoning (3.54), and aesthetics (3.54). All of these ratings fell in the category "More than average value," as defined by the author.

Students rated the activity program as having average or above value in contributing to all of the educational needs listed in the Cooperative Study inventory. Teachers rated the values of activities somewhat higher than did students, but the correlation of .84 between teachers' and students' ratings indicates close agreement.

Hamilton's study presents objective evidence that students and teachers believe the extraclass program makes important contributions to educational needs. Other studies and many statements by educators and prominent laymen support this conclusion. If activities have made the transition from "fads to fundamentals," it has been due in no small degree to the conviction of students, teachers, and laymen that they provide important educational experiences.

Values in Implementing Educational Theory

A third factor contributing to the growth of extraclass activities has been their effectiveness in implementing educational and psychological theory. Psychologists and educators have learned much about individual differences, motivation, transfer of training, retention, and youth interests during the twentieth century, and much of what has been learned supports the case for extraclass activities as effective media for learning.

Although youth exhibit many common characteristics and needs, they vary widely in capacities, interests, and attitudes toward education. Ex-

---

[6] Homer H. Hamilton, "The Educational Value of Pupil Activities," *Texas Study of Secondary Education,* Research Bulletin No. 29 (Austin: University of Texas, January, 1960).

[7] Cooperative Study of Secondary School Standards, *Evaluative Criteria* (Washington: The Study, 1950), pp. 35–45.

traclass activities, based on student interests, have proved more adaptable to individual differences than have most formal courses. Clubs, athletics, publications, and social affairs provide many opportunities for students to explore and develop interests and talents. Theory holds that motivation is a requisite condition for learning and that interest and purpose are two of the most effective means of securing motivation. Since high interest and purpose are characteristic of extraclass activities, it follows that activities serve to motivate learning. Moreover, student participation, relationships to out-of-school situations, and opportunities for recognition that are inherent in the extraclass program satisfy other important conditions for learning.

Extraclass activities also make direct and positive contributions to the social purposes of education. Statements of educational objectives, from the Seven Cardinal Principles to the Imperative Needs of Youth, hold that schools should develop such outcomes as civic responsibility, economic competence, and social understanding. Experience has demonstrated that student councils, clubs, social affairs, team sports, and committee work lend themselves well to the achievement of these purposes.

Still another value is the influence of student activities in holding students in school who otherwise might drop out. In so doing they implement the popular American view that all educable youth should complete the secondary school on a voluntary basis. Research shows that students who have completed high school took part in a significantly greater number of activities than did dropouts during the same period of schooling.[8] The relationship between the activity program and educational theory is not forced and one may logically assume that it has been a substantial factor in the growth of activities in the secondary school.

Increased Leisure Time for Adults and Youth

With the exceptions of such groups as teachers, doctors, clergymen, and nurses, Americans have more leisure time today than at any time in the history of the nation.

> From 1890 to 1937, the average work week of factory employees in the United States decreased from about 60 to 42 hours; in the building trades, from 55 to 39; in steam railroads, from 60 to 48; and in anthracite and bituminous coal mining, from 60 to 35.[9]

The average work week for production workers in manufacturing declined from 43.4 hours in 1945 to 38.6 hours in 1958.[10] Prior to the urban

---

[8] Paul E. Opstad, "Non-Scholastic Factors Associated with Drop-Outs in Iowa High Schools," unpublished Ph.D. dissertation, State University of Iowa, 1958, pp. 60–65.

[9] Newton Edwards and Herman G. Richey, *The School in the American Social Order* (Boston: Houghton Mifflin Company, 1947), p. 484. (Quoted from *Technology in Our Economy*, Temporary National Economic Committee, p. 167.)

[10] U.S. Bureau of the Census, *Statistical Abstract of the United States: 1958* (79th edition) (Washington: Government Printing Office, 1958), p. 227.

movement and the mechanization of many household services, children were required to spend much of their out-of-school time doing chores; today there are few work responsibilities for children around the typical urban home. Because adults have more free time, among other reasons, they have become increasingly interested in entertainment and have supported school activities in the interest of securing good entertainment. And because students have fewer work responsibilities, schools have expanded their extraclass programs in order to keep youth off the streets and to occupy their free time with constructive leisure-time pursuits.

Public Interest and Pressures

One index of the popularity of school activities among the American people is the amount of space they receive in newspapers. A study at Michigan State University in 1952–53 reported the amount of newspaper space devoted to different types of school news. The sample included 8 out of 56 daily newspapers and 42 out of 291 weekly newspapers in the state. From November, 1952, to October, 1953, the daily papers gave 77,785 lines of space to schools, 65 per cent of which was devoted to extraclass activities.[11] School people may decry this emphasis in the press, but it indicates what experienced newspaper people believe is news about the schools and, therefore, the degree of public interest in activities.

Illustrative of the public interest and pressures that stem from the activity program is the situation which developed in a midwestern state in 1957, when a bill was introduced in the state legislature to abolish the state high school activities association because it had declared a star basketball player ineligible. The bill was defeated, but a number of important political figures became involved before the issue was settled. Local pressure on the schools in connection with activities is commonplace, and the situation with respect to the turnover among coaches, at both college and high school levels, is notorious. Public interest is a potent, albeit not always constructive force in shaping the student activity program. Certainly the school administrator cannot treat such interest casually.

The high school principal may become disillusioned with extraclass activities because of the many problems involved in their administration, but he would be naïve to regard lightly the factors that have contributed to their growth. Activities have become established as an inseparable part of secondary education because of their appeal to student interest, their values in meeting educational needs, their values in implementing educational theory, the increased leisure time possessed by Americans, and public interest and pressures.

These factors have been at work in varying degrees to extend activi-

[11] Benjamin Fine and Vivienne Anderson, *The School Administrator and the Press* (New York: Arthur C. Croft Publications, 1956), p. 5.

ties in American high schools for over one hundred years. The issue of activities versus no activities is academic. The challenge to administrators in the contradictions that sometimes emerge is to (1) develop with students and patrons a sense of perspective concerning the role of activities in an educational program, and (2) exhibit leadership in determining purposes and sound policies for the conduct of the activity program in their schools.

Functions and Purposes of the Extraclass Program

Thirty-odd years ago the Lynds, commenting on school activities in Middletown, wrote:

> The high school, with its athletics, clubs, sororities and fraternities, dances and parties, and other extracurricular activities, is a fairly complete social cosmos in itself, and about this city within a city the social life of the intermediate generation centers. . . . Today the school is becoming not a place to which children go from their homes for a few hours daily, but a place from which they go home to eat and sleep.[12]

Where do student activities fit into the general scheme of formal education? What are their functions and purposes in secondary schools? The observations made by the Lynds in 1929 are certainly no less apropos today. Indeed, in many schools activities now occupy more of the students' time than they did thirty years ago. One of the most urgent tasks facing administrators and teachers in directing the classroom as well as extraclass program is stated cogently in the Rockefeller Report on Education:

> If we are to meet these pressures, our schools will need greatly increased public support and attention, and much more money. *But they also need something besides money: an unsparing re-examination of current practices, patterns of organization and objectives.*[13]

The pertinence of this statement to the extraclass program has been demonstrated many times in the conflicts and excesses that have occurred over the years. Each school staff in cooperation with local citizens has an obligation to draft a statement of policies and functions for the extraclass program if the latter is to contribute in any real measure to the purposes of the school. The authors hold that activities provide many opportunities for valuable educative experiences, but that these experi-

---

[12] Robert S. Lynd and Helen M. Lynd, *Middletown* (New York: Harcourt, Brace and Company, 1929), p. 211.

[13] Rockefeller Report on Education, *The Pursuit of Excellence — Education and the Future of America*, America at Mid-Century Series (Garden City, N.Y.: Doubleday and Company, 1958), p. 21. (Italics ours.)

ences should supplement and enrich the experiences of organized classroom instruction, not substitute for them. We believe that the following statement of functions, drafted by Miller, Moyer, and Patrick, provides a useful guide for any school faculty in formulating goals for extraclass activities:

General Functions of Cocurricular Activities:
a. Contributions to Students
   1. To provide opportunities for the pursuit of established interests and the development of new interests.
   2. To educate for citizenship through experiences and insights that stress leadership, fellowship, cooperation, and independent action.
   3. To develop school spirit and morale.
   4. To provide opportunities for satisfying the gregarious urge of children and youth.
   5. To encourage moral and spiritual development.
   6. To strengthen the mental and physical health of students.
   7. To provide for a well-rounded social development of students.
   8. To widen student contacts (with people, ideas, and ways of doing things).
   9. To provide opportunities for students to exercise their creative capacities more fully.
b. Contributions to Curriculum Improvement
   1. To supplement or enrich classroom experiences.
   2. To explore new learning experiences which may ultimately be incorporated into the curriculum.
   3. To provide additional opportunity for individual and group guidance.
   4. To motivate classroom instruction.
c. Contributions to More Effective School Administration
   1. To foster more effective teamwork between students, faculty, and administrators and supervisory personnel.
   2. To integrate more closely the several divisions of the school system.
   3. To provide less restricted opportunities designed to assist youth in the worthwhile utilization of their spare time.
   4. To enable teachers to better understand the forces that motivate pupils to react as they do to many of the problematic situations with which they are confronted.
d. Contributions to the Community
   1. To promote better school and community relations.
   2. To encourage greater community interest in and support of the school.[14]

The long experience of secondary schools with student activities suggests that these are appropriate and attainable purposes. For example,

[14] Franklin A. Miller, James H. Moyer, and Robert B. Patrick, *Planning Student Activities* (Englewood Cliffs, N.J.: Prentice-Hall, Inc., 1956), pp. 13–20.

the contributions of high school activities in discovering and strengthening interests in a career have been observed many times by parents and veteran teachers. The authors are well acquainted with a midwestern newspaper executive who decided on a career in journalism as a result of his work on his high school paper. No members of his family had any connection with a newspaper. He would be the first to agree that his high school newspaper experience was no more valuable, perhaps even less valuable, to his career than the organized courses he pursued. But he is convinced that he would not have learned about the possibilities in newspaper advertising, developed an interest in it, or discovered his talent for that type of work had he not served on his high school newspaper staff.

Administrative and Organizational Policies for the Extraclass Program

Special-interest groups seem to be attracted to school activities the way politicians are attracted to a TV camera. Some groups want to help youth, some want publicity, and some want to be entertained. The interests of these groups frequently conflict, and often are not consistent with the views of board members, teachers, and students as regards the role of activities in the high school program.

Because of these diverse interests, administrators, teachers, and board members need to agree on basic policies for the conduct of the educational program. But education is an exceedingly complex enterprise and new problems develop which do not fit neatly into a set of policies. This is especially the case in the field of extraclass activities. For example, a faculty and board may agree that the extraclass program should not disrupt regular classroom instruction. But, without consultation, some well-intentioned organization may propose to raise funds to send the high school band to a distant pageant or bowl game and to take the students on a two-weeks tour of historic shrines en route. The question arises as to whether this violates the policy of noninterference with regular instruction or is a fine opportunity to supplement classroom experiences. If the board and faculty approve the proposal, what course should they pursue if several other civic clubs decide to sponsor similar trips for other student groups?

In the interest of maintaining perspective in the conduct of the educational program, local boards and faculties should settle on a course of action which they propose to follow with respect to certain types of problems. However, it is impossible to anticipate every conceivable set of circumstances which may develop. Therefore, policies should be regarded as guides rather than as a fixed set of answers for the management of an activity program.

It is desirable also that policies for the management of activity programs be determined in relation to the characteristics and needs of students in local communities. Nevertheless, many secondary schools encounter similar problems, and policies that have proved to be sound for a large number of schools often are applicable to a local situation. The following recommendations have been compiled from several sources. Some have been adapted from statements by regional accrediting bodies, some from state associations, and some from local schools. We present them as guides and not as universally applicable standards.

1. *Each sponsored activity should serve valid educational purposes.* The purpose of any school activity should be to contribute to the educational growth of students. Some activities may be primarily recreational in form, but as long as they serve socially valid objectives, they have a place in the school program. On the other hand, when a school activity or organized group serves primarily to promote the self-interests of its members, or when its aims and proceedings conflict with the purposes of the school, it becomes a detriment.

Occasionally, extraclass groups wander far afield from their original goals and become strictly amusement or prestige social clubs. When the "Y-teens" becomes a social sorority and the "Hi-Y" a fraternity, their members have lost sight of the intents of these organizations and have defaulted their right to continue under the sponsorship of a public high school. When athletics becomes chiefly entertainment for fans and is given precedence over other aspects of the school in recognition, time, and finances, it becomes negative rather than positive in its educational impact.

In order to permit a faculty to coordinate, maintain balance in, and evaluate the extraclass program as a whole, each group of student and faculty supporters of a specific activity should be expected to draft a statement of its purposes. This should be done before authorization is granted for its organization and should be called for at intervals throughout its operation. When, and if, the participants and sponsors of an activity persist in departing from its purposes or the purposes come in conflict with sound educational values, the activity should be disbanded or reorganized.

2. *Student interest and desire should be essential conditions for initiating and continuing an extraclass activity.* The principal justification for extraclass activities is to provide desirable and effective learning experiences which cannot be, or usually are not, supplied as well in most organized courses. Two of the basic differences between extraclass and classroom programs are that learning in extraclass activities is largely

voluntary and motivated by common adolescent interests, while learning in the classroom is largely teacher-directed and is motivated by adult purposes. There are notable exceptions, but these differences are characteristic.

Students may learn many valuable things through activities which they initiate and in which they participate on a voluntary basis. Motivation for learning under such circumstances is largely intrinsic; students make an effort to learn in order to discover answers to problems and to secure experiences that they regard as important to them. Although learning may be as effective when motivated by extrinsic as by intrinsic factors, concomitant outcomes such as general attitudes toward school and work are usually more favorable when learning is intrinsically motivated.

Extraclass activities originated in schools because of student interest and desire. These are the special qualities that make such experiences effective in education. If students need to be pressured into taking part in certain extraclass affairs and if teachers dominate students in these situations, the main values of extraclass experiences are lost. If, for example, most of the boys in a school do not want to play football, there is little virtue in trying to pressure them into playing football. Interest and desire are requisite conditions for sports as well as for other activities.

However, some activities, such as student councils, hobby clubs, publications, and service organizations, have as their main objectives citizenship training, service, and opportunities for students to explore and develop special talents. In some schools the potential values in certain of these activities may not be immediately apparent to students, and an activity may well be proposed by the faculty to meet educational needs that teachers regard as important.

To a considerable extent, the interest of students in an activity grows out of their previous experiences or their observations of things in which adults or other students engage. If students have had no opportunity to learn about an activity and faculty members believe that it would serve an important purpose, teachers quite properly should attempt to stimulate interest in it. If the expense is not too great, the activity may be given a trial run in an effort to develop student interest. However, if students do not become interested after an exploratory period, the faculty will accomplish little by continuing to promote it.

Although student interest and desire are important, it does not follow that they are sufficient conditions in themselves to justify offering a particular activity. An activity must also meet other criteria, such as offering opportunities for constructive learning, being socially acceptable, and being reasonably free from danger to participants. The interest of some boys in drag racing hardly qualifies drag racing as an appropriate activity for school sponsorship. Secret fraternities and sororities, all-night parties, and unsupervised skip days belong in the same category. Experience has shown that the most successful long-term procedure for dealing with problems raised by student participation in socially undesirable or dangerous activities is to promote interest in educationally sound substitutes.

3. *Sound balance should be maintained among student activities and between the extraclass and classroom programs.* The extraclass program should be balanced and provisions made for the educational needs of all students. In too many schools, activities which entertain, receive extensive publicity, and bring in substantial revenue are promoted at the expense of others which could serve more students. A case in point is the typical athletic program, in which interscholastic football, basketball, and baseball are given most of the time and energies of coaches, most of the publicity, and most of the financial support. As a result, such activities as intramural sports, tennis, golf, swimming, and wrestling are not made available in a majority of high schools.

Band, dramatics, and musical shows are usually sponsored in secondary schools of all sizes and types, but orchestras, subject clubs, service clubs, and hobby groups are given very little attention and financial support. It often happens that students who are given the most attention and recognition are those who have talents and interests in a few entertainment-type activities.

If it is a valid principle of education that course offerings should serve all students, it is a valid principle that the extraclass program should serve all students. Most adolescent boys are interested in, and will profit from, participation in sports. The first concern of the school in athletics, therefore, should be to provide a comprehensive and well-balanced program of intramural competition. Varsity competition for boys who are gifted in athletics has a legitimate place in the total sports program, but this phase of athletics should grow out of a broad base of competition for all boys.

Similarly, students interested in such things as photography, literature, debating, art, stamp collecting, and electronics should be provided an opportunity to join with other students with similar interests in developing their talents. These youngsters need recognition, experience, and the leadership of a competent faculty sponsor as much as do the outstanding athlete, the talented musician, and the dramatics star.

The most difficult problem facing the administration in securing good balance in the activity program is finance. Taxpayers and boards of education usually are reluctant to approve the expenditure of tax money for the support of extraclass activities. The burden of securing revenue for the program has had to be carried largely by activities that attract paying customers. Consequently, these are the activities that have been given priority with respect to facilities and trained faculty personnel.

It would be wishful thinking to assume that a school administrator could come into a community and correct long-standing abuses within a short period of time. He can be assured that he is not going to reform overnight the tastes of rabid sports fans or enthusiastic patrons of marching bands. However, in most communities he should be able to educate the faculty, student body, parents, and board of education to recognize the values in a comprehensive and balanced program of activities. With such support he should be in a position to shift some of the financial base for nonentertainment types of activities from gate receipts to other sources of revenue, including tax funds. A broad financial base will go far toward reducing the pressures for attracting paying customers and toward eliminating the abuses that develop from overcommercialization of a few activities.

Over a period of time it is possible for administrators and teachers to obtain recognition and support for the less spectacular activities from the public. Science fairs, hobby exhibits, balanced news stories in school publications, recognition assemblies, and similar methods may be successful in accomplishing this purpose. In answer to the inevitable "It can't be done," the fact that it is being and has been done in a substantial number of communities stands in rebuttal.

4. *Participation should be open to all students who have a genuine interest and the special abilities needed.* Membership and participation in various activities should be limited only by the interests, educational needs, and abilities of students. The American public high school was established to extend educational opportunities to all youth who had the desire and the ability to profit from them. Over a period of 140 years the principle of free public secondary education for all youth regardless of economic status, race, or creed has become solidly established in most states. In implementing this principle many states provide not only tuition-free secondary schools but also free transportation and free textbooks.

One inconsistency between practice and theory is the restriction on extraclass participation due to the expense to students. Other inconsistencies result from the election of members by certain organizations and inflexible scholastic requirements for eligibility. Some school administrators take the position that a student should not be permitted to engage in certain school-sponsored activities if he doesn't have the money to pay the costs. Apparently these administrators are unmindful of the fact that the same arguments were invoked by the opponents of free tuition, free textbooks, and free transportation. It is a strange sort of logic to argue that the school should make it possible for all students to study English, algebra, or physics regardless of the economic situation of their parents, but that such educational experiences as clubs, social events, or bands should be available only to those who can afford them.

Selectivity in the extraclass program based on economic status reflects a fundamental weakness in the method of financing activities in most schools. Where the activity program receives no tax money and must be self-supporting, some administrators have permitted expediency to obscure purposes. If an activity cannot be provided without prohibitive costs to some students, it should not be sponsored by a public school. The most logical answer, if such activities seem worthwhile and the school budget is overburdened, is to secure financial support through sponsorship by civic groups or through fund-raising activities such as work days, festivals, or similar joint student endeavors.

A more flagrant violation of the tenets of democratic education is the practice of permitting students in some organizations to select their own members after the manner of secret lodges or exclusive social clubs. Social and class discriminations do exist in adult society, but they have no place in a public school dedicated to the education of the young in the ideals and values of a democratic society.

Adherence to democratic principles in student participation in extraclass activities does not imply, however, that there should be no selection. Some types of activities require special talents. A student who has no aptitude for music will contribute little to the concert band, and a boy who is puny is likely to get maimed in a varsity football scrimmage.

But all students should have an opportunity to participate in activities in which they have the requisite ability and interest. If the boys who have limited athletic ability want to play football, the school should do the best it can to provide an intramural program. Similarly, if students with little musical talent want to participate in music, the school might well organize a music appreciation or choral group which is open to all interested students.

Ideally, decisions as to whether students should or should not share in certain activities should be made in terms of what is best for the student and the school. Rigid scholastic eligibility requirements frequently do an injustice to students and assume that activities are simply icing on the cake rather than solid educational food. It may not be any more desirable to bar a student from baseball because he is failing in history than it would be to bar him from history because he is failing in trigonometry. Whether or not it is desirable depends upon the ability, interests, and conduct of the student concerned. If he has adequate intelligence and is simply indolent and attempting to ride on his reputation as an athlete, he should be held to a scholastic performance consistent with his ability. If he has low scholastic ability but is making a sincere effort in his courses, and athletic participation is making an important contribution to his personal development, then a scholastic requirement which bars him makes little sense.

Admittedly, this is a theoretical point of view. In practice, all state high school athletic or activity associations require that participants in interscholastic athletics must be passing in a certain number of subjects or have a certain grade-point average. This is not a common practice, however, in other types of extraclass activities. The scholastic requirements for athletics were made necessary by the many abuses that existed before they were adopted.

The figures on eligibility requirements for participation in other activities indicate much lack of agreement. For example, a study by Sanders shows that 82 per cent of the schools in his sample required that students be passing a certain minimum number of courses to be eligible for instrumental music, but only 19 per cent had a similar requirement for vocal music![15] This is an interesting and paradoxical practice and may be peculiar to one state. Unfortunately, recent studies of requirements in other states are not reported in the literature.

The authors recognize the practical considerations involved in setting certain minimum state eligibility requirements for interscholastic athletics. Similar conditions do not exist, however, in other extraclass activities. We support the view expressed by a junior high school principal who said, "We have no eligibility except to say that we expect them to be doing as well as can be expected. . . . We try to take the positive approach through homeroom teachers, coaches, directors, counselors, etc., before dropping a child from an activity."[16] The authors believe that except for interscholastic athletics, eligibility should be determined by what, in the judgment of staff members, is best for the student and the activity.

5. *All students should be encouraged to participate in the extraclass program, but overparticipation by a few should be discouraged.* If the experiences provided in extraclass activities are of consequence, all students should benefit and, therefore, all students should participate in them. It does not follow, however, that all students should be required to take part or that no restrictions should be placed on the extent of participation by individuals.

With few exceptions, it would seem desirable to keep student involvement on a voluntary basis. One of the most important assets of extraclass activities is the interest of students growing out of their freedom of choice. The youngsters are there because they want to be there. At least this is true for all but homerooms and assemblies, where it is essential to reach all students for guidance and administrative purposes.

In order to retain the value of spontaneous interest and to involve a maximum number of students, the faculty of each school will need to

---

[15] Stanley Sanders, "Survey of Eligibility Requirement for Participation in Extracurricular Activities," *The Iowa Center for Research in School Administration, Research Report No. 4,* State University of Iowa, June 24, 1960, pp. 3–4.
[16] *Ibid.,* p. 6.

plan a comprehensive program appropriate for the needs and interests of most students. For a large majority of students, the matter of securing participation should require little effort. For a few, however, skilled guidance may be necessary to get them to take part in the program. These are usually the ones who need it most — the potential dropouts, the delinquents, and the isolates. Recognition and awards for participation have been employed successfully by many schools to stimulate participation.

One of the perplexing problems in administering the activity program is that of discouraging overparticipation by a few students. It is perplexing because it is difficult to determine when a student is overparticipating. Some exceptionally able students seem to thrive on an educational diet that includes a large number of activities, and their academic work does not appear to suffer. On the other hand, unusually high participation in the extraclass program may take adolescents away from their homes more than is desirable and may limit their experiences in other worthwhile community affairs.

Of equal concern to school faculties is the fact that overparticipation by a few able and popular students reduces opportunities for others. To meet this problem a number of high schools have classified activities as "majors" or "minors" and have limited the number in each category in which a student may engage during any one semester. For example, serving as a student council officer, a publications editor, a member of the cast of an important dramatic production, or a varsity team captain may be classified as a major activity, while serving as a member of an intramural team, a homeroom officer, a newspaper reporter, or a band member may be defined as a minor activity. A maximum limit, such as a combination of five majors and minors, four majors, or six minors, may be set for any one student during a semester. The exact limits should be determined jointly by faculty and student representatives in each school.

Other schools use a point system to limit the amount of participation. Weighted point values are assigned to each activity, and students are limited to a certain total number of points during a semester or year. Some schools also use this system to encourage participation by granting a school letter or some other award when a student has earned a certain point total, regardless of the nature of the activities in which he engages. The point system is much more complicated than the major-minor system and involves extensive clerical work. It is also difficult to assign appropriate point values to various activities and positions.

Since students vary so much in their capacities, interests, and needs, it is the view of the authors that the most effective way to control overparticipation is individual counseling. Systems become rigid and may not permit a program that is appropriate for an individual student. Recommended limits may be useful in counseling, but the counselor should be free to exercise his best judgment in recommending a suitable extraclass program for each of his counselees.

6. *The extraclass activity program should serve the mores and educational needs of the local community.* An activity which departs from or defies local mores is likely to be injurious to the school program as a whole and promote antagonisms between students, faculty, and laymen in the community. If the students and faculty are convinced that a certain activity is desirable but it appears to deviate from long-standing customs, conventions, and beliefs in the community, an effort should be made to persuade representative citizens to consider its merits and to approve it on a trial basis. Often the most productive approach is to conduct a series of small-group discussion meetings with students, faculty, and parents. If agreement cannot be reached after a reasonable effort has been made to educate the elders of the community, action should be deferred until the time is more propitious.

By way of illustration, adults in some communities in which there is a dominant religious group may be opposed to social dancing, girls' sports, and/or modern music. But students may be intensely interested in one or all of these, and may actually be participating in them outside of the local community and school. The faculty may be convinced that it would be far better to provide these activities under school auspices than to have students forced into unsupervised situations in order to secure the experiences that they desire and believe they need. Certainly this situation involves important educational issues, and the faculty has the right and responsibility to attempt to persuade the public to shift its position. But the faculty and students cannot defy public opinion without weakening support for the school program and dividing the community into quarrelsome factions. Even though the board of education may agree with the students and faculty, the negative impact on the community may far outweigh the advantages gained in pursuing the issue.

Consideration should also be given to educational needs of the community in planning the extraclass program. If a town is limited in musical, dramatic, and other cultural opportunities, the school may well emphasize these areas. In communities lacking recreational facilities, the school — over a period of years — may educate future adult citizens to appreciate the values in community recreation and assume leadership in securing such facilities.

The school also may aid in perpetuating distinctive customs and traditions of the community through its activity program. Certain national groups often bring colorful as well as educational dances, folk songs, and celebrations with them to America. It is a serious loss to our cultural life if these traditions are permitted to fade away in two or three generations.

7. *Extraclass activities should supplement and be articulated with other phases of the educational program.* Most extraclass activities sponsored

by a school should supplement its classroom and guidance programs. Notable exceptions are such purely social and recreational affairs as parties and dances. More than thirty years ago Fretwell wrote, "Wherever possible, extracurricular activities should grow out of curricular activities and return to them to enrich them."[17] After decades of empirical testing, Fretwell's thesis appears to be as appropriate for secondary schools today as it was when he stated it. Subject clubs, assembly programs, intramural sports, newspapers, and forensics have proved to be valuable supplements to formal class instruction over the years.

Through the science club, for example, students may pursue individual and small-group research projects for sustained periods of time. These operate under unstructured conditions in which students learn because they are curious and are permitted to follow their curiosity. The teacher assumes the role of a consultant rather than a director. Classroom instruction, on the other hand, serves a special and essential function in directing systematic study and practice under necessary time limitations and with larger groups of students. Because of the interest and self-motivated activities of students in clubs, their projects may be used effectively as demonstrations in science classes or to motivate systematic study.

Debate, dramatics, and journalism supplement the English program; intramurals motivate the program in physical education; work on the student council enriches social studies; and a ham radio club may give new meaning to industrial arts. Each of these activities also helps students discover and develop educational and occupational interests and thereby supplements the guidance program.

Some educators contend that extraclass activities should be converted to classroom activities with credit, fixed-time assignments, grades, and similar administrative accessories. This has happened, and is happening, in several fields such as music, speech, journalism, and electronics. As stated in a preceding section, the authors believe that the formalization of activities can be overdone. Much of their value depends upon their spontaneity, freedom, and self-direction. Extraclass and classroom activities can be mutually beneficial through close articulation, but this does not require amalgamation.

Articulation also needs to be effected with respect to such administrative matters as scheduling, practice periods, physical facilities, publicity, and teacher loads. For example, administrative practices which permit certain popular activities to disrupt classroom instruction frequently or demand a disproportionate share of the teachers' time defeat the purposes of activities. Such practices tend to warp the students' sense of educational values and erode the morale of the faculty.

[17] Elbert K. Fretwell, *Extra-Curricular Activities in Secondary Schools* (Boston: Houghton Mifflin Company, 1931), p. 2.

8. *Lines of responsibility should be well defined; extraclass participants should recognize that the legal authority for their organization and functions is vested in the board of education and faculty.* If all of the participants in an activity are students, if the activity uses school facilities, and if it is associated with the school in the eyes of the public, it is a school activity and should be subject to school policies and control. Each student activity derives its authority from, and is under the control of, the board of education. Most boards properly delegate much of their authority in this field to the faculty and hold the members responsible for the successful conduct and direction of the program.

Students and some community groups do not always understand the administrative framework within which activities must operate. Misunderstandings develop most frequently in relation to those sponsored by an outside organization such as the band mothers, Monday morning quarterbacks, and civic and patriotic clubs. The aims of these organizations may be commendable, but frequently their members have no conception of the difficulties and conflicts they promote within the school. It may be a commendable undertaking for the Junior Commercial Club to sponsor an all-star high school basketball game to raise money for a charity, but it commits the school to join in other equally worthy community projects, and collectively, these affairs disrupt the instructional program. The rapidly increasing volume of such externally sponsored enterprises seriously interferes with the basic functions of the school.

Student council members sometimes become confused with respect to their rights, privileges, and functions. Upon occasion, they have been known to develop a legislative complex and have undertaken to legislate on such things as the curriculum, school discipline, and teaching methods, which are not their proper responsibilities. They may properly advise with the faculty on such matters, and they should communicate the views of students to the faculty; but they should not legislate on them.

Many of these points of confusion may be anticipated and should be clarified by means of written statements of faculty and board policies and rules of procedure. Most activities should be chartered by the student council acting upon authority granted by the faculty and board of education. A charter should be given only upon the basis of an appropriate constitution and set of bylaws submitted by potential members of a proposed organization and should clearly state the lines of responsibility for the organization in relation to the board, faculty, and student council. A few student activities, of course, do not lend themselves to a formal charter. Varsity athletics, band, assemblies, and dramatics should operate under plainly stated board and faculty policies, but a formal charter would have little purpose.

The faculty and board, acting through the administrative head of the school, should retain veto power over proposed actions by student organizations. However, the frequent exercise of the veto will soon destroy the sort of student-faculty rapport and student initiative that a faculty is trying to build through the activity program. Therefore, the principal should rarely permit himself to be placed in the position of having to veto student proposals. The faculty adviser should consult with the principal when he observes that students are considering action in conflict with school policy. They should then take steps to avoid the sort of action that would require a veto.

Faculty and administration cannot always accept action taken by members of an activity group, and in this circumstance the principal will need to exercise his veto power. He should, of course, give his reasons to the student organization in order to preserve as much of the positive relationship between the students and the faculty as possible.

9. *Participation in extraclass organizations and most events should be limited to students currently enrolled.* In the interest of providing for and encouraging participation by regularly enrolled students, and of exercising responsible control over student conduct, only *bona fide* students should take part in most extraclass activities. Certain commonsense exceptions, such as community service projects in which laymen and students cooperate, the admission of adults to school entertainments, and some types of social events, will be necessary. But usually the general policy should be followed. Surely, participation in athletics, musical organizations, clubs, plays, and most social events should be limited to regularly enrolled students. The primary justification is to provide as much opportunity as possible for regular students to benefit. If nonstudents are admitted, *bona fide* students may be denied the chance to get experience or they may be discouraged from competing for certain positions. Although state athletic association regulations limit participation in interscholastic athletic events to enrolled students, many other activities are not regulated by a state association. Therefore, controls must be exercised by local authorities.

The need to supervise the conduct of members of school organizations is another important reason for limiting participation to enrolled students. Outsiders may not recognize the authority of school officials and may engage in undesirable behavior and influence younger students to do the same. Problems most frequently arise in connection with dances and parties. Occasionally, exceptions may be appropriate for certain social affairs, but if so, admission should be by invitation, and the invited guests should understand that they will be expected to observe the same standards of conduct as students.

A further reason for excluding outsiders is that participation by mature and experienced performers in some events and productions makes it almost impossible to evaluate the growth made by students and creates a misleading impression of the quality of work being done.

10. *Each extraclass activity should be supervised by competent and interested faculty members.* A few years ago the head of a famous boys' home was reported to have said, "There is no such thing as a bad boy." He was widely quoted by sincere but rather unrealistic supporters. Presumably the same generalization would hold for girls. But anyone who has had extensive experience with adolescent boys and girls knows that some of them, if they are not bad, persistently behave badly. Moreover, many of them who are not bad get mixed up in unfortunate situations under the pressures of the gang.

Most high school students may be trusted to behave in conformity with desirable social standards most of the time. But when adolescents are together and unsupervised, unpredictable situations develop. Some boys suddenly get an urge to show off, the gang meets another gang which challenges them, someone bets that his car will outrun another car, and accidents happen. Consequently, any social event, group meeting, athletic contest, or other activity which is held under the auspices of a school should be supervised by one or more teachers and/or administrators.

The most important reasons for faculty supervision are (1) to provide mature leadership in order to direct student activities toward desirable goals, (2) to protect students from injury or impetuous acts that may involve them in serious trouble, and (3) to insure that the position of the school is properly interpreted when controversial situations rise. In the interest of providing opportunities for effective learning, it is desirable to give adolescents as much freedom and responsibility as they demonstrate they can assume in the conduct of their own affairs; but this can, and should, be done only under competent supervision. A really skillful supervisor will guide but not dominate the activities and thinking of students. He will permit them to risk mistakes, provided that they are likely to learn from their mistakes and that no serious damage is likely to result.

A faculty member need not be an expert in a specialized field such as electronics or creative writing in order to succeed as a supervisor of an activity, but he needs to be interested, willing to learn, and skillful in working with students. If an expert layman is available, and if he is the sort of responsible person with whom parents want their children to be associated, he may well serve as consultant to a group. But it should be clearly understood that the teacher, not the lay consultant, is the responsible supervisor of the group and the official representative of the school.

Some laymen question the policy of requiring faculty supervisors for all activities, arguing that any expert layman is a competent teacher. But long experience has demonstrated that many laymen are not successful as teachers. Furthermore, teacher-supervisors are in a better position than a layman to interpret school policies and to coordinate the learning activities in an extraclass project with other phases of the school's program. In addition, the use of faculty sponsors lessens the likelihood of the exploitation of students. Many schools have had unfortunate experiences with lay specialists who have volunteered their services in such fields as athletics, music, dramatics, dancing, boys' clubs, and the like. Too often it has developed that they have been using the school for self-advancement and exploiting talented students to build a reputation for themselves.

Although a faculty sponsor need not be an expert in a specialized field to be a successful activity adviser, he must share the interest and enthusiasm of students. In some fields, of course, such as athletics, music, and dramatics, the coach or director will have to have expert knowledge in order to command the respect of students. But in activities such as service or hobby clubs students will usually accept the leadership of a sponsor who is genuinely interested and willing to learn with them. If no teacher with a sincere interest in a certain activity is available, the activity has little chance of success. Adult leadership often is the cement that holds the activity together and gives it proper direction.

11. *Activity sponsors should be appointed and supported by the administrative head of the school.* One of the key issues in the selection of sponsors for activities is whether they should be appointed by the administration or elected by students. The most common as well as the recommended practice is for the principal to appoint all sponsors. This policy (1) increases the probability that the sponsor will be qualified to work with a particular group of students, (2) permits the administrator to balance teacher loads, and (3) avoids the sort of popularity competition among faculty members that frequently results from student election of sponsors.

Since the administrative head of a school is responsible for the success of its educational program, it is essential that he have an opportunity to select and to organize his faculty team. He is in a much better position than the students to know the over-all needs of the school and how individual faculty members can best serve the activity program.

Bill Johns may be the best man on the faculty to serve as adviser to the newspaper staff, but he may also be the best man to get the boys' service club back on the right track. Furthermore, the newspaper may be well established and have an excellent student staff, and Betty Miller may be interested and well qualified to sponsor it. Even though Bill Johns is the choice of the newspaper staff, the principal appoints Betty Miller because he needs Bill for the service club and Betty can be depended upon to do a capable job with the paper.

Teaching loads and preferences also should be considered in the assignment of sponsors. Here again, the principal is in a much better position than the students to know the conditions and problems involved. In the interest of good staff morale and of the well-being of individual faculty members, teaching loads should be made as reasonable and equitable as possible. If activity sponsors are elected by students, the factor of teacher load is usually lost sight of in favor of personal popularity.

The preferences of teachers for certain activities should be one of the important considerations in their assignment. Administrators will have more valid information relative to a teacher's interests than will students. Furthermore, if teachers are elected they usually are hesitant to express their preferences because of a desire not to show favoritism toward a certain group of students. Nevertheless, most teachers do have pronounced preferences in line with their training and experience, a factor which usually affects their enthusiasm and effectiveness in working with students in an activity. The administrator may find it impossible to give each teacher his first choice of an activity, but he can usually manage to give him his second or third choice.

If faculty sponsors are to provide the type of professional direction necessary to the success of extraclass activities, they must be assured of the support of the administrative head of the school when strains and stresses develop. Some activities invite considerable pressure because they are in the public eye and involve frequent competitions and/or public performances. Other activities may happen to attract a few students who are difficult to supervise. When conflicts develop which require the faculty sponsor to take a firm but unpopular stand, he must be assured of the backing of the administrator and, through him, of the board of education. This is not to suggest that the administrator should support a teacher right or wrong, but if the sponsor is clearly wrong and has done a serious injustice to a student or group of students, the administrator should be willing to help him correct the injustice with as little loss of professional prestige as possible. If the teacher is right and has upheld the policies and objectives of the school in dealing with a problem, the principal must stand behind him regardless of the pressures that are brought to bear. Otherwise the administrator will lose the confidence of his faculty, and his entire educational program will suffer.

Questions and Group Projects

1. Secure a description of student activities sponsored by an English grammar school such as Eton or Harrow and compare that program with a typical program in a large public high school in your state.

2. Interview several high school graduates and secure their opinions as to the values of extraclass activities to them.

3. Interview a random sample of high school seniors from four to five different schools. Secure their opinions on (1) values, (2) costs, (3) eligibility requirements, and (4) methods of selecting members of student activities.

4. Secure copies of faculty and board of education policies for extraclass activities from four or five different schools and discuss their appropriateness in light of the aims of extraclass activities.

5. Secure copies of the eligibility requirements of the activities association or associations in several states and make a comparative analysis of them.

6. Prepare a case study description of a controversy over some phase of extraclass activities in a high school in your state. Describe the community, the school, the events leading to the controversy, the composition of the conflicting groups, the debate, and the actions that resulted. Draft a critique of the procedures employed by the school administrators in this situation.

7. Assume that you are principal of a high school of 500 students and the board of education has refused to finance from tax funds any part of the athletic program other than the salaries of coaches. Prepare a case to be presented to the board for the allocation of some tax money for your athletic program.

8. Make a survey of the extent of participation by students in activities in any high school in which you have access to the records.

9. Should local school faculties attempt to persuade students to participate in activities in which they have shown no interest? If so, describe the circumstances and the reasons.

10. Make an analysis of the news stories about schools carried in five daily newspapers during four different one-week periods during the school year. What conclusions may be drawn from this analysis?

Selected References

Cooperative Study of Secondary School Standards. *Evaluative Criteria.* Washington: The Study, 1950. Pp. 35–45.

Douglass, Harl R. *Organization and Administration of the Modern High School.* Boston: Ginn and Company, 1954.

Fretwell, Elbert K. *Extra-Curricular Activities in Secondary Schools.* Boston: Houghton Mifflin Company, 1931.

Hamilton, Homer H. "The Educational Values of Pupil Activities," *Texas Study of Secondary Education,* Research Bulletin No. 29, Austin: University of Texas, January, 1960.

Johnston, Edgar G., and Roland C. Faunce. *Student Activities in Secondary Schools.* New York: The Roland Press Company, 1952.

Kilzer, Louis R., Harold E. Stephenson, and H. Orville Nordberg. *Allied Activities in the Secondary School.* New York: Harper & Brothers, 1956.

Lynd, Robert S., and Helen M. Lynd. *Middletown.* New York: Harcourt, Brace and Company, 1929.

McKown, Harry C. *Extra-Curricular Activities.* New York: The Macmillan Company, 1952.

Miller, Franklin A., James H. Moyer, and Robert B. Patrick. *Planning Student Activities.* Englewood Cliffs, N.J.: Prentice-Hall, Inc., 1956.

National Association of Secondary School Principals. "Vitalizing Student Activities in the Secondary School," *The Bulletin* of the NASSP, February, 1952, Vol. 36.

Rockefeller Report on Education. *The Pursuit of Excellence — Education and the Future of America,* America at Mid-Century Series, Garden City, N.Y.: Doubleday and Company, 1958.

Tompkins, Ellsworth. *Extraclass Activities for All Pupils.* U.S. Office of Education, Bulletin No. 4. Washington: Government Printing Office, 1950.

U.S. Bureau of the Census, *Statistical Abstract of the United States: 1958* (79th Edition). Washington: Government Printing Office, 1958.

CHAPTER 9

Administration of Major Types of Extraclass Activities

The growth of the activity program in American secondary schools has paralleled the rapid rise in enrollments during the twentieth century. The types of activities most frequently found in contemporary high schools are those listed by the Cooperative Study of Secondary School Standards:[1]

      1. Pupil participation in school government.
      2. Homerooms.
      3. The school assembly.
      4. School publications.
      5. Music activities.
      6. Dramatics and speech activities.
      7. Social life and activities.
      8. Physical activities for boys.
      9. Physical activities for girls.
    10. School clubs.

With the possible exception of homerooms, each of these areas is, in the view of the authors, essential to a balanced extraclass program. Some, to paraphrase George Orwell, are more extraclass than others, depending upon local circumstances. Speech, publications, and music are being made credit courses in an increasing number of schools, while clubs, as-

[1] Cooperative Study of Secondary School Standards, *Evaluative Criteria* (Washington: The Study, 1950), pp. 195–205.

semblies, social affairs, and sports operate chiefly as extraclass activities. Course work doubtless gains something when activities are brought into the classroom, but extraclass activities lose something when they are formalized as credit courses. Two of the most important assets of activities have been their appeal to student interests and the high degree of student participation which they induce.

Since the planning and management of the activity program is one of the major duties of a high school principal, he will need to be familiar with trends, purposes, and administrative problems related to each of the broad extraclass fields. Consequently, it is our purpose in this chapter to describe trends in each of the main types of student activities, call attention to successful administrative practices and policies, and suggest sources for more detailed information.

Student Participation in Government

Student participation in government is the heart of the extraclass program. It embraces those activities in which the entire student body has an opportunity to participate in planning and managing extraclass affairs and in matters of student citizenship. The term may be somewhat cumbersome, but it has a precise meaning. It suggests that students should be given an opportunity to help plan and manage some of their own school affairs, but it does not suggest that the government of the school should be turned over to students. The legal responsibility for the control and management of local schools is delegated by each state to boards of education, who, in turn, delegate much of it to professional staffs. For educational purposes, a professional staff may desire to share some of its authority and responsibility with students. The extent of the sharing depends upon the maturity of students, their interest in assuming responsibility, and their knowledge and skill in using authority. These conditions are not static, and as students develop, the amount of responsibility delegated to them may be extended.

Although the student council has emerged as the key organization in programs of student participation in government in many schools, the two are not identical concepts. The council is a body of representative students elected to perform certain functions in a broad program of student participation. However, students also may take part in planning and managing extraclass affairs on a town meeting basis, as members of *ad hoc* committees, or as members of a homeroom. The student council may be the most effective organization for achieving the purposes of student participation, but it is not essential to the achievement of those purposes. A number of schools have a functioning program of student participation in government without a student council.

Purposes

The central aims of student participation in government are to promote the best interests of the school and to provide opportunities for students to develop desirable civic qualities and know-how. The program takes citizenship education beyond the realm of theory and makes possible direct and active experiences under circumstances that have many elements in common with life outside the school.

A study conducted by the National Association of Secondary School Principals reports that principals regarded the following as the chief purposes of the student council:[2]

To furnish citizenship training	48%
To allow students to participate or manage extracurricular affairs	16.4%
To promote student-faculty relationships	15.5%
To promote general welfare	12.1%
To provide pupil expression	4.3%
Miscellaneous	3.7%

Held has proposed the following aims and objectives for the council:[3]

AIMS AND OBJECTIVES OF THE STUDENT COUNCIL

A. Pupils
  1. To train for citizenship through participation in school government.
  2. To develop leadership qualities.
  3. To provide a clearinghouse of student opinion.
  4. To provide an opportunity to participate in school activities.
  5. To provide an opportunity for pupil self-expression.
B. School
  1. To develop in the student body a high morale and sense of pride in the school.
  2. To promote better student-faculty relations.
  3. To provide a channel to reach the student body more effectively.
  4. To conduct social affairs.
  5. To organize school activities.
  6. To conduct various campaigns.
  7. To help solve school problems.
C. Community
  1. To represent the student body in various civic committees.
  2. To assist in various community drives and campaigns.
  3. To assist in reducing delinquency.
  4. To develop good public relations.

---

[2] "The Student Council in the Secondary School," *The Bulletin* of the NASSP, October, 1944, 28:20.
[3] Warren H. Held, "What Are the Aims, Objectives, and Powers of the Student Council?" *The Bulletin* of the NASSP, April, 1958, 42:88–90.

Types of Councils

Although there are other types of organization for a program of student participation, a large majority of schools prefer some form of council. The National Association of Student Councils, organized in 1931, reported 283 members in 1943–44 and 6,413 in 1954–55.[4] The total number was undoubtedly higher, since some schools with councils did not belong to the Association. Ludwig conducted a study of 345 high schools in nine midwestern states in 1961–62 and found that all of them had some type of organized program of student participation in government.[5] Two general types of councils are sponsored in American secondary schools: the first is a *student* council composed entirely of elected student representatives but with one or more faculty advisers; and the second is a *school* council, which includes both student and faculty representatives. Usually the principal is an ex officio member of the latter.

The *student* council is by far the more common, but the *school* council is gaining in popularity. The latter has the merit of providing an organization which encourages direct planning and exchange of views by students and faculty members. One important limitation of the *school* council is that teachers may tend to dominate the proceedings and thereby discourage student initiative and interest.

Numerous adaptations in the form of organization for the student council are made in secondary schools over the country. Some schools employ a bicameral council modeled after our national or state legislatures; others use a model of state or national government, with executive, legislative, and judicial branches; and still others have a unicameral type of organization. Most of the rest have modifications of these three basic types. Officers of the council may be elected in a general student election or by the council from its own membership.

The authors believe that the unicameral council, with representatives elected from homerooms and officers elected at large by the student body, is the most satisfactory type for most schools. Its organization is simple, and the homeroom, as the basic unit for representation, is small enough to permit all students to take an active part in the conduct of student affairs. The council membership should not be too large to permit effective discussion and action. Miller, Moyer, and Patrick found in a nation-wide study that student councils ranged in size from twenty to one hundred members and that the average size was fifty-two.[6]

---

[4] Gerald M. Van Pool, "A History of the National Association of Student Councils, 1931–56," *The Bulletin* of the NASSP, October, 1955, 39:78–153.

[5] Merlin A. Ludwig, "A Survey and Evaluation of Current Practices and Problems in Scheduling Co-curricular Activities in Public Secondary Schools in Nine Midwestern States," unpublished Ph.D. dissertation, State University of Iowa, 1962, p. 295.

[6] Franklin A. Miller, James H. Moyer, and Robert B. Patrick, *Planning Student Activities* (Englewood Cliffs, N.J.: Prentice-Hall, Inc., 1956), p. 231.

Projects

A persistent problem related to the functioning of student councils has been their tendency to become occupied with unimportant things. In some schools the council meets merely for the sake of meeting, and upon occasion it undertakes projects that contribute little to good student-faculty rapport. In the absence of substantial projects the council may become hardly more than an exclusive political science club. Some projects such as conducting elections, making up a budget, and planning and scheduling social affairs are perennials, but these are not sufficient to challenge a group of bright and energetic students for a full year.

Councils may constructively engage in promoting desirable attitudes toward scholarship, promoting good relations with neighboring schools, providing community and school service, improving student citizenship and school spirit, raising funds for activities, assisting in planning the activity budget, developing good faculty-student relationships, sponsoring student foreign exchange programs, engaging in community welfare services, chartering new organizations, and sponsoring programs to encourage or to control student participation in activities. These projects assume different characteristics in different schools, and it is difficult to describe a particular project that would be suitable for all schools, or even for one school over a period of years. There are, however, some excellent suggestions in the yearbooks of the National Association of Student Councils and in some of the recent special reference books on student activities and councils. The National Association of Student Councils, which is sponsored by the National Association of Secondary School Principals, publishes an informative magazine for student councils entitled *Student Life*.

One of the more controversial questions involved in a program of student participation has to do with the student council's serving as a policing agency and/or court. The authors subscribe to the point of view that council members should not be expected to police or to take punitive action against their fellow students. We believe that most adolescents are too inexperienced to assume these functions and that they may become badly confused with respect to their authority in relation to that of the faculty. Certainly the council can, and should, be effective in working with the faculty to develop constructive social attitudes and desirable standards of conduct among all students. But the responsibility for disciplining students is delegated by the public to teachers upon the assumption that they have the maturity of judgment and wisdom to exercise it judiciously.

Administrative Guides

Some form of student participation in government has been in operation in European secondary schools since the early Greek period and in

American schools since the late eighteenth century. Over the years school administrators have developed some working precepts which, though not qualifying as principles, should serve as useful guides to administrators who are interested in establishing a council or some other type of student participation.

1. *A program of student participation should grow out of student interest and desire.* A faculty may suggest that students study and investigate the possibilities in a program, but it should not be launched before the student body is ready and understands its purposes. Otherwise, misunderstandings and disappointments are likely to develop, with a consequent lack of constructive service.

2. *The program should function under a written constitution.* The constitution should define lines of responsibility, spheres of authority of the faculty and student body, functions and duties of the central body, functions and manner of selection of student representatives and officers, and relationships between the central body and other activities. Teachers and students should find it helpful to study constitutions from other schools, but they should develop their own working instrument. A model constitution is included in the handbook published by the National Association of Student Councils.

3. *Adequate and competent faculty supervision should be provided.* The number of faculty advisers and their qualifications should be such as to insure competent and sympathetic supervision of the program from year to year. Advisers should provide mature direction but should not dominate the program.

4. *All students should have representation in the central organization.* It is important that the basic groups from which representatives are chosen should, in combination, include all students and that each group should be small enough to encourage direct and active participation by all students at the grass-roots level. The entire student body should participate in the direct election of officers.

5. *A program of student participation should be developed gradually.* It takes time to arrive at teacher and student understanding of the purposes, functions, and responsibilities of a program of student participation. Usually it is most effective to begin with a few committees and to undertake only a limited number of projects during the early stages. The successful completion of one or two important projects will go far toward developing confidence in the program.

6. *Projects and problems undertaken should be considered important by students.* A student organization that meets merely for the sake of meeting or is limited to leaf-raking and paper-picking projects is of little value and its members may develop negative attitudes toward the school. The central body should select problems of real significance to students and get something done.

7. *The principal should retain veto power but should rarely be placed in the position of having to exercise it.* As stated in Chapter 8, the principal is the official administrative head of the high school and at times may be required to exercise his authority in terms of his experience and best judgment. The frequent use of his veto power, however, will defeat the purposes of a program of student participation. With competent faculty advisers, he should rarely have to veto student action. But it should be understood that he has the authority and responsibility to do so when he believes such action necessary.

8. *The council, or an alternative type of central organization, should be given power to grant charters to other student organizations.* A charter clarifies lines of responsibility and defines the position of the council, or its counterpart, in representing the interests of all students. In addition, the chartering process makes it possible to review the purposes of an organization and to avoid needless duplication. When a group of students have thought through the questions raised in preparing a charter, they are more likely to organize a purposeful and constructive activity than they would without going through this process.

9. *Good communication should be established between the central student organization and all students and faculty members.* Student participation cannot promote good citizenship and good student-faculty rapport without effective means of two-way communication. Regular reports to and from homeroom units or designated classes and to and from faculty meetings are indispensable to unity and direction in the program.

10. *Student representatives and officers should meet desirable standards of citizenship and scholarship.* Two important purposes of the program of student participation are to promote good school citizenship and to develop leadership. These can best be achieved through the example set by student leaders. Since student officers and representatives are presumed to be leaders, they may reasonably be expected to meet desirable standards of citizenship and scholarship. It is not important that all student representatives be top scholars, but certainly none should be scholastic laggards.

Homerooms

The homeroom is rapidly becoming more a part of group guidance than the extraclass program. Although it originated with the extraclass program well before the guidance movement had gained momentum, many of its major functions have always been in the area of guidance. As its name suggests, the homeroom was first conceived as a home within the school for students. It was to be a place where they would be able to get well acquainted with at least one teacher and he with them. It was to be a place also where students could become well acquainted with a small group of classmates and could consider personal and school problems within the friendly and informal setting of this group.

In addition, the homeroom was expected to function as a basic unit in the program of student participation in government. From this small unit, representatives to the council were to be elected and matters of school citizenship and the management of school activities were to be considered. The homeroom was to be a group of students small enough to permit each one to have a direct part in the management of student affairs. From it ideas would emerge to be transmitted to the council and the faculty, and the deliberations of the council and the point of view of the faculty were to be reported through it to the students. Thus, it promised to be the basic unit for participation in management of student affairs.

Gradually, however, attempts were made to formalize the homeroom. Manuals and teachers' guides were developed following protests by teachers that they were hard pressed to occupy the time allotted to homeroom periods. Many teachers found that student interest began to lag after the first few weeks of the school year, and they devoted more and more of the time to supervised study. Teachers in many schools regarded the homeroom as an extra assignment and resented the additional load.

By the late 1930's most faculties had abandoned the homeroom as an educational medium and it was converted to an administrative unit. It survived in many schools as a convenient organization for checking attendance, making announcements, collecting money, selling tickets, conducting registration, and similar routine procedures. Usually it met for about ten minutes each day, although occasionally the period was lengthened when the principal had some important business to present. Generally it continued to serve as the basic unit for the election of representatives to the council.

In the late 1940's and early 1950's some interest was revived in the homeroom as an appropriate unit for group guidance. It continued as an administrative unit, but the period was lengthened to thirty or forty minutes as needed for special guidance purposes such as administering standardized tests, securing pupil information, carrying out preliminary registration, and presenting guidance information. In most schools now employing some type of homeroom, it is a hybrid administrative, extra-class, and group guidance unit.

Although no recent nation-wide data are reported in the literature, Ludwig reported that in 1961–62, 62 per cent of the 345 midwestern high schools in his study scheduled a homeroom period.[7] And Lounsbury, in a study of 251 junior high schools in 1953, found that 93 per cent had homerooms.

The following summary statement by Miller, Moyer, and Patrick appears to be representative of the status of the homeroom in most states:

---

[7] Ludwig, *op. cit.*, p. 292.

MAJOR TYPES OF EXTRACLASS ACTIVITIES

One of the most controversial activities in the co-curriculum program is that of the home room. Theoretically the home room should be the co-curriculum's basic activity; in practice it is often one of the least popular organizations in the program. . . . It is an organized concept that should work but fails to live up to its potentialities in many schools. As an indication of this problem, the national survey on which this book is based revealed that not one school recommended the home room as worthy of special mention. Of course, one should not infer from this that all home rooms are inferior.[8]

If the homeroom is to be made a constructive part of the educational program of the school rather than merely a place for taking care of administrative routine, the authors suggest that the following conditions should be met in its organization and administration:

1. An in-service teacher education program should be conducted to develop an understanding of the philosophy and procedures of homeroom activities.

2. There should be clear evidence that a majority of teachers understand what their responsibilities will be, and that they believe a homeroom program has merit before it is initiated.

3. Adequate materials and guides should be developed cooperatively by teachers, counselors, and supervisors for use in homerooms.

4. Assignment of pupils to homeroom sections should be made on a heterogeneous basis within each grade level in order to promote social understanding and democratic attitudes.

5. Homeroom advisers generally should be assigned to the same group of students through their entire three or four years in the school.

6. The teacher-pupil ratio in each homeroom should be small enough to permit teachers and pupils to become well acquainted. A ratio not exceeding one to thirty is recommended by the Cooperative Study of Secondary School Standards.

7. Information needed in counseling students should be made readily available to homeroom advisers.

8. Students in homerooms should be given extensive opportunities to participate in the organization and implementation of the program. Officers should be elected and programs and business conducted by democratic procedures.

9. The student council or its counterpart should be made up of elected representatives from the homerooms.

10. Adequate time should be provided for homeroom activities in the daily schedule, but time allocations should be flexible and adjusted to the requirements of the program. Probably a daily period of ten to twelve minutes will be adequate, with the understanding that this may be increased to thirty or forty minutes when needed.

---

[8] Miller, Moyer, and Patrick, *op. cit.*, p. 172.

Assemblies

The modern school assembly evolved from the religious chapels of seventeenth- and eighteenth-century secondary schools. From the chapel exercise it developed into a meeting for administrative purposes and then into a combined educational and entertainment medium with extensive student participation.

Purposes

The general purposes of school assemblies as proposed by various writers and as suggested by the types of programs reported in the literature are to (1) supplement the educational experiences of the classroom, (2) develop good student morale and school spirit, (3) aid in guidance, (4) provide wholesome entertainment, (5) recognize student achievement, and (6) aid in the organization and administration of the school.

The primary function should be educational. Not only is it desirable for a majority of programs to be informational, but as many students as possible should be given an opportunity to be active participants in order to develop poise and to have experience in expressing themselves before an audience. In view of the increasing opportunities for high school students to observe professional entertainment of one sort or another via television, it is becoming more difficult to present school assembly programs that command audience interest. Under the circumstances, a somewhat greater percentage of outside speakers, films, and lyceum programs may be in order for school assemblies than has been customary in the past. But well-presented student dramatic and musical productions and stimulating forum discussions on problems that are of genuine interest to students usually are well received.

Administrative Guides

The following guides for the conduct of assemblies has been compiled from suggestions by experienced school administrators and from criteria proposed by various writers and professional organizations: (1) Most school assembly programs should be planned jointly by teachers and students. (2) A central planning committee composed of student and faculty representatives should plan the assembly schedule for the year and assume much of the responsibility for its administration. (3) Assembly programs should be planned to serve all of the educational objectives of the school. (4) Extensive participation by students should be a major goal of the over-all program. Student chairmen should preside over most assemblies. (5) A sustained effort should be made to develop good audience attitudes and courteous conduct as an integral part of the program. (6) Some assembly programs should provide for audience participation, *e.g.*, group singing and forum discussions. (7) Adequate provisions should be made for assemblies in the school schedule. (8) No charge for admission should be made to students for assembly programs, except for an occasional benefit program to raise funds for some worthy cause. (9) All assembly programs should be evaluated by a central planning committee. (10) Adequate faculty supervision should be provided to insure good programs and good audience situations.

Suggestions and examples of programs are included in the general references on extraclass activities listed in the bibliography at the end of this chapter and in such periodicals as *School Activities,* published by the School Activities Publishing Company, Topeka, Kansas, and *The Bulletin* of the National Association of Secondary School Principals.

School Publications

Most of the publications sponsored in American secondary schools are of four types: (1) newspapers, (2) handbooks, (3) yearbooks, and (4) magazines. The school newspaper first appeared in high schools around 1850. The executive secretary of Quill and Scroll, honorary high school journalism society, estimates that a school paper is now published in approximately one-half of the secondary schools of the nation, and in some states the figure is as high as 90 per cent.[9] In the late 1940's Hess estimated that 15,000 high schools sponsored some 30,000 publications at an annual expenditure of over sixteen million dollars.[10] Although no recent national data are reported in the literature, the school yearbook appears to rank second in terms of the number of schools sponsoring it, the handbook third, and the school magazine fourth.

In a majority of schools, publications are strictly extraclass activities, but in 36 per cent of the schools in Ludwig's study, the school paper was sponsored as a joint project of a journalism class and an extraclass staff.[11] The student handbook usually is a project of the student council, and the magazine normally is sponsored and directed by the English department.

The Newspaper

Historically, the school newspaper developed out of students' interest in news about themselves; currently it is supported largely by that interest. It also serves as a record of the school year, an educational project for the staff, an effective means of interpreting the school to parents and patrons, and a means of fostering *esprit de corps.*

In 1955, Benz states, 49.2 per cent of school papers in Iowa were mime-

[9] Lester G. Benz, "The Status of Journalism in Iowa High Schools," unpublished master's thesis, State University of Iowa, 1956, p. 24.
[10] Ellsworth Tompkins, *Extraclass Activities for All Pupils,* U.S. Office of Education, Bulletin No. 4 (Washington: Government Printing Office, 1950), p. 24, footnote quoting Walter E. Hess, Managing Editor of NASSP.
[11] Ludwig, *op. cit.,* p. 304.

ographed or multilithed, 31 per cent were printed as a page in the local commercial newspaper, and 17.6 per cent were printed on a regular printing press as independent school papers.[12] National data are not available but probably do not vary greatly from these figures. The independently printed school paper is the most attractive and satisfactory type, but it is also the most expensive. A duplicate-processed school paper is far better than none and can be made readable and attractive. In small communities a school page in the weekly town paper may be an asset both to the school and to the local paper, although problems of control and working relationships with the editor may arise.

Benz reports that a slightly larger percentage of school papers (28.7 per cent) are published monthly than weekly (26.7 per cent).[13] If at all possible, the paper should appear weekly or biweekly; otherwise it loses its value as a *news* medium. Few things are more vapid than old news stories.

The three major administrative problems in sponsoring a school paper are (1) financing, (2) supervision and control, and (3) maintaining high quality. Financing is usually accomplished by subscriptions and the sale of advertising. Although some administrators frown on the sale of advertising, most merchants seem to believe that they get their money's worth from advertising in school papers, and it provides students an opportunity for sales and layout experience. Since the newspaper usually is a valuable educational activity, tax funds should be made available to make up any deficit resulting when reasonable subscription rates and advertising sales do not provide sufficient income to meet production costs.

The supervision of the school paper should be directly under a competent and responsible faculty adviser. However, a board of publications composed of members of the student council and the faculty may be desirable to assist the faculty adviser in formulating policies and in business management. Policies on such matters as review of editorials and news stories should be established, and applicants for student staff positions should clearly understand them before they are appointed. Students sometimes confuse freedom of the press with freedom to write and print anything they choose. In commercial papers, freedom of the press is enjoyed by the publisher, but he establishes policies for his staff. In school papers, students sometimes do not understand that the school is the publisher. A publications board may be extremely helpful in defining lines of responsibility with the student staff, developing policies, lending support to a hard-working faculty adviser, and settling differences of opinion.

Over a period of years, the quality of the school paper will depend primarily on the adviser. On the other hand, finances, working time, and continuity of the student staff also affect the quality of the paper and

[12] Benz, *op. cit.*, p. 25.
[13] *Ibid.*, p. 26.

these are responsibilities of the principal. A journalism class offered in the eleventh and twelfth grades may help in securing continuity on the student staff and a scheduled period in the school day for production work usually pays dividends in terms of quality.

The Yearbook

Although school administrators disagree on the value of a yearbook, most students seem to feel that the school would be incomplete without one. If students want a yearbook badly enough to pay for it and do the work, there are few good reasons why they should not have one. But if it has to be financed by donations from local merchants under the guise of advertising and if some English or journalism teacher has to do most of the work, it is scarcely justified.

The costs to students can be eased if multilith printing is employed and if the covers are plain instead of ornately tooled. Several companies now multilith school yearbooks and do excellent work.

The principal value of a yearbook is its memory-book appeal to students, but under an imaginative adviser and staff it can be made a good medium for creative writing and art work. If it also tells the story of the entire school rather than a few popular activities and events, it may serve as a valuable historical record.

Student Handbook

The handbook is primarily a service publication for incoming students. The better handbooks do not contain advertising and often are financed by an appropriation from the board of education, since they are employed in orienting new students to the school. One of the most frequent criticisms of handbooks is that they are usually so small that they are difficult to read and to locate when needed. To be most serviceable, the handbook should be at least five by eight inches in size.

The publication of a handbook or its periodic revision provides an appropriate project for the student council. An excellent handbook — that of Shaw High School, East Cleveland, Ohio — came to the attention of the authors. Major topics included in it are a greeting and foreword by the principal, history of the school, annual events and school calendar, guide to rooms, assemblies, attendance and other regulations, graduation requirements, grading system, school records, interesting places in the school, the student council, athletics, clubs, music, courtesy ideals, and school songs and cheers.

The Magazine

Although published by relatively few high schools, the school magazine often contains the best creative writing to be found in any school publication. The magazine is not burdened with the necessity of selling itself through gossip columns, "guess who" sketches, tired jokes, and class prophecies. An excellent example of a high school literary magazine is *The Writers Rendezvous,* published annually for over twenty-five years by the Little Rock, Arkansas, Central High School. It is put out under the direction of the English department and contains many creative prose pieces and poems written by students in English classes. A unique feature of *The Harvest,* school magazine of the Wahlert High School, Dubuque, Iowa, is the fact that the several issues during the year are so planned that they can be bound into an attractive book at the end of the year.

Music Activities

It is almost impossible to distinguish between the extraclass and classroom programs in music because of the overlap in personnel and instruction. For example, band may be scheduled during a regular period and carry academic credit, which qualifies it as a regular course, but the band may also compete in contests and play at athletic events, which are primarily extraclass affairs. Some students participate in glee club without credit as an extraclass activity and some enroll for credit as a part of their regular study load. This section will be directed primarily to extraclass administrative problems in music rather than to the scope and nature of the entire program.

The purposes of extraclass music activities are the same as those for the organized course program except for harmony, history of music, or other theory classes. The Music Educators' National Conference defines the purposes of music education as follows:

A. The primary purpose is to disseminate the cultural aspects of music as an art.
B. A second purpose . . . is to help pupils develop understanding of other peoples through acquaintance with their music.
C. . . . to develop in each child knowledge and appreciation as well as skill in music.
D. . . . to educate children in the use and worth of music in the home, church, and community.
E. . . . to encourage its use as a means of recreation, as an avocation or a hobby.
F. . . . to encourage and explain its use not only as a cultural experience, but also as a means of relaxation and release from tensions of everyday living. . . .
G. . . . to identify the child gifted in music and guide the development of such giftedness so that the individual may realize his potential so that such talent may be shared with society.
H. . . . to use it as a means of developing social relationships, desirable conduct, feeling of responsibility, and group cooperation.[14]

[14] "Music — A Vital Force in Today's Secondary Schools," *The Bulletin* of the NASSP, Part One, March, 1959, 43:5–6.

MAJOR TYPES OF EXTRACLASS ACTIVITIES

The most common extraclass music activities, as reported by Miller, Moyer, and Patrick, are group singing (assemblies), choruses, music clubs, band, orchestra, operettas, contests, and festivals.[15]

Difficult administrative problems sometimes grow out of an overemphasis on public entertainment and contests. Unfortunately, some music teachers have a limited understanding of the place of music in a comprehensive educational program. They seem to believe that music competitions, concerts, festivals, and related activities should be given priority over other phases of the school program and over a program of general music education. Practices such as taking students from other classes to prepare for special music affairs, making long trips to participate in demonstrations for music educators, or participating in big spectaculars such as bowl games and national carnivals are questionable but fairly common.

One indication of loss of perspective concerning the relative values of music and academic classroom instruction is reflected in the payment of higher salaries to music teachers than to teachers of academic subjects. Ernst, in a nation-wide study of music programs in large cities, reports that "Opinion of music directors was about equally divided over the matter of granting extra pay to secondary school music teachers."[16] Apparently the practice of paying music teachers more than other high school teachers is commonplace, and it is controversial even among music educators.

There are other persistent problems in the administration of music activities:

1. The overemphasis on bands and a corresponding neglect of instruction for all. Price reports that in 943 high schools — all members of the North Central Association in 1950 — three times as many offered band as offered orchestra.[17] This situation reflects an overemphasis on the entertainment aspects of school music, especially in the extraclass phases of the program. Unfortunately, many high schools offer no music instruction at all for a majority of students.

2. Scheduling music activities so as to avoid conflicts with other activities and classes. Large schools are able to schedule music classes and organizations during regular periods in the daily schedule, since they have duplicate sections in academic courses and a large enough enrollment so that their music groups do not depend upon the same student personnel in order to be able to function. Ludwig reports that 80 per

---

[15] Miller, Moyer, and Patrick, *op. cit.*, pp. 384–96.

[16] Karl D. Ernst, "A Study of Certain Practices in Music Education in Cities of 150,000 Population," *The Bulletin* of the NASSP, Part One, March, 1959, 43:92. (Abstract of Ed.D. dissertation, University of Oregon, 1955.)

[17] David E. Price, "An Analysis of Some of the Musical Experiences Provided for Students in the Tenth, Eleventh, and Twelfth Grades in Public Secondary Schools Approved by the North Central Association," unpublished Ed.D. dissertation, University of Colorado, 1950.

cent followed this practice.[18] Small ensembles and clubs in large schools often are scheduled during the activity period or at irregular times outside of school hours.

The problem is quite different in small high schools. Ludwig found that 39 per cent scheduled band and 57 per cent scheduled chorus during the activity period.[19] It is usually impossible to clear a period for students from four different grade levels in small schools without interfering with other classes. Many students in these schools must participate in both vocal and instrumental music groups if these organizations are to have sufficient membership to permit effective work. In addition, the same students are likely to be essential to the athletic, dramatics, and forensic programs and may be carrying a schedule of five academic classes.

Consequently, the large music groups in small schools must meet outside of the regular school day or during an activity period. Probably the most feasible answer is to schedule band in the morning before school or during the noon hour and vocal groups during the activity period and on alternate days with physical education. Meetings after school are extremely difficult to arrange because rural students must usually return home on the buses and several boys are certain to have conflicts between music and athletics.

In schools of medium size, a combination of periods within and outside of regular school hours may be worked out. Lickey bases the following suggestions on his long experience in a six-year high school in Missouri, which enrolls about 900 students:

> Let orchestra alternate with band the same period each day. First semester, during the football season, let band meet three periods a week and orchestra twice. . . . Keep the orchestra, band, and chorus periods free of one section classes. Place in these periods only those classes that seem to draw few musicians.[20]

3. Granting credit. The matter of credit for extraclass participation in music is complicated by the fact that there is so much overlap in student personnel. For example, some students participate in band for credit and some participate without credit. The same situation exists in several other quasi-formal music activities.

For those who desire or need credit, the most common practice is to grant one-fourth of a unit per year for a music group that meets at least two periods per week for thirty-six weeks. The Music Educators' National Conference recommends one-half unit of credit for music classes which meet daily throughout the school year.[21] The North Central As-

[18] Ludwig, op. cit., p. 304.
[19] Ibid.
[20] Harold L. Lickey, "Scheduling the Music Program in a Small or Middle-Sized High School," *The Bulletin* of the NASSP, Part One, March, 1959, 43:104–5.
[21] "Music — A Vital Force in Today's Secondary Schools," *The Bulletin* of the NASSP, Part One, March, 1959, 43:16.

sociation requires 275 minutes per week for 36 weeks for a full unit of credit in activity-type classes.[22]

4. Determining the place of contests, festivals, and trips in the music program. Although the festival idea has been gaining some following at the expense of contests in a few states, regional and state contests are still extremely popular, and apparently a large majority of secondary schools in the nation participate in them. Although there are no accurate national statistics to back up the foregoing conclusion, it has been one of the persistent activity problems studied by administrators of North Central Association high schools for several years.

The concern of the Association is reflected in the Contest Committee's report of 1951, in which it stated,

> The Committee believes that contests in music tend to emphasize specialization in music rather than the general education aspects. It is recommended, therefore, that more emphasis be placed upon the festival idea. . . . Interscholastic music contests should be discontinued.[23]

The Music Educators' National Conference also devotes one complete section of a recent report to festivals and contests. The report states,

> Festivals and contests offer the opportunity for school organizations to broaden their experiences in music. They offer students the opportunity to work toward specific performance objectives, to see and hear other organizations perform, and to have the advantage of competent judgment and criticism about the work that the groups and individuals are doing. Although festivals and contests have the same purposes, they are distinct in their organization and procedures; *and it would seem from the fact that organizations are more and more frequently taking part in festivals or in modified contests, that the festival better achieves these purposes than does the contest* . . .[24]

The authors agree with this point of view and hold that a shift to festivals would eliminate many of the undesirable practices which now attend preparation for, and participation in, music contests. Some music teachers now spend an excessive amount of time polishing a few numbers and working with a few talented students in preparation for contests. The results are a limited repertoire for music groups and the neglect of a balanced music program to serve the needs of all students. If the pressures to make as many "one" ratings as possible in contests were removed, music teachers would be in a much better position to develop a balanced program.

[22] North Central Association, "Policies and Criteria for the Approval of Secondary Schools" (Chicago, Commission on Secondary Schools, 1960), p. 22.

[23] North Central Association of Colleges and Secondary Schools, "Recommendations of the Contest Committee of the North Central Association," *North Central Association Quarterly,* January, 1951, p. 263.

[24] "Music — A Vital Force in Today's Secondary Schools," *The Bulletin* of the NASSP, Part One, March, 1959, 43:26–28. (Italics ours.)

Speech and Dramatics

Although speech gained admission to the high school program as an extraclass activity like music and publications, it has become established as a classroom subject in many schools. Speech was one of the first branches of extraclass activities to be initiated by students in secondary schools. In 1961–62 Ludwig found that of the 345 midwestern schools studied, 88 per cent sponsored speech activities.[25]

Johnston and Faunce classify extraclass activities in speech as *forensic* and *interpretative*.[26] Forensic activities include debating, extempore speaking, group discussion, student senate, and oratory. The interpretative program embraces such activities as long plays, short plays, declamation, choral reading, interpretative reading, and radio and television productions. Each of these has an important place in a balanced high school speech program.

Speech activities serve the individual student in developing poise, the ability to work cooperatively with others, the ability to communicate effectively, skill in the use of reference materials, the ability to organize ideas logically, and the ability to do creative work. They have value to the school, as an institution, in stimulating public interest and promoting student *esprit de corps*.

The administrative problems in extraclass speech are much the same as those in the field of music. The chief problem is the great proliferation of speech contests, which many colleges, civic organizations, women's clubs, and commercial firms tend to promote. A few speech contests have educational value, but the law of diminishing returns sets in soon after the first ten or twelve during any one school year. In addition to the loss of a great amount of school time and the expense involved, participation in a large number of contests greatly increases the load on speech teachers. Since the normal reaction in competition is to try to win, the program of basic speech activities suffers because of the need to put a high polish on a few talented students for contest purposes.

One means employed successfully in some schools for controlling overemphasis on all contests, including speech, is the organization of an advisory committee of parents and teachers to recommend a maximum limit on the number of contests and a list of approved contests for the school year. Such a committee should serve strictly in an advisory capacity to the board of education. If a school has a citizens advisory committee, the contest committee might well be a subcommittee of this larger organization. The approved list of national contests published by the National Association of Secondary School Principals in *The Bul-*

---

[25] Ludwig, *op. cit.*, p. 294.
[26] Edgar G. Johnston and Roland C. Faunce, *Student Activities in Secondary Schools* (New York: The Ronald Press Company, 1952), p. 224.

letin each fall provides a valuable guide for local schools in considering national contests.[27]

Financial support is another problem in the extraclass speech program. The dramatics program may pay its way, but other aspects of the speech program, such as debate, oratory, and group discussion, do not attract many paying customers. Speech activities have important educational values and, if necessary, should be supported from tax funds as well as from extraclass income.

The following criteria for "Dramatics and Speech Activities," prepared by the National Study of Secondary School Evaluation, are well-developed guides for the administration of this phase of the extraclass program:

1. Opportunity is provided for students to write and to produce their own dramatic productions.
2. Dramatic activities provide opportunity for practice in a variety of stagecraft activities.
3. Student dramatic activities are presented to the community.
4. Dramatic activities encourage attendance at good plays in local theaters.
5. Provision is made for participation in formal or prepared presentations such as addresses, debates, and radio programs.
6. Provision is made for student participation in informal and extemporaneous speech activities.
7. Students markedly lacking ability or confidence to express themselves are provided speech activities to meet their particular needs.
8. Dramatic and speech activities provide for participation by many students as well as participation by talented performers.
9. The dramatic and speech activities are coordinated with curricular experiences in English.
10. Equipment . . . and materials are provided for dramatic and speech activities.
11. Financial returns from dramatic and speech activities are subordinate to the educational values.[28]

Social Life and Activities

School parties, dances, festivals, picnics, and social clubs have been a part of student life since the days of the early European grammar schools. When such activities have not been permitted in the school, students have merely shifted their base of operations outside the school, and this has created new problems. The central issue is not whether

---

[27] National Association of Secondary School Principals, "Approved List of National Contests and Activities for 1962–63," *The Bulletin* of the NASSP, September, 1962, 46:216–26. (List published each fall.)

[28] National Study of Secondary School Evaluation, *Evaluative Criteria* (Washington: The Study, 1960), p. 250.

young people should engage in these activities but whether the school should sponsor and supervise them.

Some laymen and educators believe that purely social affairs do not belong in a school program and that the entire responsibility for providing them should be assumed by the home and other community agencies. Affairs of this kind detract from the intellectual purpose of the school, they argue, and overburden the faculty with duties of supervision.

Supporters of a social program in the school maintain that many students come from homes where they do not have opportunities for desirable social experiences and that the school is an appropriate institution for sponsoring wholesome social activities for all youth. Proponents maintain also that it is far better to conduct such affairs under the supervision of the school than to force students into unsupervised situations in order to satisfy their desires for social experiences. Many parents and teachers believe that school social events are valuable means of developing democratic attitudes and relationships, since students from all social levels participate in them.

The school cannot reform the social behavior and alignments of adults, but it is in a position to organize and sponsor social affairs for youth that develop democratic attitudes, encourage the timid, and develop good manners among the rowdies. Social activities may be regarded as fads and frills by those who believe that the only function of the school is intellectual training, but the secondary school is working with boys and girls whose emotional and social adjustment often affects their attitudes and achievement in the classroom. Equally important, their attitudes and behavior as members of the community are affected by these factors. It is a distinct loss to society as well as a personal tragedy when any student drops out of school or becomes a delinquent, especially if he is a potentially fine scholar. Often when these things happen, it is due in no small measure to the fact that the student has failed to gain recognition and acceptance among his schoolmates. The authors recognize the danger of overgeneralizing on such matters, but research shows that many delinquents are intellectually superior children.[29]

We believe that the following suggestions for the organization and implementation of a program of social activities should contribute to its effectiveness in serving the needs of all students and in developing desirable attitudes and standards of behavior:

1. The program of social activities should be planned to serve and to encourage the participation of all students.

2. Most school social functions should be limited to students registered in the school. Occasional exceptions may be made for invited guests for certain types of functions.

[29] Austin L. Porterfield, *Youth in Trouble* (Potishman Foundation, 1946).

3. No student should be prevented or discouraged from taking part in school-sponsored social events because of costs. If a formal activity entailing considerable expense to students is desired by a large majority of students, an effort should be made on a confidential basis to assist students who need help to get some part-time work.

4. The program for any one year should include a variety of activities — recreational games, picnics, dances, dinners, and parties.

5. Effective supervision should be provided for all social affairs. Parents should be encouraged to assume joint responsibility with the faculty for supervision.

6. The school code for student conduct should include standards for social affairs. Parents, students, and teachers should cooperate in formulating such standards.

7. The program of social activities should be planned jointly by students, parents, and faculty.

8. Provision should be made for instruction in matters of etiquette, dress, and conduct for various types of social functions.

9. Exclusive organizations such as fraternities and sororities should be prohibited. These organizations are illegal in most states, but even though they are not banned by state law, they have no place in a secondary school concerned with developing wholesome social values and democratic attitudes.

Physical Activities — Athletics

The United States is a sports-loving nation. The pride and joy of many communities are their high school athletic teams. Upon occasion, normally rational and solid citizens, including educators, become highly irrational over schoolboy sports.

The great interest of adults and students in school athletics may be explained partly by the love of excitement and the drama of sports events, partly by our frontier tradition of physical competition, and partly by the increased leisure time enjoyed by the American people. More important, a great majority of parents, patrons, students, and educators believe that there are positive educational values in athletics for our type of society.

Values

In light of the evidence, the thesis that athletics builds character better than do other types of school activities appears to have been overworked. Athletics does, however, provide a setting which permits the right type of coach to establish close rapport with a group of boys through their great interest in sports. If the coach is a man of character, he has a fine opportunity to build character. This is not to say that the music teacher, debate coach, or dramatics instructor cannot be equally effective in working with students in their fields, but the coach works with boys at a certain stage of development when athletics has a powerful attraction for them.

Presumably there is something droll about a coach's building character, especially when he has a losing season, but any high school teacher who does not build character is in the wrong profession. The faculties of the great public grammar schools of England may have been laboring under illusions for the last three centuries, but they have maintained extensive sports programs primarily for their value in character education.

The Educational Policies Commission in a bulletin on athletics declares, "We believe in athletics as an important part of the school physical education program. We believe that the experience of playing athletic games should be a part of the education of all children and youth who attend school in the United States."[30] Expressions of faith in the worth of athletics as reflected in the long-time programs in English schools and endorsements by such groups as the Educational Policies Commission lend strong support to the view that athletics has important values for participants and schools. Supporters of school athletics hold that the program (1) educates for worthy use of leisure time — for physical, recreational interests and skills; (2) contributes to physical fitness and bodily strength, which, in turn, contribute to the physical health of the individual; (3) provides opportunities for many students to gain recognition and status among fellow students; (4) contributes to the mental health of participants by providing relaxation, play therapy, and recognition; (5) develops physical coordination; (6) develops attitudes and skills in team play which have direct carry-over values for our way of life.

In addition, it may be claimed quite logically that a sound athletic program serves the school by (1) building *esprit de corps* among students; (2) stimulating interest in the school among the adults of the community; (3) providing associations with other schools which broaden the educational experience of students, teachers, and patrons; and (4) bringing many patrons to the school who otherwise might not have occasion to visit it and to get acquainted.

Problems

The most serious problem in high school as well as college athletics is overemphasis on winning. Certain unfortunate practices such as the following have become all too common: (1) Coaches and administrators

[30] Educational Policies Commission, *School Athletics — Problems and Policies* (Washington: National Education Association, 1954), p. 3.

are discharged because of losing seasons even though they may be competent teachers, (2) coaches often are paid higher salaries than academic teachers, (3) students are indoctrinated with a false sense of values with respect to the importance of athletics and winning, (4) key athletes are used by coaches when they are not physically fit to compete, (5) coaches tend to devote their attention to a few physically gifted athletes and neglect a broad program for all students, (6) men are employed as coaches for girls' teams, (7) too much time is lost from school for championship meets and long trips, and (8) star athletes are proselyted by large high schools and colleges.

These practices result largely from pressures exerted on the schools by dominant individuals and groups, but they also stem from the loss of educational perspective on the part of school administrators and coaches. Some coaches and administrators permit abuses because they are obsessed with winning, but fortunately the number in this category is small. Others suffer abuses because they are ineffective in developing rational support for their educational program among citizens in the community. Still others have the ability and perspective but have not been in their positions long enough to bring the situation under control.

There are wide differences among communities in attitudes toward athletics. In some with a long history of athletic fanaticism, the school administrator will wisely go about the business of building a sane philosophy of athletics and support from responsible citizens rather gradually. Otherwise, he may find that he no longer exercises educational leadership in the community, since he is no longer in a position of leadership. Most assuredly he will have to develop basic policies for an athletic program before he can hope to gain support.

Guides

The authors suggest the following administration guides in the interest of maintaining a sound high school athletic program:

1. The program should be based on a clear statement of athletic policies formulated and adopted through cooperative action by representative citizens, the board of education, and the professional staff.

2. Publicity and recognition for athletic accomplishments should not be emphasized at the expense of other school activities. The school administrator cannot control the news stories prepared by mass media, but he can do much to educate commentators, reporters, and editors about schools. Certainly he can influence practices with respect to publicity and recognition within the school.

3. Coaches should be given classroom teaching assignments and status as teachers. They should be selected on the basis of their competence as teachers as well as their competence as coaches. Their coaching assignments should be regarded strictly as extraclass activity assignments

and should be made on the same basis as the assignments of other teachers to activities. If a coach is not satisfactory as a coach he should be shifted to another activity, but he should have the same tenure on the faculty as any other teacher.

4. Coaches should be paid on the same scale as other teachers with the same training and experience. The argument that coaches spend more hours out of school working with students than most other teachers may be true, but other teachers spend many out-of-school hours reading papers, planning instruction, and doing committee work. The teaching load of a coach should be adjusted to compensate for his long hours, but to pay him a higher salary not only implies that the school board and administration regard coaching as more important than teaching in other fields but also sets up the coach as a target for disgruntled taxpayers.

5. The interscholastic athletic program should grow out of a broad base of physical education and intramural sports for all students. The varsity interscholastic program should not be emphasized to the detriment of the basic program. Provisions should be made for programs for students of different abilities, maturity, and interests.

6. The athletic program should be financed in part from tax funds and in part from admission charges. It should not be required to pay all of its way from gate receipts. This is the source of many of the abuses in interscholastic sports, at both high school and college levels. As long as athletics has to make its own way and in some schools pay the freight for certain other activities, the program is forced to woo cash customers, and cash customers, being human, pay to see a winning team. If the athletic program has real educational merit, it should be underwritten by the board of education in the amount that gate receipts fall short of the expenditures required for a comprehensive and balanced program.

7. The health and physical well-being of participants should be given top priority in the athletic program. Most schools now require that all students desiring to take part in athletics have a physical examination and the approval of a doctor before being permitted to participate. This should be a uniform requirement in all schools and for all branches of athletics. The school should provide the best equipment available to insure that students will have the greatest possible protection against injury.

8. The school should make arrangements for adequate insurance to cover medical expenses in the event that a participant is injured. In most states, group insurance coverage is made available at a nominal cost through the state activities association.

9. Insofar as facilities permit, interscholastic athletic contests should be scheduled on Fridays or Saturdays so as to avoid additional midweek conflicts with home study and other educational activities.

10. A statement of permission should be secured from the parents of a student before he is allowed to participate in the athletic program. It should be recognized that there is greater danger of injury in competitive sports than in most other phases of the school program and parents should be apprised of this fact and indicate their willingness to share responsibility.

11. All athletic events should be well supervised by faculty members. The principal, or one of his assistants, and some teachers should be present at all athletic contests. Problems may arise precipitately and some official representative of the school should be present to minimize the likelihood that students or spectators may become involved in unfortunate incidents during the excitement of the competition.

12. A positive program should be conducted to develop attitudes of good sportsmanship upon the part of all students plus desirable competitive relations with other schools.

Junior High School Athletics

In the bulletin on school athletics referred to earlier, the Educational Policies Commission makes the unqualified recommendation that junior high schools should not engage in interscholastic athletic competition. Conant made the same recommendation in his 1960 report, *Education in the Junior High School Years*.[31] However, many school administrators, coaches, and parents do not agree and some heated debates have developed on this issue in recent years.

The main argument in opposition to interscholastic competition in junior high schools is that it adds to the existing overemphasis on secondary school athletics. If good balance is to be maintained between the academic and athletic programs, it is time to contain, rather than expand, interscholastic athletics. Some educators and laymen argue that interscholastic competition for junior high school students is likely to be injurious to their health, but no conclusive evidence is available on this point.

The supporters of interscholastic competition claim that junior high school boys love sports competition, and if the school does not provide a program, they will gang up on sandlots and compete without proper supervision and equipment. This appears to be a sound argument for a comprehensive intramural program in the junior high school, but not for an interscholastic program. The pressure for interscholastic competition at the junior high school level has come largely from college and senior high school coaches and rabid fans who are primarily interested in grooming junior high school boys for varsity competition in the senior high school.

[31] James B. Conant, *Education in the Junior High School Years* (Princeton, N.J.: Educational Testing Service, 1960), p. 42.

The authors are in general accord with the views of the Educational Policies Commission and Dr. Conant on this issue. Probably there would be no detrimental effects from an interschool game or two at the end of the intramural season, but we believe that a full schedule of interscholastic contests in the junior high school tends to result in greater imbalance between athletics and scholastics. Furthermore, we believe that such competition would be likely to subject the junior high schools to the same sort of pressures for winning teams that now plague the colleges and senior high schools. If this happens, it may be anticipated from experience in the senior high schools that coaches will tend to neglect an intramural program for all students in order to concentrate on the development of a few boys with athletic promise.

School Clubs

History and fiction record that youth have been getting together in some manner for fun, companionship, or competition since people first began to live in communities. Twentieth-century psychologists have employed the term "gregariousness" to describe this form of behavior, and in recent years the rather saccharine term "togetherness" has become a synonym. Regardless of terminology, most youth exhibit a strong affinity for the companionship of their peers and there is little that adults can, or should, do about it except give it some direction.

Undirected, youth often have drifted into gangs and gotten themselves into an uncommon amount of trouble. Directed, they have joined forces in many constructive services and recreational organizations. It took about a hundred years, however, for American administrators and teachers to recognize the educational potential in the gregariousness of adolescents. Sub-rosa clubs persisted on the fringes of secondary schools throughout the nineteenth century, but not until the early 1900's did they receive any encouragement as means of supplementing the curriculum. Following World War I, the club movement gained momentum rapidly. It is now solidly established as a part of the activity program.

Not all high schools should sponsor an extensive club program, however, nor should all students belong to a school club. The role of clubs in the high school is largely a supplementary one. If a need exists for a certain type of educational experience, if a number of students are interested in doing something about it, and if a capable and interested sponsor is available, the organization of a club should contribute to the school program. But if these conditions cannot be met, and if a club is promoted primarily to satisfy some teacher or prominent layman, the prospects for its success are poor.

Student interest and faculty support are the first essentials for the success of any school club. This is not to suggest, if the initial response of students to a proposed organization is apathetic, that no attempt should be made to promote it. But if after a reasonable effort has been made to sell a club idea, student reaction remains indifferent, the project may as well be abandoned. A club just for the sake of a club is likely to be a liability to the school and an imposition on student and faculty time.

The need for a club program will depend to a considerable extent on the amount of student participation in other types of extraclass activities in a particular school. In small high schools, the percentage of students engaged in music, athletics, forensics, dramatics, and other activities may be so high that there is little need and little time for an extensive club program. In large schools, however, often less than 30 per cent of the students participate in other activities, and a club program may serve as the most successful means of enlisting a large majority of students in the extraclass program.

Assets

The special virtues of school clubs are that they enable a high percentage of the student body to take part in the extraclass program and that they provide a wealth of opportunities for students to learn through experiences with projects and the management of club affairs.

Clubs also make possible the enrichment of course work, the advancement of specialized interests and talents, the acquisition of skills in cooperative group action, and service to the school and community.

Types

Most clubs now found in secondary schools may be classified under the following headings:

1. *Service*, embracing such organizations as library assistants, stage crews, Hi-Y, Y-teens, secretarial services, pep squads, traffic safety, hospitality, and audio-visual operators.

2. *Subject area*, including science, civic, world affairs, Future Farmers, Future Homemakers, Quill and Scroll, GAA, foreign languages, creative writers, literary, Future Engineers, Distributive Workers, Future Teachers, and woodturners.

3. *Hobby*, represented by photographers, philatelists, numismatists, craftsmen, ham radio operators, model plane builders, astronomers, puppeteers, gourmets, travel, movies, gardeners, and similar groups.

4. *Social and recreational*, which embraces such groups and activities as social dancing, chess, bridge, folk dancing, group singing, fishing, boating, archery, and mountain climbing.

5. *Honors*. Some honors organizations are not active clubs, but several

do have officers and conduct projects. Included are the National Honor Society, Quill and Scroll, National Forensic League, Lettermen's Club, Girls and Boys Leadership, and similar organizations.

Administrative Problems

The most common problems associated with the administration of club programs seem to be (1) securing faculty support and competent sponsorship, (2) avoiding clannishness and social class cleavages, (3) keeping the club program sensitive to student interests, (4) keeping costs to students nominal, and (5) arranging for suitable times and places for meetings.

Staff Support

The quality of a club program in a local school will be about as good as the degree of interest and enthusiasm shown by staff members, individually and collectively. The first requirement in building a solid program, therefore, is to secure faculty support. If the administrator makes no effort to promote clubs, it is improbable that any sizable number of teachers will be moved to initiate a program. If he is extremely aggressive, there is danger that some teachers will react negatively or merely go along to avoid criticism.

Probably the best procedure is to begin with a few clubs and gradually build a comprehensive program. There are certain to be a few faculty members in any school who have the interest and skill necessary for the successful sponsorship of clubs. Given a chance to work with a few enthusiastic students and strongly backed by the administration, these teachers should get the club program off to a good start. Gradually other groups of students should become interested and other teachers impressed with the success of the pilot program. At this stage it ought to be possible to expand with a minimum risk of overemphasis.

It would be highly desirable for a sponsor to possess all of the noble virtues, but at going rates for teachers this expectation is a little unrealistic. The sponsorship of a club is an added responsibility for any teacher and the first requirement is availability. If, in addition to availability, the administrator can find desire, leadership, sympathy, and experience embodied in one teacher, he has about all he can hope for in a club sponsor. Availability and desire will be enhanced to a considerable extent by giving teachers their preferences in club assignments. It is unlikely that each sponsor can be given his first choice, but certainly he can be given his second or third choice.

Discrimination

A possible by-product of high school clubs, and an explosive one, is social discrimination. To a large extent snobbery reflects the attitudes and class structure of adults in the community. Youth tend to imitate their elders in basic social (and political) views, and the problems of the school administrator are made no easier by the fact that some parents encourage their children to band into social cliques.

The most vicious form that this may take in a school is racial discrimination, followed closely by economic snobbery and neighborhood clannishness. Secret fraternities and sororities have been the chief offenders in promoting social class division, but these are now illegal in most states, and school authorities should move quickly to bring legal action if they appear. More subtle, and therefore more difficult to deal with, are the school clubs which originate as recreational, service, or hobby groups and gradually assume the characteristics of exclusive social organizations. The girls' pep squad may appear to be a group of cheerleaders but actually functions as a social sorority. The key factor is usually the manner in which members are chosen. If new members are elected by current members, the organization will tend to become exclusive and social divisions will develop within the student body.

When undemocratic social segregation infiltrates the club program, the administrator has two choices: (1) to ignore it or (2) to change it. In either event he has trouble. If he ignores it, he not only gives tacit approval to the undemocratic values that result but invites open revolt on the part of the students and patrons against whom the discrimination is directed. Furthermore, he risks losing the respect of some of his more intelligent and fair-minded teachers.

If he undertakes to change it, he is almost certain to arouse the opposition of certain "influential" students and parents. His most likely chance for success is to secure the support of the board of education and his faculty and then take the issue directly to parents and students. A number of principals who have had the determination to face up to this problem have worked out a plan of gradual change in cooperation with a citizens committee or the PTA and, within a reasonable period of time, have been successful in effecting desirable changes. The story of a constructive approach to the sorority problem in the Ramsey Junior High School in Minneapolis is reported by Miller, Moyer, and Patrick.[32]

Student Interest

Student interests change and clubs wear out. Fifteen years ago there was a rash of aeronautics clubs in high schools following World War II; the current demand is for rocket clubs. Twenty or thirty years ago foreign language clubs were uncommon; today high schools without any are becoming uncommon.

Some clubs, such as the lettermen's club, honor society, library assistants, GAA and science club, generally persist year after year, but others come and go as adolescent interests shift. Since student interest is

[32] Miller, Moyer, and Patrick, *op. cit.*, pp. 291–92.

the principal motivation for learning in clubs, the program should be evaluated frequently to determine whether interest in certain organizations is beginning to lag. Declining interest may be due to the development of new interests, outmoded activities and procedures, or inept sponsors.

It is the responsibility of the school administrator to note shifting interests and encourage appropriate changes. A joint faculty-student advisory committee may be exceedingly helpful in identifying problems and making suggestions. Sometimes a shift in sponsors may be the answer, sometimes a new club is needed, and sometimes an existing club should be disbanded. There is no virtue in continuing a club merely for the sake of tradition.

Costs to Students

Since it is a purpose of the club program to reach as many students as possible, the costs to members should be kept nominal. If a club is engaged in construction projects which individual members retain upon completion, it is only reasonable that they should purchase the materials used. However, if a club is working on a group project that will benefit the school as well as provide worthwhile experience for the students, the school should share the costs either through a board allocation or by a grant from the general activity fund.

Expensive organizations such as an equestrian club requiring the ownership of a horse or a travel club requiring the ability to finance a long and costly trip, which exist in some public as well as private high schools, tend to aggravate class prejudices and to embarrass the youngsters and parents who cannot afford them. If students are interested in an expensive club project such as a long trip (e.g., a summer trip to Mexico City by the Spanish Club) and the project has the approval of the faculty and parents, long-term plans should be worked out for financing it. Members may gain valuable experience by cooperating in legitimate money-raising projects so that the expenses for all members can be paid from club funds.

Time and Place of Meetings

Ideally all school clubs should meet during the school day, but so should all classes and other activities. It should be possible, however, for most clubs to meet during the activity period at least twice each month. Of the 75 per cent of the schools with clubs in Ludwig's study, 35 per cent scheduled them after school and 20 per cent in an activity period.[33] If at all possible, club meetings should not be held in the evening except when the members are working on a special project which requires the use of school facilities not available at any other time. Evening meetings

[33] Ludwig, *op. cit.*, pp. 291 and 303.

present supervisory difficulties, impose on the time of busy sponsors, and tend to conflict with home study and other activities.

All but a few very special types of meetings should be held on the premises of the school to permit effective supervision. Exceptions may be justified for field trips and certain other unusual learning opportunities.

Extraclass Finances

Activity financing has developed into a relatively big and complex business in most schools. A survey by Brogue and Jacobson,[34] in the late years of the depression, showed activity budgets as high as $75,000 in some high schools, and recent reports from individual schools indicate that budgets have almost tripled during the last twenty years.

The management of extraclass finances is complicated because of the involved relationship of student activities to classroom instruction, the great variety of sources of income, and the lack of agreement on a system of control and accounting. As noted previously, the distinction between extraclass and classroom activities is becoming more and more difficult to make. Such activities as band, intramural sports, publications, and clubs are both extraclass and classroom ventures within the same school. It is also difficult to allocate costs for activities. All activities use the physical facilities of the school and are supervised by teachers. And such costs are paid from tax funds. At the same time, much of the operating cost for student activities is paid out of income from admissions, fees, dues, sales, and services.

The special responsibilities which the high school administrator must assume in the management of extraclass finances include (1) organization and control, (2) budgeting, (3) securing adequate support, (4) purchasing, (5) disbursements, and (6) accounting. Each of these will be considered in some detail in Chapter 18, on business functions.

QUESTIONS AND GROUP PROJECTS

1. Send a postal card questionnaire to the student body presidents of fifteen or twenty high schools of different size in your state. Inquire about their student council organization — size, functions, membership, projects, etc.

2. Should a program of student participation in government be modeled after the local city government? Should it include all branches?

3. Prepare a paper defending or rebutting the thesis that all student body and class officers and all student council members should be required to have above-average grades in order to be eligible for office.

[34] Ellen P. Brogue and Paul B. Jacobson, "Student Council Handbook," *The Bulletin* of the NASSP, March, 1940, 24:153.

4. Interview several homeroom teachers from four or five different secondary schools to get their appraisal of the homeroom. How do their opinions compare with the results of the study by Miller, Moyer, and Patrick?
5. Interview several high school students from four or five different schools to get their reactions to the number, types, and quality of assembly programs in their schools.
6. Examine ten or twelve high school yearbooks from different schools. What unique features are to be found in individual books? Are these books worth the time, money, and effort that they cost?
7. Should all materials to be published in a school newspaper be approved by a faculty sponsor?
8. Interview a random sample of parents of high school band members from several different schools. Get their views on the positive and negative values of having their children participate in band.
9. Organize some research teams from the student council or senior problems class of the high school with which you are most closely associated and have them interview high school students in some neighboring schools to compare their out-of-school and in-school social and recreational activities. Report the findings to the class.

Selected References

American Association for Health, Physical Education, and Recreation. *Physical Education for High School Students.* Washington: The Association, 1955.

Brammell, P. Roy. *Guiding Home-Room and Club Activities.* New York: McGraw-Hill Book Company, 1949.

Educational Policies Commission. *School Athletics: Problems and Principals.* Washington: National Education Association, 1954.

Fedder, Ruth. *Guiding Home Room and Club Activities.* New York: McGraw-Hill Book Company, 1949.

Forsythe, Charles Edward. *Administration of High School Athletics.* New York: Prentice-Hall, Inc., 1954.

Johnston, Edgar G., and Roland C. Faunce. *Student Activities in Secondary Schools.* New York: The Ronald Press Company, 1952.

Kilzer, Louis R., Harold H. Stephenson, and H. Orville Nordberg. *Allied Activities in the Secondary School.* New York: Harper & Brothers, 1956.

Ludwig, Merlin A. "A Survey and Evaluation of Current Practices and Problems in Scheduling Cocurricular Activities in Public Secondary Schools in Nine Midwestern States," unpublished Ph.D. dissertation, State University of Iowa, 1962.

Miller, Franklin A., James H. Moyer, and Robert B. Patrick. *Planning Student Activities.* Englewood Cliffs, N.J.: Prentice-Hall, Inc., 1956.

National Association of Secondary School Principals. "Health, Physical Education, and Recreation in the Secondary School," *The Bulletin* of the NASSP, May, 1960, Vol. 44.

———. "Music — A Vital Force in Today's Secondary Schools," *The Bulletin* of the NASSP, Part One, March, 1959, Vol. 43.

———. "A Speech Program for Secondary Schools," *The Bulletin* of the NASSP, January, 1954, Vol. 38.

National Association of Student Councils. *A Handbook for Student Councils.* Washington: National Association of Secondary School Principals, 1950.

National Study of Secondary School Evaluation. *Evaluative Criteria.* Washington: The Study, 1960. Pp. 241–57.

Strang, Ruth. *Group Activities in College and Secondary School.* New York: Harper & Brothers, 1941.

Thompson, Nellie Zetta. *Utilizing Assemblies.* New York: E. P. Dutton and Company, 1952.

CHAPTER 10

The Library as an Instructional Center

If the general level of instruction in secondary education is to be raised, the level of instructional resources must be raised. This is the main purpose of a school library. Other aspects of a school — teachers, curriculum, and guidance — may be more important, but the library plays an essential role in instruction and merits more than casual attention from the school administrator.

A national committee on school library standards states the case for the library as follows:

> Whatever form the soul-searching regarding the education of youth may take, sooner or later it has to reckon with the adequacy of the library resources in the schools. Any of the recommendations for the improvement of the schools, currently receiving so much stress and attention, can be fully achieved only when the school has the full complement of library resources, personnel, and services. This fact holds true for the multi-track curriculum, ability groupings in subject areas, the expanded and intensified science program, the toughening of the intellectual content of all courses, advanced placement and accelerated programs, the development of the disciplines of critical thinking, the teaching of reading, the provision of a challenging education for superior students, the meeting of needs of all students no matter what their abilities may be, ungraded elementary school classes, and similar practices and proposals.[1]

---

[1] American Library Association, *Standards for School Library Programs* (Chicago: The Association, 1960), p. 3.

In school, students learn from each other, from teachers and books, and from laboratories and shops. It is difficult to demonstrate that one type of experience contributes more than another. Much depends upon the individual and his purpose.

Students also learn by themselves through reading, observing, reflecting, and experimenting. Except in the realm of social relationships, these may be the most productive ways of learning. Carl Sandburg put it this way: "Da Vinci, Milton, Shakespeare, Jefferson, and Lincoln . . . didn't have television, but they had books. Most of all they had creative solitude. They weren't afraid of loneliness."[2] Libraries provide books and an atmosphere which lends itself to reflective thinking. Good scholarship in an era of greatly expanding knowledge requires access to and ability to use the means of communicating knowledge. It may be unrealistic to expect most adolescents to master any great portion of the world's knowledge, but it is also unrealistic to expect them to develop a great taste for knowledge in surroundings that stimulate little appetite for it. If educators and laymen are seriously concerned about the enrichment of educational experiences for high school youth, they must contribute more than verbalism to the support of our typically neglected school libraries.

Although the teacher is the key to quality in classroom instruction, even the best classroom teacher is severely handicapped without good working tools: books, periodicals, pamphlets, films, tapes, indexes, and the like.

The high school administrator cannot be an expert in all things, but he must be sufficiently well informed in each of the major aspects of the educational program to select competent personnel, to stimulate its development, and to evaluate progress.

Definition and Role of the School Library

The school library is the service and materials center in the high school program. It is for the use of students, teachers, counselors, supervisors, and administrators. It aids students by guiding their reading, stimulating their desire to learn, and assisting them to become self-directive in their pursuit of knowledge. It serves professional staff members by cooperating with them in planning the curriculum, keeping up with developments in instructional materials and equipment, securing professional reading materials, and guiding the learning activities of students.

A good school library is *not* simply a large room with books on rows of shelves, it is *not* a place for students to socialize, and it is *not* a special appendage to a school. It is the hub of the instructional program and its staff is a *bona fide* part of the faculty.

[2] *The Press-Citizen*, Iowa City, Iowa, November 16, 1960, p. 1.

In the words of one group of librarians,

> ... The school library, in addition to doing its vital work of individual reading guidance and development of the school curriculum, should serve the school as the center for instructional materials. Instructional materials include books — the literature of children, young people, and adults — other printed materials, films, recordings, and newer media developed to aid learning.[3]

Although large school systems may provide a special division of audio-visual instruction, every good school library should include some audio-visual materials and equipment in addition to many types of printed matter. The contemporary secondary school must draw heavily on a materials center to meet the educational requirements of its students and staff, and the modern school library is a resources and service center.

In summary, a functional school library is

1. *A service agency* — working with students and teachers in implementing the educational program.
2. *A teaching agency* — helping to guide the learning of students.
3. *A materials center* — providing all types of materials for learning.
4. *A reading center* — providing a suitable place for reading along with a comprehensive and organized collection of materials.[4]

The Present State of School Libraries

The school library should be and do all of the things proposed in the preceding section, but the typical high school in the United States is small, and small high schools usually have no qualified librarian and very little in the way of a library collection. Usually, library services are more adequate in large schools, but even in many of these funds are short and facilities limited.

A nation-wide survey of 2,830 school systems reports that the per-pupil expenditures for library materials in 1953–54 was only $1.05 and that the average number of books per pupil in school libraries was only 4.8. Of these 2,830 school systems, 5 per cent had no library service, 47 per cent were served from classroom collections only, 36 per cent had a centralized library, and 11 per cent had some other type of library service. Of the 16,785 high schools studied, 94 per cent had a central library and 91 per cent had someone acting as a librarian. However, of the 30,753 librarians employed in all of the school systems, only 51 per cent were trained in library work.[5]

[3] American Library Association, *op. cit.*, p. 11.
[4] Mary Peacock Douglas, *The Teacher-Librarian's Handbook* (Chicago: American Library Association, 2nd ed., 1949), pp. 3–4.
[5] Nora E. Buest and Emery M. Foster, "Statistics of Public School Libraries, 1953–54," *Biennial Survey of Education in the United States* (Washington: Government Printing Office, 1957).

In another national study, over one-third of the urban secondary school teachers rated the available library materials in their subject fields as "poor" or "only fair," while only one-fifth rated them "excellent." At the same time, almost all (99 per cent) of these teachers reported that they had some type of central library in their school.[6]

The Role of the Administrator

In order to serve students and teachers well the library needs knowledgeable support from administrators and supervisors. First, the library requires well-trained professional people to give it direction, and in most schools, boards are not likely to be sensitive to this need unless administrators make a strong case for library services.

In addition, a library needs materials, appropriate quarters, and faculty cooperation in order to become a really functional instructional center. A professional library staff can organize and catalog available materials, meet the faculty more than halfway in providing assistance, encourage students to use the library facilities, and call the needs of the library to the attention of the administration. But librarians cannot secure necessary funds, provide space and equipment, work with curriculum committees, and coordinate audio-visual and reading services without the assistance of administrators who understand the role of the library in a comprehensive educational program.

The principal is the key administrator in the operation of the library in his school, but the superintendent must persuade the board and the public that school libraries are just as vital to the educational program as other more publicized services. The superintendent must also prepare the budget, develop a system-wide organization for coordinated library and audio-visual services, formulate policies, and coordinate the planning of physical facilities.

The principal, on the other hand, works directly with the library and its staff. Not only must he interpret and implement system-wide library policies; he also must keep the superintendent informed about the progress and needs of the library in his school. More important, the interest and leadership of the principal will influence to a great extent the use made of library services by teachers and students.

Characteristics of Good School Libraries

Judging from the professional articles and speeches on the subject, school librarians seem convinced that most school administrators are not

[6] National Education Association, Research Division, "Library Services," *Research Bulletin,* October, 1958, 36:76–81.

sufficiently familiar with the qualities of a good school library to provide adequate leadership in the development of library services. A recent study of the treatment of the school library in textbooks used in courses in school administration confirms the librarians' opinion. Copeland and Shaw conclude from their study that

> (1) Although the library is considered an important phase of the secondary school program, authors of textbooks fail to give the type of treatment commensurate with its significance.
> (2) Textbooks used for professional preparation of school administrators are insufficient in content [on the library] to meet the needs of persons who are in administrative and supervisory positions.[7]

Although it would be unrealistic to undertake an extended treatment of the technical aspects of school libraries in a textbook on school administration, this section provides a summary of essential characteristics as recommended by various organizations and authors in the field. We believe that these will prove useful as guides for high school principals in planning and supervising library services.

Staff

In many years of conducting school surveys and evaluations, the authors have seen some poor libraries in schools with librarians, but they have never observed a good library in a school without a librarian. A casual collection of books, periodicals, and general references in a special room probably contributes something to the instructional program of a secondary school, but not much. To make such a collection effective, someone on the staff needs to organize and catalog it, prune it, build it up in the right places, know how to select the best materials for the money, keep essential records, and assist students and teachers in its use. These are the special tasks of the school librarian, and special training and experience are required to do them well.

Duties. Since the most important single factor in the success of a school library is the professional staff, the most important single thing that the administrator can do is to secure well-qualified personnel. This requires more than a superficial knowledge of what a good librarian should be expected to do. A review of professional books and articles on the subject suggests the following major areas of responsibility for school librarians: (1) developing and organizing a good collection of materials; (2) administering, supervising, and coordinating instructional materials; (3) working cooperatively with faculty members to secure good utiliza-

---

[7] Emily A. Copeland and Leander J. Shaw, "The Library as Presented in Selected Textbooks of Secondary School Administration and Supervision," *The Bulletin* of the NASSP, March, 1957, 40:81–92.

tion of library services; (4) working closely with students in encouraging and guiding their use of library facilities; (5) participating with other faculty members in curriculum planning; (6) working with people and agencies in the community to develop support for and to supplement the school library; (7) keeping adequate library records; (8) maintaining the collection in most usable form and husbanding the resources of the library; (9) evaluating the library services.

From the foregoing list of duties it is apparent that a school librarian needs to be much more than a technician, keeper of books, and guardian of silence. Although he must have technical know-how in selecting, ordering, classifying, and cataloging books and other reference materials, he must first of all be a teacher who is able to stimulate and guide pupils and work effectively with other teachers in developing and implementing the curriculum.

The capacity of the librarian to understand students and to encourage and guide their use of library materials is a major factor in the success of a school library. The librarian needs to develop a rapport with students which will prompt them to visit the library often and voluntarily, but at the same time he needs to maintain an atmosphere that encourages the constructive use of library facilities. He should be friendly, sympathetic, and somewhat more informal than the teacher in the classroom. But he also should be able to maintain favorable conditions for reading and study.

The technical aspects of assembling, organizing, and servicing the library collection require considerable time and training. Involved are selecting materials for purchase, ordering and processing new materials, making up index cards, shelving, and filing. The collection should be evaluated regularly and obsolete materials discarded.

The growing use of audio-visual materials in class instruction requires that the librarian be familiar with such materials and the equipment necessary to their use. If there is a separate division of audio-visual instruction in the school system, the high school librarian usually should assume the task of coordinating the use of facilities and services in his building with those of the central bureau.

It is important also that the school librarian work with public librarians in coordinating school and community library services. He should become familiar with community resources which might be available and contribute to the instructional program of the school. In his community relations he cannot afford to overlook the importance of developing interest and support for the school program and for its library. He should participate in organizations and enterprises which are devoted to the cultural and educational life of the community and, through these associations, interpret the purposes and needs of the school library to the public.

Numerical Adequacy. The number of trained librarians required to perform all of these tasks will depend to a large extent on the size of the school and its organization. In a small high school of 200 or fewer students, the North Central Association requires one part-time librarian who devotes at least one-third of his time to library duties — exclusive of study halls and related assignments. The Association requires a half-time librarian in schools enrolling 200 to 499 students and a full-time librarian in schools of 500 and over. It recommends a full-time professional assistant librarian for each 1,000 students or major fraction thereof and a ratio of one clerical assistant for each 750 students.[8] These standards were adopted in 1960 after extended study and discussion by administrators of the 3,600 member schools in nineteen states. However, they are considerably lower than the following recommendations by the American Library Association:

(1) *For the first 900 students or fraction thereof* (The minimum enrollment recommended for a full-time librarian and for a half-time clerk is 200 students): One librarian for each 300 students or major fraction thereof if the head librarian has no administrative responsibility for audio-visual materials. . . .

(2) *For each additional 400 students or major fraction thereof:* One librarian, if the head librarian has no administrative responsibility for audio-visual materials.[9]

The ALA also recommends that if the head librarian has partial responsibility for audio-visual materials, the number of librarians should be increased by 25 per cent, and in case of full responsibility for these services, by 50 per cent.

Although the American Library Association maintains that its recommended standards are minimal for a really good library program, they are beyond the financial resources of many high schools. The authors believe that the librarian-pupil ratios of the North Central Association, which are similar to those of the Southern Association and of various state departments, are realistic and that their general adoption would contribute to a substantial upgrading of the general level of high school libraries.

Training and Experience. The National Study of Secondary School Evaluation states that the professional members of the school library staff should have (1) a broad general education equivalent to the baccalaureate degree, (2) professional courses in education required for a teacher's certificate, (3) successful teaching experience or experience in an organ-

---

[8] North Central Association of Colleges and Secondary Schools, "Policies and Criteria for the Approval of Secondary Schools" (Chicago: Commission on Secondary Schools, 1960), p. 18.

[9] American Library Association, *op. cit.*, pp. 54–55.

ized internship program, and (4) advanced professional preparation leading to a knowledge of such fields as reading instruction, curriculum development, guidance services, mass communication, and research.[10]

The Southern Association of Colleges and Secondary Schools[11] requires at least twelve hours in library science for librarians in small high schools and thirty hours for librarians in large schools, while the North Central Association requires fifteen hours of library science for all school librarians regardless of the size of the school.[12]

Although a fifth year of professional training is as desirable for school librarians as it is for high school teachers, the current supply is so short in many states that it may be several years before this can be achieved. The school librarian needs at least fifteen to twenty hours in library science, but he also needs training in guidance, curriculum planning, and the teaching of reading. If he is expected to assume some responsibilities for the administration of audio-visual materials, he doubtless could profit from some course work in that field.

In addition, there are important advantages in a librarian's having had some classroom teaching experience. Although a clever person may learn to work reasonably well with students and teachers within a year or two on the job, he is not likely to develop a real knowledge of the problems of teacher-pupil rapport, providing for individual differences, the many demands on a teacher's time, and related teaching problems unless he has had some firsthand experience with them in classroom instruction. Neither is he likely to develop a genuine understanding of high school students — their attitudes, backgrounds, diverse abilities, peer group relations, and ambitions — without having worked closely with them in classroom and extraclass situations.

Then too, if library services are to be most effective, the librarian will need to join with teachers, counselors, and administrators in curriculum improvement. This requires more than a passing acquaintance with the types of professional and instructional materials used in curriculum work. It calls for an understanding of the nature of instruction and the ability to work with teachers as a professional colleague.

Professional Status. Other than securing adequate financial support, the most difficult problem confronting administrators in upgrading school libraries is that of finding well-qualified librarians. In many states the supply is far below the demand. Colleges and universities with facilities for training school librarians report that it is difficult to enlist students in their programs. One reason is that librarians have been loaded with too much clerical work and other routine assignments. In too many schools

---

[10] National Study of Secondary School Evaluation, *Evaluative Criteria* (Washington: The Study, 1960), p. 259.
[11] As quoted by Douglas, *op. cit.*, p. 12–13.
[12] North Central Association, *op. cit.*, p. 19.

they have been regarded as semiprofessional people, occupying a position somewhere between a clerk and a teacher.

Librarians should be placed on the same salary schedule as other teachers and given the same status with respect to tenure, retirement, and other fringe benefits. They should serve on faculty committees, participate in faculty meetings, and enjoy the same opportunities for advancement as other faculty members.

Equally important, certain peripheral assignments which have long been given to school librarians should be discontinued. Chief among these is the practice of assigning the librarian to more study-hall duty than is assigned to other teachers. Not only does this interfere with the librarian's professional functions, but for most librarians a steady diet of study-hall duty is an extremely enervating experience. If it is necessary to combine the library and study hall in the same room owing to lack of space, the librarian should not be expected to be both librarian and study-hall supervisor.

Student Assistants. Students may provide valuable services and obtain excellent experience as assistants in the library. However, they should not be expected to take the place of professional personnel or experienced adult clerks. Library work offers unusual opportunities for learning about all types of resource materials and for making important contributions to the school. Frequently, the student library assistants are organized as an extraclass club, so that they may enjoy group recognition plus worthwhile cultural and social experiences.

Organization and Management of the Collection

Like other school services, the quality of the library depends to a great extent upon adequate financing and efficient organization and management. Instructional materials need to be carefully selected, classified, cataloged, made easily accessible, and well maintained. Financial requirements must be determined, a budget prepared, and the money so used as to get the most for the funds available. A continuous evaluation of library materials should be made in relation to their contributions to the instructional program. Although these are primarily functions of the librarian, the principal, as responsible head of his school, must keep informed and make certain that they are carried out.

Size and Nature of the Collection. A well-trained school librarian should be familiar with the extent and the general nature of library collections recommended for schools of different sizes and types. Research studies and recommendations by professional organizations — the American Library Association, various state departments, and regional accrediting associations — provide useful guides, but adaptations must be made according to the special characteristics of a local school. Teachers vary in their emphasis on supplementary materials, students vary in their intellectual interests and capacities, audio-visual services are organized in different ways, curriculum offerings differ from school to school, and physical facilities are far from uniform. All of these must be taken into account in planning the library collection for a specific school.

The American Library Association recommends the following minimum collection of printed materials:[13]

For schools enrolling 200 or fewer students: (1) at least 6,000 books for a school of 200 (proportionately fewer for smaller schools); (2) a magazine collection of at least ten to fifteen titles; (3) an up-to-date reference collection with a variety of dictionaries, one encyclopedia, a world atlas, and an almanac; (4) a selection of pamphlets, pictures, and other vertical file materials; (5) such filmstrips and recordings as will be used several times during the school year.

For schools enrolling more than 200 students: (1) books: minimum in schools of 200–999 students, 6,000–10,000; in schools of 1,000 or more, 10 books per student; (2) magazines: senior high schools, 120 titles in the general magazine collection and five titles in areas of librarianship and instructional materials; (3) at least three to six newspapers; (4) an extensive collection of pamphlets covering a wide range of subjects.

With respect to the collection of professional materials for the faculty in a school of 200 and over, the Association suggests: (1) books: at least 200–1,000 titles, the number depending upon the needs and the size of the faculty and the availability of other collections of professional materials in the community; (2) at least twenty-five to fifty professional magazine titles; (3) other instructional materials as needed.

The size of the collection of supplementary materials will depend upon the needs and enrollment of the school, and the type and number of reference materials purchased for classroom use will depend upon local school policy.

The Association makes the following recommendations on audio-visual materials: (1) a sufficient number of all types of audio-visual materials for use in the classroom, in the school library, and at home; (2) films used six or more times a year; (3) filmstrips and recordings used more than once a year.

Building the Budget and Financial Management. The same principles and policies apply to budget making for the library as for other aspects of the educational program. The superintendent is responsible for the final draft to be submitted to the board for approval, but he will need to rely heavily on recommendations from principals and librarians in individual schools. In large systems, the library budget requests for all schools may be coordinated by a director of library services.

---

[13] American Library Association, *op. cit.*, pp. 25 and 103.

The librarian in an individual school should consult with each teacher and special services head (e.g., guidance coordinator) to determine their library needs for the coming year. The librarian and principal should make necessary adjustments in light of available funds.

The minimum amounts recommended by the American Library Association to maintain the high school collection are as follows:[14]

Printed materials: (1) funds for regular library books: in schools having 200–249 students, at least $1,000 to $1,500; in schools having 250 or more students, at least $4.00 to $6.00 per student; (2) additional funds as required for encyclopedias, unabridged dictionaries, magazines, newspapers, pamphlets; also funds for rebinding and supplies and equipment; (3) professional collection for the faculty: a minimum of $200–$800, depending on the needs and size of the faculty and availability of other collections.

Audio-visual materials: (1) not less than 1 per cent of the total per-pupil instructional cost ($2.00 to $6.00) for the acquisition of audio-visual materials; (2) funds for supplies and equipment.

Once the budget has been approved by the board of education, the librarian should have the main responsibility for its implementation.

Administrators in large high schools with an adequate collection of materials may logically question the continued expenditure of $4.00 to $6.00 per pupil per year as recommended by the American Library Association for such materials. For example, in a school of 2,000 students, an expenditure of $4.00 per pupil would add from 1,500 to 1,700 volumes to the collection each year. It is highly unlikely that half of this number of volumes would be lost or would need to be discarded annually. Consequently, the per-pupil expenditure would have to be scaled to the rate of loss and discard or the problem of shelf space would soon become critical.

Selecting and Ordering Materials. The selection of books and other materials for the high school library should be a joint enterprise of teachers, librarian, and principal, with the librarian serving as chief expediter and liaison person. When it comes to the point of more teacher requests than money, the principal should help make decisions. But the librarian should be given major responsibility for this task.

Periodically, the book collection should be checked against the lists in the *Standard Catalog for High School Libraries* (New York, H. W. Wilson Company) and *A Basic Collection for High Schools,* prepared by joint committees of the National Education Association, the National Council of Teachers of English, and the American Library Association and published by the latter. Similar guides are available for audio-visual materials and periodicals.

[14] *Ibid.,* p. 25.

In many schools it has been difficult to persuade teachers to take the time to make a careful selection of books for instruction in their classes. A good librarian should be able to enlist the cooperation of most faculty members in this important task, but he may need the support of the principal from time to time. Students also should be encouraged to make suggestions for the purchase of books and periodicals.

Newspapers, magazines, pamphlets, films and filmstrips, pictures and slides, recordings, and realia are also indispensable to a good instructional materials collection. Teachers should be encouraged to assist the principal and librarian in selecting them. Several state departments of education publish recommended lists of magazines.

The librarian should be given authority to place orders throughout the school year rather than concentrate on annual or semiannual orders. This permits him to adapt his purchases to shifting needs in the school program and to take advantage of market conditions.

In large school systems, economy and efficiency in ordering and processing materials may be effected through the centralized facilities of the directors of library and audio-visual services.

Classifying, Cataloging, and Record Keeping. The classification and cataloging of the library collection is a technical job and should be the responsibility of the librarian. The Dewey Decimal System of classification is generally recommended for high school libraries, since it is most widely used in public and college libraries and a knowledge of it will have carry-over value for students.

Some older books on library and school administration recommend that librarians keep an accession record of all books, but many library education people now regard this as waste motion, since a well-organized library will have other records such as the annual inventory, shelf lists, and card catalogs.

An annual inventory is necessary in order to determine what books have been lost, are in need of repair, or should be discarded. In schools with a large collection — over 6,000 to 8,000 volumes — it may not be possible to make more than a partial inventory each year.

Card catalogs for books, audio-visual, and flat file materials are necessary for effective use of the school library. The book catalog should be organized with an appropriate number of separate cards for each book — main entry cards filed by author's name and added entry cards which include subject cards and title cards. Printed sets of cards are available for most books from the H. W. Wilson Company, the Library of Congress, and some library supply houses. The time saved for the librarian to perform other important duties makes the purchase of these printed cards an economical investment.

Card catalogs for audio-visual and flat file materials should be developed by the local library staff. The cards should be grouped by subject and filed alphabetically by title. A *Readers' Guide to Periodical Literature* will be essential for effective use of the magazine collection.

Again, in large school systems economies can be effected by processing books for the various school libraries in the central department of library services. The school librarian should prepare an annual report of circulation, service activities, finances, and maintenance for the principal and central office.

Pruning the Collection. It may be painful to an economy-minded school administrator to throw books away, but he will have to do it each year in the interest of getting maximum utilization out of the library collection and shelf space. There is not much justification other than utilization for a library collection.

In schools that have not had an organized library, pruning is one of the first steps in building a usable collection. First, all high school textbooks should be either moved into the classroom collections or thrown away. All of the old ones should be discarded. Second, a hard look should be taken at books that are more than ten years old. Those that in the opinions of teachers and the librarian are obsolete should be discarded. Finally, all books that are badly worn or damaged should be pulled out of the collection for repair or discard. If the repair cost is likely to approach the cost of a replacement, a book should be junked.

All books with old publication dates, of course, are not obsolete. Certain classical and historical volumes, if still in good repair, may be valuable assets to the high school collection.

Circulation and Lending System. As noted earlier, the chief purpose of a school library is to get maximum utilization by students and faculty members. This requires not only a well-selected functional collection and considerable promotion by the librarian but also a system which makes it convenient for students to borrow books.

At the same time, the lending system must be designed to minimize losses and to keep books in circulation so that they are available to all students who need and want them. A record of circulation is necessary for the evaluation of library services, and the lending or charging system provides the base for this record. Since it is assumed that every *bona fide* pupil and teacher in the school is a qualified borrower, a borrower's card or number should not be necessary except in very large schools. To avoid excessive losses and damage a system of nominal fines will probably be required in most schools.

Simple and effective systems for checking books in and out of the library and for keeping records are described in various librarian's manuals such as the handbook by Mary Peacock Douglas.[15]

[15] *Op. cit.*

Library Services

To be of any great value to the instructional program of the school, the instructional materials collection must be housed in the school and designed for school purposes. There is no cheap way to provide adequate school library services. It may be possible to make some use of community library facilities and bookmobiles, but at best, these supplement the school facilities and cannot substitute for them.

It is both possible and desirable for the school librarian and the community or county librarian to collaborate in coordinating services and collections, but they serve different clienteles with different needs and interests. School library facilities must be available *where* and *when* students need them. Most materials will be needed in school during study periods or immediately before or after school.

Some public library materials such as fiction may be used conveniently by students, but special references in science, languages, mathematics, occupations, and social sciences must be selected in relation to the curriculum and located in the school where they will be most accessible. The public library probably cannot justify acquiring this type of material, and even if it could, it would not be readily accessible to class groups when they most require it.

The services of the school library should be closely related to the educational program of the school and should be considerably more specialized than those which reasonably might be expected from a community library. The American Library Association recommends the following policies and services for students and teachers to provide for optimum use of library materials:

1. The school library is available for use by individual students and by class groups throughout the school day.

2. The school library is open before and after school for use by students and teachers. Unless local conditions dictate otherwise . . . , the school library is open at least one-half hour before classes begin and at least one hour after classes end.

3. All materials are made easily available for use in the library by students and teachers. Good library service provides the library patron with the convenience of being able to examine and use in one location all types of materials that he needs for his particular purposes; and a good program of guidance in the school library entails referral to and use of all forms of communication.

4. Collections of materials from the school library are continuously sent to the classrooms for short-term loans, ranging in length from one class period to several weeks.

5. Materials are sent to some classrooms for long-term or permanent loans.

6. The resources of the school library are easily available for home use.

The policies of the library for the circulation of materials are liberal and flexible, geared always to provide the best service possible for students and teachers. With the exception of some very expensive or unique reference works, all printed materials in the school library may be withdrawn for home use by teachers and students.[16]

Instruction in the Use of the Library. If students are to make good use of school library facilities, they need to know the nature of such facilities, how they are organized, and how to locate them. These things can be taught relatively quickly and perhaps most effectively by direct instruction. However, they should be taught early in the student's high school career so that he can profit from them over a maximum period of time.

Where and by whom they should be taught depends upon the organization of the curriculum, the school schedule, and the availability of faculty members who know *what* should be taught and *how* it should be taught. Library instruction might be included in first-semester English courses, in homerooms, or in special short-term courses for that purpose.

Although regular English teachers or homeroom advisers may provide some of the instruction, the school librarian should collaborate closely with them in planning the program and in the laboratory sessions in the library. On the other hand, the librarian may assume full responsibility for teaching a short course, for units within a regular English course, or for a series of homeroom lessons.

Stimulation and Guidance of Students in Use of Materials. Classroom teachers are in a position to have more influence than other staff members in stimulating and guiding students in the use of library services. If teachers assign supplementary references, research papers, and reports as a regular part of their instruction, students will be strongly motivated to use the library for resource purposes.

But the librarian can do much to encourage voluntary reading by calling attention to new materials through displays and bulletins, presenting dramatic skits in assemblies and homerooms, and writing reviews for the school paper. Also, sympathetic and friendly assistance to students in locating and in interpreting materials will go far toward persuading them that the library is an interesting and stimulating source of help rather than an impersonal dispensary of books.

Curriculum Planning. Because of his knowledge of available instructional and professional publications and of the reading interests of students, the school librarian should be a valuable member of faculty curriculum planning committees. For instance, a science curriculum committee may be concerned with locating suitable reference materials for a low-ability group in tenth-grade biology. Through his professional peri-

---

[16] American Library Association, *op. cit.*, pp. 87–90.

odicals and catalogs the librarian may well have knowledge of some of these materials that the science teachers have not seen reviewed in their own professional journals or bulletins. Also, he may be better trained than most classroom teachers in judging the suitability of specific reference materials for different groups of students. Then too, the librarian usually has access to various lists of audio-visual and similar types of supplementary materials, which may save curriculum committees a considerable amount of time in searching for such resources.

Assistance to Individual Teachers. Not the least important task of the school library is that of helping individual teachers locate supplementary references and professional aids for classroom use. Frequently, classroom teachers are so occupied with regular teaching duties, extraclass assignments, and guidance functions that they do not have time to search for new references and teaching aids in revising or building unit plans. It is a valuable service to the teacher if the librarian can assist in locating digests and reviews of materials on certain topics. At the same time, this type of service generally influences teachers to encourage students to greater use of the library.

Library Quarters and Physical Facilities

A good school library requires appropriate and adequate quarters and equipment. Students will be *attracted* to a library that has plenty of room, pleasant decor, good lighting, and good sound control. They will *use* a library in which materials, functional facilities, and comfortable places to read are readily accessible.

Location

The library should be located near departmental areas that normally make the most use of it, such as English, social studies, science, and home economics. It should be located away from noisy areas such as shop, physical education, and music facilities. In schools with study halls the library and study hall should be near or adjacent to each other.

Size

The North Central Association states that

> In schools enrolling up to 1,000 pupils, the library should be large enough to accommodate at least eight per cent of the student body, but not less than forty pupils.
> In schools enrolling from 1000 to 1999 pupils, seven per cent, but not less than 80 pupils.
> In schools enrolling 2,000 or more pupils, five per cent, but not less than 140 pupils.[17]

[17] North Central Association, *op. cit.*, p. 19.

The amount of floor space in the main reading room should be from twenty-five to thirty square feet per student. The minimum in small schools, therefore, should be 1,000 square feet in the reading room plus rooms for the librarian's office, work and storage, and conferences. The capacity of any one reading room should not exceed 125 students. Large schools, of course, will need more than one reading room.

Functions to Be Housed

The National Council on Schoolhouse Construction states that the special functions for library quarters which should be provided for in their design include (1) a reading and circulation center, (2) a workroom, (3) storage space and book stacks, (4) conference room or rooms, (5) space for screening or listening, or the audio-visual area, and (6) office space for the librarian.[18]

Equipment

The reading room should be furnished with tables and chairs for students, open shelving for books, magazine racks, newspaper racks, card catalogs, a circulation desk, a librarian's work desk, files for pamphlets and other flat materials, bulletin boards, book trucks, and storage cabinets and stands for general reference materials — dictionaries, atlases, encyclopedias, and the like.

Student tables should be large enough for comfortable use and chairs should be sturdy and designed to encourage good posture. Shelving should be open and should not exceed seven feet in height. It should be located around the walls, in alcoves, or both. Approximately eight books per linear foot of shelving is the average capacity. Most sections of shelving should be three feet long, eight inches deep, and adjustable in height. A limited number of shelves should be ten to twelve inches deep.

Special Rooms and Equipment

Audio-Visual Room. In schools in which the audio-visual services are organized as a part of the library, a special storage and viewing-listening room is needed. It should be equipped with storage cabinets for films, filmstrips, slides, records, and tapes. It should have several different types of projectors (e.g., for sound film, filmstrip, opaques, etc.), tape recorders, record players, TV receivers, screens, and similar equipment. The audio-visual room should be acoustically treated.

Workroom. A workroom for the library staff is essential, and an absolute requirement in the workroom is a sink with running water. In addition, there must be shelving for new books to be processed and old

---

[18] National Council on Schoolhouse Construction, *Guide for Planning School Plants* (Nashville: The Council, 1949), p. 91.

books to be repaired, cupboards with doors for back issues of magazines if a special storage room is not available, storage spaces for tools and supplies, a workbench, a typewriter, a secretarial desk and chair, and work stools. Adequate lighting and several electrical outlets should be provided.

Conference Room. At least one special room, large enough to accommodate a minimum of ten to twelve students and preferably large enough for a full class section of twenty-five to thirty students, located next to the reading room, is highly desirable. It will be used by student committees working on projects, by classes for instruction in use of the library, and by other classes engaged in special activities which require ready access to audio-visual and/or special reference materials.

Storage Room. In small schools the workroom and storage room may be combined, but in large schools a separate storage room will be necessary for back numbers of magazines, bulletins, and catalogs. Also, expensive and/or rare editions of books, charts, maps, pictures, and similar materials should be housed in the storage room. It should be equipped with shelving, cabinets, files, and a work table.

Carrels for Teaching Machines. Some new libraries are being equipped with a bank of carrels for the individual use of students in working with teaching machines and for independent study. Since the design and use of teaching machines is still in the experimental stage, it is impossible to predict just what type of physical facilities will be most appropriate. But the experimental results to date suggest that school administrators and architects should give consideration to their space requirements in the design of new libraries.

Questions and Group Projects

1. What are the major purposes of a high school library? Interview ten or fifteen high school students in three or four schools to learn their views on what services they believe their school library should and does provide. How do the views of the students compare with the purposes for school libraries as stated by librarians?
2. Examine the training program for high school librarians as described in the catalogs of fifteen or twenty universities and teachers colleges. What are the most common requirements as listed in these catalogs?
3. Visit four or five high school libraries. (a) Is the library used as a study hall? (b) When do most students use the library? (c) What percentage of the student body can be seated in the library? (d) What departments make the greatest use of the library? (e) Who teaches students how to use the library? (f) What responsibilities does the librarian have for audio-visual aids?

4. Investigate and discuss the extent to which a nearby community library affects the need for a central high school library.

5. Examine some floor plans for new high school buildings. What are the trends in size, location, and room arrangement for high school libraries as reflected in these plans?

6. Write a paper on the desirability of requiring high school librarians to qualify for a teacher's certificate and to have a year or two of teaching experience.

Selected References

American Library Association. *A Basic Book Collection for High Schools.* Chicago: The Association, 6th ed., 1957.

―――. *Standards for School Library Programs.* Chicago: The Association, 1960.

Buest, Nora E. *School Library Standards,* U.S. Office of Education, Bulletin 1954, No. 15. Washington: Government Printing Office, 1954.

Douglas, Mary Peacock. *The Teacher-Librarian's Handbook.* Chicago: American Library Association, 2nd ed., 1949.

Fargo, Lucile F. *The Library in the School.* Chicago: American Library Association, 4th ed., 1947.

Mahar, Mary Helen. *Certification of School Librarians.* Publication of the U.S. Office of Education. Washington: Government Printing Office, 1958.

National Council on Schoolhouse Construction. *Guide for Planning School Plants.* Nashville, Tenn.: The Council, 1949.

National Education Association, Research Division. "Library Services," *Research Bulletin,* October, 1958, Vol. 63, No. 3.

―――. Department of Audio-Visual Instruction. *The AV Instructional Materials Center.* Washington: The Association, 1954. No. 3.

National Study of Secondary School Evaluation. *Evaluative Criteria.* Washington: The Study, 1960.

Standard Catalog for High School Libraries. New York: H. W. Wilson Company, 7th ed., 1957. Annual and cumulated.

Wofford, Azile. *The School Library at Work.* New York: H. W. Wilson Company, 1959.

IV

Staff Organization and Relationships

The strength of a school is the quality of its faculty. Good teachers can be expected to produce good results. But even good teachers can be helped to achieve their best through effective organization and the creation of favorable working conditions. It is the job of the administrator to organize the efforts of teachers so as to produce the best results possible from their combined talents as well as to encourage successful teaching by individuals. There is no magic formula, however, to insure success in building a strong staff. In some cases, it is the initial selection of teachers who show considerable promise that is crucial. In others, in-service procedures and techniques enable teachers to grow professionally on the job. And in all cases, the administrator can improve the chances for the success of teachers by creating conditions within the school which support high job satisfaction on the part of the staff.

Part IV is concerned with the selection and utilization of the staff and the use of in-service procedures and techniques to improve teacher effectiveness and to enhance democratic staff relationships. Chapter 11 deals with staff organization. Special attention is given to factors affecting teacher morale in Chapter 12. In Chapter 13 there is a review of various in-service procedures and techniques which can be used in developing democratic staff relationships. Chapter 14 suggests criteria and procedures useful in selecting teachers.

CHAPTER 11

Staff Organization and Utilization

Webster defines "chaos" as "any confused collection or state of things; complete disorder." In contrast, "organized" means "to become systematized or constituted into a whole of interdependent parts." To be organized is to be systematized. To be without system or organization is to be in a state of chaos. So it is with any social institution, business enterprise, or activity which depends upon the combined efforts of individuals to achieve its purpose.

Some advocates of democracy in administration suggest having only a minimum of formal structure in schools. There is danger, however, in having so little organization that the result is a laissez-faire type of operation. The authors do not believe there is any inherent conflict between a formal plan of organization and democratic principles of administration. On the contrary, democracy is highly dependent upon the cooperative efforts of all parties concerned and on an atmosphere in which individuals may exercise freely their creative abilities. Lack of organization, which results in confusion or substandard performance on the part of a staff, is more undemocratic than is a systematic operation which enables a school to function smoothly and with purpose.

Individuals within a group must know its "ground rules." It is quite apparent that, in the absence of a specific plan which clarifies "who is responsible for what and to whom," there is likely to be a great deal of confusion, uncertainty, and conflict. A faculty cannot be expected to work together systematically if duties and responsibilities are not defined.

In planning an organization suitable for the administration of a school, it is necessary to consider staff relationships both from a formal and from an informal viewpoint. In general, formal structure is needed to distinguish lines of authority within the staff and to provide for an orderly distribution of tasks to be performed, whereas informal organization is concerned with defining the working relationships within the faculty and with how authority is exercised. For example, schools A and B may have identical charts of formal organization, but the principals may use patterns of organization quite different in their consultation and communication with the faculties. Principal A might decide to make decisions with little, if any, consultation with his staff. Principal B might also choose to make final decisions, but he wishes to have a system whereby he consults regularly with his staff before coming to a decision. Although the formal plan of organization is the same in both instances, the informal procedures and plans for faculty communication result in quite different rapport. In this chapter consideration will be given to formal plans of organization and staff utilization. A discussion of informal plans of organization is reserved for the next two chapters.

Line and Staff Organization

Basic to all patterns of organization of school staffs is some form of line and staff relationships. Hunt and Pierce indicate that schools have adopted this plan from both the military and industry.

> ... The most common form of organization is the line and staff structure in which the "line" is administration's channel of authority. It is a time-honored concept of administrative effectiveness, early adopted by the schools from the military and industrial spheres.[1]

Authority generally passes in a direct line from one official down the line to subsequent positions. Line school officials are administrators to whom power or authority has been delegated by the board of education. According to Griffiths, "A line officer is also a 'generalist,' with competence in many areas, as contrasted with the specialist, who is an expert in one area."[2] The most simple pattern of line authority is illustrated in Figure 16.

In this plan, the board of education receives its authority from the local electorate and has authority over the superintendent, teachers, and pupils, but it delegates the power of administrative actions to the superin-

---

[1] Herold C. Hunt and Paul R. Pierce, *The Practice of School Administration* (Boston: Houghton Mifflin Company, 1958), p. 335.
[2] Daniel Griffiths, *Human Relations in School Administration* (New York: Appleton-Century-Crofts, Inc., 1956), p. 306.

tendent of schools. Similarly, the superintendent delegates authority to teachers to make decisions with respect to the pupils. Lines of authority are clear and direct. This is the system of organization generally used in very small schools in which there is only one administrator.

FIGURE 16

Line Type of Organization

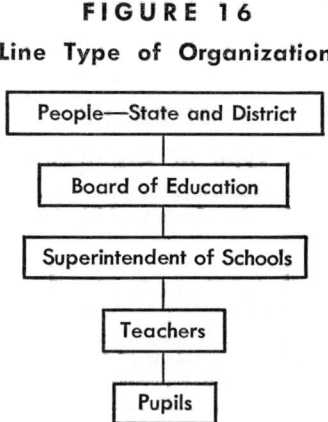

As a school increases in size, the line relationship of authority must be extended to include additional administrators or other officials, but the basic principle of delegation of authority in a direct line is the same. Figure 17 shows an organization for a somewhat larger school, but it still retains direct line relationships. Note, however, that the lines of authority are divided in this case. There is one line from the superintendent to the high school principal and another to the elementary school principal. This division emphasizes the fact that the high school principal has *no* authority over the elementary school principal nor does the elementary school principal have any authority over the high school staff. However, the superintendent retains direct authority over both unit administrators.

A rigid adherence to a line type of organization in which individuals at different levels are not free to consult with each other is to be avoided. Schools which want to encourage freedom of communication between individuals often indicate such a relationship by the use of dotted lines on the chart of organization, as in Figure 17.

Establishing "line" authority does not complete the organization of most schools. Consideration must be given also to "staff" officials. A staff officer is a specialist who acts as adviser or consultant to other members of the organization, in either a formal or an informal way. Results may be achieved through committee action, publishing results of local research, demonstration teaching, individual counseling of teachers, or whatever approach is most effective in a particular situation. The main point is that staff personnel are people with special skills or knowledge who assist other members of the organization in the operation of the school program. For example, a reading specialist consults with all teachers and principals in the school system on instruction in reading. His major interest is to improve the teaching of reading throughout the school system. Similarly, a director of pupil personnel serves in an advisory capacity to administrators, counselors, special education consultants, and teachers with respect to improving all phases of pupil personnel services in the system.

FIGURE 17

Line Type of Organization

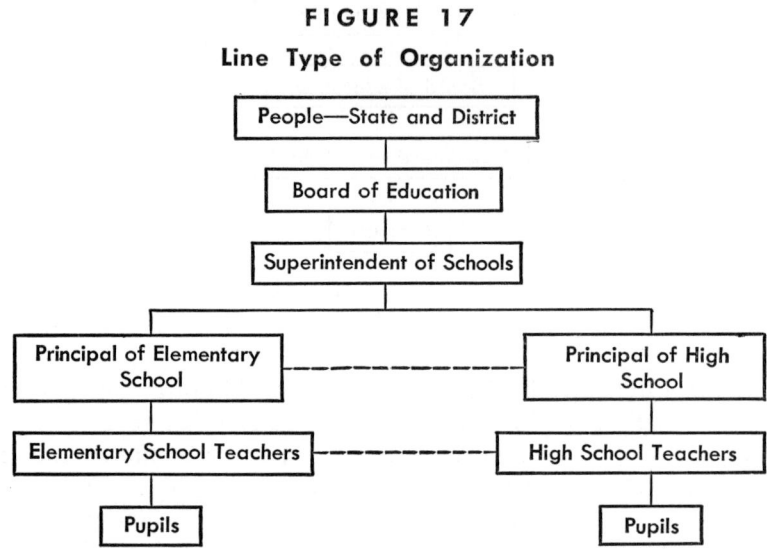

Staff personnel usually have no line authority within an individual school unit, such as the senior or junior high school. The principal should be responsible for his unit, and staff officers should work through the principal on specific problems in his school. Authority rests with the principal, not the staff person. There may be instances, however, in which a staff official has general competences and advises line officers. Such an individual is usually given a special assignment which necessitates some line responsibility in order to achieve its objectives. An assistant superintendent in charge of instruction is in this position.

Titles of staff personnel vary from school to school and usually give clues to the positions they designate. For example, one school may have a staff person with the title Coordinator of Mathematics, while another school employs a supervisor with the title Director of Mathematics. The former title implies a consultative and cooperative working relationship, whereas the latter seems to indicate a line authority relationship. Efforts should be made when establishing a plan of organization to assign titles to all positions which are descriptive of the role expectations of the position.

Figure 18 illustrates a plan of organization including both line and staff officials.

FIGURE 18

Line and Staff Organization

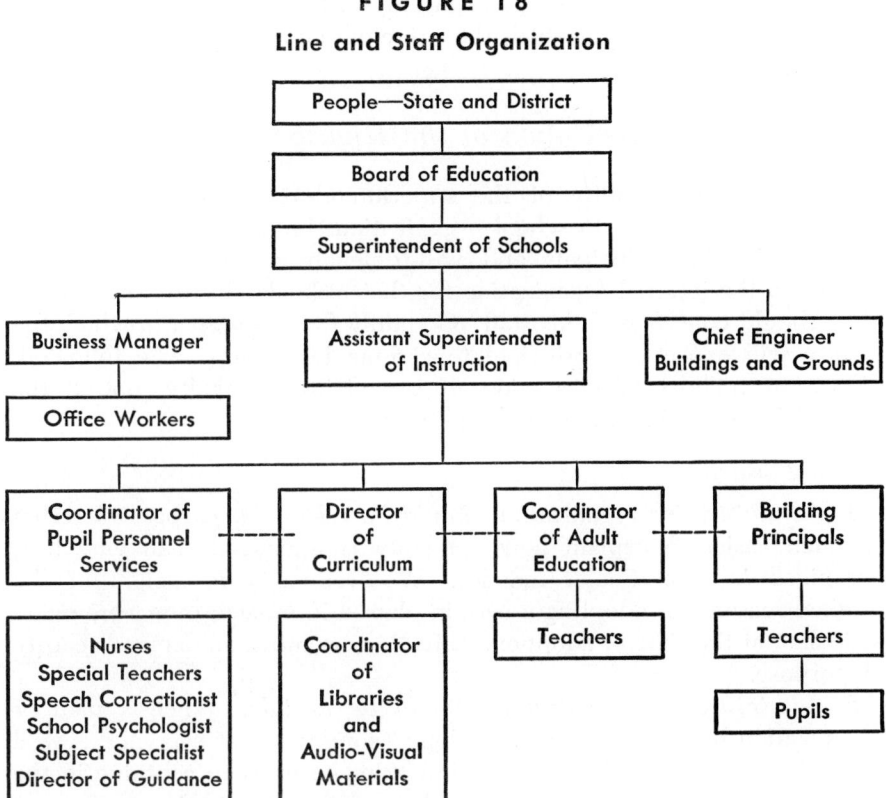

The following advantages are claimed for line and staff organizations: (1) Relationships between individuals are clearly defined; (2) responsibilities and authority of individuals are established; (3) it is an efficient way to organize for action; and (4) the principal is held responsible, together with his staff, for the successful operation of his unit. There are some disadvantages, however, which can be anticipated: (1) It is oriented toward an authoritarian plan of organization; (2) line officials can become "bottlenecks" for action; (3) loyalty up the line is required, with no assurance of loyalty down the line; and (4) communications tend to flow down much more easily than they move upward. Disadvantages such as these can be minimized through the use of supplementary plans introducing advisory councils and cabinets.

Patterns of organization become increasingly complex as the school system expands and there is a need to indicate multiple relationships among members of the organization. It is not the purpose of this discussion, however, to review the more involved patterns of school system organization. Our intention has been only to identify the basic line and staff relationships within which the principal and his staff are expected to operate.

Organization of the High School

It is the responsibility of the superintendent of schools to make decisions with respect to school organization, but usually he will work closely with his principals and will delegate authority to them to decide on the internal organization for their schools. In turn, each principal should consult with his staff. Certainly this is an area in which the faculty will expect the principal to assume leadership. The following discussion reviews various ways of organizing a faculty, noting the strengths and limitations of each pattern.

Guiding Principles

1. *Administrative organization should be related to purpose.* It often is much easier to explain how a faculty is organized than why it is organized in a particular manner. We frequently lose sight of the original reasons for adopting a certain plan — if, indeed, they were made articulate at the time of adoption. Effective organization demands clarity of purpose.

2. *Administrative organization should be flexible.* When a plan of organization has been in operation long enough so that everyone is well acquainted with its details, the easiest thing to do is to continue in the same old way regardless of new problems or conditions. However, conditions and people do change. What was appropriate at one time may be entirely inappropriate at a later date. An organization that is going to make good sense in terms of students, teachers, and community must be capable of adaptations.

In many respects, flexibility and the ability to change are dependent more upon the attitude of the administrator than upon the details of organization. Any pattern of organization can be changed if the people who control the system really want it changed. An awareness and acceptance by the principal of the need for flexibility to meet new conditions will help considerably in preventing his becoming so emotionally attached to a particular plan as to make it virtually impossible even to consider change.

3. *Administrative organization should be as simple as will serve the needs of the group.* High schools with very small staffs, i.e., five to ten

teachers, have little need for elaborate plans of organization. It is relatively simple to coordinate the activities for a faculty of this size. At least such things as advisory councils and departments are unnecessary.

A larger school, however, can become seriously involved with red tape in its operations. A few years ago the automobile industry made cars so large and powerful that they became known as "gas guzzlers." They were entirely too large and powerful for the needs of most people. Similarly, complicated and oversized school organizations can become "energy guzzlers," consuming more time and energy merely to maintain the system than can be justified by the results. Unfortunately there is no magic formula by which a principal can determine the precise amount and complexity of organization needed in his school. He must use his best judgment and take advantage of periodic evaluation of the organization by the faculty to uncover any unnecessary or defective parts and to keep it as simple as will serve the needs of the staff.

4. *Administrative organization should make provisions for both vertical and horizontal articulation.* In order to provide opportunities for communication, planning, and a sequential development between grade levels, some type of vertical organization is in order.[3] An effective instructional program at any grade level must be related both to the experiences of the learner in previous grades and to those planned for later grades. An illustration of vertical organization is a plan which uses coordinators of subject fields or special services, i.e., in English, mathematics, science, guidance, libraries, etc. Any system which organizes the staff in such a way as to require coordination of the curriculum content of two or more grades is achieving some vertical articulation.

Horizontal organization, on the other hand, cuts across subject lines and encourages communication and planning between teachers of the various subjects and services. Typical of such a system is a school in which teachers work together in committees to plan the learning experiences in all subjects on a grade-level basis, i.e., Grade 10, Grade 11, or Grade 12.

An effective plan of organization for a high school must provide for both vertical and horizontal articulation as well as the other principles of organization mentioned above in order to coordinate the efforts of the entire staff. Unfortunately, no one plan meets all of these conditions. It is necessary, therefore, to utilize a variety and/or combination of plans within a single high school.

Departmental Organization

A common organization for medium and large high schools is the departmental plan. Usually each major subject field or service constitutes a

[3] The reader is referred to Chapter 5 for additional discussion on the problem of articulation.

department, i.e., English, social studies, science, mathematics, foreign languages, health and physical education, music, art, vocational and industrial arts, guidance, and any other major area. The departmental plan is common in large high schools; according to findings of a study by Brandes, there were department heads in more than three-fourths of the larger high schools studied in California.[4]

The primary purpose of departmental organization is to effect vertical articulation. Its major strength is its use of teachers in their specialized subject fields to plan the sequence of subject matter and learning experiences for all grades of the high school. Sometimes departments are system-wide, i.e., kindergarten through Grade 12, rather than confined to just the secondary school. Faculties that feel systematic subject-matter instruction is an important part of the educational program usually find a departmental plan much to their liking.

In a departmental plan, someone is designated as the department chairman and assigned the responsibility for coordinating the work of the department. He may or may not have line authority, depending upon the views of the superintendent and the principal. If the chairman does have such authority, he is usually expected to supervise the teachers in his department. If he does not have line authority, he is expected to serve as a staff consultant to other teachers in the department. A knotty problem in many schools is how to provide adequate time from teaching for the chairman to perform his duties as head of the department. Unless the school is willing to give him time for research, classroom visitation, preparation of instructional materials, and other supervisory functions, it is unreasonable to expect any substantial instructional leadership from him.

The method of choosing a department chairman is also a controversial issue. Because the departmental type of organization usually follows subject divisions, the chairman should be one of the best prepared teachers in his field. But he should be skilled also in coordinating the efforts of others so as to establish a cohesive working group within the department. The practice of selecting the teacher with the longest service as chairman of the department leaves much to be desired. The individual should be chosen for his qualifications to provide leadership and to coordinate the work of other teachers, not merely on the basis of seniority. Some schools rotate the chairmanship among all department members. This practice is questionable also, because many teachers are neither interested in serving as chairman nor qualified to do so.

Election of a chairman by other members of the department has the advantage of securing a person who is most acceptable to teachers in

---

[4] Louis H. Brandes, "Administrative Policies and Practices in Larger California Three and Four Year High Schools," *The Bulletin* of the NASSP, May, 1956, 40:46–52.

the department. This plan is used successfully in a number of schools. Or again, the principal may appoint a chairman for a definite term with the provision that the person may be appointed for successive terms, as are other administrative or supervisory personnel, depending upon his success in the position. This system encourages careful screening of a candidate's qualifications prior to the appointment, which provides greater assurance that the chairman will be selected on the basis of his competence. Selection either by department members or by the administrator appears to be superior to the length-of-service methods or the system of rotation.

A serious limitation of the departmental plan of organization, if used exclusively, is its lack of provision for horizontal integration between subject fields. Under a departmental plan teachers have a strong tendency to become highly specialized, often becoming insensitive to the interests of students and teachers in other fields or having little concern for general school objectives. Some schools compensate for this limitation by supplementing it with some type of horizontal organization — an advisory council or cabinet, for example. It is the function of such a council to serve as an advisory and coordinating body through which individual departments participate in planning all areas of the school program. If the departments are required to clear their recommendations with the council prior to implementing them, there is some assurance that departments will operate in harmony to further the total interests of students and faculty. Other informal plans of organization are discussed in Chapter 13. These are useful also in supplementing departmental organization.

FIGURE 19
Departmental Plan of Organization

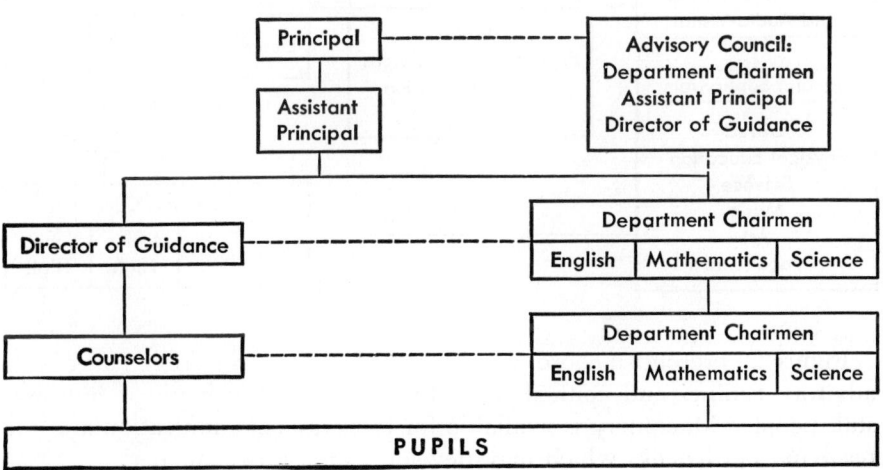

Figure 19 illustrates how a high school might be organized using a departmental plan plus an advisory council. For sake of simplicity, only three departments are shown in the chart. Actually, as many additional departments would be included as are appropriate for a particular school.

FIGURE 20

**Coordinate Line and Staff Organization
with Cabinet and Advisory Councils**

(medium-sized school system)

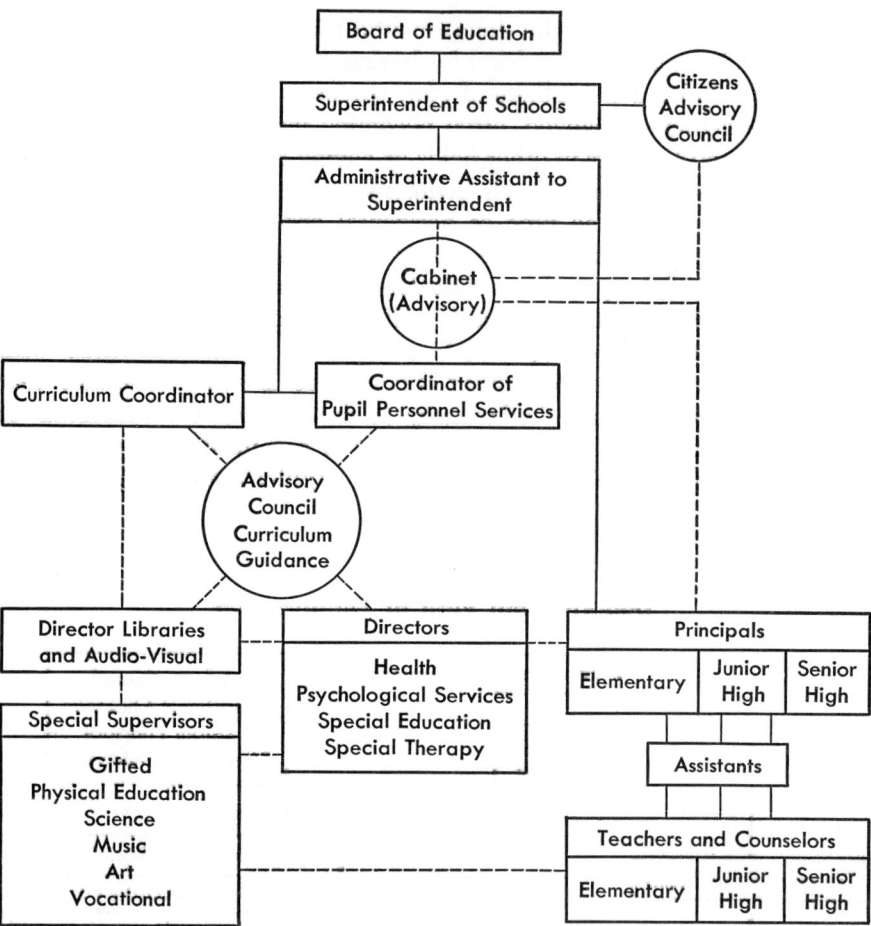

Figure 20 presents a coordinated line and staff organization, using both advisory cabinet and council plans to coordinate the work of line and staff people. Machinery is available for two-way communication and for resolving bottlenecks which may develop in the line sequence.

Committee Organization

Use of some type of committee organization is popular in many agencies and institutions. Committees are employed extensively in all branches of government, church bodies, boards of education, business and industrial concerns, and other organizations large enough to necessitate some form of systematic arrangement. In fact, it is almost axiomatic that when three or more Americans get together someone will organize a committee. Three types of committees usually are characteristic of the committee system.

Standing Committees. A standing committee is one which continues from year to year, usually with members appointed for a specific term. It performs as part of the parent organization to consider problems related to a particular function and reports its recommendations to the full membership for action. A high school faculty might have standing committees with responsibility for faculty meetings, guidance, general education, college preparatory education, school-community relations, extraclass activities, or other areas which necessitate continuing study and action by the staff.

The general method of operation is for the faculty to refer all appropriate questions or problems to the committee for study and recommendations. An important point in the committee structure is that the faculty is the parent body of the committee, and the committee derives its authority and direction from the faculty. All committee recommendations should be referred to the faculty for final disposition. Retention of final authority by the parent group prevents standing committees from becoming authorities unto themselves and aids also in providing for horizontal articulation inasmuch as all committee reports are made to the entire faculty for action.

Administrative responsibilities are sometimes assigned to a standing committee, but usually it is considered wise to separate administration from the work of a standing committee. The principal, with or without the aid of an advisory council, should be responsible for administering the policies established by the faculty and its standing committees.

Another pitfall to be avoided is the persistence of standing committees beyond the point where they have any worthwhile function. Once the original need for a committee has ceased to exist, the committee should be discontinued. It is necessary also to guard against overlapping functions of standing committees. Care must be exercised in defining clearly the specific purposes of each, and the total number of standing committees should be kept at a minimum.

Special Committees. A special committee, sometimes called an *ad hoc* committee, is appointed to fulfill a particular function. Its term should be determined by the length of the time needed to perform the assigned task. Special committees should be disbanded just as soon as their tasks have been completed. Any faculty group may appoint a special committee, and the authority and direction of the special committee is located in the group from which it is appointed.

Use of special committees is illustrated in the procedures recommended for use of the *Evaluative Criteria*.[5] When a faculty chooses to utilize this document for curriculum evaluation, it assigns a series of special committees to carry out the necessary study for the faculty's deliberations. Each individual committee makes its evaluation of the area assigned to it and presents its report to the total staff. These results are either accepted or modified by the staff. When the evaluation of each area is completed, the committee assigned to that section has completed its task and is dismissed.

Special committees are used almost universally in schools and are considered an excellent means of organizing for faculty action. The concern with committees in this discussion is as a system of organization, not primarily with the details of operation. However, a number of suggestions and principles for the successful operation of special committees as they contribute to democratic staff relationships are discussed in Chapter 13. Suffice it to repeat here that the principal will need to select committee members who are competent, especially the chairman, and who can work together cooperatively. Also the committee's functions should be well defined.

Committee of the Whole. There are times when a faculty wishes to study, discuss, and come to some conclusions with respect to a problem as a committee, but it does not wish to take official action as a faculty. In situations like this, the entire faculty can be made a committee of the whole so that it functions as a committee rather than as a faculty. No doubt faculties often act in this manner without realizing that they are working as a committee. But if a group is organized formally on a committee basis, it should be alert to the possibilities of convening officially as a committee of the whole.

Grade-Level Organization

Organizing the staff on the basis of a single grade level stresses a horizontal relationship within the faculty. In this plan, all teachers of ninth-grade classes make up one working group, and all teachers of tenth, eleventh, and twelfth grades make up similar groups. The plan encourages teachers to become specialists for a particular age group. There is an excellent opportunity to relate subject matter to specific needs of each grade when teachers of all subjects taught in that grade coordinate

[5] National Study of Secondary School Evaluation, *Evaluative Criteria* (Washington: The Study, 1960).

their instructional plans. Such conditions provide a maximum opportunity for the correlation of subject matter.

The major limitation in using grade-level organization exclusively is the lack of provision for vertical communication. There is danger that teachers of ninth-grade students will plan their instructional programs with little or no specific information about, or concern for, what the students will do when they move to Grade 10. Subject matter might be repeated in various grades with little thought given to its sequential arrangement. Teachers also appear to lack enthusiasm for working on problems outside of their own subject fields. Undoubtedly, these limitations have restrained high school principals from using this plan to any great extent. It can be effective, however, as a supplementary plan for considering problems which are quite unique to a particular grade level. Elementary schools have made greater use of a grade-level organization than have high schools.

The grade-level plan is rather well adapted to a large high school in which a number of teachers are assigned to teach at a single grade level. In smaller schools, most teachers will have classes involving more than one grade level, and often in the very small high school only one teacher teaches in each subject field and he must teach all grade levels in the high school. Very little formal organization is needed in the very small school other than a single line and staff relationship and the use of a few special committees.

Schools-within-Schools

American secondary schools attempt to serve all youth of secondary school age through a system of comprehensive high schools. This has resulted in an increasing number of large high schools, i.e., having 1,000 or more pupils. Whether a school is large or small is not important in itself. The important thing is whether students obtain a good education. Many laymen and educators believe that small schools, more often than large schools, provide for individualized attention and for the development of desirable social attitudes. In small schools teachers know each student and take a personal interest in him, and all students gain valuable group experiences through extraclass activities. But the curriculum offerings are limited, teacher turnover is high, and facilities and special services, such as guidance, are usually limited.

The large high school, on the other hand, offers a broader curriculum, makes better provisions for individual differences in academic ability, has a better-trained and more stable faculty, has better library and laboratory facilities, and supplies more adequate special services.

Some large school faculties believe it is possible to combine the best features of large and small high schools within the framework of a large school organization. In the "schools-within-a-school" and "house" plans a large school is divided into two or more small, semi-independent schools, each with its own faculty for general education, including a coordinator and counselors. The students remain in their separate houses or sections of the building for their general education courses but share teachers and facilities in specialized areas such as music, art, physical education, industrial and vocational education.

There are two basic plans for dividing the school: vertical and horizontal. The vertical plan includes a cross section of the student body, Grades 9 through 12, as a school. A complete high school is established, including extracurricular activities. Typically, each division has about 250 to 500 pupils. An advantage of including all grades is that a relatively complete variety of activities is available to the students. It is possible also for teachers to teach at more than one grade level. In a horizontal plan of organization, division is according to grade level; i.e., all ninth-grade students are together, and all other grades are grouped in like manner. Many of the student activities are then conducted by grade level.

The individual houses are integrated into a single school by having all students and teachers participate in all-school activities without reference to their individual units. Varsity athletics, concert musical groups, and other performing groups are organized to represent the entire school. Faculties are united through periodic meetings of the total group, interschool committees, and interschool councils or cabinets in order to coordinate the solving of problems which relate to the whole faculty.

Examples of two high schools organized on a cross-sectional basis are found in Fairfield, Connecticut. The Andrew Warde High School, according to Headmaster Daniel Fitts, is divided into four small schools with about 350 students in each, while Roger Ludlow High School is divided into only two house units.[6] Each of these units enrolls students from all four grades. The students remain in the same houses and homerooms for their entire four-year program.

Each house has a staff of eighteen to twenty teachers with an administrative headmaster and a guidance headmaster. Students take all of their required general courses and popular electives within their own house but may enroll in some specialized courses, such as advanced academic and vocational courses, with students from other houses. Each house has its own program of extraclass activities, but some activities such as varsity athletic teams include students from all of the divisions.

After one year of operation, Fitts reported the following advantages as judged by the Fairfield faculties:

> 1. Decentralized administration permits an intensive supervisory program *and its follow-up* — the proof of a supervisory program.

[6] Daniel B. Fitts, "The House Plan as a New Concept is Secondary School Organization," *The Bulletin* of the NASSP, March, 1958, 43:155–63.

2. Closer relationships *at the House level* among the teacher, administrator, guidance team members.
   a. Housemasters who are still teaching a class are close to the teachers' problems in the House.
   b. A faculty meeting at the House level where the team of twenty people get together to discuss programs and problems is not the unwieldly activity that a staff meeting of eighty-six people becomes on a school-wide basis.

3. Pupil response to a survey of the closeness of teacher-pupil relationships shows improvement in terms of numbers of positive responses compared to that of last year.

4. Participation by students and staff is increased by the addition of House level activities to a total school program.

5. Parent-school relationships are closer as evidenced by the constant flow of parents for conferences — especially at House level.[7]

The Citrus Union High School at Azusa, California, is organized on a house-grade plan. The total enrollment was around 2,000 in 1957. According to Michael, each grade is organized as a small school with its own faculty and physical facilities. Each grade unit is housed in a wing of the plant in which its classrooms, administrative and guidance offices, student lounge, and shop facilities are located. The acceptance of this plan is evidenced by the fact that the people of Azusa voted funds to build a second high school organized on the same pattern.[8]

Michael reported briefly on the well-known "New School" plan, which has been in operation in his school at Evanston, Illinois, for more than twenty-five years. This is a small school unit of about 250 students within the large Evanston Township High School. It provides a core curriculum for students who elect to take that type of program.[9]

The schools-within-a-school plan as it is being employed in Fairfield, Azusa, Evanston, and several other large communities is based upon the conviction that there are important advantages in both small and large high schools. It is the judgment of most teachers and administrators in these schools that the major advantages of each can be captured within a large school by use of a "house" unit type of organization.

Staff Utilization

One of the most important aspects of organizing the high school staff has to do with teacher assignments and staff utilization. It is here that the principal comes to grips with day-to-day realities with respect to

[7] *Ibid.*, pp. 162–63.
[8] Lloyd S. Michael, "Innovations in Organization," in Francis S. Chase and Harold A. Anderson, editors, *The High School in a New Era* (Chicago: University of Chicago Press, 1958), pp. 235–36.
[9] *Ibid.*, p. 237.

the psychology of learning, educational theory, and the resources of the school and community. Pupil-teacher relationships and the quality of instruction depend to a great extent upon conditions surrounding teacher assignments. The two major problems which concern high school principals in the matter of staff utilization are (1) securing a reasonably equitable distribution of teacher loads and (2) utilizing the staff so as to secure the most efficient and productive instruction.

Teacher Load

A number of factors must be considered when the high school principal attempts to equalize teaching loads: the number of different subjects to be taught, class size, total number of pupils taught, responsibilities for supervision of extraclass activities, study hall supervision, administrative responsibilities, number of classes per day, and total clock hours devoted to teaching.

The foregoing factors are all quantitative in nature, but equalizing teacher loads also involves qualitative factors. Teachers differ in their ability to carry assigned responsibilities. For example, some teachers find working with a group of slow-learning students quite easy and stimulating; to others this type of assignment is depressing. A large group of students might be handled quite easily in a class such as physical education or music, but the same size group would be completely unrealistic for art classes. The number of papers to be read and graded in English classes may require many hours of homework, whereas teaching some other subject may demand much less time for such tasks.

At times, it may be necessary to assign teachers to fields for which they have had only the minimum formal preparation, and this means considerable extra work for the teacher. In addition, adequacy of materials, supplies, clerical assistance, and other conditions peculiar to a local school affect teaching load. It is virtually impossible for a principal to achieve a situation in which all teachers have the same teaching load. Sometimes rather large inequities develop, over which the principal has little control at the time. In spite of such complications, the task of assigning duties to teachers has to be done. A principal must exercise his best judgment in these matters in an effort to bring about the best possible conditions for teaching and learning.

Unfortunately, the research evidence available on optimum teacher loads is inconclusive. But teachers and administrators have had considerable experience and have made frequent recommendations. Also, some states have legal requirements which must be observed, and accrediting associations usually provide criteria which may guide administrators of member schools. In 1960, for example:

Thirty-four states have a standard for teaching load. Maximum teaching load permitted varies from five to seven periods, the mode being six periods of actual teaching plus responsibility for the study hall or for other activities that may be assigned. Twenty-three states use student-teacher ratio. The typical standard in states having a quantitative requirement reads, "The pupil-teacher ratio shall not exceed 30 to 1." Fifteen states use class size. The maximum varies from 35 students to 50. Colorado has a maximum for inexperienced teachers of 25 students per class.[10]

The North Central Association of Colleges and Secondary Schools reccommends limiting the average pupil-teacher ratio to twenty-seven to one.[11] Opinions of teachers with respect to class size is in substantial agreement with the above legal requirements and those of the North Central Association:

> Two findings of Tompkins, who reported the results of a questionnaire sent to 576 teachers in 193 high schools which represented a sampling of all public secondary schools of five hundred or more students, are pertinent. His teachers regarded a class of 11 or 13 students too small, and a class of 32 to 33 students too large for efficient instruction. For them, an ideal class consisted of 25 students. The most frequently mentioned justification for smaller classes was more adequate time for individual attention; the second one, the opportunity for the teacher to check the progress of students more closely.[12]

Although most schools have an over-all pupil-teacher ratio that meets the above standards, not infrequently individual teachers are assigned to an unusually large number of pupils per day. Attention was given to this possibility by the North Central Association when it established a criterion limiting the number of pupils assigned to one teacher to 170 per day.[13] This limit does not apply, however, to physical education, music, and study halls. Undoubtedly some school people regard 170 pupils per day as an unreasonably large number of different pupils for a teacher to instruct, but this appears to be a realistic maximum in light of current conditions. For example, Lambert and Iwamoto summarized a number of status studies with respect to trends in teacher loads and reported,

> In 1929–30, about 10 percent of the teachers taught more than 160 students daily; in 1932–33 the figure was almost 21 percent. . . . A national survey in 1950 showed the average number of students taught

[10] Sam M. Lambert and David Iwamoto, "Teaching Load," *Encyclopedia of Educational Research* (New York: The Macmillan Company, 3rd ed., 1960), p. 1497.
[11] The North Central Association of Colleges and Secondary Schools, "Policies and Criteria for the Approval of Secondary Schools" (Chicago: Commission on Secondary Schools, 1960).
[12] Lambert and Iwamoto, *op. cit.*, p. 1500.
[13] North Central Association, *op. cit.*

by each teacher in the secondary school to be 129 in rural areas, 169 in urban, and 152 for the two combined. Nearly 20 percent of these teachers were working with 200 or more different students.[14]

It is noteworthy that the trend in total number of pupils taught per day has been increasing. No doubt one of the factors related to this increase is the corresponding rise in the number of larger high schools in the United States. Pupil-teacher ratios in larger schools tend to be quite uniform each period during the day, so that larger numbers of pupils are served. "A national survey in 1957 reported that the median class size in the nation's secondary schools was 26.9. The rural median was 21.0 students, and the urban median 28.8 students."[15]

Class size and the total number of pupils taught per day are not settled issues in secondary education; there may be major changes in the near future, especially if present experimental programs are successful. But at the present time, the authors recommend that the high school principal attempt to keep class size at an over-all pupil-teacher ratio of twenty-five to one and total number of pupils at not more than 170 a day for any one teacher, except in large-group activities such as physical education, music, and study halls. This recommendation is based on opinions of teachers that it is very difficult, if not impossible, to provide adequately for individual differences or to give individual attention to students in large classes. Furthermore, the experimental programs with team teaching provide for small discussion sections under assistant teachers; thus the over-all staff-pupil ratio is approximately the same as that recommended by state and regional accrediting agencies.

Another factor to be considered by the principal in making teacher assignments is the number of different subject preparations per day. Theoretically, a teacher's preparation should be different for every class if individual differences among pupils are being taken into account. However, it is more time consuming to make preparations in two or three subject fields as well as to make adjustments in the level of content or other adaptations within the same subject. A national survey of the Research Division of the National Education Association revealed that "secondary-school teachers of two subjects spent an average of 47.6 hours, but teachers of three or more subjects spent an average of 49.8 hours, per week at their work."[16]

Small schools face the most difficult problems in this regard, since it is practically impossible to staff the usual subjects in such schools without assigning every teacher to two or more fields. An important advantage of larger schools is that most teachers teach in only one subject field. Assignments to teach in more than two subject fields should be avoided if possible. If the administration finds it necessary to use a

[14] Lambert and Iwamoto, *op. cit.*, p. 1498.
[15] *Ibid.*
[16] *Ibid.*, p. 1499.

teacher in more than two subjects, his other school responsibilities should be reduced. A study by Romine shows that a large majority of teachers are assigned to only one or two fields:

> The replies of 2,128 teachers [in Colorado] showed that about 53 percent of all teachers were assigned in a single field; approximately 33 percent in two fields; 12 percent in three fields; and 2 percent in four or five fields. Assignments involving more than two fields were rare in the larger schools.[17]

It is desirable that teachers be assigned to teach those subjects in which they have major preparation. This practice would mean less preparation time for the teacher and a better-qualified teacher in the classroom. All too frequently, teachers who have been asked to teach temporarily in their minor subjects are never reassigned to their major fields. A careful analysis should be made each year of each teacher's preparation and teaching assignments in an effort to secure the best possible use of each faculty member's qualifications and the best possible conditions with respect to teaching loads.

Some teachers find that their responsibilities in extraclass activities and committee work have become a major part of their teaching load. This is especially the case in schools which require all athletic coaching and sponsorship of student activities to be in addition to a full classroom schedule. Some schools reduce the amount of regular teaching to compensate for extra responsibilities in other areas. If this practice is not followed, extra pay usually is provided for sponsoring or coaching in major activities. A more detailed discussion is found in Chapter 9, but the point we wish to emphasize here is that some method of equalizing teacher load is necessary where teachers have heavy extraclass duties.

Douglass Teaching Load Formula

There has been considerable interest on the part of some educators, particularly Douglass and his associates, in establishing a formula to be used in calculating teacher load. Such a formula does provide a rough means of comparing teacher loads on a quantitative basis, both within a school and between schools. A principal might find it helpful in adjusting assignments of teachers who appear to have unusually light or heavy assignments.

Opinions among principals differ, however, on the value of the Douglass formula as a single index of teacher load. Usually an administrator's reservations are directed toward certain features of the formula, particularly the use of subject coefficients which assume differentials in time required by teachers of different subjects in preparation, paper work, handling materials, and so on. Additional criticisms are that some of the items in the formula are based on unreliable estimates of time spent

[17] *Ibid.*

in certain activities, that use of the formula entails some pointless mathematical operations, and that the formula is fairly complicated to use. However, a little experience in using the formula often reduces the principal's objections to its complexity.

TABLE 20

Subject Grade Coefficients for Use in the Teaching Load Formula

Grade Level	7 and 8	9	10–11–12
English	1.0	1.1	1.1
Art	1.0	.9	1.0
Home Economics	1.0	1.0	1.1
Music	.9	1.0	1.0
Mathematics	1.0	1.0	1.0
Agriculture	—	—	1.3
Industrial Arts	.9	.9	1.0
Physical Education	.8	.9	.9
Health	.9	1.1	1.2
Commerce	1.0	1.0	1.0
Social Studies	1.0	1.1	1.1
Foreign Language	1.0	1.0	1.0
Science	1.0	1.1	1.1

Source: Harl R. Douglass, *Modern Administration of Secondary Schools* (Boston: Ginn and Company, 1957), p. 97.

Of the various teacher load formulas developed, Douglass's appears to have the most evidence to support it. The authors recommend its use as a supplement to the principal's judgment in making teacher assignments and not as a sole basis for determining teacher load. It is possible to apply the formula without using the subject coefficients, if an administrator has serious reservations about their validity. Following is the Douglass Teacher Load Formula with a description of the variables included in it:[18]

$$TL = SC\left[CP - \frac{Dup}{10} + \frac{NP - 25CP}{100}\right]\left[\frac{PL + 50}{100}\right] + .6PC\left[\frac{PL + 50}{100}\right]$$

TL = units of teaching load per week.
SC = subject coefficient used for giving relative weights to classes in different subject fields.
CP = class periods spent in classroom per week.
Dup = number of class periods spent per week in classroom, teaching classes for which the preparation is very similar to that for some other section, not including the original section.

[18] Harl R. Douglass, *Modern Administration of Secondary Schools* (Boston: Ginn and Company, 1957), pp. 96–97.

STAFF ORGANIZATION AND UTILIZATION

NP = number of pupils in classes per week.
PC = number of class periods spent per week in supervision of the study hall, student activities, teachers' meetings, committee work, assisting in administrative or supervisory work, or other cooperations.
PL = gross length of class period, in minutes.

In addition to the general definition of terms in the formula, Douglass suggests the use of certain variations for special types of classes:

> In applying the formula to classes requiring no reading and no marking of written work (for example, physical education or music), the term pertaining to the number of pupils should either be divided by 2 or, better still, be omitted entirely.
> In applying the formula to double-period classes in science laboratory, household arts, typewriting, and art or shop of various types, the following procedure should be employed:
> 1. Count each double period as two periods (CP).
> 2. Count each double period as one unit of duplicate preparation over and above any other allowance made for duplicate preparation.
> 3. Count the number for each half of double period.[19]

The following example illustrates the application of the Douglass formula in calculating the teaching load for one teacher, who had teaching and cooperative work assignments as follows:

Chemistry, 1 section, 26 pupils.
Biology, 2 sections, 27 and 29 pupils.
General Science, ninth grade, 2 sections, 35 pupils in each section.
A science club meeting, 60 minutes per week.
Department meetings and faculty meetings, total of 60 minutes per week.
PTA and other special meetings, average 45 minutes per week.

Calculations:

$$TL = SC\left[CP - \frac{Dup}{10} + \frac{NP - 25CP}{100}\right]\left[\frac{PL + 50}{100}\right] + .6PC\left[\frac{PL + 50}{100}\right]$$

$$= 1.1\left[25 - \frac{10}{10} + \frac{(152)(5) - 25(25)}{100}\right]\left[\frac{55 + 50}{100}\right] + .6\left[\frac{165}{55}\right]\left[\frac{55 + 50}{100}\right]$$

$$= 1.1[25 - 1 + 1.35][1.05] + .6(3)(1.05)$$

$$= 31.2$$

Future Developments in Staff Utilization

One of the most extensive programs to study the problems related to staff utilization has been conducted by the Commission on the Experimental Study of the Utilization of the Staff in the Secondary School.

[19] *Ibid.*, p. 97.

Organized in May, 1956, under the direction of the National Association of Secondary School Principals, and supported by grants from the Fund for the Advancement of Education, the Commission has been particularly concerned with the quality of teaching and its dependence upon the supply of well-prepared teachers. One of the basic assumptions of the Commission is as follows:

> Unless changes are made in the use of teachers we now have and are likely to obtain in the next few years, the present trend to increase class sizes, eliminate courses, and employ more and more teachers with inadequate preparation will become accepted policy; such developments will cause deterioration in the quality of education.[20]

A further assumption of the Commission has been that "experimental studies should be undertaken to learn better ways of utilizing the teachers we have and may be able to obtain so that quality of education can be improved."[21] The method of operation of the Commission has been to sponsor studies and innovations in practices by secondary schools throughout the United States. Specific projects have emphasized particularly changes in class size and/or schedules, team teaching, changes in personnel, and use of mechanical aids.

Changes in Class Size and/or Schedules. A direct challenge to the traditional concept of class size and the schedule has been the experimentation in large-group instruction, individual study, and small-group instruction.

Large-group instruction usually involves groups of 100 or more. It is intended that large groups should be used when new topics or new concepts are being introduced, or when general explanations of a subject are needed. A lecture is given by a teacher who is especially effective at this type of procedure, and extensive use of audio-visual aids is made.

A major claim made for large-group instruction is that it makes more efficient use of the teacher's time. Under the usual plan of dividing 100 students into four groups of twenty-five each, a teacher must spend four periods presenting material which could be presented in one period under a plan of large-group instruction. It is not proposed that all classes should be organized as large groups; large-group instruction should perhaps be used about 40 per cent of the time. The amount of large-group instruction should vary, too, according to subject, at different stages in the handling of a subject, and in accordance with student interest and maturity. In addition, different members of the teaching team

---

[20] J. Lloyd Trump, *New Horizons for Secondary School Teachers* (Urbana, Ill.: Commission on the Experimental Study of the Utilization of the Staff in the Secondary School, NASSP, 1959), p. 31.

[21] *Ibid.*, p. 32.

may assume responsibility for lectures as their special interests and competence in particular topics dictate.

Small-group instruction, supplementing large-group instruction, provides students with an opportunity to discuss ideas, to seek further information, and to pit their ideas against those of others. It is proposed that discussion groups should contain no more than twelve to fifteen students in order to assure participation by all members of the group. The teacher's role in the small group is intended to be that of counselor, consultant, and evaluator. Approximately 20 per cent of a student's time should be devoted to small-group instruction.

The remaining 40 per cent of a student's course time should be used in independent study activities, or study in groups of two or three, with a minimum of faculty supervision. In terms of staff utilization, the teachers are expected to serve primarily as consultants during this phase. Pupils and teachers should be able to confer and plan activities appropriate to the needs of individual students during this part of the school day. According to Trump, "Students will read, listen to records and tapes, view, question, experiment, examine, consider evidence, analyze, investigate, think, write, create, memorize, make records, visit, and self-appraise."[22] They will be free to use the libraries, museums, laboratories, project and materials centers, or any similar facilities available in the school. A major objective of individual study is to promote increasing responsibility for self-direction in learning.

In Figure 21 the Commission on the Experimental Study of the Utilization of the Staff in the Secondary School visualizes how instruction might be organized.

Team Teaching. A major problem in implementing instruction in large-group, small-group, and individual study plans is that of organizing teachers to work together effectively. This concern has done much to stimulate experimentation in the use of team teaching. Another problem to which it is hoped that team teaching may be the answer is the failure of existing organizational patterns to make full use of the special talents and abilities of the professional staff. The basic idea of team teaching is to organize the faculty in groups of teachers who work together in planning the learning experiences for a particular group of students. There are at least four types of teacher teams described in the literature: the team leader type, the associate type, the master teacher-beginning type, and the coordinated type.[23]

[22] J. Lloyd Trump, *Images of the Future* (Urbana, Ill.: Commission on the Experimental Study of the Utilization of the Staff in the Secondary School, NASSP, 1959), p. 10.

[23] Luvern L. Cunningham, "Team Teaching: Where Do We Stand?" *Administrator's Notebook* (Midwest Administration Center, University of Chicago), April, 1960, Vol. 8, No. 8.

FIGURE 21
Proposed Organization of Instruction

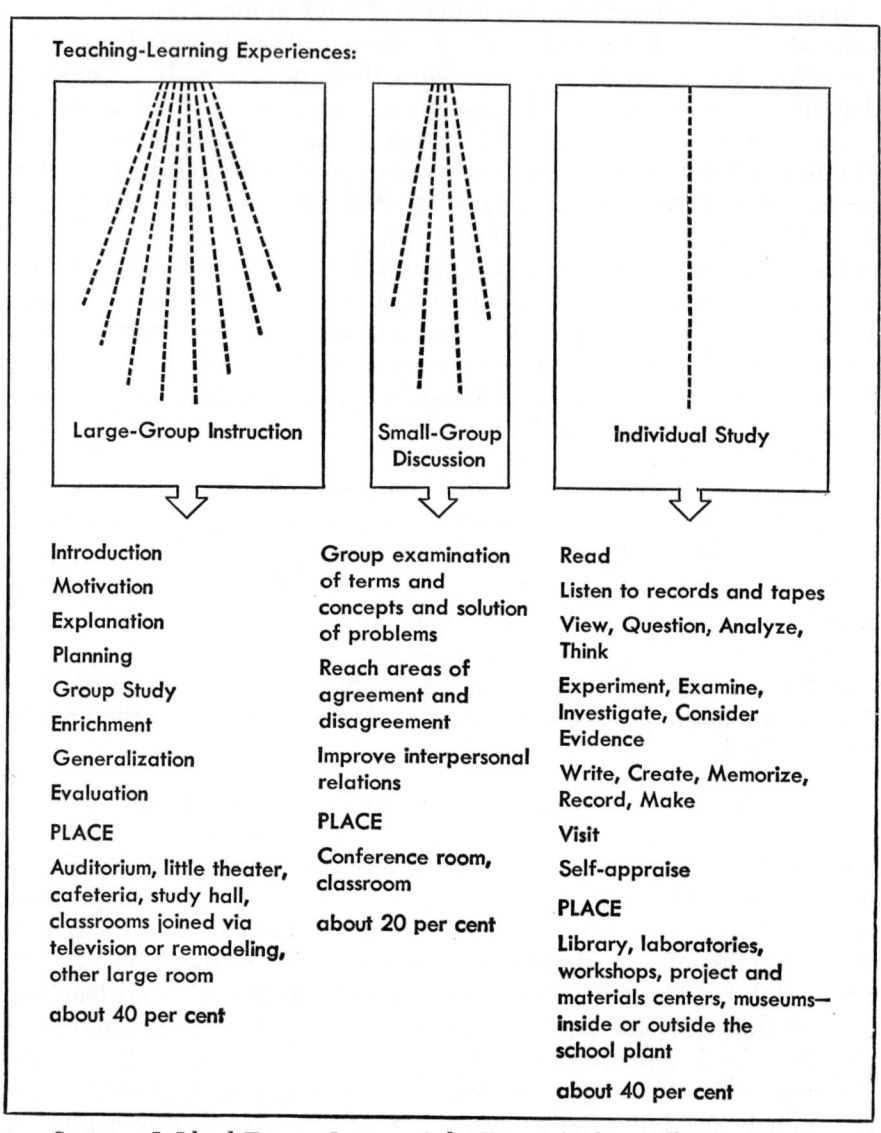

Source: J. Lloyd Trump, *Images of the Future* (Urbana, Ill.: Commission on the Experimental Study of the Utilization of the Staff in the Secondary School, NASSP, 1959), p. 9.

1. In the *team leader type,* one person is designated as the "leader" of a group of two or more teachers. It is his responsibility to coordinate the work of the other members of the team. A team might include personnel with varying degrees of professional preparation and experi-

ence, and it might include representatives from only one subject or from several subject fields. For example, four teachers of tenth-grade English could be assigned as a team for 120 pupils. One teacher is appointed team leader or coordinator of the group. The four teachers are expected to plan the learning experiences for their 120 pupils in such a way as to utilize the special talents and strengths of the individual members of the team. With all 120 pupils scheduled for English at the same time, the team could determine when it wants large-group instruction, small-group activities, or individual study. Be it noted that this device does not reduce the pupil-teacher ratio, but it does provide flexibility in the use of teacher talents.

2. An *associate type* of team is formed when two or more teachers are given responsibility for a particular group of pupils, as in the team leader type of organization. The basic difference is that no one person is appointed as coordinator of the group. The associate plan is relatively informal, with leadership of the group emerging out of the situation or problem before the team. Cunningham reports,

> Teams in this classification are usually two or three member teams. Some have non-professional adults or students assigned to them. At the high school level associate teams are sometimes composed of teachers from just one subject area and sometimes more than one. Practices are not at all uniform, but most of these teams work with large classes and a premium is placed upon opportunities to work with sub-groups of teachers.[24]

3. The *master teacher-beginning teacher type* makes it possible to work with a larger group of students at one time or to have a smaller group separated from the larger group for special attention. Sometimes one teacher lectures to the entire group, freeing the others to do research, study, or prepare materials for the next session. A major advantage in this plan is the opportunities it provides for inexperienced teachers to mature and develop under the guidance of a master teacher. Usually teams organized on this basis have teachers within the same subject field. A key to the success of the plan is the degree to which teachers assigned to a team are able to work together cooperatively.

4. A *coordinated team type* is in many respects merely a variation of other types of team teaching. The team comes together to do cooperative planning, but there is no joint responsibility for a specific group of pupils. Each teacher retains responsibility for his own group of pupils. The teamwork comes merely from the fact that teachers with similar teaching assignments plan and work together on mutual problems. Some of the features of team teaching employed by such groups include combining classes in the auditorium, cafeteria, or other areas for lectures, and the switching of sections during certain periods or for certain topics in

[24] *Ibid.*

order to capitalize on special strengths of particular teachers. According to Cunningham, "It is questionable whether this should be included as a team type. The relationships appear to be so loose and informal that little can be expected from an organization of this character."[25]

It is too soon to assess the ultimate effect that current innovations in team teaching will have. Results will have to be evaluated in a variety of situations. Whether or not team teaching turns out to be a permanent organizational pattern remains to be seen. In any event, high school principals are encouraged to experiment within their own schools on the problems of staff utilization and should be well informed of the results of experimentation in this area.

Changes in Personnel. One of the more controversial proposals concerning staff organization is that made by Trump in *Images of the Future*. He advocates having teachers classified according to various levels of professional competence. The proposal is based on the assumptions that there will not be an adequate supply of highly qualified teachers in the immediate future and that a plan of differentiation between teachers, combined with the team teaching concept, is a possible solution to the problem. According to Trump, there would be teacher specialists, general teachers, instruction assistants, clerks, general aids, community consultants, and staff specialists.

Teachers would be assigned to different tasks according to their individual abilities, preparation, and experience. Teacher specialists would be primarily large-group instructors who have demonstrated their effectiveness in this type of teaching. General teachers, usually with less experience than teacher specialists or perhaps not interested in teaching as a long-term career, would serve primarily as observers and consultants in small-group discussions.

Other personnel — instruction assistants, clerks, general aides, and community consultants — with less preparation and experience than teacher specialists and general teachers, would assist the professional teachers in many of the more routine duties necessary to the instructional process. Such assistance would free the professional teachers to concentrate their time and energy on the preparation of appropriate materials or other tasks demanding the attention of well-qualified teachers.

Staff specialists would be professional workers providing such services as guidance, counseling, research, health, and aid to exceptional children. These people would function much as in present organizations.

In many respects, organization of the staff on the basis of level of preparation and experience is very similar to the system used by colleges and universities, in which the faculty is organized according to various ranks: professor, associate professor, assistant professor, instructor, and student assistant. It is a plan of utilization which is based on acceptance

[25] *Ibid.*

of the idea that some teachers are better qualified to perform certain teaching activities than are others. It seems improbable that this plan will be used extensively in secondary schools in the immediate future, especially in light of the strong position teacher organizations have taken against merit provisions in determining salary. Any plan which establishes different levels of teachers must recognize these differences in salary levels. It may be that teachers in schools of the future will accept the idea of merit as a desirable factor in salary determination, but until they do, there seems to be little chance of establishing a system of staff organization based on different levels of teachers.

Mechanical Aids. Undoubtedly teachers in the future will make greater use than at present of mechanical aids of all kinds, i.e., tapes, television, radio, films, records, teaching machines, etc. The development of television and teaching machines as instructional aids holds considerable promise for better staff utilization.

The chief virtue of television, insofar as staff utilization is concerned, is its potential for instruction of large numbers of pupils by a single instructor of superior talents. Television has other assets, particularly the possibility of increasing motivation on the part of the learner; but of overriding importance is its ability to bring the influence of one outstanding teacher or one program to bear on large groups of students. This is especially valuable in subject fields in which there are severe shortages of qualified teachers.

Particularly dramatic has been the attention recently given to the use of teaching machines. A teaching machine is a mechanical device that serves as an individual tutor. It presents questions or information to the learner, carefully planned to provide small, overlapping tasks which are performed one at a time. The machine records the learner's answers and then presents the correct answer each time he responds. A major advantage of the machine is that it enables a student to proceed at his own rate of learning. Failure is minimized because the student need not proceed until he masters a particular concept. Rapidly growing is the use of tape recorders to aid in the teaching of foreign languages. A foreign language laboratory, equipped with enough machines so that every pupil has an opportunity to drill on listening and speaking skills in the language being studied, has become standard equipment in many high schools.

From the viewpoint of staff utilization, use of teaching machines has an important implication in that the machines can take the place of the teacher as a "drillmaster." Machines also have an infinite amount of patience, and the learner may repeat a learning exercise as often as is necessary. There is evidence that learning which is dependent upon drill can be taught just as effectively by a machine as by a teacher. Thus the teacher may use his time in working with individual pupils or in other instructional activities rather than in quizzing pupils and grading papers. Although teaching machines will probably have no great effect in reducing the pupil-teacher ratio, they do appear to be changing the way teachers spend their time in the classroom. It should be noted that research indicates that programmed textbooks are as effective as machines for these purposes.

Questions and Group Projects

1. Make a diagram of the administrative structure of a high school you know well. It is suggested that you interview the principal, department chairmen, or other administrators in the school to check the accuracy of the diagram.

2. Assume that you are the new principal of a high school which has had no departmental organization. You decide you would like to establish such a plan, but the faculty is reluctant to go along with you. However, the faculty has agreed to review your suggestions. In light of these conditions, what reasons could you give for the establishment of a departmental plan of organization?

3. Some people believe small high schools are better than large high schools. Others claim that advantages of small high schools can be secured within a large school through appropriate organization. How is this possible to achieve?

4. Using the Douglass Teaching Load Formula, calculate the teaching loads of all teachers in one high school.

5. Do you believe team teaching will become general practice in high schools during the next ten years? Present arguments in support of your position.

6. To what extent are television and teaching machines likely to replace teachers in high schools? Discuss the reasons why you think as you do.

Selected References

Cornell, F. G. "Organization Is More Than a Line Chart," *School Executive*, September, 1957, 77:83–86.

Cronin, J. M. "What's All This About Teacher Aids?" *California Journal of Secondary Education*, November, 1959, 34:390–97.

Cross, Eva A., and Ruth S. Ford. "Progress Can Have Priority," *NEA Journal*, January, 1958, pp. 26–28.

Douglass, Harl R. *Modern Administration of Secondary Schools*. Boston: Ginn and Company, 1957.

Douglass, Harl R. "1950 Revision of the Douglass High School Teaching Load Formula." *The Bulletin* of the NASSP, May, 1951, 35:13–24.

French, Will J., Dan Hull, and B. L. Dodds. *American High School Administration.* New York: Rinehart and Company, Inc., 1957.

Frost, Norman. "What Teaching Load?" *American School Board Journal,* March, 1941, 102:43–45.

Griffiths, Daniel. *Human Relations in School Administration.* New York: Appleton-Century-Crofts, Inc., 1956.

Hunt, Herold C., and Paul R. Pierce. *The Practice of School Administration.* Boston: Houghton Mifflin Company, 1958.

Jung, Christian A. "Revision of the Douglass Teaching Load Formula," Ed.D. dissertation, University of Colorado, 1950.

Lambert, Sam M., and David Iwamoto. "Teaching Load," *Encyclopedia of Educational Research.* New York: The Macmillan Company, 3rd ed., 1960, p. 1497.

Lumsdaine, A. A., and Robert Glaser. *Teaching Machines and Programmed Learning.* Washington: National Education Association, 1960.

National Association of Secondary School Principals. "Progressing Toward Better Schools," *The Bulletin* of the NASSP, January, 1960, Vol. 44, No. 252.

National Education Association, Research Division. "The Status of the American Public-School Teacher," *Research Bulletin,* February, 1957, 35:3–63.

———. "The Teacher Looks at Teacher Load," *Research Bulletin,* November, 1939, 17:221–70.

———. "Teaching Load in 1950," *Research Bulletin,* February, 1951, 29:3–51.

Pettit, Maurice L. "Determining Teacher Load," *American School Board Journal,* March, 1954, 128:34.

Quambeck, Martin, and Harl R. Douglass. "Teacher Loads in High Schools," *Nation's Schools,* February, 1935, 15:37–39.

Romine, Stephen. "Subject Combinations and Teaching Loads in Secondary Schools," *School Review,* 1949, 57:551–58.

Spalding, H. G. "What Is an Adequate High-School Staff?" *The Bulletin* of the NASSP, January, 1952, 36:46–57.

Tompkins, Ellsworth, "What Should You Demand of a High School Principal?" *School Management,* September, 1960, 4:34.

Tompkins, Ellsworth. *What Teachers Say About Class Size.* U.S. Office of Education, Circ. 311. Washington: Government Printing Office, 1950.

Trump, J. Lloyd. *Images of the Future.* Urbana, Ill: Commission on the Experimental Study of the Utilization of the Staff in the Secondary School, NASSP, 1959.

CHAPTER 12

Staff Morale

Morale, like love, is a powerful force, and it is about as easy to describe. People write about it, talk about it, and give advice about it, but there remains the difficulty of analyzing it or predicting its status. Some groups have it and some don't. Whatever it is, it makes a remarkable difference in the behavior of groups. There is considerable evidence to support the view that good morale is among the most important ingredients in the success of any group enterprise over an extended period of time.

A significant series of studies relating to morale was conducted by the Western Electric Company at its Hawthorne Works near Chicago between 1924 and 1940.[1] In these studies, various changes were made in the physical conditions of an experimental group of workers in order to improve productivity. A control group continued to work under less favorable conditions. An unexpected outcome of these studies was that productivity of both groups increased, and that of the experimental group remained high when the physical conditions were returned to their previous state. One conclusion was that a human factor i.e., the way people feel about their work, was operating, and it made a significant difference in their productivity. Apparently workers who were made to feel important and had a favorable attitude toward their work were more productive than they had been previously.

School administrators have personnel problems similar to those of industrialists. Although good morale may be regarded as a desirable end in itself, if only to make people feel congenial and important, high teacher morale is important also as a means to better teaching. True, it is

[1] F. J. Roethlisberger and W. J. Dickson, *Management and the Worker* (Cambridge, Mass.: Harvard University Press, 1943).

easier to obtain evidence with respect to productivity of workers in an industrial plant than in a school, but there is some evidence that high morale in schools produces results similar to those found in the Western Electric studies.

A study conducted in twenty Iowa high schools demonstrated that there is a significant relationship between high student achievement and high teacher morale.[2] The twenty high schools were divided into two groups of ten each. One group ranked in the upper quartile of schools in their student achievement on the Iowa Test of Educational Development, and the second group ranked in the lower quartile. The level of teacher morale was ascertained in all twenty schools by the teachers' responses on a multiple-choice scale and also by personal interview. The mean morale score of teachers in the first group of schools was significantly higher than the mean score of teachers in the second group. The difference was significant at the 5 per cent level.

In a similar study of the relation between quality education and the morale of teachers in selected elementary schools in Orange County, Florida, Stosberg found that

> . . . the morale tendency of teachers varies with the quality of the educational program in the school. The teachers in schools with high quality educational programs responded with higher morale tendency scores than the low quality schools in this study. . . .[3]

The evidence points consistently to the fact that teacher morale and good educational achievement are closely related — in other words, where teacher morale is high, student achievement is high and teaching is good.

If he accepts this evidence, the administrator will do everything possible to bring about those conditions conducive to high morale in his staff. As administrators identify and eliminate conditions which create morale problems, they may expect improved teaching and learning in the classroom. This chapter is devoted, therefore, to a discussion of the factors affecting teacher morale and their implications for administrative practice.

Definition

The majority of definitions of morale describe it as a mental condition and cite various factors affecting it. Webster calls it

> A condition as affected by, or dependent upon, such moral or mental factors as zeal, spirit, hope, confidence, etc.; mental state, as of a body of men, an army, and the like.

[2] Lester W. Anderson, "Teacher Morale and Student Achievement," *Journal of Educational Research,* May, 1953, pp. 693–98.
[3] William Kenneth Stosberg, "A Study of the Relation Between Quality of Education and the Morale Status of the Faculty," *Dissertation Abstracts,* July–September, 1958, 19:72.

G. Stanley Hall made the following statement concerning a definition of morale:

> What is morale? No two conceptions of it are alike. It can be no more defined than energy, or life, or soul. All we can do is to try and describe it, to feel, and to guide it. When and where it is strongest it makes the individual "fit" for any task. It also gives him a sense of solidarity with his comrades seeking the same end, and enables him either to do or to suffer in a common cause.[4]

A more comprehensive definition than most was drafted at a conference of ten psychologists at Cambridge University in England in 1940. They identified three aspects of morale, but the following definition, with emphasis on group aspects, is most applicable to a school staff:

> [The group emphasis] Morale refers to the condition of a group where there are clear and fixed group goals [purposes] that are felt to be important and integrated with individual goals; where there is confidence in the attainment of these goals, and subordinately, confidence in the means of attainment, in the leaders, associates, and finally in oneself; where group actions are integrated and cooperative; and where aggression and hostility are expressed against the forces frustrating the group rather than toward other individuals within the group.[5]

A statement by the American Association of School Administrators describes morale from the administrative viewpoint:

> ... Morale is a disposition on the part of persons engaged in an enterprise to behave in ways which contribute to the purposes for which the enterprise exists. When this disposition is strong, morale is said to be high. It manifests itself in a tendency to subordinate personal considerations to the purposes of the enterprise, to work as a member of a team for the accomplishment of common goals, and to derive satisfaction from achievements of the organization. When the disposition toward the achievement of common purposes is weak, morale is said to be low. Low morale is characterized by behavior that is obstructive or noncontributory to the common purposes, by failure to derive personal satisfaction from group achievement, and by a tendency to elevate personal interests above the purposes of the enterprise.[6]

It is often possible when visiting a school to sense high morale in a faculty. Members speak with pride about their school. Students are proud of their school and display an attitude of seriousness and purpose toward their studies. Teachers show evidence of new approaches to

---

[4] G. Stanley Hall, "Morale in War and After," *Psychological Abstracts*, 1918, 15:361.
[5] Irwin L. Child, "Morale: A Bibliographical Review," *Psychological Bulletin*, 1941, 38:393–94.
[6] American Association of School Administrators, *Staff Relations in School Administration*, Thirty-Third Yearbook (Washington: National Education Association, 1955), p. 15.

instructional problems. The noon hour sessions in the faculty lounge are relatively free of grousing. There is evidence that the staff has been keeping pace with new materials and ideas in curriculum, and the relationships between administrators and teachers are friendly and characterized by mutual respect. Faculty morale is likely to be at its best when teachers feel secure, understand where they are trying to go, are loyal to the school and their colleagues, and feel that what they are doing is important.

Factors Affecting Morale

Among professional people such as teachers it would seem reasonable that good morale could be expected without special administrative effort. But teachers have the same emotions as anyone else. Good morale has to be cultivated in schools as well as in other group enterprises. And the key person in building it in a school is the principal. He must understand the desires of his faculty and the factors bearing on their job satisfactions. He must do everything within reason to provide the best climate possible for good morale. A first step is to identify the factors affecting morale. Specific administrative practices taking these into account can then be developed. The emphasis in this chapter is on identifying these factors, while consideration is given to specific techniques for promoting cooperative working relationships in Chapter 11.

Agreement on Purposes

In the interest of promoting morale a faculty needs to know where it is going in education. Morale is affected positively or negatively depending upon whether or not the faculty is agreed on its objectives. Recognized objectives give direction to the activities of an enterprise, and it is much better, from a morale viewpoint, if the activities of the faculty have purpose and are directed toward specific goals. The opposite situation is to have teachers working aimlessly, not knowing just what they really are trying to accomplish. In general, people feel greater satisfaction in their work when they see a direct relationship between what they are doing and what they are trying to achieve. It makes considerable difference in a teacher's attitude, for instance, if, when asked to chaperone a school party, he regards it as an opportunity to contribute to the social development of young people and does not think of it merely as a baby-sitting chore.

In times of tension it is especially important for teachers to know what their objectives are and where they stand on educational issues. The quality of classroom teaching or the content of the curriculum is often a subject for debate in a community. In either case, the objectives to be achieved must be considered if one is to make intelligent observations about the school. A faculty that has clarified its goals is much more likely to act positively under pressure than is a faculty that has not given thoughtful consideration to where it is going. It is too late for a faculty to think straight on its purposes if it waits until it is forced to face an issue by outsiders. For example, some organized groups have put considerable pressure on teachers to refrain from dealing with controversial issues such as communism and local politics. Whether or not a faculty is willing to bow to such pressure often is related to how wholeheartedly it has accepted the development of critical and independent thinking as a worthy objective of secondary education. If this is considered an important purpose, the faculty is likely to take a firm position. It also follows that teachers will feel more confident about their position, and consequently have better morale, when issues of this kind have been thought through and a statement of purposes has been prepared before a situation of extreme stress develops.

Not only should the staff define the school's objectives, but it is desirable that individual teachers be in general agreement with them. A major concern of the principal is to coordinate the interests of individual staff members in the development of general aims. This task is complicated by the fact that a high school faculty is a collection of specialists in the various subject fields, and a considerable part of their success as teachers is dependent upon their enthusiasm for and understanding of the specific objectives related to the teaching of their subjects. It is unlikely, for instance, that a band director who is not interested in promoting music in the school will ever develop a band of high quality. Similarly, the athletic coach is expected to be enthusiastic about sports, and the teacher of English is looked to as a leader in stimulating the reading of good literature. Although special interests are bound to be present, morale will be higher if all teachers recognize that the overall objectives of the school are of prime importance and do their best to support them. It is a sign of good morale when teachers are willing to reconcile individual goals with those of the staff as a whole.

There are usually a few prima donnas on a faculty who feel that they should receive special consideration in everything they do. The principal will need a great deal of patience and skill in dealing with these individuals to make certain that interests which are not acceptable to the faculty as a whole are reoriented in such a way that serious divisions do not result. This does not imply, however, that anyone should be denied the opportunity to convince others of the logic of his ideas. But it does imply that the principal must see that a dissenter observes general policies until such time as he can convince the rest of the faculty of the merit of his ideas. To make sure that teachers have a chance to express their views, good means of communication must be established.

Cooperative Determination of Policy

The nature of the process by which teachers express themselves and policies are developed may be just as important to faculty morale as the final policy. Involving teachers in the solution of problems relating to their work is advocated by most researchers who have investigated morale. In fact, they mention no factor in morale as frequently as this one. The findings of a follow-up study made by Schultz of 776 graduates of the University of Illinois who entered teaching revealed a cooperative approach used by administrators in practically every situation where teachers were classified as being most satisfied.

> One hundred per cent of the most satisfied teachers were of the opinion that teachers in their schools are given an opportunity to express themselves on school problems and 98 per cent felt that they are given sufficient voice about school plans and policies related to their work. Conversely, only 23 per cent of the least satisfied teachers felt teachers in their systems are given an opportunity to express opinions on school problems and only 19 per cent were of the opinion that they are given sufficient voice about school plans and policies related to their work.[7]

One of the major reasons for the involvement of teachers in policy formulation is that teachers are the ones who eventually must implement policies. If policies are not acceptable to teachers, either they will find ways of circumventing them or they will not make a sustained effort to achieve them. On the other hand, policies which incorporate teachers' views are likely to be implemented with good effort.

Although it is recommended by the authors that the principal have teachers participate in policy formulation, it is not to be inferred that the faculty should *determine* policy. As pointed out in Chapter 11, the legal responsibility for policy decisions rests with the board of education. Faculty members must respect the legal framework of the school, and they must recognize also that employees of a school cannot expect to be an autonomous group. Some boards of education do delegate authority to establish policies to the administration and faculty in such areas as methods of instruction, curriculum development, and discipline. But even in these fields faculty members should recognize that legally the board of education is still responsible for determining policy.

Teachers must recognize, too, that administrators are charged by the board with formulating administrative policies. This is their job and they should see that it is done. Conflicts arise, however, when either administrators or the faculty insist on formulating policies without con-

[7] R. E. Schultz, "Keeping Up Teacher Morale," *Nation's Schools*, October, 1952, 50:55.

sultation with others. Differences of opinion have a reasonably good chance of being resolved satisfactorily if teachers can work with the administrators in planning policy. In contrast is the procedure whereby policies are developed by the board and/or administrative staff and are made known to teachers at the same time, or after, the policies have been invoked. Teachers' opinions are then invited after the fact. Conflicts of purpose often result when teachers lack information or have misconceptions about the basis for the establishment of a policy. There is no adequate substitute for face-to-face communication between administrators and teachers in developing school policies.

If the principal demonstrates by his own actions that he is willing to work cooperatively with teachers and that he believes it is important for them to reciprocate, the teachers will probably stand more solidly in support of policies than they will if policies are handed down from above. However, he must be sincere; teachers easily detect inconsistencies between the principal's verbalizations and the way he acts.

Utilization of Talents and a Sense of Achievement

The need to feel a sense of achievement in one's work is basic to morale for people in all fields, but it is especially crucial to professional persons. Teachers are professional workers. Most of them are intelligent, talented, sensitive, and ambitious people who want to believe that they are accomplishing something of consequence. They want to feel that they are exerting a positive influence on their students and that they are continuing to improve in their own professional skill and knowledge as teachers. In order for a teacher to develop professional drive, he must feel that he has been successful in the past and has a reasonably good chance of being successful in the future.

Many teachers have received public recognition both in academic and in extraclass activities in their student days. It is probable that as undergraduates they participated in a variety of activities. For such people, teaching may become a bore or a "dead end" if they go through the same old routine day after day or if they believe their efforts are not appreciated. In many instances, if the principal is alert to the problem and makes an effort to provide teachers with adequate recognition and opportunities to utilize their abilities, the development of such attitudes can be forestalled. Fortunately, there are many assignments in a high school which challenge professional excellence and offer wide scope for the exercise of teachers' talents.

The least that a principal can do is to give recognition and express his appreciation for work well done. There is little reason to withhold commendation when teachers have done a good job. Principals can emphasize the positive contributions of their teachers without becoming unctuous. If done in good taste, it may be effective to give recognition publicly. Certainly a written note of commendation, with a copy sent to the superintendent, should not embarrass the recipient and usually will be appreciated. Realization that a job well done will receive acknowledgment generally contributes to good rapport with the administration, and good teacher-administrator rapport contributes to good instruction. The principal who employs a constructive approach is much more likely to strengthen faculty morale than the principal who constantly criticizes.

Professional assignments often make a marked difference in a teacher's chances for success. Since not all teachers are endowed with the same abilities, principals should make every reasonable effort to assign the right task to the right person. It is hardly necessary to repeat that all teachers should be assigned to their major subject fields. Teachers have a greater sense of security and confidence if they know they are adequately prepared in their subject than if they have to struggle to keep a chapter ahead of the students, not an unusual experience for teachers who are improperly assigned.

Special consideration also should be given by the principal to making extraclass assignments. Teachers sometimes express a strong desire for a particular assignment but lack adequate training or experience to direct it successfully. It is usually a serious mistake, from a morale standpoint, to ask a teacher who does not have adequate preparation to sponsor an extraclass activity such as a play or the school paper, which requires expert direction and is to be judged by an adult audience. Chances for success under such circumstances are limited and the results may be demoralizing to both the students and the teacher. Granted that interest is invaluable, it is no substitute for training and experience for such assignments. On the other hand, a person with inadequate preparation initially might be appointed to assist a teacher who has been successful in the undertaking, and in this way have an opportunity to exploit his interest and to develop competence under experienced leadership. Certain activities, of course, do not demand expert faculty direction; in fact, students may learn more if they depend upon their own resources. All that is needed in these activities is mature supervision.

Not only should extraclass assignments be in keeping with the teacher's interests and abilities, but the total teaching load should be reasonable so that he is not forced to take shortcuts in his preparation and instruction which may result in less than his best teaching. The variables to be considered in determining teacher load are discussed in detail in Chapter 11.

The role and nature of a going in-service program, which is fundamental to professional growth, is dealt with in Chapter 13. Here we wish only to emphasize that the development of faculty talent is not something that can be left to chance or be considered as an incidental aspect of school administration. Frequently the success of the principal is judged by the effectiveness of his in-service leadership.

Confidence in and Respect for Administrators

The attitudes that a group holds toward its leaders have an important bearing on morale. Morale is enhanced if teachers respect their administrators, feel that the administrators are competent, and believe that they, the teachers, will be treated fairly and in a professional manner. Generally, the principal represents the teachers and the school in relations with the public and at professional meetings. In many respects, the reputation of the school and its teachers is strengthened or weakened by the way the principal represents them.

Teachers will respond to a principal's leadership in professional activities with more enthusiasm if he leads by example rather than exhortation. The following testimony from a teacher reflects the high regard felt for a principal who demonstrated her willingness to participate in professional activities:

> They [teachers] soon realized that their principal never asked them to do anything which she was not willing to do herself. She not only encouraged them to improve their professional status by doing in-service work, she enrolled in classes with them. She led the way to membership and participation in professional organizations by becoming active in local, state, and national associations.[8]

This type of leadership helps to convince the faculty that the principal is genuinely interested in their progress and is not giving mere lip service to it.

A very serious staff morale problem was encountered by one of the authors in a high school in which the faculty requested the principal to arrange a curriculum workshop. The superintendent of schools and the board of education supported the request by underwriting the complete cost of the program. Everything appeared to favor a successful session. However, as the program moved along, it became increasingly apparent that the teachers were spending a great deal of time discussing the principal. This was easy to do, because he never attended any of the work sessions. Unfortunately, the faculty became convinced that the reason he stayed away was that he had nothing to contribute. One year later the principal's contract was not renewed, chiefly because his teachers no longer had confidence in his competence. Much of this feeling was prompted by his unwillingness to work with them in the curriculum workshop.

[8] M. L. Bradford, "Building Morale from the Principal's Viewpoint," *School Executive,* July, 1951, 70:46.

Just the opposite attitude was in evidence during a convention of high school principals. A number of principals were discussing the eighteen recommendations made in an address by Dr. Conant on junior high schools.[9] One principal mentioned that he had been favorably impressed with the suggestions in the talk but was convinced that his faculty was doing most of the things recommended by Dr. Conant. Acting on this conviction, he immediately prepared a memorandum to his faculty, reporting on the talk, assuring his teachers that he was pleased and proud that they were already doing most of the things outlined, and telling them he was eager to get back to the school to discuss with them the ideas advanced by Conant at the convention. It is genuine concern of this type that bolsters faculty confidence in the professional leadership of an administrator.

At the same time, conflicts among members, differences of opinion on professional matters, and errors in judgment are likely to occur even in faculties which have good morale. The conduct of the administrator in these situations should be characterized by impartiality, a willingness to look at all sides of an issue, and the exercise of professional ethics. There is no substitute for fair play in winning and keeping the confidence of teachers. The word spreads rapidly if this is not forthcoming, and the morale of the staff can be quickly undermined.

An "open door" policy which makes the principal readily available also may contribute to good staff morale. A principal would not be human if he did not feel more inclined to discuss problems with some teachers than with others. But there is no place for favoritism in administrator-faculty relations. At times it may be quite inconvenient for the administrator to talk with a teacher. But he should recognize that, from a morale viewpoint, when a teacher wants to see him, it is exceedingly important to make the teacher feel that he is not imposing on the principal's time. No doubt sometimes a conference must be postponed, but if so, an appointment should be made with the teacher as soon as possible. Teachers respect a principal who is willing to listen to their problems and to do his best to assist them.

Occasionally a situation arises in which a teacher is unjustly criticized by parents, other teachers, or pupils. Teachers are extremely sensitive about the attitude of the principal when this happens. There must be no doubt in their minds that the administrator will defend them from unjustified attacks. Tracking down the source of malicious rumors, false accusations, or loose talk is difficult, but every effort should be made to do so before the teacher's reputation has been damaged. If teachers realize that the principal will not waver in his support of them under such conditions, it contributes substantially to their morale.

[9] James B. Conant, "Some Problems of the Junior High School," *The Bulletin* of the NASSP, April, 1960, 44:310–21.

Good Relationships Within the Faculty

An individual's confidence in the ability of his colleagues, in the professional ethics of the group, and in the knowledge that he will receive fair treatment from his associates is an important factor in his morale. Most people want to be "one of the gang" or to have a sense of status in the group. Campbell maintains that

> The essentials for morale stem from an individual's basic urge to have a fullness of relations with a closely knit group of colleagues and friends. Fullness of relations means on the one hand that individuals want to belong, to be secure, and to be inspired by the group, and on the other hand, they want freedom to exercise personal creativeness uncoerced by autocratic controls. These two ambivalent desires must be harmoniously blended if there is to be high morale in any organization. . . .
>
> . . . The things which people achieve together give greater satisfaction than the things which individuals achieve alone. When the process of group thinking is operating at its highest level each person contributes to the thinking of every other person until the many ideas are synthesized into a larger whole.[10]

Earlier in this chapter attention was called to the importance of cooperative problem-solving by the faculty. The authors hold that such procedures are a productive means of promoting group solidarity. But the principal must be alert to note any "isolates" from the group. If a teacher is being overlooked or withdraws from group activities, it is the principal's responsibility to try to analyze the reasons and to do what he can to include the teacher in group enterprises. In some cases, individual conferences with the person may be in order. In other cases, the situation may be improved by an appropriate assignment or by recognizing some particular achievement of the teacher. The specific means for getting him to work with the team depend on the situation and the individual.

Some faculties become demoralized by the presence of troublemakers, gossips, or generally obnoxious persons. The patent answer to this is careful selection of faculty personnel. But sometimes undesirable characteristics are difficult to detect or do not develop until after an individual has been hired. Here is a real test of a principal's skill as an administrator as well as of the extent of his patience. He must make an honest effort to help the person improve his relationships with his colleagues. Merely ignoring the situation generally results in increasing discontent among the faculty. One malcontent may eventually injure the morale of an entire staff. If all efforts to work with the individual through conferences, reassignment, attention to his complaints, and other reasonable approaches have failed, he may have to be dropped in the best inter-

---

[10] Clyde M. Campbell, "Security and Freedom — Requisites for Morale," *School Executive*, July, 1951, 70:41.

est of the school program. A surgeon has to resort to amputation in severe cases, and a principal has to recommend the discharge of a teacher when the occasion demands it. Dismissal of any teacher is a disagreeable task, but the administrator must be prepared to take such action when necessary.

Social affairs may be obvious devices for promoting group *esprit de corps*, but they work and should not be overlooked as a means of creating solidarity among teachers. Although it is difficult to make specific recommendations concerning the principal's role in purely social staff activities, such events can be effective avenues for developing desirable relationships among teachers and between teachers and the principal. Certainly, the latter can contribute much to the success of these occasions without dominating them. If he is pleasant and relaxed and tries to get around to visit with everyone, other faculty members tend to relax and enjoy themselves.

Community Relations

In general, people in the United States are gregarious and place considerable value on being accepted by others. Teachers are no exception. Unfortunately, it is not unusual for teachers to experience difficulty in making social acquaintances outside their professional circle. They usually are held in high regard for their important contribution to the community as teachers, but there are often reservations in accepting them in community affairs apart from school activities. Merely being "in" the community does not mean being "of" it. This frequent lack of general acceptance of teachers as social peers has been a stubborn limitation in the development of good faculty morale.

It is not entirely the teachers' fault that they have found it difficult to enter into the social life of the community. In past years, they have been forced out of normal social activities because of restrictions written into their contracts: no smoking, no drinking, no dating, no dancing, no card playing, no married teachers — and many more "no's" depending upon the collective prejudices of a board of education. There was unquestionably a double standard of social behavior, since the same activities and modes of behavior that were prohibited for teachers were perfectly acceptable in some of the "best" homes in the community, including those of members of the board of education. When a teacher had to pull down the shades of his home to have a smoke, enjoy a cocktail, or play a game of cards, it followed that his social activities were seriously limited. This was the social climate for many teachers only a few years ago.

Fortunately, there have been changes. Undoubtedly the scarcity of qualified teachers since World War II has forced many boards of education to eliminate discriminatory regulations and to adopt a more liberal attitude toward the social life of teachers. But although formal restrictions have been reduced, it does not follow that most teachers have won desirable social status. They do have greater freedom in their personal social activities, but the situation leaves much to be desired. The school administrator is in a position to influence members of the community to accept teachers as social equals and to apply the same standards as for any other respectable citizen. Usually, the principal may expect to gain most support in this matter from parents. He should try to get parents to invite teachers to their homes and to join them in civic and social affairs. It is probable, however, that many parents will need some assurance that the teachers *want* to be involved in community affairs. A strange sort of reserve frequently exists between parents and teachers which is difficult to break through and can be dissolved only as they are associated in informal social affairs and work together in community projects.

By the same token, teachers should be encouraged to show an interest in civic affairs other than those related to the school. It is characteristic of teachers to talk shop with laymen at nonschool functions or to limit their conversations to other teachers who may be present. An effort should be made to get teachers to expand their acquaintance by visiting with laymen and by developing interests in a variety of affairs. This is of course a delicate matter to discuss privately with an individual teacher, but it can be freely talked over in a group meeting. There may be considerable merit in encouraging a faculty to discuss community social relations on the same basis as other professional problems, since they are clearly linked to faculty morale.

Physical Health

An individual who has sufficient energy and physical health to perform his daily tasks without undue fatigue generally will have better morale than a person who is in poor health and becomes easily exhausted. The American Psychiatric Association says, "The individual who is in good physical health and who carries out the elementary health rules is capable in general of developing and maintaining much better morale than the man who is ailing."[11]

A school administrator cannot assume responsibility for the health of staff members, but there are some things related to teacher health over which he has some control. For instance, demands upon a teacher's time and energy can become excessive when a school attempts to provide a comprehensive program of studies and a diversified extraclass program without an adequate number of teachers. Some protection must be given against teaching loads which are unreasonably heavy. This is a more serious problem in smaller schools than in larger ones, since the former

[11] American Psychiatric Association, *Psychiatric Aspects of Civilian Morale* (New York: Family Welfare Association of America, 1942), p. 47.

often try to imitate the latter and provide a program too diverse for the staff to handle. The result is exploitation of teachers. The principal has a responsibility in this matter and should limit the school program to those areas which can be provided without overloading teachers.

It is important in the interest of their physical and mental health for all teachers to have rooms which are well lighted, adequately heated and ventilated, and of sufficient size to permit constructive instructional conditions in all classes. An increasing number of schools are providing faculty lounges to give teachers an opportunity for a few minutes of relaxation away from students. Another facility appreciated by teachers is a faculty dining room where they may eat in a relaxed atmosphere and enjoy a break from their contact with students. A desirable provision is a teachers' workroom equipped with typewriters, duplicating machines, desks, files, and professional literature needed in preparing materials for classes. Adequate clerical and secretarial service for teachers also lightens the teaching load and permits them to devote more time to creative work and to their major function of teaching.

It is recognized that the principal cannot provide facilities without financial support, but he must be aware of the need for favorable teaching conditions if anything is to be done about them. It is up to him to call to the attention of the superintendent of schools any substandard working conditions and to seek improvement.

Sick leave policies and hospitalization insurance which make it possible for teachers to rest when they are ill are a must for schools concerned about the health of teachers. Unfortunately, some schools allow no sick leaves and make deductions from the teacher's salary to pay for a substitute when it is necessary for the regular teacher to be absent. A policy of this type encourages teachers to continue in the classroom even when ill, since they feel that they cannot afford the loss in salary. There is little doubt that both health and morale are affected adversely under these circumstances.

Promoting the health interests of teachers through good facilities and working conditions is an important factor in high morale. Whatever the principal can do to provide such conditions will be rewarded by greater effectiveness on the part of the faculty.

Economic Security

Few people would question the influence of economic status on morale. A teacher whose income fails to provide the necessities of life for himself and his family cannot be expected to be in the best frame of mind for teaching. In recent years, a number of teachers have been forced to take part-time jobs after school. Some even work a full eight hours on the evening shift of a local firm. Summer employment also continues to be a major concern of teachers.

There has been considerable progress, however, in stabilizing teachers' salaries by the general adoption of salary schedules. At least, teachers are not forced into a position of individual bargaining every year, a practice which often rewarded the aggressive personality and penalized the teacher who was too shy to make an issue of his salary. Support for the importance of a good salary schedule is demonstrated in the results of a study by Harap. Twenty schools were surveyed to determine major factors relating to morale, and the following conclusion was reached: "The most frequent suggestions for improvement of morale showed that a good salary scale and reasonably small classes were the most potent in creating satisfactions."[12]

The superintendent of schools and the board of education carry greater responsibility in salary matters than does the high school principal. However, any support the principal can give teachers in improving their economic status will have a positive influence on morale.

Positive Teacher-Student Relationships

At the heart of the teaching-learning process is the relationship of teachers and students. It may be possible for a teacher who is antagonistic toward students to do informative teaching, but it is doubtful that any teacher can be effective in securing outstanding results without a good working relationship with students. Just as the morale of the teachers is related to the quality of their instruction, so is the morale of the students related to the quality of their achievement. Factors discussed in this chapter as basic to principal-teacher relationships and their resulting effect on morale are applicable generally to teacher-student relationships.

Although there is no substitute for a basic interest in students, it is possible to aid teachers to work more effectively with students through adequate guidance and counseling service. The importance of providing special personnel in this area is now widely recognized, and schools appear to be moving rapidly toward achieving a much more favorable counselor-pupil ratio than has been true in the past. Dr. Conant's recommendation that there be one counselor for every 250 students[13] and the provisions in the National Defense Education Act[14] have given a big impetus to the development of guidance services in secondary schools. Such services should make it easier for teachers to handle both behavior and academic adjustment problems within the classroom. No doubt schools will devote an increasing amount of attention to assisting students in selecting courses appropriate to their interests and abilities, which, in

---

[12] H. Harap, "Many Factors Affect Teacher Morale," *Nation's Schools*, June, 1959, 63:56.

[13] James B. Conant, *The American High School Today* (New York: McGraw-Hill Book Company, 1959), pp. 44–46.

[14] U.S. Office of Education, *Guide to the National Defense Education Act of 1958* (Washington: Government Printing Office, rev. ed., 1959).

turn, should help to create a better situation for both teachers and students.

The example set by the principal in working with student organizations such as the student council and in dealing with individual students has a large influence on the kind of general faculty-student rapport which will prevail throughout the school. If he establishes good relations with students, some of this rapport is certain to carry over into classes and other school activities. But if he is unable to achieve a good relationship with students, teachers also will find it difficult to achieve.

Encouraging teachers to participate in case conferences in which they share information and ideas on specific student problems can be helpful in developing their awareness of the importance of effective relationships with students. Teachers need assurance also that the principal is willing to assist and support them in handling difficulties which arise in their classes. There should be no doubt in their minds concerning his position if they are to feel confident in dealing with student problems. A more comprehensive discussion of student behavior, discipline, and the development of citizenship is presented in Chapter 15.

Some faculty conferences on instructional and curriculum problems should be pointed toward developing good rapport with students in classroom and out-of-class situations. There is no way of separating good teaching from good teacher-student relationships. As the principal and his faculty give joint consideration to all phases of the learning process they should achieve better morale, both for teachers and for students.

Personal Problems of Teachers

Most teachers are mature and intelligent people and can and should work out their own personal problems satisfactorily. Sometimes a person finds that things pile up to such a point that they become overwhelming; his morale suffers and his work suffers. It would be unrealistic to try to present an inventory of teachers' personal problems. For the most part they do not differ from those experienced by other workers.

But there are a few nonprofessional problems that appear to be more common among teachers than among other groups. For example, housing is a perennial problem facing teachers, particularly in smaller communities in which there are few good rentals. Beginning and single teachers find it difficult to locate suitable apartments, and in many cases wind up living in a bedroom with kitchen privileges if they are lucky. It is depressing to a person who has been accustomed to a good home and to the run of a house to be unable to secure adequate housing. Assistance given a new teacher in locating a comfortable place to live before he starts to work can be a morale builder. A principal may be extremely helpful to teachers by encouraging people in the community to call his office if there are rentals available and thereby build up a file of good leads for teachers to investigate. He is not, and should not be, in the real-estate business, but any help he can give in this matter will pay off in morale dividends.

At times a teacher may become upset over family problems. A man who is having marital difficulties, financial reverses, or other complications of a personal nature may develop serious morale problems. Obviously, the principal cannot be expected to be a "junior psychiatrist," but he can serve as a friend and counselor. If he is a good listener he is worth a lot to a faculty, for sometimes teachers need to discuss personal problems with someone who is sympathetic.

Although the principal should be aware of the importance of working with teachers when personal problems detract from their effectiveness as teachers, a word of caution is in order. He will need to know when *not* to become involved. Being oversolicitous could be most damaging to his relationships with teachers even though his intentions were the best. If he is to err, it is better to err on the side of too little rather than too much attention.

Morale of the Principal

The factors which affect the morale of the principal are similar to those which influence the morale of teachers. In a study of morale at the administrative level in twelve schools conducted by the Cooperative Development of Public School Administration, Barry has this to say:

> The administrators in the high morale group of schools studied felt they were important in their communities, held in high esteem, and had an appropriate share in determining policies under which their schools operated. They appear to stress communications to a degree greater than those from the low morale schools, and they always seem to encourage staff development to a greater extent. Their peculiar strengths and weaknesses are considered more often, and they operate in a warmer, more personal atmosphere than their counterparts. They also apparently feel greater sense of encouragement and achievement and seem to be slightly better satisfied with the material aspects of their positions. . . .
>
> The lower morale schools are definitely slower in the adoption of many of the innovations in education. . . .[15]

The significance of good morale on the part of administrators is that it helps staff morale. Information from the CDPSA study supports this conclusion:

> If there is excellent morale at the leadership level, we think there is ample evidence to support the assumption that there will be good faculty and teacher morale. With good morale in these groups, faculty and administration, we firmly believe that the education of children in those schools will be of a better quality in every measureable area.[16]

[15] F. S. Barry, "CDPSA Looks at Morale," *New York State Education*, October, 1955, 43:22.
[16] *Ibid.*, p. 20.

These findings suggest that if the high school administrator follows the suggestions concerning faculty morale presented earlier he will derive satisfaction from his job as well as contribute to good morale in his faculty. Studies indicate that from rational efforts to develop good morale, better staff relationships, greater accomplishments, fewer problems, and greater job satisfaction may be expected than if little attention is given to morale. Generally, good morale produces more effort to achieve common goals, greater awareness of the broad purposes of education, and greater educational achievement.

Questions and Group Projects

1. Assume you are the new principal in a high school in which the faculty is known to have poor morale. How might you determine the status of staff morale?
2. Why is it difficult for an administrator to be certain of the current status of faculty morale?
3. Select a teacher you know who you feel has high morale. Try to analyze why.
4. Select a teacher you know who you feel has low morale. Try to analyze why. Compare the factors you have identified in this situation with those you identified in the previous question.
5. Have you ever observed a sharp rise or fall in the morale of a faculty? If you have, what factors do you think caused such a marked change?

Selected References

American Association of School Administrators. *Staff Relations in School Administration.* Thirty-Third Yearbook, Washington: National Education Association, 1955.

American Psychiatric Association. *Psychiatric Aspects of Civilian Morale.* New York: Welfare Association of America, 1942.

Anderson, Lester W. "Teacher Morale and Student Achievement," *Journal of Educational Research,* May, 1953, pp. 693–98.

Bailard, V. "Teachers' Mental Health: Principal of It," *Clearing House,* January, 1954, 28:283–84.

Barry, F. S. "CDPSA Looks at Morale," *New York State Education,* October, 1955, 43:20–22.

Benjamin, Harold. "Developing and Maintaining Morale of Teachers," *University of Pennsylvania Bulletin,* June 30, 1947.

Bradford, M. L. "Building Morale from the Principal's Viewpoint," *School Executive*, July, 1951, 70:45–46.

Burton, William H. "The Teacher's Morale as an Important Factor in Teaching Success," *California Journal of Elementary Education*, May, 1938, Vol. 6, No. 4.

Burton, William H., and Leo J. Brueckner. *Supervision, A Social Process*. New York: Appleton-Century-Crofts, Inc., 1955, pp. 555–59.

Campbell, Clyde M., "Security and Freedom — Requisites for Morale," *School Executive*, July, 1951, 70:41–42.

Chase, F. S. "Factors for Satisfaction in Teaching," *Phi Delta Kappan*, November, 1951, 33:127–32.

Coffman, W. E. "Teacher Morale and Curriculum Development," *Journal of Experimental Education*, June, 1951, 19:305–32.

Diettert, A. E., and C. C. Diettert. "What Can the Principal Do for Staff Morale?" *American Teacher*, February, 1953, 37:10–11.

Ferguson, H. A. "School Solutions: Improving Teacher Morale," *Journal of Education*, September, 1951, 134:173.

Hall, G. Stanley. "Morale in War and After," *Psychological Abstracts*, 1918, Vol. 15.

Harap, H. "Many Factors Affect Teacher Morale," *Nation's Schools*, June, 1959, 63:55–57.

Hocking, W. E. *Morale and Its Enemies*. New Haven, Conn.: Yale University Press, 1918.

Hunter, E. C. "Attitudes and Professional Relationships of Teachers, A Study of Teacher Morale," *Journal of Experimental Education*, June, 1955, 23:345–52.

Jones, J. J. "Teacher Morale and Administration," *Clearing House*, January, 1958, 32:291–92.

Juckett, E. A. "Staff Morale," *The Bulletin* of the NASSP, December, 1950, 34:158–66.

Lautenschlager, H. "Role of Principal as a Morale Builder," *Peabody Journal of Education*, March, 1957, 34:258–62.

Lewin, Kurt. "Experiments on Autocratic and Democratic Atmospheres," *The Social Frontier*, 1938, Vol. 4, No. 37.

Lowe, J. "Five Steps to Higher Morale," *School Executive*, September, 1954, 74:54–55.

Pepper, N. H. "Holding Your Teachers," *The Bulletin* of the NASSP, May, 1948, 32:116–20.

Redefer, F. L. "Teacher Morale and Quality of Education," *Nation's Schools*, February, 1957, 59:53–55.

Roethlisberger, F. J., and W. J. Dickson. *Management and the Worker.* Cambridge, Mass.: Harvard University Press, 1943.

Schultz, R. E. "Keeping Up Teacher Morale," *Nation's Schools,* October, 1952, 50:53–56.

Wiles, Kimball. *Supervision for Better Schools.* New York: Prentice-Hall, Inc., 2nd ed., 1955. Pp. 50–75.

CHAPTER 13

Developing a Democratic In-Service Program

Democracy has been called everything from "mobocracy" to the "noblest of all social relationships." Certainly it is a term that is difficult to define, and consequently it is widely abused. Despite the fog and abuse, we are persuaded that it is a highly useful term and conveys a meaning for Americans and their ways of doing things that cannot be conveyed as well by any other word.

In education, "democratic" has come to be regarded as the antonym of "autocratic" or "authoritarian." Autocracy, according to Webster, means self-derived power and uncontrolled authority or supreme government by an individual. Democracy, on the other hand, means government by the people, government in which the supreme power is retained by the people and exercised either directly or indirectly through a system of representation.

This is the meaning of democracy as we see it in the conduct of school affairs. In our use of the term "democratic faculty relationships," we have in mind a faculty organization in which administrators and teachers serve as public employees appointed by the representatives of the people. Within the faculty body the administrator acts as coordinator and executive officer, but power to operate the educational program is delegated by the board of education to the faculty and exercised either directly by faculty action or indirectly through its representatives, including administrators. The power held by a faculty is defined by the people through state statutes and by policies and regulations of local boards of education. Power in schools, therefore, resides in the electorate of each state. It is delegated to, and shared with, the people who actually operate the schools.

The term "democratic" often is used in the sense of "cooperative" in describing relationship among individuals in a group. It seems to us that this is overworking a good adjective, which thereby loses much of its force. Consequently, when we mean a cooperative relation we will use the term "cooperative," and when we mean power held by the people and exercised directly or indirectly through faculty representatives we will use the term "democratic."

Participation of the staff in policy formulation must be carried on within a democratic framework which is both legal and cooperative in spirit. A study by the Educational Policies Commission involving visits to ninety high schools resulted in a statement of principles which provides a framework for democratic administration and cooperative staff relationships:

1. The ideal of equality of educational opportunity through education largely determines the structure of the school system in the United States, and provides a fundamental criterion of efficiency in school administration.

2. Educational policy in the long run, is determined by the people, through the exercise of the franchise. The people, however, place the authority to control educational policies in the hands of a lay board.

3. The lay board selects a chief executive officer and holds him responsible for presenting policies and programs to the board for discussion and approval, and for carrying out these policies and programs after the board has approved.

4. Educational policies should be formulated initially by the professional staff of the school system, through a cooperative process capitalizing on the intellectual resources of the whole staff. This participation in the development of educational policy should not be thought of as a favor granted by the administration, but rather as a right and an obligation. After policies have been developed by the staff, they should be submitted to the board of education for final review and approval.

5. When a policy has been so formulated and approached, every member of the school system for whom it has implications becomes responsible for carrying it into effect. This responsibility is centered in the superintendent through whom account must be rendered to the board and the public.

6. The superintendent will require that board policies be carried out throughout the school system, but he will place large responsibility in the hands of the principals as to details of policy and means to be employed. The principals, in turn, will allow a large degree of freedom to individual teachers. The aim of administration is to secure cooperation in working for common objectives while encouraging resourcefulness and ingenuity on the part of all.

7. The right and duty of teachers to take part in formulating educational policy is closely related to one of the basic purposes of American education. Our schools are organized for the purpose of educating children, young people, and adults for participation in a democratic society. Any significant realization of this purpose will require independent thinking, a large degree of cooperative endeavor, and broad sympathy and understanding on the part of all who are enrolled in educational institutions. Certainly these virtues may not be expected to abound among those who are taught unless they are found also in the experiences of teachers. Surely in no area may teachers more certainly exercise independence of thought, cooperation in action, and social understanding than in their daily professional work. It is sound procedure to provide for active participation of teachers in the development of policy.

8. Back of the professional staff, back of the board of education stand the people as the ultimate judges of educational policy. In a democratic school system, therefore, the board and staff will seek the cooperation of parents and other citizens in developing the educational program. It is essential that the professional staff of the school system be supported in its work by the participation of intelligent citizens in the development of curriculum and in determining educational objectives.

9. The persons who control the school budget thereby determine school policy. Therefore the control of the budget must be in the hands of the same persons who control policies, namely, the board of education.[1]

Included in the above statement by the Educational Policies Commission is the suggestion that a major role of the principal is to develop the processes and structure by which the faculty can influence school policies and that teachers have a *right*, as well as an *obligation*, to share in policy formulation. It is emphasized, however, that any attempt by the professional staff to *determine* policy is contrary to the legal and democratic function of the board of education.

Although the emphasis in this discussion is on the development of cooperative working relationships within a faculty, the authors recognize that principals can go too far in seeking consultation. For example, some administrators feel guilty if they make any decisions without first consulting the faculty. Such an attitude is just as undesirable as to have a principal impose his authority and decisions on the staff without ever seeking to involve them in making the decisions. Often the principal should use his own judgment on a course of action. After all, one of the reasons he was appointed to the position of principal was that the superintendent and the board of education felt he had the ability to exercise good judgment and to make decisions in harmony with established policy. It is not contended that policies derived in a cooperative manner are, ipso

[1] Educational Policies Commission, *Learning the Ways of Democracy* (Washington: National Education Association and American Association of School Administrators, 1940), pp. 331–32.

facto, better than those derived by an individual. What the authors wish to emphasize is that policy recommendations arrived at cooperatively are likely to serve better the purposes of the faculty than are policies determined without such involvement of the staff.

There is little doubt that practice lags behind theory in school administration. Thus some principals who have accepted the philosophy of democratic administration have not been able to translate it into practice. The following discussion is intended, therefore, to illustrate how selected group activities of the faculty might be planned so as to incorporate a democratic philosophy of administration and cooperative working relationships within the staff. The beginning principal should recognize, however, that there are additional approaches to these same group activities which are perfectly acceptable, and experimenting or trying out techniques to improve working relationships of the staff is to be encouraged.

Faculty Meetings

Regular meetings of the faculty are recommended as providing the staff with opportunities to participate actively in making decisions affecting the school. These are occasions when all members of the staff get together as a group to work on professional problems. Usually teachers have only a very limited chance to associate with one another and to discuss their mutual problems because conference periods come at various times during the school day. It is surprisingly difficult for teachers to find out what their colleagues really think on issues confronting the school.

For example, one of the problems common to many faculties is determining the most effective ways to individualize instruction, especially for the academically talented students. A discussion or study of this question by a faculty might reasonably be expected to result in some innovations in current practices, an interest in surveying practices in other schools, or an agreement to continue in much the same manner as has been done in the past. In any event, the staff should have a chance to clear signals on such problems, and the faculty meeting is the logical way to provide this opportunity. If for no other reason, faculty meetings are desirable because they do allow an exchange of ideas on various professional matters. They are also the only occasions when teachers from all subject fields share plans — when there is some assurance that special interests will be blended with the general interest or viewpoint of the staff. Thus, it is reasonable to expect that faculty meetings will contribute to greater unity within the staff and more enthusiastic support of policies resulting from the group's action.

The general faculty meeting is used widely by principals. Practically every high school has at least two such meetings during the school year, and most schools have several. Most administrators do not hesitate to call a meeting whenever they feel a problem ought to be discussed or there is a need to report some administrative action to the teachers. Although faculty meetings are recommended highly and used frequently, it would be naïve to assume that all of them achieve significant results. Unfortunately, teachers often express the opinion that faculty meetings are of little value to them in solving instructional problems. Not uncommonly they resent being asked to give their time for these meetings.

There is some justification for negative feelings about faculty meetings, because principals generally have not given adequate attention to planning them. Heywood reviewed results of a research study by Cook and Full in which five desirable standards were established for the conduct of faculty meetings.[2] These standards were as follows:

1. Faculty meetings must be concerned with teachers' professional needs and must be focused on educational problems growing out of the immediate school environment,
2. Faculty meetings must be concerned with problems having broad educational import,
3. Faculty meetings must be well planned and teachers should participate in the planning,
4. Teachers must prepare for faculty meetings, and
5. Informal participation should characterize the discussion in faculty meetings.

Surveying 240 schools to see how well the above standards were being met, Cook and Full reported that school systems failed to meet four out of five of the standards.[3] It seems apparent that, once more, practice is not consonant with theory. The following suggestions on planning and conducting faculty meetings are made in the interest of increasing their value to participants and developing democratic staff relationships.

Focusing Meetings on Problems of Real Educational Concern

If faculty meetings are to make a genuine contribution to the professional growth of teachers, attention must be focused on problems of real educational concern. That many principals have been negligent in this matter is indicated by Heywood's study, which found less than 8 per cent of schools devoting faculty meetings to important educational problems.[4] The following might be considered such problems: How may students be motivated to achieve up to their potential? What is the role of the classroom teacher in a guidance program? Should students be grouped ac-

---

[2] Stanley J. Heywood, "What's Wrong with Faculty Meetings?" *Administrator's Notebook* (Midwest Administration Center, University of Chicago), December, 1952, Vol. I, No. 5.
[3] *Ibid.*
[4] *Ibid.*

cording to ability? Contrasted to problems of this type are: What is the schedule for taking tickets at the basketball games? What should we do if students come to class without notebook paper? When are the report cards due?

Unfortunately, too many faculty meetings are concerned with questions of the second type. Such questions need to be answered, but they can be handled through written bulletins or announcements by the principal. Any administrative announcement or detail that can be effectively taken care of through written means should be eliminated from faculty meetings. Time available for group work is too limited to dissipate it on matters which can be resolved individually or by other means.

Faculties that have been complacent about instructional matters for some time are not likely to respond with enthusiasm the first time they are given an opportunity to consider problems of real educational concern. Quite the contrary; they probably will try to duck such involvement. Patience by the administrator, especially the beginning principal, will be needed. It may well be that he will have to start with problems of immediate concern to the local staff, regardless of how minor they are, and then move gradually to questions of increasing significance. For example, there is almost always interest in pupil discipline. This perennial topic can serve as a springboard for future topics of greater educational import.

Teacher Participation in Planning Meetings

Faculty meetings need advance planning by the staff to make certain that they will not bog down and that the problems discussed will reflect the genuine interests of the group. Use of a planning committee selected by the faculty is an excellent way to increase the probability that the meetings will represent the concerns of the faculty. In spite of frequent recommendations favoring such an approach, Cook and Full found a serious lack of advance planning involving faculty members in the schools surveyed:

> In 43 per cent of the schools teachers did not know more than a day ahead that there would be a faculty meeting. In over one-fifth of the schools teachers learned of the meeting on the day it was to be held. In 58 per cent of the schools the principal did all the planning for faculty meetings. Cooperative planning was employed in only 10 per cent of the schools. . . .[5]

Obviously there is considerable room for increased participation of teachers in planning faculty meetings. It is little wonder that teachers have been less than enthusiastic over staff meetings. An administrator who insists on deciding what items will be included on the agenda, when the meeting will be held, who will serve as chairman, and how the meet-

[5] *Ibid.*

ing will be run is missing an excellent opportunity to further cooperative relationships with his faculty, and he is jeopardizing the chances for successful meetings.

Teachers have a right to participate in planning their meetings. When a principal dominates the planning, he is assuming that they are *his* meetings instead of the *faculty's* meetings. In most meetings it is desirable for the principal to regard himself as a professional colleague of teachers, and as such he should have a voice in determining the nature of the meetings. His ideas should receive consideration with those of the other teachers, but should be judged on their merits rather than on the official status of the principal. Occasionally, a meeting dealing with organizational and administrative problems may be necessary, in which case the principal should assume his role as status leader. But these meetings should be infrequent.

Election of Chairman by Teachers

Although it is common for the principal to chair the teachers' meeting, it is a mistake for him to insist on this prerogative. Teachers should elect their own chairman. A principal who serves as chairman often falls into the unfortunate practice of dominating the discussion of the group. He is in a much more favorable position, from the point of view both of developing cooperative staff relationships and of presenting his ideas on issues, if he does not act as chairman. For example, assume that a meeting has been planned to solicit faculty opinion on how the counseling program may be made more effective. Specifically, the counselors are anxious to develop a system by which teachers may conveniently refer individual students to them when it appears as though the counselors can be of assistance. If the principal insists on being chairman and then talks twenty to thirty minutes on how he thinks the job should be done before anyone else has an opportunity to present a plan, he will discourage teachers from expressing their ideas, especially if they differ from his. In addition, he violates the functions of chairman by dominating the discussion rather than encouraging others to speak. In this instance, the counselors will undoubtedly end up with no more ideas on what the teachers think than they had prior to the meeting.

The same meeting conducted by a chairman other than the principal might result in greater expression of ideas by the faculty. The principal would be in a more appropriate position to express his views as a member of the group. Of course any individual can dominate a discussion, but a skillful chairman can control this tendency quite well by recognizing other members of the group who wish to speak. At least, in this instance the principal would not be able to control the entire discussion.

Although there are these dangers to be guarded against, it does not follow that the principal should be overlooked as a possible chairman. If the teachers really prefer him as chairman, he should assume the position and perform the required duties in the best possible manner.

We recommend that the chairman be elected for a limited term so that no one begins to think that he "owns" the job. Some faculties go to an extreme and elect a different person for every meeting. Others rotate the position among all teachers. It is doubtful that changing chairmen so frequently or insisting that all teachers take their turn is desirable. A successful chairman needs to develop specific skills, and this takes a little time and practice. But the group would do better to err on the side of changing too frequently than be placed in the embarrassing situation of being burdened for a long time with an incompetent or domineering chairman. It is much easier to elect a new chairman periodically than to remove one. The latter course is especially difficult when it is the principal who is the unpopular chairman. A reasonable approach might be to elect a chairman to serve one semester. This assures the faculty of the opportunity to review their choice semiannually.

Time of Meetings

It is impossible to establish a time for faculty meetings which will be satisfactory to all teachers, but the schedule of meetings should be made as convenient as possible to the majority. Typically, staff meetings are held after school on Tuesday or Wednesday. Some faculties meet before classes start in the morning, at night, on Saturday mornings, or on school time. There are advantages and disadvantages in all of these possibilities.

After-school meetings have the advantage of not interfering with regular classes; teachers are present in the building and normally can be expected to remain long enough to attend a meeting. A disadvantage of meeting after school is that teachers are tired and so find it difficult to discuss issues enthusiastically, and the time available is relatively short. There is the inevitable clash also with extraclass activities, especially athletics. Some schools avoid such conflicts by refraining from scheduling any extraclass activities one afternoon per week.

The question of whether or not all teachers, including athletic coaches and directors of other extraclass activities, should be required to attend faculty meetings which meet after school has troubled many principals. Failure of the coaches, or any other group of teachers, to attend the meetings suggests that they are receiving preferential treatment. Most teachers resent such partiality, and this feeling diminishes the effectiveness of the meetings. The implication is that if a meeting is important for one, it should be important for all, including coaches. If teachers consider the meetings worthwhile they will want to attend.

But even though the meetings are interesting and helpful to the teachers, in some cases there will be a genuine conflict of professional commitments. It is doubtful that requiring attendance at all meetings works in the best interests of good staff relationships. Therefore, attendance at most meetings should be voluntary. Nevertheless, the principal should encourage attendance and do his best to eliminate conflicts. He should at least set an example by attending all staff meetings himself.

One of the best solutions to the attendance problem is to schedule meetings on school time. Each period can be shortened ten to fifteen minutes to allow an hour at the end of the day, or the pupils can remain at home for a day while the teachers spend the entire time in professional meetings. The practice of taking a full day should not be used frequently; probably two or three times a year would be the maximum. Some schools dismiss students for one afternoon a month or bimonthly. Any plan which includes the dismissal of pupils from classes must be approved by the board of education because it involves legal aspects and general school policies, and the purpose of the meetings may be misunderstood by the community if it is not supported by the board.

Evening or Saturday meetings are possibilities to avoid competition with other school affairs. However, this is not an ideal answer, since part-time jobs or other community affairs might cause conflicts. Some teachers may feel, too, that this demand on their time is an imposition. On the other hand, it is reasonable to have occasional evening and Saturday meetings when a relatively long block of time is needed to give proper consideration to a problem.

Schools that are very large and use an overlapping schedule for classes need at least two general meetings in order to include all teachers conveniently. These schools run the danger of having two faculties operating independently of each other unless special provisions are made to bring them together. Utilization of released time, evenings, or Saturdays, or asking one group to come back in the late afternoon, is about the only way to get the entire staff together for one meeting. Some principals in schools of this type have very few general staff meetings, resorting instead to a series of smaller group conferences. For example, the administrator may set up a meeting every period in the day, inviting all teachers to attend during their conference period. These meetings help keep the principal in touch with his teachers, but they take a great deal of his time, and they are not the same as a general faculty meeting.

In light of the fact that there is no ideal time to hold faculty meetings, it is suggested that a combination of all approaches, i.e., meetings after school, before school, evenings, Saturdays, and on school time, be considered, and that the final choice of the meeting time be left to the group, assuming that satisfactory administrative arrangements can be made.

Atmosphere of Meetings

Teachers appreciate a relaxed, informal atmosphere for their meetings, and they prefer furniture designed for adults, not children. When meetings are held immediately after school, refreshments may be served. This provides a period for informal visitation before concentrating on the business at hand, and it gives the "good humor boys" an opportunity to share their best jokes. Ten to fifteen minutes spent in this manner will do much to create a receptive atmosphere for the meeting.

It is especially important that a place with comfortable furniture be available. Few things irritate adults more than being forced to sit for an hour or more at desks designed for teen-agers. Most schools find the tables and chairs used in the home-making room, the library, or the cafeteria reasonably adequate. Movable tables and chairs make it possible to arrange the group in a square or semicircle so that everyone is in a face-to-face relationship and can be seen and heard easily. The least satisfactory arrangement is a regular classroom, the study hall, or the auditorium.

Length and Frequency of Meetings

Usually meetings held after school are planned for sixty to seventy-five minutes, including the refreshment period. Longer meetings are likely to result in lack of attention and negative reactions. If it is necessary to plan meetings of greater length in order to give proper attention to a problem, arrangements should be made for a special meeting at a different time, but the faculty should be consulted and express approval of the plan.

Many faculties have scheduled meetings every week, others every two or three weeks, and still others only once a month. Weekly meetings are too frequent if teachers are expected to participate in other special committee and departmental meetings. Some teachers are enrolled in university extension classes, which also are time consuming. It is difficult to plan good meetings every week, and they may become routine administrative affairs when held that frequently. No doubt there is merit in advance scheduling for the entire year, but the authors recommend that general meetings be scheduled no more often than every two weeks.

Miscellaneous Suggestions for Faculty Meetings

1. Staff members should have a copy of the proposed agenda at least two days prior to the meeting.

2. Teachers should have an opportunity to suggest changes or additions to the agenda at the beginning of the meeting. The agenda should be adopted at each meeting.

3. It is desirable to work for consensus of the group rather than voting on issues. However, some issues may require immediate action and may be highly controversial. Under such circumstances a vote may be necessary to get something done.

4. A variety of procedures is desirable: speakers, panel discussions, demonstrations, social meetings, buzz sessions, brainstorming, and other activities appropriate to specific problems being studied. Teachers get bored with "the same old stuff!"

5. The chairman or leader must be well versed in group processes.

6. A series of meetings on a central theme, such as guidance, the dropout, or some other instructional problem, can be very effective.

7. Policy recommendations and decisions by the group should be followed by administrative action.

8. In most cases, the principal should accept the decision of the group as representative even though he differs with it. Occasionally he may find it necessary to call for a reconsideration and, rarely, he may be compelled to veto a faculty action.

There is no assurance that faculty meetings will be successful in spite of all the precautions and suggestions made on this topic. There is no substitute for the ability of the administrator to create good personal relations with his teachers. But the faculty meeting is well established in most secondary schools, and it does provide an opportunity for the faculty to study its problems as a group and to have a voice in determining policies which affect them. In this respect it is basic to democratic staff relationships. Used properly, it can be an effective group technique, but used improperly, it can be a damaging one.

Educational Workshops

Along with the increased acceptance of a democratic philosophy of administration has come a corresponding interest in and need for the development of administrative procedures, techniques, and activities which are in harmony with that philosophy. One such is the educational workshop, an organized professional activity which has grown steadily in favor since its introduction at Ohio State University in 1936. Its popularity stems partly from the fact that it stresses cooperative working relationships between teachers and between administrators and teachers. Consequently, the high school principal may find it profitable to use a workshop procedure.

Nature of an Educational Workshop

Although the term "workshop" has gained wide acceptance in the educational literature, there is no single definition for it and no standard pattern for operating a workshop. This does not mean, however, that definitions or descriptions are lacking. A study of the workshop as an in-service procedure by the North Central Association of Colleges and Secondary Schools reported a number of definitions. Following are some typical statements and concepts of an educational workshop:

> A workshop is a technique whereby the democratic process of solving problems is utilized. It provides an atmosphere conducive to concentration for exhaustive study of specific problems, and gives opportunity to pool experience and findings.
> A workshop is an informal gathering of interested people composed of a self-guided program, dealing with special interests and aided by ably prepared assistants. It is a process of solving a problem and stimulating professional growth through democratic means of group interaction.
> A workshop is a group experience desired by participants, in which the group shares in the planning, process, techniques, and evaluation. The group selects its own leaders and knits itself into a social entity through shared experiences, living, and social and recreational activities.[6]

A workshop is intended to be a means by which a group of teachers work together cooperatively in the identification and solution of educational problems. This alone does not make the workshop distinctive from other group methods of problem solving; its distinctiveness lies rather in the way it functions and in the attitude of the participants. The following discussion identifies certain characteristics of the educational workshop which seem to have the greatest bearing on its success as an in-service procedure.

Workshop Procedures and Facilities

A basic ingredient in democratic staff relationships is free and open communication among staff members. Workshops are ideal in providing maximum opportunities for teachers to discuss issues with other teachers. Discussion groups, small enough to assure all a chance to express their thoughts, are a typical feature. A great deal of interaction takes place also in the informal and recreational activities which are usually a part of the workshop. Some of the more successful workshops are held at camp sites or lodges where the participants eat, work, play, and live together for a period of one to two weeks. Granted that not all workshops can be planned for an uninterrupted week or two at a camp site; nevertheless, a number of informal activities can be arranged using typical school facilities.

As we have pointed out in Chapter 12, "Staff Morale," it is desirable for teachers to work together toward common goals. In an effective workshop, one of the first things the group does is agree on where it is trying

[6] James R. Mitchell, "The Workshop as an In-Service Education Process," *North Central Association Quarterly*, April, 1954, 28:428.

to go and why. This is done usually in small buzz sessions, which may involve considerable discussion in order to define problems clearly. Following a compilation of suggested problems, each participant is asked to pick the one in which he is most interested. Real motivation for attacking problems should result if the thinking of the group is centered on issues that all have had a hand in selecting.

After the individual makes his choice, he joins others who have chosen this problem, and they form a small study or discussion group. If there are too many interested in the same topic to keep the group small, additional groups may be formed on the same problem. Thus each person has an opportunity to concentrate on a problem he feels is important, to work cooperatively with others, and to get some satisfaction from group attainment.

One of the strong features of the workshop process is its flexibility. Although many suggestions may be made on how a workshop might operate successfully, there is no set procedure that *must* be followed. The group can adapt its activities to the particular problem and to its membership. The workshop loses much of its uniqueness if it is highly structured in advance. On the other hand, some preplanning is desirable, providing it is done according to the wishes of the group. This point was stressed in the North Central Association study report:

> There is almost complete agreement in one item, "the workshop was not totally unplanned." It would seem that all parties to the workshop, the participant, the leader, and the sponsor, favor some planning in advance of the initial meeting of the workshop but the major portion of the planning in conjunction with the workshop groups should be done at its early sessions.[7]

Preplanning need not make the workshop any less sensitive to the wishes of the group; indeed, it is an attempt to anticipate its needs and to prepare accordingly. For example, an abundance of good reference material should be available for use by the study groups. Workshops that do not provide for reference material may become little more than a series of debates. It is easy for participants to express opinions on issues, but real progress in solving a problem is dependent upon getting the facts pertinent to the problem. If such information is available in the educational literature, it should be readily available for use by the study group. Librarians cannot be expected, however, to provide materials unless they have some idea of the general nature of the problems to be studied and a reasonable amount of time to collect them. Preplanning is especially important if the workshop is to be held in a place remote from libraries. Some schools find it helpful to hold the problem-census part of the workshop well in advance of the work sessions. It should be pos-

[7] *Ibid.*, p. 433.

sible to identify problems in the spring of the year to be studied in the fall workshop. The problems can still be revised at the time of the workshop, but greater success is likely if they have been defined in advance and materials are available when needed.

Consultants, usually college professors or outstanding teachers, often are employed to contribute specialized knowledge, to advise or counsel with individuals, or to serve as keynote speakers for general sessions of the workshop. They can be of real service if they have been chosen for their knowledge or skill in relation to a particular problem rather than merely for the sake of having well-known names on the program. To get the most good from the services of a consultant, he needs to know in advance the problems to be considered, since he too will have to prepare carefully if he is to do a good job. It usually is necessary to schedule the date with the consultant well in advance of the workshop date to be certain of his availability. An ideal situation would be to have several consultants available after the group has had its first meeting and defined its problems. Unfortunately, this is not realistic, for consultants are not that readily obtainable for workshop purposes. Just as some preplanning is called for so that the librarian may secure materials, so advance arrangements must be made in order to secure consultants who are prepared to assist with specific problems of the workshop.

Involving workshop participants in the evaluation of its activities is important both as the workshop progresses and at its completion. Major outcomes of the workshop process should be a contribution to the development of self-direction on the part of the teachers and the ability to judge the adequacy of their own actions. These will provide a guide for future action and enable individuals to locate their weaknesses and to adapt their activities. Evaluation of the workshop often is made both by individual participants and by an evaluation committee which is concerned with improving the over-all operation.

Facilities needed for the workshop include a meeting room large enough for the general sessions of the entire group and a number of rooms for smaller groups to work on their special problems. A resource materials center or library should be in a location convenient to the smaller work groups. As in the case of faculty meetings, it is a must to have furniture which is comfortable for adults. Camp sites which have been developed especially for group meetings of this type usually have excellent recreational facilities. Although such facilities are highly desirable and add much to the success of the workshop, it is just as important to have comfortable places for the work groups, because the primary reason for the workshop is to *work* on educational problems and not merely to have a change in routine. When the workshop is held in a school building, adequate meeting rooms are available, but the recreational possibilities offered by a camp are missing. Special attention should be given under these conditions to making sure that recreational activities are included as a part of the workshop. It may be necessary to supply transportation to recreational areas, but this should not be a serious problem.

In summary, a statement made by a respondent to the North Central Association study is especially descriptive and seems to encompass many of the characteristics discussed:

> A true workshop is not like a formal class where students come together at intervals, listen to lectures, receive assignments to work out, etc. The organization, purpose and goal, procedures and outcomes are different. It is a matter of learning by doing. It is a give and take affair for working out some practical problems common to all. It is the same idea we have in getting children to be interested in and see the purpose and goal and procedures as they together, under teacher guidance, plan, try, check-up, or evaluate, make corrections when needed, continue to work toward a goal, see how much is achieved, and how to improve.
>
> It is a group of teachers in a workshop who through a variety of ways (conversation, conferences, consultation with instructors, observations, investigations, use of books and any other way possible) work out a problem they have chosen to study. The responsibility for learning is that of the student. The aim is to develop self-confidence, make use of his ability, take part in what is being done, and thus achieve more than he otherwise could.
>
> I attended a two weeks' workshop in 1938, at New York University that was one of my most interesting summer experiences and one of my most profitable ones. We worked, ate, mingled together for recreation, lived together — a group of fourteen. We stayed at a nearby hotel. We spent the forenoon at the University and the afternoons and evenings visiting places around New York City — libraries, cathedrals, museums, slums, Chinatown, large stores, courts, ball games, theaters — special trips of all kinds. It was a wonderful workshop, a wonderful learning experience for everyone in the group.[8]

Although the above description is concerned with a workshop operated by a university, the characteristics are much the same as one would expect in a workshop organized by any high school faculty. Some of the activities and details will vary according to the locale, but the basic pattern of operation can be made very similar to the one described.

Considerable attention has been given to describing the characteristics of a workshop because the term has been badly misused. Some people have chosen to call any type of conference, institute, seminar, faculty meeting, study group, or other activity a workshop. This is unfortunate because it creates misunderstanding and confusion with respect to the special characteristics of a workshop. Even though workshops should be flexible enough to serve the needs of the group, they do have qualities

[8] *Ibid.*, pp. 429–30.

which distinguish them from other group activities. Workshops are not panaceas, nor are they replacements for conventional college courses, institutes, or other in-service activities. They serve different purposes and operate in the sort of situation described in the foregoing paragraphs.

Planning a Workshop

Responsibility for coordinating all group activities of the faculty rests with the principal. He must have ideas on how the job can be done in a cooperative manner. It is important, therefore, that he understand the problems of planning a workshop. The following suggestions present some of the more common procedures used in such planning. In order to be specific, assume that the faculty and principal have agreed at a faculty meeting in February that they need more time to work on some curriculum problems than is available in regular faculty meetings. They would like to have a week's workshop for this purpose before the opening of school in the fall. What should be done prior to that time, and who should do it?

1. The teachers should elect a planning committee, sometimes called a steering committee, to work with the principal in planning the workshop. This committee will need to be very active during the remainder of the school year so that most of the plans are complete before teachers leave for the summer recess. The planning committee must answer the following kinds of questions: (a) Where should the workshop be held? (b) How will it be financed? (c) What problems will be studied? (d) What materials and resources should be made available? (e) Should outside consultants be used? If so, who should they be? (f) What recreational and social activities should be included? (g) Should laymen be invited to join the workshop? If so, who? It is desirable that the planning committee bring its recommendations to the faculty for approval and suggestions before deciding these questions.

2. The planning committee should conduct a problem-census session with the faculty. Every teacher should have an opportunity to state the problems he wishes to study. The committee should make a list of all problems, stating them exactly as the teacher stated them. The list should be duplicated and made available to the faculty. Following a discussion for clarification of the problem statements, the teachers should indicate their preferences for study.

3. An analysis should be made of the teachers' preferences of problems. This will provide the information necessary in securing resource materials and special consultants. It should be recognized that this is a tentative selection of problems and some shifting may take place at the time of the workshop. Invitations to consultants should be extended as soon as the major problems to be studied have been identified in order to secure, insofar as possible, the first choices of the faculty.

4. Housing and financial arrangements should be made early enough so that they can be announced to the faculty prior to the closing of school.

5. The faculty should elect a chairman of the workshop.

The above planning should take place before the actual convening of the workshop. When the faculty arrives to start the workshop, there still will be a number of arrangements to be made. The original planning committee should continue in this capacity throughout the workshop, but the faculty should be very much involved now in making decisions which will affect the nature of the activities. No doubt some shifts in interest will have occurred since the problems were identified in the spring, but most of the teachers will probably be interested in their original choices. Those who wish to change should be allowed to do so if adequate materials and consultants are available. It will be necessary to appoint certain special committees: a recreation committee, an evaluation committee, a publications committee, and a materials committee. Any unusual or unforeseen problems should be handled by the planning committee.

In general, the workshop should be organized on a pattern of general sessions and small-group sessions. It is at the general sessions that keynote speeches are given, reports presented, discussions held which have general implications, and plans made which require group approval. In the small-group sessions each teacher works on his problems cooperatively with others interested in the same problems. A detailed description of how the various group sessions operate would be too lengthy for this discussion. The reader is referred to an excellent treatment in *The Workshop Way of Learning* by Earl C. Kelley.[9]

The authors believe that the workshop is an excellent technique for attacking school problems in a manner which is consistent with democratic principles. Workshops are intended to be democratic ventures involving both teachers and administrators. Consideration should be given to the use of workshops — or at least to the incorporation of their basic concepts — as the principal and his faculty develop cooperative staff relationships and good-quality education.

Preschool Conferences

The practice of having the faculty report for a work session on school matters a week or so before school opens has grown in popularity during recent years. Placing the work session just prior to the opening of school has a big advantage in terms of getting teachers when they are fresh and

[9] Earl C. Kelley, *The Workshop Way of Learning* (New York: Harper & Brothers, 1951).

ready to focus their thinking on broad educational problems. It has another desirable feature in that problems not solved completely can be carried into the faculty deliberations during the remainder of the year. Part of the time may be spent also in orienting new teachers to the administrative routine and policies of the school, and new teachers will have an opportunity to establish relationships with other teachers before they become too involved with their own classroom activities.

Additional salary should be allowed proportionate to the length of time teachers are expected to work beyond their normal contract period. Schools have been moving gradually toward a ten-month contract for all teachers. Where this is in force, the preschool conference is considered part of the normal contract period.

The objectives, problems, and goals of the preschool conference are usually defined by the faculty during the preceding spring semester. Its manner of operation is not unique, since it typically employs a workshop method, but it is an excellent means for developing cooperative staff relationships.

Faculty Committees

One of the most universally used devices to enlist the faculty in the over-all affairs of the school and in policy formulation is the faculty committee. When there is a job to be done that needs the thinking of more than one person, a committee may well be the best means of handling it. Committees are employed in seeking answers to numerous school problems. They carry on curriculum studies, survey communities for local resources, plan faculty picnics, recommend a new salary schedule to the faculty, organize plans for meeting the needs of students, and do an almost endless number of things related to the instructional program of the school. In general, the use of faculty committees is an effective means by which teachers can participate in policy formulation. It also has offered teachers a way to improve their professional competence. The use of committees in administration has long been associated with democratic concepts. In many respects, committees have become the teachers' voice, and when this is the case they serve as excellent vehicles in the development of democratic staff relationships.

If participation in a committee undertaking is to contribute to the betterment of faculty morale and staff relationships, it must be a satisfying and successful experience. Although there is no way of assuring complete success in any committee enterprise, it is possible to anticipate some of the more common problems and to establish some guides which will help assure its success.

1. The specific task to be performed by the committee should be identified by its parent group, namely, the faculty. If the faculty cannot define

the task, certainly the committee will not be able to. Unless the problem and prerogatives of the committee are understood by all, there is bound to be confusion, misunderstanding, and a probable rejection of the committee's recommendations. But when the committee has a definite assignment from the faculty, it can address itself to the task effectively and with a minimum of confusion or misunderstanding.

For example, periodically there will be teachers who are convinced that secondary education is not "rigorous" enough. They propose, with some emotion, that "something must be done about it." After considerable discussion, no one seems to know what should be done, so it is agreed that a committee should be appointed to investigate the problem. No doubt a committee can study such a problem profitably, providing the faculty can be more definitive in its concerns. Does it want the committee to evaluate current teaching practices? Does it want a comparative study of student achievement with other schools? Or does it want the committee to investigate community opinion on the problem? Similarly, the faculty needs to decide whether it wishes to give the committee authority to make changes in the curriculum or wants the committee merely to make recommendations. The point is that the faculty has an obligation to define its specific concerns and to establish the ground rules so that the committee can proceed with confidence and with its purpose well in mind.

2. Appointment of teachers to a committee should be made only if they are willing to accept the assignment. Ideally, teachers should volunteer to serve on a committee when they are particularly interested in the problem at hand. Certainly, volunteers should be sought from the faculty and given the opportunity to serve. But some people who are willing and have the interest to serve are too timid to volunteer for anything. The high school principal should do his best to spot these individuals and invite them to be members of the committee.

In all cases, teachers should be consulted and agree to work on the committee before being assigned to it. People who feel they have been "railroaded" into a job are not likely to be productive members of the group. If teachers are not sufficiently interested in a problem to serve willingly, chances are the problem is not of great enough importance to the faculty to warrant committee study.

3. Committees should be used only when there is reasonable assurance that a group decision will be better than the decision of an individual. If the problem before the group is such that an individual teacher can secure the necessary information and recommend a course of action acceptable to the faculty, there is no reason to involve a committee. There is no advantage, for instance, in assigning a committee to prepare an analysis of the results of the standardized testing program. This is a

technical task which should be assigned to someone who has the requisite knowledge.

Similarly, there is no particular point in asking a committee to build the schedule of recitations for the high school. This too calls for technical knowledge and skill which might better be supplied by one individual working alone. However, the person with such an assignment should not be above seeking assistance and advice from other members of the faculty; it is just that he has the responsibility for completing the task. Committee work by a faculty is difficult enough to arrange at best, and any unnecessary use of the teachers' time is unjustified. Too many committees can result in serious administrative confusion.

4. The principal should accept work assignments willingly along with other faculty members. Too many administrators make the error of getting the faculty involved in committee activities and then making a fast retreat to their offices to take care of the daily routine. One cannot expect the faculty to show enthusiasm for committee work if the principal is unwilling to assume his share as a working member of the group. In contrast, a willingness by the principal to take part in the work of the committees will encourage others to do the same.

5. Committees should be encouraged to continue their deliberations until the best possible solution to the problem has been determined. Teachers often are extremely sensitive to the attitude of the principal. Naturally there will be a letdown if a committee feels that the principal is only incidentally concerned with its activities. When the committee loses its motivation, it is likely to bog down before completing its task. Goals not achieved have a depressing effect on teacher morale and a negative influence on the development of cooperative staff relationships. It is imperative, therefore, that the interest of the principal in the progress of committees should be made evident.

6. The principal should see that committee proposals are given a chance to be implemented just as soon as circumstances permit. This is one of the crucial tests of the sincerity of the administrator in the committee system. When he decides to use a committee, he takes a calculated risk that the committee will advance some proposals with which he may not agree. He must be willing to remain open-minded on issues if he chooses to operate through committees. For instance, the faculty may support a committee recommendation to try a new grading system. If this is a practice the principal has not supported — in fact he may have opposed the idea in the faculty discussions — he must still be sure that it gets a fair trial. There is probably nothing more discouraging to the faculty than to have their recommendations fail to get an opportunity to succeed.

It is not contrary to this precept, however, for the administrator to retain a veto power over committee recommendations, especially those which are related to administrative practices, for he is responsible for the final consequences of the actions taken. But the veto should be used with extreme caution, and only when the principal is convinced that serious damage to the school would follow the implementing of a committee's proposal. If the principal frequently refuses to accept the recommendations of the group, there will be serious deterioration in the quality of committee planning. Committee work becomes a mere formality under such conditions. Teachers are most reluctant to give their time and energy to study a problem if they know in advance the administrator already has decided on the answer to it.

7. Adequate recognition should be given to a committee whenever its proposals have been utilized successfully. The solution to the problem should be clearly acknowledged as the result of committee and faculty study and not an achievement of the administration. Having received recognition for a job well done, members will be more receptive when considering future committee assignments.

One of the most important functions of a school principal is to stimulate effective group action by the faculty. There is substantial agreement in the literature that the use of faculty committees is of material help in this task. Like any other group technique, it is not necessarily the "best" answer, but it is a very useful device.

Administrative Advisory Councils

An administrative advisory council is a special-purpose committee organized to transmit the views of the faculty on specific administrative problems to the administrator of the school and vice versa. It is a liaison group between principal and faculty. It serves as an important vehicle for action and reaction, opinion and counter-opinion, comment and constructive criticism. Thus it provides another opportunity for teachers to have a voice in school policies. An advisory council is usually understood to be *advisory* and not a policy-forming group. This limitation seems to encourage even freer expression of opinion than if the group were expected to make policy. However, administrative policies determined in light of the discussions in an advisory council are likely to reflect many of the desires of the staff. The council may be a particularly effective two-way communication device in large schools, where it is virtually impossible for the principal to have frequent personal contacts with all teachers. Through a representative group of the faculty, the principal can keep in touch with the thinking of members of the staff and they with his.

Many of the administrative policies and decisions made by the administrator should reflect faculty opinion, and these can be considered appropriately with the advisory council. For example, in a large high school the council may be very helpful in such policy matters as articulating courses with the junior high, deciding whether detention should be used in discipline cases, whether interscholastic competition should begin in Grades 7 and 8, the handling of instructional supplies, easing pressures of committee meetings on the faculty, scheduling special workdays for teachers, and similar items which need not be discussed with the whole faculty but which should reflect their concern.

Membership on the advisory council most often is partly ex officio, i.e., department heads, assistant principal, counselors, and chairman of the curriculum committee, and partly elected from the ranks of classroom teachers. In some schools all members are elected by the faculty. The main point to be stressed is that members should be individuals who are in a position to know the concerns and feelings of the faculty, but they should also be familiar with the administrative procedures and processes of the school. Membership should not be so large as to make the council cumbersome.

It is common for the principal to meet once a week with the administrative advisory council, or at least biweekly. Ordinarily, the frequency of meetings and the amount of business carried on will depend upon the extent to which the principal encourages the group to speak freely. The considerations discussed earlier in this chapter concerning the administrator's attitude toward committee recommendations are applicable to his relations with the administrative advisory council. If he receives the recommendations of the council favorably, the council is likely to be a constructive force in improving administrative policies and in furthering the democratic process within the faculty. If he engages in autocratic abuse of the council or attempts to make the council into "errand boys" or a privy council for maneuvering the faculty, the result will certainly be strained staff relationships or mere indifference.

Individual Conferences

Although the major emphasis in this chapter has been on group techniques for building democratic and cooperative staff relationships, we do not intend to discount the importance of favorable face-to-face relations of the principal with teachers. No group process can substitute for the administrator's ability to work cooperatively with others. The reader is referred especially to the discussion in Chapter 12 on staff morale, for the administrator must understand the broader setting in which democratic relationships are developed. Nevertheless, a brief description of one of the major characteristics of individual conferences is presented here to emphasize the importance of the principal's efforts to establish a close working relationship with each of his teachers.

In past years, it was common for administrator-teacher conferences to be conducted as if a *superior* person were passing on his knowledge and experience to an *inferior* worker, the purpose being to improve the teacher. This point of view has changed considerably in recent years and the conference now characteristically focuses on problem solving — instead of being "teacher centered" it is "problem centered." This concept is fundamental to the development of democratic relations with the staff. Burton and Brueckner stress the nature of the problem-centered philosophy in their description of such a conference:

> An individual conference is (or should be) a meeting between two persons equally interested in improving a situation. The views and facts of each party are necessary to complete the picture. Exchange of facts and ideas is focused on problem-solving and not on one of the persons in the conference. Aid and assistance will inevitably result, but the giving of aid will flow in both directions.[10]

There may have been some justification earlier for the principal to direct his attention primarily to the improvement of the teacher inasmuch as many teachers had less than four years of college education. This situation was even more prevalent in the elementary grades. No doubt there were many schools in which the principal was much better prepared than most of his teachers, and he was expected to pass on the benefits of his training and experience to them.

At the present time, high school teachers are generally required to have a bachelor's degree as a minimum, and in some states or communities to have substantial graduate credit or a master's degree. It is becoming more common to find faculty members in larger schools with a doctor's degree. In general, teachers should be viewed as well-trained, professional workers in education. As long as this is a valid assumption, individual conferences should be based on a cooperative relationship between two professional people, equally interested and concerned about an educational problem.

Following is an illustration of a "teacher-centered" approach to a problem as contrasted with a "problem-centered" approach. Miss Peterson, a teacher of algebra, came to the office of her principal and asked to talk over a situation which had developed in one of her classes. The principal listened carefully as she described the trouble she was having with a pupil named Carl. She explained how Carl was always disrupting the class with annoying or what he thought "cute" remarks. There was nothing particularly bad about Carl; it was just that all of the other pupils were begin-

---

[10] William H. Burton and Leo J. Brueckner, *Supervision, A Social Process* (New York: Appleton-Century-Crofts, Inc., 3rd ed., 1955), p. 168.

ning to anticipate his remarks and they would all laugh every time Carl said anything, which was often.

In this case the principal replied immediately to Miss Peterson, "Well, apparently you are doing something wrong, or you are failing to do something you should be doing. Let's see if we can figure out what it is. I tell you what I will do. I will visit your class personally to analyze the situation for you." This is of course the "teacher-centered" approach, and it implies that Miss Peterson is not competent. It suggests also that if she were competent she could figure out what was wrong herself.

Another approach to the same situation finds the principal saying to Miss Peterson, "There must be some important information about Carl that will help us to analyze this situation, for he has been in our school since the fourth grade. Suppose we get his cumulative record to see if there are any clues there that might help us." In this instance, attention is directed immediately to gathering facts which might be helpful to both Miss Peterson and the principal in attempting to figure out how to deal with *Carl's* problem rather than with Miss Peterson's problem.

This illustration is not at all atypical of the problems which frequently are the subject of individual conferences with teachers. In situations like this the principal must understand the democratic nature of a problem-centered approach. There must be respect for the other person's intelligence. Acceptance of such an attitude enables the principal to concentrate on mutual problem solving with his teachers rather than establishing a "superior-inferior" relationship. It is recognized, however, that sometimes the teacher is indeed the problem. In such cases, the relationship is bound to be different from the one just described.

Application of the problem-solving point of view is useful in many situations in which the principal will find himself, e.g., classroom visitations, case conferences, parent-teacher-student conferences, and other face-to-face meetings with his staff. Individual techniques must be developed which are appropriate to each situation, but whatever the technique employed, it should be based on getting the facts and information necessary for joint solution of the problem. Such an approach will make a positive contribution to the development of democratic and cooperative staff relationships.

Questions and Group Projects

1. Assume you are a new principal in a school with twenty teachers. Prior to your administration, the faculty was required to attend a faculty meeting every Tuesday afternoon which usually continued until six o'clock. Would you continue to follow the established plan? Give the reasons for your answer.

2. What is the difference between laissez-faire administration and "democratic" administration?

3. Prepare a questionnaire designed to solicit faculty opinion concerning the effectiveness of faculty meetings. With the permission of the principal, circulate the questionnaire among the faculty of a high school. Summarize suggestions for improvement resulting from your survey.

4. Assume the class is a faculty. Select one person to serve as principal, put him in charge of planning a faculty meeting with the class, and at a future time convene the "faculty meeting."

5. Draw up detailed plans on how you think an ideal workshop or preschool conference should be run.

6. Organize a debate on the topic "Resolved: the high school principal should retain veto power over faculty decisions."

7. Plan a role-playing activity in which one person is the high school principal and the other is a teacher. They are to have a conference following a visit by the principal to the teacher's classroom. Let other members of the class analyze the discussion to determine whether or not it is "problem centered" or "teacher centered."

Selected References

Adams, Harold P., and Frank G. Dickey. *Basic Principles of Supervision.* New York: American Book Company, 1953.

Anderson, Lester W. "How Faculty Committees May Produce," *Education Digest,* October, 1956, 22:21–23.

Bartky, J. "Participation in Democratic School Administration," *Educational Administration and Supervision,* December, 1957, 43:449–57.

Burnright, R. "Democracy and the Committee Method," *Educational Forum,* March, 1958, 22:325–28.

Burton, William H., and Leo J. Brueckner. *Supervision, A Social Process.* New York: Appleton-Century-Crofts, Inc., 3rd ed., 1955.

Cove, W. H., and J. B. Peyton. "Guidelines and Ground Rules for a Curriculum Committee," *The Bulletin* of the NASSP, February, 1959, 43:30–35.

Educational Policies Commission. *Learning the Ways of Democracy.* Washington: National Education Association and American Association of School Administrators, 1940.

Hendrix, H. "Decision Making? Who Is Responsible?" *School Executive,* February, 1957, 76:77.

Heywood, Stanley J. "What's Wrong with Faculty Meetings?" *Administrator's Notebook,* Midwest Administration Center, University of Chicago, December, 1952, Vol. 1, No. 5.

James, H. T. "Committees in the Administrative Process," *American School Board Journal*, February, 1960, 140:23–25.

Kelley, Earl C. *The Workshop Way of Learning*. New York: Harper & Brothers, 1951.

Leach, Kent W. "What Is the Role of the Principal in Democratic Administration?" *The Bulletin* of the NASSP, April, 1958, 42:7–10.

Manlove, D. C. "Organizing the Faculty for Curriculum Improvement," *The Bulletin* of the NASSP, February, 1959, 43:57–60.

Mitchell, James R. "The Workshop as an In-Service Education Process," *North Central Association Quarterly*, April, 1954, 28:421–57.

National Education Association. "Some Workshops That Have Worked," *NEA Journal*, May, 1959, pp. 20–25.

Rounds, L. E. "Channel for Staff Opinion; Professional Advisory Committee," *School Executive*, August, 1959, 78:34.

Scudder, Hazel J. "A Staff Organizes for In-service Education," *NEA Journal*, May, 1956, p. 26.

Secor, L. J., and J. P. Anderson. "What Administrative Practices Contribute to Better Principal-Faculty Relationships," *The Bulletin* of the NASSP, April, 1958, 42:162–64.

Seyfert, W. C. "Experiences in Faculty Self-Determination," *School Review*, November, 1953, 61:458–67.

Wiles, Kimball. *Supervision for Better Schools*. New York: Prentice-Hall, Inc., 2nd ed., 1955.

Winetrout, Kenneth, and John C. Robertson. "Workshops in Education," *The Bulletin* of the NASSP, February, 1947, 31:41–47.

CHAPTER 14

Selection of the Staff

The cornerstone of good education in any high school is its faculty. Fine buildings and equipment, specialized services, adequate custodial and clerical services, and all the other factors which help to provide a favorable environment for learning mean little if the learning experiences are directed by incompetent teachers. Chandler and Petty are emphatic on this point: "A competent staff with a sound educational philosophy, working with virile and dynamic leadership, is an element in the school administrative process for which there is no satisfactory substitute."[1]

Communities make a large financial investment in their teachers. Salaries are usually the largest single expenditure in a school system. For example, of the local educational expenditures in the United States for the school year 1957–58, 47.4 per cent went as salaries to instructional staff members (Table 21). Benson points out also that salary expenditures often account for as much as 80 per cent of a school budget.

> Inevitably, salaries constitute something over 50 per cent of local school expenditures. In a system that is not currently undertaking a school construction program, it would not be unusual, as a matter of fact, to find that all salaries represent more than 80 per cent of the school budget.[2]

---

[1] B. J. Chandler and Paul V. Petty, *Personnel Management in School Administration* (Yonkers, N.Y.: World Book Company, 1955), p. vii.

[2] Charles S. Benson, *The Economics of Public Education* (Boston: Houghton Mifflin Company, 1961), p. 15.

Frequently, the public schools are the largest business in a community, the teachers its largest single investment. From a business point of view, it is one of the best investments a community can make providing it gets its money's worth through a return of high-quality education. It is the school administrator's responsibility to see to it that a good return is realized. An administrator who selects good teachers, uses their talents efficiently, organizes them effectively is a valuable asset to a school system.

TABLE 21

Distribution of Local Educational Expenditures by Function or Object, 1957–58

Distribution	Amount ($million)	Per Cent of Total
Total expenditures in local school districts	13,456	100.00
Current expenditures	10,261	76.3
Administration	330	2.5
Instruction	6,901	51.3
Salaries of instructional staff	6,368	47.4
Salaries of clerks	127	0.9
Textbooks	102	0.8
School library books	32	0.2
Supplies and other expenditures	272	2.0
Operation of physical plant	924	6.9
Maintenance of physical plant	378	2.8
Fixed charges (retirement, rent, etc.)	715	5.3
Other elementary and secondary services (attendance, health, transportation, food, etc.)	890	6.6
Community services	41	0.3
Summer schools	5	—
Adult education	37	0.3
Community colleges	40	0.3
Capital outlay	2,853	21.2
Interest	342	2.5

Source: U.S. Office of Education, Department of Health, Education and Welfare, *Biennial Survey of Education, 1956–1958*, 1961, Chap. II. Taken from Charles S. Benson, *The Economics of Public Education* (Boston: Houghton Mifflin Company, 1961), p. 14.

It is essential, therefore, that high school principals give competent leadership in the selection of teachers. Anyone involved in this process must be concerned with three basic questions: (1) Who selects the teachers? (2) How can teaching success be predicted? and (3) What procedures should be followed in selecting teachers?

Who Selects Teachers?

Boards of education have the legal authority to elect or appoint *all* employees of the school district. In a democratic society committed to local control of education this authority must be retained by the board. Boards of education are dependent, however, upon professional administrators for assistance in the selection process. Teacher selection is not a policy matter; it is an administrative task which demands considerable insight into the learning process, a knowledge of the intricacies of the administrative structure, and the ability to make good judgments on the qualifications of applicants as they relate to specific staff needs.

At times a board may delegate authority to the superintendent or his representative to sign contracts with teachers — generally, only when a large number of teachers must be employed and an immediate decision is needed in order to secure the services of particular teachers. Even under such circumstances, the board must retain its legal authority by confirming the appointment at a later meeting of the board. Administrators should be certain to check the exact legal provision in their state for this type of action, since education is a state function and there are some variations among the states in these matters.

Superintendents of schools typically are the ones who recommend candidates to the board of education for appointment. Screening of the applicant's qualifications usually is delegated to the superintendent. He is expected to judge the applicant in terms of the requirements of the vacancy and the policies established by the board. In larger school systems, the superintendent calls upon other administrators to assist him in screening and in carrying out other administrative tasks related to it; but the final selection of teachers to be recommended to the board is up to the superintendent. In small school systems, the superintendent is likely to assume complete responsibility for all selections. No doubt the reluctance of many superintendents to allow the selection of teachers to get very far away from them is indicative of the importance of the task.

Although the major responsibility for choosing the staff has been retained by superintendents, there is evidence that principals are becoming involved increasingly in this phase of school administration. Keller has summarized the principal's role in the selection process:

> Only in recent years has teacher selection become identified as an administrative function shared by high-school principals or department heads. In small school systems the school superintendent has kept major responsibility for recommending teaching candidates to the board of education. In larger systems a centralized personnel department has handled this function. In both instances consultation with high-school principals has grown, partly with greater professionalization of the position and

partly with the lengthening period of appointment. High-school principals increasingly take responsibility for initial screening of candidates through review of credentials, interviews, and visitations at work. Leaders in the field recommend strongly that the head of the school in which the teachers are to be employed share in their nomination and selection.[3]

The increased activity on the part of principals in the selection of teachers is a desirable development, because it is the principal and his assistants who will supervise and work most closely with them. Logically, therefore, he should have some voice in the process. Final decisions in this matter, however, are *not* his prerogative. He merely recommends candidates for consideration by the superintendent of schools.

In very large school systems, associate or assistant superintendents in charge of personnel are often assigned responsibility for screening applicants for the entire school system. It is not unusual in these situations for the principal to be unaware of who the teachers for his school will be until final appointment and assignments have been made.

Sometimes department heads, or other individuals within the school other than those already mentioned, are asked to assist in selecting teachers, but usually as consultants or advisers to the other administrators mentioned.

How Can Teaching Success Be Predicted?

Basic to the selection of teachers is the ability to predict the probable success of a candidate. Many approaches have been used in setting up criteria for prediction of success in teaching. Attempts have been made to establish high correlations between supervisors' judgments of teaching success and certain personal qualifications such as intelligence, scholastic achievement, marks in student teaching, reading comprehension, and similar traits which can be measured or identified with reasonable objectivity. Researchers have tried to identify personality or social traits that students, administrators, parents, or other interested observers believe to be necessary for successful teaching. An indication of the number of studies designed to predict teaching success is found in Levin's summary on this topic:

> It is no accident, therefore, that for the last twenty-five years educational bibliographies have been replete with studies variously called teacher competence or teacher effectiveness. A bibliography compiled in 1950 by Dumas and Tiedeman lists no less than a thousand studies. . . .[4]

[3] Robert J. Keller, "Secondary Education — Organization and Administration," *Encyclopedia of Educational Research* (New York: The Macmillan Company, 3rd ed., 1960), p. 1250.
[4] Harry Levin, "A New Perspective on Teacher Competence Research," *Harvard Educational Review*, Spring, 1954, 24:98.

Results of one of the most comprehensive studies to determine significant teacher characteristics and to develop objective measures that might be used in evaluating and predicting teacher behavior were published by the Educational Policies Commission.[5] This study, organized in 1948, included approximately 100 separate research studies and over 6,000 teachers in 1,700 schools and 450 school systems which participated in various phases of the investigation. Although the results of this study have extended substantially our understanding of behavior characteristics of teachers, and certainly they are helpful in the selection of teachers for specific situations, no claims are made by the author for using the results as a general basis for selecting teachers.

It would seem reasonable to expect that such a large quantity of research on a problem would have produced criteria for success which could be used with considerable confidence by administrators. Unfortunately, this is not the case, for the authors of this book have not been able to locate any studies in the literature that take the guesswork or personal judgment factor out of the selection process. According to the Committee on Criteria of Teacher Effectiveness of the American Educational Research Association,

> The simple fact of the matter is that, after 40 years of research on teacher effectiveness during which a vast number of studies have been carried out, one can point to few outcomes that a superintendent of schools can safely employ in hiring a teacher or granting him tenure, that an agency can employ in certifying teachers, or that a teacher-education faculty can employ in planning or improving teacher-education programs.[6]

A major handicap in determining criteria for predicting success in teaching is the lack of agreement on what a "good" teacher is. Most individuals have their own value judgments in this matter. Further, what constitutes success in one teaching position may not be considered successful in a different community or in a different position within the same school. According to Levin, there appears to be no immediate hope for removing this factor as a major deterrent to predicting teacher success:

> When a supervisor or principal or observer is asked to identify for the researcher the good teachers, we are likely to have among our group of "goodness" as many different kinds of people as we have frames of reference of identifiers. It is little wonder, consequently, that there is little consistency in the results or that the studies are not replicated later. For it is highly improbable that a later researcher will be able to gather a group for study which he could be sure has been selected on comparable criteria of goodness. In other words, when, as a first step, we start to work

[5] David G. Ryans, *Characteristics of Teachers* (Washington: American Council on Education, 1960).

[6] H. H. Remmers, et al., "Second Report of the Committee on Criteria of Teacher Effectiveness," *Journal of Educational Research*, 1953, 46:657.

with "good" or "poor" teachers we undoubtedly have a *potpourri* of many kinds of goodness and badness — all of them legitimate. It is small wonder, therefore, that we can achieve no meaningful research results based on such a group of subjects.[7]

Granted that there is no conclusive proof of a general factor or combination of factors which will insure teaching success, some studies, nevertheless, show low but positive correlations between certain attributes and what some supervisors, professors, and administrators have chosen to classify as successful teaching. There is also considerable information available as to what pupils, parents, administrators, and other interested people "think" is necessary for success in teaching. The authors recognize too that teachers are often selected in terms of an administrator's personal biases or of what he believes will make a successful teacher in a specific situation. Even though there are many limitations on our ability to predict teaching success, the job of selecting teachers still has to be done. It is important, therefore, that administrators at least be aware of what information is available from research and what opinions people have to offer for assistance in this matter. Consequently, the following discussion presents those characteristics or ideas mentioned in the literature most often and thought to have some degree of usefulness for administrators or other individuals who are responsible for the selection of teachers.

Intelligence

The field of education and teaching is concerned with the development of intellectual talents, which is an extremely complex process. It seems logical to expect that anyone involved in such an undertaking should be reasonably intelligent. This point of view is generally accepted by authorities in personnel management and is expressed in typical fashion by Chandler and Petty:

> Teaching is a complex profession. The teacher must have the mental ability necessary for him to provide civic and educational leadership. Only those who possess a relatively high degree of intelligence should be encouraged to prepare for teaching.[8]

Additional support is found in a study by Carlile comparing the intelligence test scores of college students with grades earned in student teaching:

> . . . The coefficients of correlation are positive. The correlation with the Detroit Intelligence Test is statistically significant but low. Its forecasting efficiency is four per cent.[9]

[7] Levin, *op. cit.*, p. 100.
[8] Chandler and Petty, *op. cit.*, p. 109.
[9] Amos B. Carlile, "Predicting Performance in the Teaching Profession," *Journal of Educational Research*, May, 1954, 47:642.

Although the evidence is not adequate to justify using high intelligence as the sole criterion, it does favor the person who scores well on intelligence tests. It might be assumed that some selection on the basis of intelligence has already operated in that the candidate has graduated from a four-year college, and it seems reasonable to assume that at least average intelligence or better is needed to earn a bachelor's degree. There may be teaching positions, however, which demand a teacher with intelligence substantially better than average, such as teaching a class of gifted or talented students. It is recommended, therefore, that consideration be given to the level of intelligence of the prospective teacher, for, other things being equal, it appears that relatively high general intelligence is desirable.

Scholastic Achievement

Administrators vary in their opinions concerning prospective teachers' level of scholastic achievement. Some say, "All I want is a good average person. I don't want any bookworms on my staff." Others take the opposite position and want only candidates who have graduated with high academic honors. Again there is no conclusive evidence that a teacher with an outstanding scholastic record will be a better teacher than one who has been an average or below average student. There is some indication, however, that the person who has done well in his academic work will be a more successful teacher than the one with a low academic record.

Carlile found that the coefficient of correlation between grades earned in student teaching and general scholastic achievement was .46, the highest single coefficient determined in his study.[10] The correlation was statistically significant, and it had a forecasting efficiency of 12 per cent.

Ryans reported in his study of teacher characteristics that those who reported themselves as having been outstanding students scored higher than other groups in the following categories pertaining to classroom behavior: friendly, understanding, responsible, businesslike, stimulating, imaginative, favorable attitude toward pupils, favorable attitude toward administrative and other school personnel, permissive, child-centered educational viewpoints, and verbal understanding.[11] The mean scores decreased in fairly orderly fashion for the "good" student, "average" student, and "poor" student. F-ratios significant at the 5 per cent level were reported.

This evidence tends to favor teachers who have had good scholastic achievement in college. At least a high scholastic record should not be discounted in a candidate for a teaching position, and apparently it should be considered an asset.

[10] *Ibid.*
[11] Ryans, *op. cit.*, p. 394.

Subject-Matter and Professional Preparation in Education

Considerable debate has taken place as to whether a high school teacher should be a subject-matter specialist or a specialist in methodology. Extreme positions have been taken on both sides of the question. There are those who believe strongly that the all-important thing in teaching high school youth is the teacher's knowledge of his subject. The logic of this argument usually centers on the idea that education is primarily concerned with intellectual development, and this means learning of facts and information, and consequently a teacher who does not know his subject cannot possibly be a good teacher.

People at the other extreme contend that the important thing is to "teach children, not subject matter," and thus it is more important for a teacher to be well informed on how students learn than to be well prepared in subject matter. These partisans argue also that teachers should be concerned with the emotional, physical, and social development of the student as well as his intellectual development.

The authors believe that a successful teacher must be adequately prepared both in subject matter and in an understanding of the elements usually included in professional education courses on child growth and development, the psychology of learning, and methods of teaching. This position is supported by Ojeman following a review of studies completed during recent years relating to successful teaching and increased understanding of child behavior:

> ... In predicting the kind of teacher who will be effective in promoting pupil growth, it seems that we have to combine several factors. Included in the list of factors thus far revealed by research are measures of competence in subject matter taught, measures of various aspects of personality, and measures of competence in teaching technique. We cannot locate the effective teacher by taking into account only knowledge of subject matter, or interest in teaching and schoolwork, or any other single factor. The effective teacher in light of our present knowledge has a combination of several factors. . . .[12]

Additional support is found in statements by Highet:

> In other words, what are the qualities of a good teacher?
>
> First, and most necessary of all, he must know the subject. He must know what he teaches. This sounds obvious; yet it is not always practiced. It means that, if his job is teaching chemistry, he must know chemistry. . . .
>
> A teacher must believe in the value of his subject as a doctor believes in health. . . .
>
> The neglect of this principle is one of the chief reasons for bad teaching. . . .[13]

[12] Ralph H. Ojeman, "Identifying Effective Classroom Teachers," *National Elementary Principal*, September, 1952, 32:138.

[13] Gilbert Highet, *The Art of Teaching* (New York: Alfred A. Knopf, Inc., 1950), pp. 13, 15.

Although Highet gives priority on subject matter, he also maintains that good teachers like and understand children:

> ... The third essential of good teaching is to like pupils. If you do not actually like boys and girls, or young men and young women, give up teaching. ...
>
> ... So if you are interested in teaching, do not even expect the young to be like yourself and the people you know. Learn the peculiar patterns of their thoughts and emotions. ... The teacher, then, must know the young as such. ... [14]

An understanding of methods is also ranked high in this very interesting discussion on teaching by Highet:

> ... Teaching has three stages. First the teacher prepares the subject. Then he communicates it to his pupils, or those parts of it he has selected. Then he makes sure they have learnt it. ... [15]

Requirements for legal certification and the standards of accrediting agencies reflect a similar position, i.e., teachers must show evidence of preparation in the subject to be taught, and also in professional education courses. These requirements commonly include a minimum of fifteen to twenty semester hours of credit in the specific subject field to be taught and the same in professional education courses. It should be recognized, however, that these are minimum rather than optimum standards. State departments and accrediting agencies recommend that teachers have substantially more than the minimum amount of preparation in both areas. The basic stand of these agencies is that high school teachers should "know their subject" but should also "know their children and how to teach." What we really want in our secondary schools is teachers who have a solid academic preparation and in addition understand youth, schools, and methods of instruction. Administrators should look for evidence on both scores in considering prospective teachers.

Personal Characteristics

The identification of personal characteristics related to successful teaching has been approached most often through surveys of opinions of pupils, parents, and administrators. As would be expected, subjective evaluations vary greatly with individuals; undoubtedly, every administrator has his own ideas as to the personal qualities necessary for success in teaching.

One of the most comprehensive surveys of public opinion with respect to desirable teacher qualifications was reported by Witty, who analyzed 12,000 letters from pupils on the topic "The Teacher Who Has Helped Me Most."[16] Four thousand of the letters were from pupils of high school age.

---

[14] *Ibid.*, pp. 27, 37.
[15] *Ibid.*, p. 74.
[16] Paul Witty, "An Analysis of the Personality Traits of the Effective Teacher," *Journal of Educational Research,* May, 1947, 40:662–71.

Table 22 presents the rank order of the twelve traits most frequently mentioned by the 4,000 high school students.

TABLE 22

Rank Order of Traits Mentioned by Pupils of Ages 14 and Higher

Trait	Frequency
Cooperative, democratic attitude	1
Patience	2
Kindliness and consideration for the individual	3
Fairness and impartiality	4
Interest in pupils' problems	5
Sense of humor	6.5
Wide interests	6.5
Good disposition and consistent behavior	9
Use of recognition and praise	9
Flexibility	9
Personal appearance and pleasing manner	11
Unusual proficiency in teaching a particular subject	12

Source: Paul Witty, "An Analysis of the Personality Traits of the Effective Teacher," *Journal of Educational Research*, May, 1947, 40:664.

Similar results were obtained in a study by McAulay in which he asked 30 school administrators, 30 parents, 30 teachers, 400 pupils, and 120 college students five questions on the qualifications of a good teacher.[17] Included among the questions was the following: "What personality traits are most beneficial to a successful elementary teacher?" Answers were in substantial agreement with the results found by Witty on high school teachers. These are the personality qualities mentioned most frequently and ranked in order of frequency:[18]

       1. Sense of humor.
       2. Patience.
       3. Tolerance.
       4. An understanding of children.
       5. A clear pleasant voice.
       6. Free from complexes.
       7. Neat in their person and surroundings.

Tiedeman studied reactions of junior high school pupils as to which teacher techniques, personality traits, and behaviorisms most generally effect either a cooperative, friendly pupil-teacher relationship or an antagonistic, unwholesome one. Some of the most frequently mentioned acts and characteristics disliked by pupils follow:

[17] John D. McAulay, "Qualifications of a Good Teacher," *Peabody Journal of Education*, July, 1954, 32:22–25.
[18] *Ibid.*, p. 23.

... It is obvious that the autocratic, dominating teacher is most disliked by junior high school pupils, followed, in order, by (2) the teacher who ridicules, uses sarcasm, nags; (3) the teacher who threatens, frightens, and punishes to secure discipline; (4) the teacher who fails to provide for individual differences of pupils; (5) the teacher who has disagreeable personal peculiarities; (6) the teacher who shows partiality to pupils.[19]

Some of the most frequently mentioned acts and characteristics liked by junior high school pupils follow:[20]

1. Teacher has a kind, friendly, cheerful disposition.
2. Teacher is glad to help children.
3. Teacher explains clearly.
4. Teacher has no pets — is fair to everyone.
5. Teacher is neat and tidy in dress and in taking care of the room.
6. Teacher has a sense of humor.
7. Teacher understands children and their problems.
8. Teacher allows children to do things for her.
9. Teacher is friendly and polite on the street or out of school.

It is generally recognized that favorable pupil-teacher relationships are a positive influence in the motivation of pupils to learn. Anything that can be done to improve motivation is worthy of consideration by high school principals as they participate in the selection of new teachers. It is important, therefore, to seek teachers who have those personal qualities that make a favorable impression on others, particularly pupils. However, some teaching positions require unusual strength of character in one area which may outweigh all others. For example, a teacher who is to teach English to a slow-learning class of tenth-grade students is almost sure to need more than the usual amount of patience and willingness to plan for individual differences. Evidence of these particular qualities should take precedence over other generally desirable qualities such as a pleasant voice and neat appearance, or over certain peculiarities. For best results in selecting teachers, priorities of personal qualities should be established with specific teaching assignments and types of pupils in mind.

At this point, the authors would add a word of caution against using personality characteristics exclusively as criteria in selecting teachers. It is necessary to keep in mind that there is no single quality or criterion which has been identified as correlating to a high degree with teaching success. Multiple criteria operate in every situation. Exceptions to the general findings should be recognized, since there are teachers who are highly successful in spite of, and in some cases even because of, unusual personal characteristics. This is an area where one outstanding quality

---

[19] Stuart C. Tiedeman, "A Study of Pupil-Teacher Relationships," *Journal of Educational Research,* May 30, 1942, 35:657.
[20] *Ibid.,* p. 664.

might compensate for a number of weaknesses. Nevertheless, the personal characteristics which pupils, parents, teachers, and administrators consistently identify as being related to success in teaching should be considered in screening applicants. The odds for success are in favor of teachers who have the greatest number of personal traits identified as being desirable over those possessing fewer of these traits.

Teaching Experience

That teaching experience is an asset is evidenced by the fact that practically all schools schedule salary increments according to the amount of teaching experience a person has gained. In past years, many of the larger school systems required some teaching experience as a prerequisite for employment. One of the main reasons was the belief that the experienced applicant would be successful.

Recently, there has been less insistence upon previous teaching experience as a condition for appointment. Elsbree and Reutter point out that "today only a small proportion of city school systems (less than 15 per cent) make teaching experience somewhere a prerequisite."[21] Administrators of larger school systems now realize that having teachers begin under their own supervisors has its advantages, since there is some question as to the benefits of teaching experience without adequate supervision. Chances appear better that beginning teachers will develop an educational philosophy and approach to teaching in greater harmony with those of the local school system if they start their professional career in that system. However, there is some danger that strict adherence to this position would result in "inbreeding" and the perpetuation of a provincial philosophy of education.

Competition for the supply of teachers since World War II has been responsible, in part, for the change in attitude by larger school systems. Many cities found they were losing teachers to suburban communities, where working conditions, facilities, and even salaries have been quite attractive.

Another argument against requiring teaching experience elsewhere is based on the view that every school should assume its share of responsibility for inducting beginning teachers into the profession. It is selfish and unfair to expect the smaller schools to do all the supervising of beginning teachers, only to have them leave as soon as they meet the experience requirement of the larger cities. The question as to whether or not the small schools should require previous experience has been an academic one. Superintendents of small schools have recognized for years that their most productive supply of teachers is from the ranks of beginning teachers. The fact that beginning teachers are paid smaller salaries

[21] Willard S. Elsbree, and E. Edmund Reutter, Jr., *Staff Personnel in the Public Schools* (Englewood Cliffs, N.J.: *Prentice-Hall, Inc.,* 1954), p. 64.

than experienced teachers has been another consideration for the small school or any other school interested in keeping the salary budget down.

Some administrators favor inexperienced teachers because they bring enthusiasm and energy to a faculty. Such teachers are anxious to be successful and are willing to carry more than their share of the load. An additional advantage in employing beginners is that it helps to maintain a balance of ages on the faculty. The number retiring in any one year is held relatively constant, and the faculty achieves stability.

Research on the relative advantages and disadvantages in requiring teaching experience has been very limited. In a study reported by Gaier, Jones, and Simpson,[22] 231 students attending a summer session at the College of Education, University of Illinois, were asked to list suggestions for meeting the following problem:

> Assume you are teaching a class of thirty students next fall. During the first week of November you notice a widespread lack of interest both in classwork and in out-of-class assignments.
>
> List specific activities you would consider doing before Thanksgiving to improve this situation.

The responses were classified in degrees of resourcefulness, as follows:

> The highest resourcefulness scores were made by those subjects with 1–3 years of experience and those with 16–21 years of experience. Lowest scores were obtained by those without any teaching experience. . . .

These results support the idea that teachers with some teaching experience are somewhat more resourceful in problem situations than are beginning teachers. It is quite apparent, however, that there is no conclusive evidence either supporting or discounting the general requirement of previous teaching experience. The decision as to whether or not to require experience should be made in terms of the specific duties involved, the desire to induct teachers early into a school system, the amount of money available for salaries, the distribution of ages within a faculty, and other factors peculiar to a particular school situation. For example, an unusual or key position may call for a teacher who has certain special abilities. When the administrator knows that a particular class is unusually difficult to control, it seems reasonable for him to seek an experienced person with demonstrated ability in this regard. Similarly, if efforts are being made to introduce additional teacher-counselors to the staff, there is reason to look for a teacher who has demonstrated success in dealing effectively with student problems.

It appears that the experienced teacher has some advantages over one without experience, other things being equal, but they are not sufficiently pronounced to rely on this as a basis for selection. Administrators will

---

[22] Eugene L. Gaier, Stewart Jones, and Ray H. Simpson, "Factors Related to Measures of Professional Resourcefulness," *School Review*, March, 1953, 61:158–62.

have to make their decision in relation to other factors and to how much a particular situation or position would benefit from an experienced teacher.

Marital Status

During the great depression of the 1930's many schools refused to employ women who were married, because there was a feeling that only one job per family was justified in light of the economic condition of the country. The supply of teachers was also more than adequate at the time. With both economic conditions improved and the supply of teachers inadequate to meet demands, the current practice is to disregard teachers' marital status. A study by Stephenson in 1953 showed that the proportion of women teachers who were married had risen to 57 per cent by that time; 82 per cent of his students at Miami University planned to combine marriage and teaching.[23]

Although it appears that marital status is no longer a major consideration in selecting teachers, Ryans reports some significant differences in mean scores in the Survey Sample when comparing single and married teachers.[24] Among the secondary teachers in general, single teachers were characterized as being more responsible, more businesslike, more democratic in classroom practices, more permissive in educational viewpoint, and higher in verbal understanding. On the other hand, married teachers had greater emotional stability.

The authors suggest that the decision as to whether single or married teachers are chosen should depend upon the balance of marital status on the present staff. Both groups have strengths which are considered desirable in the teaching situation.

Age

In Ryans' study of teacher characteristics, substantial differences were found between different age groups:

> There appears to be little doubt about the existence of significant differences between teachers comprising different age groups with respect to a number of teacher characteristics. Among 60 different F tests computed with the data for these teachers, 45 of the sets of differences between means were found to be significant at or beyond the .05 level. Generally, scores of older teachers (55 years and above) showed this group to be at a disadvantage compared with the younger teachers, except from the standpoint of . . . systematic and businesslike classroom behavior and . . . indicative of learning-centered, traditional educational viewpoints. Younger teachers generally attained higher scores relative to the other scale.[25]

[23] Chester M. Stephenson, "Married or Single Elementary Teachers?" *Ohio Schools,* December, 1953, 31:426.
[24] Ryans, *op. cit.,* pp. 392–93.
[25] *Ibid.,* p. 390.

Generally speaking, it appears that selection of teachers under fifty-five years of age is advantageous to a staff. On the other hand, if there is a need to provide an atmosphere characterized by a more businesslike and traditional educational viewpoint, it would be logical to seek older teachers. A reasonably wide distribution of ages seems desirable so that students may benefit from association with both young and more mature teachers. The natural course of events assists in this matter, however, inasmuch as teachers over fifty-five are much less likely to be seeking new teaching positions, and most of the new teachers available will be in the younger age group.

Sex

Differences between men and women in the teaching situation do exist at the secondary school level. Ryans found that women generally score significantly higher than men on scales measuring classroom behavior characterized as understanding, friendly, responsible and businesslike, stimulating and imaginative, favorable toward pupils, favorable toward democratic classroom practices, permissive in educational viewpoint, and high in verbal understanding. But, men teachers in the secondary school scored significantly higher than women on emotional stability.[26]

The decision as to whether to select a man or a woman teacher must be related to the situation and not based merely on sex. If the situation is one which demands considerable emotional stability, a man might be more desirable, other things being equal. If the particular behavior strengths of women teachers seem to be called for, selection of a woman is indicated.

The authors feel there is logic also in having a balance of men and women on the total staff of a school system. There is some virtue in having a substantial number of men teachers on the high school faculty to compensate for the proportionately large number of women usually found on the faculty of the elementary school. Adolescent boys seem to need the influence of male teachers.

Fortunately the percentage of men teachers in public secondary schools has been increasing in recent years — from 40 per cent in 1947–48 to 50.4 per cent in 1957–58, as is shown in Table 23.

Some communities pay a salary bonus to attract men teachers. No doubt this is necessary where salaries are unusually low inasmuch as a man is more likely to be head of a family and cannot afford to teach at the same salary as a single woman teacher. However, in communities where salaries are reasonably adequate, serious morale problems can develop over differentials in salary based on sex. Continuing efforts should be made by the administration, therefore, to secure good salaries for all teachers rather than paying male teachers a bonus.

[26] *Ibid.*, p. 391.

SELECTION OF THE STAFF

TABLE 23
Number of Teachers in Public Secondary Schools, by Sex, School Years 1947–48 to 1957–58

School Year	Total	Men	Women	Per Cent Men
1947–48	305,739	122,258	183,481	40.0
1949–50	324,093	142,043	182,050	43.8
1951–52	343,060	154,315	185,745	45.9
1953–54	374,618	173,267	201,351	46.3
1955–56	410,203	202,030	208,173	49.3
1957–58	459,525	231,817	227,708	50.4

Source: U.S. Office of Education, *Biennial Survey of Education in the United States* (Washington: Government Printing Office, years indicated).

Employment of Local Teachers

Policies relating to employing local residents as teachers vary from giving priority to home products to prohibiting their employment. In the absence of any research evidence supporting either position, this factor should not be given undue consideration in the selection of teachers. Every effort should be made to find the best candidate regardless of place of residence. Probably the employment of a high percentage of local residents should be avoided in order to prevent excessive inbreeding of philosophy and methods. Some schools have adopted policies declaring that relatives of members of the board of education are not to be employed. A policy of this type discriminates against such people, but it does protect board members from what can be rather embarrassing situations.

The practice of paying lower salaries to local residents, especially married women, than to teachers from outside the community is extremely unwise. It has a demoralizing influence on the staff, and it makes salary rather than professional qualifications the primary consideration in the selection of teachers.

Teacher Tenure

The adoption of tenure for teachers has been a growing practice both locally and state wide. Most teachers give considerable weight to tenure in seeking a job. They prefer a school system in which they have assurance that teachers will not be dismissed on the whims of a few people in a community. Although the net effect of tenure is undoubtedly to improve working conditions for teachers, it does add an additional concern to administrators and boards of education. Removing a teacher who has achieved tenure status is rather difficult, both legally and emotionally. Few issues can arouse more ill will within a community than the dismissal proceedings against a teacher. An experience or two of this type usually will convince an administrator of the need to be reasonably certain that a teacher has the qualifications desired prior to employing him or granting him tenure. It is much better for everyone concerned to refuse to employ a person initially than to dismiss him at a later date.

What Procedures Should Be Followed in the Selection Process?

It was pointed out earlier in this chapter that responsibility for the selection of teachers belongs to the superintendent of schools, and the responsibility for election of teachers rests with the board of education. But it also is the task of the administration to establish procedures necessary to accomplish the final election of the staff, and there is a logical sequence of actions which should assist administrators in making the best possible choices: (1) development of job specifications, (2) announcement of the vacancy, (3) searching for able candidates, (4) preliminary review of applications, (5) testing of applicants, (6) interviewing of selected applicants, (7) observation of candidates in teaching situations, (8) recommendations for appointment, (9) appointment by the board, and (10) issuing of a contract.

Development of Specifications

Written specifications should describe both the nature of the position and the qualifications of the person who is to fill it. The specifications should be drawn up prior to any formal announcement that a vacancy exists, because they are basic guides for all future considerations of applicants. Typical of the recommendations of specialists in the field are these presented by Chandler and Petty:

> In advance of the employment of personnel planning must indicate the use to be made of their services, the position of the persons in the organizations plan, and the way in which their services are supposed to contribute to the ultimate objectives of the organization.[27]

Any unusual qualifications needed for the position should be included in the specifications. For example, if the teacher will be expected to serve as an adviser to the senior class or as a homeroom teacher, it is reasonable to consider only applicants who have had some training or experience appropriate to counseling with students and who are interested in the students' social and emotional development as well as their intellectual achievements. These duties and qualifications should be stated in the specifications. Any administrative responsibilities required of the teacher should be included also.

[27] Chandler and Petty, *op. cit.*, p. 12.

It is desirable when a vacancy occurs on the high school faculty that the superintendent of schools consult with the high school principal in planning for the replacement, especially in the writing of the job specifications. Similarly, if the situation permits, the principal should ask the help of his staff in defining the position to be filled. In some large schools a faculty committee works with the principal in the selection process. Advocates of such a committee suggest that this is a logical extension of democratic principles of administration and that the faculty should have a voice in the choosing of new members. Opposition to the use of a selection committee is usually based on the following: (1) A teacher committee is not responsible, officially; if errors are made the administrator is held responsible; (2) many teachers object to being placed in the position of judging future colleagues, although they would like to have a voice in selecting members in their department, especially in larger schools, and (3) details of selecting a person become unnecessarily complicated and time consuming if applicants must deal with a committee as well as with the administrators.

The authors suggest that although it is not desirable to use a selection committee for every vacancy, the principal should seek consultation with any faculty member who can help him improve the quality of selection. Such assistance is most appropriate at the point of preparing written specifications. The idea is to secure as accurate a description of the position as possible, and any aid the staff can give should be sought and utilized.

Announcement of the Vacancy

The purpose of formally announcing a vacancy is threefold: (1) to make known the exact specifications of the position, (2) to announce the qualifications being sought, and (3) to invite institutional placement bureaus, private placement agencies, and individuals to submit names and credentials for consideration.

From the school's point of view, the announcement should have a reasonably wide circulation so that a substantial number of qualified teachers may be considered. In order to secure the best of service by placement agencies, the following suggestions are recommended:

1. Identify the specific subject or subjects to be taught. If you are seeking a teacher of physical science, for instance, do not ask just for a science teacher. Name the actual sciences to be taught — chemistry, physics, earth science, or others intended for this assignment.

2. State the number of classes to be taught — e.g., three classes of chemistry, two classes of physics, and one class of ninth-grade general science.

3. Specify the teaching major and minor field or fields desired. For a combination of subjects, such as English and social studies, indicate in which subject a major is required.

4. State the grade level, i.e., junior high school, senior high school, or specific grade.

5. Identify the degree requirements and state whether or not teaching experience is necessary.

6. Specify extraclass responsibilities. If coaching is involved, be sure to name the sport.

7. Include a copy of the salary schedule or identify the base salary and whether or not there is a differential for men and women.

8. Include a short sentence giving the size and location of the city.

9. Be sure to inform the placement bureau when the position is filled.

10. Always inform the placement agency when you employ one of its candidates.

11. Supply the agency with enough job specification sheets so that a copy may be sent to all individuals expressing interest in the position.

12. Be sure to include information on how and to whom applications should be made.

Some schools include with the job specifications literature about the school, community, housing, living conditions, churches, and other factors which might be of importance to a prospective teacher. Such information is helpful both to the prospective teacher and to the school, for it is a waste of everyone's time and energy to have someone apply and receive consideration only to find late in the screening process that certain conditions in the community make it undesirable for the applicant.

Searching for Able Candidates

Good teachers are always in demand, but the competition for them is especially keen during periods of teacher shortages. Currently there is no oversupply of well-qualified teachers, nor are prospects encouraging for any substantial change in the immediate future. For example, the fall statistics for 1960 revealed that there were 24,300 teachers with substandard credentials employed full time in public secondary schools.[28] It is apparent that under these conditions administrators need to be aggressive in searching for teachers if they want to secure top-quality people.

Many large and medium-sized school systems send a representative regularly from their personnel department to visit college placement offices throughout the United States in order to secure teachers. Others seek the assistance of all teachers employed in the system to recommend good prospects known by them. The point is that a school system cannot expect to merely announce its vacancies and have an endless stream of applicants at its door. The exceptions, of course, are the school systems

---

[28] Samuel Schloss and Carol Joy Hobson, *Fall 1960 Statistics on Enrollments, Teachers, and Schoolhousing*, publication of the U.S. Office of Education (Washington: Government Printing Office, 1960), p. 2.

which have unusually high salary schedules or are located in communities recognized as highly desirable places in which to live and work.

We do not suggest that a school will have no applicants if it does not develop elaborate recruiting schemes and practices. But administrators must be sensitive to the need for actively and continuously recruiting applicants rather than merely relying on the announcement of a vacancy if they are interested in securing the best possible candidates.

Preliminary Review of Applications

It should be the responsibility of the administrators to make a preliminary review of all applications received. This means checking the qualifications of the applicants which can be determined objectively. Usually these items are a matter of record and contained in the credentials furnished by the placement agencies. For instance, it is possible to determine whether or not the applicant meets the specifications prepared previously with respect to degrees, major and minors, academic achievement, experience, age, sex, and any other items of this type regarded as minimum requirements of the position.

All applicants who meet these requirements should be listed and considered for further screening. Applicants who do not pass the preliminary screening should be so notified and have their credentials returned to the placement agencies. From a public relations point of view, it is important also to acknowledge immediately all applications received. This may be done quickly and easily if a postcard or form letter has been prepared in advance which recognizes receipt of the application and tells what disposition will be made of it.

It is a very common practice for school systems to develop their own application form and require all applicants to complete it. Use of such a form has the advantage of securing similar information from all prospective employees.

Testing of Applicants

The purpose of testing applicants is to secure objective estimates of their intelligence, special abilities, knowledge of their special subject, and knowledge in the professional education field. Schools that utilize a testing procedure either prepare their own examinations or use regular standardized examinations prepared by testing companies. Applicants usually are required to come to the school or city on a designated date to participate in the examination. However, some schools use the results of the National Teacher Examination, which is administered periodically in different centers throughout the United States. All applicants who write the examinations are ranked according to the test scores. It is determined locally what relative weight shall be given to each examination or whether or not all candidates who receive a particular score or above are to be considered for further screening.

Use of written examinations as a part of the screening process is far from being a settled issue among school administrators, although tests have been used extensively in industry and government. Arguments favoring the examinations are as follows: (1) All candidates can be compared on a common basis, i.e., intelligence and academic achievement; (2) standardized examination results reduce personal bias and unprofessional influence by providing a reasonably objective estimate of ability; and (3) the tests give credit to teachers who are well prepared academically.

Administrators opposed to the use of examinations as a screening process usually make the following objections: (1) There is no conclusive evidence that the characteristics tested are valid predictors of teaching success; (2) tests are expensive; (3) it is inconvenient for applicants to take examinations; (4) testing complicates and delays the screening process unnecessarily; and (5) testing implies a certain distrust of the records and recommendations of teacher training institutes.

As in all debates, there is some support for both sides. An important argument relates to the validity of tests in predicting teacher success and their ability to measure intelligence and academic achievement. Those who doubt the ability of tests results to predict teaching success are correct on the basis of information now available. We cannot yet identify the qualities highly correlated with teaching success, as was indicated earlier in this chapter. The use of tests to compare general ability and knowledge of subject matter, however, is defended by Arthur L. Benson, Director, Teacher Examinations, Educational Testing Service:

> On the question of the validity of tests for predicting teaching effectiveness, the agnostic is right. We simply do not have the answer, and neither those who denounce tests nor those who laud them can do so on the basis of sound research. . . .
>
> . . . The appraisal of a candidate's knowledge of certain specialized professional fields [is] more validly and reliably evaluated by well-constructed objective tests prepared by specialists on these fields than by any other known appraisal technique. . . .
>
> . . . In summary, the charge that tests are not valid is without support. The validity of tests for predicting teacher effectiveness is unknown, and will remain so until more rigorous criteria of teacher effectiveness are developed. On the other hand, the validity of tests for appraising certain knowledges and abilities of prospective teachers has been repeatedly demonstrated by research, and further rational controversy on this issue seems pointless. . . .[29]

[29] Arthur L. Benson, "Testing Procedures in the Administration of Educational Personnel," *Education,* December, 1954, 75:245–46.

Whether or not a school system decides to use standardized tests will depend upon personal opinions as to the relative importance placed upon a teacher's ability and knowledge in specialized fields. Schools that include intelligence and knowledge of subject matter as criteria for selection will find the use of examinations helpful. Schools that do not choose to include such criteria for selection would incur unnecessary expense and waste time using examinations. It seems as though the matter of expense, delay in screening, and inconvenience to applicants are of minor consequence if the school really finds the information helpful in selecting the best person for the position.

The authors recommend testing as a part of the screening process in schools which have a relatively large number of candidates for the various vacancies. If the school is small, with few applicants for each position, testing is probably impractical.

Interviewing Selected Applicants

Use of a personal interview as one of the later steps in the selection process is almost universal. In spite of all the data contained in formal credentials plus the information gathered by tests or other instruments, there are a number of personal qualifications which cannot always be identified in a teacher's credentials, and they might be highly important for a particular position. Consequently, there appears to be no substitute for a personal interview. In many cases it has carried as much weight as any other single aspect of the selection process. Administrators place a great deal of confidence in their ability to select teachers on the basis of a talk or visit with them. Berry notes the relative importance of the interview in the selection process:

> The interview is not an infallible instrument but we dare not neglect it when we select personnel. As yet, we have not developed instruments for measuring personal qualifications that can take its place. In a brief employment interview, often only one-half hour or less, impressions of personality are given that make or break an applicant and guide the employer in selecting a well qualified or poorly qualified person. . . . When the interview is well done and is used along with certain diagnostic measures, it is generally considered to be the most important method in personnel selection.[30]

If the personal interview is going to continue to play such an important part in the selection of teachers, and there appears to be no indication to the contrary, it should be well planned in order to serve its purposes most effectively. Basically, the interview is a conversation between the applicant and the interviewer or interviewers with two major purposes: (1) to allow the employer to determine whether or not the applicant

[30] Aubrey L. Berry, "Art of Interviewing Teachers," *Nation's Schools*, June, 1955, 55:63.

possesses those personal qualities or other characteristics established in the specifications for the position and (2) to allow the applicant to determine whether or not the position will be personally satisfactory to him. The interview must be a two-way affair in which there is a free exchange of ideas and points of view. It is a waste of time to use the interview to discuss items which are a matter of record and can be secured by examining the credentials of the applicant or a brochure about the school and community. Ideally, the interview should focus on questions or issues intended to reveal attitudes or personal characteristics not revealed in other ways.

It is generally considered wise to have more than one person interview a candidate and then combine their reactions into a composite rating. Both the principal and the superintendent should interview the applicant whenever possible. Additional interviews with the department chairman, special supervisors, assistant principals, or other administrative personnel are desirable. At times, candidates must be interviewed at a considerable distance from the community, in which case it is not practical to have more than one administrator do the interviewing.

Care should be exercised in questioning a candidate so that answers are not suggested by the interviewers. For example, to say, "I think that talented students should be taught in homogeneously grouped classes. Don't you agree with me?" encourages an applicant either to enter into a debate or merely to agree with the interviewer rather than to state his point of view. It is important to remember that one purpose of the interview is to provide the applicant an opportunity to express himself; there is no need for the interviewer to deliver a lecture.

Adequate time should be scheduled for the interview so that all concerned will feel relaxed rather than as though the time taken for discussion were an imposition on the interviewer. Interruptions should be avoided during the scheduled period. It is most disconcerting to have an interview broken constantly by telephone conversations or by a secretary running in and out of the office.

Some candidates may have traits which produce a "halo" effect so that the interviewer does not give adequate attention to all qualities being sought. For example, an attractive woman might impress a male interviewer favorably because of her appearance in spite of other attributes which are serious limitations. Attention to the criteria prepared in advance will assist in focusing questions and observations on other factors considered to be important. Some schools use a rating form which includes all characteristics specified. Each interviewer is requested to rate the person on all traits observed. We do not wish to imply that outstanding traits should be overlooked or deprecated. On the contrary, due credit should be given for strong features providing they are characteristics appropriate to the needs of the position.

SELECTION OF THE STAFF

TABLE 24

Selected Items Discussed in Less Than 20 Per Cent of the 106 Initial Interviews

Subject	Total Questioned	Per Cent
Type of work experience	20	18.8
Teaching philosophy	15	14.2
Your interest in children	12	11.3
College grade-point average	10	9.4
Professional ambitions	8	7.5
Preparation and qualifications which you believe will help you in the teaching profession	8	7.5
Why you want to teach	7	6.6
Honors, college distinctions	6	5.7
How much you enjoy working with people	5	4.7
Per cent of expenses earned in college	3	2.8
Personal traits which you believe will help you as a teacher	1	0.9
Travel experience	0	0

Source: Richard A. Siggelkow, "Meaningful Interviews with Beginning Teachers," *Nation's Schools*, June, 1954, 53:45. Copyright 1954 by The Modern Hospital Publishing Co., Inc., Chicago.

Closing an interview is especially important from the applicant's point of view. Naturally, he is interested in knowing the outcome of the interview and what the next steps are in the selection process. The administrator should make it a point to tell the candidate exactly what he may expect as a result of the interview. He must also make certain that any commitments or promises made to the candidate are fulfilled promptly.

Extensive research on the extent to which interviews are conducted according to the above suggestions is very limited. One study was made, however, of the content of 106 initial interviews between school administrators and prospective teachers at the Teacher Placement Bureau, University of Wisconsin.[31] In this study four criteria were considered important to a successful interview:

1. Does the prospective employer give teaching candidates the opportunity to express themselves adequately and present their own views?
2. Does he conserve valuable time during the interview by not discussing items with which the candidates are probably already familiar?
3. Does he acquaint candidates with information about typical living conditions and other matters of personal concern to them as future members of his community?
4. Does he attempt, through key questions, to gain some insight into the individual's philosophy?

[31] Richard A. Siggelkow, "Meaningful Interviews with Beginning Teachers," *Nation's Schools*, June, 1954, 53:43–46.

STAFF ORGANIZATION AND RELATIONSHIPS

TABLE 25

The 25 Most Frequently Discussed Items During Initial Conferences with 35 Hiring Officials

Item	Times Reported	Per Cent
Specific classes and grades candidate is to teach[a]	104	98.0
School enrollment	95	89.6
Extra class or cocurricular assignments[a]	83	78.3
Size of classes candidate is to teach[a]	83	78.3
Population of the community[a]	83	78.3
Condition of physical plant[a]	70	66.0
Location of community	70	66.0
Room facilities (school)[a]	70	66.0
Number of teachers[a]	64	60.4
Typical living conditions for teachers[c]	64	60.4
Transportation facilities[a]	59	55.7
General educational and cultural level of population[a]	54	50.9
Enrollment trends[a]	50	47.2
Practice teaching experience[b]	46	43.2
Size of community in which candidate was raised[b]	44	41.5
Financial ability of community to support schools[a]	44	41.5
Number of new teachers in school[a]	42	39.6
Dominant nationality groups[a]	40	37.7
Philosophy of the school[a]	40	37.7
Other schools in community[a]	39	36.7
Cost of room and board[a]	39	36.7
Recreational opportunities[a]	36	33.9
Churches in community[a]	35	33.0
Dominant vocational group[a]	35	33.0
Engagement or marriage plans[b]	34	32.1

[a] Introduced into discussion by both candidates and hiring official, but initiated more frequently by hiring official.
[b] Asked by hiring official only.
[c] Introduced into discussion by both candidate and hiring official, but initiated most frequently by candidate.
Source: Richard A. Siggelkow, "Meaningful Interviews with Beginning Teachers," *Nation's Schools*, June, 1954, 53:45. Copyright 1954 by The Modern Hospital Publishing Co., Inc., Chicago.

Administrators who could answer yes to these questions were definitely in the minority. An analysis of the topics actually discussed in the interviews revealed that administrators need to give greater attention to their interviewing technique, because the percentage of questions asked that would allow for observation of personal qualities was relatively small. The data contained in Table 24 reveal that many of the items which would enable a candidate to demonstrate personality characteristics were discussed in less than 20 per cent of the 106 interviews. Similarly, the data in Table 25 reveal that the twenty-five most frequently discussed items during the interviews were concerned primarily with matters of an informal character which could have been handled through other means or were probably already known by the candidate.

Interviewing of applicants for teaching positions undoubtedly will continue for many years to come. It can be an effective means for gathering information about candidates not available in any other way. The interview's usefulness can be increased considerably, however, if it is planned and executed with this specific purpose in mind.

Observation of Candidates in Teaching Situations

Following the interviews, the candidates should be ranked in order of preference for final screening. If at all possible, the final screening should include a visit to the classrooms of the top-ranking candidates by one of the administrators in order to observe them in their regular teaching situations. The visit should serve mainly as a final check on whether or not all other indications of the person's desirability as a teacher are corroborated in his actual teaching. In addition, attention should be centered on his teaching skill and ability to establish good teacher-pupil rapport and a favorable environment for learning. Observations of this type will be important as a supplement to information and observations secured through the other steps in the screening process.

Permission to visit a teacher's classroom should be secured in advance from the principal of the school. Arrangements should be made with the teacher also as to an appropriate date for the visit. Efforts should be made to have visiting conditions as favorable as possible so that the teacher will not be surprised or emotionally upset because she was unaware of the intended visit.

Use of a visit to teachers as part of the screening process will cause some delay in the final selections, and it will increase the expense of the process, but it should aid considerably in the selection of the best candidate for the position.

Recommendations for Appointment

It is the responsibility of the principal to recommend to the superintendent the teacher who he thinks meets the specifications for the position. This recommendation should be arrived at after thoughtful consideration of all applicants. Some principals recommend more than one person as meeting their standards and the superintendent chooses from those recommended. Others name the applicants in order of preference. Any of these practices is acceptable as long as the principal's preferences are indicated to guide the superintendent.

Upon receipt of the recommendations of the principal, the superintendent of schools makes his choice for recommendation to the board of education. If the superintendent is not in agreement with the principal on the candidates submitted, he should state his differences of opinion and return the names to the principal for further consideration.

Appointment by the Board of Education

The board of education receives recommendations for appointment from the superintendent and either appoints the teachers recommended or requests additional names from the superintendent if none of the candidates is acceptable to the board. Only in most unusual circumstances, such as the serious illness of the superintendent, should the board appoint someone *not* recommended by the superintendent. But even in such situations the board should not initiate the appointment of a teacher. Some other staff employee should represent the administration and recommend the person to the board. Some administrators provide for the final selection by the board by recommending more than one person as being acceptable, but the desirability of this procedure will depend upon the agreement of the superintendent and the board on final selection.

Action of the board in approving the candidate should be recorded in the minutes of the board, and such action should be taken only in an official meeting of the board. Securing approval of a candidate individually from members when the board is not in session makes the legality of the action open to question. Administrators should be aware of the legal requirements in the appointment procedures within their particular state so that they will not place the members of the board in embarrassing positions by requesting them to take action improperly.

Issuing a Contract

A contract approved by the board of education should be issued to the teacher immediately after the appointment. It is recommended that immediate notification of the fact that a contract is being mailed should be communicated to the teacher by telephone or telegram so that there is no chance of his being lost to some other school just because of delay in letting him know of his appointment. Teachers will appreciate the demonstration of concern and consideration by the school officials in taking such special action. Issuance of the contract should then be done according to the legal provisions of the state in which the school is located. This action completes the selection procedure.

QUESTIONS AND GROUP PROJECTS

1. Inquire about the extent to which principals are involved in the selection of teachers by consulting some of the secondary school principals in your county. From your results, does it appear that secondary school principals play a major role in this process?
2. Why is it considered undesirable for the board of education to handle the screening and interviewing of teacher applicants?

3. Describe what you would consider to be an ideal procedure for selecting a teacher in your own major subject field.
4. Organize a debate within the class on which is more important in teaching: knowledge of the subjects or methods of teaching.
5. How can you best determine whether a person has personal qualities which will make for success in teaching?
6. Prepare an announcement of a vacancy for a teaching position.
7. Prepare a brochure describing your school and community, including such information as you feel a prospective teacher would desire.

Selected References

American Association of School Administrators. *Staff Relations in School Administration.* Thirty-third Yearbook. Washington: National Education Association, 1955.

Barr, A. S. "The Measurement and Prediction of Teacher Efficiency," *Journal of Experimental Education,* June, 1948, 16:203–83.

Benson, Arthur L. "Testing Procedures in the Administration of Educational Personnel," *Education,* December, 1954, 75:244–51.

Benson, Charles S. *The Economics of Public Education.* Boston: Houghton Mifflin Company, 1961.

Berry, Aubrey L. "Art of Interviewing Teachers," *Nation's Schools,* June, 1955, 55:63–66.

Black, Willis J., and M. Jerome Page. "Recruitment and Selection of Elementary Teachers," *Review of Educational Research,* June, 1958, 28:198–205.

Carlile, Amos B. "Predicting Performance in the Teaching Profession," *Journal of Educational Research,* May, 1954, 47:641–68.

Chandler, B. J., and Paul V. Petty. *Personnel Management in School Administration.* Yonkers, N.Y.: World Book Company, 1955.

Clark, Alfred H. "Interviews, Conferences, and Oral Examinations as Techniques in Administration of Educational Personnel," *Education,* December, 1954, 75:252–58.

Doll, Ronald C. "High School Pupils' Attitudes Toward Teaching Procedures," *School Review,* April, 1947, 55:222–27.

Elsbree, Willard S., and E. Edmund Reutter, Jr. *Staff Personnel in the Public Schools.* Englewood Cliffs, N.J.: Prentice-Hall, Inc., 1954.

Fields, Harold. "Group Interview, A New Testing Technique," *School Executive,* December, 1950, 70:48.

Gaier, Eugene L., Stewart Jones, and Ray H. Simpson. "Factors Related to Measures of Professional Resourcefulness," *School Review,* March, 1953, 61:158–62.

Gowan, J. C. "Use of Adjective Check List in Screening Teaching Candidates," *Journal of Educational Research,* 1956, 49:663–72.

Griffiths, Daniel E. *Human Relations in School Administration.* New York: Appleton-Century-Crofts, Inc., 1956.

Highet, Gilbert. *The Art of Teaching.* New York: Alfred A. Knopf, Inc., 1950.

Levin, Harry. "A New Perspective on Teacher Competence Research," *Harvard Educational Review,* Spring, 1954, 24:98–105.

McAulay, John D. "Qualifications of a Good Teacher," *Peabody Journal of Education,* July, 1954, 32:22–25.

Michael, William B., Earle E. Herold, and Eugene W. Cryan. "Survey of Student-Teacher Relationships," *Journal of Educational Research,* May, 1951, 44:657–73.

Moore, Harold E., and Newell B. Walters. *Personnel Administration in Education.* New York: Harper & Brothers, 1955.

Murray, Thomas. "Should Letters of Recommendation Be Abolished?" *Nation's Schools,* June, 1949, 43:47.

Ojeman, Ralph H. "Identifying Effective Classroom Teachers," *National Elementary Principal,* September, 1952, 32:130–38.

Remmers, H. H., *et al.* "Second Report of the Committee on Criteria of Teacher Effectiveness," *Journal of Educational Research,* 1953, 46:641–58.

Ryans, David G. *Characteristics of Teachers.* Washington: American Council on Education, 1960.

Ryans, David G. "Interview in Teacher Selection Can Be Improved and Used Effectively," *Nation's Schools,* June, 1949, 43:45–46.

Ryans, David G. "Investigation of Teacher Characteristics," *Educational Record,* May, 1954, 47:695–703.

Ryans, David G. "Local Selection, Placement, and Administrative Relations," *Journal of Educational Research,* 1949, 19:210–18.

Scates, Douglas E. "Good Teachers: Establishing Criteria for Identification," *Journal of Teacher Education,* June, 1950, 1:137–41.

Schloss, Samuel, and Carol Joy Hobson. *Fall 1960 Statistics on Enrollments, Teachers, and Schoolhousing.* Publication of the U.S. Office of Education. Washington: Government Printing Office, 1960.

Siggelkow, Richard A. "Meaningful Interviews with Beginning Teachers," *Nation's Schools,* June, 1954, 53:43–46.

Stephenson, Chester M. "Married or Single Elementary Teachers?" *Ohio Schools,* December, 1953, 31:426.

Tiedeman, Stuart C. "A Study of Public-Teacher Relationships," *Journal of Educational Research,* May, 1942, 35:657–64.

Weber, Clarence A. *Personnel Problems of School Administrators.* New York: McGraw-Hill Book Company, 1954.

Witty, Paul. "An Analysis of the Personality Traits of the Effective Teacher," *Journal of Educational Research,* May, 1947, 40:662–71.

V

Student Relationships

Much of the high school principal's job is occupied with relationships between students and the school, such as the development of mature behavior on the part of students. Skill in handling the concomitant problems comes with insight into adolescent psychology, as well as some practical know-how in dealing with misbehavior. Chapter 15 discusses the nature of self-discipline and the means of fostering it in teen-age students. Consideration is given also to deciding on school policies and procedures with respect to discipline. Corrective procedures are discussed, including legal provisions for such practices as corporal punishment and suspension and expulsion of students. A number of administrative guides having to do with discipline are suggested; they deal with such matters as the school's relationship with law enforcement officers, support of teachers in discipline cases, and the principal-parent relationship.

Chapter 16 takes up school records and reports, offering suggestions for planning an efficient and effective system of records. In addition, some of the basic types of records are presented along with recommendations concerning their use. Special consideration is given to certain key records such as the cumulative record, the permanent record, transcript of credits, marks and reports to parents, and attendance records. Various administrative procedures are suggested also as they relate to problems associated with pupil personnel records.

CHAPTER 15

The Principal's Role in Discipline

More than two thousand years ago Socrates was moved to make the following protest about the deportment of the youth of his day:

> The children now love luxury; they show disrespect for elders and love to chatter in the place of exercise. Children are now tyrants, not the servants of their households. They no longer rise when elders enter the room. They contradict their parents, chatter before company, gobble up dainties at the table, cross their legs, and tyrannize over their teachers.[1]

Elders have been protesting ever since. Now, as in the days of ancient Greece, youth continue to distress adults with brash and disrespectful conduct. There are built-in differences, physiological and psychological, between older and younger people which make it difficult for them to fully understand each other. As a result, teachers have been challenged by discipline problems ever since students were organized in groups for instructional purposes, and they are likely to continue to experience difficulties in developing socially acceptable behavior by youth. The problem is complicated by the fact that discipline is not a problem for which there is a permanent solution. Just when it appears as though Johnny has licked his problems, he graduates and a new Johnny comes along with the same problems. The process of teaching good behavior has to start all over again.

[1] National Education Association, Research Division, "Teacher Opinion on Pupil Behavior, 1955–56," *Research Bulletin*, April, 1956, 34:53.

Rational laymen recognize that educating youth to behave in a socially responsible manner is an immensely complex task and must be shared by the home, church, government, school, and other institutions and agencies. Nevertheless, the public, through local actions and legal decisions, has indicated that it expects teachers to act *in loco parentis* and by extension delegates to teachers the authority and responsibility to discipline.

The importance attached to good discipline in the schools is reflected by the spate of articles by laymen on the subject. Representative of the view expressed in many of these essays is the following excerpt:

> Educational *discipline*, in the pre-space era, suffered from a softening of the spine comparable to the sogginess of the curriculum. And what is frustrating in the end, is the entire process we call education. . . . A new philosophy is demanded by the times. School is neither a playpen, a social agency, nor a prison. It is a right — the right to an education.[2]

In addition, studies of factors related to the failure of teachers have reported that the most frequent reason for dismissal is inability to discipline students. Griffith's statement, based on a study in 1958, is typical of the findings of most of the studies:

> As in earlier studies of teacher dismissal, this study shows that inability to control pupils remains a major factor in teacher dismissal. . . . And again, the major reason for dismissing . . . teachers was the inability to control pupils placed in their charge. Of 283 dismissals, 39.5% were dismissed for this reason.[3]

Although it is undoubtedly true that some of these teachers were dismissed because of unreasonable requirements imposed by local individuals or groups, nevertheless the importance attached to managing the conduct of youth in school cannot be viewed lightly by members of the profession. One of the popular criteria for the success of a high school principal is his ability to maintain good standards of student conduct; if he lacks this ability he is in serious trouble.

Most school administrators recognize the fact that principals are pressured daily to deal with discipline problems. Teachers find the principal their most dependable source of assistance in dealing with difficult cases. Students recognize him as the authority of the school as well as a friend and counselor in matters of misbehavior on their part. Members of the board of education and the superintendent of schools expect to be kept

---

[2] Howard Whitman, "Throw the Rowdies Out," *Better Homes and Gardens*, September, 1959, pp. 34 ff.

[3] LeRoy H. Griffith, "Reasons for Teacher Dismissal in Public Secondary Schools of Iowa," unpublished Ph.D. dissertation, State University of Iowa, 1958, p. 155.

informed on serious discipline problems, but for the most part they delegate to the principal the responsibility for these matters in his school. The police, juvenile courts, and other community agencies look to him as the liaison person in the school with whom they will work most closely in dealing with juvenile problems. Whether he likes it or not, most people look upon him as the "disciplinarian" of the school. The principal cannot disregard matters of discipline, and is obligated to do as much as possible to develop a positive program in his school.

Definition of Discipline

Basic to all questions of discipline in the school is the need to agree on what we mean by the term and what kind of discipline we want in our schools. One of the serious complications in defining discipline is the fact that most people have widely divergent views on the subject. To some, discipline means the ability to control the behavior of individuals. Others see it as conformity to rules and regulations. Memories of the "birch rod" and physical punishment still persist in the minds of some adults as representing school discipline. Even Webster has a variety of definitions, including the following:

1. Teaching; instruction.
2. That which is taught to pupils.
3. Training which corrects, molds, strengthens, or perfects.
4. Punishment; chastisement.
5. Control gained by enforcing obedience or order, as in a school or an army.
6. Rule or system of rules affecting conduct or action.
7. To develop by instruction and exercise; to train in self-control or obedience to given standards.

For years discipline in schools meant punishment for the violation of rules and the enforcement of regulations imposed upon students by the authorities of the school. Webster recognizes these concepts of discipline but points out that discipline can be characterized by a process of education designed to improve and perfect behavior; furthermore, discipline may have as its goal obedience to rules and regulations based on self-control or self-discipline. Present-day educators are in general agreement that, although discipline in the school still involves the establishment of rules and regulations, the major emphasis should be on securing a high degree of self-discipline in students.

As society has become increasingly complex, and as fates of nations depend more and more upon the exercise of reasoned judgment in human relations and international affairs, the need to help future citizens of the world develop behavior controlled from *within* rather than imposed from without has become critical. Sheviakov and Redl reflect present-day attitudes in their support of this viewpoint:

> Problems of discipline and self-control assume a new significance and realism in today's world. In a complex civilization, the individual often has to subjugate his personal inclinations, whims, comforts, even some of his liberties to bigger goals than personal ones. In the uncertainty of a "divided world" where peaceful coexistence of conflicting philosophies of life may at any time be terminated by armed conflict, the individual must be ready to renounce for the good of the group even his wish to survive. If the democratic philosophy is to flourish, our ways of living and believing, the ideals of generations must be preserved. For this we need children and young people who cherish these ideals above all and who, therefore, are ready to endure privation and to exercise the utmost self-control.[4]

School discipline in harmony with the above viewpoint has the following characteristics: (1) Student behavior is largely self-controlled, (2) authority is vested primarily in humanitarian principles rather than in a person, (3) obedience to rules and regulations is based on an understanding of the reasons for such requirements rather than on accepting someone's word for them, (4) school activities and classroom experiences are designed to provide opportunities to develop socially acceptable behavior, and (5) emphasis is on treating behavior problems according to the background of individual students.

Ideals and principles are necessary guides in planning a program aimed at achieving self-discipline, but someone has to see to it that appropriate practices are implemented. In the case of school discipline, it is the principal who is the responsible person. The following discussion is intended, therefore, to describe the role of the principal in matters pertaining to school discipline and to recommend certain practices which research and experience support.

Establishing Policies and Procedures

There is no very logical reason why school officials should wait until difficult situations arise to begin to think about the best way to handle discipline problems. In general, the establishment of policies and procedures relating to discipline help to (1) diminish the possibility of extreme behavior in a crisis situation, (2) encourage a united front on discipline, and (3) increase the degree to which disciplinary actions may be executed intelligently.

[4] George V. Sheviakov and Fritz Redl, "Let's Look at Discipline," *Discipline for Today's Children and Youth* (Washington: Association for Supervision and Curriculum Development, National Education Association, 1956), p. 1.

Board of Education Policies

High on the list of priorities of positive disciplinary procedure is the establishment of policies by the board of education. These will provide the general framework within which the individual units of the school system must operate. It is imperative that teachers, administrators, and students know the board's attitude in these matters, since everyone concerned may become confused if recommendations or actions by the staff are not in harmony with those of the board. Without some agreement on policy to guide faculty action, administrators and teachers are shooting in the dark and their decisions will probably not have the support of the board. Illustrative of general board policies on discipline are those established by the Board of Trustees of the Salinas Union High School District, Salinas, California:

> The board of trustees of the Salinas Union High School District, in support of the aims of public education, believes that behavior of students attending public schools shall reflect standards of good citizenship demanded of members of a democratic society. Self discipline (responsibility for one's actions) is one of the important, ultimate goals of education. The board of trustees believes, also, that while education is a right of American youth, it is not an absolute right. It is qualified first by eligibility requirements and secondly by performance requirements. As regards to performance requirements, our courts speak of education as a limited right or a privilege. That is, *should a pupil fail to perform those duties required of him upon attendance in public schools, he may be excluded from school.*

The board thereupon adopted a four point policy.

> 1. Students shall respect constituted authority. This shall include conformity to school rules and regulations and those provisions of law which apply to the conduct of juveniles or minors.
>
> 2. Citizenship in a democracy requires respect for the rights of others and demands cooperation with all members of the school community. Student conduct shall reflect consideration for the rights and privileges of others.
>
> 3. High personal standards of courtesy, decency, morality, clean language, honesty and wholesome relationships with others shall be maintained. Respect for real and personal property, pride in one's work and achievement within one's ability shall be expected of all students.
>
> 4. Every student who gives evidence of a sincere desire to remain in school, to be diligent in studies, and to profit by the educational experiences provided will be given every opportunity to do so and will be assisted in every way possible to achieve scholastic success to the limit of individual ability.[5]

---

[5] Donald P. Shock, "How to Put Teeth in a Discipline Policy," *School Management*, April, 1959. Reprinted by permission from *School Management*. Copyright 1959 by School Management Magazines, Inc.

Faculty Policies

Once the board of education has established general policies, it is the responsibility of the professional staff to define supporting policies and procedures to be followed in each building unit. The approach recommended by the authors in establishing discipline policies is the same as that for establishing other faculty policies, namely, the use of committees, faculty discussions, and other related procedures discussed in Chapter 13. Although the faculty is expected to set up supplemental policies on student behavior, it is desirable that students and parents participate in discussions preceding their formulation so that they will have an opportunity to influence the policies, rules, and regulations within which they must operate. The student council and Parent-Teacher Association are logical sources for securing student and parent representatives.

Student Codes

In addition to statements prepared by the faculty, some schools find it valuable to have students develop a "code of ethics" or "code of behavior." A favorable feature of a code of ethics is that it provides a positive statement of principles concerning behavior, and it implements the general idea of developing self-discipline rather than discipline based on external controls. An example of a code of ethics developed by students with suggested actions corresponding to each principle is the Bill of Rights and Duties of the Barrington Consolidated High School, Barrington, Illinois:[6]

BILL OF RIGHTS AND DUTIES

1. Because it is my right to elect student representatives to govern the student body . . .   it is my duty to elect those who can lead us wisely and to give them my full cooperation.

2. Because it is my right to have free speech, assembly, press, and religion . . .   it is my duty to allow others the same privilege.

3. Because it is my right to have free education and to choose subjects which interest me . . .   it is my duty to use my privilege to the best of my ability.

4. Because it is my right to act with freedom . . .   it is my duty to conduct myself so that I will not interfere with others.

5. Because it is my right to participate in school activities . . .   it is my duty to do my best in these activities and to uphold the name of the school at all times.

---

[6] *The Roundup*, student handbook, Barrington Consolidated High School, Barrington, Ill., p. 3.

6. Because it is my right to use school and public property . . .   it is my duty to care for and respect this property.

7. Because it is my right to enjoy all of these rights . . .   it is my duty to accept the responsibility of preserving these rights.

Rules and Regulations for Students

Although it is a goal of education to develop self-discipline on the part of high school students, educators realize the need for specific rules and regulations to guide student conduct. Teaching self-discipline is a gradual process to be achieved through a gradual reduction in the number of rules and regulations imposed in maintaining a favorable learning environment.

General recognition of the need for rules and regulations is evidenced by the fact that practically every student handbook examined by the authors from hundreds of high schools contains them. Board of education policies, faculty policies, and codes of ethics often are missing, but rules and regulations are standard features. Rules frequently deal with the following topics:

1. Locks and lockers
2. Hall permits
3. Use of halls between periods
4. School property
5. Noon driving
6. Reserved parking
7. Smoking
8. Assemblies
9. Cafeteria behavior
10. Study halls
11. Student lounge
12. Fire drills
13. Attendance and absences
14. Tardiness
15. Homework
16. Makeup work
17. Report cards
18. School parties

There is considerable variation in the degree to which different schools spell out their rules and regulations, but most schools tend to be specific in their statements. Typical is the following concerning student behavior during school assemblies:

Assemblies

Any group wishing to give an assembly should inform the Assembly Committee of the nature of the program and set a tentative date for its presentation. If the committee approves the program it will definitely set the date and clear the assembly with the Clearing House Committee. The Assembly Committee has the power to refuse permission for the presentation of poorly prepared or undesirable assemblies.

Assembly Conduct

Because we wish our assemblies to be above criticism, the Student Council asks you to comply with this behavior code. Students and faculty are asked to:

1. Attend assemblies on time;
2. Take seats promptly and stay seated until dismissed;
3. Stay for the entire program unless special permission to leave is obtained from a member of the Ushers Club;
4. Refrain from excessive applause such as whistling, stamping feet;
5. Refrain from applause at assemblies having religious significance;
6. Refrain from using the rails and seats for foot rests;
7. Refrain from eating, throwing things, or causing unnecessary disturbance;
8. Give courteous attention to all people kind enough to appear before us.

The Ushers Club and Monitors with the cooperation of the faculty will seek to solve problems arising from the failure of individuals to abide by the code.[7]

Similar rules and regulations should be developed for those problems for which the faculty and students feel the need for guidance and control. Such problems will vary considerably from school to school. Although it is desirable to keep rules and regulations to a minimum, some are necessary in high schools, and they usually are most effective when drafted cooperatively by faculty and students.

Counseling

The achievement of self-discipline is dependent upon the ability of the individual to assess the consequences of his own behavior and to act accordingly. This, in turn, is a major objective of a counseling and guidance program. Individual counseling is a positive approach to discipline, which stresses the belief in developing every human being as a unique personality. It stands in contrast with negative approaches which use various forms of punishment for misbehavior.

No doubt the principal, and/or the assistant principal, will be expected to carry a good bit of the load in such counseling. He should not be expected, however, to assume the total responsibility for it. All professional personnel, i.e., teachers, counselors, and administrators, must share in counseling pupils in discipline matters. Some teachers and counselors feel strongly that they should have no hand in this type of counseling. Their argument is that it works against them in establishing rapport with students and handicaps them in other counseling situations or in working effectively with the students in the classroom.

The authors recognize that counselors should not become tagged as the "disciplinarians" of the school and that teachers should not be expected to do a great deal of individual counseling. On the other hand, discipline which is based on the philosophy of developing self-control cannot be isolated from the total experiences of the pupil in the school,

[7] *Through the Doors of Mt. Pleasant High*, Mt. Pleasant High School Student Council, Mt. Pleasant, Mich., p. 9.

including his relationships with counselors and teachers. A positive approach to discipline through individual counseling by the entire staff is aimed at long-range gains rather than mere control of behavior or the doling out of punishment for violations of rules.

Corrective Procedures

Punishment for the violation of rules and regulations is an accepted practice in most societies in which there is a desire to live an orderly life. And even in a democratic society, relying heavily, as it does, upon self-control by the individual, it is necessary to establish laws which, if violated, carry some form of punishment. When a motorist is arrested for exceeding the speed limit on the highway, he fully expects to be punished through the assessment of a fine. The offender may resent getting caught, but he is still likely to support the idea that unless there are traffic laws and they are enforced, it would be impossible for people to drive with any degree of safety. It is understood also that if a relatively light fine does not improve his driving, a more severe form of punishment may be imposed upon him such as the revocation of his right to drive an automobile. Schools must employ the same psychology. For instance, when a student deliberately "skips" school or knowingly violates other established rules, he expects to receive some type of punishment as soon as his action is detected by the school officials or his parents.

Knowledge of the fact that there are punishments for misbehavior is a substantial influence in controlling pupil behavior in the school, and no doubt it will continue to be so used by high school faculties. But there are limitations in punishment as a form of treating misbehavior. One of its most serious limitations is that it is a negative approach based upon fear of reprisal rather than on the positive concept that a person should behave in a certain manner just because it is the right thing to do. Another limitation is that, unless the form of punishment is chosen wisely and with discrimination, it may work against other desirable objectives of the school. For example, teachers are concerned with bringing pupils to want to attend school. But they often support detention after school as punishment for minor misbehavior. The contradiction here is that the thing they would like pupils to desire, i.e., attendance in school, is used as punishment. This produces a conflict of values in the mind of the student; he is not sure whether attendance in school is a reward or a punishment. Still another form of the same problem is the practice of using extra study assignments as punishment. An occasional form of punishment is requiring the miscreant to write a theme. Certainly a teacher of composition must find this repugnant. At least, he is well aware that it does not increase the student's interest in written composition. Probably the most serious limitation is that punishment is directed at symptoms rather than causes of misbehavior. A positive program of discipline needs to include techniques for treating the causes of misbehavior as well as controlling the symptoms.

Recognizing individual differences in pupils is just as important in disciplinary action as it is in providing differentiated learning experiences in the classroom. What is effective punishment for one person may be entirely ineffective for another. A principal should beware of having so many automatic penalties in his school that there is no flexibility to exercise judgment in individual cases. Frequently, for instance, an automatic penalty of one-half hour of detention is imposed for a pupil's first case of tardiness. No doubt this plan has served to emphasize the importance of getting to school on time and to control mass tardiness, but for pupils with a record of chronic tardiness the penalty has little value. Tardiness in such cases is merely symptomatic of some other problem — perhaps a health problem, perhaps a family situation. In any event, automatically requiring these offenders to stay after school is not appropriate treatment. It is necessary in such cases to learn as much as possible about each individual and attempt to correct the cause for his tardiness rather than to automatically assess a fixed penalty. The point is that when punishment is used, it must be appropriate to the individual and not applied indiscriminately.

An effort should be made to avoid the use of sarcasm and ridicule with teen-age students. Possibly a sarcastic remark will squelch most students and force them to conform to the wishes of the teacher. Similarly, making the behavior of a teen-ager look ridiculous before his peers is effective in securing conformity. But both of these forms of punishment are in direct conflict with democratic values and modern psychology. Sheviakov and Redl are emphatic in their condemnation:

> ... Shaming Johnny before the class seems effective — at the moment. Modern psychology and our democratic philosophy, however, are all against this method. Why? (a) It ruins the morale of the individual and of others in the group. (b) It destroys respect for authority as others feel resentment of the teacher's attack upon Johnny, or fear that they will be next. (c) The teacher shows by example that we do not have to respect others when we are angry with them. This method does not pay in the long run, since it diminishes the strongest motive for learning self-discipline — self-respect. ...
>
> ... Individuals are not punished as examples to the group. Because each personality is of value, in his own right, he is not used as a "lesson." Such a practice denies the uniqueness of individuals. Punishment — or a term which reflects a truer concept — the re-education of each child, must be based upon analysis of the causes of his behavior and consideration of plans suited to his own needs.[8]

[8] Sheviakov and Redl, *op. cit.*, pp. 10–11.

When punishment is used, it must be appropriate to the nature of the offense and to the individual. In addition, it must be administered and used in such a manner that it does not violate the over-all aim of helping students gradually achieve a high degree of self-discipline. Punishment may be a useful aid providing it is used skillfully by principals and teachers who are aware of its limitations as well as its strengths. Granted that it may be helpful in controlling pupil behavior, it is not a cure-all for school discipline problems. At the secondary school level punishment, at best, is a supplement to other approaches in developing self-control and responsible conduct.

Corporal Punishment

Corporal punishment is discussed separately from other forms of punishment because it raises some special problems. Teachers and administrators have used corporal punishment for hundreds of years. By this time it should be a settled issue, but it continues to be controversial among teachers and parents. It is the authors' opinion that the use of corporal punishment is not appropriate in dealing with high school students. Teen-agers are generally beyond the point where physical punishment is a remedy for misbehavior in school. However, since corporal punishment is still in evidence in some secondary schools, it seems necessary to consider the implications of its use.

The legal question of whether or not a teacher may physically punish a pupil has been settled in a majority of the states in favor of the teacher. Generally, it is legal for teachers to employ corporal punishment unless there are specific state laws or local regulations by the board of education prohibiting it. According to Robert H. Hamilton, Dean of the College of Law, University of Wyoming, the general attitude of the courts is as follows:

> . . . Assuming that corporal punishment is not prohibited by statute or regulation, the courts have said that a teacher is, within reasonable bounds, the substitute for the parent, exercising authority delegated to the teacher, and under such delegated authority may inflict corporal punishment upon the pupil. . . .[9]

Although the majority of states and boards of education allow the use of corporal punishment, it is still necessary for the principal to determine whether or not his state or district sanctions it. For instance, a teacher or principal who used physical punishment upon a pupil under the assumption that it was legal, only to find in a court case that the principal had failed to check local and state provisions in advance, could be found guilty of assault and battery. The high school principal cannot afford to expose himself or his teachers to such a situation.

[9] Robert R. Hamilton, *Legal Rights and Liabilities of Teachers* (Laramie, Wyo.: Laramie Printers, Inc., 1956), pp. 35–36.

Aside from the *right* to administer corporal punishment, additional factors must be considered in specific cases. There is no automatic assurance, for instance, that a jury or a judge will rule in favor of a teacher merely because he has the legal right to administer physical punishment to his pupils. Also under scrutiny will be the intent of the teacher, the seriousness of the misbehavior, and the physical condition of the pupil. Teachers are expected to administer punishment without malice or anger. If a teacher deliberately sets out to do bodily harm to a pupil, a jury will probably not condone his action. Brutality in any form is unlikely to be supported by the courts. Corporal punishment must be applied without anger and with no intent to inflict injury. According to Hamilton, the following conditions are considered by the courts in ruling on corporal punishment cases:

> . . . From the purely legal point of view, even in states in which corporal punishment is permitted, a teacher who resorts to it assumes substantial legal risks. He is bound, under the law, at least to:
> 1. Act from good motives, and not from anger or malice.
> 2. Inflict only moderate punishment.
> 3. Determine what the punishment is in proportion to the gravity of the offense.
> 4. Convince himself that the contemplated punishment is not excessive, taking into account the age, sex, size and physical strength of the pupil to be punished.
> 5. Assume the responsibility that the rule he seeks to enforce is reasonable.[10]

It seems apparent that, although the teacher generally has the legal right to resort to corporal punishment, there are pitfalls enough to cause even the most aggressive individual to think twice before striking a pupil. Unfortunately, sometimes teachers have no intention of inflicting physical punishment, but their tempers wear short and they get involved before they realize it. Let us consider the hypothetical case of Bill Smith, who has a class of slow-learning pupils in Grade 8. Actually Bill has never enjoyed teaching this group of youngsters; college preparatory students have always been his first choice. As a matter of fact, the only reason he agreed to teach this class was that the principal promised to find someone else to take it over at the second semester. Mr. Smith tried diligently to teach his pupils to the best of his ability, but at times he felt that he had reached the limit of his patience.

One morning Bill had an argument with his wife at the breakfast table which left him in a very disagreeable mood. When he was ready to leave for school, he found that the battery of his car was dead. As a result, Mr. Smith arrived at school ten minutes late feeling quite upset.

[10] *Ibid.*, p. 36.

But in spite of his feelings, everything went along reasonably well until the period just before lunch, when he was confronted with his slow-learning class. This was the day that three of his most difficult pupils decided to disrupt the class continuously with their chatter. It was too much for Bill. He grabbed the first boy he could get his hands on and proceeded to shake him vigorously. Unfortunately, Mr. Smith became so violent in his shaking that the boy tried desperately to free himself and in so doing fell against a desk, breaking his leg in the fall.

In this instance the teacher did not plan to use corporal punishment in his classes, but under the tension of the situation, plus the preceding annoyances earlier in the morning, he lost control of his emotions and thus became involved in a possible case of assault and battery. Whether such a case ever gets to court depends upon how much the parents become aroused or how effective the principal is in resolving the conflict. Although the authors are opposed to the use of corporal punishment with high school pupils, occasions like this do arise. It is important, therefore, that teachers be informed on the conditions under which corporal punishment is legal or illegal. In this way the involvement of teachers, pupils, and parents in some rather touchy situations can be kept at a minimum.

Expulsion and Suspension

Teachers and school administrators generally have the reputation for leaning over backwards in favor of pupils when it comes to recommending expulsion or suspension from school. This is as it should be, because any act which takes away anyone's opportunity for continued education is a serious matter and should not be taken lightly. But there are times when the rights of one person must be taken away in order to protect the rights of others. Legal support of this position is well established, according to Edwards:

> The right to attend the public school is not absolute. No pupil has the right to attend if his presence in the school impairs its efficiency or interferes with the rights of other pupils. Consequently, it has been held that a pupil who is mentally ill or physically defective may be excluded from school.[11]

State legislatures generally have recognized this and have established specific statutes for the expulsion and suspension of students. Typical is the Michigan law covering these situations:

> The board may authorize or order the suspension or expulsion from school of any pupil guilty of gross misdemeanor or persistent disobedience, or one having habits or bodily conditions detrimental to the school, whenever in its judgment the interests of the school may demand it.

[11] Newton Edwards, *The Courts and the Public Schools* (Chicago: University of Chicago Press, 1946), p. 506.

This entire matter of suspension and expulsion of pupils is a delicate one both from the point of view of human relations and from that of the legal implications. It is vital for the principal to recognize that the *legal* authority in such matters rests with the board of education. At times principals overlook this fact, assume that they have such authority, and inform pupils that they are expelled. This is an error which can cause considerable embarrassment to the principal if his actions are appealed to the board of education. However, the board may choose to delegate some of its authority to the principal, in which case it usually delegates authority for suspension but retains authority for expulsion. This is a reasonable position and allows the administrator to handle severe cases, while protecting the pupil from a hasty decision by one individual.

There is an important difference between suspension and expulsion. *Suspension is a temporary severing of a pupil's membership in the school whereas expulsion is the permanent severing of a pupil's membership in the school.* Normally, suspension is used in cases in which the school authorities have not given up on the pupil but feel that continued membership in school is contingent upon the pupil's performing certain acts of restitution or committing himself to improved conduct before he can be readmitted to school. For example, in cases of truancy it is common practice to *suspend* the pupil from school until his parents appear with him for a conference with the principal. Here suspension is used to emphasize the seriousness of the offense, to provide an opportunity for a conference with the parents, and to secure a pledge of cooperation from the pupil and his parents that the offense will not be repeated. It is not unusual for some pupils to receive more than one suspension during their high school careers. On the other hand, most pupils consider suspension a serious matter and try not to repeat the offense that incurred it. A high school may have several cases of suspension during a school year, but expulsion is rather rare.

Procedures involving suspension and/or expulsion need to be established in advance and reviewed thoroughly with teachers. If this is not done, teachers sometimes commit the school to action prematurely through lack of understanding of the implications in such cases. Members of the board of education also appreciate working with administrators and teachers who handle disciplinary problems in a rational and systematic manner. In cases of suspension, the authors recommend that the principal (1) verify and document all facts in the case before taking final action; (2) consult with the pupil's parents prior to taking final action; (3) notify the superintendent of schools of the suspension immediately by telephone or direct conversation and follow this with a written summary of the situation and actions taken; (4) notify the parents in writing of the action taken by the school and the reason for this action; (5) indicate to the pupil and the parents what courses of action they should follow to secure reinstatement; (6) report all actions in the case to the faculty.

In cases of expulsion, the procedures to be followed are much the same except that final action is taken by the board of education. This means that the principal should prepare a written recommendation of expulsion to the superintendent, who is responsible for presenting it to the board. It is not uncommon for the pupil to be under suspension during the period in which his status is being reviewed by the board. Final action in expulsion cases should be reported by the superintendent to the principal, who should then transmit the decision to the pupil and his parents and teachers.

Treatment of Group Offenses

Sometimes the principal is confronted with flagrant misbehavior by a large group of students — a gang fight at a football game, a student strike, an unauthorized "skip" day. It is extremely hard to deal effectively with students in a large group, especially when the group is at the height of emotion. At best, these are delicate situations, and the principal must exercise extreme care in handling them. A general rule to follow is to try to contain the action of the group until negotiations can be carried on with its leaders. Often the principal has difficulty in controlling an aroused group unless he can get the cooperation of student leaders. The group will be much more likely to respond to a student leader during a revolt than to the principal. The authority of the latter has been defied already and loyalty has been established to peer leaders.

Illustrative of the problems involved is a case in which approximately 200 students decided to strike in protest of a decision by the high school principal and his staff to discontinue a student "skip" day. The setting was a typical midwestern community of 15,000 people with a high school enrollment of 1,000 students. For many years there had been a traditional "Hobo Day" in spring, when all students were given a holiday. It was the custom on this day to dress like hobos and meet in a large picnic area for a day of roughhouse activities, including a tug of war across a river and a cage ball game between the juniors and the seniors. It was not unusual for a student to have most of his clothing torn away during the day's activities, and there was a great deal of ramming around in automobiles. A rather hectic atmosphere prevailed.

Not surprisingly, these doings were looked upon with considerable disfavor by the faculty. On the other hand, "Hobo Day" did have a long tradition in the community. However, the faculty and the high school principal decided to discontinue it without consulting the students or offering a substitute type of activity.

At first the students seemed to accept the idea, but within a week some of their leaders began to complain. The crisis came within a week following the principal's announcement. At noon, when students were returning to school, a small group of student leaders persuaded approximately 200 students to go to a park directly across the street from the school. Within fifteen minutes a strike was organized and in operation.

It took the form of a protest parade down the main street of the town to the chant of "We want Hobo Day!" A police officer met the group and asked the reason for the commotion. Their explanation was enough, and he proceeded to clear traffic for the group. After all, he too remembered "Hobo Day" and was sympathetic to the cause. It is not difficult to imagine the reaction of the businessmen and other adults who observed the parade. Immediately the telephone of the superintendent and the principal began to ring. "What in the world is going on down there?"

The students' parade finally halted outside the high school building with the students continuing their chant. At this point the principal locked the doors of the school and told the students that unless they returned to classes within ten minutes they would all be expelled. The students did not take the threat very seriously, and finally the principal, realizing that he could not possibly deal with a mob by shouting at it from his window and that the community would not accept a mass expulsion of students, invited the leaders of the group to come forward and negotiate the situation. Within five minutes after the principal agreed to discuss the problem with them, the student leaders had all students back in their classes. The obvious errors in handling this situation were that (1) no students were included in discussions of the reasons for discontinuing "Hobo Day" and (2) the principal threatened the entire group with expulsion, a threat which obviously could not be carried out.

In contrast, the solution was achieved by (1) dealing directly with a few leaders of the group and (2) providing the students an opportunity to deliberate with the administration.

Not all principals are confronted with group misbehavior quite as dramatic as a student strike, but many do get involved in attempts to discipline an entire student body. Use of a "disciplinary assembly" in which the principal takes the entire group to task is not uncommon. Most of the time students will tolerate this approach, but there are always students in the group who are not guilty of the acts for which they are being berated, and they resent this type of treatment. It is the opinion of the authors that a more effective way of handling group discipline is to work through the student leaders, whether they are an organized group such as the student council or simply the active leaders in a particular case.

Outside assistance, such as the police, is sometimes needed to control an explosive situation. Whenever the school opens its activities to the general public — its athletic events, for example — it is a good idea to have policemen on hand; they are trained to handle emergencies which might arise in public gatherings, and frequently misconduct at public affairs sponsored by the school involves non-students rather than the student body.

No one can anticipate all types of large-group problems, and there is no substitute for having resourceful people at the scene. But the principal can anticipate that sooner or later he will deal with a discipline problem involving a large group of pupils.

Administrative Guides in Discipline

Space limitations have made it necessary to limit this discussion largely to the most important administrative problems confronting the high school principal in the matter of discipline. Following are a number of miscellaneous problems which fall in this category.

Relationship with Law Enforcement Officers

Some high school students get involved in unlawful acts, and there are times when law enforcement officers find it necessary to pursue students to school to question them about their activities. Administrators must be prepared to work with law officers in these instances. It is important that the principal anticipate such problems and call on the local chief of police in order to exchange ideas and work out a cooperative relationship. Most law enforcement officers are pleased to have such contact because it is helpful to them in carrying out their duties.

Special consideration is due the matter of interrogation of students by the police. In general, the principal should insist that all contacts with students in the school be made through his office. In addition to knowing who is in the building and for what purpose, he knows that there is a legal question associated with the interrogation of pupils. According to an opinion of the Michigan attorney general, school officials have no right to allow a pupil to be questioned without the consent of his parent or guardian:

> The board of education of a school district is without authority to adopt a rule which would permit law enforcement officers to interrogate children without authorization of parent or guardian. School authorities cannot lawfully waive the privilege of the child against self-incrimination relative to the processes of law enforcement and the interrogation of the child by law enforcement officers. Only the parent or guardian can waive the privilege against self-incrimination of the child.[12]

[12] Michigan Attorney General Opinion No. 3537, August 23, 1960.

In the matter of pursuit, the law also is specific:

> Law enforcement officers are empowered to arrest a person without a warrant in the case of a felony where the officer has reasonable cause to believe that the person, including minor children, has committed a felony or for a misdemeanor committed in the officer's presence. A rule of the board of education of a school district which would permit law enforcement officers to remove a student from the public schools only upon presentation of a warrant is not in accordance with law.[13]

Other situations may arise in which there is potential conflict in the way school officials and law enforcement officers want to handle a particular case. But the above interpretation of the legal relationship between the two groups covers most of the circumstances in which the school will be directly involved. There will be times, however, when a law enforcement officer does not know the law in cases involving pupils in school, or deliberately attempts to bypass established procedures. In this case the principal must be firm in protecting the pupil's legal rights. It is important, therefore, to have readily available a written agreement between the school and the chief of police which specifically states how these cases must be handled.

Support of Teachers

Probably nothing is more destructive of faculty morale than a feeling on the part of teachers that the principal will not support them in cases of conflict with students or parents over discipline. Needless to say, the high school principal cannot afford to leave any doubt in the minds of the faculty on this score. There will be times when the teacher has been indiscreet or has used very poor judgment, but even then the principal must support the teacher's right to insist on good behavior by the pupil.

On the other hand, there are occasional incidents in which a serious injustice is done to a pupil by the teacher. Sometimes the teacher goes beyond his authority or imposes a penalty far more severe than is warranted by the offense. For example, he may announce to a student that he is *expelled* from school. A teacher has no legal authority to make such a decision. In such a case the principal may still back the teacher's desire to have the pupil punished, but he cannot possibly uphold the pronouncement that the pupil will be expelled from school.

Another type of situation arises when the teacher has already administered an unreasonable form of punishment, such as requiring a pupil to kneel on bare knees in a corner for two hours. This is a medieval form of punishment and cannot receive the principal's support, but he must support the teacher in her right to maintain order in the classroom. Fortunately, most teachers are reasonable in their relationships with their pupils, so the principal should not find it difficult to stand with

[13] *Ibid.*

his faculty in discipline matters. It is worth repeating, however, that the principal must be on his guard constantly in backing teachers in discipline cases, for unless teachers have confidence in his support of them, maintaining a good program of discipline in a school is a lost cause. When a teacher is clearly wrong and a serious injustice has been done to a student, the principal should make every effort to persuade the teacher to revise his action in order that the principal does not appear to be overruling the teacher.

Irate Parents

When an irate parent appears on the scene, it is usually because he feels some teacher has mistreated his child. The principal is responsible for protecting teachers from the sudden appearance in the classroom of a parent ready to avenge the wrong done his child. Whether or not the emotions of the parent are justified, the fact is that he is angry and eager to demonstrate the point. Fortunately, a parent usually is not well enough acquainted with room assignments to go directly to the teacher with whom he wishes to exchange blows, either physically or verbally. He is likely to come to the principal's office with a demand to see the teacher in question. It would be an obvious mistake for the principal or his secretary to say, "His room is 202, just down the hall to the right!" This would send the parent on the way to almost certain arrest for assault and battery or disturbing the peace. The principal should contain the action of the parent while he is in such an emotional state.

A helpful procedure to follow is to invite, or insist, that the parent come into the principal's office to discuss the matter. This may take a little persuading, because his anger is not directed at the principal; he is out to "get" the teacher. If at all possible, the principal should try to persuade the parent to sit down and tell him about the problem. However, little good is achieved if he tries to argue with an irate parent! The parent should be encouraged to talk freely without contradiction until he has had the opportunity to get his grievance off his chest. Once the emotion has been expressed, parents are usually willing to resort to a more reasonable course of action.

If an extremely wrathful parent finds the teacher in question without the assistance of the principal and proceeds to do what he set out to do, namely, punch the teacher in the nose, the principal should not hesitate to have the parent arrested for assault and battery. Even if the parent does not attack the teacher but causes considerable disturbance in the classroom, consideration should be given to having him arrested for disrupting the normal operation of the school. The point is that no one has the right to disrupt the school, distract teachers, or attack school personnel. It is the principal's responsibility to do whatever is reasonable and necessary, within the limits of the law, to assure teachers and pupils that they will not be subject to such disturbances.

Questions and Group Projects

1. Organize a debate on whether or not pupil behavior in school is better or worse now than it was twenty years previously.

2. Make a collection of written policies by boards of education and/or faculties. Compare their viewpoints on discipline.

3. Prepare what you consider an ideal set of rules and regulations for pupils in high school.

4. Describe the most serious case of pupil misbehavior you have observed personally. How was it handled by the teacher and/or high school principal? What recommendations would you make for dealing with a similar problem in the future?

5. Visit your local police station and discuss with the officer in charge what he thinks is the best way for principals and law officers to work together on pupil cases involving the law.

Selected References

Barnes, A. F. "How Laurel Organized a Discipline Policy," *American School Board Journal,* May, 1960, 140:20–21.

Barnes, E. H., and K. Barnes. "Learning Discipline," *Illinois Education,* December, 1960, 151:151.

Baumgardner, H. "Some Elementary Principles of Discipline," *School Review,* September, 1955, 63:347–48.

Bell, J. W., and A. S. Green. "Discipline, A Case for Administrative Support," *American School Board Journal,* September, 1957, 135:36–37.

Chamberlain, R. J. "Role of the Principal in Discipline," *The Bulletin* of the NASSP, September 1959, 43:139–43.

Cortale, M. J. "Counselors and Discipline," *Personnel and Guidance Journal,* January, 1961, 39:349–51.

Cutts, N. E., and N. Mosely. "Four Schools of School Discipline," *School and Society,* February, 1959, 87:87.

Edwards, Newton. *The Courts and the Public Schools.* Chicago: University of Chicago Press, 1946.

Garber, L. O. "When Is Corporal Punishment Lawful?" *Nation's Schools,* April, 1960, 65:100.

Garrison, K. C. "Study of Student Disciplinarian Practices in Two Georgia High Schools," *Journal of Educational Research,* December, 1959, 53:153–56.

Hamilton, Robert R. *Legal Rights and Liabilities of Teachers.* Laramie, Wyo.: Laramie Printers, Inc., 1956.

Havighurst, R. J. "Functions of Successful Discipline," *Educational Digest,* September, 1952, 18:7–9.

Haymes, James L. *Discipline.* New York: Bureau of Publications, Teacher's College, Columbia University, 1949.

Krug, Othilda, and Helen L. Beck. *A Guide to Better Discipline.* Chicago: Science Research Associates, 1954.

Langdon, Grace, and Irving W. Stout. *The Discipline of Well-Adjusted Children.* New York: The John Day Company, 1952.

Morse, William C. "The School's Responsibility for Discipline," *Phi Delta Kappan,* December, 1959, 41:109–13.

National Education Association. "Corporal Punishment," *Research Bulletin,* October, 1958, 36:88–89.

National Education Association. "Discipline in the Public Schools," *Research Bulletin,* December, 1957, 35:152–55.

National Education Association. "Discipline: Symposium," *NEA Journal,* September 1958, 367–81.

National Education Association, Research Division. "Teacher Opinion on Pupil Behavior," *Research Bulletin,* April, 1956, Vol. 34. No. 2.

Olivia, Peter F. "High-School Discipline in American Society," *The Bulletin* of the NASSP, January, 1956, 40:1–55.

Olsen, L. R. "Effective Disciplinary Practices of Secondary School Administrators," *American School Board Journal.* February, 1957, 134:41–42.

Punke, N. H. "Corporal Punishment in the Public Schools," *The Bulletin* of the NASSP, September, 1959, 43:118–38.

Salmer, A. M. "How Effective Is Detention?" *California Teacher Association Journal,* November, 1956, 52:35–37.

Sheviakov, George V., and Fritz Redl. *Discipline for Today's Children and Youth.* Washington: National Education Association, Association for Supervision and Curriculum Development, 1956.

Shock, Donald P. "How to Put Teeth in a Discipline Policy," *School Management,* April, 1959.

Vredevoe, L. E. "Practices in School Discipline," *American School Board Journal,* July, 1959, 139:19–21.

Witzel, F. F., R. E. Emery, and S. Crockett. "How to Develop a Desirable Student Behavior Policy," *The Bulletin* of the NASSP, April, 1961, 45:209–14.

CHAPTER 16

Pupil Personnel Records and Reports

In any high school, large or small, rural or urban, the principal is called upon to gather data, to expedite communication, and to furnish information about students or former students. For example, an applicant for a position in business wants to verify the fact that he is a high school graduate, as much as ten, twenty, thirty, or even forty years after graduation. Information about applicants for positions involving the national security is requested by a federal investigator. Seniors need an official record of their credits, grades, and test scores in order to apply for admission to college. Professional organizations and agencies frequently seek data from the school for research purposes. A teachers' or citizens' committee may need information about students in order to study curriculum problems. Counselors need student information accumulated over the years in order to do their job well. And county, state, and federal agencies must have reports related to legal matters in the operation of the school, such as average daily attendance, as a basis for financial aid.

A well-planned and carefully maintained system of pupil personnel records is essential if the high school principal is going to meet the numerous requests for information about his students and his school. In general, the purposes of the pupil personnel record system are (1) to record the achievement and growth of a student during his school career; (2) to provide information necessary in preparing reports required by the local board of education, the state, and various professional boards and associations; (3) to report information to parents with respect to the progress of their children in school; (4) to provide pertinent information and data necessary for research relating to students and the school; (5) to provide information needed by teachers and counselors in working with students; and (6) to provide information needed by higher institutions and employers about former students of the high school.

Guiding Principles

During the early period of the American high school, records were simple or, in many cases, practically nonexistent. According to Traxler,

> ... A century and a half ago few high schools kept any records at all. Largely through the efforts of Horace Mann, the Daily Register was introduced into the schools of Massachusetts in the 1830's and its use gradually spread throughout the country. . . .[1]

Since Horace Mann's day the number and complexity of pupil personnel records have increased greatly, although many small rural high schools still maintain relatively few student records. In too many cases, however, records have been adopted on a very haphazard basis. Frequently they have "just grown," with little reference to any guiding tenets other than those of expediency. Statements of principles cannot assure the development of adequate records, but records which are developed according to such principles are likely to be more adequate than they would be otherwise. The following points are presented, therefore, as guides in building a system of pupil personnel records for a modern high school.

1. Each record should serve a clearly defined purpose. If, for instance, the faculty intends to individualize instruction, it is necessary to have information about each student for use by teachers. Such a record should be evaluated according to how useful the information is for instructional purposes. On the other hand, some records have strictly administrative purposes, such as the collection of tuition. There is little value in cluttering up a record of this kind with test information about a pupil. All that is needed is his name, place of residence, attendance record, and other details related to the collection of the tuition.

Although some school records call for information that is rarely used, a more serious weakness is that they do not include significant data which are needed. For example, the rating of a student's special aptitudes from his elementary teachers is essential in forming ability

---

[1] Arthur E. Traxler, *Techniques of Guidance* (New York: Harper & Brothers, rev. ed., 1957), p. 183.

groups in the secondary school, but this information often is missing on his cumulative record card.

2. Only information that will be used should be included in school records. To collect anything else is a waste of time. Pupil records should contain the kind and amount of data, however, necessary for teachers who seek to adapt instruction to student needs. If the faculty accepts the idea that the most important purpose of records is to aid in the instruction and guidance of each student, adequate supporting information must be available. But unless it is used in pertinent research and to better school practice, its collection dissipates the time of staff members.

It is easy to lose sight of the original purposes of certain records and to maintain them long after their intended use has been served. This sometimes happens when there is a change in administrators. One principal may establish a special record which he finds useful, but his successor may not be interested in or need the information it contains. Being new, he may hesitate to discard established records until he is sure they are unnecessary. In the meantime, he will probably install a few records of his own without weeding those of the first principal, because he has neglected to determine whether or not they are needed.

3. Pupil records should be coordinated within a school system. It is a common weakness to allow each unit, i.e., elementary, junior high, senior high, and junior college, the privilege of designing its own records. Although each unit may have unique purposes, there is information about pupils which should be cumulative from kindergarten through junior college — for example, the health record. Similarly, marks earned and results of standardized tests in all grades are useful in counseling with a student at any point during his school career. The cumulative student record will be considered in more detail later in this chapter. Suffice it to point out here that there are important facts about the student and his achievement which should move along from one school unit to the next. Consequently, representatives from each unit of the school system should plan jointly what should be included in the cumulative record.

4. Few clerical demands should be made upon teachers to maintain pupil records. Use of professional personnel to perform clerical duties constitutes a false economy. Teachers cannot be freed completely from these duties, because some items such as student marks and ratings on reports to the principal require professional judgment in the recording process. But the recording of marks and routine student information on report cards and permanent office records can be assigned to clerical workers.

5. All records should be as simple as will serve the purpose intended. Sometimes pupil personnel records are so complicated as to discourage their use. Some principals appear to be fascinated by involved code systems supposedly invented to simplify the use of records. But these

can become so intricate that the intended efficiency is lost. There may be virtue in condensing information into a few well-chosen symbols, but there also is virtue in keeping information simple enough so that teachers and counselors will not throw up their hands in despair as they try to decipher the code.

6. Repetition of information on pupil records should be reduced to a minimum. Often vital statistics about the pupils, their families, and other pertinent background data need not appear on more than one form. Implementation of this principle is helped by having a record system which is cumulative for the entire school system so that a number of items do not have to be recorded each year.

7. Personnel records of pupils should be readily accessible to the faculty. If the principal insists on having the pupil records located in his inner office, there will be times when a teacher would like to use the files but finds the principal in conference. Rather than disturb such a meeting, the teacher may leave without using the records and may not have time to come again to secure the information. Some schools follow the practice of having homeroom teachers maintain the records for their pupils and store them in their homerooms. Such a plan still makes the records relatively inaccessible to other teachers. A better procedure is to centralize the storage of all records intended for general teacher use in the counselor's outer office and/or in the principal's outer office.

8. Pupil personnel records must be revised as school practices and needs change. Although a faculty usually does not change its practices drastically in any one year, a gradual change takes place over a period of years — witness the gradual acceptance of increased counseling and guidance services in modern, comprehensive high schools and the significant advances in the use of standardized tests. If one considers only these two developments, it is apparent that today's pupil records must be substantially different from those of twenty years ago. Administrators must be alert to the fact that a periodic review and adaptation of pupil records is necessary.

9. Long-term and frequently used record forms should be durable. If a system of pupil personnel records is continuous and cumulative, the records will be used many times during a student's career. Transferring the accumulated information from a record which is wearing out to a new record requires a great deal of time. It is better to select durable material that will last the entire time a pupil is in school. In the long run, this will result in considerable economy.

10. Records should be housed so as to prevent loss and tampering. There are hazards to the maintenance of any record system — fire, theft, or unauthorized changes by individuals. In order to prevent such things from happening, records should be stored in a place which is fireproof and secure. A minimum precaution in all schools is to store the perma-

nent records in a fireproof vault. If a vault is not available, it is desirable to maintain duplicate records containing the most important items of information and to store each set in a place safe from the risks that the other set is subject to.

Types of Records

The number of different pupil records used in high schools in the United States is unknown. Even if there were enough interest and resources available to make a complete inventory, it is doubtful that it would be worthwhile. Hundreds of different records are employed in schools, because most states delegate considerable control of education to local communities, and as long as faculties differ in educational theories and practices, variations in the types of records are to be expected.

Efforts have been made, however, to standardize some records. A Committee on Uniform Records and Reports in 1912 made recommendations intended to improve records at that time.[2] The Committee on School Records and Reports in 1927 revised the 1912 report and made its own proposals with respect to school records. Although both committees were concerned with standardizing records, they expressed a strong commitment to the principle of local determination.

> The procedures described and the forms produced in this bulletin are intended to be suggestive rather than prescriptive. Final prescription as to just what records should be kept and what reports should be made cannot be made at this time. Definite prescription and more complete uniformity must wait upon further research and experience. . . .
> Rather than uncritically adopting any particular set of record forms, whether found in this bulletin or developed by other agencies, a school system should evaluate in the light of best theory and its own peculiar needs several alternative sets of forms.[3]

More recently, the National Association of Secondary School Principals designed record forms which have been recommended for national use by the American Association of Collegiate Registrars and Admissions Officers and the Joint Committee on School-College Relationships. In addition, several state departments of public instruction have designed records which are recommended for general use within their respective states. Other committees, such as the Committee on Personnel Methods of the American Council on Education, have given attention to individual records appropriate to their own special interests.

[2] National Education Association, Department of Superintendence, *Report of the Committee on Uniform Records and Reports*, U.S. Bureau of Education, Bulletin 1912, No. 3 (Washington: Government Printing Office, 1912).

[3] National Education Association, Research Division, "School Records and Reports," *Research Bulletin*, 1927, 5:230–31.

These efforts have been particularly helpful in providing model forms for use in developing local records, and some principals have adopted the records recommended. Responsibility for selecting or developing records must remain with the principal and his staff so that the records will be in harmony with local instructional practices. Nevertheless, it is important for the prospective principal to be acquainted with records which are basic to most schools and also to know what types of records other schools have found most useful. The following discussion is directed, therefore, to what is considered the core of a record system for any secondary school. Included in the core of the pupil personnel record system are the following: (1) pupil cumulative record, (2) permanent school record, (3) attendance records, (4) registration and classification records, (5) reports to parents, (6) reports to colleges and employers, and (7) consumable records for day-to-day management and operation.

Cumulative Record

Purposes of the Cumulative Record. The pupil cumulative record is a development of the last thirty years. Even the term was unfamiliar prior to the 1930's. Since that time, however, schools generally have adopted a guidance viewpoint toward their pupils, which, in turn, has demanded records providing the information needed in guidance activities. According to Bollenbacher, cumulative records are needed to

> (a) aid in identifying scholastic strengths and weaknesses of individual students and in planning appropriate school programs; (b) aid in identifying personal and social adjustment problems; (c) aid teachers in getting acquainted quickly with new students; (d) provide information necessary for parent conferences; (3) serve as a basis for reports to other schools, colleges, and prospective employers, and (f) serve as records for archival purposes.[4]

Some confusion still exists in the use of the term "cumulative records." Used in a nontechnical sense, it can mean any record which adds to the general accumulation of information about a pupil. Thus any permanent record of a pupil's progress through the school system would be considered to be a cumulative record. Used in a technical sense, "cumulative record" has become more specific in its meaning. It should be considered as "the newer type of record forms in which emphasis is placed on objective measurements and personality data as contrasted with the older type of permanent record that was confined largely to attendance, school marks, and credits. . . ." In this discussion, the cumulative record will be considered as a continuous record, or combination of records, containing significant information regarding a student's growth as he progresses from kindergarten through the secondary school.

[4] Joan Bollenbacher, "Student Records and Reports — Elementary and Secondary," *Encyclopedia of Educational Research* (New York: The Macmillan Company, 3rd ed., 1960), p. 1439.

Basic Concepts Related to Cumulative Records. Certain basic concepts pertinent to the cumulative record should be considered — for instance, that every pupil is a growing personality and that his growth is a continuous process from the day he enters school until the day he graduates or leaves for other reasons. The cumulative record helps to provide an over-all description of the individual student for use by teachers, counselors, and administrators. It also fills in a number of the details which may be called for by external agencies.

Education is continuous, even though for administrative purposes it has been organized into segments. A cumulative record is intended to improve articulation between the various units of the school system, i.e., elementary and junior high, junior high and senior high, and senior high and junior college or college. It is based on the concept of continuity in education, with each unit of the school system receiving the benefit of information on the student's record from other units. There are those who argue that the pupil should receive a "fresh start" when he enters a new unit of the school, but this implies that teachers, counselors, and principals are likely to discriminate against pupils who have had difficulties previously. Acceptance of this viewpoint depreciates the status of teachers to a position below that of a professional. The authors believe that we have progressed beyond the point where such conditions prevail, and that the cumulative record should be passed along as a continuous report through the entire career of the student.

Changed behavior and personality development are important outcomes of a pupil's experiences in schools. Evidence of growth along these lines is as important as marks, test results, and credits.

Information Included in the Cumulative Record. What information should be included in the cumulative record? There is no definitive answer to this question, because each faculty will have need to adapt its program to the characteristics of its pupils. The record should be as broad and detailed as necessary for wise faculty use, but it should not be cluttered up with irrelevant data. Although there is considerable variation among schools, some items of information are common to most cumulative records. For example, Segel, in a study of the records of 177 school systems, classified the items included into seventeen categories and tabulated the frequency of occurrence of each type of item.[5] The following items appeared most frequently: scholarship (marks), school progress, attendance, entrance and withdrawal, home conditions and family history, intelligence test results, social and character ratings, and health history. These items represent a minimum amount of information which should be included in the cumulative record in all schools. In a sense, one might

---

[5] David Segel, *Nature and Use of the Cumulative Record*, U.S. Office of Education, Bulletin 1938, No. 3 (Washington: Government Printing Office, 1938).

regard them as the basic items of information which teachers and counselors need in working with students. Additional items should be determined by the faculty as it plans instruction, guidance, and student activities.

Some writers suggest that the cumulative record should contain only information which is objective in nature. The reason usually given is that if data based on observation and/or opinion are accepted, teachers will record judgments about pupils which may be biased. An additional reservation is that teacher opinions are likely to reflect the values of the individual teacher rather than general opinion of the faculty; consequently, the cumulative record might provide data which will work an injustice upon the student. Contrary to this viewpoint is the idea that if items are restricted to objective data, a great amount of helpful information with respect to the behavior and personality development of pupils will be lacking. The danger of misuse of subjective data is not so much in the recording of such information as in the misinterpretation of it. To protect against such misuses it is suggested that interpretations be made only by personnel who are qualified by training and experience to do this. Fortunately, teachers and counselors are now being prepared to interpret such data, and chances are good that the situation will continue to improve. Schools are encouraged to include information of a subjective nature in the cumulative record even though the largest share may well be objective. The main consideration is to secure as comprehensive a picture of the pupil as is possible, including observations of his behavior and personality.

Type of Record (Card, Envelope, or Folder). The advantage of using a separate card for each special purpose, such as standardized test results, marks, personality ratings, etc., is the flexibility in use of the records, because a teacher interested in reviewing only one part of a pupil's record can do so without tying up the entire record. A major disadvantage in using a series of cards is that there is no way to secure a quick overview of a pupil's record, and frequently principals are in need of a convenient comprehensive picture. In addition, it is easier to lose part of a student's record when cards are used.

Greater security of records is obtained when an envelope packet is used. On the other hand, it is more difficult to sort through materials stored in an envelope than those contained in a folder. The same major disadvantage of the card type of record holds for the envelope type, that is, a quick overview of the total record is not easily made.

Most commonly used is the folder type of record. It has the advantages of easy access to materials and of a quick summary of a pupil's record, assuming the recording of pertinent information is kept up to date. A busy administrator, counselor, or teacher can see the over-all record at a

FIGURE 22

Cumulative Personnel Record

CUMULATIVE PERSONNEL RECORD
Copyright, 1946 NATIONAL ASSOCIATION OF SECONDARY-SCHOOL PRINCIPALS
1201 SIXTEENTH STREET, N. W., WASHINGTON 6, D. C.

PRINT: LAST NAME | FIRST & NICKNAME IN ( ) | MIDDLE | SEX (CIRCLE M F) | DATE & PLACE OF BIRTH | EVIDENCE

19 7	19 8	19 9	YEAR / GRADE / AGE AS OF SEPT. 1	19 10	19	19	19	
			HOME ADDRESS					TO-TAL CRED-ITS BY SUB-JECTS
			HOME TELEPHONE					
			TOTAL DAYS OF SCHOOL / TOTAL DAYS ABSENT / TOTAL TIMES LATE					
			SCHOOL ATTENDED					
			COUNSELLOR					
UNITS CRED.	UNITS CRED.	UNITS CRED.	ACADEMIC ACHIEVEMENT	UNITS CRED.	UNITS CRED.	UNITS CRED.	UNITS CRED.	
			ENGLISH (ENGLISH)					
			LANGUAGE					
			MATHEMATICS					
			SCIENCE					
			SOCIAL STUDIES (SOCIAL STUDIES)					
			OTHER SUBJECTS					
			HEALTH & PHYSICAL ED.					
			MAJORS PASSED / MINORS PASSED / AVERAGE / TOT UNITS CREDITS					
TEST / MO / SCORE / % ILE	TEST / MO / SCORE / % ILE	TEST / MO / SCORE / % ILE	TEST RECORD	TEST / MO / SCORE / % ILE	TEST / MO / SCORE / % ILE	TEST / MO / SCORE / % ILE	TEST / MO / SCORE / % ILE	
			ACADEMIC APTITUDE USE M.A. & I.Q. IF PREFERRED					
			READING					
			ACHIEVEMENT & OTHER TESTS					
			INDEX COLUMN					

1. MOTIVATION																			
2. INDUSTRY																			
3. INITIATIVE																			
4. INFLUENCE & LEADERSHIP																			
5. CONCERN FOR OTHERS																			
6. RESPONSIBILITY																			
7. INTEGRITY																			
8. EMOTIONAL STABILITY																			

PERSONALITY ESTIMATE

SIGNIFICANT HEALTH CHARACTERISTICS — HEALTH

HOURS, KINDS, EARNINGS — WORK

IN AND OUT OF SCHOOL, SUMMERS, E.G., ATHLETICS, CAMPING, HOBBIES, SCOUTING, CLUBS, ETC. — INTERESTS & ACTIVITIES

DATA EXPLAINING EXTREME VARIANCE BETWEEN TESTING RESULTS & ACTUAL ACHIEVEMENT IN CLASS — TESTS VS. ACCOMPLISHMENT

EDUCATIONAL & VOCATIONAL — PLANS

PHOTO & DATE

GUIDANCE NOTES

FATHER—GUARDIAN, COMPLETE NAME, OCCUPATION, EDUCATION

MOTHER COMPLETE NAME, OCCUPATION, EDUCATION

BROTHERS, NAMES & BIRTHYEARS

[S]ISTERS, NAMES & BIRTHYEARS

SCHOOL LEAVING: DATE & REASONS:

POST-SCHOOL DATA:

PHOTO & DATE

LANGUAGE SPOKEN AT HOME

Copyright, 1946

Source: National Association of Secondary School Principals, 1201 Sixteenth Street, N.W., Washington 6, D.C.

glance. When using a folder, it is possible also to include many inserts or supplementary materials which may be summarized at a later date or be discarded when they no longer are pertinent. A disadvantage of the folder type is that one person using the folder ties up the entire record of a student. Further, the clerical work to keep summaries up to date is considerable and summarizing data on the folder often requires judgments by the professional staff, which means that clerks cannot be assigned the entire task of recording information.

It is not intended to imply here that a school must confine itself to using only one type of record. Many schools combine the card type with an envelope or a folder. In this case supplementary records can be inserted in the folder or envelope and then summarized later. The combination of the card and folder types has a number of advantages over a single form for use as a complete cumulative record.

Model Forms. Although local schools are encouraged to design their own cumulative record, it may be helpful to examine models prepared by others. Usually some sections on the models are applicable for local use even though an entire form may not be appropriate. Space does not allow the presentation of a large number of sample forms, but a school can obtain forms from other schools for examination. Most principals are quite willing to assist other administrators in such studies. In addition, colleges and universities often have collections of the forms in their curriculum materials centers. Traxler includes a particularly good discussion of model forms from several school systems in his book on guidance techniques.[6]

Widely used and copied is the form developed and distributed by the American Council on Education. Another form, developed by a committee of the National Association of Secondary School Principals and recommended by the Association, is a six-year record including the following categories: academic achievement, test record, personality estimate, health, work experience, interests and activities, explanation of extreme variation between test results and actual achievement in class, educational and vocational plans, attendance, home background, follow-up, and guidance notes. A strong feature of this form is the arrangement of items, which lends itself to ease of reading. The form is available in an envelope, card, or folder type. The one shown in Figure 22 is the folder form.

Permanent Record

The permanent record contains information about students which becomes their official record in the school, and it is that part of a student's school record which remains in the school permanently. If

[6] Traxler, *op. cit.*

a former student of a school requests his record, the information he is likely to receive is that which is recorded on the permanent record. Therefore, the minimum amount of information which should be included is the following: name of a student, dates attended, final marks and credits earned in each subject, and date of graduation or of withdrawal.

How much additional information a school may wish to keep on the permanent record depends upon whether or not the cumulative record is retained permanently. If it is, there is less justification for developing an elaborate permanent record. If it is not, additional data about the pupil's achievement similar to those recorded on the cumulative record should be made part of the permanent record.

The permanent record is not used frequently by teachers and counselors. It is an office record. Removal of the permanent record from the principal's office should not be allowed, since there is a danger that it may be lost or misplaced. Duplicate sets of records usually are a waste of time and energy except when a duplicate serves a highly important purpose. But in the case of the permanent record, a duplicate is highly desirable if it is stored in a different place, preferably in another building. Large school systems frequently keep one set in the central office and one in the principal's office to insure that there will be a duplicate in case of loss by fire or other disasters. A fireproof vault is ideal as a storage place, but if one is not available a fireproof filing cabinet will serve.

The permanent record prepared by the National Association of Secondary School Principals is shown in Figure 23 as an example of a typical form. It includes more than the minimum amount of information needed on a permanent record. There is some space available for a brief summary of the student's participation in extraclass activities, intelligence test results, achievement test results, attendance record, personality and health record, home and family information, vocational preference, college or position attained, and rank in class. Much of this information duplicates that normally included in the cumulative record, but the amount of space devoted to it is very small. Consequently, only a very brief summary of these various items can be included, and it should not be considered an adequate substitute for the cumulative record.

Rank in Class

Practically every permanent record contains a place to record the student's rank in class. Traditionally this has been used as an over-all indicator of achievement in high school. It has been used especially for college admissions. In recent years the Joint Committee on School-College Relations of the National Association of Secondary School Principals and the American Association of Collegiate Registrars and Admissions Officers have tried to standardize the way rank in class is calculated, and at their 1957 meeting in Chicago they recommended the following:

FIGURE 23

Permanent Record Form

Name

SCHOLASTIC RECORD

Subject	Gr. / Yr.	9 19 1S 2S	10 19 1S 2S	11 19 1S 2S	12 19 1S 2S	Extra 19 1S 2S	No. Wks.	Credits
English								
Lang.								
Math.								
Science								
Soc. Studies								
Other Subjects								

Notes

Specify laboratory periods, variations in time allowance for subjects, or any other information needed to interpret this record. Such other information as Regents grades, College Boards and record of a fifth year may be entered in the Extra column. If a school does not use marks, enter here an estimate of success achieved.

PERMANENT RECORD

School City

Last Name First Name Middle Name Sex Race Birthplace Month Day Year

Entered from Date Age Class Curriculum Adviser

Parent or Guardian Occupation Nationality Address Telephone No.

EXTRA CLASS ACTIVITIES

Date	Activity	Honors or Offices	Pts. Crs.

INTELLIGENCE-TEST RECORD

Date	Name of Test	Form	Score	%-ile Rank	MA	CA	IQ

ACHIEVEMENT-TEST RECORD

Date	Name of Test	Form	Score	Class Norm.	%-ile Rank	Subject Age

Was Graduated Date Rank No. in Class

Left Date Reason

ATTENDANCE RECORD

Semester	1	2	3	4	5	6	7	8	9	10	Totals
Days Present											
Days Absent											
Times Tardy											

PERSONALITY RECORD

Symbols: (1) High; (2) Above Av.; (3) Av.; (4) Below Av.; (5) Low

	1st yr.	2nd yr.	3rd yr.	4th yr.	5th yr.	Summary
Motivation						
Industry						
Initiative						
Influence & Leadership						
Concern for Others						
Responsibility						
Integrity						
Emotional Stability						

General Health

Significant Limitations

Home conditions Parents Living No. Brothers No. Sisters

Vocational Preferences

College or Position Date

Credits Sent to Date

Source: National Association of Secondary School Principals, 1201 Sixteenth Street, N.W., Washington 6, D.C.

1. Marks for all subjects for which unit credit or fractional unit credit is given, whether passed or failed, should be recorded and used in computing class rank.

2. All students in the class should be included in determining the class rank.

3. The following four-point system based on quality of achievement should be used in computing rank-in-class average (grade-point average) for each student. For example, this shows how one year of a student's record can be rated:

Key	Units	Final Mark	Points
A — 4 points per unit	1	A (Passing)	4
B — 3 points per unit	1	B (Passing)	3
C — 2 points per unit	0.5	B (Passing)	1.5
D — 1 point per unit	1	C (Passing)	2
F — 0 points per unit	1	D (Passing)	1
	0.5	F (Failing)	0
	5		11.5

Thus, the student's rank-in-class average for one school year based on the record above $= \frac{11.50}{5}$ or 2.30 (two decimals). This statistic also is called grade-point average.

4. Schools with a different marking system should adopt the basic principles involved in this plan.

5. Exact class rank should be determined at the end of the first semester of the senior year.

6. Rank in class, or at least approximate rank, should also be made at the end of the junior year by those secondary schools which have students applying for admission to colleges granting tentative admission upon completion of three years of secondary school work.

7. Rank in class should be regarded not as the only statistical measurement but as one of many criteria to be used in the college admission process.

Having determined the grade-point average for all years spent in high school for each student, the principal is then ready to calculate the actual rank in class, as follows:

1. He arranges all grade-point averages in descending order, e.g., 3.89; 3.75; 3.50; 3.50; . . . to the lowest.

2. He assigns the highest grade-point average rank 1, the next highest rank 2, and so on down the list.

3. Ties are assigned the highest rank for the numbers tied. For example, if there are three students with a grade-point average of 3.50 and ranks 1 and 2 already have been used, all three students should be ranked 3. The next highest grade-point average should be ranked 6.

Following is an example of how to rank twenty students after their grade-point averages have been calculated and arranged in descending order.

Grade-point average:	3.89	3.75	3.50	3.50	3.50	3.00	2.75	2.75
Rank in class:	1	2	3	3	3	6	7	7

2.00	2.00	2.00	1.68	1.50	1.45	1.25	1.00	1.00	1.00	0.90	0.50
9	9	9	12	13	14	15	16	16	16	19	20

Many schools continue to designate the students ranked 1 and 2 as the valedictorian and the salutatorian. The authors have no quarrel with this practice providing principals do not try to carry out the grade-point average calculations to four and five decimals in order to resolve ties. One of the suggestions above for calculating grade-point average should be observed in such cases, i.e., carrying out the calculation to only two decimal places. If students are tied for these important honors, it is much better to bestow similar honors on more than one student than to split hairs in determining grade-point average.

Transcript of Credits

Every high school must be prepared to issue a transcript of credits for each student. This is the official statement of credits and marks earned for each subject during the time the individual was a student in that school. Rank in class and the number of pupils in the class are also included. It is good practice for the high school to adopt an official seal which can be affixed to the transcript in order to make it valid.

One of the most frequent uses of a transcript of credits is for entrance into college. College admission officers generally require a transcript along with an application for admission. In recent years, colleges have become progressively more selective since many colleges and universities do not have facilities to permit them to admit all applicants. Consequently, admission officers are recommending that high schools include an additional fact sheet along with the transcript of credits to assist them in judging a prospective student. The fact sheet should contain information such as the following:

Community — population, cultural backgrounds, unusual or special characteristics, and location.
School — description, enrollment, size of classes, accreditation, annual expenditure per student for operating costs, and faculty.
Guidance personnel.
Curriculum.
Grading system — use of letters or numerical system carefully explained.
Ability grouping.

Testing program.
Median IQ for school enrollment — test forms, norms used.
Class rank — how determined.
Graduating class for a specific year — size, median IQ, number participating and median scores in CEEB's, other test information used, number and types of colleges attended.
Advanced placement program, if any.

Figure 24 shows a transcript of credits recommended for use by the National Association of Secondary School Principals. Figure 25 shows an additional fact sheet used by Ann Arbor High School, Ann Arbor, Michigan.

Marks and Reports to Parents

School marks provide a basis for (1) pupil promotion, (2) counseling of students, (3) predicting future success, (4) providing research data, (5) rewarding students for work well done, (6) admonishing lazy students, (7) selecting scholarship winners, (8) selecting students for admission to college, (9) informing prospective employers of the academic achievements of students, and (10) informing parents of the progress of their child in school. Marks and reports to parents are intended to be helpful to all concerned. In general, the issue is not so much whether such evaluations are important as how they may be made more effective. In other words, the practice of giving marks and issuing report cards is well established, but opinions differ on what should be included in the reports and what the basis for determining marks should be. The following discussion reviews some of the more common methods for determining and reporting marks.

Percentage System. Pupil progress is traditionally indicated by per cents (95, 90, 85, 80, 75, 70), letter grades (A, B, C, D, F), and numbers (1, 2, 3, 4, 5). The percentage system is based on the premise that there is an absolute standard of achievement and teachers can measure how close to perfection students are able to come. For example, a student who receives a mark of 85 per cent is supposed to have mastered 85 per cent of the content. The basic weakness in the percentage system is that high school achievement cannot be defined in such absolute terms. How, for instance, can a teacher determine whether a student knows all of the United States history that he should know? Not only is it impossible to define subject matter so definitely, but it is also unrealistic to assume that teachers can measure achievement accurately enough to distinguish in per cents. In recognition of these limitations, use of the percentage system for assigning marks has decreased considerably in recent years.

FIGURE 24

Transcript of Credits

Secondary-School Record
(REVISED)

Name, in full .... Birth Date .... Sex ....
                    Last Name   First Name   Middle Name   M. or F.

Home Address ....
                         Number and Street   City   State

Name of Parent or Guardian .... School accredited by ....

Entered .... Was graduated ⎫
         Name of School   Will be graduated ⎬ ....
                                                          Withdrew   ⎭   Month   Year

....
Month   Year   Location of School

Class periods are .... minutes, ... times a week, ... weeks a year. Passing mark is .... College recommending mark ....

1. List your complete marking system, highest to lowest: .... Honor marks ....
2. List other secondary schools by years attended: ....

Are all failing marks for each year listed? ☐ yes ☐ no

CLASS RECORD

Check (✓) all subjects where no marks are given.
Star (*) all subjects in progress.

Notes

A **unit** represents the study of a subject a full school year four or five times per week.
One **unit** equals two credits unless otherwise defined.
Use **extra** column for extra school year.
Use **exams** column for special exams as Regents, *etc.*

Subject	Grade → Year → 19	1st Sem 9	1st Sem 10	1st Sem 11	1st Sem 12	Extra	Standard Exams	Units or Cred.

English
Lang.
Math.

Check Special Lab Periods Yes No

Science
Social Studies
Other Subjects

TEST RECORD

Name and Form of Test	Year Given	Score	%-ile Gr. Level	Basis*

Mental Ability
Reading
Achievement
Others

ADDITIONAL INFORMATION

*Give available interpretation of tests on an enclosure.

Total number of units school requires for graduation ....

Applicant ranks ☐ exactly ☐ approximately .... in a graduating class of .... students.

School computed above rank in class by using official record beginning with .... grade and ending with .... semester in .... grade:

☐ Marks weighted as recommended by NASSP and AACRAO
☐ Includes all subjects given school credit
☐ Major or full-time subjects only
☐ College preparatory students only

Date .... Signature .... Title ....

This **Standardized Form** prepared and recommended for national use by the Joint Committee on School-College Relations of the National Association of Secondary-School Principals (NASSP) and American Association of Collegiate Registrars and Admissions Officers (AACRAO).
Copyright, 1958 by the National Association of Secondary-School Principals of the NEA, 1201 Sixteenth Street, N. W., Washington 6, D. C. All rights reserved. This blank, or any parts thereof, may not be reproduced except by permission.

(Figure 24, continued)

Personality Record (Confidential)
(REVISED)

Room ....
Grade ....

PERSONAL CHARACTERISTICS OF .... Last Name .... First Name .... Middle Name

School .... Town or City .... State ....

The following characterizations are descriptions of behavior. It is recommended that where possible the judgments of a number of the pupil's present teachers be indicated by the use of the following method or by checks:

```
                            1              M (5)                       2
Example: MOTIVATION   |    | √    |     | √√√√√ |              |      | √√
                   Purposeless  Vacillating  Usually Purposeful  Effectively motivated  Highly motivated
```

M (5) indicates the most common or modal behavior of the pupil as shown by the agreement of five of the eight teachers reporting. The location of the numerals to the left and right indicates that one teacher considers the pupil *vacillating* and that two teachers consider him *highly motivated*. If preferred, the subject fields or other areas of relationship with the pupil may be used to replace the numerals.

1. MOTIVATION	Purposeless	Vacillating	Usually Purposeful	Effectively motivated	Highly motivated
2. INDUSTRY	Seldom works even under pressure	Needs constant pressure	Needs occasional prodding	Prepares assigned work regularly	Seeks additional work
3. INITIATIVE	Merely conforms	Seldom initiates	Frequently initiates	Consistently self-reliant	Actively creative
4. INFLUENCE AND LEADERSHIP	Negative	Co-operative but retiring	Sometimes in minor affairs	Contributing in important affairs	Judgment respected— makes things go
5. CONCERN FOR OTHERS	Indifferent	Self-centered	Somewhat socially concerned	Generally concerned	Deeply and actively concerned
6. RESPONSIBILITY	Unreliable	Somewhat dependable	Usually dependable	Conscientious	Assumes much responsibility
7. INTEGRITY	Not dependable	Questionable at times	Generally honest	Reliable, dependable	Consistently trustworthy
8. EMOTIONAL STABILITY	Hyperemotional / Apathetic	Excitable / Unresponsive	Usually well-balanced	Well-balanced	Exceptionally stable

Significant school activities and special interests or abilities. List membership and offices held in school activities.

Significant limitations (physical, social, mental):

Additional information which may be helpful, such as probable financial needs or work experience:

Principal's Comments and Recommendations

1. Specific statement concerning the applicant's fitness for acceptance by this college or employer:

2. Principal's estimate of applicant's future success, based on the purpose of this application.
☐ Little success   ☐ May encounter some difficulty   ☐ Average   ☐ Above average   ☐ Superior

3. Specific recommendation   ☐ Recommended   ☐ Not recommended for this college or position   ☐ Prefer not to make recommendation

Date .... Signature .... Title ....

This Standardized Form prepared and recommended for national use by the Joint Committee on School-College Relations of the National Association of Secondary-School Principals (NASSP) and American Association of Collegiate Registrars and Admissions Officers (AACRAO).
Copyright, 1958 by the National Association of Secondary-School Principals of the NEA, 1201 Sixteenth Street, N. W., Washington 6, D. C. All rights reserved. This blank, or any parts thereof, may not be reproduced except by permission.

Source: National Association of Secondary School Principals, 1201 Sixteenth Street, N.W., Washington 6, D.C.

FIGURE 25

Additional Fact Sheet Used by Ann Arbor High School, Ann Arbor, Michigan

SCHOOL CHARACTERISTICS AND PROFILE — CLASS OF 1961   October, 1961
ANN ARBOR HIGH SCHOOL
601 West Stadium Boulevard, Ann Arbor, Michigan
Telephone Area 313-663-2431

Nicholas Schreiber, Principal   *Paul Meyers, Assistant Principal and Coordinator Guidance*
Mrs. Frances Hughes, Class Adviser   *Mr. Albert Gallup, Class Adviser*   *Mr. Frank Reed, College Consultant*

COMMUNITY CHARACTERISTICS. Population estimate: 68,000. Location: 45 miles west of Detroit; site University of Michigan with enrollment over 25,000; an important scientific and industrial research center; light manufacturing plants employing more than 6,000; average annual income per household in 1959 estimated at $9,847. (Source of information: Sales Management Survey of Buying Power.)

ANN ARBOR SCHOOL SYSTEM. Twenty-one elementary schools, three junior high schools, one high school; total enrollment 12,771, professional staff 660. Tax base: State equalized evaluation, $281,408,108; Tax levy for operation, $16.30 per $1,000 state equalized evaluation; Annual expenditure per student in system, $431.

ANN ARBOR HIGH SCHOOL. Comprehensive three-year high school; 1961-1962 enrollment 2,181. The school day includes a homeroom period of 25 minutes and six class periods, 55 minutes each. Accredited by University of Michigan and North Central Association. Building completed at cost of $6,000,000; situated on 177-acre campus.

Faculty — 113 members; Degree: Ph.D.—2; Master—89; Bachelor—22.

Curriculum — Seven curricula; college, university, stenographic, retailing, general office, industrial, general, special education for mentally retarded.

Accelerated, Enriched and Advanced Placement Courses — English, mathematics, French, German, Spanish, chemistry, physics, American history.

Guidance—Ratio of students to professional guidance personnel, 240-1; Class advisers (educational counselors)—6; Special consultants (social workers) — 2; College consultant — 1 (⅓ time); Vocational guidance consultant—1 (⅓ time); Nurse (health consultant) — 1; Diagnostician (part-time); Full-time equivalency—9 teachers.

Extracurricular Activities — Wide range including clubs, interscholastic athletics (boys), intramurals, student government, service committees, speech, music, publications.

Requirements For Graduation — Quantity: 17½ units in grades 9-12; Quality: At least one-half C's; Prescribed units include English 4, social studies 2, math 1, science 1, physical education 1½.

Grouping in Academic Subjects according to educational plans and ability, four major ability groupings.

College Recommendation Standards—University of Michigan and comparable institutions — "C+," all other—"C."

Class Sizes — All academic classes average under 27 per section; Pupil-teacher ratio on North Central Association formula, 20.1—1.

Enrollment — Class 1962, 594; Class, 1963, 721; Class, 1964; 783; Post-graduates and special students — 83. Total 2,181.

Testing Program — Ninth Grade   Eleventh Grade   Twelfth Grade
     Differential Aptitude   PSAT   CEEB
     California Test Mental Maturity   NMST   California
     California Reading   CEEB   Reading
     Schorling 100 Problems   Wechsler
     Ann Arbor Spelling   (as recommended)

GRADUATING CLASS OF 1961 — 630.

Curriculum Followed	Number	Percent
College or University	413	65.6
Business	53	8.4
Industrial	5	.8
General	150	23.8
Certificate of Attendance	9	1.4

Distribution of Marks—Entire school (second-semester—college preparatory, academic subjects)

Mark	Percent	Mark	Percent
A 95-100	14.5	D 65-74	12.9
B 85-94	34.2	E Below 65	3.3
C 74-85	34.6		

Grade Point Average distribution in class rank by quartiles (A = 3, B = 2, C = 1, D = 0)
    $Q_1 = 1.75$ Median = 1.30 $Q_4 = .95$

College Board Results (315 taking SAT)

Range	Verbal	Math
800-		
700-799	17	37
600-699	58	65
500-599	91	115
400-499	94	72
300-399	50	25
200-299	5	1
Median	510	505

I.Q. Distribution

	Entire School		Class 1961	
Above 141	21	1.	2	.03
126-140	151	7.5	49	7.8
111-125	660	32.2	208	33.1
91-110	922	44.8	302	48.
76- 90	257	12.5	59	9.4
75 or below	41	2.	9	1.5
Median = 106.8			107.3	

Advanced Placement Examination, May, 1961

Physics	6	French	8	
Am. history	9	Spanish	5	
Math	27	German	8	
Chemistry	8	English	22	
		Total = 93		

Advanced Placement Examination Results

5 Highest Honors	6
4 Honors	17
3 Creditable	32
2 Pass	37
1 Fail	1
	93

College Attendance. 54% are continuing their education in 60 different institutions of higher learning: 80% in Michigan institutions and 20% in out-of-state institutions.

Scholarships and Grants — Seventy members of the class received scholarships or grants.

(Figure 25, continued)

October, 1961

ANN ARBOR HIGH SCHOOL
Ann Arbor, Michigan

BRIEF EXPLANATION OF ACCELERATED AND ADVANCED PLACEMENT COURSES

ac = accelerated
AP = Advanced Placement

Symbols	Taught Grade	Awarded Units	Course Description
MATHEMATICS			
	Junior High	1½	Algebra 1, 2, 3
1ac, 2ac	10	1½	Geometry 1, 2, Solid geometry
3ac, 4ac	11	1	Algebra 4, plane trigonometry plus special topics
5ac, 6ac	12	1	Introduction to analytic geometry and calculus
3AP, 4AP	11	1½	Algebra 4, topics in modern algebra, introductory analytic geometry, plane and spherical trigonometry
5AP, 6AP	12	1½	Introduction to integral and differential calculus with applications to analytic geometry and physical problems
FRENCH			
3ac, 4ac	10	1	Intermediate college grammar and selected contemporary reading
7AP, 8AP	12	1	Review of college grammar, oral-aural practice, exercises in translation and extensive selected readings from the Middle Ages to the present.
SPANISH			
3ac, 4ac	10	1	Intensive oral practice; selected readings from representative Hispanic-American writers; thorough study of grammar; considerable writing practice
5ac, 6ac	11	1	Same as above
GERMAN			
3ac, 4ac	11	1	Intensive study of grammar and idioms, considerable writing of original German; oral and aural approach. Content of courses 31 and 32 at the University of Michigan covered
ENGLISH			
4ac	10	1	Chronological survey of American literature. Critical study of the essay. Extensive reading and themes
5ac, 6ac 7ac, 8ac	11	1½	Survey of English literature with special units in American drama and modern American poetry. Extensive reading and themes
AP, AP	12	1½	Largely a composition course. Critical study of poetry. Extensive reading and themes
AMERICAN HISTORY			
3AP	11, 12	1	Fourteen areas are covered during the year, tracing American History from 1750 to the present day. Greater emphasis placed on political and economic theory with special attention to the development of American thought and social influences. Extensive reading
CHEMISTRY			
1ac, 2ac		1	Thorough coverage of traditional material. Also included: gas laws and their derivation. Van der Wall's forces, crystalline structure, electron energy levels, chemical equilibrium, standard solutions and volumetric analysis, qualitative and quantitative analysis, and radioactivity and nucleonics.
PHYSICS			
1ac, 2ac	12	1	The Physical Science Study Committee course is studied in its entirety. The PSSC text and laboratory guide are utilized. The main areas studied are the Universe, Optics, and Waves, Mechanics, and Electricity and Atomic Structure. Course emphasis is understanding the basic laws of physics with a minimum of applied physics and technology, mathematical techniques of trigonometry, and to some extent calculus, are utilized in problem solving and equation derivations.

Five-Point Letter or Numerical Scale. Both the five-point letter scale and the five-point number scale are intended to show relative achievement among students rather than mastery of a certain amount of content. In such systems students are ranked according to achievement scores or the teacher's estimate and then assigned a category with a description of its meaning. The usual definitions for letter or number marks as follows:

Mark	Definition	Mark
A	Superior	1
B	Above average	2
C	Average	3
D	Below average	4
F	Failing	5

"Superior" means superior in achievement as compared to other members of the class. Other meanings or definitions can be assigned to these symbols if they help in communicating with parents. Teachers feel more competent to make judgments based on relative standards than on absolute standards, and parents generally have been willing to accept a system based on judgments of relative achievement.

Some faculties prefer fewer categories for classifying student achievement, so they use only two marks, S and U — S for satisfactory and U for unsatisfactory achievement. Having only two categories simplifies the marking from the teacher's viewpoint, but parents usually want to know just "how satisfactory" or "how unsatisfactory" are the achievements of their child. Sometimes schools meet this objection by using S—, S, S+, U—, U, and U+. Thus the degrees of differentiation are about the same as in the five-point scale. It is recommended, therefore, that high schools evaluate academic achievement on a five-point rather a two-point scale.

Normal Curve. Most marks assigned by teachers are arbitrary or subjective to some extent. In order to increase the reliability of these judgments, statisticians and psychologists have urged that marks be assigned on the basis of a "normal" curve. This recommendation stems from the fact that measurement of large numbers of human traits and abilities yields data that approximate the normal probability distribution, i.e., a bell-shaped curve. Under this system, a fixed percentage of marks is assigned to each letter grade, i.e., 7 per cent A's, 23 per cent B's, 40 per cent C's, 23 per cent D's, and 7 per cent E's. The exact percentages for each letter grade may be varied according to local policies, but the percentage of E's and A's is the same, the percentage of D's and B's is the same and the largest percentage of students receive C's under this plan.

It is true that for large numbers of students and over a long period of time, measures of student achievement tend to approximate a normal curve distribution. But according to Good, there are two basic fallacies in attempting to use the normal curve for assigning marks:

> ... the assumption (1) that the distribution of marks must be symmetrical, and (2) that the units on the base line must be equal. The mere fact that the measurements tend to approximate normal distribution does not support either of these assumptions; the marks may still be distributed in any way we choose — it depends upon what meaning we wish to convey. The first of these two fallacies is illustrated in Figure A, and both are involved in Figure B.[7]

Two Inferior Systems of Assigning Marks

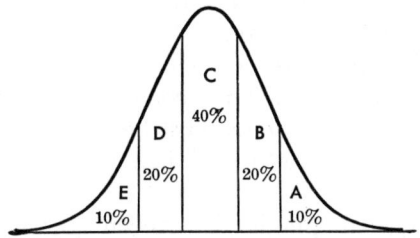

Figure A—Symmetrical Assignment of Marks on the Basis of Certain Arbitrary Percentages.

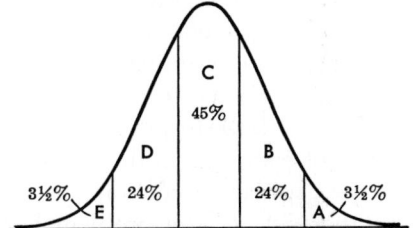

Figure B—Symmetrical Assignment of Marks by the Use of Equal Base-Line Units.

The issue involved in using the normal curve is not whether marks can be distributed symmetrically or according to a fixed percentage but what the marks mean. Is it reasonable, for instance, to decide that 10 per cent, or any other fixed per cent, of students must be called failures? In cases where students are selected to succeed, such as in an advanced or accelerated class, it becomes completely unrealistic to assume that a fixed percentage must fail. The objection to a fixed rate of failure does not mean that some students should not fail, but it does imply that settling in advance on a fixed percentage of students to be failed is unfair. For that matter, it is unfair to determine the percentage for any category of marks in advance, particularly in small classes.

We suggest, therefore, that the idea of a symmetrical distribution of marks must be modified for any one class, depending upon the criteria used for selection, and a more realistic interpretation made of the percentage of students who should be identified as failures. Use of the normal curve in analyzing the total distribution of marks over a number of years should provide data helpful to a faculty when studying its marking

[7] Warren R. Good, "The Assignment of School Marks," *School of Education Bulletin*, The University of Michigan, May, 1947, 18:121.

policies, but strict adherence to the normal curve is not appropriate for all schools and/or all classes within a school. In addition, use of the normal curve, as well as the percentage system, usually ignores outcomes other than measurable mastery of knowledge. Thus it is necessary to supplement marks with other forms of reporting to give a more nearly complete picture of a student's total achievement.

Marking on Ability. One issue which often comes up when a faculty discusses marks is whether they should be assigned on the basis of comparison with the class in general or in terms of the individual's ability. Modern educational theory has emphasized adjusting instruction to the ability of the learner. Under this concept, it is logical to report a student's achievement in relation to his potential. But there are those who object to marking a student A in mathematics if he scores below the average of the class on examinations or other measures of achievement even though he works up to or above his own ability. They contend that this is misleading both to pupils and to parents; students must be exposed to the type of competition they will face in the adult world, i.e., competition with the general population.

Another side of the problem has been highlighted in recent years in the increased use of grouping for programs of instruction designed for the academically talented. These special programs, such as the advanced placement program, accelerated classes, honor programs, and other similar plans, have created special marking problems. It does not seem reasonable, for instance, to insist on five levels of marks (A, B, C, D, E) in a course in which pupils are selected because of outstanding ability and high achievement in the past. Neither does it seem fair to jeopardize the chances of a good student for admission to the college of his choice merely because his marks are below those of students who were enrolled in classes less demanding than the special program in which he participated. This can happen if teachers insist on using traditional systems for assigning marks in special programs.

If a student desires to participate in a class such as the advanced placement program, it is common practice to require a previous record of B or A in that subject as one criterion for selection. In addition, it is assumed that all participants will continue to achieve at a high level. Anyone not capable of doing high-quality work should not be chosen in the first place. Obviously some adjustments in the marking system are necessary in these situations. Some schools which practice grouping have adjusted their traditional marking plans in accordance with one of four plans: fixed limits, weighted honor points, classified, or dual.

Under the system of fixed limits, marks are limited to each grouping of students. For example, assuming a school has three levels of grouping, X, Y, and Z, the following marks could be assigned to each group.

Group:	X	Y	Z
	A	B	C
	B	C	D
	C	D	F
		F	

Any pupil in Group X would be assured of receiving a mark no lower than C whereas students in Group Y would receive a mark no higher than B, and those in Group Z would receive a mark no higher than C.

Advantages of the fixed limits system include the following: (1) There is some differentiation for different ability groups, recognizing that students in different groups should not be graded on the same scale; (2) excessive clerical work is not demanded of teachers; and (3) it tells parents, students, and colleges where the student stands in comparison to all students in a subject and not just in his ability section. Disadvantages include the following: (1) It compares students from one ability level to another without any common measures of achievement; (2) consideration is not given to different materials used in the various groups; (3) there is too much overlapping of marks between groups; (4) low-ability students tend to get discouraged, realizing that they cannot earn a mark above a C no matter how hard they work; and (5) indolent students in the high group are not failed even though they deserve to be.

In the system of weighted honor points different honor points are assigned to marks depending upon the ability group, with the highest ability group receiving the highest honor point value. Following is a typical assignment of honor points under this plan:

Group:	X	Y	Z
A	6	5	4
B	5	4	3
C	4	3	2
D	3	2	1
E	0	0	0

Although students in each group would receive the full range of marks, students in Group X have an advantage over those in Groups Y and Z when rank in class is calculated because of the higher honor point value assigned to it. Similarly, students in Group Y have an advantage over students in Group Z.

The advantages of the weighted honor point system include those of the fixed limit plan, but in addition, (1) a full range of marks at each level recognizes effort and allows for unusual cases; (2) it is suited to research and predictions; (3) students in middle and low groups can earn a top grade; (4) honor points provide a means for differentiating marks among the three groups; and (5) different scales allow for differences in instruction among the groups. Disadvantages of this plan include: (1) Parents, employers, and college registrars have difficulty in interpreting the meaning of the marks without access to local norms; (2) there is no common measure between the groups; and (3) it is not useful in single-section electives and other nongrouped courses.

Under the classified system marks are designated according to the group to which the student is assigned. If, for example, there are three groups X, Y, and Z, each mark includes the group in which the mark was earned; an A would be reported as A_x, A_y, or A_z. Some schools choose to number the groups, i.e., 1, 2, and 3. In this case, the mark would be A_1, A_2, or A_3.

Advantages of the classified plan include those of the weighted honor points system, but in addition, it is more easily understood by parents, employers, and colleges.

The dual system for reporting marks combines grading according to ability and relative achievement in comparison with all students enrolled in a subject by giving two achievement marks instead of attempting to combine both evaluations in one mark. Under this plan, one mark is given on relative achievement based on departmental examinations of the general educational development type and certain other common measures such as themes. A second mark is assigned according to achievement in relation to the individual's ability. For example, a student with an IQ of 92 who scored at the fiftieth percentile on the departmental examination might be assigned a C for his achievement in relation to the total population, but he would receive an A in relation to his ability.

It appears to the authors that the dual system for assigning marks answers most of the criticisms of the other systems. (1) It is not difficult to interpret, (2) it indicates both relative achievement and individual progress, (3) it can be used for research and prediction, and (4) it can be used for most courses. However, it does present the problems of demanding more of the teachers' time for clerical work and of establishing a valid index of each student's ability.

Reporting Behavior and Work Habits. In addition to reporting academic achievement, teachers are in a favorable position to observe students' work habits and social behavior. If, for instance, a student is receiving low marks because he is consistently turning in incomplete work, or if he is showing considerable improvement in his general attitude toward his studies, most parents want to know it. Some teachers object to reporting on behavior and work habits because they cannot always document their remarks with test results or other objective data. Such reports do force teachers to make subjective judgments, but even without the support of objective data, the opinion of teachers in these matters is the best source of information available to parents. Honest errors in judgment usually will be tolerated by parents and there is more to be gained by making such judgments than by ignoring behavior for fear of making an error. A word of caution is in order, however; positive comments should be made when deserved as well as negative comments. It is important to give attention to what is wrong, but it is just as important to give attention to what is right. On the other hand, objective data to support observations of behavior should not be neglected; teachers should be encouraged to gather as much objective evidence as possible to back their observations.

A practical objection by some teachers to reporting on behavior and work habits is the amount of time it takes. Consequently, many schools have included checklists describing behavior and work habits on their report cards. Teachers need only to check those items which best describe the pupil. If none of the descriptions is appropriate, a note can be added. Use of such checklists reduces considerably the clerical burden of reporting pupil behavior to parents.

Letters and Parent-Teacher Conferences. Report cards are at best impersonal and hardly an adequate answer in communicating a student's progress to his parents. Some schools substitute letters and/or parent-teacher conferences for the traditional report card.

A well-written letter or a conference is more effective than a report card. But in some respects this is merely a theoretical issue because of the practical problem of finding the time to write letters or to have individual conferences with parents. For example, Miss Smith has 150 different pupils per day in her English classes. Assuming it takes at least twenty minutes to gather pertinent data and to write a letter or have a conference with a parent, Miss Smith would have to spend a minimum of 20×150 or 3,000 minutes (50 hours) to perform this duty. If she were to do this six times per year, 300 hours (seven and a half weeks on the basis of a forty-hour week) would be devoted to parent reports. Obviously, a plan requiring this amount of time is completely unrealistic. It is not implied, however, that there is no place for these techniques in high school. Many high schools do have regularly scheduled parent-teacher conferences. But students are excused from classes, and appointments are made by the parents with the homeroom teachers. Such a plan is practical since there are only about thirty pupils per homeroom teacher, but it still does not provide an opportunity for the parent to confer with each teacher of his child.

If letters are used, it is suggested that all teachers should be encouraged to write to the parents whenever something particularly significant occurs rather than at fixed intervals.

Letters to parents and parent-teacher conferences are effective ways to communicate with parents concerning the progress of their children. In high schools, however, they should be supplementary to regular report cards, not substitutes for them.

Frequency of Reports to Parents. Traditionally, high schools report to parents six times during the school year. However, some schools have reduced reports to four per year in order to lessen the clerical work involved. Reporting only four times a year is adequate providing there is an interim report on students who are having difficulty. It is not in the best interest of the student who is having trouble to allow a period as long as nine weeks to pass before advising him and his parents of this fact. A mid-quarter report to those who are not achieving satisfactorily gives them a chance to improve before the official marking period is ended. It is recommended, therefore, that schools report to parents only four times per year, but that teachers be responsible for continuous evaluation of pupil progress during the time between marking periods and report any serious difficulties pupils appear to be having in the interim.

Model Report Card. The actual form or design of report cards varies from school to school. This is as it should be; each school should include information it feels is important and in a manner acceptable to its patrons. The report card shown in Figure 26, used by Tappan Junior High School, Ann Arbor, Michigan, does have many excellent features which might be helpful to administrators and their faculties in planning a card appropriate to their schools. For instance, it includes the following: (1) achievement in subjects as compared to other pupils in the class, (2) achievement in relation to own ability, (3) a checklist of behavior or work habits, (4) space for parents or teachers to write comments, and (5) explanation of the symbols used.

Diplomas

All high schools issue some type of diploma to a student when he graduates. The format of most diplomas is the same, but there is some difference of opinion on whether or not all students should receive the same diploma regardless of the curriculum completed. Most schools use only one type of diploma, but some of the larger schools with multiple curricula label the diploma as Academic, General, Vocational, or Certificate of Attendance. The latter is awarded to those students who attended the required number of years but were unable to achieve a prescribed grade-point average.

Some supporters of differentiated diplomas argue that in order to preserve the standing of the high school in the opinion of the public, only students who achieve well in the academic subjects should receive a regular diploma. Employers are sometimes critical because some high school graduates who seek employment with them cannot perform certain basic skills as well as high school graduates in the past. Others feel that the diploma no longer means much, because absolute standards are no longer required for graduation.

FIGURE 26
Report Card Used by Tappan Junior High School, Ann Arbor, Michigan

SEVENTH GRADE

Explanation of Report
Your child has a "mark" "M" and a "rating" "R" in each subject. The "mark" shows his achievement compared with other pupils. The "rating" reveals his achievement in relation to his own ability, as well as can be estimated. Both marks are important, even though they are different in meaning. "N" or "Teacher's Notation" explains something more about your child's achievement or adjustment.

Explanation of Marks
The A, B, C letter marks stand for the pupil's achievement as compared with other pupils.
A Very much above average
B Above average
C Average
D Below average, barely passing
E Failure, no credit
I Incomplete work due to absence

RATINGS: The rating in each subject shows how well he is doing in relation to the teacher's estimate of his ability.
G good   M medium
P poor

Teacher's Notations
1. Fails to bring necessary materials
2. Very inattentive
3. Uncooperative
4. Poor oral participation
5. Poor attendance
6. Fails to complete assignments.
7. Discourteous behavior
8. Low test scores
9. Poor use of time
10. Works very hard
11. Completes assignments
12. Capable of doing better
13. Good work habits
14. Helpful group member
15. Cooperative Attitude
16. Good self-control
17. Accepts responsibility
18. Shows improvement
19. _____
20. _____

Homeroom Teacher _____ Pupil's Name _____ Homeroom _____

Marking Periods	1		2		3		4		Final
	M	R	M	R	M	R	M	R	
UNIFIED STUDIES									
ENGLISH SKILLS	N								
MATHEMATICS	N								
HOMEMAKING	N								
SHOP	N								
SCIENCE	N								
ART	N								
GENERAL MUSIC	N								
BAND	N								
ORCHESTRA	N								
CHORUS	N								
PHYSICAL EDUCATION	N								
	N								
STUDY HALL NOTATION Teacher:									
HALF DAYS ABSENT									
TIMES TARDY									

On the other side of the argument are those who feel it is unfair to label students according to varying degrees of academic performance. A parent may be willing to admit that his son is not as bright, academically, as some other child, but he is unwilling to have such a tag attached to him on commencement night.

An increasing number of schools are meeting this problem by issuing only one diploma but printing a transcript of credits on the back. This practice is to be commended, for it allows employers to consider the entire record of graduates. In addition, it is possible to issue each pupil a transcript of credits reduced in size so that he can carry it in his billfold for ready reference when applying for a position or any other time when he has reason to refer to his high school record.

Attendance Records

All but a few southern states now have laws for compulsory attendance in school, usually to age sixteen and in some cases to age eighteen. However, educators have never been able to legislate motivation for students to attend school. High school administrators are faced with the task, therefore, of keeping an accurate record of the attendance of each student. In addition to the compulsory attendance laws, some states calculate the amount of money a school receives from the state on the basis of student attendance. This usually motivates the principal to encourage regular attendance by students and to maintain records as accurately as possible.

The basic records used in accounting for student attendance are the teacher's class register and the office attendance record. The teacher's class register is one of the earliest records maintained in schools. Its exact form varies according to legal requirements and preference. Usually, however, the teacher records date of enrollment, absences, date of withdrawal, tardiness, and other pertinent data in a class book. Practically every teacher has had experience with such a record and is familiar with the procedure for maintaining it. From time to time, the principal may have to remind teachers of the necessity for keeping these records accurate and up to date; some teachers get careless in clerical duties of this type.

As a rule, the official attendance register, normally a card type of record, is maintained in the office of the principal. At the end of each day a clerk in the office records all absences of students on their cards. Figure 27 shows a typical card.

Calculating Average Daily Attendance. At the end of each semester, a summary is made for each student of the number of days he was enrolled in school and the number of days he actually attended school. A total is made for all students on these two items, i.e., days enrolled and days attended. The Average Daily Attendance (A.D.A.) is calculated by dividing the total student days attended by the total student days enrolled and multiplying this quotient by 100.

$$\text{A.D.A.} = \frac{\text{Total student days in attendance}}{\text{Total student days enrolled}} \times 100$$

FIGURE 27
Typical Attendance Record Card

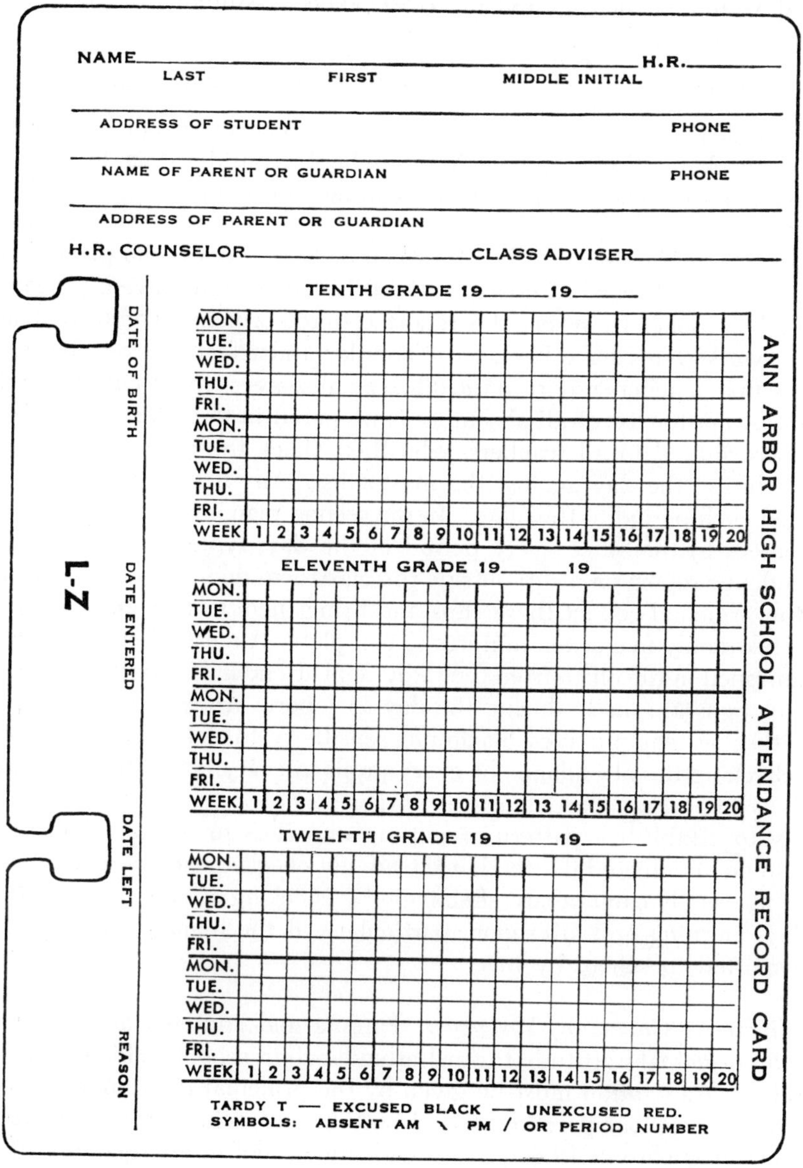

NAME _____ H.R. _____
     LAST   FIRST   MIDDLE INITIAL

ADDRESS OF STUDENT   PHONE

NAME OF PARENT OR GUARDIAN   PHONE

ADDRESS OF PARENT OR GUARDIAN

H.R. COUNSELOR _____ CLASS ADVISER _____

L-Z — DATE OF BIRTH — DATE ENTERED — DATE LEFT — REASON

ANN ARBOR HIGH SCHOOL ATTENDANCE RECORD CARD

TENTH GRADE 19____ 19____
(MON./TUE./WED./THU./FRI./MON./TUE./WED./THU./FRI.) WEEK 1 2 3 4 5 6 7 8 9 10 11 12 13 14 15 16 17 18 19 20

ELEVENTH GRADE 19____ 19____
(MON./TUE./WED./THU./FRI./MON./TUE./WED./THU./FRI.) WEEK 1 2 3 4 5 6 7 8 9 10 11 12 13 14 15 16 17 18 19 20

TWELFTH GRADE 19____ 19____
(MON./TUE./WED./THU./FRI./MON./TUE./WED./THU./FRI.) WEEK 1 2 3 4 5 6 7 8 9 10 11 12 13 14 15 16 17 18 19 20

TARDY T — EXCUSED BLACK — UNEXCUSED RED.
SYMBOLS: ABSENT AM \ PM / OR PERIOD NUMBER

Source: Ann Arbor Senior High School, Ann Arbor, Michigan.

For example, if a school has 300 students enrolled for the full 180 days normally included in the school year, the total number of student days enrolled would be 300 × 180 or 54,000 days. Assuming the total days actually attended by these 300 pupils to be only 50,000, the A.D.A. for this year would be $= \frac{50,000}{54,000} \times 100$ or 92.6 per cent. Many principals place a great deal of emphasis on regular attendance in school and keep a daily check on their A.D.A. Many schools consider this to be their barometer for determining how well things are going.

Reporting Absentees. The classroom or homeroom is the place where attendance is checked. Consequently, it is necessary to have a procedure whereby absence from school is reported to the principal's office by teachers. Two systems have been most popular and effective over the years. In the first, teachers report to the office all absentees from their first-period class. A master list of all absentees is prepared in the office immediately and distributed to all teachers, who then check the attendance in each class during the day against the master list. Any new absentees are reported each period to the office. In the second plan, every teacher reports absentees to the office every period of the day, typically by placing an attendance report on a slip outside the classroom door. Student assistants to the principal collect these slips and bring them to the office; this process takes only five to ten minutes to complete. A master list of absentees is compiled in the office from the individual attendance reports. Additions or deletions are made during the day as reports are received.

Either system provides maximum sensitivity to determining absences by checking the attendance of every pupil in every class during the day. This is important, particularly in larger schools where some pupils are likely to establish a pattern of cutting one class or a study hall which would go undetected if attendance were not checked each period. Smaller schools usually can operate effectively by checking attendance only twice a day, morning and afternoon, particularly if the majority of pupils are transported to school by bus.

Principal's Check of Absences. Parents and students are influenced by the principal's attitude toward attendance in school. This means that careful consideration must be given by the principal to attendance problems. An excellent practice, aimed both at improving attendance and at encouraging parents to cooperate with the school in attendance matters, is to telephone the home of every absent pupil the first day of absence. Such calls should be made by the principal, his assistant, or a trained secretary, and not by a clerk. Problems encountered in these home contacts can be delicate in terms of public relations and should not be delegated to a clerk. Not only does the practice of calling the home demonstrate the school's concern for the child's welfare, but it also helps to identify any truancy at the earliest moment. In addition, it gives the school a chance to offer its assistance in cases of long-term illness. Parents generally appreciate this, although occasionally there will be parents who resent the school's being so inquisitive about their affairs. However, most parents are willing to cooperate with the school, and the pattern is soon established where the parent anticipates a call when his child is absent, or he will take the initiative to report the absence to the school.

Truancy. Truancy is absence from school for reasons other than illness or special situations approved by the school. Most cases of truancy merit careful consideration by school authorities. A truancy case should be looked upon not as a law enforcement procedure but rather as an opportunity to provide special counseling and guidance to a pupil who obviously has some irresponsible or negative attitudes concerning attendance in school.

The authors recommend the use of trained visiting teachers rather than "truant officers." There may be cases in which a law officer is also needed, but in most schools truancy is better dealt with by the principal or his assistants. The manner in which the contacts, with both the parents and the student, are made may determine how satisfactorily the pupil responds. People who have been with him in other school situations and who have knowledge about his total school relationship are in a better position to work with him when he has been truant than are "truant officers" who only apprehend offenders.

Most principals soon become adept at spotting truancies. All that is needed in some cases is to examine the list of absentees, and when two or three known "buddies" are absent on the same day, it is likely that something irregular is happening. Routine telephone calls on all absences as suggested previously will identify the majority of truancies, but where both parents work it may be necessary to make late afternoon or evening calls. If a home has no telephone, a representative of the school should visit the home. It is important to locate the truant child just as soon as possible in order to keep his absence to a minimum and also to help prevent other acts of delinquency which sometimes accompany truancy.

After a case of truancy has been confirmed, many schools suspend the offender from school until such time as the parents accompany him to school for a conference with the principal. This procedure is not always the best one to follow — home conditions or other circumstances must be considered — but usually it is effective to insist on a parent-student-principal conference before the student is readmitted to school. This achieves four major objectives: (1) The school's concern for regular attendance is emphasized, (2) cooperation of the parent and the school is enhanced, (3) responsibility for assuring regular attendance in school

STUDENT RELATIONSHIPS

is placed on the student and parent, and (4) an opportunity is provided to identify any problem which either the parents or the student feel concerning their relationship to school.

If reasonable assurance is given in such a conference that the truancy will not be repeated, the student should be readmitted to school. After he has returned to classes, his case should be referred to counselors for a follow-up on problems leading to the truancy.

FIGURE 28

Form for Reporting Absence

ANN ARBOR HIGH SCHOOL—Ann Arbor, Michigan

REPORT TO PARENTS OR GUARDIAN H.R. ___ Grade ___

_____ returned to school today after an absence during _____

He/she states the reason for absence as follows:

_____

_____

An excused/unexcused class admission blank has been issued in accordance with the policy of the Board of Education and the Ann Arbor Senior High School.

You will find the school always willing to cooperate in the best interest of your child. If further information is desired, please call 3-0551 the Attendance Office.

Sincerely,

Date_____   _____
                                Class Advisor

Source: Ann Arbor Senior High School, Ann Arbor, Michigan.

Excused and Unexcused Absences. A large majority of absences from school are due to illness and should be excused, but some should not be excused even though they are not considered cases of truancy. For example, a mother insists on taking her daughter out of town to visit an aunt; another one says this is the only day she can take her daughter shopping for new clothing. Such occasions hardly justify absence from school and generally are not regarded as acceptable excuses. The most appropriate penalty would seem to be to make up the time missed.

Traditionally, students have been required to bring a written note from their parents to the high school principal to explain the reason for being absent from school. The student is then given a permit to rejoin his classes. The permit usually indicates whether or not the absence was excused or unexcused. The serious deficiency in this procedure is that many students forge their parents' signatures, often just because a parent is not available to write the note. A number of schools recognize that a note from the parent is not always needed and are willing to accept a statement from either the parent or the student. The authors recommend this practice, especially in schools which follow the suggestions previously made for identifying truants. An excellent follow-up to the student's statement is to send a card to the parents such as the one shown in Figure 28.

The principal's office can become a real bottleneck each day if all absentees must present themselves to the principal for readmission. It is better to delegate authority for readmitting students either to the home-room teacher or to the teacher of the first-period class. Only unusual cases need by referred to the principal. This minimizes the delay in getting pupils back in class and often teachers can confer with the pupil about his absence and are in a better position to judge whether or not it should be excused than is the principal.

Tardiness. Tardiness is handled in much the same way as absence in most schools. The tardy student is required to get permission from the principal or an assistant to be admitted to class. Many schools also establish certain penalties such as loss of assembly privileges or assignment to a retention room after school for tardiness. These rather mild penalties seem to serve adequately except in cases of chronic tardiness, which require more careful attention through counseling and enlisting the aid of the parents.

Miscellaneous Consumable Forms

Every high school has numerous miscellaneous forms: library permit, student schedule change blank, change of address blank, emergency information form, car registration, hall pass, etc. They are usually designed to suit the needs of individual schools and so vary in style and content. Space does not permit a discussion of all possible records and forms of this type, most of which are available from school supply houses. The principles discussed earlier in this chapter are appropriate to the employment of such forms. It is especially important that a form serve a useful purpose and not demand an excessive amount of teacher or secretarial time.

Implications of Automation

The development of machines for processing data has considerable promise for reducing the clerical work necessary to maintain school records and for speeding up the processing that must be done. The advantages are especially significant for large high schools. At the present time, the greatest use of these machines is in building the schedule of recitations for the school (see Chapter 6). However, some companies have developed forms and procedures for keeping records of the school census, attendance, registration, report cards, and program evaluation which also are worthy of study. Particularly helpful are the ease and speed with which machines can prepare various student lists, making it possible to secure class lists, homeroom lists, grade lists, etc., with a minimum investment of time and energy by school personnel. Printing of report cards is another task in which some schools have found machine processing helpful.

Machines for data processing are expensive and most school systems cannot afford to rent all the necessary equipment but must rent time on the machines at a central service place. This requires a certain amount of foresight in order to have the services of the machine available when needed. Some delay is likely unless the administrator plans carefully or unless the school is located near a center that has enough equipment to service the school with little advance notice.

Small and medium-sized schools may find little advantage in machine processing of data. In some cases, it may be faster to have clerks perform the necessary tasks. Whether a school should utilize the services of data-processing machines depends upon a careful analysis of the comparable costs and convenience as between clerical processing and machine processing. In addition, attention is called to the fact that it is not necessary to do everything by machine processing, and a certain amount of clerical work still is needed to prepare material for use by the machines. But the principal of a large high school should investigate the possibilities of utilizing the services of a data-processing center, since the gains can be substantial. Improvements and new developments in this field will probably continue at a rapid rate, and all administrators should keep informed about them.

Questions and Group Projects

1. Make a collection of all the forms used by the principal of a school.
    a. What is the purpose of each form?
    b. How effectively is it achieving its purpose?
    c. What recommendations would you make for its improvement?
2. Design a cumulative record which you feel would serve effectively in a school having a well-established philosophy of adapting instruction to the individual.
3. Calculate the rank in class for the following students:

Student	Grade-Point Average	Student	Grade-Point Average
A	3.97	G	2.50
B	2.25	H	2.25
C	1.50	I	2.25
D	3.50	J	3.50
E	3.25	K	1.90
F	2.75	L	3.45

4. Make a survey of the opinions of the parents of pupils in a school to determine what information they want to have included on report cards.

5. Visit the office of the county superintendent of schools in your county to determine what reports must be made to his office during the year and the due date of each report.

Selected References

Ahman, J. S., and M. D. Glock. *Evaluating Pupil Growth.* Boston: Allyn and Bacon, 1955. Chap. 17.

Bollenbacher, Joan. "Student Records and Reports — Elementary and Secondary," *Encyclopedia of Educational Research.* New York: The Macmillan Company, 3rd ed., 1960. Pp. 1437–42.

Casey, J. E. "Evaluating Pupils in Terms of Improvement," *School and Society,* 1958, 86:263–65.

Elicker, Paul E. "Record Forms for Secondary Schools," *The Bulletin* of the NASSP, November, 1947, 31:39–48.

Jansen, Udo H. "Marking and Reporting Procedures in the Secondary Schools of Texas," *Texas Study of Secondary Education,* Research Bulletin No. 32. Austin: University of Texas, 1960.

Keller, I. A. "Evaluation of the Dual Grading System," *The Bulletin* of the NASSP, March, 1955, 39:38–45.

McDonnell, K. A. "A Dual Mark for Reporting Pupil Subject Accomplishment," *American School Board Journal,* 1955, 131:19–20.

National Committee on Cumulative Records. *Handbook of Cumulative Records.* U.S. Office of Education, Bulletin 1944, No. 5. Washington: Government Printing Office, 1944.

National Education Association, Department of Superintendence. *Report of the Committee on Uniform Records and Reports,* U.S. Bureau of Education, Bulletin 1912, No. 3. Washington: Government Printing Office, 1912. P. 46.

National Education Association, Research Division. "School Records and Reports," *Research Bulletin,* 1927, 5:227–346.

Segel, David. *Nature and Use of the Cumulative Record,* U.S. Office of Education, Bulletin 1938, No. 3. Washington: Government Printing Office, 1938.

Strang, Ruth. *How to Report Pupil Progress.* Chicago: Science Research Associates, 1955.

Traxler, Arthur E. *Techniques of Guidance.* New York: Harper & Brothers. rev. ed., 1957.

Van Dyke, L. A., and J. N. Sparks. *Four-State Survey of Secondary School Marking Practices,* Research Digest No. 2. Iowa City: Iowa Center for Research in School Administration, January, 1960.

Wrinkle, W. L. *Improving Marking and Reporting Practices.* New York: Rinehart and Company, 1947.

Yeager, William. *Administration and the Pupil.* New York: Harper & Brothers, 1949.

VI

Management and Community Relations

Although the secondary school principal's major professional interests and energies should be directed toward work with his faculty to improve instruction, someone has to manage the store. In a small or medium-sized high school the principal has to direct, or handle in person, most of the business and managerial operations that support the instructional program. And in large high schools assistant principals are expected to perform this task.

In a public school system the supporting public quite properly expects to be kept informed about the progress of the educational program and the management of public funds for education. In addition, it wants to have an opportunity to exchange views with educators on the ends and means of public education. Providing these services as they relate to the high school is an important part of the job of being a principal. Therefore, the purposes, nature, problems, and techniques of school-community relations have been made the subject of Chapter 17.

Chapter 18 deals with the business management of secondary schools. The duties of high school administrators in budgeting, accounting, purchasing, storing, and inventorying supplies and equipment are described, along with those of preparing long- and short-term plans for educational services.

The management of the high school's central office and the preparation of summary reports on the operation and progress of the school's educational program are the subjects of Chapter 19. Even though these are workaday tasks and many of them should be delegated, the principal must assume responsibility for organizing, programming, and supervising them, and in a small high school he must perform many of them himself.

Chapter 20 deals with the role of the principal in school plant planning. Not many principals will have an opportunity to participate in planning a new plant, but many will have occasion, in cooperation with their faculties and superintendents, to plan expansions and remodeling projects to keep pace with mounting enrollments and new curriculum developments. In combination, these tasks represent a major responsibility.

CHAPTER 17

The Secondary School and Community Relations

In the United States, continued community support for any public institution must be earned. In the case of the public schools, support over the years is largely dependent upon the quality of education provided. It would seem to follow that, if teachers and administrators were to concentrate on the business of running a good school, the matter of community relations should take care of itself. Unfortunately, things do not work out quite that neatly in a large pluralistic society.

Although good community relations depend largely upon good public service, they also depend on the public's being well informed about institutions and their services. If the public schools are to do well the things they are expected to do, the people must be sufficiently aware of their needs to provide adequate funds and to maintain a favorable climate of opinion for their support. But competition for tax dollars and public favor is intense. Furthermore, the general public is composed of many smaller publics — each with special social, economic, and political interests. A school may be successful in demonstrating to its own clientele that it is doing an excellent job of teaching children, but it must also persuade local tax leagues, retired farmers, city hall politicos, and a variety of patriotic societies.

The terms "public relations" and "community relations" frequently are used interchangeably. The authors have no desire to shoot at sparrows, but the popular view of public relations carries a "hard sell" connotation. Thus it has little appeal for most teachers since they have had little training and less experience in such matters. At the same time, teachers generally are conscious of the interrelationships of a school and its community. And if public relations is viewed broadly, as it is in the following statement, there seems to be little point in quibbling over fine distinctions between the two terms. The Commission on Public Relations of the American Association of School Administrators states,

> ... public relations involves far more than "publicity" or interpretation. It means genuine cooperation in planning and working for good schools, with the public giving as well as receiving ideas. It becomes a two-way process, a two-day flow of ideas between school and community which provides the basis for mutual understanding and effective team work.[1]

Although the authors are partial to the term "community relations," the preceding view of public relations, with its emphasis on a two-way flow of ideas between school and community, mutual understanding, and effective teamwork, impresses us as sound. Consequently, the two terms will be used synonymously.

The board of education and the superintendent of schools are charged with the primary responsibility for developing cooperative community relations for a school system. But boards and superintendents cannot do the job alone. They need help — in these times they need a large amount of help — from other people who know and understand the needs of instruction in the schools.

The people who know these needs best and who are in closest touch with the people who care most — parents and students — are the teachers and principals in individual school units. It may seem incongruous to them to be expected to take time from teaching in order to develop public understanding and approval of what they are doing and what they need, but if they do not assume a reasonable share of this responsibility, they are certain to be handicapped in their teaching. More important, students are certain to be handicapped in the type of education they receive.

Growing Importance of School Public Relations

The United States has had a great tradition and a great faith in public education. It still has, but both the tradition and the faith have been severely strained during the past decade. Disturbed by criticisms and local problems, people sometimes lose sight of the cause-and-effect relationship between free public education and the preservation and strength of a free society. Their memories may need to be refreshed upon occasion by such cogent statements as the following from Washington's farewell address: "In proportion as the structure of government gives force

---

[1] American Association of School Administrators, *Public Relations for America's Schools*, Twenty-Eighth Yearbook (Washington: The Association, 1950), p. 13.

to public opinion, it is essential that public opinion be enlightened." How? "Promote then, as an object of primary importance, institutions for the general diffusion of knowledge."[2] And more recently from the United States Supreme Court's *obiter dicta* in the Brown case in 1954:

> Today education is perhaps the most important function of the state and local governments. Compulsory school attendance laws and the great expenditures for education both demonstrate our recognition of the importance of education in our democratic society. It is required in the performance of our most basic public responsibilities. . . . It is the very foundation of good citizenship. Today it is the principal instrument in awakening the child to cultural values, in preparing him for later cultural training, and in helping him to adjust normally to his environment. In these days it is doubtful that any child may reasonably be expected to succeed in life if he is denied the opportunity of an education.[3]

Henry Steele Commager, commenting on this historic declaration, writes,

> This argument, with its brief but comprehensive references to the relation of education to citizenship, culture, special skills, and social adjustment, is an echo of a long series of statements, proclamations, and arguments, that began in the 1630's, and have re-echoed down the corridors of our history.[4]

But sometimes people forget, their vision becomes blurred, and they indulge in rash actions. A few local school districts, such as Virginia's Prince Edward County, abandoned their public school systems over the integration issue with seeming disregard for our national welfare and our constitutional form of federal government. In so doing, Prince Edward County denied over 1,700 Negro children the opportunity for formal education while providing private schools, supported largely by state grants of tax funds, for 1,400 white children.[5]

In many of our large cities increasing numbers of parents have elected to send their children to nonpublic schools. Some of them have sought to avoid having their children associate with children from different social, economic, religious, and racial groups, and some have become distrustful of the quality of public education. As the number of parents refusing to patronize the public schools has risen, support for an adequate program of public education has been weakened. More important,

---

[2] As quoted in Educational Policies Commission, *The Unique Functions of Education in American Democracy* (Washington: National Education Association, 1937), p. 18.

[3] 347 U.S. at 493.

[4] Henry Steele Commager, "A Historian Looks at the High School," in Francis S. Chase and Harold A. Anderson, editors, *The High School in a New Era* (Chicago: University of Chicago Press, 1957), p. 3.

[5] Irv Goodman, "Public Schools Died Here," *The Saturday Evening Post*, April 29, 1961, 234:32–33 f.

the pressures for granting tax funds for the support of nonpublic schools has increased at both state and national levels. If tax funds are employed for nonpublic schools, the public schools, already suffering from a lack of adequate support, are certain to be further handicapped.

As noted in Chapter 4, the quality of public education has been the target for a mounting volume of criticism during the past decade. Certain critics have claimed that public schools are retrogressing and that private and church schools provide a better quality of education than do public schools. That these claims are not based on fact has been established through numerous objective studies such as those cited in Chapter 4.

Criticism is essential to maintaining the quality and integrity of public institutions in a democracy. But a great flood of critical articles, without an adequate presentation of the facts, needs, and accomplishments of public institutions, tends to weaken or destroy the latter. In the case of an institution indispensable to the national welfare, such as public education, our republic and way of life are in turn weakened.

The urgency of telling the story of public education is further accentuated by the growing intensity of the competition for tax funds among public agencies. Each branch of the military services sponsors professional dramatizations and spot advertisements on television and radio to tell its story and to appeal for tax support. Each also employs a large corps of professional writers and public relations experts to present its needs to the public. Similar procedures are employed by many other federal, state, and local government agencies.

Teachers, school administrators, and board of education members may find such public relations campaigns distasteful, but they are naïve if they believe that the public schools can prosper in the struggle for public support by doing no more than going about the business of teaching school. The authors share the view of many other citizens that the employment of Madison Avenue techniques by government agencies is a waste of public funds which are badly needed to provide constructive public services. But one of the facts of life in our large, busy, and complicated society is that the institutions that fail to reach the public with a full accounting and with a clear presentation of their needs fare poorly in the competition for public support. They also suffer the greatest damage to prestige when organized attacks are directed against them.

Nature of the Problem

Since public schools are created, patronized, and maintained by the people, they must have the moral and financial support of a great majority of the people in order to provide sound education. It would seem axiomatic that the second condition should follow the first. But the American public is made up of many sub-publics. Some of them have a direct and active association with the schools and some do not. The only continuous and direct contact that a large number of people have with public education is the payment of taxes.

Although the benefits of public education are in evidence all around us, many people fail to reflect upon them. Older people whose children have completed their formal schooling lose touch with the public schools. Other groups, such as patrons of nonpublic schools, have very little firsthand knowledge of public education. Not infrequently, they are disposed to believe criticisms and rumors which are intended to discredit it.

The point is not that some people are critical of the public schools, but that it is imperative to acquaint all groups of people with the facts about them. The first requirement in good school-community relations is to maintain the best educational program possible with the resources provided, and the second requirement is to establish effective two-way communication with laymen to learn their views and to inform them about the nature and needs of the public schools.

The business of communicating with the people about education is a two-way process of interpretation between the public and the personnel of the schools. It involves (1) providing the information that people want, (2) learning what laymen expect the schools to do, and (3) informing the public what the schools need in order to do well the job they are supposed to do.

Information Desired

What people want to know about their schools varies from community to community and from period to period. However, the items most consistently appearing in the annual reports of boards and superintendents to the public, reflect the things that the people generally are interested in or at least have continued to ask about. Fine and Anderson list the following items as typical of those included in annual reports:[6]

>Descriptions of the instructional program
>>Elementary school program
>>Junior high school program
>>Senior high school program
>>Adult education
>>Extracurricular program
>
>The Staff
>>In-service education
>>Professional study groups
>>Non-instructional personnel

[6] Benjamin Fine and Vivienne Anderson, *The School Administrator and His Publications* (New London, Conn.: Arthur C. Croft Publications, 1957), pp. 22–23.

Enrollments
    Current and projected
School buildings
    New building features
    Capital outlay construction
Public support
    How the public makes good schools possible
    Community councils
    Lay-professional study councils
A look at the future
    Enrollment
    Classroom needs
    Teacher needs
    Teachers' salaries
    Bond funds
    Revenue needs
Budget and finance
    How the school dollar is used
    Financial report for the school year
    The operating and maintenance program
    Capital improvements made during the year
    Salary schedules

Elsewhere in their handbook, Fine and Anderson emphasize that the public is especially interested in the achievements and activities of students. Patrons want to know how well students do on standardized tests, how the graduates get along in college, what honors and scholarships students have won, how they fare in extraclass competitions, what unusual projects and experiments they have conducted, and what the alumni are doing.

Expressions from the People

Good school-community relations require two-way communication. Not only do laymen want to know what goes on in the schools, but they want to inform the schools what they would like to have them do. In small communities this may be a relatively simple and direct process. However, it is difficult for the people in large communities to become articulate about education. Frequently special-interest groups presume to speak for all of the people when in reality they are speaking for only a small minority. Consequently, school staffs should make it possible for representative groups of people to make their views on education known.

Two-way communication may be implemented through such media as teacher-parent conferences, PTA meetings, discussion groups, citizens advisory committees, and public opinion polls. These methods will be discussed more fully in the section on "Procedures and Media."

Presenting Needs

Because many people have little direct relationship with the schools, they do not know what is required to operate good schools. They fail to understand the terrific competition from business and industry that the schools face in securing and holding competent people in teaching. They have little knowledge of the extreme variations in abilities and interests among students and of the special training of teachers and the type of equipment and materials required to work with a heterogeneous body of students. They may see or read about the accomplishments of students in athletics, music, and dramatics and be willing enough to spend money for stadiums, gynasiums, and auditoriums. But in demanding good academic achievement, they often fail to associate scholastic results with libraries, laboratories, guidance programs, and well-trained teachers.

Consequently, board members, administrators, teachers, and parents — the people who know what is required to educate children — must assume responsibility for informing as many local patrons as possible about the needs of the schools. Experience has demonstrated that this cannot be done simply by printing budget proposals in the newspapers once a year. It must be a year-round process employing a wide variety of approaches and techniques. As many people as possible need to be persuaded to visit the schools and to see what is involved in educating children. In addition, continuing information must be presented through mass media, discussions with community groups, and citizen committees.

Responsibility and Coordination

A community is composed of a cluster of social-economic groups and institutions, and a school is composed of a variety of students, teachers, and nonprofessional personnel. The number of groups and individuals and the complexity of their relationships tend to vary substantially with the size and nature of the community. Although basically school-community relations are much the same in large and small communities, the methods and problems of communicating with various publics become progressively more complex as the size of the community increases.

Regardless of the size of the community, the number and diversity of groups and individuals involved in school-community relations produce problems of conflicting interests, proper balance, accuracy of information, and means of communication. If relations are to be maintained at a high level of effectiveness, all personnel directly associated with the public schools must recognize and be willing to help meet these problems.

Principal's Responsibilities

Working with his own staff and the superintendent's office in furthering good school-community relations is one of the professional responsibilities of a high school principal. Although the extent and specific nature of his duties in this field of administration vary with the policies and organization of the central office, frequently a principal who is actually the administrative head of his school is called upon to perform the following tasks:

Develop Staff Appreciation of the Importance of Good Community Relations. Some teachers either do not recognize the connection between good education and good community relations or regard such relations as being the responsibility of administrators and board members. Whether he wants to be or not, the teacher is a key person in school-community relations. By virtue of his daily association with students and frequent contacts with parents and other laymen, he is continuously shaping attitudes toward the school. Consequently, the teacher's sense of responsibility toward his role in community relations is a pivotal factor in the success of the program. If he is concerned, well informed, friendly toward parents and patrons, and fair and sympathetic in his dealings with students, it is probable that he will have a positive influence on community attitudes. If he is indifferent, aloof from the community, and inconsiderate in his relations with students and parents, he is likely to alienate many parents and patrons.

Since teachers receive little training in community relations in their undergraduate preparation, most of their attitudes and know-how in this field must be learned on the job. Probably the principal can be most helpful through individual conferences, but some types of problems lend themselves well to group study and discussion. Also, custodians, secretaries, and bus drivers have many community associations and actually may influence public opinion more than teachers do. Consequently, the principal should work as closely with them as with the faculty in seeking to develop an understanding of their role in interpreting the school.

Interpret System-Wide Policies and Develop Supplementary Policies with His Staff. As noted earlier, many people become involved and many diverse problems are encountered in the relations between a school and its publics. For example, who should speak for the schools on major controversial issues? If several staff members presume to act as spokesmen and their statements are contradictory, the faculty will appear to be divided and the educational program is likely to suffer.

By way of illustration, in a community near the home of one of the authors a controversy recently arose over the location of a proposed new high school building. In the local paper two board members and the superintendent were quoted as favoring a particular site, another board member and the high school principal stated a preference for a second site, and two high school coaches issued statements in support of a third site. Consequently, the people of the town became divided primarily over the location of the school. In the first election the proposition to authorize bonding the district for a new building was defeated. A policy with respect to public statements from the official school family undoubtedly would have helped the school bond issue to pass in this instance.

Policies with respect to such matters as discipline, citizens advisory committees, publicity for activities, teacher-parent conferences, and the like are also essential in building effective school-community relations. Within his own staff, the principal must assume responsibility for interpreting system-wide policies, making sure their implications for the educational program are understood, and working out supplementary policies needed in his school.

We are not proposing a gag rule for staff members. But we are proposing that an agreement on controversial issues should be reached within the staff before statements are made to the public. After an official position is taken by the staff, a statement should be issued through the principal, the superintendent, or the board of education. This question will be considered more fully in a later section.

Secure, Present, and Interpret School Information for Staff Use. If members of the staff are to be effective in communicating with laymen about the schools, they will need adequate and reliable information. One of the tasks of a principal is to see that they get it. Information on enrollments, financial status of the school, personnel, plant facilities, curriculum, special services, student achievement, evaluation data, and the like should be made available to the staff through the principal. Without such information, individual staff members are handicapped seriously in their discussions with the public.

Develop a Coordinated and Positive Program for Community Relations. Media and procedures will be described in a later section. Suffice it here to emphasize the responsibility of the principal for developing a well-coordinated program. A successful principal will need to be well versed in the use of such means as mass media, informal staff-patron contacts, teacher-parent conferences, advisory and planning groups, student activities, open-house programs, and faculty and student participation in community groups.

Effect Two-Way Interpretation of Educational Problems Between School Personnel and Patrons. Two of the chief ingredients of good school-community relations are mutual understanding and teamwork between school personnel and laymen. These require careful organization and the selection of appropriate vehicles for joint work and planning. School people ought to know how parents and patrons view education and the program of the local schools, and parents and patrons ought to know what the educators are attempting to do, what their problems are, and what facilities they need in order to do their jobs well.

In small school districts, two-way communication can be carried on in informal face-to-face discussions and in group meetings of patrons and teachers. However, in large metropolitan districts, it is impossible for school personnel to reach a high percentage of laymen through personal contacts. Furthermore, large meetings are unwieldy and do not lend themselves to a free exchange of ideas. Consequently, a combination of procedures must be resorted to in order to get representative expression and participation from members of various sub-publics. PTA meetings, citizens advisory councils, televised discussions, public forums, teacher participation in civic groups, and neighborhood coffee hours have been used successfully. The task of organizing and maintaining interest in these activities should be assumed by the principal of each school in his section of the community.

Coordinate Activities with Elementary Schools. Contradictory information, duplication of effort, and conflicting policies between elementary and secondary units place a strain on school public relations. Many parents with children in high school also have children in elementary school, and the patrons of a high school are also the patrons of one or more elementary schools. Frequently, one or more junior high schools serve the same area. Conflicts and contradictions between the staffs of these units are quickly sensed by the public.

Where two or more schools in the same system serve the same territory, the problem of resolving conflicts and avoiding duplication in school events requires coordinated planning. Most serious is conflict in viewpoint and educational philosophy. The public has good cause to be disturbed and a little disgusted when elementary and secondary school staffs in the same system contradict each other on questions of educational policy. The cause of good community relations certainly is not strengthened when parents at a high school PTA meeting are urged to support the offering of remedial courses in the basic skills because the elementary schools promote all students regardless of their achievement.

Elementary and secondary principals and their faculties need to get together on these matters. Calendars for PTA meetings and other events should be coordinated as much as possible; unnecessary duplication of questionnaires, polls, and other data-gathering projects should be eliminated; and conflicts in educational philosophy and policies should be reconciled.

Principles and Policies

A many-sided and inconstant relationship such as that between a school and the publics which make up its community needs direction based on precedent and ground rules if its influence on public education is to be constructive. On the other hand, it is a relationship that is likely to deteriorate under rigidly imposed regulations. Fine-edged distinctions between the freedom of individuals and the best interests of the school come into play. And such factors as freedom of speech, freedom of the press, institutional integrity, majority rule, and minority rights continuously interact.

Because of the complex and sensitive nature of these relationships, few schools have attempted to formulate statements of principles and policies to give direction to staff activities in public relations. One of the deterrents has been the possibility that policies may be interpreted too rigidly to permit the school to meet extraordinary situations. At the same time, there is danger that policies may infringe on the right of individual staff members to dissent from board and administration views.

However, many schools have found themselves in deep trouble because they lack guiding policies for community relations. Greater than the danger that policies may interfere with some rights of some staff members is the risk that lack of policies may result in weakened community support for the schools and thereby interfere with the opportunities of students to get a good education.

The authors are persuaded that, somewhere between inflexible regulations and no policies at all, a board and its professional staff should be able to formulate a set of guides which will strengthen school-community relations.

No prefabricated set of principles is likely to be appropriate for very many local schools, but the following list, authored by the Commission on Public Relations of the American Association of School Administrators, is useful:

1. School public relations must be honest in intent and execution.
2. School public relations must be intrinsic.
3. School public relations must be continuous.
4. School public relations must be positive in approach.
5. School public relations should be comprehensive.
6. School public relations should be sensitive to its publics.
7. The ideas communicated must be simple [that is, presented clearly, concisely, and in understandable form].[7]

With the possible exceptions of items 2 and 7, these statements need little expansion. By "intrinsic" the Commission means that the substance

[7] American Association of School Administrators, *op. cit.*, pp. 17–33.

of public relations employed by a school should be its educational program, not the instruments employed or external materials. For example, if a report is elaborate and ornate, its form tends to become the center of attention rather than its content. This not only may detract from its effectiveness in communicating information but may provoke a negative reaction from discriminating readers.

Expanding the seventh statement, the Commission emphasizes that the language and style of school communications should be simple — that profound ideas may be simply stated. In the words of Chancellor Adenauer of West Germany, no amateur in public relations, "As soon as you are complicated, you are ineffectual."

Although materials about the schools sometimes must deal with complex ideas and complicated facts and figures, the simpler the style and method of presentation, the better the chance of its being understood by a large number of people. Pictures, graphs, sketches, dramatizations, and anecdotes make materials more interesting and understandable. The function of communications about the schools is to communicate, not to exhibit the writer's vocabulary. Although the use of technical terms may be justified at times, the less pedagese the better.

Policies with regard to local school-community relations are both necessary and hazardous. They are necessary to secure accuracy, coordination, and balance. And they are hazardous because the relationships involved are volatile, complex, and fine-edged.

One of the recurrent problems is that individuals may be poorly informed or careless about the accuracy of information that they present to the public. Closely related is the matter of coordination. When a large number of people interpret an institution to the public, repetitions, gaps, and conflicting views are likely. It is not possible to eliminate all "foot-in-mouth" performances, but careful organization and agreement on areas of responsibility should help considerably. The most nebulous question involved is the extent of freedom of individual staff members to voice public dissent from board and administration views. In system-wide matters the board of education and/or superintendent are responsible for determining the official position of the schools. In an individual high school, the principal and/or a majority of the faculty determine the position of the school — within board policies.

There are no clear-cut answers to this question. The authors support the position that members of the staff have the right to express disagreement with board and administrative views but not to represent themselves as official spokesmen for the schools. Neither do they have the right to attempt to promote political pressures opposing an official board action. Mass news media are justified in reporting board and staff discussions, and the public has the right to know the issues involved in the operation of the schools. But after official decisions are made, it is not ethical for staff members to employ pressure tactics to force changes.

Such behavior could lead to a breakdown of representative and responsible administration of the schools as well as fragmentation of the educational program. Educational practices would then be determined largely by whoever could muster the greatest number of influential supporters.

If balance is to be maintained in the school's program, as high a degree of balance as possible must be maintained in public relations. Typically, those divisions of a school that receive the greatest amount of publicity receive the most support. It is necessary only to compare the salaries of athletic coaches in most high schools and colleges with those of librarians and academic teachers to be convinced of the validity of this observation.

More important, however, is the matter of students' attitudes. If school publicity and public interest emphasize contests and neglect scholarship, students tend to develop a distorted sense of values.

The need for policies relevant to accuracy of information, coordination of efforts, balance among divisions and departments, and responsible professional relationships arises in most school systems and in most individual schools. Other policies may or may not be germane to a particular school or system. The problems most commonly covered in statements of policies which various local schools have drafted for their own situations are the following:

1. Teacher-student relations — especially with reference to discipline and supervision of extraclass affairs.
2. Teacher-parent relations.
3. Relations with representatives of mass news media.
4. Relations with local business enterprises.
5. Controversial issues in the classroom.
6. Relations among teachers, central office, and board.
7. Teacher relations with colleagues.
8. Religion in the schools — matters of public ceremonies, religious holidays, religious symbols, etc.
9. Staff responsibilities toward such teacher-citizen organizations as the PTA.
10. Organization, responsibility for, and channeling of news releases.
11. Handling complaints from parents and patrons.

Procedures and Media

The major tasks in developing sound relations between a high school and its community are (1) organizing and planning a program, (2) securing information about the community, and (3) providing for two-way communication between the school staff and laymen. The effectiveness of various procedures and media will depend largely upon the makeup of the community, the experience and abilities of the staff, and the problems encountered.

Organizing and Planning a Program

Although the greatest impact any school has on its community will be made through its day-by-day work with students, supplementary relationships need to be developed to reach certain groups and to meet special situations. Of the various supplementary relationships, the personal and informal association of staff members with laymen in social and business affairs is likely to be most influential. Since the effectiveness of interpretations in these informal situations will depend largely on the attitudes and alertness of individual staff members, the principal can do little but keep his staff informed on school matters and attempt to make them aware of the importance of good relations. Possibly conferences to consider background materials and situations which may be anticipated in various groups and in contacts with community leaders may prove helpful to the staff. But there are no stock techniques. The individual staff member is on his own and his sense of personal responsibility and attitude will determine much of his success in interpreting the school.

On the other hand, news stories, parent conferences, open-house events, entertainments, exhibits, published reports, and demonstrations lend themselves to planning and preparation. One device that some principals have found useful, both as a memory tickler and as a means of organizing the activities of the staff, is a news and programs calendar. Although each principal will need to develop his own, the following outline for the first and last few weeks of the school year may suggest some items and procedures appropriate for those periods:

August	NEWS AND PROGRAMS CALENDAR
Last two weeks of summer recess	News story on anticipated enrollments. Announcement for radio, TV, and newspapers on registration procedures and dates. News stories on new staff members. Stories on curriculum changes — new courses, services. Stories of plans for preschool teachers' conference — speakers and consultants. Stories on graduates going to college. Football practice — schedule, prospects. Announcements about textbooks, fees, work certificates, etc.
September	
Opening week	Actual enrollment figures — stories on transfer students, exchange students, etc. Announcements and stories on organization of extra-class activities — music, clubs, paper, etc. Participation in Labor Day program by students.

Second week	Stories on interesting vacation experiences of staff. Sale of activity tickets. Stories on first football game — pep rally, etc. Calendar of school events for first semester. Social events for new teachers. Organization — election of class officers and student council. Organization of faculty committees.
Third week	First PTA meeting — election of officers. Stories on instructional innovations — e.g., language laboratory, honors program, remedial classes. Stories on new materials and equipment. Plans for parent-teacher advisory council. Stories on fire drill and traffic safety. Second football game — band stories. Stories on plans for speech and dramatic events.

. . . .

May

First week	Preregistration and counseling information. Commencement schedule — stories on speakers and program. Stories on senior class events. Stories on honor banquet — speakers. Stories on school yearbook. Final PTA meeting — review of year. Stories on senior play.
Second week	Junior-senior prom. Awards assembly. Home economics tea for mothers. Stories of teacher changes. Final report of curriculum council studies. Stories on track and baseball. Stories on scholarship tests. Stories on college scholarships.
Third week	Baccalaureate services. Summer school program. Announcements for closing of school year — textbooks, fees, report cards, examinations.
Fourth week	Commencement stories. Reports to parents. Teachers' summer plans. Summer office hours. Summer music program. Summer school enrollment. Review of school year for press.

Securing Information

It is axiomatic that if a school staff is to achieve effective community relations it must have a thorough knowledge of its community. Under our system of local control, the principal and his staff must know the views of the several publics about schools, the important educational needs of the community, the supplementary resources for education available, the basic mores and value systems of the sub-publics, and the power structure of the community.

To find time to study these things without neglecting their basic responsibility of providing good instruction presents problems for local faculties. However, much of the knowledge needed in community relations is also needed in planning and improving the curriculum — community study for one purpose serves other purposes.

In a small and relatively homogeneous town the principal and teachers will not need to devote a great amount of time and effort to becoming acquainted with the community. But in a city with many publics careful organization, systematic procedures, and some expert assistance will be required to accomplish that purpose. The principal will need to rely heavily on the central office staff to keep him informed on community-wide developments and factors. However, in the area served by his school he should be the best-informed person in the system and should keep the central staff informed.

From the point of view of the high school staff, probably the most useful information about the community will be that outlined in the *Evaluative Criteria* (Section B):[8]

II. Basic Data Regarding the Community
    A. Population Data for the School Community
    B. Occupational Status of Adults
    C. Educational Status of Adults
    D. Financial Resources
    E. Financial (for private schools)
    F. Rural Pupils
    G. Composition of the Community
III. Community Agencies Affecting Education
    A. Educational Agencies
    B. Recreational Opportunities
    C. Civic Organizations
    D. Health and Sanitation Facilities

In addition, teachers need to know the power structure of the community. What groups, organizations, and individuals exercise the greatest influence on public opinion and on political action? These, of course, will vary widely with the political and economic composition of communities

[8] National Study of Secondary School Evaluation, *Evaluative Criteria* (Washington: The Study, 1960), pp. 39–48.

and with individual personalities. However, certain studies of community structure provide some valuable clues to their identification. For example, according to a study by Woodward and Roper, the distribution of people on a general social participation scale takes the form of a J-curve.[9] Approximately 55 to 60 per cent of adult residents fall in the lowest quarter of participation, 25 to 30 per cent in the next quarter, 10 per cent in the third, and 5 per cent in the top quarter.

Participation in community affairs tends to increase with level of income and amount of formal education. The Valley City studies found that people with some college education had average participation scores 60 per cent higher than people with only a high school education and 250 per cent higher than those who did not continue beyond the ninth grade. Also, people with an income of $10,000 a year or more had average scores one-third higher than those whose incomes were in the $4,000 to $10,000 bracket and twice as high as those with an income of under $4,000.[10]

Levels of community influence tend to be related to socioeconomic groups. For example, the Valley City studies show that political leaders had the highest average influence score and educators the lowest. The average scores for eight groups were as follows: politics, 7.20; labor, 6.20; civic, 6.16; recreation, 5.64; local government, 5.55; business, 5.41; religion, 5.33; and education, 5.00.[11] The Yearbook Commission of the American Association of School Administrators comments,

> Thus the leadership of any given community will not be a cross section of the population, but will tend to represent certain occupations, income and economic levels, and certain organizations. Because each of these variables involves particular values and points of view, there will be a tendency for decisions to be made in a given direction. Implications for the school administrator are clear. So far as community leaders affect school policies, the effect may well be in a given direction. Policies of one kind will receive support; others will be opposed.[12]

The authors recognize that these influences are very real and that certain local groups tend to dominate school policies. However, it does not follow that patterns of influence cannot be changed. Teachers who are cognizant of the influences in their communities may do something about them. If it is apparent that particular dominant groups are opposed to needed improvements in the school program, strategies may be developed to change the attitudes and traditional positions of their

---

[9] Julian Woodward and Elmo Roper, "Political Activity of American Citizens," *American Political Science Review*, 1950, 44:876.

[10] As reported by the American Association of School Administrators, *Educational Administration in a Changing Community*, Thirty-Seventh Yearbook (Washington: The Association, 1959), pp. 58–59.

[11] *Ibid.*, pp. 66–67.

[12] *Ibid.*, p. 66.

members. At the same time, support may be built up in other groups. Organizations such as the PTA, whose membership cuts across traditional alignments, may be enlisted to aid in changing the views of the opposition and in strengthening the position of supporting groups.

Valuable information also may be secured through surveys. Those most likely to produce information needed in the community relations program are (1) surveys of school building needs in relation to enrollment trends; (2) surveys of curriculum trends — national and in surrounding schools; (3) follow-up studies of former students — graduates and dropouts; (4) public opinion polls on educational questions; (5) surveys of employment opportunities and trends — local and regional; and (6) surveys of recreational interests and facilities — local and regional.

School building surveys should be conducted through the superintendent's office, but the high school principal may be called upon to supply some basic data about his students, building needs, and curriculum plans. He also may play a valuable role in learning the views of the people about building proposals in the area served by his school.

Information about curriculum trends and developments in other schools often is vital in discussing local curriculum practices and needs with various community groups. For example, if the local high school faculty proposes the introduction of ability grouping, parents and patrons will want to know what the trends are and what the experience of other schools has been. Since procedures for securing curriculum information have been described in Chapter 5, they will not be expanded upon here.

Public opinion polls help to determine the attitudes of a cross section of the population toward school issues. Although this procedure has little value for a small community, it may be exceedingly helpful in a large complex community. The Denver Public Schools have employed a public opinion survey at regular intervals for several years. Good suggestions for the design and use of opinion polls in education may be found in several publications by Hand.[13]

Follow-up studies of graduates and dropouts may be used to secure basic information about the effectiveness of the school program and as a means of keeping in touch with former students. Present residence of former students, the success of graduates in college and in jobs, their marital status, recreational pursuits, civic activities, views on the value of school experiences, and the like may be included on the survey. Procedures for conducting follow-up studies have been outlined in Chapter 7, on guidance.

Communicating and Planning with Laymen

Laymen form many impressions of schools through information gained from students and through informal relations with teachers. Unfor-

[13] For example, Harold Hand, *What People Think About Their Schools*, Illinois Inventory of Parent Opinion (Yonkers, N.Y.: World Book Company, 1948).

tunately, what they learn from these sources is sometimes incomplete or misleading. In addition, large segments of the population such as retired persons or other people without children in the schools may not be reached through such casual personal contacts. If the schools are to reach all community groups with full and accurate information and learn their views on education, more reliable means of communication must be employed.

Procedures for establishing communication between the schools and the public are of two broad types: (1) informative and (2) deliberative. *Informative* procedures include the use of mass news media, exhibits and demonstrations, conferences, special reports, bulletins and newsletters, programs and entertainments, and speeches. *Deliberative* procedures involve the use of various organizations through which laymen and teachers may exchange views and pool their thinking on school problems. Parent-teacher organizations, citizens advisory councils, general conferences, and *ad hoc* citizen-teacher committees are likely to be the most productive for these purposes.

Mass Media. The most effective means of reaching a large number of people with information about the schools is through newspapers, television, and radio. However, what is news to newsmen is not always news to teachers and administrators. Consequently, the school administrator must be able to work with newsmen and interpret news from their point of view. The most important single factor in success in enlisting good coverage through mass media is the day-by-day working relationship between school personnel and program directors, editors, and reporters. The strength of this relationship will depend largely on the confidence each has in the integrity of the other. If administrators and teachers expect fair treatment at the hands of the mass media, they will need to be candid with reporters. Although reporters cannot reasonably expect school people to seek them out with stories which are unfavorable to the school, they have every right to expect that staff members will give them the facts when they request them. It will aid the cause of good working relationships also if school personnel prepare news releases in a form and style appropriate for use by news media.

According to Fine and Anderson,

> When editors get a story from a school or college, or indeed from any other individual or institution, this is what they ask:
>
> Is it timely?
> Is it important?
> Is it newsworthy?
> Is it written in good newspaper style?
> Is it broad?
> Is it of enough general interest for the paper?[14]

[14] Fine and Anderson, *op. cit.*, p. 99.

These authors also studied the opinions of one hundred typical editors in all parts of the country on what school administrators should do to handle school news more effectively. The following suggestions were made by the editors:

1. Give the press advance notice of coming school events.
2. Be willing to take time off to give the reporter enough background facts to help him do a thorough job.
3. Hold regular periodic press conferences so the newspapers can get an overview picture of the school program.
4. Maintain an "open" school policy — no censorship — to help the press understand the many programs of the school system.
5. Recognize that news is perishable and should be given to the papers as soon as it occurs.
6. Permit the editors to determine the amount of space that stories should get. Accept the editor's judgment without a fuss.
7. Set aside a definite time — each day or week — for the school administrator to meet with the press reporter assigned to the schools.
8. Give the reporters access to all school records (unless confidential) as the police do for reporters covering the police beat.
9. Tell the editor the whole story and let him decide what to print and what to omit.
10. Learn the techniques of the press and understand the newspaperman's point of view concerning news.[15]

In general, these suggestions also apply to relationships with representatives of radio and television stations. There are, of course, many types of mass media and many types of newsmen. Most of them are conscientious and trustworthy. Usually the school will benefit if staff members work with them openly, frankly, and cooperatively. However, it doesn't follow that school people need to be naïve in dealing with news people; a wise administrator will know his newsmen.

Television is a powerful medium for presenting certain types of educational information. Actual classroom scenes, music and dramatic productions, panel discussions, and interviews are televised to good advantage by many schools throughout the nation. The possibilities in educational television are extensive — not only for teaching but also for community relations. In these times, any school administrator in a community large enough to have television facilities is guilty of negligence or myopia, or both, if he does not use them.

Although the tasks of planning, coordinating and preparing school materials for television usually are assigned to a special division in the central office, much of the success of educational television depends upon the cooperation of principals and teachers in reporting news and in participating in programs. The directors and technical experts can do much to prepare smooth productions, but the real substance and

[15] *Ibid.,* p. 100.

personnel must come from the classrooms. Not the least important aspect of television in school-community relations is that it permits many people to see and to get to know the teachers, students, and administrators.

Exhibits, Demonstrations, and Open House. Either televised or live, exhibits and demonstrations are good vehicles for showing the public what the schools are doing. The number of schools presenting science fairs, classroom demonstrations, school exhibits, physical fitness pageants, and demonstrations of how Johnny is taught to read has vastly increased during the past few years. People have a consuming curiosity to see how things are done — whether it is putting an astronaut in flight, making motion pictures, or teaching children the three R's. And the best way to inform them is to let them see it firsthand.

American Education Week is an especially opportune time for local school exhibits, visits, and demonstrations. Because of the nation-wide publicity immediately preceding and during this week, even people who do not have children in school become school conscious and are disposed to take time to visit the local schools if given an opportunity.

There is nothing unethical about using a little patent psychology. Two sure-fire ways to get a crowd of people to attend a local event are to feed them and get their children into the act. The first may not always be practical for a school exhibit, but the second is both practical and desirable. Some schools combine the two. There are few parents so indifferent — or with such important business deals — that they will not attend a school event in which their child is performing or his handiwork is being displayed. This, of course, is the purpose of a school exhibit: to show the work of as many students and to draw as many parents as possible.

Conferences. Face-to-face relationships between parents and teachers may contribute materially to school-community cordiality and to the education of children. To be most productive, the student should participate in the conference at some stage. Conferences may be group or individual or a combination of the two.

Regularly scheduled parent-teacher conferences to supplement report cards or other types of written reports to parents are now widely employed by elementary schools. Education is a joint undertaking of the home and the school calling for close cooperation between parents and teachers. Many elementary schools now schedule individual teacher-parent conferences twice a year and a few schedule them more frequently. Recognizing the success of these conferences at the elementary level, junior high schools and a few senior high schools are beginning to use them. At the secondary level, the conference usually takes place with the homeroom teacher, who secures pertinent information about each student from other teachers and counselors.

Secondary schools generally schedule individual teacher-parent conferences once a year, at midyear, or twice a year, at midsemester. Some schools set aside a block of four or five days and concentrate conferences in this relatively short period; others space them over a period of two or three weeks. A number of schools include students during a part of the teacher-parent conference so that plans and problems may be considered from the viewpoint of all three.

Group conferences also may be helpful in strengthening parent-school understanding. In secondary schools, parents of students in each grade meet with the administrators and teachers to discuss plans, procedures, and problems. Often individual conferences follow the group session.

Special Publications, Bulletins, and Reports. Although bulletins, newsletters, and special reports are prepared and distributed more frequently by the superintendent and his central staff than by principals, certain publications of this type have a place in the high school's program of community relations.

Among those which have been employed successfully by secondary schools in all sections of the country are curriculum guidebooks for parents and students; student handbooks; brochures on the guidance program, college days, etc.; newsletters to parents — periodic and special; principal's annual report; student publications — newspaper, yearbook, etc.; PTA handbook; and brochures on extraclass activities.

Student publications have been described in Chapter 9. Curriculum guidebooks usually include descriptions of various curriculum programs and courses — with illustrative programs and procedures for registration. The curriculum guide is one of the most important publications issued by the high school and merits careful preparation. If at all possible, it should be printed and well illustrated.

The principal's annual report is described in some detail in Chapter 19. Although it is addressed to the superintendent and may be incorporated in whole or in part in *his* annual report, news people often are interested in some sections of the principal's report as source material for school stories. Such groups as the PTA and citizens advisory council may have occasion to refer to it for basic data about the high school. Consequently, if it is done well it may contribute substantially to good community relations.

Programs, Entertainments, and Commencement Exercises. These are the old reliables of public relations. They probably date back to colonial days and have lost none of their appeal to modern parents. Rather than suffering from the competition of television they have been adapted to this new medium. Although they appeal mostly to parents, relatives, and fellow students, programs and entertainments are a source of both information about the instructional program and enjoyment. In some schools certain special productions such as plays and variety shows have become traditions in the community. However, programs are more effective than entertainments for revealing the quality of instruction in the school since they are adaptable to many different subject fields and permit the participation of many students.

Commencement exercises hardly qualify as entertainment, but they employ a liberal portion of academic pageantry and a bit of showmanship. Even without the pageantry and showmanship, commencements hold considerable fascination for parents and relatives of the graduates. And whether contrived or not, they influence school-community relations.

Some administrators and writers in the field of extraclass activities have developed a strong aversion for traditional commencements and advocate a so-called modern type, featuring a student pageant or forum. The authors suggest that if most of the people in the community want their commencements traditional, it would be well to make them traditional; if they want them modern, let them be modern. The issue is not of sufficient consequence to warrant a running feud with a substantial number of patrons.

In most communities school patrons like their commencements well organized, with the spotlight on the graduates and the speeches short. Often patrons judge the professional competence of a principal by the way he manages commencement exercises. In the interest of good public relations, it would seem prudent for the principal to devote the time and attention to commencement exercises required to make them impressive and stimulating ceremonies. More important, they should be happy and memorable occasions for the graduates.

The PTA. Of the several types of deliberative agencies which bring teachers and parents together to work on educational problems, the PTA is one of the oldest and has one of the most impressive records of service to public education. Despite many jokes about tired mothers and the PTA, and despite some misdirected efforts by local associations in a few communities, the PTA has excellent potential for implementing desirable school-community relations. Any school requires the organized cooperation of parents in these days of intensely conflicting pressures and competing agencies for public funds. And the PTA, as a long-established national organization, has much to offer in the way of guides and policies for local parent-teacher relationships.

Among the advantages claimed for the PTA by its supporters are the following: (1) It promotes better acquaintance and working relations between teachers and parents. (2) It is a channel of communication of educational views and ideas to and from the school and various publics in the community. (3) It promotes public understanding of school needs and enlists public opinion in support of a sound educational program. (4) It provides leadership for local associations of parents and teachers through its well-developed organizational structure and policies. (5) It helps to coordinate the joint efforts of local school systems in securing better educational support from state and national sources. (6) It aids in awakening large numbers of parents to their responsibilities in educating children. (7) It advises the school staff and board of education on educational needs of the community as viewed by parents. (8) It studies educational issues and trends and aids in informing laymen on these matters.

The PTA had its beginning in 1897 as the National Congress of Mothers and became the National Congress of Parents and Teachers in 1924. From about four million members in 1946, it had increased to over twelve million by 1962, and the number of local units had grown from about 26,000 in 1946 to around 44,000 in 1962. There are associations in all fifty states and the District of Columbia. It is a thoroughly democratic organization and its dues are so nominal that any parent can afford to belong. Although it has always been concerned with problems of children which extend beyond formal schooling, it has worked consistently at local, state, and national levels to strengthen public education. The program of the National Congress has five objectives: (1) to promote the welfare of children and youth in home, church, and community; (2) to raise standards of home life; (3) to secure adequate laws for the care and protection of children and youth; (4) to bring into closer relation the home and the school, that teachers and parents may cooperate intelligently in the training of the child; and (5) to develop between educators and the general public such united efforts as will secure for every child the highest advantage in physical, mental, social, and moral education.

Like any civic organization, problems sometimes appear in local PTA's in the absence of competent leadership. Some local associations lose sight of their proper functions and relationships to the board of education by undertaking to raise funds for certain parts of the school program and by legislating on matters that are the legal responsibility of the board. Others become social clubs for mothers and have leaned too heavily on school personnel for programs and entertainment.

But these things are not in keeping with the purposes and policies of the state and national organizations and are not likely to develop if local groups secure competent lay leadership and intelligent cooperation from members of the teaching profession. Other types of parent organizations may serve a local school reasonably well, but a strong and well-designed national organization such as the PTA has many important advantages.

The PTA is an independent organization. Although local chapters are usually associated with a school, they may function independently. If a local high school does not have a PTA, however, it is proper for the principal and teachers to take the initiative in stimulating interest among parents and in securing organizational materials from the state association. Once the local association gets under way, teachers should take an active part but should not attempt to dominate it.

Early in the organizational stage, it should be made clear that the PTA is *not* an alternate board of education, it is *not* a fund-raising organization for the school, and it is *not* a political pressure group. It is intended to work for the welfare of children, for parent education, and for good working relationships between teachers and parents.

Citizen Advisory Councils. Henry Toy, former Executive Director of the National Citizens Commission for the Public Schools, reported that there were about 17 communities with citizens committees on education in 1949, and about 15,000 in 1957.[16] More recent estimates place the total at about 20,000. Most of these committees serve in an advisory capacity to the board of education and are concerned with the over-all program of the local school system. Consequently, if a system-wide advisory council is functioning and the high school has a PTA, there would appear to be little purpose in another such organization in the high school.

The authors believe that citizens advisory councils may play and have played an important role in public education in America. We are fully in sympathy with the point of view that laymen and teachers should work closely on matters of educational philosophy, over-all curriculum design, and community support. On the other hand, we see no virtue in piling up citizen advisory groups to the point that an advisory committee is needed to advise advisory committees on what they are supposed to do. We are persuaded that a school PTA can and should do everything that an advisory council can do in working with the staff of an individual school.

On a system-wide basis, however, a citizens advisory council may be extremely helpful in advising with the board and professional staff and as a liaison between the school system and the citizen groups whom members of the council represent. Some members of the high school staff and PTA should serve on the central advisory council.

There is some disagreement among educators as to whether advisory councils should be organized on a continuing rather than an *ad hoc* basis. A study by Lehman in Michigan reports that only 6 per cent of the members of permanent advisory committees believed that their committees should be disbanded.[17] On the other hand, in a study by Schooling in Missouri less than 3 per cent of the school administrators surveyed expressed the belief that use should not be made of temporary committees before permanent advisory committees were organized.[18]

---

[16] As reported by Roderick F. McPhee, "The Administrator and Lay-Advisory Committees," *Administrator's Notebook,* Midwest Administration Center, University of Chicago, May, 1957, 5:1.

[17] Charles F. Lehman, "A Study of Interpersonal Role Perceptions of School Administrators, Board of Education Members, and Lay Citizens Committees in Michigan Public Schools," unpublished Ph.D. dissertation, University of Michigan, 1956.

[18] Herbert W. Schooling, "The Use of Lay Citizens Advisory Committees in Selected Missouri Public Schools," unpublished Ed.D. dissertation, University of Missouri, 1954.

Schools have used *ad hoc* or temporary committees of citizens as long as committees have been an institution in America. And that dates back to the 1600's, when visiting committees of laymen used to inspect the old Latin-grammar schools. Temporary committees of parents and teachers have a long record of valuable services to schools and have been used with increasing frequency since mid-twentieth century. Even in schools with permanent PTA and advisory council organizations *ad hoc* committees may have an important place.

In recent years, temporary committees of laymen have been most active in securing community support for new buildings, better salary schedules for teachers, and additional educational services such as guidance and special classes for exceptional children. They also have worked on special problems relating to the curriculum and youth needs. Local temporary committees have helped to develop improved report cards, enriched curriculum offerings, codes of student conduct, better recreational facilities for youth, better balance in extraclass activities, expanded summer school programs, and the like. Two important advantages of an *ad hoc* organization over a continuing council are that it does not waste the time of busy people between major projects and more laymen are given an opportunity to participate in school affairs over a period of years.

Personal Public Relations of the Principal

The functions of the high school principal in the field of community relations include not only planning, securing information, and providing two-way communication but also active personal associations in the community. As pointed out in Chapter 2, the public regards the principal as the professional leader of the high school and as its official representative and spokesman in community affairs.

In the relationship of any institution to the public, firsthand acquaintance with official representatives of the institution has tremendous value in building confidence and understanding. Some of the most successful retail corporations and public utilities companies encourage their local managers to take an active part in community affairs for this reason. This is also why politicians make so many public appearances at athletic events, plowing contests, and any other large public gathering where they may be seen and shake a lot of hands.

The authors do not suggest that the high school principal adopt the public relations strategies of large corporations and politicians. The public rather enjoys the obvious attempts of these people to court its favor, whereas equally obvious efforts by educators would be considered in bad taste. At the same time, school administrators need to get out of their offices and meet people in order to establish good rapport.

Within the limits of good taste and the time that he can afford to spend away from the school, the principal should try to meet as many people as possible or at least permit them to see him and get to know who he is. Probably his most effective contacts will be made at school events because these give him an opportunity to meet a cross section of people who are interested in the school. At the same time, a reasonable number of speaking and television engagements, plus participation in a service club, some church activities, and membership in various community youth agencies, are important in establishing personal ties with the public.

Needless to say, these activities can get out of hand. In large schools, the principal must rely on other members of his staff and in small schools he and the superintendent should agree on a division of duties. There are also such items as domestic tranquility and his responsibilities as a father to be taken into account. Therefore, the principal must learn to concentrate his efforts where they will count most and occasionally answer invitations with a discreet "no." He may well reflect upon the fact that the best speakers run out of speeches or audiences or both sooner or later, and it is better that it be later.

Questions and Group Projects

1. What distinction should be made between public relations and community relations as associated with public schools?

2. Tabulate the frequency of and time allocations for television programs sponsored and presented by branches of government (i.e., military, local, state, and federal), as listed in a local TV guide over a two-week period. How do the schools compare in total time allocations and frequency of presentations?

3. Examine five or six daily newspapers over a period of one month. How many column inches of space are devoted to school news? What portion of this space is devoted to each major area, e.g., curriculum, students, and extraclass activities?

4. Make tape recordings of five or six school television programs. Play these back in class and criticize them.

5. What are the purposes of school-community relations? How well do the news stories and television programs examined in 3 and 4, above, serve these purposes?

6. What are the principal areas of misunderstanding, misinformation, and distortion about public education? What are some effective means of clarification?

7. Should teachers be free to make any statements they choose to the public about board and administrative policies? Should they be free to seek to muster public support for some phase of their field of interest in opposi-

tion to board and administrative policies — e.g., should a coach who seeks to take athletes out of class for special practice sessions carry his case to the people?

8. Prepare a plan for a one-year series of teacher and parent conferences for a junior high school of about 750 students in an industrial city of around 100,000.
9. Make an analytical study of the composition, method of selection of members, tenure, accomplishments, and questions of conflict for three or four citizens advisory committees in public schools in your area.
10. Make a similar study of several local PTA organizations.

Selected References

American Association of School Administrators. *Educational Administration in a Changing Community.* Thirty-Seventh Yearbook. Washington: The Association, 1959.

———. *Public Relations for America's Schools.* Twenty-Eighth Yearbook. Washington: The Association, 1950.

Bernays, Edward L. *Public Relations.* Norman, Okla: University of Oklahoma Press, 1952.

Campbell, Roald, and John A. Ramseyer. *Dynamics of School-Community Relations.* Boston: Allyn and Bacon, 1955.

Drieman, David. *How to Get Better Schools.* New York: Harper & Brothers, 1956.

Fine, Benjamin, and Vivienne Anderson. *The School Administrator and His Publication.* New London, Conn.: Arthur C. Croft Publications, 1957.

———. *The School Administrator and the Press.* New London, Conn.: Arthur C. Croft Publications, 1956.

McCloskey, Gordon. *Education and Public Understanding.* New York: Harper & Brothers, 1959.

Moehlman, Arthur B., and James A. Van Zwoll. *School Public Relations.* New York: Appleton-Century-Crofts, Inc., 1957.

National School Public Relations Association. *Feel Their Pulse.* Washington: Education Association, 1956.

Nolen, Barbara, and Delia Goetz. *Writer's Handbook for the Development of Education Materials.* Publication of the U.S. Office of Education. Washington: Government Printing Office, 1959.

Sumption, Merle R. *How to Conduct a Citizens' School Survey.* Englewood Cliffs, N.J.: Prentice-Hall, Inc., 1952.

Tompkins, Ellsworth, editor. "Public Relations for Secondary Schools," *The Bulletin* of the NASSP, September, 1960, Vol. 43.

CHAPTER 18

Business Functions and Responsibilities of the Principal

The conduct of a modern comprehensive program of secondary education involves a large number of business procedures. For the most part, these are responsibilities of the superintendent and his office staff. But superintendents need supporting information and help from principals and teachers. And in each building unit there are many business matters that must be attended to by the professional personnel most directly associated with them.

For example, if a senior high school principal and his faculty decide to recommend team teaching in some department, the superintendent must know the number of teachers, classroom facilities, textbooks, and other instructional materials required before he can make an intelligent budget recommendation to his board. The most reliable source for such information is the staff directly responsible for implementing the program — the principal and teachers.

Most superintendents agree that principals should be relieved of as much business routine as possible so that they may devote a major share of their time to the educational program. But in most school systems an operational gap exists between theory and practice, and principals find themselves responsible for a growing volume of business tasks.

In some schools the principal spends an inordinate amount of time on business matters because he lacks adequate administrative and clerical help. In other schools this happens because the principal is an inept manager. The responsibility for remedying the former situation rests with the board and the superintendent of schools. But if the principal has adequate administrative and clerical help and continues to become entangled in a mass of business details, the situation reflects his inability to delegate or his lack of knowledge of administrative procedures, or both.

Any description of the business functions of high school principals is complicated by the fact that these duties vary widely from school to school. School size, type of central business organization, the superintendent's concept of the principalship, and the nature of auxiliary services enter into the definition of a principal's duties. In one school system the superintendent may prefer to use his principals chiefly as clerks and "keepers of order"; in another he may expect them to provide substantial educational leadership.

However, in some areas of business management all *bona fide* principals have like responsibilities, and principals in schools of similar size have many common business duties. Most high school principals are expected to have a hand in the following business operations:

General Operations

1. Budget planning
2. Procuring supplies and equipment
3. Distributing materials
4. Taking inventory
5. Storage of materials
6. Food services
7. Student transportation
8. Rentals and fees

Extraclass Activities Operations

1. Budgeting
2. Securing financial support
3. Purchasing
4. Handling receipts and disbursements
5. Accounting
6. Storing and inventorying
7. Reporting
8. Miscellaneous managerial duties

These two broad types of business functions are the central topics of this chapter.

General Operations

In a survey conducted in 1961–62, Salisbury found that principals in 267 North Central Association high schools reported various degrees of responsibilities for fifteen different items related to the general business operations of their schools.[1] The numbers and percentages of principals

[1] Arnold W. Salisbury, "Business Management Responsibilities of High School Principals," unpublished study, Cedar Rapids, Iowa, Public Schools, mimeographed, 1962.

TABLE 26

Major Business Functions and Responsibilities of High School Principals for General Operations (Exclusive of E.C.A.)

Functions and Responsibilities	Per Cent by Size of School									Total	
	I 1,000 and Over		II 500–999		III 250–499		IV 249 and Under			
	Number	Per Cent	Number	Per Cent	Number	Per Cent	Number	Per Cent	Number	Per Cent
1. Budget making	65	97.0	76	96.2	73	93.6	37	86.0	251	94.0
2. Food service operation	19	28.4	25	31.6	16	20.5	10	23.3	70	26.2
3. Development of specifications for purchase of instructional materials and equipment	53	79.1	62	78.5	67	85.9	36	83.7	218	81.6
4. Purchase of instructional materials and equipment	49	73.1	65	82.3	62	79.5	35	81.4	211	79.0
5. Storage of instructional materials and equipment	63	94.0	68	86.0	72	92.3	37	86.0	240	89.9
6. Inventory of instructional materials and equipment	63	94.0	75	94.9	73	93.6	42	97.7	253	94.8
7. Distribution of instructional materials and equipment	63	94.0	75	94.9	71	91.0	37	86.0	246	92.1
8. Development of specifications for noninstructional materials and equipment	42	62.7	44	55.7	45	57.7	24	55.6	155	58.0
9. Purchase of noninstructional materials and equipment	30	44.8	36	45.6	38	48.7	23	53.5	127	47.6
10. Storage of noninstructional materials and equipment	45	67.2	41	51.9	45	57.7	26	60.5	157	58.8
11. Inventory of noninstructional materials and equipment	36	53.7	44	55.7	41	52.6	29	67.4	150	56.2
12. Distribution of noninstructional materials and equipment	38	56.7	42	53.1	41	52.6	26	60.5	147	55.0
13. Collection of fees	60	89.6	75	94.9	61	78.2	29	67.4	225	84.3
14. Transportation of pupils	16	23.9	20	23.3	18	23.1	15	34.9	69	25.8
15. Control of rental of building	34	50.7	29	36.7	29	37.2	20	46.5	112	41.9

Source: Arnold W. Salisbury, "Business Management Responsibilities of High School Principals," unpublished study, Cedar Rapids, Iowa, Public Schools, 1962.

reporting each type of responsibility are shown in Table 26. Approximately the same percentage of principals of smaller schools reported each type as did principals of larger schools. Budget planning, taking inventory, distributing instructional materials, developing specifications for instructional materials, and collecting fees are the five areas of participation reported by the highest percentage of principals. On the other hand, fewer than 50 per cent of the principals had responsibilities for the transportation of pupils, rental of the building, food service operations, and purchase of noninstructional materials. In addition, all secondary school principals have responsibilities for the business management of extraclass activities, but since these represent their most common business duties, they will be considered as a separate business function.

Eight of the fifteen business responsibilities of principals, apart from extraclass activities, have to do with financial planning and management. They range from participation in budget planning and the purchase of supplies and equipment to the collection of fees and the rental of the building. For the most part, principals have only supplementary and consultative duties in connection with the general financial operation of their schools. Most fiscal functions are delegated to the superintendent by the board of education and are performed by him or by his central office staff. On the other hand, there is a trend toward more extensive participation by principals and teachers in these matters, especially in planning the budget.

Budget Planning

A good school budget relates educational plans to financial plans. It should include both long-term and short-term educational plans plus estimates of receipts and of expenditures for the next fiscal year and for a period of several years.

The high school principal and his faculty frequently are asked to assist in formulating educational plans as a part of the budget and, to some extent, in making up estimates of the amount of money required to finance them. However, they usually have few, if any, responsibilities for estimating revenues. The actual drafting of the system-wide budget is the task of the superintendent and his administrative assistants. Its final approval, of course, is up to the board of education.

The principal of the high school and his faculty may perform a valuable service in budget making by developing plans for future curriculum offerings, instructional procedures, guidance services, and other aspects of the educational program of their school. To be most helpful, these plans should be both long- and short-term and should be well supported by statements of purposes, reasons for change, summaries of pertinent research and experience, and similar information needed by the superintendent and board to make intelligent decisions in the allocation of avail-

TABLE 27

Functions and Responsibilities of High School Principals in Planning the General Budget

Functions and Responsibilities	Per Cent by Size of School									
	I 1,000 and Over		II 500–999		III 250–499		IV 249 and Under		Total	
	Number	Per Cent	Number	Per Cent	Number	Per Cent	Number	Per Cent	Number	Per Cent
1. Provide some budgetary information	65	97.0	76	96.2	73	93.6	37	86.0	251	94.0
1.1 For certificated personnel	55	82.0	60	75.9	55	70.5	25	58.1	195	73.0
1.2 For noncertificated personnel	46	68.6	39	49.4	39	50.0	24	55.8	148	55.4
1.3 For equipment needs	65	97.0	76	96.2	73	93.6	37	86.0	251	94.0
1.4 For instructional supplies	60	89.6	77	97.5	71	91.0	39	90.7	247	92.5
1.5 For noninstructional supplies	50	74.6	46	58.2	43	55.1	30	69.8	169	63.3
1.6 For food service operation	29	43.3	29	36.7	14	17.9	13	30.2	85	31.8
1.7 For building and equipment	47	70.1	31	39.2	31	39.7	20	46.5	129	48.3
1.8 For pupil transportation	13	19.4	18	22.8	19	24.4	15	34.9	65	24.3

Source: Arnold W. Salisbury, "Business Management Responsibilities of High School Principals," unpublished study, Cedar Rapids, Iowa, Public Schools, 1962.

able funds. The principal also may be expected to prepare estimates of personnel, building space, equipment, and supplies necessary to implement the plans which he and his staff have developed.

The specific budget items for which high school principals are called upon most frequently to make estimates are shown in Table 27. Over 60 per cent of the principals help formulate budget plans for certificated personnel, equipment, instructional supplies, noninstructional supplies, and building space needs and maintenance. On the other hand, less than one-third of the principals are involved in budget planning with respect to food services and pupil transportation.

It may be seen from Table 27 that some differences exist in the budget duties of principals of large schools and small schools. For example, 43 per cent of the principals of schools of 1,000 or over have some budgetary responsibilities for food services, while only 18 per cent of the principals of schools enrolling 250 to 499 students have these responsibilities. For the most part, high school principals share budget planning about equally with other officials or they have only minor consultative roles.

In formulating budget requests, the principal will need to confer with the members of his staff and solicit plans and estimates of needs from each department and special service as early as January or February. If there are no department heads, departmental committees or individual teachers may be invited to submit plans and needs. Conferences also should be held with the librarian, guidance coordinator, activities director, school nurse, and other special services personnel. Requests should be based on an inventory of departmental equipment and supplies plus plans and needs for the forthcoming year and for a projected long-term period.

Following receipt of requests and plans, the principal organizes them into a comprehensive and coordinated budget proposal to be submitted to the superintendent. Undoubtedly the principal will find it necessary to make adjustments in the original proposals and requests from staff members in the interest of maintaining good balance in the program of his school. And probably he will need to establish some order of priorities for certain plans. The format of the principal's budget draft should be similar to that employed by the superintendent's office.

After his budget proposals have been acted upon by the superintendent and board and he is informed of the amounts allocated to each division of his program, the principal should confer again with members of his staff concerning any adjustments which have to be made. Needless to say, the entire budgetary procedure demands considerable skill, tact, patience, and good judgment upon the part of the principal. It is almost inevitable that requests for funds will exceed anticipated revenue, and adjustments will have to be made in harmony with the best interests of the total school program.

Management of Instructional Materials and Equipment

The management of instructional supplies and equipment is the most common business responsibility of the high school principal. It was reported among their duties by about 95 per cent of the principals in Salisbury's study.

In general, the principal must assist his teachers in getting the supplies and equipment that they need for instruction when and where they need them, but in conformity with the policies and procedures established by the board and the superintendent. The principal also must keep records of encumbrances against his budget, manage the storage and distribution of goods in his building, and maintain a continuing inventory of supplies and equipment.

Purchasing. In a well-administered school system, all purchases of supplies and equipment for the high school other than for extraclass activities are made through the superintendent's office in accordance with board of education policies.

A purchase may be initiated by a principal and his teachers for instructional and administrative items to be charged against board funds. But this calls for a requisition, which, in substance, is a request to the superintendent to make a purchase. Principals and teachers do not have authority to order things directly from merchants in the name of the school. Nevertheless, some teachers are careless about such matters and occasionally order goods without authorization. If this occurs only once or twice and the amounts are small, perhaps the best thing for the principal to do is to recommend payment after an effort to make the procedure clear to the teacher involved. But if it happens several times, the teacher should be held responsible for payment.

For budgetary and accounting purposes, supplies and equipment are put in separate categories. Although it is difficult to classify certain articles, *supplies* are generally regarded as items which are consumed in the process of instruction or administration — such things as paper, chalk, groceries for home economics, and chemicals. *Equipment* includes articles which are not immediately consumed in the operation of the school and which cost more than a minimum figure, usually ten dollars. Furniture, typewriters, shop machinery, and similar items which are not an integral part of the building are classified as equipment.

The chart on page 502, prepared by Roe, describes the way most purchases of items to be used for instructional purposes should be made.[2]

In purchasing instructional supplies and equipment, the principal serves first as a consultant to the teacher with regard to the need for and quality

---

[2] William H. Roe, *School Business Management* (New York: McGraw-Hill Book Company, 1961), p. 133. Used by permission.

1. The Idea — Teacher gets an idea for equipment to help her.
2. Consultation — Teacher goes to colleagues, consultants, and administration for advice on feasibility of idea and how it can be implemented.
3. Requisition — Principal approves and sends through requisition to purchasing agent.
4. Coordination — Purchasing agent sees that this is not a routine request, so he sends it to the audio-visual director and assistant superintendent for instruction.
5. Staff Action — Audio-visual director and assistant superintendent agree that the idea is good, check on budget, fix responsibility for control, set up experimental procedures, and approve requisition.
6. Investigation — Purchasing agent uses his knowledge and contacts to determine the experience of other users and of suppliers; he sets up possible specifications.
7. Standardization — Meets with teachers to see if certain specifications can be agreed on and if standardization is possible; here he serves as consultant.
8. Specifications — Sets up specifications in line with meetings.
9. Bids or Quotations — Checks with all possible sources to get the best buy.
10. Purchase Order — Purchasing Officer and designated co-signers sign purchase order in quadruplicate. One copy each goes to vendor, warehouse, purchasing agent, and accounting office.
11. Follow-up — Purchasing agent makes a follow-up if equipment is not received when due.
12. Receipt of Goods — Warehouse receives goods, checks according to specifications, and returns purchase order with o.k.
13. Payment — Purchasing agent and board of education approve purchase for payment, and accounting office pays.
14. Accountability — Goods are sent to the department which is held accountable for equipment.
15. User Receives — Teacher picks up equipment at designated place.
16. Quality Control — Equipment is used experimentally and tested under different conditions.

of the article. He also checks to see if any of the articles are on hand and informs the teacher as to the state of the high school budget — whether funds are available. If he decides to request the item, he makes out and signs a requisition, which is forwarded to the superintendent's office.

If and when the article is purchased, it is sent to the high school, where the principal or his representative inspects it and acknowledges its receipt. It is then delivered to the teacher. The acquisition should be properly recorded on the principal's inventory list and as an encumbrance against his budget.

Many large school systems now use standardized order lists for supplies and equipment. Usually these are printed on separate forms for each department or service and the principal or teacher merely fills in the quantity desired opposite the item. The principal then signs the form and sends it to the business office as a requisition. However, some materials or pieces of equipment do not lend themselves to such lists and the purchasing agent will need a statement of specifications from the teacher and/or principal. The trade name and catalog number from the supplier's catalog are generally adequate, but certain special items, such as an unusual piece of science apparatus, may require more complete specifications.

A perennial problem is the matter of patronizing local merchants, who often feel the school has an obligation to do business with them. This can become rather touchy in some communities, and the principal should be informed of and follow board policy. Usually he becomes involved only in the purchase of merchandise for student activities, but the question may arise in connection with other goods. Most boards make it a policy to buy from local merchants when the service, quality, and price are as good as elsewhere. But many boards now take the position that they represent the interests of all taxpayers in conducting school business and have no special obligation to local merchants if, by patronizing them, school costs will be increased.

Receiving, Storing, and Distributing Supplies. Even though a school system has a central supply department and warehouse, goods delivered to the high school must be checked and stored in the school. The principal must see to it, through a custodian and/or secretary, that goods received correspond to their requisitions and invoices and that a minimum of loss occurs. Any damage or discrepancies should be noted on the invoice.

A common problem in storage is deterioration of some types of supplies, such as paper. The storeroom should be kept clean and dry to prevent as much loss as possible. Shelves and bins should be numbered to correspond with the school's continuing inventory list so that items can be readily located. Supplies on hand should be stored in front or on top of newly received goods so that they will be used first. Items such as lumber for the shop, food for home economics, and science supplies should be stored in a space provided in the departmental area and a member of the department assigned responsibility for them.

In schools which furnish or rent textbooks to students, the process of storing, distributing, and accounting for them is a demanding task. If each book has not been numbered and stamped with a form for recording the names of students to whom it is issued, this must be done upon delivery to the school. An effective procedure is to record the receipt of all textbooks in a ledger by title, authors, publisher, quantity, and copyright date. Some schools employ a card catalog for this purpose. An individual textbook card or loose-leaf ledger sheet should be made up for each student, and all books which are issued to him should be entered on this form. Space can be provided to record charges for rental, loss, or damage for each book. This record should be surrendered to the student when he finishes school and his account is closed.

Textbooks may be distributed through a central book room, in homerooms, or in each class. Distribution in classes is likely to be most economical and feasible but may result in some inaccuracies. Textbooks may be checked in at the close of the school year in the same manner and damages and losses assessed and recorded on the student's card.

The principal or some member of his staff should manage the entire business of processing, storing, issuing, and accounting for textbooks. Storage must be in a safe dry room which is kept free of insects and rodents. After the books are checked in at the close of the school year, badly damaged ones should be discarded and the inventory list brought up to date. The cost of repairing badly damaged books is so high that most schools find it less expensive to replace them with new ones.

Inventorying. Of the principals surveyed in Salisbury's study, about 95 per cent reported responsibilities for taking inventory of instructional supplies and equipment in their buildings and about 56 per cent for noninstructional materials (Table 26). Once the original list of supplies and equipment is made up, keeping it up to date is not difficult. But the compilation of the original list is a time-consuming task. Incoming principals should check the equipment inventory list as soon as possible after assuming their duties.

Some large school systems have an inventory department in the central business office which places inventory number tags on all movable equipment in each school and on new equipment when it is delivered. In the absence of a central inventory department, the principal of each school should arrange to have each piece of furniture and other equipment (e.g., typewriters, shop machinery, projectors, etc.) in his building tagged with an inventory number.

Specialists in school business management recommend that schools use a continuing inventory system. Under this system, an inventory clerk (e.g., custodian, assistant principal, or secretary) makes an entry for all supplies and equipment when they are delivered. When any item of equipment is lost or discarded, it is deducted from the inventory list at the time.

However, a continuing inventory system does not eliminate the necessity of making an annual check on supplies and equipment. The best time to do this seems to be shortly after the close of the school year so that a count of supplies and equipment on hand will be known when it is time to make up requisitions for the new school year. Separate lists of supplies and equipment for each room and office in the building should be prepared, and teachers and secretaries should check the lists against the actual supplies and materials on hand and record differences between the room and office lists and the actual count. Some schools assign a team of office secretaries and custodians to the job of making the annual count of furniture in order to relieve teachers of that much busywork. However, in science, industrial arts, business, art, and music departments, a teacher or the department head may need to take the inventory of equipment because of the many specialized articles used. Some large schools employ machine accounting systems for taking inventory and have a separate card for each item of equipment. The inventory card shown in Figure 29 may be used in maintaining a continuing inventory of equipment. The

FIGURE 29

Typical Inventory Card

INVENTORY CARD LAKE SIDE COMMUNITY SCHOOL DISTRICT School _____ Washington Senior _____					
Item: Student desk chair, steel and wood					
Date Received	Quantity Received	Unit Cost	Received From	Location	Inventory Numbers
7/24/62	42	$32.50	General Stores	Rooms 224, 231	86–201 to 86–243
8/16/62	–4	—	Discarded— Poor Cond.	Rooms 103, 105	86–011, 022, 118, 121

negative number under "Quantity Received" shows that four student desks were discarded. The totals for each type of article may be quickly computed from these cards if they are properly indexed.

Food Services and Student Transportation

Few principals have more than incidental responsibilities for food services and student transportation. In general, they see that student conduct is supervised during the noon hour and that students are educated on matters of safety on buses. Salisbury's study shows that 28 per cent of the principals of large high schools and about 20 per cent of the principals of small high schools had some responsibilities for the business management of food services. Only one-fourth of the principals reported business duties in connection with student transportation.

Food Services. The provision of food services in schools has become big business during the past twenty-five years. The federal government's program for furnishing surplus commodities and reimbursing schools for hot-lunch programs has introduced some complicated business procedures. In addition, menu planning, securing personnel, maintaining hygienic standards, and handling receipts and expenditures require someone who is well qualified. Since principals need to devote as much of their time as possible to the instructional program, they should not be expected to assume responsibilities for the cafeteria.

Most school systems either employ a food services manager or contract with a private catering firm to operate the school cafeterias. However, the preparation and dispensing of food must be synchronized with the rest of the school's program. The principal has to schedule lunch-hour shifts to fit the capacity of the cafeteria and work out time schedules with cafeteria personnel. In some schools, he may be expected to supervise the sale of lunch tickets, arrange for the noon-hour supervision of the cafeteria area, and serve as a liaison man between the customers and the management.

The principal needs to be knowledgeable about hygienic standards for food services, and should consult with the superintendent when problems arise in this respect. He must keep informed on the quality of meals being served and bring student representatives and the cafeteria management together on this perennial issue.

Student Transportation. The high school principal's duties with respect to student transportation are limited largely to cooperating with bus drivers in educating students on matters of safety and courteous conduct, supplying the superintendent's office with student data, making periodic reports on the transportation operation in his school, and arranging for transportation for special events such as field trips and athletic contests.

Of these, the problem of student safety and conduct is by far the most important. However, this is a matter of student citizenship and discipline rather than business management and is discussed in Chapter 15. The principal may be called upon to secure certain data and to make reports on student transportation to the superintendent's office. Information may be needed on the residence of students who are to be transported, their ages, location of feeder routes, and the like.

In small school systems, the principal may confer informally with the superintendent about loading and unloading, the competence of bus drivers, the suitability of routes, and related matters. But in larger systems the superintendent may call for periodic written reports from principals on these items. The use of buses for special educational trips and for extraclass events should be arranged through the principal's office. He will need to work out schedules for these trips as far in advance as possible and requisition buses and drivers from the superintendent's office so that they will be available when and where they are needed. The principal also arranges for faculty supervision on such trips and for establishing rules for student conduct.

Business Management of Extraclass Activities

A major share of the business functions of high school principals has to do with managing the extraclass activity program. In his 1962 study of 267 North Central schools, Salisbury found that from 65 to 85 per cent of the principals of these high schools reported business functions in nine categories related to student activities. In general, more of the principals of small high schools reported making assignments for ticket sales, arranging for supervision of public events, and engaging officials and judges for competitive activities while fewer indicated responsibilities for finances than did principals of large schools. The number and percentages of principals reporting each function are shown in Table 28.

Organization

The type of organization required for the conduct of extraclass business affairs depends to some extent on a school's definition of extraclass activities. The general business organization for the activity program is usually geared to the system of financial accounting, and this, in turn, should be adapted to the types of activities included under the category "extraclass."

The activities over which there is some dispute are student merchandising (student stores) and rentals and fees for articles used for instructional purposes, such as musical instruments. Some schools regard these as a part of extraclass business and some classify them as a part of general operations. There are logical arguments on both sides, but the authors take the position that these two operations are not actually student activities and therefore should not be included with the business management of the extraclass program.

In determining the type of organization and in fixing controls for the business management of extraclass activities the main purpose of the school — to provide the best possible educational opportunities for students — should never be lost to sight. The system should facilitate, not impede, the educational program. If the machinery gets in the way and if educational decisions are being made by bookkeepers rather than by educators, the system is poorly designed. The specific objectives of the

TABLE 28
Responsibilities and Functions of Principals for Activity Fund Management

Functions and Responsibilities	I 1,000 and Over		II 500–999		III 250–499		IV 249 and Under		All Schools	
	Number	Per Cent	Number	Per Cent	Number	Per Cent	Number	Per Cent	Number	Per Cent
1. Budgeting funds	58	86.5	66	83.5	46	58.9	23	53.5	193	72.3
2. Securing financial support	53	79.1	62	78.5	49	62.8	29	67.4	193	72.3
3. Purchase of supplies and equipment	54	80.6	64	81.0	54	69.2	32	74.4	204	76.4
4. Accounting	56	83.5	60	75.9	37	47.4	21	48.8	174	65.1
5. Storage and inventory	57	85.0	66	83.5	52	66.6	31	72.1	206	77.1
6. Reporting on funds to central office	57	85.0	65	82.3	47	60.2	23	53.5	192	71.9
7. Arranging for ticket sellers and takers	47	70.1	70	88.6	70	89.7	40	93.0	227	85.0
8. Arranging for police and supervision of events	50	74.6	72	91.1	72	92.3	33	76.4	227	85.0
9. Engaging officials and/or judges	38	56.7	60	75.9	61	78.2	30	69.7	189	70.8

Source: Arnold W. Salisbury, "Business Management Responsibilities of High School Principals," unpublished study, Cedar Rapids, Iowa, Public Schools, 1962.

business organization are (1) a sound program within the limits of the available funds, (2) accuracy and integrity in accounting for funds, (3) prudent expenditure of funds, (4) full reporting of the use of funds to the public, (5) sound allocation of funds to different activities, (6) proper care of supplies and equipment, (7) good control and management of activities.

Legal control of all extraclass funds and business affairs is vested in the board of education. In some states, such as Oklahoma and Pennsylvania, this has been clearly defined by state law; in many other states, by court decisions. The courts and specialists in school administration seem to agree that activity funds are public funds regardless of their source. Hamilton states, "You would be well-advised to place all funds in the hands of the board and let it approve and pay all bills. . . . Let those the law charges with responsibility of protecting and disbursing such money discharge that responsibility."[3] Knezevich and Fowlkes say, "By implication the board of education has control over student body activity funds even though the laws may be silent on the matter. The school board has control over all public funds within the school district unless the law states to the contrary."[4]

But this does not imply that principals, teachers, and students may not be delegated considerable responsibility for conducting the business affairs of student activities. The board should develop policies and procedures and within this framework, principals, teachers, and students should plan and implement the extraclass program. Much of the bookkeeping may be done in the central administrative office, but students, with the counsel of their principal and sponsors, may raise money, assess dues, keep organization records, initiate certain purchases, and manage supplies and equipment.

The authors subscribe to the view that in both large and small schools the system should be unified and centralized. The budget should be planned as a complete budget for all activities, and all funds should be deposited in a single bank account. A staff member should be appointed as the central treasurer and should be responsible for receiving all monies and for writing all checks or approving invoices for payment by the business manager of the school district. We believe that a centralized business system for activities is not only more efficient than a decentralized system but also keeps the business and educational functions more unified and takes some of the pressures off students in handling finances. The management of activities business provides valuable learning experiences

---

[3] R. R. Hamilton, "The Legal Status, Control, and Use of Athletic and Other Extra-Curricular Funds," *The Bi-Weekly School Law Letter*, Vol. II, September 18, 1953, pp. 57–60.

[4] Stephen J. Knezevich and John G. Fowlkes, *Business Management of Local School Systems* (New York: Harper & Brothers, 1960), p. 189.

for students, but the system should be so well organized that it discourages carelessness and removes most of the temptation in handling school funds.

The extent of student participation will vary with the type of activity. For social events, clubs, class projects, and assemblies, for instance, students should assume an important role in budgeting, raising funds, recommending expenditures, keeping records, and caring for equipment and supplies.

Activities which involve interscholastic relations or regular class instruction and which require expert knowledge in securing supplies, equipment, and special services should involve only nominal student participation. Business management for music activities, athletics, school publications, and speech and dramatics must be assumed primarily by the administrator and faculty directors and coaches, since substantial contracts and the procurement of expensive equipment are involved. But students can and should assist. In large high schools a central activities committee, composed of both student council and faculty representatives, may serve in an advisory capacity to the principal. Because of the opportunities for valuable educational experiences, the committee should meet with the principal and faculty sponsors to formulate the budget and draw up policies and procedures for raising and expending activity funds.

A chart for the business management of extraclass activities is shown

FIGURE 30

Organizational Chart for Business Management of Extraclass Activities in a School System with a Unit Type of Organization

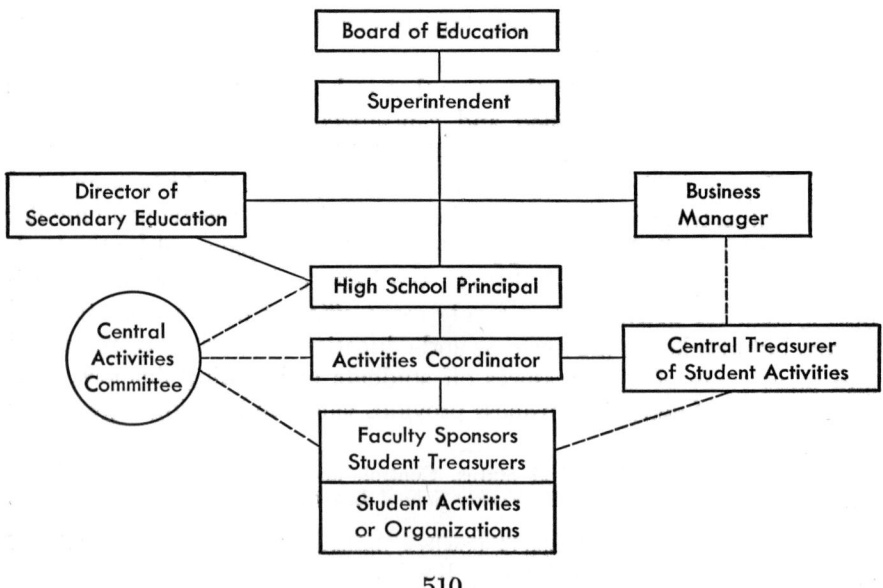

in Figure 30. The organization shown is the unit type, which is based on the assumption that business procedures are auxiliary to the educational program. This plan makes the principal the responsible administrative head of the high school. As such, he is in a position to design the activities business operation within his school so that it serves the educational program — within general policies and guidelines established by the board of education. The organization provides for student participation in managing the business affairs of their activities and recognizes the key role of faculty sponsors in the conduct of the activity program. Some of the bookkeeping and banking may be done through the school district's business manager, but the high school treasurer should handle all monies from student affairs in his school, keep complete records, and make disbursements. Needless to say, he should be bonded and his accounts audited regularly. As a matter of good business, any incoming principal or treasurer would do well to insist on an audit of activity funds before he assumes his duties.

Management of Extraclass Finances

The management of extraclass finances involves (1) budgeting, (2) securing funds, (3) handling receipts, (4) purchasing, (5) disbursing monies, and (6) accounting. In its handbook *Financial Accounting for School Activities* the U.S. Office of Education recommends the following:[5]

1. The general administration of school activity fund accounting should be governed by rules and regulations prescribed by the board of education of the school district.

2. The board of education should designate a person (usually the superintendent) to implement all policies and rules pertaining to the supervision and administration of funds in schools under his jurisdiction.

3. One person should be designated (usually the principal) to be responsible for funds in each individual school.

4. Expenditures for school activities should be carefully planned with the resources of the activity, which would make the use of a budget control of receipts and expenditures desirable and sometimes necessary.

5. Persons handling the school funds should be bonded through the regular school district procedures, and the bond should be in an amount sufficient for adequate protection of the funds of the school.

6. An annual audit should be made of all school activity funds by trained and recognized auditors.

7. Regular financial reports should be made to the administrative head of the school and to the board of education.

[5] U.S. Office of Education, *Financial Accounting for School Activities* (Washington: Government Printing Office, 1959), pp. 51–52.

Either a centralized or a decentralized system may be employed for activity fund accounting. The centralized system calls for all monies and records of the several funds to be handled through a central activities treasurer. The decentralized system sets up individual fund accounts for different activities such as athletics, student council, band, and the like, and each organization has its own treasurer and back account.

The U.S. Office of Education handbook recommends a centralized system, and our descriptions and recommendations will assume the use of that type.

Budgeting. It is difficult to keep a business or a school activity solvent, the program well balanced, and the people who run it honest over an extended period of time without a well-planned budget. In the absence of a budget for activities, students and teachers become careless in incurring liabilities, the principal is forced to go begging for money, and misunderstandings develop with respect to the allocation of funds. More serious, many activities may be short-changed and their educational programs impaired if sound financial planning is lacking.

In its general form, the budget consists of estimated receipts from all sources and estimated financial needs for each activity or organization for the fiscal year. The fiscal year recommended for school activities is from September 1 to August 31. A sound activities budget should also include a section on short- and long-term plans.

The principal has the responsibility for planning the activity budget for the high school. Administrative assistants, teachers, and students should assist in planning and the board should pass on it, but the principal must see that the job gets done.

The principal should initiate budget planning by reviewing the financial situation of each activity with its coach, director, or sponsor. A few weeks before the end of the school year he should request sponsors to submit short- and long-term plans, estimates of receipts, needs for their activities, and an inventory of supplies and equipment on hand. In addition, he or the superintendent should estimate receipts from such general sources as the sale of activity tickets, dues, gate receipts, guarantees, and board allocations.

The estimated receipts and financial needs for each activity should be reviewed by the principal and tentative allocations of funds made. The total allocations should equal or be less than the total estimated receipts determined by taking four- or five-year averages and adjusting them for known changes for the ensuing year (e.g., increase in price of football tickets, smaller number of guarantees from basketball, and similar changes). Unused balances for the current year should be transferred to the general fund and treated as estimated revenue in making allocations.

Students will gain valuable experience if they participate in some phases of the process. Sponsors of clubs, classes, and the student council should confer with student members in making preliminary estimates, and the student council may well do much of the planning for all-school affairs like dances, parties, assemblies, and service projects.

After the principal and/or his assistants have made tentative allocations to each organization in light of its estimated needs and estimated income, these allocations should be reviewed with each sponsor, coach, and director. Some revisions may be necessary at this point. The complete activities budget should then be put into proper form for transmittal to the superintendent's office and the board of education for revision or approval.

In schools in which the practice has not been followed previously, some resistance may develop with respect to transferring unused balances from specific activities to the general fund at the close of the year. Activities monies are public funds and do not belong to a particular organization. Sponsors and students must be led to recognize that a balanced and sound activity program for everyone depends upon equitable financial support for each activity. Football, for example, earns money because the school sponsors it, provides the facilities, and pays the salary of the coach. Therefore, the income is school income and should not be earmarked for a specific activity. By the same token, if an activity happens to have a poor season financially, the school must be prepared to make up the deficit from other sources. There are, of course, a few logical exceptions to the no-earmarking policy, such as money earned by a class for its junior–senior banquet or a senior trip, in which the amount that a group will be permitted to spend is limited to the sum they earn for that purpose. These accounts should be classified as "clearing accounts" and should not be included in the regular activity budget.

The U.S. Office of Education handbook on student activity accounting sets up the following classifications for receipts and expenditures:[6]

RECEIPTS
10–40 Series

10. Activity Incomes.
    11. Admissions.
    12. Prorated Share of General Activity Tickets.
    13. Dues and Fees.
    14. Sales.
        14-a. Books and periodicals (including publications).
        14-b. Confections, foods, and beverages.
        14-c. Other merchandise.
    15. Student Rentals from Materials.
        15-a. Rental from books.
        15-b. Rental from equipment.

[6] *Ibid.*, pp. 3–19.

MANAGEMENT AND COMMUNITY RELATIONS

RECEIPTS
10–40 Series (Cont.)

16. Advertising.
17. Guarantees.
18. Other Activity Income.
20. Grants from the School District.
30. Gifts from Other Sources.
40. Other Receipts.

Total Anticipated Receipts ———————

Balance from Previous Year ———————

Total Estimated Cash Assets ———————

ACTIVITY EXPENSE
100–200 Series

Regular Expenditures Accounts

100. Activity Expense.

110. Basic Operating Expenditures.

. . . . .

120. Supplemental Operating Expenditures.

. . . . .

200. Capital Outlay (Initial or additional equipment).

The suggested groupings for accounting purposes, which would also be followed in budgeting, are as follows:

1. *Student Organization Fund.* This includes clubs, class organizations, societies, and similar organizations.

2. *Athletic Fund.* Interscholastic and intramural.

3. *Merchandise Fund.* For merchandising activities such as school stores, canteens, and concession stands. (Not regarded as a part of the extraclass activities budget in most schools.)

4. *Publications Fund.* For the newspaper, yearbook, and handbook.

5. *Instructional Fees and Rentals Fund.* This includes activities primarily of a classroom nature and would not be considered as "extraclass" in most budgets.

6. *Miscellaneous Fund.*

For any of the above funds the budget estimates might well be set up in the following form:

ATHLETIC FUND
Regular Accounts

Receipts (10–40 Series)
10. Activity Income
    11. Admissions
    12. Prorated Share of General Activity Tickets
    13. Dues and Fees
    16. Advertising
    17. Guarantees
    18. Other Activity Income
20. Grants from the School District
30. Gifts from Other Sources

Expenditures (100–200 Series)
100. Activity Expense
    110. Basic Operating Expenditures
        111. Personal and Contracted Services
        112. Supplies
        114. Other Activity Expense
            114-a. Advertising
            114-b. Guarantees
            114-c. Travel Expense
    120. Supplemental Operating Expenditures
        121. Health Services
            121-a. Personal and Contracted Services
            121-b. Other Expense
        122. Pupil Transportation
            122-a. Personal and Contracted Services
            122-b. Other Expense
        123. Operation of Plant
            123-a. Personal and Contracted Services
            123-b. Other Expense
        124. Maintenance of Plant
            124-a. Personal and Contracted Services
            124-b. Other Expense
        125. Fixed Charges
            125-a. Employer Contributions to Retirement Systems
            125-b. Insurance
            125-c. Rental
200. Capital Outlay (initial or additional equipment)

Total Estimated Expenditures _____
  Recapitulation, 1960–61
    Total Estimated Cash Assets _____
    Total Estimated Expenditure _____
    Estimated Balance _____

Financial Support. Most high schools secure funds for the extraclass program from tax monies, admissions, dues, fees, sales, guarantees, and gifts from outside sources. Tax funds are provided primarily for such things as physical facilities, equipment, and salaries of sponsors and coaches. However, some boards allocate additional tax monies to the activity program for operating costs. Miller, Moyer, and Patrick summarize a nation-wide survey of activities programs in 1956: "The replies to our questionnaire study have been encouraging. They show that an increasing number of schools are getting at least some subsidization for the activities program from school district funds, but the number of such schools was still relatively small."[7]

It is evident from an examination of financial statements for individual schools and the few recent articles on the subject in the professional literature that operating funds for activities in most schools are derived largely from non-tax sources. Admissions, fees, dues, guarantees, and sales account for most of these revenues. There is considerable logic in the argument that student activities should be partially self-supporting so that students may develop a sense of financial responsibility and an understanding of the costs of education. Many school districts are forced to levy a stiff tax in order to finance buildings, instructional supplies and equipment, and salaries. It seems reasonable, therefore, that student activities should pay a part of their own way from admissions and student earnings and thereby lighten the tax load for public education.

The extent to which the earnings and fees from activities should carry the cost of the program depends upon keeping faith with the following educational criteria: (1) Fees and assessments should be kept nominal so that all students have an equal opportunity to participate; (2) fund-raising procedures should have desirable educational values for students; (3) the buying public should feel that they are getting full value for their money and have confidence in the integrity of the methods employed; and (4) over-emphasis on income-producing activities should be avoided.

These conditions are difficult to meet, and it is highly probable that tax funds will have to supply a part of the support of the extraclass program. Therefore, the professional staff should try to present to board members and patrons the case for using tax funds for the *difference* between the cost of an educationally sound activity program and the revenue from appropriate fund-raising enterprises.

No comprehensive studies of fund-raising activities to help defray the costs of the student activity program have been reported in the literature since the 1940's. But current extraclass financial statements for several local schools indicate that the most important change since

[7] Franklin A. Miller, James H. Moyer, and Robert B. Patrick, *Planning Student Activities* (Englewood Cliffs, N.J.: Prentice-Hall, Inc., 1956), p. 149.

that period has been an increase in the number of schools using a student activity ticket.

The most productive and commonly employed means of securing funds for student activities in 543 schools studied by Stout were as follows:[8]

Sources of Income	Per Cent of Schools
1. Gate receipts from programs, plays, etc.	95
2. Athletic gate receipts.	93
3. Sales of candy, soft drinks, etc.	80
4. Ticket sales through community canvasses.	51
5. Sale of advertising and publications.	46
6. Bazaars, fairs, and carnivals.	40
7. Sale of scrap paper, old clothes, etc.	34
8. Class assessments, fees, and dues.	34
9. General student activity ticket sales.	29

In 1955 Strahan made a study of activity costs for students in the same state and found that 77.1 per cent of the schools used a general activity ticket — as compared to the 29 per cent reported by Stout in 1942.[9]

The general student activity ticket has several attributes that commend it as the best single method of securing non-tax funds for activities: (1) It assures the activity program of a relatively certain and stable revenue from year to year. (2) It facilitates advance planning of the budget. (3) It reduces the cost of individual events to students. (4) It encourages all students to attend school events. (5) It permits a sales campaign limited to the student body. (6) It can be sold on an installment plan so that practically all students can afford to buy it.

Usually the activity ticket provides for admission to all athletic, music, and dramatics events and frequently it includes a subscription to the school paper. Costs vary widely from school to school depending upon prices and the events included. Some schools require the purchase of an activity ticket, but since a few students may not be able to afford it or may have legitimate reasons for not attending most evening events, the better policy is to make the purchase of an activity ticket voluntary.

Other means of raising funds reported in Stout's study would seem to be appropriate if they are not overworked. However, raffles, bingo parties, tag days, and the like, which amount to soliciting contributions, are not appropriate for schools and imply that the activity program is

[8] Minard W. Stout, "Administration of Extra-Class Activity Finances in Public High Schools in Iowa," unpublished Ph.D. dissertation, State University of Iowa, 1943, p. 47.

[9] Donald F. Strahan, "An Analysis of Expenditures of Pupils in Attendance in Certain Secondary Schools in Iowa," unpublished Ph.D. dissertation, State University of Iowa, 1956, p. 125.

something "extra" attached to education rather than an integral part of the program.

Purchasing. All purchases which encumber the activity fund should be channeled through the central treasurer and should have a requisition signed by a designated administrative official of the school in order to prevent unauthorized buying and to provide an accurate record. In large school systems, purchases involving large sums, such as new band uniforms, should be approved by both the principal and an official in the central business office. In these schools, also, the principal usually delegates responsibility for approving the general run of purchase orders to an assistant. In small and medium-sized schools, the superintendent or principal commonly approves all purchase orders.

Student officers, sponsors, coaches, and directors usually initiate purchases. When a decision to purchase is reached, the faculty sponsor and/or student treasurer should make out a requisition form in triplicate, sign it, and then secure the signature of the proper administrative official. One copy of the requisition should be retained by the sponsor, one should go to the school's central treasurer, and one should go to the merchant from whom the purchase is made. The signed requisition form sent to the vendor becomes a purchase order. This procedure provides a check to make certain that an organization is not incurring liabilities beyond its budget and provides an accurate record upon which to make payment.

All local merchants and out-of-town firms with whom the school does business should agree that no orders will be honored which encumber the school activity fund without a properly signed requisition.

Handling Receipts. Money collected by student treasurers of organizations, ticket sellers, and other persons authorized to receive funds should be deposited as soon as possible, accompanied by a deposit slip, with the school's central treasurer. The deposit should be acknowledged by issuance of a prenumbered receipt or ticket, signed by the treasurer, to the person making payment. Receipts should be made up in duplicate or triplicate form.

The central treasurer should bank all receipts daily in an officially designated school depository. A duplicate deposit slip should accompany each deposit and be signed by the bank teller.

The school administrator is ultimately responsible for making sure that all monies received by students and staff members as a part of the activities program are handled without loss and that an accurate accounting is made. Carelessness in this area of the business procedure is little short of obtuseness. In addition, it may tempt students or cause them to become careless in money matters. School administrators who manage activity funds out of their vest pockets are not only risking their own careers but are doing students and teachers a great disservice.

Disbursing Funds. All but petty cash payments from the activity fund should be made by checks issued by the central treasurer. Most schools need a petty cash fund to pay for very small items such as delivery charges on packages, stamps, or purchases that must be made immediately to meet some emergency. Needless to say, these disbursements should be kept to a minimum and should be recorded in a petty cash book.

All other payments should be made only upon the basis of signed requisitions with an attached invoice showing that goods or services have been received and, in the case of merchandise, found in good condition. Checks issued in payment for goods or services should be numbered and entered in a disbursement ledger.

Accounting and Bookkeeping. The accounting procedures recommended in the U.S. Office of Education handbook include the following: (1) keeping a fund balance record, (2) registering receipts and expenditures, (3) recording the distribution of receipts, (4) recording the distribution of expenditures, (5) maintaining subsidiary activity records, (6) reconciling the bank statement with the balance in the activity books, (7) preparing a monthly financial statement for each fund, (8) preparing a monthly financial statement for all funds, and (9) preparing an annual financial statement.[10]

These steps are recommended in recording receipt and expenditure transactions:

1. Steps to be followed in recording receipts:
   a. Issue receipts.
   b. Deposit money, using duplicate deposit slip and Analysis of Deposit form.
   c. Record receipt in appropriate Fund Balance Record.
   d. Record receipt in Receipts and Expenditures Register.
   e. Record receipt in appropriate Receipts Distribution Ledger.
   f. Record receipt in Subsidiary Activity Ledger (if used).

2. Steps to be followed in recording expenditures:
   a. Process Activity Purchase Order for payment.
   b. Issue check.
   c. Record expenditure in appropriate Fund Balance Record.
   d. Record expenditure in Receipts and Expenditure Register.
   e. Record expenditure in appropriate Expenditure Distribution Ledger.

[10] U.S. Office of Education, *op. cit.*, pp. 55–60.

3. Summary statements to be prepared:
   a. Reconcile the bank statement.
   b. Prepare Monthly Financial Statement of Each Fund.
   c. Prepare Monthly Summary Statement of All Funds.
   d. Prepare an Annual Financial Statement of Each Fund.
   e. Prepare an Annual Summary Statement for All Funds.

The key forms shown in Figures 31 through 36 are recommended in the U.S. Office of Education handbook,[11] as are additional forms briefly described with recommended procedures for using them. Principals attempting to develop or revise an accounting system for the activity program in their schools will find this handbook especially helpful.

The annual summary report for the activities program may well take the same form as the monthly statement shown in "Monthly Summary Statement for All Funds." The annual report is simply a summary of the monthly reports and should be included in the principal's annual report on the entire activity program. Its preparation should be a responsibility of the central activities treasurer.

FIGURE 31

Official Receipt

YOUR SCHOOL		No. _1_ (1)
Received from _John Smith, Class of 1960_ (2)		
Source of Income _Gate Receipts, Play, Class of 1960_		
Fund (3)	Account (4)	Amount (5)
Student Organization	11, Admissions	$490.00
Student Organization	1030, Fees and Deductions	10.00
	Total	$500.00
	Signed _John Doe_	
Date _10/2/58_	Title _Central Treasurer_	

Source: U.S. Office of Education, *Financial Accounting for School Activities* (Washington: Government Printing Office, 1959), pp. 60–87.

[11] *Ibid.*, pp. 60–87.

FIGURE 32

Activity Purchase Order

ACTIVITY PURCHASE ORDER

Your School
Yourtown, U.S.A.   No. __40__ (1)

Date __9/1__ 19__58__

Purchased from __Any Supply Company__ (2)
Address __1010 Main Street, Yourtown, U.S.A.__
Charge to __Student Organization__ Fund, __Dramatic Club__ Activity (3)
Date Wanted __10/1/58__   Terms __2%__ (4)
Deliver to __Your__ School

Quantity	Unit	Description	Unit Cost	Total Cost
1	ea.	Tape Recorder A-1011	$153.06	$153.06
		Less discount of 2%		3.06
				$150.00

Joyce Rogers
Activity Treasurer

George Robinson
Activity Sponsor

W. E. Jones
Principal's Approval

Source: U.S. Office of Education, *Financial Accounting for School Activities* (Washington: Government Printing Office, 1959), pp. 60–87.

FIGURE 33
Fund Balance Record

Date	Deposit Number	RECEIPTS Receipt Numbers	Amount Each Deposit	Cumulative Deposits	Date	Check No.	EXPENDITURES Payee	Fund	Amount Each Check	Cumulative Checks	Cash Balance
(1)	(2)	(3)	(4)	(5)	(6)	(7)	(8)	(9)	(10)	(11)	(12)
1958					1958						
10/1											$1,000.00
					10/2	21	A.B.C. Publishing Co.	S.O.	$20.00	$20.00	980.00
					10/4	22	John Jones	A.	75.00	95.00	905.00
					10/6	23	John Doe (Establish Petty Cash)	S.O.	10.00	105.00	895.00
					10/8	24	Acme Costume Co.	S.O.	50.00	155.00	845.00
10/9	10	1-3	$1,000.00	$1,000.00							1,845.00
10/15	11	4-5	50.00	1,050.00							1,895.00
					10/17	25	Jones Publishing Co. Mdse.		350.00	505.00	1,545.00
					10/17	26	General Novelty Co.	S.O.	100.00	605.00	1,445.00
					10/18	27	City Newspaper	S.O.	15.00	620.00	1,430.00
					10/20	28	State Tax Commission	A.+ S.O.	30.00	650.00	1,400.00
					10/24	29	Clay Supply Co.	S.O.	150.00	800.00	1,250.00
10/28	12	6-8	690.00	1,740.00							1,940.00
					10/28	30	George Jackson	S.O.	25.00	825.00	1,915.00
10/30	13	9	750.00	2,490.00							2,665.00
					10/30	31	John Doe (Replenish Petty Cash)	S.O.	6.02	831.02	2,658.98
10/30	14	10-11	60.00	2,550.00							2,718.98

Source: U.S. Office of Education, *Financial Accounting for School Activi-*

Receipts Distribution Ledger

Student Organization Fund

No.	Date	Rec. or Vou. No.	Amount	Received From	For	REGULAR RECEIPT ACCOUNTS							CLEARING RECEIPT ACCOUNTS			
						10. Activity Income					Grants	Total Regular Receipts	Taxes and Deductions	Inter-fund Transfers	Petty Cash	Total Clearing Receipts
						Admissions	Pro-rated Activity Tickets	Dues and Fees	Sales	Other Activity Income						
						11	12	13	14	18	20		1030-a	1090-a	1100-a	
(1)	(2)	(3)	(4)	(5)	(6)	(7)						(8)	(9)	(10)	(11)	(12)	(13)
1	1958 10/1	1	$500.00	Class of 1960	Play	$490.00							$490.00	$10.00			$10.00
2	10/9	3	100.00	Student Council	Programs	100.00							100.00				
3	10/15	5	25.00	Dramatic Club	Dues			$25.00					25.00				
4	10/17	7	600.00	Class of 1959	Carnival	196.00			$392.00				588.00	12.00			12.00
5	10/18	8	50.00	X-Roads	Dues, Profit, sale of magazines			50.00					50.00				
6	10/20	V-1	400.00	Class of 1959	Interfund transfer										$400.00		400.00
7	10/20	V-2	100.00	Interfund Transfer for Student Council	Shore Honorial Activity Tickets		$100.00						100.00				
8	10/30	11	10.00	John Doe	Close out Petty Cash											$10.00	10.00
			$1,785.00			$786.00	$100.00	$75.00	$392.00			$1,353.00	$22.00	$400.00	$10.00	$432.00

Source: U.S. Office of Education, *Financial Accounting for School Activities* (Washington: Government Printing Office, 1959), pp. 60–87.

FIGURE 35

Expenditures Distribution Ledger

Student Organization _____ Fund

No.	Date	Check or Vou. No.	Amount	Payee	For	REGULAR EXPENDITURE ACCOUNTS							CLEARING EXPENDITURE ACCOUNTS		
						10. Activity Expense				Operation of Plant	Capital Outlay	Total Regular Expenditures	Taxes and Deductions	Petty Cash	Total Clearing Expenditures
						Supplies	Purchases of Mdse.	Other Activity Expense						
						112	113	114	123	200		1030-b	1100-b	
(1)	(2)	(3)	(4)	(5)	(6)	(7)				(8)	(9)	(10)	(11)	(12)
	1958													
1	10/2	21	$20.00	ABC Publishing	Books	$20.00					$20.00			
2	10/6	23	10.00	John Doe	Establish Petty Cash								$10.00	$10.00
3	10/5	24	50.00	Acme Costume Co.	Costume Carnival			$50.00			50.00			
4	10/7	26	100.00	General Novelty Co.	Carnival		100.00				100.00			
5	10/18	27	15.00	City Newspaper	Advertising			15.00			15.00			
6	10/20	28	22.00	State Tax Comm.	Tax							$22.00		22.00
7	10/24	29	150.00	Ony Supply Co.	Tape Recorder					$150.00	150.00			
8	10/28	30	25.00	George Jackson	Custodian				$25.00		25.00			
9	10/30	31	6.02	John Doe	Replenish Petty Cash			6.02			6.02			
			$398.02			$20.00	$100.00	$71.02	$25.00	$150.00	$366.02	$22.00	$10.00	$32.00

Source: U.S. Office of Education, *Financial Accounting for School Activi-*

Monthly Summary Statement for All Funds

RECEIPTS AND EXPENDITURES BY FUND

Fund	Balance 10/1/58	Regular Receipts	Clearing Receipts	Regular Expenditures	Clearing Expenditures	Balance 10/31/58
Student Organization	$ 275.00	$1,353.00	$432.00	$366.02	$ 32.00	$1,661.98
Athletic	250.00	392.00	8.00	75.00	8.00	567.00
Merchandise	200.00	750.00		350.00	400.00	200.00
Publications	100.00	25.00				125.00
Instructional Fees and Rentals		50.00				50.00
Miscellaneous	175.00		40.00		100.00	115.00
Total	$1,000.00	$2,570.00	$480.00	$791.02	$540.00	$2,718.98

RECEIPTS BY SOURCE AND PURPOSE

BALANCE, 10/1/58 .... $1,000.00

Regular Receipts:
- Admissions $1,178.00
- Prorated Share Activity Tickets 100.00
- Dues and Fees 125.00
- Sales 1,167.00
- Total Regular Receipts $2,570.00

Clearing Receipts:
- Taxes and Deductions .... $ 30.00
- General Activity Tickets 40.00
- Transfers from Other Funds 400.00
- Petty Cash 10.00
- Total Clearing Receipts .... $ 480.00
- Total Receipts $3,050.00
- TOTAL RECEIPTS AND BALANCE $4,050.00

EXPENDITURES BY SOURCE AND PURPOSE

Regular Expenditures:
- Personal and Contracted Services .. $ 75.00
- Supplies 20.00
- Purchases of Merchandise 450.00
- Other Activity Expense 71.02
- Operation of Plant 25.00
- Capital Outlay 150.00
- Total Regular Expenditures .... $ 791.02

Clearing Expenditures:
- Taxes and Deductions .... $ 30.00
- General Activity Tickets 100.00
- Transfers to Other Funds 400.00
- Petty Cash 10.00
- Total Clearing Expenditures .... $ 540.00
- Total Expenditures $1,331.02
- BALANCE, ALL FUNDS 10/31/58 .... $2,718.98

We hereby certify to the best of our knowledge and belief that this financial report reflects the true condition of these funds.

John Doe
(Central Treasurer)

W. C. Jones
(Principal)

Source: U.S. Office of Education, *Financial Accounting for School Activities* (Washington: Government Printing Office, 1959), pp. 60–87.

Other Activities Business Functions

In addition to the financial management of student activities, principals commonly are expected to supervise the storage and inventory of supplies and equipment, make periodic reports on the financial condition of the program, handle such chores as arranging for the supervision and policing of public events, engaging officials, and the like.

Storage and Inventory. For the most part, the problems and procedures for the storing and inventorying of activities supplies and equipment are the same as those described in the preceding section on "General Operations." One difference in most schools is that the inventory need not be submitted to the central business office. It becomes a part of the principal's record of the assets of the extraclass program for his school. However, if substantial amounts of board funds are expended for activities items, the principal usually will be expected to follow the same business procedures in relation to the central business office as for the instructional and administrative operation of his school.

The three activities for which storage and inventory become sizable tasks are dramatics, music, and athletics. Each of these departments will need separate storage facilities located so that they are convenient to their base of operations. Suitable forms should be drafted for inventory purposes and the heads of each department made responsible for directing the inventory. An athletic director has been employed in an increasing number of schools during the past few years and in these schools he should be made responsible for the storage and inventory of athletic goods. The use of student managers to assist in taking care of supplies and equipment has been commonplace in athletics and dramatics for many years. It provides an excellent opportunity for students to get some good experience, but the burden of responsibility placed on students should be reasonable. Final responsibility for the care of and accounting for supplies and equipment must be assumed by the faculty sponsor, director, or coach of each activity.

Reporting. Together with the annual financial statement for all activities, the principal should prepare or have prepared a comprehensive annual report on extraclass supplies and equipment owned by the school. Copies should go to the student council, members of the faculty, and the superintendent of schools. In small schools, the principal probably will need to compile this report, but in larger schools the activities director may be made responsible for its preparation.

Providing for Supervision and Policing of Public Events. Events such as athletic contests, public concerts, and plays require faculty supervision, and if crowds are large, some police services will be needed for parking and taking care of emergencies. Faculty members and principals should not be expected to handle disorders among spectators at public events. This is a job for police, and if the city will not provide adequate personnel, the school may be required to employ special police. The working relationships between the school and the local police should be negotiated by the superintendent and board.

Ticket sales, supervision of students, and similar tasks in conjunction with public events may be assigned to faculty members. It is a responsibility of the principal to arrange for these services and to see that related business transactions are handled efficiently. Assignments that require the continued use of faculty members who are experienced and competent should be paid for out of board of education funds and should be made a part of the written contracts with the teachers so employed.

Engaging Officials and Judges for Contests. Interscholastic contests require the services of officials and judges, and since these people are usually paid from activity funds, the principal or an assistant is responsible for engaging them. In large high schools the athletic director should assume primary responsibility for engaging officials for athletic events. But in small schools, the principal will need to attend to this matter. A complicating factor in engaging officials is securing people who are acceptable to each competing school. Usually, this requires considerable communication by correspondence or telephone. One advantage in belonging to an interscholastic conference is that its secretary may be delegated to compile a list of approved officials, and agreements can be reached for securing persons for specific contests at conference meetings. Thus each school can engage officials well in advance of the season or special event.

Needless to say, the payment of officials should be made in the same manner as other payments from the activity fund — by a check made out by the central treasurer. It is incredible that some school administrators still pay officials and judges directly out of cash receipts without making a record of the transaction, but some of the authors' acquaintances who do officiating insist that this does happen in small schools. If true, it would seem to indicate extreme carelessness.

Questions and Group Projects

1. Interview several superintendents in school systems of different size to learn what special functions they expect principals to assume in budget planning.
2. Secure printed or mimeographed copies of several school system budgets. What are the major sections of these budgets? What items are most frequently included for the secondary schools?

MANAGEMENT AND COMMUNITY RELATIONS

3. Interview several principals from both large and small high schools. Compare their responsibilities for purchasing, storing supplies, and inventorying.

4. Write a paper comparing the advantages of a free textbook system and a rental system.

5. Secure materials from your state department of education and the U.S. Office of Education on the operation of the hot-lunch program in schools and the aid provided in the form of surplus commodities and cash payments. Then visit several school cafeterias and check prices, quality of meals, and management problems. Summarize your reactions to this program.

6. Debate in class the proposition "All activity funds, regardless of source, should revert to the general activity fund at the close of the fiscal year and be rebudgeted."

7. Discuss the merits of a centralized and a decentralized system of activity fund management and accounting.

8. Interview members of several high school student councils to learn the extent to which members of the council participate in raising and budgeting extraclass funds.

9. Review articles on the use of activity tickets in financing extraclass activities. What activities are usually included, what sales plans are used, and what policies are followed with respect to required and optional purchases?

10. Interview several high school principals to learn how they secure revenue for financing the activity program in their schools. Also secure copies of forms used in managing the business of the extraclass activity program. Summarize your findings and write a critique of practices as revealed in your study.

Selected References

Burke, Arvid J. *Financing Public Schools in the United States.* New York: Harper & Brothers, 1957.

Douglass, Harl R. *Modern Administration of Secondary Schools.* Boston: Ginn and Company, 1954.

Grieder, Calvin, Truman M. Pierce, and William E. Rosenstengel. *Public School Administration.* New York: The Ronald Press Company, 1961.

Hamilton, R. R. "The Legal Status, Control, and Use of Athletic and Other Extra-Curricular Funds," *The Bi-Weekly School Law Letter,* Vol. II, September, 1953.

Jennings, William E. "Student Central Fund Used to Teach Money Management," *Ohio Schools,* January, 1960, 38:32–33.

Knezevich, Stephen J., and John G. Fowlkes. *Business Management of Local School Systems.* New York: Harper & Brothers, 1960.

Mort, Paul R., Walter C. Reusser, and John W. Polley. *Public School Finance.* New York: McGraw-Hill Book Company, 1960.

National Education Association, Research Division, "Fiscal Authority of School Boards," *Research Bulletin.* Washington: The Association, 1950.

Reason, Paul L., and Alpheus L. White. *Financial Accounting for Local and State School Systems.* Bulletin 1959, No. 22. Washington: Government Printing Office, 1959.

Roe, William H. *School Business Management.* New York: McGraw-Hill Book Company, 1961.

U.S. Office of Education, *Financial Accounting for School Activities.* Washington: Government Printing Office, 1959.

CHAPTER 19

Office Management and Program Accounting

In many respects a principal's office is a cross between a modern traffic control center and an old-fashioned country store. It is a combination control center, business enterprise, informal meeting place, information bureau, conference center, and seat of authority. Students and parents expect its atmosphere to be warm and friendly, but they also expect it to function with dispatch and efficiency. And many teachers who take pride in cultivated clutter in their own offices are quick to criticize disorder and inefficiency in the front office.

The principal's office is the hub of the school's program and of relationships between the school and the public. Many laymen form strong impressions of the character of the school from the tone, appearance, and services of its office.

Students also form lasting impressions of the school from their associations with the central office and the people who work there. For many students, members of the office staff serve *in loco parentis.* The principal and his secretaries answer their questions, listen to their problems, advise them, help retrieve their lost articles, admonish them when they need it, and assist them when they are in trouble.

The organization and direction of office services is another facet of the job of being a high school principal. However, it should occupy only a minor share of his time. Once the organization is established, much of the routine should be taken over by assistants and clerks so that the principal may concentrate on faculty relations, planning, and direction of the instructional program. On the other hand, he is obligated to see parents, students, and teachers who have problems that require his attention, and representatives of colleges and commercial concerns frequently call on legitimate business. Consequently, a part of the principal's job of office management is that of organizing his own time so that he will be able to accommodate people who need to see him.

Office Services

As is true with other school functions, the types of services provided or facilitated by the principal's office depend to a large extent upon the size and organization of the high school. However, in a school in which the principal is the actual administrative head, the following managerial and secretarial tasks usually are performed by him and his office staff:

1. *Communicating* — exchanging information by such means as intercom systems, bulletins, telephone, correspondence, and face-to-face conferences.
2. *Processing materials* — typing, duplicating, etc.
3. *Handling correspondence and mail* — preparing and filing letters for professional staff and processing staff mail.
4. *Procuring supplies and equipment* — for both the professional and non-professional staffs.
5. *Administering attendance* — checking, recording, and clearing student attendance.
6. *Directing the daily program* — control and necessary adjustments in the daily schedule and movement of students.
7. *Administering records* — maintaining, storing, summarizing, and supplying information.
8. *Preparing reports* — the principal's annual report, reports to the state, reports to accrediting agencies, financial summaries, and the like.
9. *Serving as control center for the operation of the physical plant* — making certain that heat, ventilation, lights, cleaning, and other services are functioning.
10. *Implementing relations with the public* — conducting business with lay visitors and providing information.
11. *Troubleshooting* — meeting emergency situations that call for on-the-spot action.

Some of these services have been described in the chapters on staff, records and reports, community relations, and business management. Some are largely self-explanatory. However, the following have not been considered elsewhere in our discussions and are sufficiently important in the management of a school to merit more than incidental attention.

Communication

The effective operation of any high school requires that everyone involved — faculty, central staff, custodians, and students — be kept informed on matters that affect the conduct and coordination of its program. The exchange of ideas in any organization depends on communication — either face to face or by telephone, correspondence, and bulletins. The importance of communication to an organization is expressed by Bavelas and Barrett:

> In an enterprise whose success hinges upon the coordination of the efforts of all its members, the managers depend completely upon the quality, the amount, and the rate at which relevant information reaches them. . . . This line of reasoning leads us to the belief that communication is not a secondary or derived aspect of organization — a "helper" of the other and presumably more basic functions. Rather it is the essence of organized activity and is the basic process out of which all other functions derive.[1]

In an organization that includes as many people as does the typical secondary school, much of the success of its operation will depend upon the principal's ability to communicate effectively with faculty, student, and supervisory personnel. The facilities of his office also should serve to expedite good communication among staff members even though the principal is not involved.

A study by Klahn shows the direction, media, and nature of communications flowing to and from the high school principal.[2] Klahn summarizes his findings, based on day-to-day logs of communications recorded by principals of selected schools, as follows:

1. Principals communicated most frequently with subordinates — 38.5 per cent of the communication was with teachers. Communication between principals and "outside" (parents and others) was the next largest category. Third in rank of percentage of contracts was superordinate positions.
2. The medium of communication most frequently used by these principals was face-to-face contact (37.3 per cent of all contacts). The emphasis on one-to-one forms of communication was further indicated by use of the telephone (30.4 per cent).

[1] Alex Bavelas and Dermott Barrett, "An Experimental Approach to Organizational Communication," *Personnel*, March, 1951, 27:27.
[2] Richard P. Klahn, "An Analysis of Patterns of Communication of High School Principals in Selected School Systems," unpublished Ph.D. dissertation, State University of Iowa, 1962, pp. 114–116.

OFFICE MANAGEMENT AND PROGRAM ACCOUNTING

3. Principals spent a composite of 55.9 per cent of their time involved in communication.

. . . .

5. Principals rated communication with their subordinates as being of greater importance than communication with coordinates or superordinates.

Although much of the direct communication by the principal is through face-to-face conferences — individual or group — he also uses daily bulletins, staff bulletins, handbooks, telephone messages, correspondence, intercom messages, and the like.

Conferences. The frequency rank of the several types of communication used by principals in Klahn's study is shown in Table 29. Some of the face-to-face conferences were group meetings — faculty meetings, conferences with citizens, administrative staff sessions, and committee meetings. But a large majority of them were informal person-to-person discussions. Outside of conferences with students, 44 per cent of the principal's communications were with members of his own staff, 28 per cent were with parents and other laymen, 22.1 per cent were with superiors on the superintendent's central staff or with the superintendent himself, and 1.6 per cent were with his fellow principals (coordinates).[3]

TABLE 29

Media Used by High School Principals in Communicating

Type of Communication	Median Frequency Per Cent
Face-to-face	37.3
Telephone calls	30.4
Memos and letters	18.0
Announcements and bulletins	13.6
Formal reports	0.7

Source: Richard P. Klahn, "An Analysis of Patterns of Communication of High School Principals in Selected School Systems," unpublished Ph.D. dissertation, State University of Iowa, 1962, p. 78.

Since principals rate communications with their own staff (subordinates) of first importance to the operation of the school and the most frequent type is face-to-face, obviously individual conferences with his staff represent one of his most common and important administrative functions. Therefore, his office should be arranged, equipped, and staffed so as to assist him in conducting these conferences effectively.

On the other hand, conferences may make excessive demands on the

[3] *Ibid.,* p. 67.

principal's time if not carefully scheduled and planned. It is especially necessary therefore, that the principal's secretary arrange his daily calendar so that he has adequate time for other supervisory and administrative duties. Needless to say, there will be days when the calendar has to be revised. Unpredictable problems develop in any school and the principal's time schedule must be flexible. Although systematic planning and scheduling of conferences is desirable, the principal's calendar should not become his master.

Bulletins. One very satisfactory way of getting announcements and messages to the staff and students is a daily bulletin distributed to homerooms or to all classes at a certain hour each day. The chief advantages of a daily bulletin are that (1) it is convenient and effective for communicating daily announcements, (2) it may be read by teachers whenever it least interferes with regular classroom or homeroom procedures, (3) it may be filed by teachers for future reference and to serve as a memorandum, and (4) copies may be bound as a day-by-day log of the events of the school year.

The principal's secretary or an administrative assistant should be responsible for compiling and editing the bulletin. However, many schools employ a corps of student office assistants for duplicating and delivery service. This practice seems to provide good experience for the students as well as economy in the service.

Telephone and Intercom Communications. Generally a large volume of telephone communications for staff and student personnel must be handled through the high school office. The chief problems are distinguishing between essential and nonessential calls and providing courteous and necessary service while keeping costs and abuses down.

The matter of community-school relations is a major consideration in handling telephone communications and warrants having the principal spend some time briefing his office personnel on procedures and methods. Parents should be requested not to telephone their children at school unless the message is essential, and teachers should not be called out of class unless the call is urgent. But many patrons call the school on business that is important to them and that may be important to the school. Whether a call is important or not, the courtesy and efficiency with which it is handled often makes a strong impression on callers.

Toll calls from the school phone frequently pose problems. Teachers, of course, should be permitted to make professional calls at school expense. But this privilege cannot be extended to students because of the costs and interference with regular school business. However, it is sometimes necessary for students to make outside calls, and the most satisfactory solution seems to be to install a toll phone in or adjacent to the main office where the clerks can supervise its use.

In medium-sized and large schools an intercom system is almost a necessity; most buildings constructed in recent years are equipped with one. Its chief value is for supplementary announcements and special messages, but some schools use it in place of a daily bulletin and to pipe educational programs to certain classes. Unfortunately, it is vulnerable to abuses and may become a nuisance. Intercoms are so convenient that some principals and office secretaries interrupt classes with trivial bulletins. In other schools, students are given easy access to the intercom system and the gadget blares away every fifteen or twenty minutes with such messages as a reminder that the junior cheerleaders will assemble at the east end of the gymnasium rather than the west end for pyramid practice.

However, the misuses of intercom systems do not negate their potential worth and convenience. It is the observation of the authors that an intercom serves as a valuable supplement to the daily bulletin in many schools and, if properly controlled, is exceedingly helpful in coordinating the daily program and in presenting certain types of educational materials.

Processing Materials for Teachers

It would be fortunate if every teacher could be provided with at least a half-time secretary to handle his correspondence, prepare tests, duplicate instructional materials, and perform other clerical tasks. But the cost of such assistance is far beyond the financial means of most school systems. Nevertheless, these tasks must be performed and teachers should be relieved of them as much as possible in order to devote their time to instruction and conferences with students and colleagues.

Even with limited finances, reasonably good clerical services for teachers can be provided with careful organization, modern equipment, and good scheduling in the principal's office. The office should be equipped with stencil-type, spirit-type, and facsimile duplicators plus a suitable workroom for their operation and for assembling and filing materials.

One of the keys to satisfactory duplicating service is good cooperation from teachers. A perennial problem is that of peaks and valleys in the work load. The demand for tests, outlines, and other instructional materials tends to pile up at the beginning and end of grading periods. If teachers can be persuaded to plan ahead and to give the office personnel a reasonable period of time to process materials, the service can be maintained at a satisfactory level. It is especially helpful if teachers can be induced to prepare their unit outlines, bibliographies, and similar materials far enough ahead so that the clerks may work on them during the summer months.

Business education students may be used to assist full-time clerks in preparing some types of materials needed by teachers. As a rule, students should not be permitted to work with test materials, and regular clerks must be held to a strict accounting for preserving the confidential nature of such materials.

Correspondence

In addition to the principal's correspondence, his secretarial staff usually is responsible for handling faculty correspondence. In a small high school the principal generally is required to share the time of his secretary with teachers. And in large schools each secretary must take care of the correspondence for several teachers.

By use of modern dictating and transcribing equipment, one secretary can attend to correspondence for about twice as many teachers as she could by means of direct dictation. Convenience is a big factor, since the teacher may dictate when he has time and the secretary may transcribe when she is unoccupied with other duties.

In medium and large high schools, it is both economical and satisfactory to provide dictating machines for members of the faculty and to organize a secretarial pool to transcribe their letters, do their filing, and provide other secretarial services. Estimating the number of machines and secretaries needed is difficult because of the wide variation in the volume of correspondence of individual faculty members. However, one dictating machine for every five or six teachers seems to be a workable ratio in high schools now using such equipment.

Direction of the Daily Program

It is one thing to draft a daily schedule for a high school on the drawing board and another thing to manage it each day. Although the school of the future may be one in which "no bells ring," at present few have developed a much better method of directing the movement of large numbers of students with a minimum of confusion and loss of time than by use of bells or some other type of sound signal.

In most schools, student movement is directed by a master clock and an electronic bell program in the principal's office. These are supplemented by special announcements over the intercom system and in the daily bulletin. If every day were the same, the bell program would not need to be changed and the whole operation would be routine and automatic.

But each day is not, and should not be, the same. Adjustments must be made to allow for special types of educational activities and emergency operations such as fire and civilian defense drills. Such adjustments require decisions which must be communicated to teachers and students. Decisions and adjustments affecting the daily program are functions of the principal and his office staff; these need to be handled efficiently in the interests of the safety of students and with a minimum loss of instructional time.

Administration of Records

With the exception of counseling records and those used by individual teachers for instruction, the principal's office is the administrative center for all of the school's records. It is the place not only where records are compiled but where most records are housed and, therefore, used. The reader is referred to Chapter 16 for a detailed treatment of records and reports.

Control Center for the Physical Plant Operation

Except in schools in which the superintendent's and principal's offices are in the same building, the latter office should serve as the control center for the operation of the high school plant. The main task is to coordinate plant operation and maintenance with the educational program of the school. This responsibility and authority should be delegated to the principal by the superintendent and board of education.

Since coordinating the use of the physical facilities of a school with its educational program frequently raises problems of staff relationships, it is desirable that the board and central administrative staff develop policies and that the principal develop regulations and procedures for the operation and maintenance of the plant.

Usually it is most effective for teachers and students to be instructed to submit requests for special custodial services to the principal and for him to reach an agreement with the head custodian on the feasibility and method of providing these services. From time to time, the principal may need to confer with members of the custodial staff to discuss problems and procedures relating to their functions, schedules, and relationships with teachers and students. Schedules for special services such as use of the building for evening rehearsals should be made and approved by the principal each week, and he should see that they reach the head custodian in time to be carried out with the personnel available.

Public Relations

As noted previously, the principal's office plays an important role in relationships between the school and the public. Perhaps the most important factor is the matter of courtesy and promptness in serving laymen who visit the school office on business. One or two secretaries should be assigned the responsibility for greeting visitors, inquiring about their business, giving them the information they desire, or referring them to the proper member of the professional staff. It is especially irritating to parents and other laymen to enter the principal's office and be ignored while a couple of secretaries chat behind the counter.

The general appearance of the office also makes an impression on visitors. Most citizens do not approve of elaborate executive suites for high school principals, but they do expect and respect an office that is dignified and attractive. The principal should not be required to devote time to the appearance of his office, but his secretary or assistant should. On the other hand, the principal must establish the standards and brief his staff on what he expects.

Troubleshooting

The potential for the unexpected is rather high when one is working with large numbers of adolescents and their parents. If a few strong-willed teachers and custodians are added, most of the ingredients for occasional trouble are present. Students suffer accidents, teachers and students come into conflict, janitors grow impatient. Elmo Jackson loses his piccolo, and Miss White is called home suddenly by an illness in her family.

Consequently, along with their other duties, the staff in the principal's office has to develop a capacity for troubleshooting. Knowing what should be done and who should be called in the case of an injury to a student, placating aroused students and parents, helping to ease the load of the custodians, locating Elmo's lost piccolo, and finding a substitute for Miss White are all in a day's work.

There are, to be sure, additional tasks for the principal's office. But in combination, the aforementioned determine the general functions and organization of the office and, therefore, the responsibilities of the principal in the role of office manager.

Personnel and Facilities

Although the principal's office should be well equipped, adequate in size, and reasonably attractive, more important are the people who staff it. The secretaries and clerks create the atmosphere and determine the efficiency of the office, and these, in turn, have an influence on student and staff attitudes. Further, they are observed by visitors to the school and thus influence the school's community relations.

Office Personnel

Except in high schools with administrative assistants to the principal, the key person on the office staff is the principal's personal secretary. Any school large enough to employ a *bona fide* principal should be large enough to provide him with a full-time secretary so that he can devote a major share of his time and attention to the real business of administration and supervision. Something may be said in support of a principal's teaching one class in a small or medium-sized high school, but there is no logical excuse for his spending time filling out attendance registers, keeping books, making out report cards, answering the telephone, and so on. These are jobs for secretaries and clerks.

A competent and pleasant secretary to the principal is indispensable to the proper conduct of the affairs of the school office. She need not possess a high degree of technical business skill, although in most schools she must be a good typist, but it is essential that she be able to deal with people competently and courteously. In addition, she must be able to manage the business affairs of the office efficiently and maintain the confidential nature of the many relationships between the principal and students, teachers, and other administrative personnel.

The demand for secretaries with personality and the ability to manage a variety of services exceeds the supply in most communities. Consequently, the salary for a principal's secretary must be competitive with salaries for good secretaries in other enterprises. Except in very small high schools, one or more assistant secretaries or clerk-typists will be needed also to handle the correspondence and to process the instructional materials of teachers.

Advanced students in business education may be assigned to do some work in the school office. They gain valuable work experience and are a welcome supplement to the office staff. Student assistants should be under the joint supervision of the principal's secretary and the business education teachers so that their experience in the office may be coordinated with their classroom work. However, in fairness to them and in the best interest of the school program, they should not be assigned to work on confidential records and correspondence. Neither should they be exploited as cheap help. Office work for students should be a *bona fide* learning experience.

Location, Design, and Equipment of the Office

Although most principals inherit an office whose location and design are relatively fixed, some will have an opportunity to plan new facilities or to remodel old ones. If the opportunity presents itself, the following guides should be helpful.

Location. Most administrators and specialists in school building construction agree that the best location for the principal's office in a single building plant is "On the ground floor near the main entrance."[4] This is convenient for the faculty for routine business and conferences, readily accessible to students, and easy for visitors to find. For a campus type of plant, the administrative building should be centrally located and easily accessible from the main drive.

Guidance and student health offices should be located in the same

[4] National Council on Schoolhouse Construction, *Guide for Planning School Plants* (Nashville: The Council, 1949), p. 86.

general area. Whether they should be immediately adjacent is a matter of some dispute, but probably of no great consequence if the suite is well designed.

The location of offices for special services near the principal's office facilitates the joint use of records, conferences between the principal and special service personnel, and joint use of special equipment, storage facilities, and committee and waiting rooms.

Design. Ideally, the principal's office should provide (1) private office space for the principal and his assistants, (2) secretarial and clerical work space, (3) waiting space for students and visitors, (4) storage and office machine space, and (5) conference and committee space.

If lack of money forces the elimination of any of these, the space for conferences and committee work may be combined with other spaces. However, since much of the staff and student planning for the school is centered in the principal's office, it is exceedingly helpful to have a room designed for group work located close to the records and secretarial personnel of his office.

Many office suites in school provide too little floor space for secretaries and clerk-typists. If necessary, the waiting room space may be reduced to provide more adequate work and filing cabinet space in the secretarial-clerical area. The need for more work space has grown and continues to grow with the increased use of electronic equipment. Transcribing, computing, punch card sorting, and other types of new equipment require space near the stations of the people who operate them.

Figure 37 shows a floor plan for an office in a high school of about 2000 students. A convenient and desirable feature of this plan is the student lobby near the office suite. The principal's, counselors', and nurse's offices are located in the same area, where records and other facilities may be jointly used.

This plan may be adapted to smaller schools by reducing the size of the large areas and the number of offices for special service personnel.

Equipment. In addition to the conventional furniture for secretaries, clerks, and administrators, the following items are needed to provide the services expected of the principal's office:

Bookkeeping machines	Intercom controls
Bulletin board	Mail trays
Cabinets, filing (some fireproof)	Post office boxes
Calendars, desk and master	Radio
Clock, master program	Telephones, desk
Computers, electric	Telephone, public toll
Dictating and transcribing machines	Typewriters, electric
Duplicating machines, stencil and spirit	Vault or safe
Duplicating machine, facsimile	Work organizer, desk

FIGURE 37
Floor Plan for Administrative Offices in a High School of 2000 Students

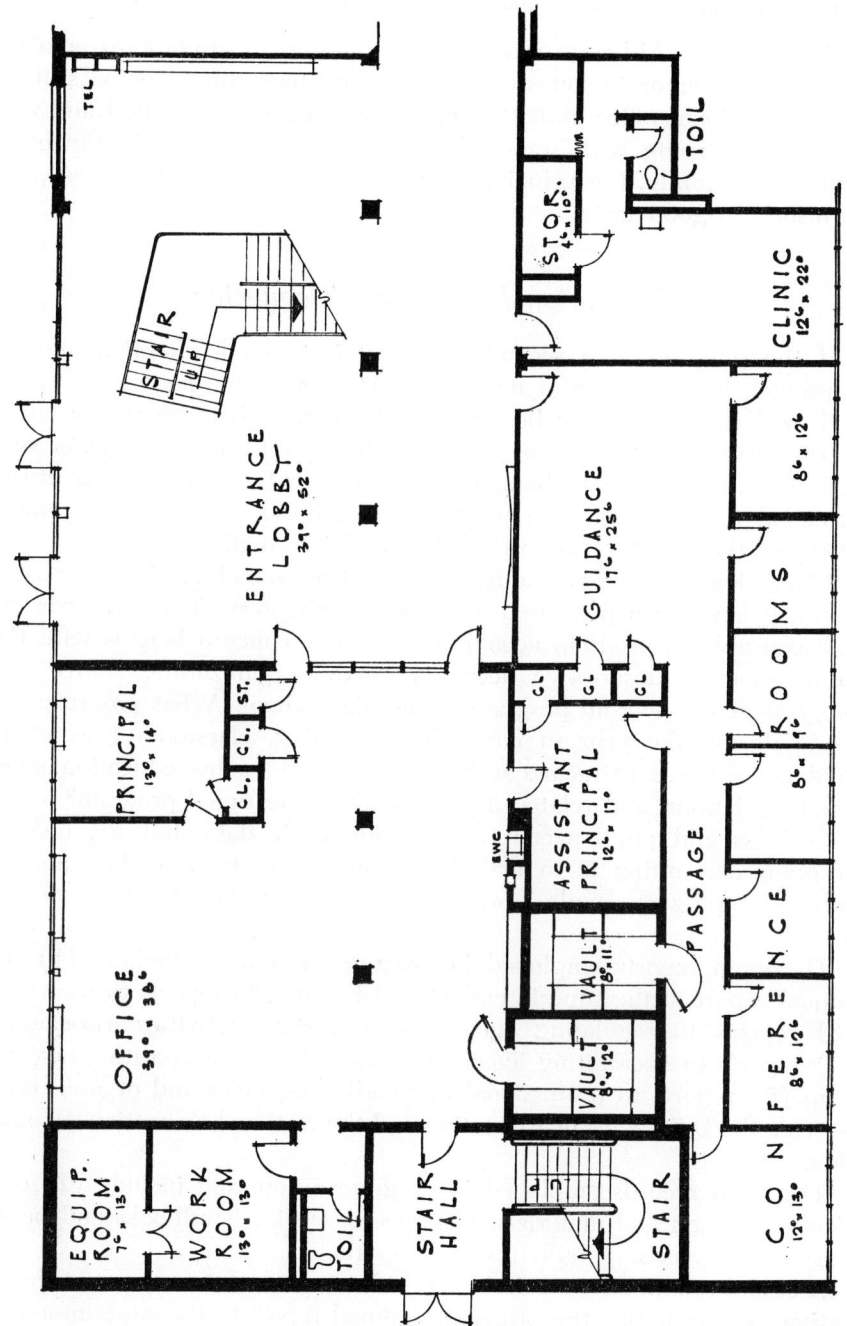

Charles Lorenz, Architect

Numerous small items such as staplers, paper cutters, paper punches, pencil sharpeners, and the like will also be needed.

Appearance. Although it is hardly desirable to attempt to emulate some of the elaborate suites of business executives, the principal's office is a professional office and it should be attractively decorated and furnished in keeping with standards for professional offices in the community. Certainly, the principal should insist that it be kept neat and furnished in good taste.

Educational Program Accounting

If the program of a secondary school is to have direction and be improved, it is a matter of no small consequence that summary reports and analyses of progress be made each year. Otherwise the program merely drifts along or moves erratically in response to pressures or special interests of staff members and laymen. It is the responsibility of the principal to coordinate the preparation of these reports and to make interpretations of the supporting data and information.

Discussions of records dealing with pupil personnel and business management have been presented in preceding chapters. These records are indispensable to program accounting, but our concern here is with the preparation of descriptive accounts of the organization, status, and progress of the over-all program of the high school. What progress was made during the year in curriculum planning, classroom instruction, guidance services, extraclass activities, in-service teacher education, community relations, and related aspects of the educational program?

Business and pupil accounting provide basic data, but the task of program accounting is to assimilate and interpret these data and to judge the progress made toward accomplishing the objectives of the school.

The main reports employed in program accounting include (1) the annual report to the superintendent and board; (2) reports to the state; (3) reports to regulating agencies — e.g., state activities association; (4) reports to accrediting agencies — e.g., regional accrediting association; (5) reports to professional fact-finding agencies and organizations — e.g., the U.S. Office of Education and the National Education Association.

The main records employed in program accounting include (1) curriculum reports and materials; (2) special service handbooks and bulletins; (3) supervisory bulletins and reports.

A casual examination of these lists indicates a certain amount of duplication. For example, the principal's annual report to the superintendent and board is a comprehensive account of the secondary school program during the school year and includes materials from each of the other reports and records. On the other hand, each of the others serves a special purpose and is needed for comprehensive program accounting.

Reports

Principal's Annual Report. The most important single record of the status and progress of the educational program is the annual report of the principal to the superintendent and board of education. Its purpose is to provide a comprehensive account of the school's educational accomplishments and of the characteristics of its student body and staff during the academic year. In some school systems the principal's report is included either in its entirety or in digest form in the superintendent's annual report. Consequently, its timing and format should be planned with that possibility in mind.

Although some superintendents and boards do not require an annual report from the principal, the value of this type of systematic review to the improvement of the school and to the professional effectiveness of the principal makes its preparation a wise investment of his time and effort.

The keys to the efficient preparation of a comprehensive annual report are (1) to design supplementary records so that they may be easily summarized for reporting purposes and (2) to enlist the assistance of department heads, counselors, secretaries, librarians, and activity directors in keeping a running account of activities and developments in their departments. These accounts should be planned so that they can be readily summarized at the close of the school year in a form appropriate for the principal's report.

An examination of thirty-two principals' annual reports by the authors for the 1960–61 school year revealed that the following items were most frequently included:

1. Letter of transmittal.
2. Summary statement by principal.
3. Student population.
   a. Total enrollments for regular academic year compared to previous years.
   b. Summer class and recreational enrollments.
   c. Number of graduates compared to previous years.
   d. Number of transfers in and out.
   e. Number of dropouts.
   f. Age-grade progress tables for students.
   g. Residence of students and previous schools.
   h. Number of pupils transported.
   i. Tuition students.
   j. Attendance data for each month and the year.
   k. Summary of honors and awards.
   l. Distribution of student population by aptitude test scores.

MANAGEMENT AND COMMUNITY RELATIONS

4. Faculty and other personnel.
   a. List of all faculty members, with degrees and colleges attended and classified by departments.
   b. Professional improvement by faculty — summer schools, institutes, conferences, travel, writing, and related activities.
   c. Faculty changes — resignations and additions.
   d. Faculty assignments.
   e. Teaching loads.
   f. List of substitute teachers and their preparation.
   g. In-service staff activities — faculty meetings, workshops, committee work, visitations, extension classes, etc.
   h. Members of office staff — changes.
   i. Members of health staff — changes.
   j. Members of custodial staff — changes.
   k. Community service activities of staff.
5. Curriculum and instruction.
   a. Total course offerings.
   b. Graduation and special curriculum requirements.
   c. Enrollments by departments and courses.
   d. Summer and advanced placement enrollments.
   e. Enrollments in ability-grouped courses.
   f. Major curriculum changes.
   g. Curriculum guides and other materials developed.
   h. Curriculum revision in progress — committees.
   i. Curriculum surveys.
   j. Curriculum conferences — consultants.
   k. Textbook lists.
   l. Use of supplemental instructional materials.
   m. Special instructional projects and activities employed by departments.
   n. Use of audio-visual materials.
   o. Results of standardized achievement tests.
   p. Analysis of semester and yearly grades by departments.
   q. Schedule of classes — first and second semesters.
   r. Experimental programs undertaken — results.
   s. Recommendations for improvement.
6. Extraclass activities.
   a. List of activities sponsored.
   b. Enrollments in each activity.
   c. Summary of activities and projects undertaken by each organization during the year.
   d. Financial statement for the year.
   e. Inventory of equipment owned by school activities association.
   f. Activity honors and awards to students.
   g. Summary of interscholastic contests and records.
   h. Summary of student council projects and membership.
   i. List of faculty sponsors by activities.
   j. Statement of needs and recommendations.

7. Guidance program.
   a. Counselors — assignments.
   b. Summary of distribution of counselors' time.
   c. Testing program and results.
   d. Follow-up study of graduates.
   e. Follow-up study of dropouts.
   f. Placements and scholarships.
   g. Group guidance activities.
   h. Experiments and studies by guidance staff.
8. Business affairs.
   a. Budget.
   b. Inventory of supplies and equipment.
   c. Report on textbooks.
9. Building maintenance.
   a. Custodial staff.
   b. Evaluation of maintenance services.
   c. Major repairs and improvements.
   d. Summary of needs and recommendations.
10. Community relations.
    a. PTA activities.
    b. News releases.
    c. Radio and television programs.
    d. Faculty talks before community groups.
    e. School visitations — parents' nights.
    f. School exhibits and programs.
11. Auxiliary services.
    a. Library — circulation, acquisitions, special services, etc.
    b. Health services — examinations, instruction, treatments.
    c. Transportation.
    d. Food services.
12. Summary and recommendations.

Reports to the State and Accrediting Associations. State departments of public education require some type of annual report from each school system in the state. Although this report is the responsibility of the superintendent of schools, usually he requests his principals to prepare those sections which call for data about their schools.

The form and information for these annual reports vary considerably, depending upon state laws and departmental regulations. However, much of the information requested by the states is the same as that called for by several of the regional accrediting associations and can be used for both. The information included in state and association reports also is needed for the principal's annual report and, with careful planning, can be organized so as to serve this purpose as well. Most frequently called for on state and regional reports are the vertical organization of the school, enrollments by classes, number of graduates, course offerings, extraclassroom activities, guidance services, preparation and assignment of the professional staff, financial data, attendance data, salaries, library, length and organization of the school day, week, and year, and similar data.

Reports to Associations for Student Activities. The state activities association, the state high school athletic association, and other regulatory agencies for student activities also require summary annual reports from member high schools. The section on activities in the principal's annual report may be designed so as to utilize the information called for in the reports to regulatory agencies and thereby save considerable time.

Reports to Professional Fact-Finding Agencies and Organizations. Several agencies and organizations have as their chief function the conduct of surveys to secure basic data needed to prepare guides and legislation for the financial support and advancement of schools. Such data form the bases for recommendations for upgrading teacher preparation, administrative practices, guidance services, school buildings, business methods, and curriculum programs.

Busy administrators sometimes lose patience with the numerous requests from organizations and agencies for data about their schools. But most of these requests are made in the interest of advancing education in the state or nation, and every administrator has a stake in, and a responsibility for, supporting these efforts. If he organizes his record system efficiently and keeps the information about his school up to date, the time required to furnish the information should not be excessive.

At the same time, the personnel of organizations and agencies have an obligation to coordinate their efforts and to design their instruments with care so as to reduce the time demands on the staffs of local schools.

Records of the Educational Program

Curriculum Reports and Records. Failure to prepare and maintain adequate accounts of curriculum work done by individual teachers and committees causes much waste motion, especially in schools which experience a considerable turnover in staff personnel. A committee may devote a great amount of time to developing plans for the revision of offerings and the reorganization of a certain department, but if no written report is prepared and key members of the committee leave, its work may soon be dissipated. Unfortunately, the memories of remaining committee members become hazy, and in the absence of records the next committee assigned to a related problem may duplicate much of the work done by the first committee.

If the assignment of a committee is important enough to justify its organization in the first place, and if it accomplishes anything of consequence, then adequate records should be kept of its proceedings and recommendations.

The reports of textbook selection committees, outlines of course guides, and copies of resource units should be filed and indexed so that continuity may be maintained in curriculum planning. New committees and new teachers should be made familiar with these resources and encouraged to use them in planning their own work. If the school has a curriculum materials center, such records should be housed and cataloged in it. The principal's job is seeing that the files are organized and cataloged and that their use is encouraged.

Service Handbooks and Bulletins. One of the most useful publications in a local school and one which also serves as a valuable record is the administrative handbook for teachers. It presents a complete but concise explanation of board policies, organization, administrative procedures and forms, staff relationships, building regulations, and student controls.

Typical of the content of such a handbook are the following:

1. Staff organizational chart.
2. Building floor plans.
3. Admission and graduation policies.
4. Schedule of classes.
5. School calendar.
6. Instructions to teachers on procedures for opening and closing the school year.
7. Philosophy and objectives of the educational program.
8. The program of studies.
9. Teachers' hours.
10. Substitute teachers.
11. Retirement plan.
12. Insurance and credit plans.
13. Tenure policies.
14. Pupil attendance.
15. Pupil discipline.
16. Intraschool traffic.
17. The grading system.
18. Report cards.
19. Clerical services.
20. Faculty meetings.
21. Faculty committees.
22. First aid.
23. Fire drills.
24. Custodial services.
25. Heat, lights, and ventilation.
26. Visitors.
27. Lost and found.
28. Cafeteria.
29. Administrative forms.
30. Business procedures.

A number of handbooks also include sections on the extraclass activity program, community relations, guidance and counseling, hall and noon-hour duty, tests and examinations, use of audio-visual and library services, and teachers' offices and rooms.

Supervisory Bulletins and Reports. Any school in which there is an active and well-conceived program for the improvement of instruction will need bulletins dealing with specific instructional areas and problems, e.g., ability grouping, remedial instruction, working with superior and talented students, developmental reading, the teacher's role in guidance, interdepartmental articulation, and programmed teaching.

These publications also become a part of program accounting and should be bound and indexed as a section of the school's records. Their value will depend in great measure on their timeliness, the skill with which they are written, and their pertinence to problems that are of genuine concern to teachers in the local school. Bulletins which deal with trivia will be viewed as trivia.

Needless to say, other records may be equally or more important to the program in a particular school. However, those described here are among the ones most frequently employed.

Questions and Group Projects

1. Discuss the proposition "Communication is the most important function of the principal's office."

2. Interview several high school teachers on three or four different occasions during one semester to learn the extent and nature of communications received by them from the administrators of the school system. Which communications do they rate as most important and why?

3. Secure samples of daily bulletins from several different high schools. Analyze their content and quality. Write a critique of their role in the daily operation of a high school.

4. Visit the offices of several high school principals. What is the ratio of secretaries and clerks to faculty members? What special equipment do they have to facilitate services to teachers?

5. Draw a floor plan of a high school office suite for a school enrolling 1,500 to 1,800 students. Assuming that you have adequate funds to include anything you like, prepare a brief prospectus supporting your plans.

6. Discuss the value of an intercom system in a high school in relation to its cost.

7. Secure several copies of the annual reports of principals to their superintendents. Make an analysis of the major items of information included and report your findings to the class.

8. Examine copies of the forms for annual reports to your state department of education and regional accrediting association. What items are called for on both? How could they be better coordinated?

Selected References

Bavelas, Alex, and Dermott Barrett. "An Experimental Approach to Organizational Communication," *Personnel,* March, 1951, 27.

Bent, Rudyard K., and Lloyd E. McCann. *Administration of Secondary Schools.* New York: McGraw-Hill Book Company, 1961. Pp. 331–44.

Douglass, Harl R. *Modern Administration of Secondary Schools.* Boston: Ginn and Company, 1954. Pp. 459–82.

Edmonson, J. B., Joseph Roemer, and Francis L. Bacon. *The Administration of the Modern Secondary School.* New York: The Macmillan Company, 1953. Pp. 154–69.

Hicks, Charles B., and Irene Place. *Office Management.* Boston: Allyn and Bacon, Inc., 1956.

Jacobson, Paul B., William C. Reavis, and James D. Logsdon. *The Effective School Principal.* New York: Prentice-Hall, Inc., 1954. Pp. 419–47.

Klavano, Robert. "The Principal — Public Relations Leader," *The Bulletin* of the NASSP, September, 1960, 44:33–38.

Merz, Albert F. "The Use of Data Processing Equipment for Education Records," *The Bulletin* of the NASSP, April, 1962, 46:7–16.

National Council on Schoolhouse Construction. *Guide for Planning School Plants.* Nashville: The Council, 1949. P. 86.

Walter, Ralph. "The School Secretary and the Faculty," *Education Digest,* May, 1949, 14:212–32.

CHAPTER 20

The Role of the Principal in School Plant Planning

The United States has been involved in an enormous school building program since the turn of the twentieth century. There was a period during the depression of the 1930's, however, when the rate of school construction slowed up considerably, and it virtually came to a halt during the 1940's when World War II consumed building materials as fast as they could be produced. But since the close of World War II, practically every community in the United States has been working feverishly to provide classrooms to cope with the population explosion which began during the 1940's and 1950's. During the years 1957–59, for instance, 141,160 classrooms were constructed.[1] Nevertheless, it was not possible to build fast enough to provide a full day's education for all children. For example, in the fall of 1960, 36 states and the District of Columbia reported a total of 685,000 pupils on curtailed sessions.[2] The extent of the building needs for the decade 1959–69 is estimated to be from 535,000 to 686,000 classrooms depending upon different birth rate assumptions.[3] Assuming a continuation of the 1955–57 birth rate, the

---

[1] U.S. Office of Education, "Ten-Year Aims in Education: Staffing and Constructing Public Elementary and Secondary Schools, 1959–69" (Washington: Government Printing Office, January 19, 1961), p. 69.

[2] Samuel Schloss and Carol Joy Hobson, *Fall 1960 Statistics on Enrollment Teachers, and Schoolhousing in Full-Time Public Elementary and Secondary Day Schools*, U.S. Office of Education, Circ. 634 (Washington: Government Printing Office, 1960), p. 3.

[3] U.S. Office of Education, *op. cit.*, p. 66.

need would be for 607,000 classrooms. The total estimate for this period is presented in Figure 38.

FIGURE 38

Accumulated Number of Needed Classrooms in the Regular Public Schools of 48 States and the District of Columbia: 1959–1969

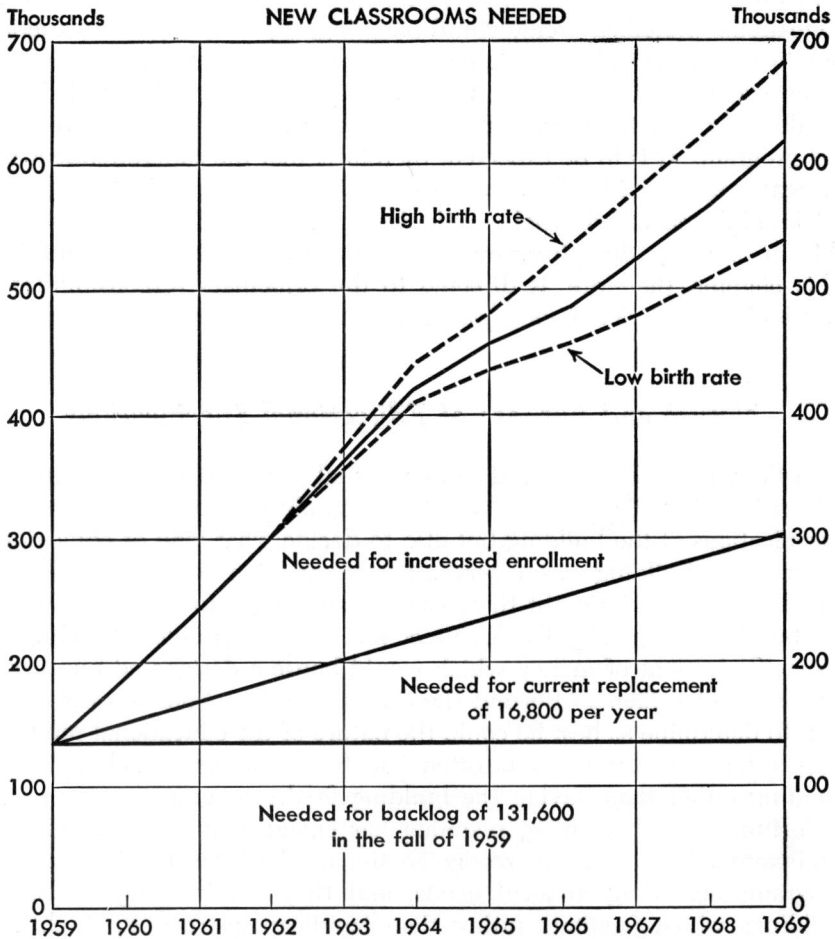

Source: U.S. Office of Education, "Ten-Year Aims in Education: Staffing and Constructing Public Elementary Schools, 1959–69" (Washington: Government Printing Office, January 19, 1961), p. 67.

Obviously many school administrators will be involved in some type of building program in the years ahead — perhaps only an addition to an older building; perhaps a completely new high school; in some rapidly growing communities, perhaps a series of buildings, elementary through the junior college. It follows that individuals preparing to be school administrators during this period will need to become well informed on the process and details required to complete a building program.

Typically, the superintendent of schools is the person responsible for the over-all planning of school buildings, but within the total building program many specialized duties can and should be delegated to other personnel. There are, for example, problems concerned with finance, educational planning, architectural planning, supervision of construction, public relations, and operational planning. One person could scarcely be an expert in all such areas; and even if he were, it is doubtful that he would have time to accomplish all the work necessary to the total building program. It is to be expected, therefore, that the superintendent will delegate responsibility in planning to various members of his staff.

The high school principal may logically be expected to assume leadership in planning the educational program to be served by his building. This chapter, therefore, is directed to the principal's responsibilities in developing educational specifications.

Nature and Purpose of Educational Specifications

In the past architects faced some unusual problems when designing a school building. They were expected not only to prepare the technical specifications of the building but also to decide what kind of educational program the building was to serve. Educators often neglected to provide an adequate description of the learning experiences to be offered within the building. Typically, the architect was asked to design a building for a specific amount of money which would house a designated number of teachers and students. Beyond these meager instructions he was on his own to determine as best he could the nature of the educational program. The result was that teachers often had to adjust their teaching to the building rather than having the building fit the program.

Fortunately, school plant planning has changed in recent years. Administrators have come to recognize the need to develop instructional programs according to local needs, and they are insisting on having buildings which facilitate rather than handicap instruction. Architects have encouraged school faculties to plan the educational program so that they can do a better job of planning. It is now generally recommended that details of the educational program be determined prior to the preparation of blueprints. Written descriptions of the program and learning experiences are called "educational specifications," and their purpose is to guide the architect in planning a functional building to house a specific program.

Contents of Educational Specifications

There is no standard list of topics which should be used slavishly in determining the contents of educational specifications. Insistence on the use of such a list would violate one of the most important concepts underlying the development of educational specifications, namely, the identification of the educational program and activities accepted and supported by a local community. Some general principles and outlines are recommended, however, to assist local schools in selecting content to be included. In one of the most comprehensive studies of the preparation of educational specifications to date, Wilson reviewed the literature on this topic and analyzed the actual documents used by local schools throughout the United States.[4] This study suggests four principles to be observed in planning educational specifications.[5]

1. All of the proposals contained in a set of educational specifications should be consistent with the recognized policies of the board of education. This recommendation presumes that the board has adopted policies concerning the educational program. If it has not, all specifications should be reviewed and approved by the board prior to submission to the architect in order to assure the architect, the local citizenry, and all interested parties that the educational practices being proposed are supported by the board of education. This procedure shows that the policies and wishes of the community, as interpreted by its elected representatives, have been considered in planning the new building.

2. All basic educational policies and philosophies expressed in educational specifications should be sufficiently broad and flexible to accommodate future trends and innovations in educational practices. Exercising this principle requires considerable thought and discussion on the part of the professional staff. Even so, no faculty can predict all future trends in education, and innovations which are exceedingly popular at the moment may prove to be less effective than anticipated when subjected to carefully controlled evaluation. Nevertheless, a faculty should have the courage of its convictions and make its best predictions of future developments so that the architect can provide for as much flexibility as possible in anticipation of them.

3. The basic information to be included in educational specifications should evolve from an analysis of classroom activities. Architects need to know what teachers and pupils plan to do. If, for example, a teacher

---

[4] Russell E. Wilson, "A Study of Educational Specifications for Planning School Buildings: Their Evolution, Preparation, and Contents," unpublished Ph.D. dissertation, University of Michigan, 1954.
[5] *Ibid.*, pp. 174–76.

of speech wishes to have his pupils present speeches from a stage within the classroom, this should be stated so that the architect can provide for such a stage.

4. Educational specifications should contain detailed descriptions of educational functions, activities, programs, groups, and equipment, so that the architect can visualize what will take place *in every class*. If a teacher of mathematics sends large numbers of pupils to the chalkboards to work problems, for instance, chalkboards will be needed on all four walls of the classroom. In contrast, the history teacher may prefer little chalkboard area because he uses the wall space to display newspaper clippings and other types of current news material. In this case, large areas of bulletin boards are in order, rather than chalkboards. Again, if a teacher has his students engage in a considerable amount of committee work, the room will need to be larger and contain a materials center, in contrast to a classroom in which little, if any, small-group or committee work is to be done.

A detailed list and description of the equipment to be used in a classroom should be made. This is important for all classrooms but especially so for classes in which laboratory equipment is needed. It makes considerable difference in the floor space and design of an industrial arts room, for instance, whether it is to be used as a general shop or as a machine shop.

The major point of the four general principles stated above is reflected in a statement by Caudill: "If the architect is given information on 'how the classroom should work' instead of 'how it should look,' he will be in a position to render architectural service."[6]

After examining a number of educational specifications used by schools and recommendations by specialists in the field of school plant planning, Wilson proposed an outline which includes specifications with respect to site and finance as well as those dealing with the instructional program.[7]

Recommended Content Outline for
Educational Specifications

I. General considerations governing the proposed school building project.
   A. Brief description of the educational plan
      1. Program considerations
         a. General statement of philosophy
         b. General characteristics of the community
         c. General characteristics of the student body
         d. General characteristics of the curriculum
         e. General relationships of this school to the school system

---

[6] William W. Caudill, *Your School* (College Station: Texas Engineering Experimental Station, Texas A. and M. College System, 1950), p. 21.
[7] Wilson, *op. cit.*, pp. 199–202.

2. Administrative considerations
   a. Description of the attendance area
   b. Description of grades and groups to be accommodated
   c. Anticipated enrollments
      (1) by grades
      (2) by years
      (3) by courses
   d. Personnel requirements
B. Brief description of the physical plan
   1. General character of the building
      a. Architectural style
      b. General type of construction
      c. General atmosphere to be created by the building
      d. Major sections or units of the building
      e. Preferred number of stories
   2. General facilities required in the building
      a. Instructional areas
      b. Noninstructional areas
      c. Community use areas
   3. General characteristics of the site
      a. Location
      b. Size and dimensions
      c. Physical description (topography, soil, etc.)
      d. Available public utilities

II. Detailed statements of the desired building spaces and educational program.
   A. Instructional spaces
      1. Required number and kinds of rooms
      2. Descriptions of the program, functions, and facilities for each room
         a. Sizes and kinds of groups to be accommodated
         b. Teaching methods
         c. Types of class activities
         d. Location and relationship to other facilities
         e. Physical arrangements and features
         f. Descriptions and lists of the equipment, furniture, and materials
   B. Noninstructional numbers and kinds of rooms
      1. Required numbers and kinds of rooms
      2. Descriptions of the functions and facilities for each room
         a. Sizes and kinds of groups to be accommodated
         b. Types of activities to be provided for
         c. Location and relationship to other facilities
         d. Physical arrangements and features
         e. Description and lists of the equipment, furniture, and materials

III. Detailed statements of the desired site arrangements and development.
   A. Instruction and recreation facilities

1. Outdoor class area
2. Organized game areas
3. Free play areas
4. Equipment requirements
   B. Arrangements for service facilities and beautifications
1. Landscaping requirements
2. Sidewalks and approaches
3. Service drives
4. Pupil transportation requirements
5. Parking requirements
   IV. Detailed statements regarding the physical details of the building.
   A. Structural details
1. Lighting arrangements
2. Floor treatments
3. Acoustical treatments
4. Wall surface treatments
5. Hardware and lock systems
   B. Mechanical systems
1. Ventilation requirements
2. Heating requirements
3. Plumbing arrangements
   C. Utility services
1. Electrical power systems
2. Communication systems
3. Fire alarm systems
4. Clock and program systems
5. Gas service
6. Water supply
7. Sewage systems
   V. Detailed statements regarding the financial plan for the project.
   A. Fund-raising program
   B. Allocations of monies
1. For professional fees and services
2. For construction contracts
3. For site acquisition and development
4. For furniture, equipment, and materials

Process of Developing Educational Specifications

One of the first things to consider in developing educational specifications is the difference between *planning for* a school building and *planning of* a school building. *Planning for* a school building means defining the kind and extent of the educational program and making long-range building plans. *Planning of* a school building means developing a school building suitable to the educational program described in *planning for* the building. It is the first concept, namely, planning for the building, that is the immediate concern of the high school administrator. The planning *of* the building is the job of the architect.

There are many ways to proceed in developing educational specifications, ranging from the use of numerous committees to the assignment of the total responsibility to one person. The size of the project will influence how elaborate the plan of organization will be, but whatever their size, good buildings do not just happen; they must be thought out carefully and thoroughly, and various groups — citizens, the board of education, teachers, and administrators — have unique contributions to make in the total plan and need to work together.

The Dearborn Plan

Of the various patterns for organizing the planning of a building, the one used in Dearborn, Michigan, has been particularly effective and is presented as a model which can be adapted to other situations.[8] This plan is in twelve steps and includes a Central Planning Group, General Committee, and various subcommittees of the General Committee. Figure 39 shows the process according to the following twelve steps:

Step 1. The Central Planning Group will be the first decision staff that works with the Superintendent of Schools from the beginning to the completion of the entire program. It has the responsibility for city-wide general planning and will develop statistical information for the individual building committees. This group will delegate to the Superintendent of Schools responsibility for contacts with the lay public in determining the hopes and anticipations of the citizens in the curriculum and building program. The Central Planning Group will make all final recommendations to the Board after thorough study of reports which come to them from the Committees in Step 2.

Step 2. The General Committee is appointed by the Superintendent through the Assistant Superintendent and is the real working body. They are charged with the responsibility of producing the thinking of the total staff in formulating educational specifications. This action is a direct responsibility of the instructional division. All phases of the school program are to be represented with special emphasis on principals, directors, and coordinators. This group must translate the educational needs of the community into the official educational program. Members of this General Committee will be consultants to the subcommittees in Step 3 and will represent subcommittees to the General Committee.

Step 3. Subcommittees will be formed to represent members of the staff to translate their special interests into the total program. These subcommittees will elect their own chairman and make written reports to the General Committee. These groups, representing every phase of the in-

[8] Dearborn, Michigan, Public Schools, *Staff Newsletter*, March, 1951, Vol. 3, No. 5.

FIGURE 39
Dearborn Public Schools
Organization for Development of Educational Specifications for School Building Projects

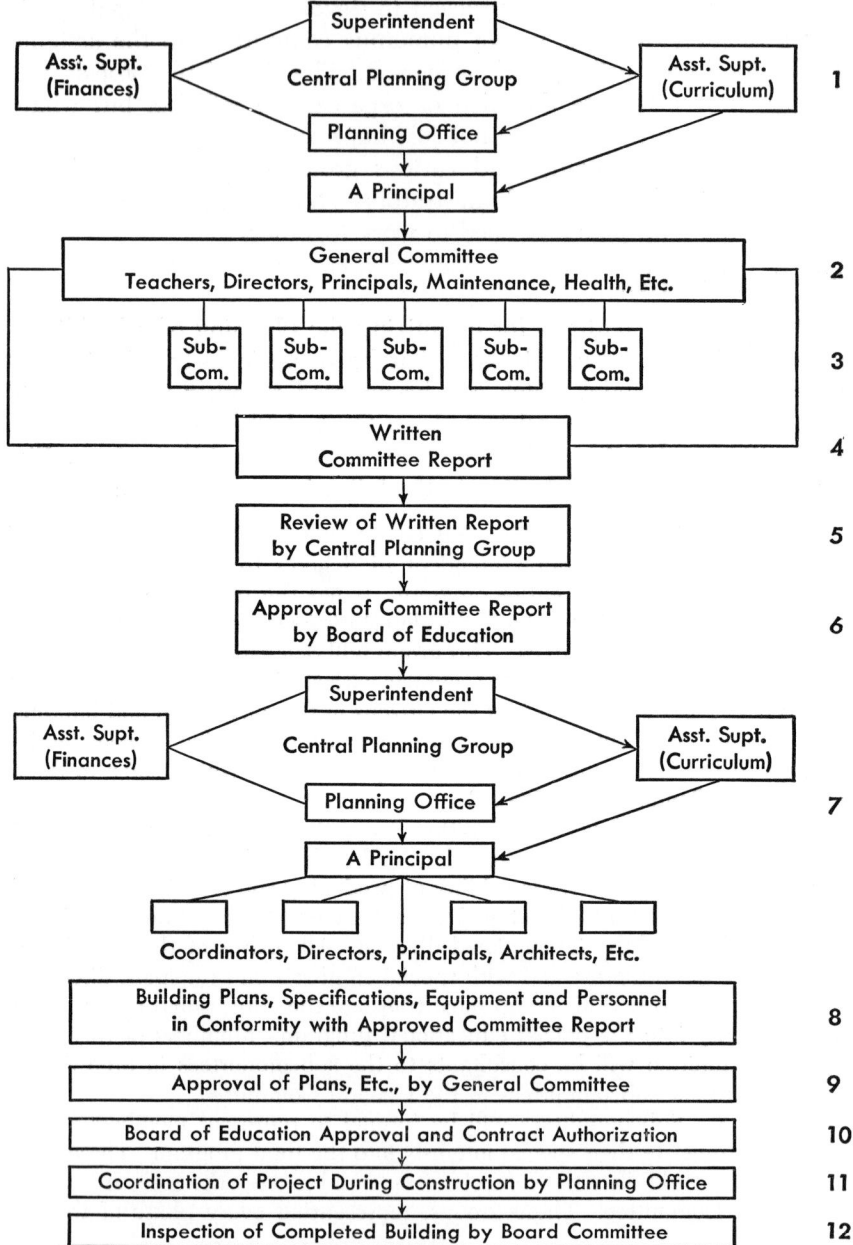

structional program, will outline the needs of the educational program. The General Committee (Step 2) will coordinate and interpret the subcommittee reports.

Step 4. The written report will consist of direct answers to questions submitted by the Central Planning Group (Step 1) and other suggestions which the committee may wish to make in writing.

Step 5. These written reports will be reviewed as fast as they are turned in to the Central Planning Group (Step 1) and either accepted or returned for further study.

Step 6. A final document will be produced from all of the written reports which will then be referred to the Board of Education as the final educational specifications for the building or buildings.

(Steps 1 through 6 finish the first phase of the program and actual work on the preliminary plans by the architects starts with Step 7.)

Step 7. The Central Planning Group will take on the responsibility for interpreting these specifications as accepted by the Board of Education to the architect.

Step 8. Production of the total completed plans including specifications, equipment, and personnel will become the responsibility of the group as outlined on the chart in Step 8.

Step 9. These final plans and specifications are submitted to the General Committee (Step 2) for approval.

Step 10. The final plans will then be submitted to the Board of Education for approval and authorization to ask for bids.

Step 11. The Planning Office will be charged with coordination of the entire project during the construction period.

Step 12. The last step will be the inspection of the completed building by the Board of Education.

In planning a secondary school building, the major role of the principal under a plan of organization like the Dearborn plan is to serve on the General Committee, usually as chairman, and to get each department or subdivision of the school to prepare specifications for their specialties. This means devoting a great deal of time to studying and discussing curriculum developments in relationship to the building facilities, including both national trends and local practices. An important by-product to drawing up educational specifications is that it provides an excellent opportunity for the faculty to bring its thinking on instructional matters up to date. Normally, teachers are highly motivated to consider such matters when they see the possibility of securing new facilities which meet their specifications.

Whether subcommittees are organized on a departmental basis or according to some other plan such as college preparatory subjects, vocational education, general education, etc., depends upon the way in which the faculty is accustomed to working together on problems. If the existing structure and procedures are utilized as much as possible, the staff will feel more competent and confident in its planning activities, especially if the general procedures have been functioning fairly well in the past. The reader is referred to Chapter 13 for additional discussion on in-service procedures. Regardless of the plan of organization used, the major objective is to have each teacher submit a detailed analysis of the objectives for his classes, the learning experiences he intends to use, and the equipment needed to implement his plans. It is the principal's responsibility to make certain that all staff members participate in the project to this extent.

Use of Special Consultants

In the Dearborn procedure there was a local faculty with which to work. Sometimes, however, communities grow so rapidly that a new school must be planned for prior to the employment of any teachers. In cases like this it is necessary to rely heavily on special consultants from other high schools, universities, and state departments of education to assist in making educational specifications. Subject-matter specialists and other special service consultants may be employed to present their ideas of a suitable program for the individual community in harmony with pertinent data about the community and student population prepared by the local administration or board of education.

If such an approach is used, one person should be designated as a coordinator for the entire task. He has the same job with the special consultants as the high school principal has with a faculty. Another approach is to employ a high school principal a year or two in advance and let him work with the special consultants in preparing the educational specifications. Although using outside consultants for developing educational specifications is not as desirable as having the faculty prepare them, it is a feasible plan under the circumstances described above. Certainly, it is far better to use special consultants than to expect the architect to do the educational planning.

Special consultants often are used even when a faculty is available to do the major planning. In these instances, the consultants are engaged for short periods to bring specialized information to the planning sessions. For example, if a decision has to be made on whether or not to recommend the installation of a foreign language laboratory, and no one on the faculty has had experience with such a laboratory, it is essential to secure advice from someone who is knowledgeable in this area.

Model of Educational Specifications

Space does not permit the presentation of a complete educational specifications document for a particular school, but a section for the mathematics-science classroom of the educational specifications prepared for the Junior High School, Van Buren Public Schools, Belleville, Michigan, is shown as an illustration of what such a document is like.[9]

MATHEMATICS-SCIENCE CLASSROOM

1.0 *General description of the space:*
    1.1–a Subjects and grade levels: The mathematics-science classroom will be used for mathematics and science in grades seven and eight; separate science and mathematics rooms will be provided for the ninth grade.
    1.1–b Other subjects: These classrooms could be used for related subjects, such as health or agriculture.
    1.2 Optimum and maximum class groups: The optimum class size is 30 pupils; the maximum class size is 35 pupils.
    1.3 Number of teaching stations: One per classroom.
    1.4 Number of pupil stations per teaching station: Each teaching station should provide 30 pupil stations.
    1.5 Names, preferred shapes, and floor areas of sub-spaces within space:

Name of Sub-Space	Preferred Shape (*)	Floor Area (sq. ft.)
7th and 8th grade Mathematics-Science Classroom:		
Classroom	Approximately square	930 sq. ft.
Work-conference room	Rectangular	120 sq. ft.
Storage room (shared by two classrooms)	Rectangular	240 sq. ft.
9th grade Mathematics Classroom:		
Classroom	Approximately square	900 sq. ft.
Work-conference room	Rectangular	120 sq. ft.
9th grade Science Classroom:		
Classroom	Rectangular	1,080 sq. ft.
Storage room (shared by two classrooms)	Rectangular	320 sq. ft.
Darkroom (shared by two classrooms)	Rectangular	80 sq. ft.
Greenhouse	Rectangular	200 sq. ft.

* If there is a minimum ceiling height for any sub-space, indicate it here.

    1.6 What is the total floor area, in square feet, of this space? 7th and 8th grade mathematics-science classroom: 1,170 sq. ft. each; 9th grade mathematics classroom: 1,020 sq. ft. each; 9th grade science classroom, 1,280 sq. ft. each.
2.0 *Functions of the space:*
    2.1 Purpose of the space:
    2.1–a Objectives to be realized: The objectives to be realized in

[9] *Educational Specifications,* Proposed Junior High School, Van Buren Public Schools (Belleville, Mich.: The Board of Education, 1960), pp. 55–56.

these classrooms include "student discovery" and exploration of the various fields of science and mathematics, as well as the development of basic mathematical and scientific skills, an ability to apply the "scientific method," and an appreciation of the importance of science and mathematics in our modern society.

2.1–b Types of skills, attitudes, and understandings to be developed: The science curriculum will endeavor to develop the habit of logical thinking through scientific investigation; it will also attempt to develop an appreciation for scientific equipment and to develop some skill in its use and care. The mathematics curriculum will endeavor to develop fundamental skills of mathematical operations and the ability to use tables, formulas, graphs, charts, and other mathematical tools.

2.2 Specific activities:

2.2–a Types of activities: The teaching of mathematics and science involves lectures and demonstrations by the teacher, student experimentation, class discussions, small group and individual activities, and, in mathematics particularly, chalkboard work and model building. Most of these activities, some active and some passive, are reasonably quiet in nature. We assume that the curriculum will involve block-time scheduling of seventh and eight grade mathematics and science in one classroom or the use of two adjacent classrooms by a team of teachers, one teaching science and the other mathematics. In the ninth grade the mathematics and science will be taught by a team of teachers, each using a room specifically adapted to that subject.

2.2–b Use of audiovisual materials: Audiovisual aids will be of considerable use in science classes and of more limited use in mathematics classes. There will be use made of motion pictures, film strips, and slides. Some use will be made of the microprojector, of an opaque projector, and of an overhead projector. Both group and individual use will be made of the visual aid materials.

2.2–c Use of reference materials: Booklets, magazines, textbooks, and reference books will be in constant use. Other materials, such as mathematical games, will also be used and should be suitably stored and displayed.

2.3 Adult education and community use:

2.3–a Adult education activities: These classrooms would be suited to adult classes in mathematics and science, as well as in agriculture, gardening, landscaping, radio and electronics, photography, basic mathematics, business arithmetic, and so on.

2.3–b Community use: In addition to adult education activities, these spaces might be used for small committee meetings, workshops, and club meetings.

3.0 *General design considerations:*
- 3.1 General description of the space:
- 3.1–a Brief description of this space and of the relationships of the sub-spaces: Each mathematics-science classroom should consist of a large classroom, approximately square, with an adjoining work-conference room and a storage room to be shared with another mathematics-science classroom. In the mathematics-science classroom there should be the following areas: a teacher-demonstration area at the front of the room, an area for seating all the pupils with space sufficient for some individual or small-group experimentation, a reference area, perimeter counters providing work space with storage. There should be as much chalkboard as possible and some bulletin board space. Small-group and individual activities should be provided for in the workroom, where experiments can be set up and kept in operation for a considerable period of time. The work-conference room should be separated from the classroom by a reasonably soundproof partition, the upper portion being glazed, so that the workroom can be observed by the teacher from the classroom. The storage-workroom, shared by two mathematics-science rooms, should provide work space for the instructor and storage for equipment and supplies which are not to be so easily accessible to pupils. Each ninth grade mathematics room should be similar to the language arts-social studies classrooms, except that considerably more chalkboard and less tackboard will be required. Each ninth grade science room will be similar to the mathematics-science rooms, with additional floor space and a larger storage room, as well as a darkroom, both of which will need to be shared by the two ninth grade science classrooms.
- 3.1–b Type or types and arrangement of pupil seating (or other working spaces): In the mathematics-science rooms either two-pupil tables, approximately 24" by 48", or smaller single tables, with matching chairs, are desired. In the ninth-grade mathematics rooms individual pupil tables and chairs will be needed. In the ninth grade science rooms large two-pupil tables and matching chairs are suggested; in addition, some movable science tables will be required. Ordinarily all pupil seating will be arranged in the usual grid, but it should be possible to divide the class into several groups and to rearrange their desks in a variety of combinations.
- 3.1–c Typical movement of teachers and pupils: It will be necessary for the teacher to move about the room so as to observe each pupil's work. Pupils will need to move to the work counters, to the chalkboard, and to the reference area. Provision should be made for aisles of adequate width.
- 3.1–d Provisions for sight lines: (Should it be possible for the

MANAGEMENT AND COMMUNITY RELATIONS

teacher to see every pupil from one position; should every pupil be able to see the teacher at the same time?) Every pupil should be able to see the demonstration table clearly. (The demonstration table should be three feet in height.) The teacher should be able to see every pupil from any point in the room, and in addition, should be able to observe the work-conference room. If inside the work-conference room the teacher should be able to supervise the classroom. The teacher should be able to see most of the classroom through the storage room door.

3.2 Lighting and light control:

3.2–a Visual environment desired: The typical visual task in the mathematics-science rooms will be the reading of text and reference books. The most difficult visual tasks will probably be reading pencil writing on ordinary notebook paper and reading handwriting upon the chalkboards. Pupils may be seated so as to face in any direction for considerable periods of time. It will be necessary for pupils to observe experiments conducted by the teacher at the demonstration desk. The visual environment should provide adequate light, whether from natural or artificial light alone or from a combination of the two, for the visual tasks described, at the same time eliminating excessive brightness differences and uncomfortable contrasts.

3.2–b Direction of natural light: Natural light from the north is preferred by the committee, but light coming from other directions, if satisfactorily controlled, will be satisfactory. (In the ninth grade greenhouse the light should come from the south.)

3.2–c Provisions for control of natural light: Each room should be provided with adequate shades and drapes for the control of natural light.

3.2–d Need to "dim out" or to "black out": It will be necessary to "dim out" all these classrooms for the use of some audio-visual aids; it will be necessary to "black out" the ninth grade science classrooms for various experiments and for the use of the microprojector or opaque projector. In general it is desirable that the rooms used for science classes be capable of being "blacked out," while this is not so important in mathematics, language arts, or social studies.

3.3 Sound and sound control:

3.3–a Acoustic environment: (Will the space be quiet or noisy? Should the space be conditioned so as to absorb or damp sound or to secure critical reverberation control?) While these classrooms will be reasonably quiet except when sound motion pictures are in use, we suggest that these classrooms be provided with sound-absorbing materials in the ceilings and walls. The conference rooms and storage rooms should be acoustically isolated from their classroom so that the activities in them will not interfere with classroom activities.

3.4   Materials, color, and decoration:
3.4–a   Appropriate materials and colors:

	Appropriate Materials	*Appropriate Colors*	*Reflection Factor*
Ceiling	Acoustic materials	White or off-white	85%
Walls	Cinder block, brick or glazed structural units	Pastels or quiet colors	20%–60%
Chalkboard	Glass	Green (black in ninth grade mathematics)	20%
Tackboard	Corkboard or cork-backed	Harmonizing with walls	30%
Floor	Asphalt or vinyl tile (vinyl tile in storage rooms and darkrooms)	Light gray, beige, or the like	30%–40%
Furniture	Wood, plastic, or fiberglass*	Natural wood, light color	40%–50%
Drapes, blinds, or shades	(Fireproof materials)	Harmonizing colors	—

* In the ninth grade any desk tops should not be black, but green or gray.

3.5   Heating, cooling, and ventilating:
3.5–a   Thermal environment: (See 5.2, below.) Even temperatures should be maintained throughout the classroom, the work-conference room, and the storage room. The work-conference room and the storage room should be separately ventilated. Provisions for maintaining adequate temperature and high humidity will be required in the greenhouse, but the adjacent spaces should not be subject to either high temperatures or high humidity.

3.6   Relationship of this space to other spaces:
3.6–a   Group or suite relationship: A pair of seventh or eighth grade mathematics-science rooms, with a shared storage room, should form a basic grouping as should a pair of ninth grade science rooms. In addition, a ninth grade mathematics room

MANAGEMENT AND COMMUNITY RELATIONS

might adjoin a ninth grade science room, in order to further a close working relationship between the two teachers.

3.6–b Location of this space (or the group or suite of which it is a part) with reference to the other spaces, groups, or suites: A pair of mathematics-science rooms should be placed across the corridor from a pair of language arts-social studies rooms. All of these rooms for a given grade should be placed in one zone. If the classrooms are arranged so that the zones are parallel (as would be possible with a finger plan or a court plan), it is suggested that the seventh and eighth grade mathematics-science rooms front upon a common area or court. This area could then provide for such activities as lawn care, making a compost pile, growing flowers and other plants, and even landscaping of the area or court.

3.6–c Location in a quiet, semi-quiet, or noisy area; use as a buffer: All these classrooms and their workshops will be relatively quiet and should be located in the quieter portion of the building; they are not well suited to serving as a buffer.

3.6–d Location with reference to site features: The mathematics-science classrooms need not be served by an access drive and should be somewhat removed from the playing fields and other noisy areas. It should be possible for science classes to make considerable use of any wooded area on the site.

4.0 *Special design considerations:*
    4.1 Modifiability:
    4.2 Safety:
    4.3 Healthfulness:
    4.4 Ease of maintenance:

5.0 *Utilities:*
    5.1 Artificial lighting:
    5.1–a Type of artificial lighting desired:
    5.1–b Light intensity recommended:
    5.1–c Arrangement and location of lighting fixtures or banks of fixtures:
    5.1–d Switching arrangement recommended:
    5.2 Heating, cooling, and ventilating:

6.0 *Special needs within the space:*
    6.1 Special lighting system:
    6.2 Special ventilation and/or exhaust systems:
    6.3 Special utilities:
    6.4 Special windows:
    6.5 Special doors:
    6.6 Special receiving facilities:
    6.7 Special waste or refuse disposal facilities:

7.0 *Chalkboards, tackboards, and provisions for display:*
    7.1 Chalkboard:
    7.2 Tackboard:
    7.3 Map and chart rails:

7.4 Book and magazine display:
7.5 Show or display cases:
7.6 Special display areas:
8.0 *Furniture and equipment:*
    8.1 Fixed, built-in, or semi-permanent furniture and equipment:
    8.2 Movable furniture and equipment:
    8.3 Special furniture or equipment:
9.0 *Storage:*
    9.1 Book, magazine, and pamphlet storage:
    9.2 Teaching aids storage:
    9.3 Equipment and/or tool storage:
    9.4 Supplies storage:
    9.5 Project storage:
  9.6 *Personal storage:*
    9.6–a Teacher's storage:
    9.6–b Pupil's storage:
    9.7 Special storage:
10.0 *Additional information for the architect, notes, remarks, etc.:*

Miscellaneous Suggestions for the Principal

1. The principal should prepare a "dummy" schedule of the classes proposed in the new building to determine the approximate room utilization and whether or not it is possible to offer the proposed program of studies. If it is not possible to schedule all classes, adjustments will have to be made either in the educational specifications or in the building plans.

2. Special efforts should be made to secure information on new instructional equipment and supplies. Representatives of educational supply and equipment companies should be invited to meet with the planning groups to demonstrate their latest materials. When equipment and supplies are selected, it is necessary to be specific in stating standards to be met by the suppliers. Administrators need to improve their buying habits; approval should not be given to purchasing supplies from one company just because it has a lower price. Equipment must meet the specifications of the teacher who will use it or else it is no bargain.

3. Visitations of the faculty and interested citizens to other new high schools with similar instructional programs and similar community characteristics should be arranged. Visits of this type frequently stimulate ideas which would never have been considered otherwise. Knowing what other communities have in their new schools, the principal will be in a better position to answer questions about them. Invariably, some individuals will imply that the building plans are more elaborate than those in other schools in the area. There is no need to guess on such matters when it is so easy to determine the facts.

4. The principal should prepare a chart of personnel interrelationships in the building. No doubt each school has developed certain ground rules

over the years concerning how various departments and teachers relate to others. This information has its place in the educational specifications. For example, it is helpful to know whether or not the art department and the industrial arts department work together on units or whether they prefer to work independently. If they wish to work together, they ought to be located in the same general area of the building. Again, what is the relationship between guidance workers and administrators? Some schools separate them; in others they share a common suite of offices.

5. Public relations need special attention during the educational planning stages. Keeping the community informed of the decisions made can be very helpful in securing its final approval of the program. Negligence in communicating with the public during this period may result in serious conflict and a lack of support by the community.

6. The principal must know what national and state standards apply to his school — both legal and nonlegal, such as those required by accrediting associations and by the state fire marshal. These standards have considerable influence in the building plans. For example, the size of a school library is determined to a large extent by the criteria of accrediting associations. A high school accredited by the North Central Association of Colleges and Secondary Schools must meet the following standard regarding the number of pupil reading stations:

> In schools enrolling up to 1,000 pupils, 8 per cent, but not less than 40 pupils.
> In schools enrolling from 1,000 to 1,999 pupils, 7 per cent, but not less than 80 pupils.
> In schools enrolling 2,000 or more pupils, 5 per cent, but not less than 140 pupils.[10]

Information of this type is very important in the planning stages if the new high school is going to meet accreditation requirements.

Legal requirements, such as fire, health, and safety codes, must be checked with extreme care, and it is the principal's responsibility to learn what these requirements are for his building and to make certain that they are being met in the proposed plans. Educators are gambling with the lives of children when they are negligent in observing fire, health, and safety codes. The state fire marshal cannot be sued for lack of safety precautions in a building, but local officials are responsibile if they have been careless in these matters.

7. The principal must play an active role in the financial campaign which usually is a necessary part of a building program. Specifically, he must be willing and able to explain the educational program intended

---

[10] North Central Association of Colleges and Secondary Schools, "Policies and Criteria for the Approval of Secondary Schools" (Chicago: Commission on Secondary Schools, 1962), p. 19.

for the new school. There may be invitations from service clubs, PTA groups, and other community groups interested in the building program, and he cannot afford to default in meeting these requests.

8. In addition to serving the architect as a guide in planning the building, educational specifications provide excellent material for in-service activities with new faculty members. A discussion of the educational specifications provides an efficient and effective means for helping new teachers become acquainted with the views and plans of veteran staff members.

No doubt there are additional ideas to be considered by school administrators who plan to launch a building program; the suggestions made here are not intended to be exhaustive. However, the major emphasis throughout this discussion has been the importance of involving all faculty members in a searching evaluation of their present educational practices as compared with the most up-to-date ideas they can gather. These ideas must be recorded and organized into educational specifications which have the considered support of the board of education and the local citizens. It then is the job of the architect to translate them into building plans. Although architects vary in the skill with which they can do this, any architect will do a better job if he has detailed specifications from the faculty to guide him.

Innovations in School Buildings

The people of the United States are extremely style conscious, and what is "high fashion" today is taboo tomorrow. Coiffures go up one year and down the next. Automobile manufacturers find it necessary to change their models every year if they are going to meet the competition of other companies. Although changes in school educational practices and school building do not occur as frequently as those in women's fashions and automobile models, there are, nevertheless, changes. The "little red schoolhouse" is a far cry from the modern consolidated school.

Because change is occurring constantly, innovations in buildings described here will not necessarily be included in future buildings. On the other hand, whenever a new building is contemplated, the innovations in school plants over the preceding decade should be carefully reviewed. The standard plan which is repeated in a school district every time another building is needed is seldom satisfactory.

1. School furniture has been designed for greater comfort and flexibility of use. Tables of varying sizes and shapes enable teachers to work with groups of different sizes.

2. Individual study areas have been designed to meet the educators'

demand for more individual study. These areas frequently are called "Q spaces" — they are places for students to raise questions with themselves and to search out the answers, i.e., places to "quest." Some schools have "Q spaces" readily accessible for use from the library, between classrooms, in the hallways, or in any location convenient for student use.

3. Language laboratories have been installed in many schools. A school without electronic equipment to teach foreign languages by means of the "aural-oral" method is seriously out of date. There has been a major revision in the method of teaching languages, and the results of studies show that a superior result is achieved if languages are taught through the spoken word initially rather than through the grammatical approach so popular for many years. Because many language teachers in the United States have not been able to speak foreign languages fluently, electronic devices have been adopted widely. Teachers of other subjects such as business education, music, and auto mechanics, in which learning and teaching take place through the medium of sound, are beginning to see possibilities in the use of this equipment.

4. Where adequate land is available, it is now common to plan single-story instead of multiple-story buildings.

5. Library facilities have been greatly enlarged. There is a growing concept of the library as a materials center, including records, tapes, and audio-visual materials of all kinds, as well as the books and magazines traditional with libraries.

6. As schools move toward a 1:300 ratio of counselors to students, additional offices for counselors are needed. Some schools now have a suite of rooms, including a reception area, testing room, and counseling rooms, for the guidance department.

7. Lounges and work areas for teachers are now included in most new buildings. Work areas are especially common in schools utilizing team teaching.

8. Use of colors and other decorating media has improved the atmosphere of schools. The aesthetic appeal has been given considerable attention in recent years.

9. A few schools have installed electrical planetariums — a logical development as we move into the space age. Certainly the study of solar systems takes on increasing importance as man contemplates travel in space.

10. Student centers including large lobbies where school parties and large-group activities can be scheduled are becoming more and more common.

11. Most new schools are being wired for television, or conduits are installed which will permit easy installation at a later date. The future of television, both closed and open circuit, looks promising.

12. Auditoriums are returning to favor in new buildings, but the trend appears to be in the direction of small facilities, i.e., 500 to 1,000 seats,

rather than extremely large facilities. Schools find it desirable to have multiple programs with smaller groups rather than making the much greater investment necessary for an auditorium which will seat an entire student body.

13. Greater flexibility in size of rooms is needed, especially in schools committed to team teaching accompanied by large- and small-group instruction. Folding or movable partitions probably will be used increasingly in schools seeking flexibility in class size.

14. Increasing use is being made of the school site for instructional purposes. Each prospective site represents an accumulation of natural resources, i.e., plants, animals, soils, water, contours, etc. Teachers concerned with subjects related to the land and its uses are planning site specifications so that development of the school grounds may make a real contribution to the educational program.

Questions and Group Projects

1. Visit three high schools, one built in the 1930's, one built in the 1950's, and one just completed. Compare features in these buildings which reflect changes in educational practices.

2. Secure a copy of your state code on fire, health, and safety for school buildings. Analyze it from the viewpoint of features you, as a high school principal, could check regularly in your building.

3. Assume you could build a high school without any restrictions with regard to cost or tradition. List features you would include in such a building.

4. Conduct an opinion survey of the teachers in a school to determine in what way the present building in which they are teaching is a handicap in implementing instructional activities which they consider to be desirable.

5. Prepare a chart of personnel interrelationships which you feel would be an ideal arrangement in a senior high school and in a junior high school. Compare the differences in your charts for these schools.

6. Prepare a list of learning activities which you think could be conducted outdoors if the site were developed properly. What are some features which could be built into a site for instructional purposes?

Selected References

American Association of School Administrators. *American School Buildings*, Twenty-Seventh Yearbook. Washington: National Education Association, 1949.

American Association of School Administrators. *Planning America's School Buildings*. Washington: National Education Association, 1960.

Bennett, H. K., P. S. Fordell, G. R. Koopman, and R. E. Wilson. "Schoolhouse Planning," *Nation's Schools*, January, 1952, 49:1.

Brubaker, C. W., and L. B. Perkins. "Space for Individual Learning," *The School Executive*, February, 1959, 78:43.

Bursch, Charles, and Helen Hefferman. *Curriculum and the Elementary School Plant*. Washington: National Education Association, Association for Supervision and Curriculum Development, 1958.

Bursch, C. W., and J. L. Reid. *High Schools Today and Tomorrow*. New York: Reinhold Publishing Corporation, 1957.

Castaldi, Basil, and M. R. Sumption. *How Safe Is Your School?* Urbana: University of Illinois, 1959.

Caudill, William W. *Toward Better School Design*. New York: F. W. Dodge Corporation, 1954.

Design for Educational Television, Planning for Schools with Television. New York: Educational Facilities Laboratories, 1960.

Dreiman, David B. *How to Get Better Schools*. New York: Harper & Brothers, 1956.

Englehardt, Nickolaus. *Planning Secondary School Buildings*. New York: Reinhold Publishing Corporation, 1949.

Englehardt, R., and N. L. Englehardt. *School Planning and Building Handbook*. New York: F. W. Dodge Corporation, 1956.

Graham, J. P. "Teachers in School Planning," *Nation's Schools*, November, 1956, 58:73–75.

Hagman, Harlan. *Administration of the School Building Program*. New York: McGraw-Hill Book Company, 1959.

Henne, Ersted Lohrer. *A Planning Guide for the High School Library Program*. Chicago: American Library Association, 1951. Section 9, "Quarters and Equipment."

Herrick, J. H., W. F. Bogner, and R. D. McLeary. *From School Program to School Plant*. New York: Henry Holt and Company, 1956.

MacConnell, James D. *Planning for School Buildings*. Englewood Cliffs, N.J.: Prentice-Hall, Inc., 1957.

Mills, George E. "Schoolhouse Planning," *Nation's Schools*, March, 1955, 55:68–78.

National Council on Schoolhouse Construction. *Secondary School Plant Planning*. Nashville, Tenn.: George Peabody College, 1957.

National Council on Schoolhouse Construction. *Guide for Planning School Plants*. Nashville, Tenn.: George Peabody College, 1958.

Perkins, Lawrence B. *Work Places for Learning*. New York: Reinhold Publishing Corporation, 1957.

Sumption, M. R., and J. L. Landes. *Planning Functional School Buildings.* New York: Harper & Brothers, 1957.

Weaver, Richard L. *Manual for Outdoor Laboratories.* Danville, Ill.: Interstate Printers and Publishers, Inc., Department of Conservation, 1959.

Wilson, Russell E. "Educational Specifications," *School Plant Studies.* Washington: American Institute of Architects, 1955.

Wilson, Russell E. "Planning the Content of Educational Specifications," *Nation's Schools,* November, 1955, 56:5.

Wilson, Russell E. "A Study of Educational Specifications for Planning School Buildings: Their Evolution, Preparation and Contents," unpublished Ph.D. dissertation, University of Michigan, 1954.

INDEX

Abilities, range in, 192–93
Ability, marking on, 450–52
Ability grouping, 62, 81, 133, 134, 143–46, 168, 173, 174, 175, 450
  in each subject, 170
  voluntary, 142
Absences, check of, 458–59
  excused and unexcused, 460–61
  reporting of, 458, 460
  truancy, 420, 459–60
Academic freedom, 65–66
Academies, 49–52
Acceleration, 146–47, 183, 450
Accounting, for educational program, 542–48
  procedures to follow in, 519–20
Accreditation, accrediting agencies, 14–16, 78, 85, 95, 98, 102, 104, 164, 169, 181, 316, 384, 545–46
Achievement, and counseling, 198–99
  evaluation of, 444–54
  and length of class period, 154–55
  recognition of, 237, 268, 336–37, 370
  sense of, in teachers, 336–38
  student, and teacher morale, 331
  of teacher candidates, 382
Action research, 121, 215
Activities, 73–74, 212, 221–23
  business management of, 507–27
  faculty sponsors for, 233, 242–44, 252, 258, 272, 274, 319, 337, 511, 513
  financial aspects of, 258, 259, 265, 270, 274, 277, 513–18
  functions of, 228–30
  growth of, 223–28, 247
  influence of, in holding students in school, 226
  in junior high school, 87
  lines of responsibility in, 240–41
  organization and administration of, 230–44
  participation in, by all students, 234–36
  size of school and, 94, 95
  types of, 247–77
  values of, 223–26
  See also Assemblies, Athletics, Clubs, etc.
Activities associations, state, 104, 241, 270, 546
Activity period, 158–59

Activity ticket, 517
Adenauer, 478
Ad hoc committee, 311–12, 485, 492
Administration, of activities program, 230–44
  of assemblies, 256–57
  of athletic program, 269–71
  of attendance, 531
  of clubs, 274
  of discipline, 420–21, 423–25
  of instructional materials and equipment, 501–5
  of records, 537
  of school-community relations, 479–93
  of school library, 288–92
  of student government, 251–53
Administrative aide, 8
Administrative records, 206
Admission to college, criteria for, 442
  early, 147
  transcript of credits for, 443
Advanced study, 40–41
Advanced placement, 81, 98, 147–48, 450
Advisory or combination curriculum, 126, 133, 134–36, 171
Advisory council, administrative, 309, 310, 370–71
  citizen, 25–26, 117–18, 120, 264, 310, 476, 485, 491–92
Age of teachers, 388, 389–90
Agriculture, courses in, 160
  mechanization in, 195
Alabama, 15
Alaska, 15
Ambridge (Penna.) Senior High School, 198
American Association of Collegiate Registrars and Admissions Officers, 432, 439
American Association of School Administrators, 17, 90, 98, 332, 468, 477, 483
American Council on Education, 432
  Psychological Examination of, 196
American Education Week, 487
American Educational Research Association, 380
American Institute of Biological Studies, 98

INDEX

American Library Association, 286, 288, 289, 290, 293
American Psychiatric Association, 342
Anderson, Lester W., quoted, 163
Anderson, Vivienne, quoted, 471–72, 485, 486
Andrew Warde High School, Fairfield, Conn., 314
Anecdotal records, 206, 207
Ann Arbor (Mich.), High School, 446–47, 457, 460
   Tappan Junior High School, 454, 455
Annual reports of the principal, 488, 543–45
Anonymity, feeling of, 94
Appraisal. *See* Evaluation
Aptitude tests, 71, 145–46
Aristotle, 222
Arizona, 14, 15
Arkansas, 15, 59
Art work for yearbook, 259
Articulation, of activities with rest of educational program, 238–39
   of administrative policies, 96–97
   and cumulative record, 434
   horizontal, 100–101, 123, 124, 309, 311, 312–13
   of secondary and elementary schools, 95–101
   vertical, 96–100, 123, 124, 307, 308, 313
Arts program, summer, 183
Assemblies, 239, 256–57
   "disciplinary," 422
   student behavior at, 413–14
Assistant principal, 11–13, 20, 22, 414
Assistant superintendent, 304, 379
Assistant teacher, 318, 326
Associate type of team teaching, 325
Athletic fanaticism, 267, 269, 271
Athletic fund, 514, 515
Athletics, 89, 159, 222, 267–72
   balance in, 233
   criticism of, 222–23
   guides to administering, 269–71
   interest in school provided by, 268, 269
   in junior high school, 271–72
   problems in, 268–69
   scholastic requirements for, 236
   values in, 267–68
Attendance, administration of, 531
   average daily, 456–58
   compulsory, 456, 469
   motivation for, 456
   records of, 456–61
Audience participation in assemblies, 256
Audio-visual materials and equipment, 282, 285, 289, 290, 291, 296, 322

Auditoriums, 570–71
Aurora (Ill.), West Senior High School, 134–35
Austin, David B., quoted, 8
Authoritarianism, 28–29, 305, 350
Autobiography, student, 206
Automation, 178, 180–81, 194, 461–62
Average daily attendance, 456–58
Awards, 237
Azusa (Cal.), Citrus High School, 315

Balance, of activities and classroom programs, 233–34, 271
   of ages on faculty, 388, 390
   of married and unmarried teachers, 389
   of men and women on faculty, 390
   in public relations, 479
   in teaching load, 175–76, 201, 244
Band, 260, 261, 262
Bargaining, of principal with teachers, 34–35
Barrett, Dermott, quoted, 532
Barrington (Ill.) Consolidated High School, 412–13
Barry, F. S., quoted, 346
Barthelmess, Harriet A., 143
Basic Collection for High Schools, A, 290
Bavelas, Alex, quoted, 532
Beard, Charles A. and Mary R., quoted, 52
Behavior, on buses, 506, 507
   code of, 267, 412–13
   and discipline, 410–23
   double standard of, 341
   reporting of, 452–53
   standards of, 266–67
   teaching of, 407, 408
Bell, Mary, 144
Bell Adjustment Inventory, 200
Bell program, 536
Belleville (Mich.), educational specifications for school in, 561–67
Benson, Arthur L., quoted, 396
Benson, Charles S., quoted, 376
Benz, Lester G., 257, 258
Berry, Aubrey L., quoted, 397
Billett, Roy O., 143
Biossat, Bruce, quoted, 71
Block-time scheduling, 89, 127, 128, 130, 152, 162
Board of education, 25, 248, 358
   approval of budget by, 498, 500, 513
   and curriculum planning, 117, 120, 122, 126–27
   and discipline policies, 411, 420, 421
   and extraclass business affairs, 509
   length of school year decided by, 181
   police services engaged by, 527
   policy formulation by, 335, 352

INDEX

principal as liaison between teachers and, 7
and school-community relations, 468
and school organization, 302
and selection of teachers, 378, 401, 402
Bollenbacher, Joan, quoted, 433
Bonner, H. R., 46
Boston English Classical School, 53
Boston Latin School, 48
Boyer, Phillip A., 143
Bradford, M. L., quoted, 338
Brandes, Louis H., 308
Bremen, Germany, 80
Brogue, Ellen P., 277
Brookline (Mass.) Public Schools, 136–40
Brown, Herbert L., Jr., 81
Brown case, 60, 469
Brueckner, Leo J., quoted, 372
Brutality, 418
Budget planning, 498–500
for activities program, 512–15
for library, 289–90
Buffalo, N.Y., 7
Building facilities. *See* Physical facilities
Bulletin of the NASSP, 166, 215, 257, 264–65
Bulletins, daily, 534, 536
supervisory, 548
Burns, Hobert W., quoted, 27–28
Burr, Marvin Y., 145
Burton, William H., quoted, 372
Business education, 135–36, 141, 160
office work by students in, 535–36, 539
Business responsibilities, 495–96
budget planning, 498–500, 512–15
in extraclass activities, 507–27
food services and transportation, 505–7
general operations, 496–507
managing instructional materials and equipment, 501–5

Calendar, daily, of principal, 534
news and programs, 480–81
school, 181, 183–85, 476
California, 15, 94
Cal Tech, 71
Cambridge University, 332
Campbell, Clyde M., quoted, 340
Cantoni, L. J., 200
Caplan, Stanley, 200
Card catalog, 291–92
Cardinal Principles of Secondary Education, 66–67, 226
Careers, interest in, and activities program, 230; *see also* Employment
Carlile, Amos B., 382
quoted, 381

Carrels for teaching machines, 297
Carroll County (Iowa) study, 192, 193
Cataloging library books, 291–92
Caudill, William W., quoted, 554
Cedar Rapids (Iowa) Public Schools, 497, 499, 508
Central High School, Little Rock, Ark., 260
Centralized system of accounting, 512
Certification, of administrators, 13–14, 15
of teachers, 384
Chandler, B. J., quoted, 376, 381, 392
Chapman, John Jay, quoted, 189
Character training, 52, 267–68
Chartering of student activities, 240, 253
Church-state separation, 49
Churchill, Winston, 30
Citizens advisory council, 25–26, 117–18, 120, 264, 310, 476, 485, 491–92
Citizenship, education and, 469
student, 248, 249, 506
Citrus Union High School, Azusa, Cal., 315
Civic responsibility, 69, 81
Class discrimination, 235, 274–75
Class register, 456
Class size, 168–69, 176, 316, 317, 318, 322–23
Classified system of marking, 452
Classrooms, 89, 170, 176, 571
Clearing accounts, 513
Clerical services, 165, 169, 326, 343, 430, 438, 453, 456, 495, 496, 535
Clubs, 239, 272–77, 288
Coaches, assignments for, 269–70
preferential treatment of, 357
salaries of, 269, 270, 319, 479
Code of behavior, 267, 412–13
Coffman, Lotus, quoted, 223
College, admission to, 147, 442, 443
articulation of, with high school, 97–100
attrition rate in, 196
community, 61, 78, 83, 85
domination over secondary school by, 54, 62
early admission to, 147
high school graduates going on to, 95
relations of school and, 432, 439
College Entrance Examination Board, 82, 148
College preparatory program, 52, 54, 62–63, 134–35
College-type schedule, 164
Colorado, 15, 93
Commager, Henry Steele, quoted, 222, 469
Commencement exercises, 489

577

INDEX

Commission on the Experimental Study of the . . . Staff . . . , 165, 169, 321–22, 323
Commission on Financing Higher Education, 196
Commission on Public Relations, 468, 477
Commission on the Reorganization of Secondary Education, 79, 83
Commission on Teacher Education and Professional Standards, 168
Committee on School Records and Reports, 432
Committee on Uniform Records and Reports, 432
Committee organization, 311–12
Committee work of teachers, 367–70
Committees, *ad hoc*, 311–12, 485, 492
  implementing work of, 311, 546–47
  of the whole, 312
"Common learnings," 127
Communication, between central student organizations and rest of school, 253
  between school and community, 120, 122, 471–72, 475–76
  between teachers and administrators, 334, 336, 370
  freedom of, and school organization, 303
  principal's office as center of, 531, 532–35
Community, activities of principal in, 7
  and activities program, 229, 238, 268, 269
  interpreting library needs to, 285
  investment of, in education, 376–77
  participation in affairs of, 483
  power structure of, 482–83
  relations of school and, *see* School-community relations
  relations of teachers and, 341–42, 474–76
  social adjustment of students as members of, 266
Community college, 61, 78, 83, 85
Comprehensive high school, 78–79, 80, 81–82, 313
Compulsory age limit, 61
Compulsory attendance, 456, 469
Conant, James B., 81, 154, 156, 190, 271, 339, 344
  quoted, 79, 82, 85, 90, 111, 128, 133–34
Conference room, library, 297
Conferences, case, 345
  group, 488
  interscholastic, 527
  parent-teacher, 453, 487–88
  parent-teacher-student, 487, 488

preschool, 185, 366–67
principal-teacher-parent-student, 371–73, 420, 459, 533–34
small-group (faculty), 358
Conflicts, of athletics and other educational activities, 270
  in dates of school events, 184, 476
  in educational philosophy, 476, 478
  in room facilities, 176
  in schedules, 173–74, 175, 179
Connecticut, 15
Consensus, working for, 360
Constants-with-variables curriculum, 125, 128, 129, 133, 136–42
Constitution, U.S., 51, 60, 65, 101
Consultants, help of, in preparing educational specifications, 560
  workshop, 363, 365
Contests, 89, 263, 264
  engaging officials for, 527
  state associations for control of, 104
Continuing inventory system, 503, 504–5
Continuity in education, 434
Conventional schedule, 152, 153–61
  activity periods in, 158–59
  criticisms of, 161
  day length in, 157
  homeroom periods in, 159–60
  laboratory and shop periods in, 160–61
  lunch periods in, 158
  opening and closing times in, 157–58
  period length in, 153–57, 160
Coombs, Philip H., quoted, 147
Cooperative Development of Public School Administration, 346
Cooperative programs for articulation, 100
Cooperative Study of Secondary School Standards, 124, 225, 247
Cooperative Trigonometry Test, 82
Cooperation, in curriculum planning, 113, 115–16, 117–18, 120
  in determining policy, 335–36
  of principal and teachers, 35–36
  in problem solving, 340
Coordinated team teaching, 325–26
Copeland, Emily A., quoted, 284
Corcoran, Mary, 196
Core curriculum, 127–28, 152, 162, 315
Cornell, Ethel, quoted, 143–44
Corporal punishment, 417–19
Correspondence, handling of, 531, 536
Correspondence courses, 169
Costs. *See* Finances
Councils, 250 (*see also* Student council)
  advisory, 25–26, 117–18, 120, 264, 309, 310, 370–71, 476, 485, 491–92
Counseling and counselors, 65, 202–3, 204, 205, 209–12, 216, 344

INDEX

counselor-student ratio, 344, 570
definition of, 209
offices for, 570
and overparticipation in activities, 237–38
in planning program of studies, 194
records kept in, 206
and self-discipline, 414–15
for tardiness, 461
for truancy, 459, 460
See also Guidance
Crawford, Dean A., 62 n., 133, 143
Creative writing, 259–60
Credit, made up in summer session, 182–83
for music, speech, etc., activities, 247–48, 262–63
by semester hours, 164
Cubberley, Ellwood P., quoted, 6
Cultural activities, 38–39
Cumulative record, 205–6, 430, 433–39
concepts related to, 434
information included in, 434–35
model forms for, 436–37, 438, 440–41
purposes of, 433
types of, 435–38
Cunningham, Luvern L., quoted, 325, 326
Cuony, E. R., 199, 208
Curriculum, advisory, 126, 133, 134–36, 171
central council on, 96–97
compartmentalization of, 94
constants-with-variables, 125, 128, 129, 133, 136–42
contribution of activities program to, 229
core, 127–28, 152, 162, 315
defined, 109–10
in early secondary school, 48–49, 50, 52, 53, 54
emphasis on societal and youth needs in, 64–65
evaluation of, 119, 122, 312
expansion and specialization of, 193–94
experimentation in, 121–22
guides to planning of, 113–18
information on trends in, 484
joint elementary-secondary committee on, 97
in junior high school, 86
in larger schools, 94, 95
leadership in improvement of, 112–13, 120
in modern high school, 72
organizational design of, 123–26
participation of librarian in planning of, 287, 294

planning of, 109–23
preparing materials for, 120–21
providing for individual differences in, 111, 142–48
reports and records on, 546–47
scope and sequence of, 123, 124
shifting of, 83
shown in schedule, 167
social conditions and, 110–11
student, *see* Program of studies
tasks in planning of, 118–23
in traditional 8–4 system, 89
types of, 125–26
Curriculum bulletin or guidebook, 171, 488
Curriculum library and materials center, 117
Curriculum Study Group (American Institute of Biological Studies), 98
Custodial services, 537

Davis, H. Curtis, 200
Dearborn plan for developing educational specifications, 557–60
Debating, 239, 264
Decentralized system of accounting, 512
Decision making, faculty participation in, 31, 35–36
Delaware, 15, 102
Delegation of tasks, 11, 12, 351
Deliberative procedures, 485
Delinquency, 197, 266
Democracy, and activities program, 234–35
in administration, 28–29, 35–36
and criticism of education, 470
in education, 350–53
in homeroom, 255
and importance of education, 80, 81, 469
in parent-teacher association, 490
responsibility and, 113
and self-control, 410
and staff organization, 301
"Demonstration" approach in curriculum change, 115
Demonstrations, 487
Denver (Colo.) Public Schools, 34, 484
Department chairmen, help of, in selecting teachers, 379, 398
selection of, 308–9
Departmental organization, 87, 88, 307–10
Depositing receipts, 518
Derthick, Lawrence, 98 n., 148
quoted, 80
Desegregation, 60, 79, 101, 469
Developmental tasks of adolescents, 65, 67, 70, 197–98, 224

Dewey, John, quoted, 29
Dewey Decimal System, 291
Dictating and transcribing equipment, 536
Dictionary of Education, 152
Diplomas, 454–56
Disbursements, 519, 527
Discipline, administration of, 420–21, 423–25
  defined, 409–10
  importance of, 408
  policies and procedures of, 410–23
  self, 409–10, 412, 413, 414, 417, 506
  by teachers or student council, 251
Discrimination, racial, 46, 275
  social and class, 235, 274–75
Discussion groups, small, class sections for, 318
  workshop, 361
Dismissal of a teacher, 341, 408
District of Columbia, 15
District reorganization, 93
Double periods, 160, 175
Double standard of social behavior, 341
Douglas, Edwin C., quoted, 148
Douglas, Mary Peacock, 292
  quoted, 282
Douglass, Harl R., 319, 320, 321
  teaching load formula of, 319–21
Dramatics, 239, 264–65
Drews, Elizabeth, 144
Driver education, 183
Dropouts, 46, 63, 94, 96, 196–97, 215
Dual system of marking, 452
DuBridge, Lee A., 71
Dubuque (Iowa), Wahlert High School, 260
Dugan, Willis E., quoted, 211
Duplicating service, 535

Early admission to college, 147
East Cleveland (Ohio), Shaw High School, 259
Economic efficiency, 68–69
Economic security of teachers, 343–44
Education, auxiliary services provided in, 74
  better products of, 71
  criticism of, 27–28, 93–94, 470
  expansion of opportunity for, 46, 50, 53, 58–60, 351
  formulation of policies in, 31, 35–36, 335–36, 351–52
  in the future, 165, 326–27, 569–71
  gains in enrollment in, 55, 56 (*see also* Enrollments)
  general, 62–63, 81, 126–31, 132
  goals of, 63–65, 66–71, 113–14, 119, 121, 127, 226, 333–34

local control over, 51, 101, 103, 126–27
need for higher standards in, 27–28
philosophy of, 18, 28, 151
relationship of activities to, 225–26, 231
retention rate in, 56, 57
social purposes of, 226
specialized, 63, 131–48
student attitudes toward, 61
  See also Secondary schools *and* Teachers
Education in the Junior High School Years (Conant), 271
Educational placement, 212–13
Educational Policies Commission, 67–69, 111, 127, 147, 268, 271, 351–52, 380
Educational specifications for new school, 552–56
  development of, 556–59
  model of, 560–67
Educational Testing Service, 127
Educational workshops, 360–66
Edwards, Newton, quoted, 226, 419
8–4 organization, 83, 88–89
Eight-period schedule, 153, 154, 156
Einheitschulen, 80
Ekstrom, Ruth, quoted, 144
Electives, 125, 130, 131, 132, 133, 135, 136, 137, 139, 140, 142–43, 193
Elementary school, 86
  high school activities coordinated with, 476
  and secondary school, articulation of, 95–101
Eligibility requirements for participation in activities, 234, 235–36
Eliot, Charles, 53, 83
Elsbree, Willard S., quoted, 387
Emmetsburg (Iowa) High School, 141–42
Employment, changes in, 194–95
  college placement offices, 394, 399
  distribution of occupations, 195
  information on opportunities in, 213
  of local teachers, 391
  part-time, for teachers, 343
England, secondary education in, 48, 80
  athletics in, 268
  "public" school in, 222
  school year in, 181
English Classical School, Boston, 53
English in core curriculum, 162
Enrichment, 147, 182, 183
Enrollments, school and course, 55, 56, 78, 171–72, 193–94
  in community (junior) college, 85

580

in minimum-size and maximum-size schools, 90, 93
in traditional and reorganized schools, 84–85
Entertainment-type activities, 233, 261
Equipment, 501, 505
library, 296
planning of, for new school, 554
of principal's office, 536, 540
storage and inventory of, 526
Erickson, Clifford E., quoted, 215
Etiquette. See Behavior
Europe, extraclass activities in, 222
school athletics in, 268
school year in, 181
secondary education in, 80, 83
Evaluation, of assemblies, 257
of clubs, 276
of curriculum, 119, 122, 312
guidance and, 205–7
of guidance program, 213–14, 215
of instructional program, 215
of library materials, 285, 288
of school achievement, 444–54
self, 206, 215
of speech and dramatics activities, 265
of workshop, 363
Evaluative Criteria, 104, 312, 482
Evanston (Ill.) "New School" plan, 315
Examinations for teacher applicants, 395–97; *see also* Testing program
Exhibits, 487
Expenditures. See Finances
Experimental programs, 121–22, 153, 165, 166, 169, 318, 323
Expulsion from school, 419–21
Extraclass activities. See Activities
Extralegal agencies, school relationship with, 103–4

Fact sheet accompanying transcript of credits, 443–44, 446–47
Faculty. See Teachers
Faculty committees, 367–70
Faculty meetings, 353–60
election of chairman of, 356–57
length, frequency, and atmosphere of, 359
planning of, 354, 355–56
preschool, 185, 366–67
problems considered in, 354–55
suggestions for, 354, 359–60
time of, 357–58
Fair play, 339, 340
Fairfield (Conn.), Andrew Warde and Roger Ludlow high schools, 314
Family problems of teachers, 346
Faunce, Roland C., 264

Federal educational agencies, 25
relationship of school with, 101–2
Feltre, Vittorino da, 48
Fennell, Edward G., 86 n., 87, 130
Festivals, music, 263
Finances, and activities program, 258, 259, 265, 270, 274, 276, 277, 513–18
distribution of educational expenditures, 377
extraclass, management of, 511–25
federal aid to education, 101–2
and new school building, 568–69
and participation in activities, 233–34, 235, 516, 517
per-pupil costs, 88–89, 90–91, 94, 282, 290
school library, 289–90
and traditional 8–4 organization, 88–89
Financial Accounting for School Activities (Office of Education handbook), 511, 512, 513, 519–20
Fine, Benjamin, quoted, 471–72, 485, 486
Fine arts program, summer, 183
Fisher Act (England), 80
Fitts, Daniel B., quoted, 314–15
Fixed limits system, 450–51
Flexible (varied) period schedule, 153, 163–64
Floating-period schedule, 152–53, 163
Florida, 15, 59
Follow-up, of committee work, 311, 546–47
of curriculum appraisal, 122–23
of graduates and dropouts, 484
records and services, 206, 211, 213–15
Food services, 505–6
Forcing a point of view on a group, 34
Ford Foundation, 147, 165
Foreign language laboratories, 327, 560, 570
Foreign language study in junior high school, 86
Forensic activities, 239, 264; *see also* Debating
Fowlkes, John G., quoted, 509
Franklin, Benjamin, 54, 61
quoted, 50, 64
Fraternities, 267, 275
French, Will, 127
Fretwell, Elbert K., quoted, 239
Froelich, Clifford P., quoted, 209
Functional leadership, 32–36
Functionalists, 69
Fund for the Advancement of Education, 147, 153, 322

INDEX

Fund-raising projects, 235, 276, 513, 516–17
Furniture, school, 569

Gaier, Eugene L., quoted, 388
Gangs, 272
Gaumnitz, Walter H., 86 n., 87, 90 n.
General activity fund, 276
General or basic education, 62–63, 81, 126–31
　aim of, 127
　in junior high school, 130–31, 132
　in senior high school, 128–30
General teachers, 326
George-Barden Act, 72, 101
George-Deen Law, 101
Georgia, 15, 102
Germany, secondary education in, 48, 80, 181
Gibson, A. J., 154
Gifted students, 70, 71, 93, 111
　acceleration and enrichment of program for, 146–47
　intelligence needed for teaching of, 382
　special programs for, 450
Girls and Boys Leadership, 274
Goldberg, Miriam L., quoted, 144
Good, Carter V., quoted, 152
Good, Warren R., quoted, 449
Government, student, 248–53, 254, 255
Government agencies. See Federal educational agencies
Grade-level organization, 312–13
Grade-point average, 442–43
Graduates from high school, follow-up of, 484
　gain in, 46, 60
Graduation exercises, 489
Graduation requirements, 128–30
Grammar school, 47–49
Gray, Stuart, 91, 92
Griffith, LeRoy H., quoted, 408
Griffiths, Daniel, quoted, 302
Grim, Mary, 87
Group experiences, 95
Group guidance, 203, 208–9, 253, 254
Group offenses, 421–23
Group work, on curriculum planning, 116
　office for, 540
　See also Committee work and Conferences
Grouping. See Ability grouping
Guidance, 65, 73, 344
　defined, 190–91
　early years of, 190
　effectiveness of, 198–200
　homerooms as units for, 208–9, 253, 254
　in junior high school, 87
　need for, 191–98
　organizing a program of, 200–205
　and participation in activities, 237–38
　physical facilities for, 216–18, 539–40
　purposes of, 189–90, 209
　in selecting courses, 172, 206, 212
　services provided by, 205–15
　and truancy, 459, 460
Guidance courses, 208

Hall, Clifton L., 50 n., 64 n.
Hall, G. Stanley, quoted, 332
"Halo" effect, 398
Hamburg, Germany, 80
Hamilton, Homer H., 225
Hamilton, Robert R., quoted, 417, 418, 509
Handbook, administrative, 547–48
　PTA, 488
　student, 259, 413, 488
Handicapped, educational provisions for, 61, 70, 71
Harap, H., quoted, 344
"Hard-core" subjects, 118
Harvard University, 48–49
Hatch, Raymond N., quoted, 191
Havighurst, Robert J., 70, 197
　quoted, 65
Hawaii, 15
Hawthorne studies in morale, 330
Health, student, and athletic program, 270
　teacher, 342–43
Health records, 206, 430
Hedge, J. W., 199
Held, Warren H., quoted, 249
Hess, Walter E., 257
Heywood, Stanley J., 354
High schools. See Secondary schools
Higher education, growth of, 196; see also College
Highet, Gilbert, quoted, 383, 384
Hill, Clyde M., 27
　quoted, 28
Hobby clubs, 273
Hollingshead, A. D., 145
Home background, 56
Homeroom advisers, 212, 255, 487
Homerooms, 89, 159–60, 248, 253–55
　checking attendance in, 458
　as guidance medium, 208–9, 253, 254
　records stored in, 431
Homogeneous grouping. See Ability grouping
Honors organizations, 273–74
Honors program, 450
Hoppock, R., 199, 208

582

Horizontal articulation, 100–101, 123, 124, 309, 311, 312–13
Horizontal organization of secondary school, 78–82
Horton, Ben H., Jr., quoted, 9–10
Hospitalization insurance, 343
Hotz, H. G., 154
"House" plan, 95, 313–15
Housing for teachers, 345
Hull, Clark L., 145
Human relationship, 68
Humanists, 69
Humanitarian principles, 410
Humor, 19
Hunt, Herold C., quoted, 302
Hutson, P. W., 199, 208

Idaho, 15
Illinois, 15, 388
Images of the Future (Trump), 326
Imperative Needs of Youth, 69–70, 226
Independence, need for, 224
Indiana, 15
Individual differences, 61–62
  activities geared to, 225–26
  and discipline, 416, 417
  provisions for, 72, 111, 142–48
Individual study, 323, 569–70
Industrial arts courses, 160–61
Information, on community, for school, 482–84
  counseling, for homeroom advisers, 255
  in cumulative record, 434–35
  for educational specifications, 553–56, 560–68
  follow-up, 214–15
  on job opportunities, 213
  in principal's annual reports, 543–46
  provided in guidance program, 207–9
  for schedule building, 167–70
  on school, for community, 471–72, 475, 476, 478
Informative procedures, 485
In-service education, 37–41, 255, 337–38, 569
Instructional fees and rentals fund, 514
Instructional leadership, 6, 34
Instructional methods and materials, 72–73
Insurance, in athletic program, 270
  hospitalization, 343
Integration, educational, 162, 309
  racial, 60, 79, 101, 469
Intelligence quotients, 56, 57, 192–93, 197
Intelligence of teachers, 381–82
Intercom system, 535, 536
Interdepartmental relationship, 100

Interpretative speech activities, 264
Interscholastic contests, 271, 527
Interviews, of dropouts, 215
  follow-up, 211
  records of, 206
  of teacher candidates, 397–401
Intervisitation, 97, 100
Intramural competition, 233, 239, 271
Inventory services and records, 205–7
Inventorying, 291, 503, 504–5, 526
Iowa, 15, 91–93, 94
Iowa Tests of Educational Development, 91, 92, 154, 155, 331
Iwamoto, David, quoted, 317–18, 319

Jacobson, Paul B., 7 n., 277
Jarrett, Richard W., 12
Jefferson, Thomas, 64
Job placement. *See* Employment
Job satisfaction, 200
Johnston, Edgar G., 264
Joint Committee on School-College Relationships, 432, 439
Joint Committee on Testing, 98
Jones, Stewart, quoted, 388
Journalism, 239, 259
Junior college. *See* Community college
Junior high school, 83, 84, 86–88
  athletics in, 271–72
  general education in, 130–31, 132
Junior-senior high school, 83, 84, 88
Justman, Joseph, 143, 144

Kalamazoo decision, 53
Kansas, 15
Keller, Robert J., 196
  quoted, 378–79
Kelley, Earl C., 366
Kentucky, 15
Khrushchev, 110
Klahn, Richard P., 532–33
Knezevich, Stephen J., quoted, 509
Knight, Edgar W., 50 n., 64 n.

Laboratory periods, 154, 160, 168
Lambert, Sam M., quoted, 317–18, 319
Language laboratories. *See* Foreign language laboratories
Large- and small-group instruction, 318, 322–23, 326, 571
Latin America, secondary education in, 80
Latin grammar school, 47–49
Leadership, by bargaining, 34–35
  cooperative, 35–36
  in curriculum planning, 112–13, 120
  in democratic administration, 28–29, 35–36
  by force, 34

functional, 32–36
  moral demands of, 27
  nature of, 28–36
  paternalistic, 35
  personal-qualities theory of, 29–30, 33
  of principal, 26–27, 30–36, 201, 228, 338, 492
  status, 30–31, 33, 356
League of Women Voters, Michigan, 26
Learning experiences, business management of, 509–10
  with business management, 526
  common, 127
  motivation for, 232, 386
  self-directed, 323
Lectures, 322, 325
Legal aspects, of activities program, 240, 509
  of appointment procedures, 402
  of corporal punishment, 417, 418
  of expulsion or suspension, 419, 420
  of new school building, 568
  of student records, 206
Legal responsibility, of board of education, 120, 127, 248
  for policy decisions, 335
Legal rights of students, 423–24
Lehman, Charles F., 491
Leisure time, and athletics, 268
  increased, 226–27
  in summer, 183
Lending system, school library, 292
Lennon, Roger T., 56 n., 193
Letter grades, 444, 448
Letters to parents, 453–54
Lettermen's Club, 274
Levin, Harry, quoted, 379, 380–81
Librarians, school, duties of, 284–85, 290, 294
  professional status of, 287–88
  student assistants to, 288
  training and experience of, 286–87
Library, school, characteristics of, 283–95
  instruction in use of, 294
  physical facilities of, 295–97
  present-day, 282–83, 568, 570
  role of, 280, 281–82
  services supplied by, 293–95
  staff of, 284–88
Lickey, Harold L., quoted, 262
Lindquist, E. F., 145
Literary magazine, school, 259–60
Little Rock (Ark.), Central High School, 260
Local control over education, 51, 101, 103, 126–27
Local merchants, patronage of, 503
Local teachers, employment of, 391
Long-period schedule, 154, 155, 163

Los Angeles, Cal., 12
Louisiana, 15, 102
Louisville, Ky., 7
Ludwig, Merlin A., 250, 254, 257, 261, 262, 264, 276
Lunch period, 158, 506
Lynd, Robert S. and Helen M., quoted, 228

McAbee, Harold V., 200
McAulay, John D., 385
McDaniel, Henry B., 205, 206, 209
McElhinney, J. Howard, 155
Machine processing of data, 172–73, 178, 180–81, 461–62
MacKenzie, Charles, 153
Mackenzie, Gordon N., 34, 35
Magazine, school, 259–60
Maine, 15, 59
"Majors" and "minors" in activities, 237
Manley, C. B., quoted, 161
Mann, Horace, 429
Mantua, Italy, 48
Marginal punch system, 173, 178, 179–80
Marital status of teachers, 389
Marks and report cards, 444–54
Maryland, 15
Mass media, 485–87
Massachusetts, 15, 48
Master teachers, 165, 169
  in team teaching, 325
Master time schedule, 171, 174–75, 176, 179
Mathematics achievement, relation of, to size of school, 94
Mathematics-science classroom, specifications for, 561–67
Matulis, Anthony S., quoted, 180
Mechanical teaching aids, 327–28; see also Audio-visual materials and Teaching machines
Mental discipline theory, 52, 62
Mental retardation, 61, 148
Merchandise fund, 514
Merchant class, rise of, 49
Merchants, local, dealing with, 503
Merit provisions in determining salary, 327
Miami University, 389
Michael, J. Lloyd, 315
  quoted, 93
Michigan, 15, 21, 26, 53, 102
Michigan State University, 227
Middle States Association of Colleges and Secondary Schools, 16, 104
Miller, Franklin A., 250, 261, 275
  quoted, 229, 254–55, 516
Minimum size of school, 89–93

INDEX

Minnesota, 15
  Ramsey Junior High School, Minneapolis, 275
Mississippi, 15, 59
Missouri, 15, 102
Mitchel, Blyth C., 56 n., 193
Mitchell, James R., quoted, 361, 362, 364
Money. See Finances *and* Fund-raising projects
Montana, 15
Morale, 13, 36, 115, 330–31
  defined, 331–33
  factors affecting, 333–46
  of the principal, 346–47
Morrill Act, 101
Mort, Paul R., quoted, 91
"Mosaic" method of filling in schedule, 175
Motivation, and activities program, 226, 232
  for attendance, 456
  committee, 369
  intrinsic, 232
  to learn, 232, 386
Mt. Pleasant (Mich.) High School, 413–14
Mowrer, George E., 155
Moyer, James H., 250, 261, 275
  quoted, 229, 254–55, 516
Mulcaster's Merchant Taylors School (England), 48
Multiple curricula, 125
Multiple-track program, 81, 133, 134, 136–40, 146
Multi-purpose university, 80, 81
Music activities, 233, 260, 261, 262–63
Music period, 159
Music Educators' National Conference, 260, 262, 263

National Association of Secondary School Principals, 17, 20–21, 22, 37, 38, 69, 86, 98, 127, 128, 153, 165, 169, 249, 264, 322, 432, 438, 439, 444
National Association of Student Councils, 250, 251, 252
National Citizens Council for Better Schools, 26
National Congress of Parents and Teachers, 26, 117, 120, 476, 484, 488, 489–91
National Council of Chief State School Officers, 98
National Council on Schoolhouse Construction, 296
National Defense Education Act, 65, 72, 102, 190, 344
National Education Association, 21, 37, 67, 125, 128, 133
  Committee of Ten of, 53–54, 83, 125
  Research Division of, 182, 318
National Forensic League, 274
National Honor Society, 37, 274
National Study of Secondary School Evaluation, 265, 286
National Teacher Examination, 395
Nebraska, 15, 102
Needs, educational, 224–26
  of society, emphasis on, 63–64
  of youth, 69–70, 224–26
  See also Development tasks
Negroes, denied public education in Virginia, 469
Nevada, 15
New England Association of Colleges and Secondary Schools, 16, 104
New Hampshire, 15, 102
New Jersey, 15
New Mexico, 15
"New School" plan, Evanston, Ill., 315
New York State, 15
  Upper Catskill Area Project in, 93
New York University workshop, 364
Newspaper, school, 239, 257–59, 488; *see also* Press
Non-degree programs, 40
Nonprofessional personnel, 165, 169, 326, 537; *see also* Clerical services
Nonpublic schools, 95, 469–70
Nonteaching assignments for teachers, 175, 319
Normal curve, 448–50
North Carolina, 15
North Central Association of Colleges and Secondary Schools, 12, 13, 16, 90, 97–98, 99, 104, 153, 154, 157, 160, 169, 181, 182, 210, 261, 262–63, 286, 287, 295, 317, 361, 362, 364, 496, 507, 568
North Dakota, 15
Northwest Association of Secondary and Higher Schools, 16, 104, 153
Northwest Ordinance, 101
Numerical scale for marking, 448

Objective data for cumulative record, 435
Objectives, of activities, 231
  of assemblies, 256
  educational, 63–65, 66–71, 113–14, 119, 121, 127, 226, 333–34
  of extraclass business organization, 507–9
  of guidance program, 189–90, 209
  of music education, 260
  PTA, 490
  of records, 429, 433
  of student government, 249
  workshop, 361–62

INDEX

Objectivity of teachers, 207
Observation, of candidates in teaching situations, 401
   judgment of student's work by, 452
   objective data to support, 453
Office, central, 530–31
   personnel and facilities of, 538–42
   services offered by, 531–38
Ohio, 15
Ohio State Psychological Examination, 155
Ohio State University, 360
Ojeman, Ralph H., quoted, 383
Oklahoma, 15
Omaha (Neb.) Central High School, 192–93
"Open door" policy of principal, 339
Open house, 487
Opening and closing times, school, 157–58
Opening week, 185
Orange County, Fla., 331
Order lists, standardized, 503
Oregon, 15
Organization, authoritarian, 305
   committee, 311–12
   departmental, 307–10
   of extraclass business affairs, 507–11
   grade-level, 312–13
   of guidance program, 202–4
   horizontal, 78–82
   of library collection, 288–92
   line and staff, 302–6
   principles in, 306–7
   of program of studies, 124–25
   of the school day, 170, 534
   of school personnel, and democracy, 301
   school-within-a-school (house plan), 313–15
   of school year, 183–85
   vertical, 82–89
Orientation of new students and teachers, 172, 185, 367
Orwell, George, 247
Otto, Henry J., 181
Overemphasis on winning, 268–69
Overlapping schedule, 157, 358
Overparticipation in activities, 236–38

Parent-teacher association. *See* National Congress of Parents and Teachers
Parents, on advisory committees, 264
   and course enrollments, 171
   irate, handling of, by principal, 425
   principal conferences with, 420, 459
   relations of teachers and, 342
   reports to, 444–54
   and supervision of social affairs, 267
   teacher conferences with, 453, 487–88

Paternalism, 35
Patrick, Robert B., 250, 261, 275
   quoted, 229, 254–55, 516
Pennsylvania, 15
Percentage system of marking, 444
Period length, 153–57, 160
Permanent record, 438–39, 445
Per-pupil costs, 88–89, 90–91, 94, 282, 290
Personal adjustment, 200
Personal qualities, of successful principals, 17–19
   of successful teachers, 384–87
Personal-qualities theory of leadership, 29–30, 33
Personal service courses, 137, 138, 139, 140, 183
Petty, Paul V., quoted, 376, 381, 392
Petty cash fund, 519
Philadelphia Public Academy, 50–51
Physical education, 159, 239; *see also* Athletics
Physical facilities, avoiding conflicts in use of, 176
   floor plan of, 170
   for guidance, 216–18, 539–40
   for housing records, 431–32, 537
   library, 295–97
   office as control center for, 531, 537
   of principal's office, 539–42
   for teachers' comfort, 343, 570
   workshop, 363–64
   See also Educational specifications for new school
Physical Science Study Committee, 98
Pierce, Benjamin, quoted, 48–49
Pierce, Paul R., quoted, 302
Placement records and services, 206, 212–13, 394, 399; *see also* Employment
Planetariums, 570
Planning, cooperation of laymen in, 484–92
   coordinated, throughout school system, 476
   curriculum, *see* Curriculum
   of faculty meetings, 354, 355–56
   for and *of*, 556–557
   of a new school building, 552–69
   of student projects, 513
   teacher-student, of assemblies and social affairs, 256, 267
   of workshop, 362–63, 365–66
Plato, 222
Play therapy, 268
Point system in activities program, 237
Poise, development of, 256, 264
Police, presence of, at public events, 526–27
   relations of school and, 423–24, 527

INDEX

Pragmatism, 28
Preregistration, 167–68, 171–72, 177, 179, 212
Preschool conferences, 185, 366–67
Press, interest of, in school activities, 227, 269
  school relations with, 485–86
Price, David E., 261
Principal, absences checked by, 458–59
  accreditation of, 14–16
  and activity program, 223, 227–28, 234, 241, 243–44, 248, 258–59, 274, 277, 345
  and advisory council, 370–71
  annual reports of, 542, 543–45
  assistant, 11–13, 20
  and budget making, 201
  business functions of, 495, 496–527
  calendar drawn up by, 181–85, 480–81
  committee work implemented by, 311, 546–47
  communication media used by, 532–35
  counseling by, 414
  and curriculum planning, 112–13, 120
  and development of educational aims, 334
  dismissal of a teacher by, 341
  economic prospects of, 19–22
  and educational specifications, 559–60, 567–69
  evolution of, 6–8
  and faculty meetings, 354, 356–57
  full-time, 10–11
  and guidance program, 198, 200–202, 209, 211
  individual conferences of, with teachers, 371–73
  and interdepartmental relationships, 100
  irate parents handled by, 425
  job opportunities for, 22–23
  leadership role of, 26–27, 30–36, 201, 228, 338, 492
  as member of school council, 250
  morale of, 346–47
  office of, 530–42
  "open door" policy of, 339
  and opening events of school year, 185
  part-time, 9–10, 11
  personal public relations of, 40, 492–93
  personal qualities of, 17–19
  and planning of school building, 552–71
  and planning of workshop, 365–66
  and policy formulation, 352
  preparation of, 13–17
  and problems of discrimination, 275
  professional growth of, 37–41
  and professional organizations, 16–17
  protection of student's legal rights by, 424
  and pupil records, 433
  relations of, with police, 423–24
  relations of, with press, 485–86
  relations of, with students, 201, 345
  relations of teachers and, 101, 334, 336–37, 340, 343, 345–46, 351
  responsibility of, for discipline, 408–9, 410–23
  route to becoming, 22–23
  schedule building by, 166–81
  and school-community relations, 474–76, 480–81, 482, 484, 488, 489
  and school library, 283, 288, 290
  and school organization, 302, 303, 304, 306–15
  selection of committee members by, 312, 368
  and selection of teachers, 378–79, 393–402
  as status leader, 30–31, 33, 356
  support of teachers by, 244, 339, 344, 345, 424–25
  teacher confidence in and respect for, 338–39
  and teacher morale, 333
  utilization of staff by, 315–28
  veto power of, 240–41, 253, 360, 370
  willingness of, to accept work assignments, 336, 338, 369
  women in position of, 13
Private-venture grammar school, 49, 50
Problem census, workshop, 362, 365
Problem solving, conferences focused on, 372–73
  democratic, 36
Processing materials for teachers, 531, 535–36
Processing school data, 172–73, 178, 180–81, 461–62
Professional education, of administrators, 13–17
  of teachers, 40, 383–84
Professional organizations, 16–17, 37–38
Program of studies, 123–24
  criteria for organizing, 124–25
  examples of, 134–41
  planning of, 172, 206, 212
  types of, 125–26
Programming courses, 177–78
  machine and marginal punch card processes of, 178–81
Projects, fund-raising, 235, 276, 513, 516–17
  leading toward curriculum change, 114–15
  planning of, 513
  student government, 251, 252, 259

INDEX

Prussian school system, 83
Public opinion polls, 484
Public relations. *See* School-community relations
"Public" schools in England, 222
Publications, school, 239, 257–60, 413, 488
Publications fund, 514
Puerto Rico, 15
Punishment, 415–17
  corporal, 417–19
  by expulsion or suspension, 419–21
  of group offenses, 421–23
  See also Discipline
Pupil personnel records, 428–29, 542
  administrative and counseling, 206
  anecdotal, 206, 207
  attendance, 456–61
  automation and, 461–62
  cumulative, 205–7, 430, 433–38, 440–41
  diplomas, 454–56
  guiding principles for, 429–32
  marks and reports to parents, 444–54
  permanent, 438–39, 445
  rank-in-class, 439–43
  test, 206–7
  transcript of credits, 443–44, 445
  types of, 432–62
Pupil personnel services, coordinator (director) of, 203, 204, 211, 212, 216, 304
Pupil-teacher ratio, 255, 317, 318
Purchasing, 501–3, 518, 521
Puritanism, 49
Purposes. *See* Objectives
Purposes of Education in American Democracy, The, 67, 127

"Q spaces," 570
Quill and Scroll, 257, 274

Racial discrimination, 46, 275
Radio club, 239
Radio stations, school relations with, 486
Ramsey Junior High School, Minneapolis, 275
Rank in class, 439–43
Readers' Guide to Periodical Literature, 292
Reading, professional, 38
Reading rooms, 296
Receipts and expenditures, activities program, 513–14, 518–19, 520, 523, 524
Recognition, of athletic excellence, 268
  of committee work, 370
  of participation in activities, 237
  of teacher achievement, 336–37

Records, housing of, 431–32, 537
  in program accounting, 542–43, 546–48
  pupil personnel, *see* Pupil personnel records
Recreation, summer, 183
  at workshops, 361, 363–64
Recreational clubs, 273
Redl, Fritz, quoted, 410, 416
Registration, course. *See* Preregistration
Relaxation, 224, 268
Remedial classes, 148, 168, 183
Remmers, D. H., quoted, 191
Remmers, H. H., quoted, 191, 380
Reorganization movement, 83–89, 93
Report cards, 454, 455, 462
Reports, of committees, 546–47
  principal's, on extraclass supplies and equipment, 526
  principal's, to superintendent, board, etc., 543–46
  supervisory, 548
Requisitions, 501, 502, 503, 518
Research, 41
  action, 121, 215
Retention rate, 56, 57
Reutter, E. Edmund, Jr., quoted, 387
Revolving schedule, 152–53, 163
Rhode Island, 15
Richey, Herman G., quoted, 226
Rickover, H. G., quoted, 79
Ridicule, 416
Ritterakademien, 48, 222
Rockefeller Report on Education, 195, 228
Rocky Mountain Project, 93
Roe, William H., 501
Roeber, Edward C., quoted, 215
Roger Ludlow High School, Fairfield, Conn., 314
Romine, Stephen, 191, 319
Room assignments, 176
Roosevelt, Franklin D., 30
Roper, Elmo, 483
Rothney, J. W. M., 200
Russell Sage Foundation, 127
Ryans, David G., 382, 390
  quoted, 389

Safety on buses, 506
Salaries, 19, 20–22, 91, 344, 376, 377
  additions to, for coaching or sponsoring, 319
  of beginning teachers, 387–88
  of coaches and music teachers, 261, 269, 270, 479
  differentials in, based on sex, 390
  preparation and, 20
  for principal's secretary, 539

INDEX

size of school and, 21
of teachers who are local residents, 391
and ten-month contract, 367
Salinas Union (Cal.) High School District, 411
Salisbury, Arnold W., 496, 501, 504, 506, 507
Salutatorian, 443
San Bernardino (Cal.) Public Schools, 202, 204–5
Sandburg, Carl, quoted, 281
Sanders, Stanley, 236
Sarcasm, 416
Schedule, block-time, 152, 162
building of, 166–81
conventional, 152, 153–61
daily and weekly, 151–52
"dummy," 567
and educational philosophy, 151
floating-period (revolving), 152–53, 163
good, criteria of, 166–67
information needed in building, 167–70
large- and small-group instruction in, 322–23
music activities in, 261–62
for school year, 181–85
team-teaching, 153, 165–66
types of, 152–53
variable, 152, 161–66
varied-period, 153, 163–64
See also Calendar
Schedule card, 177, 178
"Scholarchs," 222
Scholastic eligibility requirements, 234, 235–36
School Activities, 257
School building program, 550–51
and educational specifications, 552–69
innovations in, 569–71
School building surveys, 484
School calendar. *See* Calendar
School and College Ability Test, 81–82
School and College Study of Admission with Advanced Placement, 147
School-community relations, 227, 467–468
handling of, by telephone, 534
importance of, 468–70
in planning for new school, 568
principles and policies of, 477–79
problems of, 470–73
procedures and media in, 479–93
responsibility and coordination in, 473–76
role of principal's office in, 531, 534, 537–38, 539
School day, length of, 157

School district reorganization, 55, 57
School of the future, 165, 326–27, 569–71
School grounds, use of, for instructional purposes, 571
School year, 181–85
Schooling, Herbert W., 491
Schools-within-a-school, 95, 313–15
Schultz, R. E., quoted, 335
Schunert, Jim, 94
Science, high school-college articulation in, 98
Science club, 239
Science fairs, 487
Scopes trial, 66
Scott, C. Winfield, 27
quoted, 28
Screening of applicants, 378, 379, 401
Secondary school modern (England), 80
Secondary schools, academies, 49–52
changed objectives of, 66–71
changed public view of, 58–66
changes in, 47
defined, 77–78
early, 6, 47–54
and government and extralegal agencies, 101–4
horizontal articulation of, 100–101
horizontal organization of, 78–82
modern, 54–58, 71–74, 80, 569–71
objectives of, 66–71 (*see also* Objectives, educational)
and other schools and agencies, 95–101
size of, 89–95
structure of, 78–89
vertical articulation of, 96–100
vertical organization of, 82–89
See also Education, Senior high school, *and* Teachers
Secretary, office, 537
for the principal, 536, 538–39
for teachers, 535, 536
Sectioning of classes, 168–69, 170, 174–75
Security, of records, 435
teacher, 343–44
Segel, David, 434
Self-contained classroom, 89
Self-control or self-discipline, 409–10, 412, 413, 414, 417, 506
Self-direction in learning, 323
Self-rating, 206, 215
Self-realization, 67–68
Self-respect, 416
Self-sufficiency, 189
Semester hours, in granting credit, 164
in teacher preparation, 169
Seminars for gifted students, 93

INDEX

Senior high school, 83, 84, 94
 advisory curriculum in, 133, 134–36
 constants-with-variables program in, 136–42
 general education in, 128–30
 See also Secondary schools
Serene, Michael, 198
Service clubs, 273
Seven Cardinal Principles of Secondary Education, 66–67, 226
Sex of teachers, 390–91
Shapiro, Daniel F., 94
Shaw, Leander J., quoted, 284
Shaw High School, East Cleveland, Ohio, 259
Sheviakov, George V., quoted, 410, 416
Shock, Donald P., quoted, 411
Shop classes, 160–61, 168
Short-period schedule, 156
Short-term courses, 40
Sick leave, 343
Siggelkow, Richard A., quoted, 399
Simpson, Ray H., quoted, 388
Single curriculum, 125
Single-section courses, 173, 174, 175
Situational leadership. *See* Functional leadership
Six- and seven-period schedules, 153, 154, 156, 157
Small discussion sections, 318
Small-group instruction, 323
Smith, Glenn E., quoted, 190–91, 215
Smith-Hughes Act, 72, 101
Snobbery, 274–75
Social clubs, 273
Social discrimination, 235, 274–75
Social environment, adjustment to, 200
 changes in, 194
 and classroom achievement, 266
Social life, 265–67
 of teachers, 341
Social stratification, 81
Social studies, 162
Socioeconomic status and community influence, 483
Sociometric charts, 206
Socrates, quoted, 407
Sororities, 267, 275
South Carolina, 15
South Dakota, 15, 102
Southern Association of Colleges and Secondary Schools, 16, 104, 287
Soviet schools, 80, 110
Sparks, Jack N., 62 n., 143, 154
Speaking in public, 39–40, 493
Special committees, 311–12
Special institutions for the handicapped, 61
Special-interest curriculum, 133
Special-interest groups, 171, 230, 472

Special services, conflicts among, 96
 offices for, 540
Specialists, staff, 303–5, 326
 use of, in preparing educational specifications, 560
 in workshop, 363, 365
Specialized education, 63, 131–48, 195
Specialized high school, 78, 79–80, 81
Specifications, educational, for new school, 552–67
 of teaching job, 392–93
Speech and dramatics, 239, 264–65
Split noon hour, 158
Sponsorship of activities, 233, 242–44, 252, 258, 272, 274, 319, 337, 511, 513
Sports. *See* Athletics
Sportsmanship, 271
Staff personnel, 303–5, 308; *see also* Line and staff organization *and* Organization, of school personnel
Staff utilization, 315–28
Staggered lunch hour plan, 158
Standing committees, 311
Standard Catalog for High School Libraries, 290
Standards, of behavior, 266–67
 in new school building, 568
 for program of studies, 124–25
Stasek, Erwin D., 199
State activities associations, 104, 241, 270, 546
State time requirements for industrial education, 160
State universities, 53
States, control over education by, 95, 101
 educational agencies of, 25, 37, 102
 funds of, for education, 102
 relationships of schools and agencies of, 102–3
 requirements of, for principals and teachers, 15, 169
 variation in per-school-child valuation among, 59
Status, high, of principal, 7
Status leadership, 30–31, 33, 356
Stefflre, Buford, quoted, 191
Stephenson, Chester M., 389
Storage, library, 297
 of supplies and equipment, 526
Stosberg, William K., quoted, 331
Stout, Minard W., 517
Strahan, Donald F., 517
Stroud, James B., quoted, 224
Student council (school council), 239, 240, 248, 249, 250–53, 254, 255, 259, 513
Student Life, 251
Student organization fund, 514

590

Student publications, 239, 257–60, 413, 488
Student records. *See* Pupil personnel records
Student teaching, 382
Students, association of, with central office, 530
  codes, rules, and regulations for, 267, 412–14
  cooperation of, in selecting library materials, 291
  cooperation of leaders of, 421, 422
  educational needs of, and activities, 224–26
  independent study by, 323, 569–70
  interest of, in activity program, 223–24, 231–33, 235, 237, 252, 272, 275–76
  interrogation of, by police, 423
  legal rights of, 423–24
  as library assistants, 288
  as managers (athletics, dramatics), 526
  as office assistants, 534, 535–36, 539
  participation of, in business management, 509–10, 512–13
  participation of, in curriculum planning, 118
  problems of, 192, 194, 208
  relations of teachers and, 93, 94, 344–45, 386
  social program for all, 266
  values held by, 479
  viewpoint of, on guidance program, 213–14
Sturges, Allen W., 153, 155, 157, 158, 159
Subject area clubs, 239, 273
Subject coefficients, 319, 320
Subject fields, relationships among, 100
  specialists in, 560
  supervisors of, 97
Subjective data for cumulative records, 435
Subjects, departmental organization of, 87, 88, 307–10
  grouping within, 145
  "hard-core," 118
  preparation for teaching of, 383–84
  required by law, 126, 132
Summer employment for teachers, 343
Summer institutes, 102
Summer instructional programs, 40, 182–83
Superintendent, business responsibilities of, 495, 498, 500, 501, 507, 513, 518, 527
  creation of position of, 7
  and curriculum planning, 112
  disciplinary role of, 421
  and guidance services, 201, 202, 211
  and length of school year, 181
  and planning of school buildings, 552
  and the principal, 9, 351, 533
  publications sent out by, 488
  and reports to accrediting associations, 545
  salary of, 19, 22
  and school-community relations, 40, 468, 493
  and school library, 283, 289
  and school organization, 303, 306
  and selection of teachers, 8, 378, 393, 398, 401, 402
  surveys by, 484
Supervision, of activities program, 241, 242, 252, 337
  of assemblies, 257
  of athletics, 271
  of clubs, 277
  of instruction, by principal, 6, 34
  longitudinal, 97
  noon-hour, 505, 506
  of public events, 423, 526–27
  of school paper, 258
  of social affairs, 267
  on trips, 507
  See also Sponsorship
Supreme Court decisions, 60, 101, 469
Supplies and equipment, management of, 501–5, 526
Suspension from school, 419–21
Surveys, 484, 546

Tabulating registrations, 172–74
Talents, development of, 233
  grouping according to, 450
  necessity of, for certain activities, 235
  teacher, utilization of, 323, 324, 326–27, 336–38
Tape recorders, 327
Tappan Junior High School, Ann Arbor, Mich., 454, 455
Tardiness, 461
Tax funds, for activities program, 234, 258, 265, 270, 516
  competition for, 470
  education supported by, 53, 60, 103
  for nonpublic schools, 470
Teacher aides, 165
Teacher-pupil ratio, 255, 317, 318
Teacher specialists, 326
Teachers, ability grouping favored by, 144–45
  and administrators, 115, 334, 336, 370
  and advisory councils, 370–71
  age of, 389–90
  application interviews with, 397–401

591

INDEX

assigned to major subject field, 175–76, 337
assistance of library to, 295
assistant, 318, 326
attitude of, as factor in articulation, 100–101
beginning, 387, 388
and budget planning, 498, 500
certification of, 384
coaches as, 269–70
committee work by, 311, 367–70
competition for, 387, 394, 473
concern for professional growth of, 18
cooperation of, in selecting library materials, 291
and curriculum planning, 113, 115–16, 120, 122
and discipline policies, 412, 420
economic security of, 343–44
educational workshops for, 360–66
and educational specifications for new school, 559–60
encouragement of ideas of, 18
evaluation of educational practices by, 559, 569
experience of librarians as, 287
exploitation of, 342–43
factors in predicting success of, 379–92, 396
and guidance program, 201, 202–3, 204, 210–11
"head," 6, 8
health of, 342–43
help of, in selecting teachers, 393, 394
individual conferences of, with principal, 371–73
in-service program for, 37–41, 255, 337–38, 569
intelligence of, 381–82
and leadership of principal, 26–27
local, 391
marital status of, 389
master, 165, 169, 325
morale of, 115, 330–31, 333–46
nonteaching assignments for, 175, 319
number of, needed, 169
open period a day for, 169
personal characteristics of, 384–87, 397
personal problems of, 345–46
physical facilities for comfort of, 343, 570
and planning of school calendar, 184
and policy formulation, 31, 35–36, 351–52
preferences of, 169–70, 244, 274, 337
preschool conferences for, 366–67
processing materials for, 531, 535–36
professional collection in library for, 290

professional preparation of, 40, 383–84
rating of students by, 206
relations among, 340–41, 350–51, 352
relations of, with community, 341–42, 474–76
relations of, with pupils, 93, 94, 344–46, 386
salaries of, *see* Salaries
and schedule making, 176
scholastic achievement of, 382
selection of, 9, 378–79, 392–402
sex of, 390–91
as sponsors for activities, 233, 242–44, 252, 258, 272, 274, 319, 337, 511, 513
with substandard credentials, 394
support of, by principal, 244, 339, 344, 345, 424–25
teaching experience of, 387–89
tenure for, 291–92
visiting, 459
See also Faculty meetings
Teaching load, 156, 169, 270, 316–19, 337, 342
balancing of, 175–76, 201, 244
Douglass formula for, 319–21
Teaching machines, 297, 327–28
Team teaching, 153, 165–66, 168, 323–26
Telephone communication, 534
Television, 169, 327, 486–87, 493, 570
Temporary (*ad hoc*) committees, 311–12, 485, 492
Tennessee, 15, 66
Tenure, 391–92
Terman, L. M., 193
Test records, 206–7
Testing of applicants, 395–97
Testing programs, student, 71, 98, 145–46, 207
Texas, 15, 59
Textbooks, basic, restriction to, 112
pruning of, 292
storing, distributing, and accounting for, 504
Thorndike, E. L., 46
Tiedeman, Stuart C., 385
quoted, 386
Toll calls, 534
Tompkins, Ellsworth, 317
Toy, Henry, 491
Traditional (vertical) organization, 83, 84, 85, 86, 88–89
Transcript of credits, 443–44, 445
Transferring students, 171
Transportation, 159, 506–7
Traxler, Arthur E., 438
quoted, 429
Trimester plan, 182

INDEX

Troubleshooting, office's role in, 531, 538
Trow, William C., quoted, 30
Truancy, 420, 459–60
Trump, J. Lloyd, 326
  quoted, 322, 323
Tuition, summer school, 183

Underachievers, 199
Uneducable youth, 61
Unicameral council, 250
"Unified studies," 127
U.S. Office of Education, 78, 85, 90, 102, 196, 511, 512, 513, 519–20
University, multi-purpose, 80, 81
  state, 53
Upper Catskill Area Project, 93
Utah, 15

Valedictorian, 443
Values, of activities program, 223–26
  of athletics, 267–68
  development of, and education, 80–82
  false, 269
  held by students, 479
  of society, emphasis on, 63–64
Van Buren Public Schools, Belleville, Mich., mathematics-science classroom specifications, 561–67
Van Dyke, L. A., 62 n., 143
Variable schedules, 152, 161–66
  block-time, 89, 127, 128, 130, 152, 162
  college-type, 164
  floating-period (revolving), 152–53, 163
  team-teaching, 153, 165–66
  varied-period, 153, 163–64
Varsity competition, 233, 270, 271, 527
Vermont, 15
Vertical articulation, 96–100, 123, 124, 307, 308, 313
Vertical organization, 82–89
Veto power of principal, 240–41, 253, 360, 370
Virginia, 15, 469
Visiting among classes. *See* Intervisitation
Visiting of other schools when preparing educational specifications, 567

Visiting teachers, 459
Vocal groups, 260, 261, 262
Vocational choices, counseling and, 199–200; *see also* Employment
Vocational education, 63, 72, 80, 160–61, 183

Wahlert High School, Dubuque, Iowa, 260
Washington, George, quoted, 468–69
Washington State, 15
Webster, A. D., 208
Weighted honor point system, 451–52
Weiss, G. A. W., 13
Wernick, Walter, quoted, 26–27
West Virginia, 15
Western Electric Company studies in morale, 330
White House Conference on Education, 70–71
Whitman, Howard, quoted, 408
Willard, Edward, quoted, 18
Winning, pressures for, 268–69, 272
Wisconsin, 15
  University of, 399
Witty, Paul, 384
Wolfle, Dael, 196
Women in administration, 13, 22
Woodham, William J., Jr., 91
Woodward, Julian, 483
Work experience, 110, 183
Work habits, reporting on, 452–53
Workroom, central office, 535
  library, 296–97
  teachers', 343
Workshop Way of Learning, The (Kelley), 366
Workshops for teachers, 360–66
  preschool, 185
  summer, 40
Writing, creative, 259–60
  professional, 39
Wyoming, 15

Yearbook, school, 259, 488
Youth inventory returns, 192, 194
Youth needs, 69–70, 224–26